MW01632235

Ask Another Question

HILCHOS MUKTZEH

Rabbi Joe Douer

First published 2021

joedouer@gmail.com
Shalzon 51/24 Jerusalem

ISBN: **9781527282889**

Published by
Targum Publishers
Shlomo ben Yosef 131a/1
Jerusalem 9380581
editor@targumpublishers.com

Distributed by
Ktav Publishers & Distributors Inc.
527 Empire Blvd.
Brooklyn, NY 11225-3121
Tel: 718-972-5449, 201-963-9524
Fax: 718-972-6307, 201-963-0102
www.ktav.com

Typesetting by Rabbi Gabriel Azoulay
Editing by Mrs Chaya Silverstone
Graphics by Mrs Chaya Murik
Sponsored in part by Merkaz HaTorah V'HaTefillah
Har Nof

Printed in Israel

This sefer

is dedicated in loving memory

of

Yosef ben Zion Douer

and

Yosef ben Mordechai Douer

Heichal Hatorah Betzion
היכל התורה בציון

Rosh Yeshiva: Rabbi Zvi Kushelevsky ראש הישיבה: הרב צבי קושלבסקי

ע״ר 580047009

בס״ד

טבת תש״פ

בא לפני תלמידי מבוגרי ישיבתנו הקדושה הרה״ג יוסף דואר שליט״א שהנני מכירו מעת לימודיו בישה״ק בהיותו עמל בתורה בצורה מופלגת, לירד לעומק הסוגיות, ולאסוקי שמעתתא אליבא דהלכתא, שזו הדרך האמיתית כמש״כ רבינו הגר״ח מוולאז׳ין זצ״ל בהקדמת ביאור הגר״א לשו״ע ״שלא להזניח ח״ו את התלמוד הק׳ המביא לידי מעשה, וזה כל פרי לימוד הש״ס להוציא ממנו הלכה למעשה וכו׳״ ע״ש.

והרב המחבר, הלך בעקבות דברי הגר״ח, ועמל להוציא לאור חיבור גדול על יסודות הלכות מוקצה, להביא הסוגיא ממקורותיה, עפ״י ביאורי הראשונים והאחרונים, מפיהם אנו חיים, ואמנם עתותי אינם בידי לעבור על הספר כולו, אבל חזקה עלי׳ דר׳ יוסף דואר שליט״א מחבר הספר שמוציא מתח״י דבר מתוקן.

והנני מברך את ר׳ יוסף דואר שליט״א שיזכה להמשיך לעמול בתורה מתוך מנוחת הנפש ללמוד וללמד לשמור ולעשות ולקיים את כל דברי התורה באהבה.

החותם לכבוד התורה
צבי קושלבסקי

צבי קושלבסקי

ראש ישיבת היכל התורה

92 Katzenelbogen St. P.O.B 43106 Jerusalem 9143002, Israel רחוב קצנלבוגן 92, ת.ד. 43106, ירושלים 9143002

Tel: +972-(0)-2-6519402 Fax: +972-(0)-2-6524402 טלפון: 02-6519402 פקס: 02-6524402

Rabbi S.F. Zimmerman
Rov of Gateshead

שרגא פייבל הלוי זיממערמאן
אב"ד דק"ק גייטסהעד

בס"ד

י"ז תמוז תשע"ט

לכ' ידידי הרה"ג הנעלה דכל מדה נכונה
הרה"ג יוסף בוער שליט"א

I read through your sefer on H' Muktza

I found it to be erudite & meticulous, yet still practical & readable for the layman. I believe it would be a great toeles to publish it for the scholar & layman alike

ויה"ר שתזכה עוד להרביץ תורה מתוך בריאות הגוף ומנוחת הנפש ונחת ממשפחתך
הכו"ח לכבוד רב
שרגא פייבל הלוי זיממערמאן

[illegible]

95 Bewick Road, Gateshead, NE8 1RR
Tel: 0191 477 1847 Fax: 0191 477 7688

אשר זעליג וייס
כגן 8
פעיה"ק ירושלם ת"ו

ב"ה

ח' ניסן [illegible]

הן ראיתי את הספר היקר על הלכות מוקצה, [illegible]
מהנעלה הרה"ג ר' יוסף [illegible] שליט"א. ספר זה [illegible] לשאלות
[illegible] שבו. הספר מצוין, [illegible]
[illegible] לכל נפש.

[illegible] שספר זה [illegible] למחבר הי"ו [illegible]
[illegible] ולהגדיל תורה ולהאדירה.

בברכה וכו'

Table of Contents

Questions

1. Reuven placed an electric fan in the sukkah for extra comfort. Can he bring it inside if it suddenly starts to rain?
2. Can Shimon move a cookbook or store catalogue?
3. Can Levi put birthday candles on his daughter's birthday cake?
4. The Cohens' nonreligious guest arrived on Shabbos with his wallet in his coat pocket. Can Mr. Cohen offer to take hang his coat for him?
5. An electric blender is blocking the way of the extra plates that Mrs. Schwartz needs for the guests. Can she move it?

1. People often fidget with cutlery at the Shabbos table. Am I permitted to do so?
2. Can I put my hands in my pockets if there are house keys inside?
3. Can I move posters in the sukkah that have *pesukim* on them?
4. Is it praiseworthy to eat with my hands instead of using cutlery on Shabbos?

1. Aharon has a box of Pesach dishes in the dining room and now needs to make more space. May he move the box?

2. Yitzchak has a very expensive vase. It's only ever been used a handful of times, since there is rarely a bouquet of flowers which is fancy enough. This Shabbos morning, guests turned up with some flowers. Can he bring the vase out in order to store the flowers (obviously without putting water inside)?

3. The kids have knocked the clock off the wall. Can I move it to a safer location?

1. One Shabbos, more guests than anticipated turned up and I didn't have enough dishes for everyone. I would like to use my Pesach set (either I will do *hagalah* afterward or I'll just buy new Pesach dishes). Even if we say that the Pesach set is *muktzeh machmas chisaron kis,* could this still be permissible?

1. After performing a bris milah on Shabbos, the mohel turned to me and asked me to pick up the knife from the table and put it away in a side room of the shul. Am I allowed to move it?

1. After lighting the Shabbos candles, do women have to drop the matches immediately (a Sephardic woman every Shabbos, and an Ashkenazic woman on Yom Tov, since with the conclusion of their lighting they immediately accept Shabbos/Yom Tov)?

2. When I eat a fruit and reach the seed or pit, can I throw it into the trash can, or must I drop it where it is?

tle, that he finished using. Must he be careful not to handle it?

2. After emptying out a packet of sugar, what should I do with the empty packet?

3. Is there any preference from the point of view of *muktzeh* to drink Coke from a bottle rather than from a can? And is an empty Coke can *muktzeh*?

1. If a shirt button broke off on Shabbos, can I move it to a safe place?

2. If the toilet seat comes off its hinges, can I still sit on it?

3. If the arm breaks off my glasses, can I continue wearing them?

4. If a screw falls out of an electric item, can I move the screw to keep it safe?

1. Does the halachah permit protestors to throw stones on Shabbos? (I'm not getting into the *bein adam l'chaveiro* - just the potential *muktzeh* involved!)

2. Are kids allowed to play in a sandbox on Shabbos?

3. A dressmaker realizes she won't have enough tablecloths for a *Shabbos sheva berachos*. Before Shabbos, can she prepare her fabric in a way to be able to use it as a temporary tablecloth?

4. Some children like to play *chamesh avanim* (Jacks) with the pits of apricots. Is that permitted on Shabbos?

Chapter 24, Part 1 - Stipulating on Muktzeh 398

1. While I know in advance that on Shabbos day I'll need to move the Shabbos candles from the table, I still want to light on the table in order to fulfill the mitzvah in the best fashion. Does it help to verbally stipulate that after the candles go out, I'll remove them?

2. Levi has a silver *chanukiah* that he lights outside his door on Chanukah. He usually brings it inside after the candles extinguish so that no one steals it. What should he do on Shabbos night in order to protect his *chanukiah*?

3. Yehudah has lights on a timer that will keep them on from 6 p.m. to 12 a.m. This suits him on Friday, but on Shabbos day he wants the lights off from 6 p.m. On Shabbos morning, can Yehudah move the switches of the timer so that the light won't turn on? (This question is more relevant on a two-day Yom Tov.)

Chapter 25, Part 1 - Muktzeh Due to a Mitzvah 420

1. Naftali wants to remove a pomegranate that's hanging as a decoration from his sukkah roof. May he do so? If yes, is he permitted to eat it now? Is it forbidden even on Chol HaMoed, not just Shabbos?

2. Can I move a decoration hanging in a sukkah? Can I put it in storage on Chol HaMoed?

Part 2 - Muktzeh Machmas Mitzvah Pertaining to a Sukkah 426

1. Dovid is going away on Chol HaMoed and wishes to dismantle his sukkah. Is he permitted to take it down on Chol HaMoed?

2. There is a custom for pregnant women to bite off the *pitom* on Hoshana Rabbah. Is this a correct custom?

3. Someone didn't listen to the *rav*'s request for everyone to take home their lulavim before Shabbos, and there's a lulav lying over several chairs. Can it be moved on Shabbos?

Preface

R*ambam* in *Yad Chazakah*[1] details eight ascending rungs regarding the mitzvah of giving charity, the highest being one who gives in a manner that facilitates the receiver to become self-supportive. We can derive a fundamental lesson from this: *Chesed* is best performed when it enables the recipient to no longer be in need of the giver. That's why Chazal called the mitzvah *gemilus chasadim* - the word *gomel* means to wean, to give enough so that a person can stand on his own two feet.

This same principle applies in imparting Torah. Although the next generation must always respect their teachers and adhere to their commands, a teacher must make his pupils self-sufficient. Otherwise, the chain of Torah from generation to generation will cease.

Writing a book with merely questions and answers does not meet this criterion. In recent decades, we have witnessed a shift in the *kollel* structure from focusing on topics of *Even HaEzer* and *Yoreh Dei'ah* to an emphasis on *Orach Chaim* and specifically Shabbos. In prewar Europe, the most important tractate a *rav* had to know was *Chullin,* dealing with the laws of slaughtering and the like. Nowadays, the most crucial tractate is arguably *Shabbos.*[2] This is particularly relevant with *muktzeh*; knowing which products exist in today's marketplace won't help you next Shabbos because even the minutest development in technology can drastically impact the halachah, from permitted to forbidden, and even carry a punishment of stoning if a Torah prohibition is transgressed.

In the same vein that we monitor the latest technological advancements with diligence and delight, we must act likewise for their respective halachic ramifications. These factors have driven me to compile this book. It's a drastic deviation from the regular English halachah *sefer* found in your local bookstore, but I feel it's the one missing the most. The aim of

1. *Matnos Aniyim* 10:7.

2. From here on in, whenever otherwise specified, the tractate referred to is *Maseches Shabbos.*

this volume is not to replace the *rav* as the final authority; rather, on countless occasions we find ourselves in scenarios that necessitate an instant answer and no one is around to help. By learning the sources behind the halachos, ideally the reader will be well versed to a high enough degree whereby he can rely on his own intuition when required. Only by learning the topic in its entirety can one strive to be self-supportive, even in areas of halachah. This is the great *chesed* I am striving to bequeath to the dear reader.

I have attempted, to the best of my ability, to present the topic in the simplest fashion, while endeavoring not to lose the depth and beauty of the Torah. This equilibrium is a treacherous path to tread and sometimes specific portions will feel too detailed and confusing. The reader is asked to be patient and remember that Torah is not something acquired in minutes, and not even hours, even when reading in English. Effort and toil are still required and only with persistence and *siyatta deShmaya* is any clarity achieved.

Each topic is preceded with practical and relevant questions, which are designed to be an aid through the *sugya,* to help readers find their bearing. I have made an effort to write the practical halachah to all the questions I have posed. The *psakim* presented have been discussed with various *talmidei chachamim*; however, the way they are presented mirror my opinion and judgment unless explicitly stated otherwise.

Shelah HaKodosh[3] impresses upon us the significance of learning *hilchos muktzeh.* He says that besides its vastness (*muktzeh* probably covers the most chapters in *Hilchos Shabbos,* all of *simanim* 308–312), it is an area even the learned can transgress. None of us intend to pick up stones to throw on Shabbos, but we can mistakenly move a vessel for no reason and transgress *muktzeh.* If, in the times of *Shelah* - where the number of household items could be counted on one's finger - he warns us that we can easily inadvertently come to move *muktzeh,* how much more so in our households today, where each cupboard alone has more *muktzeh* items

3. In his commentary on Shabbos, end of chapter *Ner Mitzvah.*

that *Shelah*'s entire house, must we be aware of *hilchos muktzeh.*[4]

Besides getting a feel as to what should and shouldn't be permissible, learning *hilchos muktzeh* is the only way to live the halachos. What does that mean?

Chovos HaLevavos[5] says that halachos must be so real to us that they become entrenched in the very nature of our lives. We're supposed to reach a level where we instinctively look at a dish in which milk and meat were cooked together as repulsive - and when we touch *muktzeh* it should feel that we've just touched burning coals! *Chasam Sofer* testifies that his father in-law, R' Akiva Eiger, lived by this realization. Once, he inadvertently moved nutshells on Shabbos. Upon realizing his error, he fainted. After awakening and seeing the shells again, he fainted once more, until someone recognized the cause behind his recurring fainting and ate the nutshells to show that they were not *muktzeh.*[6] R' Akiva Eiger clearly felt the pain of touching *muktzeh.*

Only through effort and toil can the Torah become part of one's self. Without the significant toil necessary to reach the true depth of any topic, it remains external. One therefore lacks the possibility of even striving for such a level.

The clarity reached in all these challenging topics would not have been conceivable without the help of all the members of the *kollel* Nezer Shlomo, in particular my *chavrusa,* who always had greater clarity to shed on every topic, Reb Jonty Hope.

I am deeply grateful for my dear, trustworthy editor Reb Moishe Reif, who meticulously combed through every sentence in this book. His corrections and additional insights significantly changed this *sefer;* without

---

4. It is said that *Chasam Sofer* would make an effort not to move items for no reason during the week. It then became natural to him and he wouldn't inadvertently move something on Shabbos for no reason.

5. Quoted in *Chasam Sofer* (*Toras Moshe*) in *Parshas Nitzavim.*

6. The credibility of the story is questionable, and we can't derive any halachos from it, but it illustrates the point.

his contributions, it would not have been legible to any audience. I also want to thank Mrs Chaya Silverstone for her editing expertise throughout this *sefer.*

I will always be indebted for everything Mori V'Rabi R' Ariav Ozer has and will teach me. The first time I merited to learn *muktzeh* was with R' Ozer. Just like with every area of Torah that flows from his mouth, he showed me the complexity and beauty behind *muktzeh*, thereby instilling in me a yearning to delve further into the topic. I am also very grateful to R' Tzvi Kushelevsky, another great teacher I was privileged to study under, and learn from his approach to understanding Gemara.

To my dear wife. It is not only during the two years in which it took me to write this book that she selflessly sacrificed a tremendous amount. She enables me to put in the hours required to learn. Since the beginning of our marriage, her sole priority has been to help me learn as much as I can, no matter the difficulty she incurs. She delights in the joy I find in my Torah learning and that joy spurs me on. For that I am forever indebted to her!

I must give gratitude to my parents, for more than just their financial support, but their continuous encouragement to continue learning and spreading Torah. Their example has instilled in me the value of giving to others, which was the impetus for this book, which serves as a tool for people to learn in-depth.

Finally, the greatest thanks I owe is to HaKadosh Baruch Hu. Day after day I saw marvelous *siyatta deShmaya* in writing this book, from a sudden difficulty arising, to a person asking me a new question that brought about a new topic to explore. HaKadosh Baruch Hu gave me the merit to sit and learn day and night, as well as special *menuchas hanefesh* while compiling this work.

Joe Douer

Tishrei 5782

Introduction to Muktzeh

What is *muktzeh* and why did Chazal institute it?

Muktzeh literally means "set aside." It is the phrase used by Chazal to refer to items they forbade moving on Shabbos. It is common knowledge that the prohibition of *muktzeh* is rabbinic. While both *Rambam*[1] and *Shulchan Aruch pasken* as such, the source for this is not so clear. The clearest indication that we find is where the Gemara[2] brings that *muktzeh* was introduced as a safeguard to protect people from carrying. Here we see explicitly that *muktzeh* is a rabbinic decree. However, we'll see several reasons why this source is not conclusive.

The Gemara[3] teaches that the prophet Nechemiah instituted *muktzeh*. Originally he forbade all utensils from being moved, even if one needed to use the item. (He made a few exceptions to the rule so that people would have what to use in order to eat the Shabbos meal.[4]) It is evident from the *pesukim*[5] that his impetus was to curb the disdain for Shabbos that was prevalent at the time: Local merchants were coming to try sell goods in Jewish towns on Shabbos, causing a laxity in Shabbos observance. Later on, when Nechemiah saw that the nation had made strides in their adherence to the sanctity of Shabbos, he mitigated the severity of his original decree, allowing various utensils to be moved.

The Gemara[6] records that Dovid HaMelech died on Shabbos. Shlomo went to ask the sages how to handle his corpse. He was worried about potential dogs that may feed from it, but he couldn't carry the corpse on Shabbos because it was *muktzeh*. Dovid HaMelech lived before Nechemiah, yet we see that in his time people already adhered to the rules

1. *Hilchos Shabbos* 24:12.
2. *Shabbos* 124a.
3. Ibid. 123a.
4. We will elaborate on this in chapter 2.
5. *Nechemiah* 13.
6. *Shabbos* 30b.

of *muktzeh* - so surely Nechemiah couldn't have been the first one to institute it. What, then, is the true source of this halachah?

Prepared Prior to Shabbos

The first Mishnah in *Beitzah* states that an egg laid on the first day of Yom Tov is forbidden to move on the next day of Yom Tov. *Rabbah*[7] explains the reasoning: We learn from the *pasuk* of [8]והיה ביום הששי **והכינו** את אשר יביאו... - "And it was on the sixth day and *they prepared* that which they brought," that the needs of Yom Tov must be prepared before Yom Tov. One cannot prepare on Yom Tov for another day of Yom Tov. But this is already learned from the fact that elsewhere the Torah tells us that we must do *melachah* before Shabbos to prepare for Shabbos, such as cooking, etc. So this extra command of "*v'hechinu*" must be teaching us that even preparations that don't involve *melachah* must be completed before Shabbos. This is called *hachanah d'rabbah.*

Rashi[9] says that *Rabbah*'s understanding of the command of "*v'hechinu*" is consistent with what *Rabbah* holds in *Pesachim,*[10] that *muktzeh* is forbidden *d'Oraisa*. *Rashi* is a lone opinion who holds that even according to the conclusion of the Gemara, *muktzeh* is learned out of the *pasuk* "*v'hechinu,*" resulting in a scriptural source for the prohibition. The other *Rishonim,*[11] however, argue that the Gemara rejects this as a source for *muktzeh* being *d'Oraisa*. Yet they still say that the prohibition the rabbis decreed was based upon the *pasuk* of "*v'hechinu*" (this is known as an *asmachta* in Talmudic literature).

Milchamos[12] writes, לא דברו חכמים במוקצה אלא כדי שיברור ויזמין לעצמו להכין מערב יו"ט ולא יצטרך למחר לחזור ולטרח בסעודה שמא יבא לעשות בה מלאכה או טלטול האסורין לו, **וסמכוהו למקרא והכינו**- "The reason the rabbis enacted *muktzeh* was

---

7. *Beitzah* 2b.

8. *Shemos* 16:5.

9. *Beitzah* 2b, s.v. לטעמיה, and *She'iltos, Emek Shelah* 7:1.

10. 47a.

11. *Rashba.*

12. At the beginning of *Beitzah.*

so people prepare before Shabbos and don't come to do *melachah* on Shabbos; they based their law on the *pasuk* of '*v'hechinu.*'"

What does "*v'hechinu*" teach us about *muktzeh*? It is a *pasuk* that discusses eating, or consumption. The commentators explain that "*v'hechinu*" teaches that something that wasn't previously prepared before Shabbos lacks *hachanah d'rabbah,* and may not be consumed on Shabbos. Based on this rule, Chazal forbade the use of any items that are inherently unprepared. They coined these items *muktzeh,* which means they are "set aside."

Forms of *muktzeh* derived from this *pasuk* are referred to as a *haktzaas hadaas,* the removal of one's intent to use. This pertains to things that don't have a function on Shabbos, such as a corpse, which without an act of preparation prior to Shabbos cannot be used. This category of *muktzeh machmas haktzaah* already applied at the time of Dovid HaMelech, which is why Shlomo was uncertain as how to move the corpse.

This type of *muktzeh,* which is based upon a lack of preparation, does not apply to *keilim* (vessels). Even a *kli shemelachto l'issur,* a vessel that predominantly has forbidden uses, can have permissible functions, e.g., a hammer can be used to break nuts. Since it still has permissible usages, one does not "set it aside" and there is no reason for it to be *muktzeh.* Only once Nechemiah came along and saw that people were lax in Shabbos observance, did he make restrictions even on *keilim* to curb people from carrying them.

Some *Rishonim* go as far as to say that *kli shemelachto l'issur/heter* are not part of *muktzeh* at all; rather, they are a new prohibition known as *gezeiras keilim,* as we will explain shortly. (This is one reason why the Gemara's inference that *muktzeh* was enacted as a safeguard to protect carrying is inconclusive, since it's not referring to the original form of *muktzeh.*) *Maharsha* is the first to make this landmark distinction.[13]

---

13. We will elaborate on this in chapter 1.

The Severity of Consuming Muktzeh

Maharsha[14] explains that the form of *muktzeh* learned from "*v'hechinu,*" namely consuming something that was not prepared, is more stringent than the form of *muktzeh* that limits merely moving items. Firstly, even Rebbe Shimon, who is more lenient regarding *muktzeh* (as we will see later), holds that there is a prohibition to consume *muktzeh* (a component of "*v'hechinu*").

Pnei Yehoshua adds another example of its severity: R' Huna[15] holds regarding consuming *muktzeh* like Rebbe Yehudah, forbidding it, while regarding moving *muktzeh* from place to place without using it, he is lenient like Rebbe Shimon. Since the problem in consuming *muktzeh* is more severe than just moving it, R' Huna is stringent like Rebbe Yehudah.[16]

Tosafos[17] says that *muktzeh* is permitted to move *l'tzorech ochel nefesh,* for the sake of cooking on Yom Tov. *Maharsha* asks how this can be. We see that the entire *Maseches Beitzah* discusses cases of food items that are *muktzeh* on Yom Tov, and we don't seem to permit moving for the sake of eating. On the contrary: We're more stringent with *muktzeh* on Yom Tov than on Shabbos.[18] He distinguishes as we've presented, that *Tosafos* was only discussing moving the *muktzeh l'tzorech ochel nefesh,* which is permitted, whereas the Gemara is always discussing consumption of the *muktzeh,* which is not permitted for the sake of cooking.

Maharsha goes on to prove that using is included in the prohibition to consume *muktzeh.* The Gemara[19] says that one can't rest a pot on top of

---

14. *Beitzah* 33a.

15. 128a.

16. This opinion is obviously in disagreement with *Maharsha,* since *Maharsha* said that even Rebbe Shimon agrees to *muktzeh l'achilah.* Maybe *Maharsha* only holds that *Tosafos* holds that Rebbe Shimon agrees, but not in the opinion of R' Huna.

17. *Beitzah* 8a, s.v. אמר רב יהודה.

18. Final halachah is that we *pasken* like Rebbe Yehudah on Yom Tov and like Rebbe Shimon on Shabbos. Rebbe Yehudah and Rebbe Shimon argue how many categories of vessels are prohibited under *muktzeh.* Rebbe Yehudah forbids many more than Rebbe Shimon.

19. *Shabbos* 33a.

stones (which are set aside for a fireplace). So we see that using *muktzeh* is considered consuming, hence it is forbidden. (This proof teaches that even passive usage is forbidden because the prohibition is not depletion, but using the *muktzeh* item as it's meant to be used.)

Iglei Tal[20] brings another proof that using *muktzeh* is considered consuming. The Gemara[21] says that cooking with *muktzeh* firewood is an *issur d'Oraisa*; If the Gemara entertains that it is an *issur d'Oraisa* it must be referring to the *issur* of consumption, as we established earlier that only this can be considered to be Torah prohibition. Even though one is just using the *muktzeh*, we see explicitly that usage is encompassed in the prohibition of consumption.[22] *Iglei Tal* then brings *Magen Avraham*,[23] who *paskens* like *Tosafos* that one can move *muktzeh* on Yom Tov if it's *l'tzorech ochel nefesh*, but it is forbidden to use *muktzeh*. Therefore *Shulchan Aruch paskens* that one can't burn wood that fell off a tree on Yom Tov. Even in a case where one isn't moving the wood, it's considered "using" the *muktzeh* and therefore belongs to the more stringent category of *muktzeh* which is forbidden and doesn't have the *heter* of *ochel nefesh*.

She'iltos writes that *muktzeh* is forbidden *d'Oraisa*. *Netziv* defends this seemingly difficult-to-understand statement of *She'iltos*: Even though the Gemara says that *muktzeh* is a rabbinic enactment, it is referring to moving *muktzeh*. When *She'iltos* says that *muktzeh* is *d'Oraisa*, he means that using it is *d'Oraisa* - it's forbidden by the *pasuk* of "*v'hechinu*" - and just moving it around was left for the rabbis to restrict. Even though we don't *pasken* like this opinion, it has still shed light on the depth behind why Chazal forbade *muktzeh*. We *pasken* that everything is only rabbinically prohibited, nevertheless there were two stages in the rabbinic decrees forbidding different categories of *muktzeh*.

---

20. *Meleches Tochen* 40.

21. *Pesachim* 47b.

22. Seemingly this proof is inconclusive because burning the firewood is "eating," i.e., depleting the *muktzeh*. We are trying to extend consumption to cases of just using without depleting. צ"ע קצת.

23. 501, section15.

The Source for the Prohibition to Move Muktzeh

If Chazal initially instituted *muktzeh* on items that intrinsically have no use - since one sets them aside and thereby they can't be used - why does that necessitate a restriction in moving the item when not using it? Surely *hachanah d'rabbah* only dictates that to *use* items they must be prepared; why can't you move items from place to place when not intending to use it, rather just relocate it?

Iglei Tal concedes that true *hachanah d'rabbah* doesn't infringe on moving *muktzeh*. However, he suggests that included in the safeguard to protect carrying[24] (stage 2) is the reason why it is forbidden to move *muktzeh* (besides what vessels Nechemiah restricted due to this *gezeirah*). *Pnei Yehoshua*[25] also entertains this idea, but asks: Why is moving *muktzeh* subject to the dispute between Rebbe Yehudah and Rebbe Shimon? If Chazal forbade moving *muktzeh* lest one comes to carry it, even Rebbe Shimon should hold that *muktzeh* is forbidden to move, since Rebbe Shimon argues on what a person sets aside, but doesn't disagree that Chazal imposed such a safeguard against carrying. Due to this question he rejects this approach that moving is forbidden due to the safeguard to protect carrying.

Based upon *Sefer Yerei'im*, we can explain the connection between *muktzeh* and safeguard to protect carrying. *Sefer Yerei'im*[26] goes through each category of *muktzeh* and explains why each contains a concern that you might come to carry it. For example, with a *kli shemelachto l'issur* whose forbidden purpose is clear in the utensil itself, using it will lead one to forget it is Shabbos and subsequently come to carry the utensil. A *kli shemelachto l'heter* doesn't have such a concern; using it won't cause one

---

24. The Gemara teaches that some aspects of *muktzeh* were insitituted to ensure that people don't come to carry items in the public domain. The more items one is allowed to handle, the more likely he might come to carry something into a public domain.

25. 44a.

26. Section 274.

to forgot that today is Shabbos, since the item can be used naturally on Shabbos.

Piskei Riyaz[27] says that all *muktzeh* is forbidden to move because of the safeguard protecting carrying, even for *muktzeh machmas gufo* like trees and stones.[28]

The above logic - that moving isn't necessarily encompassed in one's *haktzaas hadaas* - can be brought out from the following understanding of Rav. Rav holds like Rebbe Yehudah regarding consuming *muktzeh*, forbidding it, yet like Rebbe Shimon regarding moving *muktzeh*, permitting it. *Ran*[29] explains how Rav[30] can make a combination between these two opinions. Rav holds that one sets aside something only from its intended purpose. Meaning, something that is meant to be consumed, the designation is from consuming it. While it is permitted to move it, moving is not included in the designation. An item that isn't used, but just moved around, according to Rav when one sets it aside the designation *does* include moving it because that is the item's intended purpose.

Applying this premise, Rav holds that on Shabbos one can move raw meat that was slaughtered, a reflection of Rebbe Shimon's opinion. This is because while the animal was alive, its intended purpose was to be slaughtered. Therefore the setting aside didn't include not moving it. Likewise, Rav forbids moving a bed which had money placed on it during *bein hashemashos*. Since this bed is only moved (the bed Rav discusses was specifically for storing money), the designation prohibits even moving it, like Rebbe Yehudah's stance.

This principle sheds light on why Rebbe Shimon agrees that something whose sole purpose is for moving, such as *mitah sheyechadah*

---

27. 17:1.

28. Yet he says it was all instituted by Nechemiah. If so, why was Shlomo not able to move the corpse? וצ"ע.

29. *Chidduhsim* on 44b at the bottom of the page.

30. As noted earlier, R' Huna also makes this distinction. R' Huna was a student of Rav. Rav explicitly said that he follows Rebbe Yehudah regarding *muktzeh*, yet R' Huna, who presumably follows the opinion of his teacher, nevertheless *paskened* like Rebbe Shimon. To reconcile this contradiction, the Gemara qualifies that Rav partially follows each opinion and so does R' Huna, his student.

l'maos (a bed designated solely for placing money), is forbidden to move. Since moving is the only active thing you do with it, the "removal of one's intent" includes moving it. Another such example[31] is blood-letting tools, whose use doesn't involve consumption, but movement. Rav following Rebbe Shimon holds that these tools are *muktzeh*. However, Rebbe Yehudah himself holds that even something that is supposed to be consumed is forbidden to be moved. He holds that despite one not *maktzah daas*, removing his intention from moving it, Chazal forbade it nonetheless.

There is a strong inference from the aforementioned *Milchamos*, who says that the reason to forbid moving is "lest one come to do *hotzaah*" - that even this safeguard is in truth forbidden due to "*v'hechinu*." In the context of explaining what Chazal were worried might occur if one doesn't prepare prior to Shabbos, he says "*Tiltul ha'assurin lo* - Forbidden carrying." Evidently that is referring to carrying. Chazal saw in "*v'hechinu*" an instruction to forbid moving *muktzeh* so that one won't come to prepare by carrying, thus violating *hachanah d'rabbah*. This is another source that the transgression to move *muktzeh* is not due to *haktzaas hadaas*.

"Setting Aside" Includes Moving Muktzeh

Other *Rishonim* explicitly argue with this. They hold that one is *maktzah daas* even from moving. The Gemara[32] discusses a woman who makes an oath not to eat from a loaf of bread. Even though the bread is forbidden to her, it doesn't become *muktzeh*; she can still move it. *Rashba* says:[33] בטילטול ודאי שרי דהא לא אקצייה מדעתיה לגמרי ואפילו לטילטול כיון דחזי לאחרים..., meaning that since she only intended to forbid *herself* from eating the loaf - she never intended to set it aside from moving and she can give it to others to eat - therefore it is not *muktzeh*. **It is clear from *Rashba*** that restrictions in moving are based upon *haktzaas hadaas*. Since in this specific scenario, the woman hasn't set the bread aside from moving, it

31. Given by *Ran* in 154b.
32. 46b.
33. 46b.

wouldn't become *muktzeh*. However, in regular scenarios the *haktzaas hadaas* would include moving.

Later on in *Maseches Shabbos* we see the same idea. The Gemara says that Rav *paskens* like Rebbe Yehudah, forbidding consuming *muktzeh*, and like Rebbe Shimon in permitting moving *muktzeh*. The *Rishonim* ask: Rav *paskens*[34] that *karki d'zuzi* (a protective sheet that is used to cover merchandise) is *muktzeh* in accordance with Rebbe Yehudah, as it is considered moving *muktzeh*. So why does Rav forbid it? *Rashba* answers: דבר שעומד לאכילה הוא דשרי לטלטל דדי לו שאוסרו באכילה, meaning that Rav held that when there is a consumable item which you have removed intent to use due to its lack of use, one only removes intent from using it, not from moving it. In that respect Rav holds that there is no *muktzeh l'tiltul* like Rebbe Shimon holds. However, for something whose use is achieved by moving, like the *karki d'zuzi*, Rav agrees that one's *haktzaah* is from the moving of it, since that's the only way that use comes about.

Ritva gives the same distinction between items one can use without moving and those that he moves to enable him to use it.[35] He then adds a cryptic comparison to a *hadas* of the four species. His intention is that the Gemara says a *hadas* is forbidden to smell on Shabbos because it is *muktzeh machmas mitzvah*. This is in contrast to an esrog, which is permissible to smell. Since a *hadas* is intended for smelling, one's *hakatzah* is from its main use; an esrog is meant to be eaten as well as smelled, so the *hakatzah* is only from eating, but he doesn't intend to include smelling in his *hakatzah*. It is clear from both *Rashba* and *Ritva* that the restriction in moving stems from a *haktzaas hadaas*.

Rabbeinu Tam also alludes to this approach. He explains that according to Rebbe Shimon the reason you can carry a *kli shemelachto l'issur tzorech gufo u'mekomo* (*tzorech gufo* is moving to use the item; *tzorech mekomo* is moving the item to vacate its space) is because anything that is potentially fit for a person to use, he doesn't set aside from using it. We see from this explanation that *Rabbeinu Tam* also understands that the

34. 19b.
35. 19b.

reason to forbid moving would be due to a conscious *hakatzah,* just that here you don't actually set it aside.

The Leniency of Graf Shel Re'i

Iglei Tal[36] explains that the practical difference between these two approaches (whether moving *muktzeh* is forbidden due to one's *hakatzah* or due to the safeguard for carrying) is whether it's permitted to move a *graf shel re'i l'tzorech tashmish,* moving a repulsive item to use it. The classic leniency of *graf shel re'i* is when a trough of excrement is bothering you, so you move it to rid the vicinity of its smell. An example of moving a *graf shel re'i* in order to use it is moving the excrement to feed an animal. If the reason is that there is even a *haktzaas hadaas* on moving, then just like Chazal permitted *graf shel re'i* to be moved, they also permitted the *use* of *graf shel re'i.* This should be true since *graf shel re'i* is actually *muktzeh,* yet we find Chazal gave it a special dispensation: Despite it being *muktzeh,* it is permitted to move due to its unpleasantness. The leniency removed the *muktzeh* status, and that includes everything, even using it. One would therefore be allowed to feed his animal from a *graf shel re'i.*[37]

However, if the restriction in moving *muktzeh* is a new enactment, all we can see from the leniency of *graf shel re'i* is that Chazal removed this new restriction. But we don't find that Chazal gave any leniencies regarding the usage of *muktzeh,* so one wouldn't be allowed to feed his animals from a *graf shel re'i.* R' Akiva Eiger permits one to feed his animals from a *graf shel re'i. Iglei Tal* notes this is concurrent with what R' Akiva Eiger holds, that moving *muktzeh* is based on *haktzaas hadaas.*[38]

---

36. Section 205.

37. This point of *Iglei Tal,* that moving and using are interdependent, is a novelty and can be disputed.

38. Which R' Akiva Eiger is he referring to? *Ran* says if one wants to use *muktzeh machmas meyus* (something *muktzeh* due to its repulsiveness) on Shabbos, he is showing that it's no longer repulsive for him, so he would be able to use it. Yet it will be subject to the dispute between Rebbe Shimon and Rebbe Yehudah whether you can remove the *muktzeh* status of an object on Shabbos or not. R' Akiva Eiger argues that even according to Rebbe Shimon it will be still be forbidden to move

Rambam's Novel Reasons for Muktzeh

Rambam[39] gives several other reasons when explaining why Chazal forbade *muktzeh*. He says that just as our speech and the way we walk must be different on Shabbos, so too our carrying must be different. Chazal were also worried that if it were permitted to come in contact with vessels whose purpose is to use for *melachah*, one might actually come to do that *melachah*. Another reason for creating *muktzeh* was that it helps make the "rest of Shabbos" recognizable. Even for the unemployed, whose "resting" may not be so clearly recognized, now their movement will be distinguishable from that of during the week.

Raavad points out that *Rambam* didn't bring down the one reason mentioned by the Gemara - to safeguard carrying! The commentators bring several explanations why *Rambam* needed to find new reasons besides this one. One reason is that carrying doesn't apply on Yom Tov and *Rambam* wanted a reason that also encompassed Yom Tov.[40] *Harerei Kedem*[41] suggests a simple answer. He says that if you look carefully, the Gemara does not actually bring the safeguard to protect carrying in order to explain *muktzeh*; rather, the Gemara explains why *tiltul shel tirchah*

---

l'tzorech mekomo because if you have just decided to move it *tzorech mekomo,* you haven't shown that it isn't disgusting. Since presently it's forbidden to use, so too it's forbidden to move, because moving and using are different enactments. While *Iglei Tal* argues that even if you don't yet in actuality have a leniency of using, you can still move it *l'tzorech mekomo* because if there is a *heter l'tzorech gufo,* included in that is a *heter l'tzorech mekomo*. It's part of the decree that once there is a leniency for *tzorech gufo,* then even for *tzorech mekomo* it applies.

39. 24:13.

40. *Rashba* says there is *muktzeh* on Yom Tov, despite no restrictions of carrying, because of a *lo plug*. (This principle means that Chazal made their ruling uniform and applicable in all scenarios, even when the reasoning for the enactment doesn't seem to apply in a particular instance.)

41. *Markeves HaMishnah* writes that only according to Beis Shammai, who doesn't hold of *mitoch* — that since Chazal waived carrying for the sake of transporting food they also permitted carrying for any purpose, did Chazal need to enact to uphold the prohibition of carrying on Yom Tov. While according to Beis Hillel, who holds of *mitoch,* all forms of carrying are *mutar*. This doesn't fit with this answer that justifies *Rambam*.

(burdensome moving) is forbidden,[42] e.g., for heavy items. Unlike the other *Rishonim, Rambam* learned the Gemara this way. Therefore he is correct in not mentioning carrying as a reason for the enactment of *muktzeh.* (This suggestion is another reason why the Gemara doesn't present a difficulty for those *Rishonim* who learn that *muktzeh* is *d'Oraisa,* as the Gemara is not actually discussing *muktzeh.*)

Summary

We follow the vast majority of the *Rishonim,* who *pasken* that *muktzeh* is *d'rabbanan.* However, Chazal based *muktzeh* on the *pasuk* of "*v'hechinu,*" which teaches us that items must be "prepared" before Shabbos if they are to be used on Shabbos. *Muktzeh* by definition means that the item was "set aside," i.e., not ready for use on Shabbos. The context of the *pasuk* is regarding eating. From this and based upon several proofs from the Gemara, the *Acharonim* established two categories of *muktzeh*: eating/consumption/using and moving. The former category is more stringent; some *Rishonim* learn that it is even *d'Oraisa.* Some learn that the reason for the latter category is a separate safeguard to protect the *melachah* of carrying, while many *Rishonim* hold that even in one's *haktzaas hadaas* he sets aside the item from moving it.

Part 2

Keilim: Gezeiras Tiltul or Issur Muktzeh?

Until now we've discussed whether the reason one can't move *muktzeh machmas gufo,* an article that is not a vessel and so is in-

42. From the mishnah in on 124, we learn that even items that are not *muktzeh* have restrictions of whether one can move them or not. Chazal didn't want one to exert himself too much on Shabbos without a justified reason.

trinsically *muktzeh* due to its lack of usage, and similar types of *muktzeh*: Is it because Chazal created a safeguard in order to protect carrying, or because of *haktzaas hadaas*? There is a similar debate regarding *kli shemelachto l'issur/heter*, both vessels whose primary or secondary use is for a *melachah* but can be used for permissible functions. The two disputes are not conditional upon each other. We mentioned earlier that the *Rishonim* differ in their understanding of *kli shemelachto l'issur/heter*. *Ran*, *Ritva*, and *Meiri* all explicitly say that *kli shemelachto l'issur/heter* doesn't belong to the regular *muktzeh* that existed before Nechemiah. *Ritva* says that people were lax in carrying, so Nechemiah curbed it by forbidding *kli shemelachto l'issur/heter*. He asks why there are leniencies to move utensils; surely there is still a worry that one will come to carry them? He explains that the same way certain utensils were not subject to any restrictions because it's impossible to spend Shabbos without them, similarly, despite the worry, Chazal permitted what necessity dictated.

According to this approach, even Rebbe Shimon should agree that *kli shemelachto l'issur/heter* is *muktzeh* since it's not relevant to his dispute with Rebbe Yehudah about when a person is and isn't *maktzah daas* (and there shouldn't even be any designation, since these are utensils that are used on Shabbos). Rather, it is a safeguard that Chazal instituted that limits their movement. *Shulchan Aruch paskens* that *muktzeh* does apply to *kli shemelachto l'issur/heter*, despite following Rebbe Shimon.

Tosafos Rid leads the opposition, holding that everything belongs to one principle of *muktzeh* based on *haktzaas hadaas*. The restrictions of *kli shemelachto l'issur/heter* are only according to Rebbe Yehudah. Rebbe Shimon holds that one can move a *kli shemelachto l'issur*, even *m'chamah l'tzel* (literally, "from sun to shade," moving the item for its protection). He must understand that it's possible to have *haktzaas hadaas* on certain uses - otherwise how would he explain why for certain needs the moving of these vessels are permitted, while for others moving is not permitted?

Meiri uses the phrase *l'tzorech Shabbos* when explaining the different leniencies one can use to move utensils, i.e., when it's for the sake of Shabbos, a utensil can be moved. This might aid in understanding *Tosafos Rid*. The conventional explanation according to *Tosafos Rid* is a person thinks not to move these items for numerous uses and thinks to move for other uses. Now we can explain that he only needs one thought and that alone explains what uses are forbidden and what uses are permitted. Merely deciding not to use an object for things that are unrelated to Shabbos results in all the limitations of not moving *tzorech gufo u'mekomo* and *m'chamah l'tzel*. E.g. deciding not to use a pen for non-Shabbos purposes causes it to be *muktzeh*, but one can still use it as a stick because that use is a Shabbos use and so was not excluded in his mind.

Tosafos Rid holds that all types of *muktzeh*, with the exception of *muktzeh machmas chisaron kis* (items that are set aside due to their high value and fragility), have leniencies of *tzorech gufo u'mekomo*. This is a lone opinion and can only be understood concurrent with what we've just presented. Namely, that if we find leniencies by *kli shemelachto l'issur/heter*, why shouldn't they apply elsewhere, since all categories of *muktzeh* are subject to the same principle?[43]

(It's interesting to note that the indication throughout *Mishnah Berurah* [especially the beginning of *siman* 308] is that all types of *muktzeh* are based on *haktzaas hadaas*, yet we don't *pasken* like *Tosafos Rid*.)

43. The *chiddush* of *Aruch HaShulchan* could fit well with *Tosafos Rid*. He says that before Nechemiah, *muktzeh* already applied to *keilim*, yet it had the leniencies of *tzorech gufo u'mekomo*. Since there was a breakdown in the observance of Shabbos, Nechemiah "upgraded" the severity of the *issur* and forbid completely all *keilim*, until the situation improved when he restored the leniencies back to what they were. In terms of people's *haktzaas hadaas*, nothing changed over the years. Originally, when they first made *muktzeh*, they modeled it based upon *haktzaas hadaas* and everything was included, even utensils (however, *Tosafos Rid* doesn't say anything about this point). In the next chapter this point will be elaborated.

Chapter 1

כלי שמלאכתו לאיסור

Utensil of Forbidden Usage

Questions

1. Reuven placed an electric fan in the sukkah for extra comfort. Can he bring it inside if it suddenly starts to rain?
2. Can Shimon move a cookbook or store catalogue?
3. Can Levi put birthday candles on his daughter's birthday cake?
4. The Cohens' nonreligious guest arrived on Shabbos with his wallet in his coat pocket. Can Mr. Cohen offer to take hang his coat for him?
5. An electric blender is blocking the way of the extra plates that Mrs. Schwartz needs for the guests. Can she move it?

It is commonly known that a *kli shemelachto l'issur* is permitted to be moved *l'tzorech gufo/mekomo,* to use it or to vacate the area it is occupying, but it cannot be moved to protect it, known as *m'chamah l'tzel.* A *kli shemelachto l'heter,* however, can be moved even *m'chamah l'tzel.* What is less known is what is what defines each category.

First, why is a *kli shemelachto l'issur muktzeh*? Surely it can still have functions on Shabbos. And does Rebbe Shimon, who generally doesn't hold of *muktzeh,* agree to that type of *muktzeh* is prohibited?

How Far Back?

During the times of Nechemiah, people were lax in their observance of Shabbos and several safeguards were enacted to protect Shabbos observance. Although most of the original restrictions were eventually removed, some remained. One was to limit the freedom of carrying a *kli shemelachto l'issur*. Abaye and Rava[1] argue to what extent the freedom was limited. Abaye holds that only *l'tzorech gufo* was permitted to be carried, while Rava, whom we *pasken* like, holds that *tzorech gufo u'mekomo* were permitted, while *m'chamah l'tzel,* moving to protect the *kli,* was forbidden.

It's certainly clear that these safeguards were made during the times of Nechemiah, yet we find an earlier source of *muktzeh* that traces back to Shlomo HaMelech. The Gemara[2] states that Shlomo HaMelech was told not to directly move a corpse, but to rely on the leniency of putting a loaf of bread on it to permit its removal. This clearly indicates that they already kept a form of *muktzeh* during that time.

Two Stages of Muktzeh

In order to explain these two early appearances of *muktzeh,* many commentators write that there were two stages in the evolution of *muktzeh.* The first enactment can be dated as far back as Moshe Rabbeinu,[3] which includes objects that themselves have no use on Shabbos and one is *maktzah daas* (removes his intent) from them entirely i.e., *muktzeh machmas gufo, muktzeh machmas chisaron kis*. This is referred to as *muktzeh machmas haktzaah*. Due to their inherent lack of use, one totally removes his mind from the item - hence Shlomo treated the corpse as *muktzeh*.

Vessels were never included in this safeguard because they have a function on Shabbos. Even if a vessel's typical use is forbidden on Shabbos, there are usually other permissible uses on Shabbos. For example, a ham-

1. *Shabbos* 123b.
2. 30b.
3. *Mishbetzos Zahav* 430:1.

mer - besides being used for nails, it can crack open nuts. Therefore, it isn't *muktzeh* due to a removal of intent, but rather due to the disrespect for Shabbos that was so commonplace that the rabbis felt it necessary to limit the movement of such vessels. The commentators refer to this second stage as *gezeiras keilim*.

Therefore Rebbe Shimon could disagree with *muktzeh* (stage 1) while still holding of *gezeiras keilim* (stage 2). This is explicit in *Ritva*: והא ודאי איתא אליבא דר״ש...דכלים שמלאכתו לאיסור לא מדין מוקצה - נגעו בהם אלא טלטול הוא שאסרו גזירה משום הוצאה - "Vessels which are used for *issur* are forbidden even according to Rebbe Shimon, since they are not forbidden because of *muktzeh*, but rather to safeguard the *melachah* of carrying." *Raavad,*[4] *Meiri Tosafos*, and *Shitah LaRan*[5] all say that Rebbe Shimon agrees to *kli shemelachto l'issur* being forbidden due to *gezeiras keilim*. *Rabbeinu Tam*[6] concurs that Rebbe Shimon agrees to *kli shemelachto l'issur*. However, he doesn't explain like we have presented, that there are two distinct categories of *muktzeh*, but rather that *kli shemelachto l'issur* is a manifestation of regular *muktzeh* that one sets aside. *Rabbeinu Tam* just holds that Rebbe Shimon agrees that one sets aside *kli shemelachto l'issur*.

Chayei Adam[7] explains that it's possible to have *haktzaah l'chatza'in*, to partially set aside an item. For example, for the item is *muktzeh* for usages he doesn't intend to use the item for, whereas for other usages that he does intend to use it for, it isn't *muktzeh*. According to *Rabbeinu Tam*, both Rebbe Shimon and Rebbe Yehudah understand that one sets aside a *kli shemelachto l'issur* for its forbidden usages, but not for what it *can* be used for. *Tosafos Rid*[8] argues, explicitly saying that Rebbe Shimon argues even on a *kli shemelachto l'issur*, and that one can move any *kli shemelachto l'issur* - even *m'chamah l'tzel*.

Shulchan Aruch[9] *paskens* like most *Rishonim* that *kli shemelachto l'issur*

---

4. Additions on *Baal HaMeor* at the beginning of *Beitzah*.
5. 36a.
6. *Sefer HaYashar*, sections 1, 2.
7. Section 66.
8. 123b.
9. 308:3.

is only permitted to be moved *l'tzorech gufo u'mekomo* and the simple implication of *Mishnah Berurah*[10] is like *Chayei Adam*, that the reason why it is forbidden to move when it is not *l'tzorech gufo u'mekomo* is due to *haktzaas hadaas* and not because of *gezeiras keilim*.

One potential practical difference between the two reasons forbidding *kli shemelachto l'issur* is the status of a non-religious person's item. He intends on making use of his *muktzeh* on Shabbos, and therefore hasn't set it aside at all. If the reasoning is an enactment of Chazal, his intended usage with these *muktzeh* items is irrelevant, but if the reasoning is based on removal of one's intent, he hasn't set it aside, as mentioned. If a non-religious Jew came to your house and has his phone or wallet in his coat pocket, it might be dependent upon this question whether you can offer to take his coat for him or not (question #4).[11]

Rashi's Take on Kli Shemelachto L'Issur

Rashi has a unique opinion about *kli shemelachto l'issur*. The Mishnah[12] writes that all *keilim* may be moved, with two exceptions. *Rashi* comments[13] that the Mishnah is according to Rebbe Shimon, the implication being that Rebbe Yehudah would forbid all of the *keilim* to be moved, even *l'tzorech gufo u'mekomo*. The Gemara says[14] that according to Rebbe Yehudah, *chatzosros* (trumpets) are *muktzeh*, while according to Rebbe Shimon they are not. *Rashi* explains: ר' שמעון דלית ליה מוקצה - "It fits with Rebbe Shimon, who doesn't hold of *muktzeh*." How do these two comments of *Rashi* fit together? It seems to be a contradiction: If Rebbe Shimon doesn't hold of *kli shemelachto l'issur*, how can the Mishnah listing the leniencies of *kli shemelachto l'issur* fit only according to him?

---

10. 308:20.

11. R' Yitzchak Berkovits used this logic in combination with other leniencies to permit taking the coat with the wallet in the pocket.

12. 123b.

13. 157a, s.v. כל הכלים.

14. 35b.

One approach is that *Rashi* distinguishes between when the *kli* has no permitted purposes at all, and when its main function is *issur* but also has some function of *heter*. A *kli* which has no function of *heter* is stricter. It belongs to regular *muktzeh* of *haktzaas hadaas,* not *gezeiras keilim,* and this only Rebbe Yehudah holds of. Whereas a *kli shemelachto l'issur* which has some permissible uses is part of *gezeiras keilim* and hence even Rebbe Shimon would agree that it is permitted only *l'tzorech gufo u'mekomo*. Obviously after the safeguards that a *kli shemelachto l'issur* has limitations of *l'tzorech gufo u'mekomo,* it'll also limit a *kli* that has no usage to only be moved *l'tzorech gufo u'mekomo*. *Chatzosros* belong to the first category, hence they are only permissible according to Rebbe Shimon, and when *Rashi* writes דלית ליה מוקצה, he is referring to the original type of *muktzeh,* which Rebbe Shimon doesn't hold of *haktzaas hadaas*.

It follows that the Mishnah that states: "*Kol hakeilim netilin b'Shabbos* - All vessels can be moved on Shabbos" is referring even to a *kli* which has no permitted purpose and the two *keilim* listed are the only exceptions to the rule. *Rashi* is correct that this is not according to Rebbe Yehudah, since Rebbe Yehudah forbids entirely any *kli shemelachto l'issur* that doesn't have any permitted uses. Therefore when *Rashi*[15] describes *kli ki'oi,* a weaver's basket, which is not *muktzeh* as "and it isn't *melachto l'issur,*" he means it is not of the type that has no permitted uses but still is certainly a *kli shemelachto l'issur*.

Kli Shemelachto L'Issur with No Permissable Usage

One of the crucial questions of this topic is whether utensils which have no permissible usage are defined as *kli shemelachto l'issur* and therefore have the *heter* of *tzorech gufo/mekomo* or not. Nowadays, many electrical appliances have such a status, having no permissible usage, so it's important to clarify whether they have the leniencies of *kli shemelachto l'issur* or not. According to *Rashi,* such a *kli* would be treated no differently than a regular *kli shemelachto l'issur,* since we *pasken* like Rebbe Shimon.

15. 113a.

(However, on Yom Tov we *pasken* like Rebbe Yehudah, so one has to be careful.) R' Akiva Eiger infers from *Tosafos* that the only reason the *chatzosros* are not *muktzeh* according to Rebbe Shimon is because they are "*chazi me'at*" - can still be used for something. If they wouldn't be fit for anything, then even according to Rebbe Shimon they would be *muktzeh*.

Baal HaMeor's Reasoning

Baal HaMeor agrees that *chatzosros* are *muktzeh*, but for a different reason. He says the *heter* of *tzorech mekomo* is conditional upon there being a *heter* of *tzorech gufo*. Since in reality these *keilim* don't have any usage of *tzorech gufo*, due to their total lack of alternative use, they will therefore also be forbidden *tzorech mekomo*. The *Rishonim* have great difficulty with *Baal HaMeor*'s reasoning. *Rashba*[16] proves from Nechemiah that these two *heterim* are not conditional upon each other, and furthermore the Gemara says[17] explicitly that the *chatzosros* are permitted to be moved according to Rebbe Shimon, despite them having no permissible use. (Presumably the Gemara means they are permitted to move out of one's way i.e., *tzorech mekomo*, and not that one is moving it *tzorech gufo*, because there is no use for it. We see the two leniencies are not conditional one upon each other.) R' Wosner[18] explains that the dispute is *l'shitasam*.

We saw earlier that *Baal HaMeor* learns that a *kli shemelachto l'issur* is a regular manifestation of *haktzaas hadaas*, and therefore one is not *maktzah daas* from the permitted uses. Therefore, if there is no practical usage, one sets it aside completely. Once it's *muktzeh*, *tzorech mekomo* will also be forbidden, since it's a *heter* which is dependent upon *tzorech gufo*. However, *Rashba* learns that *kli shemelachto l'issur* is part of *gezeiras keilim*. A utensil never gets an identity as *muktzeh machmas daas*, but it is identified as a *kli shemelachto l'issur*, and even if you have no permissible usage you can still move it *tzorech mekomo*.

---

16. 154b.

17. 36a.

18. *Shevet HaLevi*, vol. 10, *siman* 59.

If we follow the *Rishonim* who have disproven *Baal HaMeor*'s principle, then the only reason to be stringent with electrical appliances which have no permissible use is based on R' Akiva Eiger's inference in *Tosafos*. However, perhaps we can refute even this. If one looks inside *Sefer HaYashar*, he says that the permissible usage of the *chatzosros* is that one can crack nuts with them! So even if we follow the stringent opinion which forbids movement when there are no permissible uses, any obscure usage that can be taken out of this *kli* will suffice to say that it has a permissible use - even if it is an absurd potential use.

What Is a Candle?

R' Yaakov Emden[19] *paskens* that a candle, which should be a *kli shemelachto l'issur*, is *muktzeh machmas gufo* since it has no permissible usages. So too there are those who want to learn that every *kli shemelachto l'issur*, even though it is a *kli*, if it has no function, it is *muktzeh machmas gufo*. However, I don't think we can conclude from his example to compare it to all types of *kli shemelachto l'issur*. He explains that a candle כיון דלא חזו למידי כיון, דאכילה ולשום תשמיש אינו ראוי - "is not fit for anything, for eating or any use it's unfit." Rather R' Emden's intention is that even during the week a candle is not considered to have an identity as a utensil. You never really use it as a utensil, so even during the week it won't have a status of a *kli*. This is in contrast to our *keilim*, which have proper usages during the week, but on Shabbos there is no permissible use and they would still be classified as a *kli* and therefore as a *kli shemelachto l'issur*.

Practically, both *Mishnah Berurah*[20] and *Magen Avraham*[21] argue with R' Emden's opinion. They both hold that candle is a *kli shemelachto l'issur*. We find that *Tosafos*[22] classifies a wick as a *kli shemelachto l'issur*. Surely it has no permissible function, yet *Tosafos* still classifies it as a *kli shemelachto l'issur*. We have no proof that an item whose sole purpose is

19. *Mor U'Ketziah, siman* 308.
20. 308:34.
21. 308:18.
22. 47a.

issur won't have the regular *heterim* of *l'tzorech gufo u'mekomo*, and if one needs to move an electric blender there are opinions which would permit so (question #5).

Are Shabbos Candles Muktzeh?

The Gemara[23] discusses two cases which differ slightly to the regular *kli shemelachto l'issur*: a candle and a *mitah sheyechadah l'maos*, a bed that was designated for storing money (one places money on it). Rebbe Yehudah (the *Amora*) holds one can move a candle *l'tzorech gufo u'mekomo*. The *Rishonim*[24] ask: Doesn't Rebbe Yehudah hold that one can't move a *kli shemelachto l'issur* at all? *Ramban* gives a famous answer: The Shabbos candles are not *muktzeh* because they are designated to beautify the Shabbos. The idea is that they become part of the essential Shabbos items and Chazal never included such items in the prohibition of *muktzeh*. *Rashba* is *mechadesh* a new idea. He says a candle is different because שהוא אינו משמש מלאכת איסור - "it doesn't aid in the performance of a forbidden task." *Ramban* quotes this answer as follows: "*V'ein osin melachah* - It doesn't do *melachah*," meaning that the candle just sits and supports the wick/flame - it isn't actively doing *melachah* itself. *Kli shemelachto l'issur* are tools that you do actual *melachah* with.

The Gemara says that according to Rebbe Yehudah, when one has placed money on a bed that has been designated to hold money, the bed becomes totally *muktzeh*. *Tosafos* explains that since you have designated it to only serve a forbidden function, it loses its status as a *kli shemelachto l'issur* and thus can't be moved at all.[25] According to Rebbe Shimon it still

---

23. 44a.

24. Found in the beginning of *Perek Kol HaKeilim* 124a.

25. In chapter 14, part 2, we will explain that a patch pocket on a shirt, which is supporting *muktzeh*, renders the shirt a *bosis* to the *muktzeh* item. If one always stores his money in his shirt pocket, that pocket is "designated for *muktzeh*," but it still doesn't render the shirt *muktzeh*. The reason is simple: Since the shirt is still functional for its main purpose (wearing it), the fact that a part of it is designated for *muktzeh* doesn't change its status. The halachah we are learning above is with cases like the bed: Where one has designated something solely as *muktzeh* and for

retains its identity as a *kli shemelachto l'issur* since it *can* be used for permissible uses. *Rif* doesn't mention this case, which implies that he held according to Rebbe Shimon, that the bed is not *muktzeh* at all. From the apparent lack of qualification in *Shulchan Aruch,*[26] *Gra* points out that it's even permitted to move the bed *m'chamah l'tzel*. Both *Levush* and R' Akiva Eiger explain that there is a similarity between a candle and this bed: With both of them, *melachah* isn't done with them, rather the *issur* sits on them. The opinions[27] that hold that a candle is not *kli shemelachto l'issur* will also hold that the bed is not *muktzeh*. (A practical example nowadays of something similar to such a bed is a laptop case. It's designated solely to contain the *muktzeh*. According to Rebbe Yehudah, even when the laptop is not inside it, the case is *muktzeh machmas chisaron kis*).

Beis Meir argues on the comparison. He differentiates that *Rashba* only said this idea regarding a candle, where the body of the candle is not in direct contact with the *issur* (the candle supports the wick which directly holds the flame). This is in contrast to the bed, which is in direct contact with the money. However, *Tosefes Shabbos* quotes an explicit *Rashba*: מטה שייחד למעות והניח עליה פעם אחת בחול, לא מקרי כשמל״א, כיון שאין המטה עושה שום מלאכה רק מעשה עץ בעלמא - "a bed that was designated for money and one placed on it during a weekday, the bed is not considered *kli shemelachto l'issur*, since the bed doesn't perform any *melachah*; it's just a piece of wood." We see explicitly that even when the utensil is directly assisting the *melachah*, as long as it itself isn't performing the *issur*, it's treated as a *kli shemelachto l'heter*.

Examples of "Assisting Issur"

The above discussion is very relevant nowadays. An empty purse is a classic example. It doesn't actively do *melachah*, yet it's only used for money. Similarly, a cookbook itself doesn't do any *melachah*, but is used for *melachah* - you check the recipe and cook. Many *poskim* treat these objects

---

no other function, the bed is no longer used for sleeping on.

26. 310:7.

27. Found in *siman* 279.

as *kli shemelachto l'issur*, however, according to *Rashba*, there would be grounds to be lenient and treat them as a *kli shemelachto l'heter*.

The Gemara discusses a *sakina deshkavsa*,[28] a meat knife used to cut raw meat. R' Shlomo Zalman Auerbach asks: Surely it's a *kli shemelachto l'heter* if its use is only for chopping permissible meats? According to the opinions that a *kli shemelachto l'heter* can't be *muktzeh machmas chisaron kis*,[29] how can the Gemara classify it as *muktzeh machmas chisaron kis*? He innovates that since this knife was used for cutting meat to sell, and selling is forbidden, it follows that the knife is assisting *issur* and can be classified as a *kli shemelachto l'issur*. This is again the same manifestation of such a type of *kli*. It itself doesn't do *melachah*, but it's used to facilitate something which is forbidden.

There is support to R' Shlomo Zalman Auerbach from *Piskei Riyaz*, who groups *tamri deiska*, dates which are set aside for selling, with other *kli shemelachto l'issur*. What *melachah* can dates do? It must be that since they are meant to do business with, they assist *issur* and can also be grouped as *kli shemelachto l'issur*. *Shulchan Aruch paskens* that a certain ladder[30] is *muktzeh*. Some explain that the reason is because it is used to tile or fix the roof, which is a forbidden activity. Since the ladder assists a forbidden function, it itself becomes *muktzeh*.

All the aforementioned cases resemble the bed of money and the candle, whereby the item is only assisting *issur*. Presumably *Rashba*, who holds that something which is assisting *issur* is not *muktzeh*, would be lenient here too. However, even though R' Akiva Eiger entertained regarding the bed of money that *Shulchan Aruch* holds like *Rashba*, in Siman 279 he says that only regarding asking a non-Jew can we rely on *Rashba*, i.e., to ask a non-Jew to move a candle once it's been extinguished. *Mishnah Berurah*[31] also writes clearly that a candle is a *kli shemelachto l'issur*, hence

---

28. From 123b.

29. We will elaborate on this in the next chapter. The basic idea is: If the only use of the item which one is careful about is permissible, we can't claim there is any designation.

30. 308:19 — a ladder leaned against the house in order to ascend to the attic.

31. 179:8.

it is forbidden *m'chamah l'tzel*. So, besides the problem involved in reading an Argos catalogue[32] and cookbook (question #2), one shouldn't move them *m'chamah l'tzel*.[33] Other examples of such *keilim* are swimsuits,[34] motorcycle helmets, gardening trousers, paint overalls, etc. Since one uses them for a task which is forbidden, they have a status of *kli shemelachto l'issur*!

Another type of *kli* which is subject to dispute whether it's grouped in *kli shemelachto l'issur* are *keilim* whose usage comes about via *issur* but don't involve one doing an *issur* to receive its benefit. Electrical items such as fans and clocks don't receive any *melachah* in order to provide benefit. Providing air and telling the time are not *melachos* and they are the function of these *keilim*, yet they only do their job because there is electricity running through them, and plugging them in and switching them on is a *melachah*. Do we say that since the ultimate functions of these items do not involve *melachos*, they are not *kli shemelachto l'issur*, or since they can only function if plugged in and their function is dependent on *issur* they will be treated as *kli shemelachto l'issur*?[35] R' Moshe Feinstein[36] writes re-

---

32. There is an *issur d'rabbanan* known as *Shitrei Hediyotos*, which forbids reading business and commerce material on Shabbos.

33. *Taz* (307:13) says that anything one can't read on Shabbos is *muktzeh*.

34. *Orchos Shabbos* (ch. 19, insight 103) notes that only due to the *minhag* not to immerse oneself in cold water do we not swim in swimming pools on Shabbos. Therefore only due to a *minhag* would swimsuits be a *kli shemelachto l'issur*. *Pri Megadim* discusses whether an item becomes a *kli shemelachto l'issur* due to a *minhag*. I found a *Levush Mordechai* that explains that since *Rema* only forbids sweeping with a broom due to a *minhag*, a broom is not a *kli shemelachto l'issur*. Mori V'Rabi R' Ariav Ozer said whether something which is forbidden only due to a *minhag* is *muktzeh* or not could depend on the reason for *kli shemelachto l'issur*. If it is based on *haktzaas hadaas*, it should be irrelevant why it is not used. If it is not used, one disassociates himself from it. While if *kli shemelachto l'issur* is based on *gezeiras keilim*, potentially Chazal only included *keilim* which are forbidden due to halachah as opposed to *minhag*.

35. There is a third possibility: what *Chut Shani* holds. Electrical items when switched on should be compared to a candle while burning, which Rebbe Shimon holds is a *bosis* to the flame and so is *muktzeh machmas gufo*. He claims similarly that the electric current running through the appliance makes it a *bosis* to the flame.

36. *Iggros Moshe* 3:49.

garding to a fan, שאין עצם מלאכתן ענין איסור כיון דנעשו באיסור אז אסור ככשמל"א - "Since they are used via *issur*, they are *kli shemelachto l'issur*." However, if you treat it as a *kli shemelachto l'issur*, then surely even a watch should be a *kli shemelachto l'issur* since it is also only functioning due to an electric battery.

One can make a distinction between electrical appliances whereby the regular usage of them involves constantly switching them on and off (e.g., a fan) and an appliance that you switch on once and let the electricity run (e.g., clock/watch, fridge). In the latter you don't play with or use the electric part of the object; you relate to a fridge as a non-melting ice box. In the former category, part of the usage of the appliance is to constantly change the electric current. There is a direct connection between the function of the appliance and the electricity; you switch a fan on and then off, changing the strength, etc. R' Shlomo Zalman Auerbach[37] is lenient by all electric items once plugged in and switched on. He says now they are *kli shemelachto l'heter*. Before they are turned on, he says their status is conditional upon his famous dispute with *Chazon Ish*. According to *Chazon Ish*'s ruling that turning electricity on is a *melachah d'Oraisa*, currently these electric items are meant to do *melachah* with and are *kli shemelachto l'issur*, but according to R' Shlomo Zalman's leniency that electricity is not a *melachah d'Oraisa*, they are all *kli heter*.[38] If one wants to bring a fan inside the house because it is getting ruined, there is room to be lenient, treating it as a *kli shemelachto l'heter* (question #1).

What Defines a Kli?

Arguably the most unclear area surrounding *muktzeh* and specifically affecting *kli shemelachto l'issur* is what defines something as a *kli*. We clearly

---

37. *Sefer Maadanei Shlomo*, p. 85.

38. However, he does recommend not to move these items because it will lead to people being lenient in *muktzeh*; they won't distinguish between electric items that have a red-hot filament, which he agrees are *muktzeh*, and appliances that don't. Even though R' Shlomo Zalman Auerbach agrees there is an *issur d'rabbanan* using electrical appliances, *muktzeh machmas issur d'rabbanan* is not *muktzeh*. We will

see from the Gemara[39] that the criteria to define a *kli* regarding *muktzeh* is not the same criteria as for *hilchos tumah*. So what is the criteria for a muktzeh vessel? The Gemara that sheds the light on this is regarding a *bikaas* (wood-chopping block). The Gemara says that it is *muktzeh* because it doesn't have a *toras kli* - "form of a *kli*." There are *poskim*[40] who learn that any object that gets depleted while in usage is not a *kli*. A *kli* needs to exist after being used;[41] accordingly, they hold that makeup, paint, poison, toothpaste, matchsticks, a bar of soap, etc., are all *muktzeh machmas gufo* since they are not *keilim*. The difficulty in this approach is that we saw earlier that *Mishnah Berurah* and *Magen Avraham* both held that a candle is a *kli* even though its usage is via consumption. How are they going to distinguish between a candle and other items that get depleted? Perhaps they understand that since a candle has a distinguishable structure, it upgrades it to a *kli*, so matchsticks would be the same.

A more simple understanding of the disadvantage of the wood-chopping block is that it's not manufactured; it is not an inherent object that is specialized for any purpose. In contrast to something that has undergone a significant process of preparation, it is visible that it is a utensil and that is coming to serve the consumer's needs, even if that service were an expendable one. A candle fits this description.[42] Matches, soap, etc., would also be a regular *kli*, and due to its use for *issur* it is a *kli shemelachto l'issur*. Therefore, if one is serving a birthday cake on Shabbos and would like to put candles on it (question #3),[43] even though it will look strange to have candles on Shabbos, it is permitted because *kli shemelachto*

---

elaborate on this idea in chapter 14.

39. The end of 123a.

40. *Shamor V'Zachor* and *Chut Shani*.

41. They bring proof from the *Mor U'Ketziah* we quoted earlier that holds that a candle is *muktzeh*. However, he doesn't say this explicitly and according to the way we explained above there is no proof.

42. I saw afterward that *Orchos Shabbos* (ch. 19, insight 25) says this same idea.

43. The source for putting candles on a birthday cake stems from Greek worshipers of the sun and moon. It is not a Jewish custom and should not be advocated (*Rema* in *Yoreh Dei'ah* 275). Birthday cakes are not subject to this problem of practicing a non-Jewish practice that has no meaning.

l'issur is permitted when it is *l'tzorech gufo.* Since paint doesn't have a form, it therefore won't be classified as a *kli* and a can of paint will be *muktzeh machmas gufo* (it's a *bosis* to the paint). R' Shlomo Zalman Auerbach is lenient even with paint, but does recommend ideally to be stringent to accommodate those who hold they are *muktzeh machmas gufo.*

Summary

A *kli shemelachto l'issur* often can have permissible usages on Shabbos. Therefore it is intrinsically different than other categories of *muktzeh* that one sets aside entirely from using. Many explain that it was a latter enactment that restricted the movement of *keilim* creating this category of *kli shemelachto l'issur,* and hence it has many leniencies, such as *tzorech gufo u'mekomo,* which we do not find by other groups of *muktzeh.* Others explain that the reason why *kli shemelachto l'issur* is *muktzeh* is no different than other *muktzeh;* it is due to *haktzaas hadaas.* However, for the permissible usages that can be extracted from this *kli,* one doesn't set this object aside.

The *Rishonim* argue whether a *kli* that has no permissible function at all is still treated as a *kli shemelachto l'issur,* or is it relegated to *muktzeh machmas gufo.* There is room to permit moving most such electrical items because even the stringent opinion agrees that an obscure usage is sufficient to be called a function of the *kli.* The consensus of the *poskim* is to treat a *kli* that it itself is not forbidden but is used for forbidden purposes, such as a candle holders, as *kli shemelachto l'issur. Keilim* whose usage comes about via *issur* but the benefit received usage doesn't involve *issur,* such as a fan or a fridge, is subject to a dispute. We gave a rule that it depends if the electricity is an integral part of the usage of the item or not, as with fridges, watches, etc. Despite only functioning due to electricity constantly being supplied, one doesn't "play" with the electricity when using a watch or fridge, so we can disassociate the present usage of *heter* with the *issur* that supplies the function, and thus they can be classified as a *kli shemelachto l'heter.* In contrast, a fan, where one constantly changes the strength of the electricity supplied, is considered a *kli shemelachto l'issur.*

Answers

1. A fan is considered a *kli shemelachto l'issur*, and Reuven shouldn't move to protect it.
2. A cookbook or store catalogue is treated as a *kli shemelachto l'issur*, and therefore can only be moved if Shimon needs its space and has a use for it on Shabbos, but not to protect it from getting damaged.
3. Since placing candles on a cake is a use of candles, Levi can put them on the cake. They are only forbidden, regardless of the reason, to move when alight; if they haven't been lit this Shabbos they are regular *kli shemelachto l'issur*.
4. The guest's coat is not *bosis* according to some opinions. Mr. Cohen can take the coat even if it has *muktzeh* items inside.
5. As long as the blender can have a use on Shabbos, even if it is very obscure, it can be still treated as a *kli shemelachto l'issur* and can be moved if it is in the way.

Appendix: Is Shaatnez Muktzeh?

Shulchan Aruch[44] brings two opinions regarding whether clothing with *shaatnez* in it is *muktzeh* or not. The *poskim* differ in explaining what the lenient opinion holds. Do they hold it is a *kli shemelachto l'heter* or a *kli shemelachto l'issur*? Its main usage, namely wearing, is forbidden.

However, the prohibition that prohibits its use is not caused by Shabbos; even during the week it is forbidden, as a Jew one cannot wear it in its present state. Nothing changes when Shabbos comes in. There are

44. 308:47.

permissible functions that *shaatnez* clothes can have, e.g., one can make a tent with the clothing. These usages existed before Shabbos and are still available on Shabbos,[45] so when Shabbos comes in, since there are no further restrictions that limit its use, there is no further *haktzaas hadaas*. Without any *haktzaas hadaas* (caused by Shabbos), there is no reason for the item to be *muktzeh*. Therefore, there is an argument that *shaatnez* clothing differs from regular *kli issur* and should be classified as a *kli shemelachto l'heter*. This is an important principle that will have further applications - that the only reason an item is designated must be due to a prohibition of Shabbos in order for it to be *muktzeh*.

45. One can make an *ohel* with the clothes in a way that won't involve any *melachah* of *ohel*.

Chapter 2

כלי שמלאכתו להיתר שלא לצורך

Utensil of Permissible Usage For No Reason

Questions

1. People often fidget with cutlery at the Shabbos table. Am I permitted to do so?
2. Can I put my hands in my pockets if there are house keys inside?
3. Can I move posters in the sukkah that have *pesukim* on them?
4. Is it praiseworthy to eat with my hands instead of using cutlery on Shabbos?

When Nechemiah originally decreed the limitations of *muktzeh,* he forbade all *keilim* from being moved, with the exception of a few essential items. Gradually, the original stringencies were relaxed. Rava holds that Chazal permitted a *kli shemelachto l'heter* to be moved *tzorech gufo, tzorech mekomo* and *m'chamah l'tzel. M'chamah l'tzel* literally means "from the sun to the shade," i.e., protecting the *kli* from being damaged by the sun.

The *Rishonim* argue whether this phrase, *m'chamah l'tzel,* is literal or not. If the term were literal, one would be allowed to move a *kli shemelachto l'heter* only for the sake of protection of the item. However, if one wants to move the item for no reason at all, it would not be encompassed in the *heter* of *m'chamah l'tzel.* The *beraisa* says that Nechemiah subsequently permitted moving a *kli shemelachto l'heter shelo l'tzorech.*

Rava explains this to mean *m'chamah l'tzel*. We see that Rava didn't leave the phrase "*shelo l'tzorech*" unexplained, rather he explained it as referring to *m'chamah l'tzel*. So, simply speaking, he isn't permitting its unrestricted movement.

Rambam [1] and *Shulchan Aruch* [2] both understand that *m'chamah l'tzel* is literal. They *pasken* explicitly that one cannot move a *kli shemelachto l'heter* unnecessarily. Based on *Meiri* [3] and *Sefer Meoros*, [4] we can understand why. The underlying principle behind what Chazal permitted was moving that is needed for Shabbos. Moving a *kli shemelachto l'heter* to protect the *kli* can be considered moving it for the sake of Shabbos, since it is possible that one could subsequently need to use that *kli* on Shabbos. If he doesn't save the *kli* now he won't be able to use it later on. In contrast, a *kli shemelachto l'issur* is not given this leniency because the chances of using a *kli shemelachto l'issur* on Shabbos are much slimmer, due to their only permitted use being for not their intended purpose. So it is more removed to view the current moving of the *kli* to protect it as a Shabbos need. [5]

What Is Considered a "Need"?

The Gemara explains that the even after the leniencies were given that allowed one to move *muktzeh* in certain circumstances, the moving of *muktzeh* unnecessarily was still forbidden. One such example brought by the Gemara [6] is that every Shabbos they would replace the bread of the *lechem hapanim*. In order to keep the bread fresh for the duration of the week, they would insert sticks between the loaves of bread, allowing air to travel between them. On Shabbos it was forbidden to place these sticks.

---

1. *Hilchos Shabbos* 25:3.
2. 308:3.
3. 124a.
4. Ibid.
5. *Aruch HaShulchan* permits moving a *kli shemelachto l'issur* even *m'chamah l'tzel*, if one knows that he will need it eventually on Shabbos.
6. *Menachos* 96a.

The Gemara explains the reason being that the gain in placing the sticks on Shabbos, as opposed to waiting until Sunday is so negligible, that the purpose does not justify the moving of the sticks, even if the sticks are a *kli shemelachto l'heter*.

Ritva and *Rashba*[7] ask that even if the gain of placing the sticks is minimal, it still does help the bread to retain its freshness somewhat. So why is this small benefit not enough to permit it? One is moving it for a purpose. They answer: Were *m'chamah l'tzel* to be permitted, so would moving the sticks be permitted because moving the sticks for a small gain is considered *m'chamah l'tzel*. Rather, the Gemara is following the opinion of the one who forbids *m'chamah l'tzel*. We can infer from the way the question is phrased a slightly different understanding as to what should be encompassed in *m'chamah l'tzel*. Just like moving it in order to protect it from the sun is a need, similarly, in order that the bread retains its freshness is also considered a need. However, if you are missing a reason, then is it forbidden.[8]

Shitah LaRan[9] argues that the phrase *m'chamah l'tzel* is not literal, it's just the way of speaking, so one can move the *kli* even without a reason. His proof is from Rava[10] - despite being of the opinion that salted meat is not *muktzeh*, nevertheless he was particular to place a knife on top of meat that he carried so that people would think he was using the leniency of *kikar oh tinok*.[11] If one can't move a *kli shemelachto l'heter* for no reason,

---

7. 124a.

8. They were moving the sticks to use them, yet despite that *Rashba* says the leniency to move them is because it is *tzorech ketzas*. Why is it not a simple manifestation of *tzorech gufo*? It must be that when one is not using a significant aspect of the vessel, it is not considered *tzorech gufo*. This is very *mechudash*, וצ"ע ואכתי.

9. End of ch. 22. (There are indications that this is also *Rashi*'s opinion.)

10. 142b.

11. *Kikar oh tinok* is a leniency given to move *muktzeh* items. If one places a piece of bread on a *muktzeh* item, he can then carry them together. Rava was worried that if he carried the meat without the knife on top, people would mistakenly learn from him to be lax in *muktzeh*, since people mistakenly thought this meat was *muktzeh*. By placing the knife on the meat, Rava's actions didn't lend room for misinterpretation because he was carrying it in a permissible fashion.

how could Rava move the knife? According to his opinion, it is unnecessary to place the knife on top of the meat, and yet Rava still did so. We can therefore deduce that there is no limitation in moving a *kli shemelachto l'heter.*[12]

Cutlery and Crockery

We mentioned that originally when Nechemiah first came along and placed restrictions upon moving items, the Gemara mentions three items that he never made rulings upon. All three are crockery items. *Tosafos* says that these three items are examples, but not an exhaustive list. Bowls, plates, and the like were obviously also allowed to be moved, the three listed are examples of *keilim* that are not receptacles[13] (*keilim* whose purpose is for storing). The logic behind *Tosafos* is that obviously there were more exceptions as to what may be moved. Cutlery and plates are a necessity, and it is highly improbable that they were included within the restrictions of *muktzeh.*

Tosafos HaRosh explains it with more reasoning. Bowls, plates, etc., are all receptacles, meaning that one doesn't do *melachah* with them; their function of storing items indicates that they are more passive *keilim.* In contrast to the three *keilim* which the Gemara lists, they are utensils - not receptacles - you do *melachah* with them. Therefore they are singled out in the Gemara because there is the additional novelty that they are per-

---

12. The proof assumes that being an important man and therefore wanting to give the correct impression that one doesn't carry *muktzeh* in any manner is not considered to be a need. The Gemara records that when Abaye carried, he did the same trick as Rava. He held sheaves were not *muktzeh,* but people mistakenly thought it was *muktzeh.* For them to not misinterpret his actions, he carried the sheaves with a spoon on top. If this assumption is true, we can ask: Then how could Abaye carry the sheaves with a spoon on top? He held that the sheaves are not *muktzeh,* so what justified moving the spoon? Abaye doesn't hold that a *heter* of *m'chamah l'tzel* was given to *kli shemelachto l'heter,* so surely he couldn't do the same as Rava? We must distinguish that that which Abaye placed on top was not included entirely in *gezeiras keilim.* We will elaborate on this shortly.

13. "*Ein lahem beis kibul.*"

mitted. However, it is apparent that for passive *keilim* there will also be no limitations.[14]

Shiltei Gibborim says the same idea as *Tosafos* - that the three *keilim* are just examples of *keilim* that are essential to eating on Shabbos. He adds that also food and *kisvei hakodesh* (Torah texts) are not part of the safeguard on *keilim* and can be moved freely. However, it's not conclusive that *Tosafos* and *Shiltei Gibborim* concur with each other practically, despite agreeing that the Gemara is not limited to only these three items. R' Elazar Moshe Horwitz says it could be true that originally these three *keilim* and those like them were not part of the enactment against *keilim* at all. However, after the final stage, when all *kli shemelachto l'heter* were permitted to be moved, they equated all *keilim*. Even cutlery and crockery were encompassed in that last stage that permitted all utensils but forbade them when there was no need at all. *Graz* suggests another reason why it is not conclusive that practically we can permit moving cutlery even for no purpose; maybe when they made an exception to these three *keilim*, they just permitted them to be moved for a regular usage, but not that they don't have any restrictions. Either of these two explanations can be true according to *Tosafos*, so perhaps *Tosafos* won't agree to *Shiltei Gibborim* that at the final stage these three *keilim* are unrestricted.

There is strong support for both of these suggestions from *Rambam*.[15] When teaching that one can't move a *kli* for no purpose, *Rambam* gives examples - bowls and cups can't be moved without any reason. These are *keilim* which *Shiltei Gibborim* claims were not part of *gezeiras keilim*, yet *Rambam* is limiting their movement. It must be either like *Graz* or R' Elazar Moshe Horwitz (or both).

Rabbeinu Chananel's Opinion

There is an inference by Rabbeinu Chananel[16] in support of *Shiltei Gibborim*. We mentioned earlier that Abaye and Rava moved

---

14. Heard in the name of R' Shmuel Arieli.

15. 25:3.

16. 142b.

non-*muktzeh* items with a *kli shemelachto l'heter* on top. Rabbeinu Chananel translates both the *kli* that Rava placed on top of the meat and the knife which Abaye placed on top as *keilim* that were one of the three exceptions listed in the Gemara. Firstly we see from Rabbeinu Chananel a refutation to *Shitah LaRan*'s proof. The placing of a *kli shemelachto l'heter* on top is not indicative that a *kli shemelachto l'heter* can be moved unrestricted, but rather it *is* forbidden to move a *kli shemelachto l'heter* unnecessarily, but certain *keilim* don't have any limitations. Abaye and Rava used such *keilim*. Secondly, we see he holds that the exceptions apply practically to us[17] because Abaye and Rava lived after the final leniency that Chazal gave and still carried these *keilim* unrestricted. According to *Graz* and R' Elazar Moshe Horwitz, by the time of Abaye and Rava there would have been restrictions even on these *keilim*.

Food and Torah Texts

Shulchan Aruch[18] follows the opinion of *Shiltei Gibborim* regarding food and Torah texts, that they can be moved unrestricted. What is encompassed in Torah texts? One can hear a strong argument that sukkah posters do not have the status of Torah texts, since one doesn't learn from them (question #3). The idea behind why food and Torah texts are more lenient is that since they are so pivotal for Shabbos, Nechemiah never placed any restrictions on them. However, a poster isn't a necessity of Shabbos; it is a poster irrelevant of what is written on it, and therefore one shouldn't be permitted to move it.

However, even if they could be treated as Torah texts, it shouldn't be permitted to move it. The reason is simple. When discussing *keilim* that should be encompassed in Nechemiah's *muktzeh*, we can say even though this is a *kli shemelachto l'heter*, it wasn't encompassed in Nechemiah's *gezeirah* due to its importance or vitality to Shabbos. However, something

17. The difficulty with this explanation is in 124a. Rabbeinu Chananel says that bowls were included in the *gezeiras keilim*. We must answer that it depends exactly what vessel it was. צ"ע.

18. 308:5.

which is *muktzeh* for a reason other than being a *kli shemelachto l'heter* will remain *muktzeh* for that reason. For example, Pesach dishes when it's not Pesach. We will discuss whether they are *muktzeh* or not.[19] The reason to permit them is not because they are a crockery item and Chazal never enacted *muktzeh* on dishes, since the reason for their potential status of *muktzeh* is due to a strong level of carefulness one acts with in their regard, causing them to be *muktzeh machmas chisaron kis*. There is no special leniency with *muktzeh machmas chisaron kis* just due to the fact that something is a dish. Similarly, sukkah posters are *muktzeh* because they have been designated for the mitzvah. Being Torah texts has no bearing at all to permit the problem of being *muktzeh machmas mitzvah*.[20]

Fidgeting

Mishnah Berurah[21] brings down two opinions about whether cutlery is included in the limitation of *shelo l'tzorech* like other *kli shemelachto l'heter*, or whether they are similar to Torah texts and food, which are permitted without any restrictions. Even if there is a limitation of "for no purpose," what does that practically encompass? Surely every time one moves an item, he is doing so for a reason! *Aruch HaShulchan* and *Chazon Ish* both permit one to move cutlery if it satisfies his nerves, which is a small need but nonetheless a need (question #1). We don't know if they would permit someone who isn't fidgeting in order to relieve his nerves, but rather he is bored at the Shabbos table and is just playing with a cup, putting his finger inside and spinning it. That is less of a need than to relax one's nerves, but maybe it still is a need. *Chasam Sofer* is quoted as to have made a special effort during the week not to move anything unnecessarily. This was to control his instincts so that on Shabbos he wouldn't move something that is *muktzeh* even if it is a *kli shemelachto*

---

19. In chapter 3.
20. *Muktzeh machmas mitzvah* is a category of *muktzeh* whereby due to the fact this item is designated for a mitzvah, and therefore one in turn is limited in what he can use the item for, he sets it aside. We will elaborate on this in chapter 25.
21. 308:23.

l'heter. Using an item to ease one's nerves is surely permitted; however, it is very plausible that just fidgeting with a *kli shemelachto l'heter* would be forbidden, for this is considered *shelo l'tzorech* - there is no positive benefit at all that is being achieved through this movement.[22]

Using a Kli Shemelachto L'Issur in Place of a Kli Shemelachto L'Heter

The Gemara brings an astounding case: Animals that were brought as offerings required flaying, removing the skin from the flesh. During the week a pole was used for this purpose, while on Shabbos it was done by using two men's outstretched arms as a makeshift pole. The reason that they didn't just use a pole like they did during the week is because a pole is a *kli shemelachto l'issur* [23] and if one can achieve the same result without using a *kli*, then moving the *kli* is considered *shelo l'tzorech*. This is a difficult idea to grasp. Surely it's much easier to flay a heavy animal on a pole as opposed to by using a person's arm. Despite that, to use the pole is still considered *shelo l'tzorech*!

Building off this Gemara, *Mishnah Berurah*[24] posits that if one has a *kli shemelachto l'issur* and a *kli shemelachto l'heter*, both of which can achieve the same result, he must use the *kli shemelachto l'heter*! *Mishnah Berurah*'s logic is that using the *kli shemelachto l'issur* is considered *shelo l'tzorech* if you could make do without it. The *poskim* discuss to what extend one must bother himself to do his task with a *kli shemelachto l'heter* as opposed to a *kli shemelachto l'issur*. For example, if the *kli shemelachto l'issur* is right in front of him and the *kli shemelachto l'heter* is in another room, does he have to go and fetch it, or can he just reckon with whatever is currently in

---

22. R' Shalom Gelber (the author of *Orchos Shabbos*) told me that one can put his hands in his pockets even if his keys are there (question #2) because he has a reason — that he's walking with his hands in his pockets. Even if the sole reason is just because he likes to walk like that, that is a sufficient reason.

23. It is a *kli shemelachto l'issur* because flaying is forbidden. Flaying is permitted just for certain *korbanos*.

24. 308:12.

his vicinity? Here is a practical application of this is: If one would like to transfer left over cholent into a small container, would he be required to take a plastic container, as opposed to a pot, which is considered a *kli shemelachto l'issur*?

The proof *Mishnah Berurah* brings from the aforementioned Gemara is not conclusive.[25] The Gemara only discusses whether to take a *kli shemelachto l'issur* or not to use a *kli* at all. The logic is that it's better not to have to move *muktzeh* if one doesn't have to. In *Mishnah Berurah*'s case, either way one will be moving a *kli* that is subject to some laws of *muktzeh*, so once there is anyway movement of something which has *muktzeh*-relevant laws, it is not conclusive that we require a person to choose to use a *kli shemelachto l'issur* over a *kli shemelachto l'heter*.

Regardless of *Mishnah Berurah*'s novel approach, we should *pasken* from the Gemara, from the case of the sticks that were forbidden to re-insert into the *lechem hapanim*, that if one can achieve a similar result without a *kli shemelachto l'heter*, he must do so. Therefore we should be required to eat with our hands and not use a knife and fork (question #4)? R' Elazar Moshe Horwitz explains that the Gemara is only halachically binding according to *Ran*, not *Rashba*. We quoted earlier *Rashba* who explains this Gemara is going according to an opinion that doesn't permit *m'chamah l'tzel*. Rabbah is of this opinion, and not according to Rava, since he holds *m'chamah l'tzel* is permitted. Therefore, using the pole as opposed to their hands can be considered a minimal need. All small needs are encompassed in *m'chamah l'tzel*. However, *Ran* doesn't change the text of the Gemara from Rava to Rabbah. Even according to Rava, who permits *m'chamah l'tzel*, one can't move the sticks. *Ran* understands that even though Rava permits *m'chamah l'tzel*, this example is not encompassed in *m'chamah l'tzel* since one doesn't need to move the *kli*. So if we *pasken* like *Rashba*, we're fine. Any beneficial usage is encompassed in *m'chamah l'tzel*, and using cutlery over ones hands surely fits this requirement. However...

---

25. Mori V'Rabi R' Ariav Ozer asked this question, and I saw in *Even Yisrael* that he too asks the same question.

Rambam paskens like *Ran*. *Rambam* forbids arranging the sticks for the *lechem hapanim* on Shabbos, which only fits with the opinion of *Ran*. According to *Rashba*, the Gemara was not *l'halachah*, since we permit *m'chamah l'tzel*. The bread retaining its freshness is considered the minimal need that is *m'chamah l'tzel*. So what is the justification to eat with a knife and fork? R' Shmuel Auerbach[26] said that nowadays every small effort causes us discomfort. Saving oneself exertion nowadays can be considered to be a need even though back then it was *shelo l'tzorech*.

Summary

Shulchan Aruch follows the opinion of those who define the leniency to move a *kli m'chamah l'tzel* as literal - "to protect the item" - but one can't move it for no reason. It is unclear what is considered "moving for no reason." Is fidgeting with cutlery included, or ultimately one has a reason why he is doing so? The reason for the leniency of *m'chamah l'tzel* is because one can move *keilim* for the sake of Shabbos. A *kli* whose main use is permitted on Shabbos is likely to be needed on Shabbos.

The stringency learned from the Gemara, that one can only use a *kli* if he cannot achieve the result with his hands, doesn't practically apply nowadays because any deviation from the normal manner is considered a large inconvenience. Food and sacred texts have no limitations. They are so essential to Shabbos that Chazal didn't place any restrictions on them. Certain crockery items were not in the original *gezeirah*, however, some hold that whatever crockery items were not encompassed in the beginning were grouped in the final leniencies that Chazal gave to move all *kli shemelachto l'heter*, so even these items are not unrestricted.

26. Quoted in *Orchos Shabbos*.

Answers

1. The *poskim* differ regarding whether fidgeting is considered a need or not. Those who are lenient have whom to rely on.

2. Similar to question #1, it depends whether or not this is considered a need. If you are walking with your hands in your pockets because you feel most comfortable walking that way, you can be lenient.

3. Any posters that are decorating a sukkah are *muktzeh machmas mitzvah,* forbidding them from being moved, even though generally Torah texts can be moved freely.

4. Nowadays, since we always take care to eat with cutlery, there is no reason from a halachic point of view to refrain from using cutlery.

Chapter 3, Part 1

מוקצה מחמת חסרון כיס

Muktzeh Due to [Concern For] Monetary Loss

Questions

1. Aharon has a box of Pesach dishes in the dining room and now needs to make more space. May he move the box?
2. Yitzchak has a very expensive vase. It's only ever been used a handful of times, since there is rarely a bouquet of flowers which is fancy enough. This Shabbos morning, guests turned up with some flowers. Can he bring the vase out in order to store the flowers (obviously without putting water inside)?
3. The kids have knocked the clock off the wall. Can I move it to a safer location?

The Mishnah[1] says that all utensils can be handled besides מסר הגדול ויתד של מחרישה - "a large saw and a blade of a plow." *Rashi* explains that these two utensils are different than the rest, since one is careful not to use them for anything other than their intended purpose. This category of *muktzeh* is known as *muktzeh machmas chisaron kis, muktzeh* due to the potential loss that may be incurred. In most cases, due to the value or delicate nature of the *kli,* one doesn't use it for any other purposes. However, even if for a reason unrelated to its value, a person is extra particular not

1. 123b.

to use a certain *kli* for any use other than what it's meant for, it will still fall into this category of *muktzeh machmas chisaron kis*. Since the level of *haktzaah* (setting aside) is greater than that of a *kli shemelachto l'issur*, it's forbidden to move such *muktzeh* even *l'tzorech gufo u'mekomo*. Rebbe Shimon, who argues on certain types of *muktzeh*, agrees that such items are *muktzeh*.

The simple reading of the above Mishnah is כל הכלים נטילין - "All utensils can be moved," meaning can be moved *l'tzorech gufo u'mekomo*, in which case the continuation: ...חוץ מן המסר הגדול, which excludes *muktzeh machmas chisaron kis*, precludes it from *l'tzorech gufo u'mekomo*, so under no circumstances can it be moved.[2]

Why Is Muktzeh Machmas Chisaron Kis More Stringent?

Rashba distinguishes between *muktzeh machmas meyus*, *muktzeh machmas issur* and *muktzeh machmas chisaron kis*. The former two are permitted *l'tzorech gufo u'mekomo*, as opposed to *muktzeh machmas chisaron kis*. Why is *muktzeh machmas chisaron kis* more stringent? Both *muktzeh machmas meyus* and *muktzeh machmas issur* are used during the week. Even something disgusting, if the situation is pressing, can and will be used. Since one uses both during the week, one is not fully *maktzah daas* from either of them when Shabbos begins, because perhaps they will end up being useful; a person doesn't use *muktzeh machmas chisaron kis* for other usages even during the week, so its *haktzaas hadaas* is far stronger.[3]

---

2. *Mordechai* has a unique opinion that permits *muktzeh machmas chisaron kis* to be moved *l'tzorech gufo u'mekomo*. He must read the mishnah as follows: "*Kol hakeilim netilin*" refers to *m'chamah l'tzel* (to protect them). It then follows that *m'chamah l'tzel* is the only restriction of *muktzeh machmas chisaron kis*. The source of *Mordechai* is *Raavya*, who just says *muktzeh machmas issur* is permitted *l'tzorech gufo u'mekomo*. *Mordechai* extrapolated from there the same is true by *muktzeh machmas chisaron kis*.

3. This idea is based on measuring the setting aside before the rules of *muktzeh* are established. One might use *muktzeh machmas meyus*, so the setting aside is not absolute. The difficulty in this suggestion is: Why should the fact that *muktzeh machmas issur* is used during the week affect one's designation from use towards

The Gemara[4] says that סיכי זיירי ומזורי כיון דקפיד עלייהו מייחד להו מקום - "launderers' pins, presses, and a clothing rod - one is particular about them and designates them a place." There are variations among the *Rishonim* what exactly these *keilim* are, but all the explanations lead to the same conclusion - one is extra careful with these objects due to their fragility not to use them for other purposes. *Tur*[5] interestingly splits the reasons behind this group of *keilim*. He starts first by saying, כלים שאדם **חס עליהם** כגון סכין **שלא יטלטלם** - "Utensils which a person *is careful not to move*, e.g., a knife." Then, after diverging to *kli shemelachto l'issur*, he continues to describe *muktzeh machmas chisaron kis* and says, כלי **שמקפיד** עלין **שלא לעשות בו אלא מלאכתו** - "Utensils which a person is *careful not to use for a task besides what they are meant for*." First he describes this *kli* as something people are careful from *moving*, and later he describes it as something people are careful not to *use*.

The truth is, we already find these different reasons in the Gemara and *Rashi*. In *Shabbos* 123a it says that a *kli* that is only used for its specific purpose due to its fragility, one is *meyached l'hu makom*, fixes it a set place, implying a total *haktzaah* even from moving. But on the next page, *Rashi* explains that you are careful not to use it for other purposes. If these are two separate reasons, we would have two different ways to determine if something is *muktzeh machmas chisaron kis*: if you don't use it for other uses due to its specialized purpose, or if you are particular that it's not moved around due to its delicacy, and you therefore are *meyached l'hu makom*, designate it a place.

This would help us clarify a complicated discussion among the latter *poskim* of whether *muktzeh machmas chisaron kis* is limited to *kli shemelachto l'issur* or even applies to a *kli shemelachto l'heter*. A *kli shemelachto l'issur*'s main use is forbidden, and therefore one can't usually use it on Shabbos. Consequently, the main use of a *kli shemelachto l'issur* which is also *muktzeh machmas chisaron kis* is forbidden regardless, and

---

Shabbos? Surely what one does during the week won't impact how he treats it during Shabbos.

4. 123a.

5. The beginning of *siman* 308.

one is careful not to use it for any other use, resulting in a strong *haktzaah*. However the uses of a *kli shemelachto l'heter* are permitted on Shabbos, so even if one is careful not to use it for any other use due to its fragility, that which it is designated to be used for can be done on Shabbos, so there is no *haktzaas hadaas*, designation due to Shabbos.[6] If there is a second reason for *muktzeh machmas chisaron kis*, that if one sets aside a specific place for an item he is careful about is, that is equally applicable for a *kli shemelachto l'heter* and it would be *muktzeh machmas chisaron kis*.

Keilim on Display

Tehillah L'Dovid[7] asks if display *keilim*, which, due to their value or fragility one doesn't use for any purpose other than being on display, are *muktzeh machmas chisaron kis*? He is referring to *keilim* that are *kli shemelachto l'heter* and could be used permissibly on Shabbos, but are normally left on display. He leaves this question unanswered. *Raaeh*[8] says that they don't become *muktzeh machmas chisaron kis* and *Tosefes Shabbos*[9] also takes that on. However, if one of the stipulations that can make something *muktzeh machmas chisaron kis* is a concern not to move it, one can even be meticulous not to move a *kli shemelachto l'heter*, and it should have the possibility to become *muktzeh machmas chisaron kis*. I think you can distinguish between different types of *kli shemelachto l'heter*. One type, due to your carefulness you *rarely use*, and another type is something you *never use*. One never intends on using display plates, vases, etc., for that function. They are still a *kli* because they have a form of a *kli*, and *Tehillah L'Dovid* says that something whose purpose is aesthetical is still considered a *kli*, similar to jewelry. Such an item one is *maktzah daas* from ever using them, despite potentially being fit to use for something permissible on Shabbos. One is very careful not to use a

---

6. This is the same principle we discussed in the appendix to chapter 1 regarding clothes of *shaatnez*, that the designation must stem from Shabbos.

7. 336:6.

8. *Beitzah* 11a.

9. 310:13.

kli shemelachto l'heter, such as a delicate tea set or an expensive serving bowl that rarely sees active service, for an unjustified purpose. However, if an appropriate occasion would occur on Shabbos, you would take them out to be used. *Tosefes Shabbos* hold that such *keilim* won't be *muktzeh machmas chisaron kis* because you could come to use them on Shabbos, so one is not really *maktzah daas*.

Perhaps we can take this a step further. Something which is *muktzeh machmas chisaron kis* due to its *yichud makom*, i.e., one never moves it, loses its identity of a *kli*. So Chazal limited its movement because the utensil is no longer meant to be used as a functioning utensil; it loses its purpose as a *kli*. However, *muktzeh machmas chisaron kis* that one is careful when using is still a *kli*, yet forbidden *l'tzorech gufo u'mekomo*. (This would also help us understand why Rebbe Shimon agrees it's like wood and stones.[10])

Tur paskens that *muktzeh machmas chisaron kis* can't be moved at all, neither *l'tzorech gufo* nor *l'tzorech mekomo*. *Nezirus Shimshon*[11] empathically argues. His claim is that since the care of *muktzeh machmas chisaron kis* is only regarding not using it, one can move it around *l'tzorech mekomo*, as movement was never included in the *haktzaah*. He doesn't distinguish between different types of care. He evidently doesn't hold of the distinction we made differentiating between a designation from total movement and a care not to use it for various other uses. According to our distinction, *Nezirus Shimshon*'s idea would be possible to entertain for *keilim* that one is careful not to *use*, not for the category of *keilim* one is careful not to *move*.[12]

---

10. I saw such an approach in *Harerei Kedem* — that in order for something to qualify halachically as a *kli*, it needs to be functioning. Even *kli shemelachto l'issur* has limited usages and therefore its identity as a *kli* is weaker. Consequently its movement is also limited. ע״ש.

11. Beginning of *siman* 308.

12. The answer to *Nezirus Shimshon*'s question on *Tur* is: Items that one is careful not to use for any purpose, he also is careful not to move around unnecessarily. This is unlike other objects that one freely moves around. Hence all *muktzeh machmas chisaron kis* is forbidden to move even *l'tzorech mekomo*.

One Category, Not Two

The implication from *Beis Yosef* is that he also didn't hold that *Tur* was setting forth a landmark principle in *muktzeh machmas chisaron kis*. *Beis Yosef* understands that it's all one category, not two types of *muktzeh machmas chisaron kis*. The proof is that when beginning the discussion of *muktzeh machmas chisaron kis*, *Shulchan Aruch* doesn't bring down the phrase *meyached l'hu makom*. He just says "careful to use" and "careful not to get dirty," which means that you are careful to use it only for their specific uses. He doesn't separate two different lists of *keilim*.

It seems like the conclusion is that the only reason for *muktzeh machmas chisaron kis* is as *Mishnah Berurah*[13] says: "careful to use." Even though *Shaarei Tzion*[14] quotes a *Beis Meir* that implies that there is an additional requirement aside for "careful to use," we also require *meyached l'hu makom*. R' Shlomo Zalman Auerbach[15] explains that if one is careful on not moving something unnecessarily, that in truth is an indication that really he is strict on not using it for other usages. The implication of the *poskim* - *Rambam*, *Shulchan Aruch*, and *Mishnah Berurah* - is that even if something like a *shechitah* knife doesn't have a designated place, it is still considered *muktzeh machmas chisaron kis*, while something that has only been put aside in a designated place won't be *muktzeh machmas chisaron kis* due to that alone.

A New Reason to Forbid Muktzeh Machmas Chisaron Kis

Despite this, *Chazon Ish*[16] has a new reason to forbid moving items that have a designated place. *Tosafos*[17] compares *kilas chasanim* (a groom's canopy) to a *menorah* (lantern). The former should be *muktzeh* because one is *meyached l'hu makom* (designates it a fixed place), similar to a *me-*

---

13. 308:3.
14. 310:19.
15. *Shemiras Shabbos K'Hilchasah*, ch. 2, note 50.
16. 43:17.
17. 46a, s.v. והא.

norah, which one also designates a fixed place, and therefore it is *muktzeh. Chazon Ish, Pnei Yehoshua,* and *Rosh Yosef* are all bothered with this comparison. *Kilas chasanim* is a *kli shemelachto l'heter* and one is not careful to not use it, so it can't be *muktzeh machmas chisaron kis* - unlike a *menorah,* which is *kli shemelachto l'issur*! *Chazon Ish* asserts that any *kli* that has been designated to never be moved loses its identity as a *kli.* Therefore one wouldn't be able to move a wall clock (question #3), which one puts up on the wall without intending to move it, because it's not considered a *kli* (it is now *muktzeh machmas gufo,* which is not part of *muktzeh machmas chisaron kis*).[18] *Rosh Yosef* gives the same answer as *Chazon Ish,* but he makes it dependent on one designating a specific place due to the value of the object. *Shemiras Shabbos K'Hilchasah, Ohr L'Tzion,* and many other *pasken* like this *Chazon Ish,* so moving a painting, wall clock etc., is problematic. R' Ovadia Yosef[19] is lenient to move paintings and the such. He doesn't hold of this new category of fixing an item in a specific place causing it to lose its identity as a *kli.*

Pesach Dishes

We have established that, according to most opinions, one can't move a clock. You can move a fancy vase that is only used rarely (question #2), because you don't truly consciously reject it from use. What about Pesach dishes during the year and *chametz* dishes on Pesach (question #1)?

There are *poskim* who argue that regarding Pesach dishes, one is very careful that they shouldn't be used at all during the year, since if they get used they are effectively ruined. Some argue that in order to qualify as *muktzeh machmas chisaron kis,* it must be that all year round one is careful not to use them unnecessarily - but one does use these dishes on Pesach. However, this claim isn't strong, as *Chut Shani* says that one's worry with Pesach dishes is that they shouldn't get ruined. This concern exists even

---

18. Besides *muktzeh,* according to some opinions there is a problem in removing items from the wall due to the *melachah* of *boneh.*

19. *Yabia Omer* 8:39.

during Pesach, just that at different times they are more likely to get ruined than at other times.

Chut Shani uses this logic to be lenient. He says that for all of its uses, e.g., eating from it, one is not careful (he would be happy to use it for eating if there would be no worry of *chametz,* since specifically he is only concerned not to use it for *chametz*). Therefore, if a need arises on Shabbos to use the Pesach dishes, one can. They're not *muktzeh machmas chisaron kis*.

Regarding *chametz* dishes on Pesach: He says that since *Shulchan Aruch*[20] requires one to store away these dishes for the duration of Pesach and they therefore can't be used, that makes them *muktzeh machmas gufo*. This is important to know if one wants to use a household item during Pesach. If his regular crockery is blocking the way, he can't move them aside.

Summary

Due to one's extreme care not to use certain items for alternative purposes other than what the *kli* is designated for, he sets it aside. Even though his main concern is for not using it, the setting aside includes not moving it, so there are no leniencies to move something which is *muktzeh machmas chisaron kis,* due to its total rejection. Some commentators understand that there are two different criteria that can cause something to qualify as *muktzeh machmas chisaron kis*: care not to use the item for other uses and care not to move the item at all. However, we understood that both of these concerns stem from the same source - as a result of one's care not to use it, he also takes care not to move it.

Simply speaking, a *kli shemelachto l'heter* shouldn't qualify as *muktzeh machmas chisaron kis* because its use that it is designated for is permitted on Shabbos. However, we brought a new principle from *Chazon Ish*: When one designates a place for an item never to be moved, it loses its identity as a *kli* and can't be moved because it is not a *kli* - it's *muktzeh machmas gufo*.

---

20. 451:1.

Answers

1. According to *Chut Shani*, Pesach dishes are not *muktzeh machmas chisaron kis*; they retain their regular status as crockery and Aharon can move the box.

2. A vase that you are careful not to use most the time is not *muktzeh* because it is still meant for its permissible function of storing items. Yitzchak has not designated the vase from ever being used again, and until that rare occasion arises he is very careful, but it remains a non-*muktzeh* vessel.

3. A wall clock is *muktzeh*; you can't move it at all. *Chazon Ish*'s principle is that something with a designated place and is never going to be moved loses its identity as a *kli*.

Part 2

ביטול ממח"כ

Removing the Status of Muktzeh Due to Monetary Loss

Question

1. One Shabbos, more guests than anticipated turned up and I didn't have enough dishes for everyone. I would like to use my Pesach set (either I will do *hagalah* afterward or I'll just buy new Pesach dishes). Even if we say that the Pesach set is *muktzeh machmas chisaron kis*, could this still be permissible?

R' Akiva Eiger[21] discusses a case where one has a *shechitah* knife, and on Shabbos he changes its designation, now intending to use it as a regular knife. Is that decision halachically significant? Can he now move the knife like a regular *kli shemelachto l'issur*? This is dependent on whether one can remove the status of *muktzeh machmas chisaron kis* on Shabbos - meaning, if one decides on Shabbos that he is no longer careful on only using an item for its specific use, and now doesn't mind using it for other uses, can he now move it freely? This is what you are effectively doing when deciding to use your Pesach dishes on a regular Shabbos.

R' Akiva Eiger brings an explicit *Tosafos*[22] that says that even in a case when the *hakatzah* is removed, it still remains *muktzeh*. *Tosafos* discusses if one has wood that he was intending to use for building material, it is *muktzeh machmas gufo* because it is not a *kli*. If on Yom Tov he decides

21. Beginning of *siman* 308.
22. *Beitzah* 2b.

he would like to use it as firewood (which is not *muktzeh* on Yom Tov because it can be used), one is retracting from the original designation. The conclusion is that one's retraction doesn't change the status and it remains forbidden. Despite this, R' Akiva Eiger leans toward being lenient, especially if you do a physical act to show that you're no longer careful, not just by changing its designation in your mind.

R' Akiva Eiger's basis to be lenient is built on the fact that generally we *pasken* like Rebbe Shimon, who doesn't hold of *migo d'iskatzi.*[23] If *migo d'iskatzi* would apply, we would be bound by the *muktzeh* status the object receives at the onset of Shabbos, since Rebbe Shimon doesn't hold of *migo d'iskatzi*, if the object changes so its status also can develop. However, *Mishnah Berurah*[24] does *pasken* that we say *migo d'iskatzi* in such cases and so since it began Shabbos as *muktzeh*, regardless of what develops it will remain *muktzeh*. (*Mishnah Berurah* is discussing a case where a *muktzeh machmas chisaron kis* breaks and you are no longer careful with moving the broken pieces). According to *Mishnah Berurah*, it should be forbidden to move these Pesach dishes (question #1).[25]

Giving Merchandise as a Gift

R' Shlomo Zalman Auerbach[26] entertains a new reasoning that could apply to our case. He discusses a case where one has merchandise which he has set aside for selling. *Rema* holds that it is *muktzeh machmas chisaron kis*, yet if one decides on Shabbos to give it to his friend, it is allowed. The reason is that he is giving to the friend to make use of the merchandise in the same way that any consumer would use it; *the purpose of the item is not changing*. In contrast, the case of R' Akiva Eiger was referring to a knife

---

23. This principle means if something was *muktzeh* when Shabbos began, its status is perpetuated throughout Shabbos even if circumstances change and it should now no longer be *muktzeh*.

24. *Se'if katan* 35.

25. We will elaborate on this point in great detail in chapter 21.

26. *Shemiras Shabbos K'Hilchasah*, ch. 20, note 83. *Chazon Ish* (42:16) explicitly argues. He says that since it's such a rare occurrence for one to take something from his merchandise, there is a definite designation from using it.

set aside solely for *shechitah,* and now *one wants to change it* and use it for cutting vegetables. A vegetable knife is physically a completely different knife, with an entirely different purpose, hence in this case R' Akiva Eiger is unsure whether you can change the purpose of the object. However, when you are still using the item for its original use, he may well agree that it is permitted. With the case of our Pesach dishes, you can say similarly that this is a plate and you still want to use it as a plate, but you don't want to restrict use anymore just for Pesach and you are willing to use it even for *chametz.* Such a change is halachically easier and permissible on Shabbos.

Avnei Nezer[27] also permits to give merchandise as a gift on Shabbos. He explains based on a *Maggid Mishnah* that the only scenario *Rambam* is referring to when he forbids using merchandise on Shabbos is when one wants to use it and then put it back - then one is careful when using it that it shouldn't get a defect. That is the care that makes it *muktzeh machmas chisaron kis.* But if one is now taking it for himself, i.e., he won't resell it, it loses its status of *muktzeh machmas chisaron kis* since he no longer is as careful as before.

Answer

1. If you remove your *kepidah* (care) towards a *muktzeh* item it is effective, provided the item is still going to be used for the same purpose it originally was meant for. Pesach plates that you are no longer careful about can be used on Shabbos, even if the change in mind occurred suddenly on Shabbos.

---

27. *Avnei Nezer, Orach Chaim* 402.

Part 3

סכין של מילה

A Bris Milah Knife

Question

1. After performing a bris milah on Shabbos, the mohel turned to me and asked me to pick up the knife from the table and put it away in a side room of the shul. Am I allowed to move it?

A bris milah knife is a classic example of *muktzeh machmas chisaron kis*; due to its specialness there is a heightened concern not to use it for anything else. So what is one supposed to do when the mohel has a bris milah to perform (question #1)? Rabbeinu Yerucham[28] holds that even once the mohel has finished doing the milah, he can still carry the knife to any place he wants. *Rema*[29] *paskens* leniently like Rabbeinu Yerucham. *Maharil* argues that the mohel must drop the milah knife immediately. *Magen Avraham*[30] explains the opinion of *Rema*. He says *Rema* holds that the knife is not *muktzeh* at all, since during *bein hashemashos* the mohel was allowed to move it to prepare for the mitzvah. Therefore on Shabbos it doesn't become *muktzeh* again, a principle known as *ein muktzeh l'chetzi Shabbos*, something can't be *muktzeh* for part of Shabbos. (We will soon discuss what this means.)

Magen Avraham himself holds that one can't move the knife after performing the bris unless he relies on the dispensation of *odo b'yado*.[31] He

28. *Nesiv* 1, 2:14.

29. *Yoreh Dei'ah* 264.

30. *Orach Chaim* 331:5 and the *Taz* in *Yoreh Dei'ah* explain very similarly.

31. Literally, "still in one's hand," this principle permits moving a *muktzeh* item freely once it has already come into one's hands.

explains even Rabbeinu Yerucham holds that the knife is *muktzeh* and only permits it to be carried while the knife is still in one's hands. Once it has been put down, it reverts back to being *muktzeh machmas chisaron kis*. Accordingly, the reason you can move the knife before the bris is because for the sake of the mitzvah there is a unique exemption.

Magen Avraham argues with the reasoning of *Rema*, saying that *ein muktzeh l'chetzi Shabbos* is not relevant in this case. *ein muktzeh l'chetzi Shabbos* only applies in scenarios where the reasoning for the *muktzeh* comes from the person's *haktzaas hadaas*; something that wasn't *muktzeh* and one decides to reject on Shabbos, the designation to not use is ineffective. (Had it occurred prior to Shabbos, it would have rendered it *muktzeh*.) However, in the case of the milah knife, *Magen Avraham* compares it to the spice crusher mentioned in *Shabbos* 123a, the halachah of which is that when it has spices in it can be moved, but as soon as the spices are finished, it reverts back to being *muktzeh*. Here too, even after the milah is over, the mohel is still careful with the knife, so it still remains *muktzeh*.[32] In order to explain *Rema*, we must say that he holds that the reason for the knife to be *muktzeh* is due to your *haktzaas hadaas*. Therefore when one knows that he will be using the milah knife this Shabbos, he no longer sets it aside.

(*Magen Avraham* rejects a notion that by deciding before Shabbos to use the knife the mohel removes the reason why it should be *muktzeh machmas chisaron kis*. From his rejection we can deduce that *Rema* holds that it's based on one's awareness/designation, hence before Shabbos one can remove the *muktzeh* status.)

Did the Mohel Know about the Bris?

Mabit[33] understands that there is a distinction between whether the mohel knew before Shabbos that there will be a milah, compared to when he is suddenly called upon to perform a milah. In the former it's obvious to

---

32. This is also what *Gra* holds, like *Magen Avraham*.

33. 3:99.

him that the halachah should be like *Rema,* namely that *muktzeh machmas chisaron kis* shouldn't be applicable because he has a usage on Shabbos which he was aware of before Shabbos came in, negating any rejection from use he would usually have. In the latter case, there is a special leniency for the sake of the mitzvah, and such a scenario is what *Shulchan Aruch* is referring to when he lists a milah knife as *muktzeh machmas chisaron kis.*

Gra evidently doesn't hold of *Mabit,* even in the scenario that *Rema* was discussing, when the mohel is aware that there is a milah before Shabbos. He still says that one can only carry the knife due to the mitzvah, however, in essence, it still remains *muktzeh. Gra* draws a parallel to this from a *Tosefta*[34] that says that immediately after finishing shaking the lulav on Shabbos, one must drop it. The lulav is *muktzeh*; it's a branch of a tree and therefore *muktzeh machmas gufo.* The reason one can carry it is because he has a mitzvah he must perform with it. From the requirement to drop it as soon as he finishes the mitzvah, we see that the need to use the lulav for the mitzvah didn't remove its *muktzeh* status entirely; rather, the *muktzeh* status is temporarily suspended to enable the fulfillment of the mitzvah. Once the mitzvah is completed, the temporary *heter* ends and the *muktzeh* status reverts back. However, *Rema* can refute the proof from lulav, saying that a lulav isn't a *kli*; its only use is for the mitzvah, so once the mitzvah is finished *Rema* would agree it reverts back to *muktzeh machmas gufo.* This is in contrast to a milah knife, which is a *kli,* and only because of one's designation from use does it become *muktzeh.* But this Shabbos he hasn't averted his attention from it, so it can be used.[35]

Maybe one can suggest an even simpler argument to understand *Gra*'s opinion that the knife always remains *muktzeh.* The underlying reason that causes a milah knife to be considered *muktzeh machmas chisaron kis* is due to his restriction not to use this knife for anything else other than milah. Therefore what difference should it make if you know there will be a milah tomorrow or not? His attitude to what he does with his milah knife

---

34. End of the second chapter of *Sukkah.*

35. We will elaborate on this point in chapter 29.

doesn't change. Just like every week he is careful not to use it for anything else, so too this Shabbos he retains that care, besides the actual milah he will be performing. It comes out that he still has a designation for other uses, which is the precise criteria for *muktzeh machmas chisaron kis*. This is certainly easier to understand according to those opinions who hold that there is *muktzeh machmas chisaron kis* even for a *kli shemelachto l'heter* - that even though one might use it for its intended use on Shabbos, since one is careful regarding everything other than its main use, therefore *muktzeh* can be pertinent.

Conclusion of Mishnah Berurah

Mishnah Berurah[36] concludes that ideally we should follow *Magen Avraham* and *Taz*, who hold that a milah knife is *muktzeh* after the mitzvah is performed. If the mohel is performing the *periah*[37] and can't take the knife to a safe place himself, he can give it to someone else to store before placing it down. (This is based on the understanding that the dispensation of *odo b'yado* extends to permitting one to give the *muktzeh* item to his friend before placing it down.) *Mishnah Berurah* does sanction relying on *Rema* if there is a real need, e.g., in scenarios when the mohel placed the knife on the table. Even though *Magen Avraham* won't allow one to pick it up anymore, if it might get stolen, one can rely on *Rema* to take it away.

Summary

R' Akiva Eiger says that since we don't hold of *migo d'iskatzi*, one can change the status of an item based on changing its designation. For example, if a *kli* is *muktzeh machmas chisaron kis* and one decides from now on that he is not going to take the same care he previously showed toward this

---

36. 310:15.
37. The stage after the circumcision when the blood is sucked out. *Metzitzah* is the tearing of the skin.

kli, it can lose its *muktzeh* status. If one wants to temporarily use the *muktzeh machmas chisaron kis,* it is not considered removing the concern and it doesn't help. One must decide from now on that he won't be careful.

This is the basis for understanding the various opinions regarding whether a milah knife is *muktzeh* after one has finished performing the milah. *Gra* holds that one is just temporarily using the knife, but still retains his caution about not misusing it, and so one must rely on the leniency of *odo b'yado* to put it away after the milah. (*Gra* himself holds that one must drop the knife because he doesn't agree to *odo b'yado.*[38]) *Rema* is lenient. He holds that when one knows he will need to use the knife this Shabbos, he doesn't set it aside - on the contrary, he designates it as a *kli* he intends to use, thereby removing its *muktzeh* status.

Answer

1. Ideally one should treat the milah knife as *muktzeh* and not move it after the mitzvah is performed. If there is a real need to move it, you can, relying on *Rema.*

38. We will elaborate on this in chapter 4.

Chapter 4

מוקצה הבא לידו

Muktzeh that Comes Into One's Hands

Questions

1. After lighting the Shabbos candles, do women have to drop the matches immediately (a Sephardic woman every Shabbos, and an Ashkenazic woman on Yom Tov, since with the conclusion of their lighting they immediately accept Shabbos/Yom Tov)?
2. When I eat a fruit and reach the seed or pit, can I throw it into the trash can, or must I drop it where it is?
3. If a child places a toy in my hand and I realize that it's a *muktzeh* toy, do I have to drop it on the floor or can I return it to the toy box?
4. If a utensil breaks on Shabbos, can I move the dangerous broken pieces to the trash can, or must I only move them away from the place where they can cause danger?

The Gemara[1] states explicitly that once one has a leniency to move a *kli shemelachto l'issur* ***l'tzorech mekomo***, a forbidden utensil in order to vacate its space. One is *unconstrained* as to where he is allowed to move the object. The novelty in this is that one could have thought that since the leniency to move the object is based on the premise that one needs the

1. 124a and 43a.

space that the *muktzeh* item is currently occupying, it would suffice to just move it away from the area required, but continuing to move it as far as he wants, once the area has been vacated, isn't justified. The *Rishonim* don't explicitly explain the reasoning for the far-reaching leniency. They just note the novelty that the Gemara is teaching us. The *poskim* argue as to which scenarios we can apply this leniency to, and from this we can try and understand this leniency.

The Extent of the Heter L'Tzorech Mekomo

Rebbe Nechemiah has a unique opinion - that on Shabbos one can only move a *kli l'tzorech tashmish hameyuchad lo,* a utensil for the specific task it is designated for, e.g., a hammer can only be moved to bang nails, not to crack nuts. The Gemara asks several questions trying to refute his ruling. One of them is: How can we clean up used dishes after a meal, since eating from them is their main purpose? Moving them in order to tidy up should be forbidden. *Rashba*[2] explains that the Gemara exclusively asked on Rebbe Nechemiah how we can move the used dishes, whereas according to the other *Tannaim,* who don't hold of such a limitation that one can only move items for their intended purpose, it's understood. This is because when one is moving dirty dishes from the table, he is not moving them *l'tzorech gufo* rather *l'tzorech mekomo,* to vacate their space. Once he has picked up the dishes to vacate the space, they now can even be moved anywhere, even to outside of the house (where they would store the dirty dishes). This is an explicit proof once that one is moving an item *l'tzorech mekomo,* he is not limited to where he must place it.

The second proof that one is unrestricted when moving *l'tzorech mekomo* to anywhere he wishes is from Rebbe Yitzchak.[3] Rebbe Yitzchak holds that אין כלי ניטל אלא לדבר הניטל בשבת - one can't move a *kli* for the sake of something that is *muktzeh,* e.g., one can't move a cup in order to cover money. Nevertheless, the Gemara finds a way that even according to

2. 124a.
3. 43a.

Rebbe Yitzchak one can move a bucket to cover an egg (that was laid on Shabbos and hence *muktzeh*). The case is when he needs to vacate the area that the bucket is currently occupying. Once one began carrying the bucket in a permissible fashion, he can continue moving it until he covers the egg. Why does moving the bucket in order to vacate its area justify moving it until the egg? It must be that once he has a leniency to move an item, he can continue moving it to wherever he wants.

Magen Avraham[4] is of the opinion that even if one picked up *muktzeh* inadvertently, he can continue to carry it and he is not required to drop it where he is. His source is from an *Agudah* brought down by *Rema*,[5] who states that if one forgot to remove his wallet from his trousers before Shabbos, he can continue to move within his house to any safe place and deposit it there. *Magen Avraham* understands that we can see from here that anytime *muktzeh* is in one's hand, even when originally it wasn't permitted to be carried, nonetheless it's permitted to continue carrying it to where you want. The simplest way to understand this stance is that the problem lies in the original handling of the *muktzeh*, the picking it up, so once one has already transgressed that problem, and we're dealing with past that stage, there is no reason for any restrictions. Therefore it's irrelevant which type of *muktzeh* we are discussing, since we're not assessing if he originally had a leniency to take it or not. This leniency is across the board. *Tzelach*[6] explaining the rule of *odo b'yado* gives this understanding: The problem with *muktzeh* is the handling/taking of the *muktzeh*.

It would follow that *Magen Avraham* would agree to a novel halachah found in *Graz*.[7] He writes that even if one intentionally picked up *muktzeh* and now he regrets this act and wants to know if he can continue to carry the *muktzeh* or if he has to put it down, he can continue carrying it.[8] (The

---

4. 306:7.
5. 266:12.
6. *Beitzah* 3a.
7. 307, at the end of *se'if* 36.
8. *Chok Yaakov* recommends that every *rav* have a room where people who are carrying *muktzeh* can deposit it safely if they come to ask the *rav* if they are allowed to continue carrying it.

reason *Magen Avraham* never discusses such a case was because he doesn't want to deal with sinners). *Shitah LaRan*[9] also implies that he is lenient regarding *odo b'yado*. He permits placing it in any place one wants, once the *muktzeh* is in one's hands.

Magen Avraham asks the following question on his view. In the times of the Gemara, the practice was that in order to announce the commencement of Shabbos, a chazzan would blow a shofar. Once the chazzan finished blowing, everyone would wait a few moments before accepting Shabbos in order to allow time for the chazzan to put away his shofar.[10] According to *Magen Avraham*, once it's in his hand, why can't he continue moving it to any place that he wants to store it, even if he's already accepted Shabbos?

From this Gemara, *Gra* proves that only when you first handled the *muktzeh* under permissible circumstances is the continuation of the moving considered permissible and thereby permitted to continue. But in the case of the shofar, it didn't start with "permission," as we will explain. *Gra* argues with the ruling of the *Agudah* that if one discovers a wallet in his trousers, he may continue walking until a safe place is found. *Gra* understands that even if when you first started handling the *muktzeh* it was permissible, it needs to be that you received a dispensation from Chazal for the moving of this item; if the item lacked any restrictions hence one began to move it, that is insufficient. Therefore, even if you started moving it on *erev Shabbos*, like in the case of the shofar, it doesn't help. Therefore, only in a case like *kli shemelachto l'issur* which, when you first started moving the *muktzeh* because of a leniency of vacating the place, did Chazal say that once we're allowing you to move it, we will not put any restrictions on where you can move it to.

The Opinion of Gra

This sheds light on the leniency of *l'tzorech mekomo*. Chazal didn't just permit vacating the space; rather, when one needs the space, they permit-

---

9. End of *Perek Kol HaKeilim*.
10. *Shabbos* 35b.

ted moving it to wherever you want. This continuous act is still part of Chazal's leniency of *l'tzorech mekomo*. *Gra* brings another proof that the start must be with "permission" from Chazal. *Shulchan Aruch*[11] *paskens* that one must drop the match once one finishes lighting the Shabbos candle (question #1). The match was in your hand when Shabbos came in, so why is one limited where he can move it to? We see from this halachah that despite having picked up something permissibly, since it wasn't a dispensation of *muktzeh* that allowed him originally to pick up the matches, the continuation of his movement can't be defined as moving with "permission." R' Akiva Eiger[12] infers from *Rashi*[13] like *Gra*, that one has to drop the matches immediately, despite it still being *odo b'yado*.

Chazon Ish[14] has a different understanding as to what *Gra* holds. He argues that *Gra* is not discussing when you picked the item up before Shabbos. If you picked up the *muktzeh* before Shabbos, then it started permissibly and is permissible to continue to move. Rather, he understands that *Gra* would agree that anytime you have a *kli shemelachto l'issur* in your hand, it would be permitted to continue carrying it, regardless of how it came into your hands. The logic is that once the *muktzeh* is in your hand, you need to vacate your hands, so the leniency of *l'tzorech mekomo* will allow you to continue moving it. All your steps are being taken to vacate the *muktzeh* from your hand. *Gra* won't permit the case of the *Agudah* because money is *muktzeh machmas gufo* and therefore will not have the leniency of *l'tzorech mekomo*.

Chazon Ish proves this from *Gra* in *Yoreh Dei'ah*, who explains that the only reason why the chazzan couldn't move the shofar is because the Gemara is going according to Rebbe Nechemiah, who doesn't hold of the leniency of *l'tzorech gufo u'mekomo*. According to *Gra*'s qualification of the Gemara, it is implicit from the Gemara that according to how we hold in halachah, namely that there is a leniency of *l'tzorech gufo u'mekomo*, it would have been permissible for the chazzan to put away the shofar. The

---

11. *Siman* 263.
12. *Siman* 308.
13. 142b, s.v. מטה על צדה.
14. 49:8.

reason must be because he picked it up before Shabbos therefore he can continue to move it, despite not having picked it up through receiving a special dispensation. Although *Chazon Ish* has a valid argument, that surely it's considered starting with "permission" when he picked it up before Shabbos, *Chazon Ish*'s explanation doesn't fit at all with *Gra* in *Orach Chaim*, which says that moving the shofar before Shabbos is not considered starting with "permission."

We must therefore try and differentiate as follows: Even if the start of your carrying was before Shabbos, when *hilchos muktzeh* didn't yet apply, whichever type of carrying you were involved with then is halachically how we will define your act, e.g., if you were moving the item to vacate its space, your act will be defined as *l'tzorech mekomo*. If you were moving the item to protect it, your act is *m'chamah l'tzel*. Therefore, when Shabbos commences, in order to determine if you can continue to carry it, we need to establish if the *kli* you're carrying has a leniency of *l'tzorech mekomo* or not. Subsequently *Gra*'s *psak*, that as soon as you've finished the milah you must drop the knife, is correct. *Gra* holds that the identity of *muktzeh* is suspended from the knife due to the mitzvah that it is required for. So even though there was permission to pick up the knife, as soon as the mitzvah is completed the permission is terminated and the *kli* reverts back to *muktzeh machmas chisaron kis*. Since one wasn't granted a dispensation to move the knife *l'tzorech mekomo*, albeit he was allowed to move it since it wasn't *muktzeh*, he now cannot continue to move it since it reverted again to being *muktzeh*.

The practical difference between our explanation and *Chazon Ish* is that when a *kli shemelachto l'issur* came into your hand on Shabbos in a forbidden way, *Chazon Ish* explicitly permits because now, when you are continuing to move it, it is considered *l'tzorech mekomo*, you now need to vacate your hands. While according to our explanation, when you first picked up the *muktzeh* the act had to have been for the sake of *tzorech mekomo* and then if that exemption would become obsolete, you could continue because of *odo b'yado*. However, the prerequisite is that the moving started *l'tzorech mekomo*. Therefore, this would not be applicable when the item originally came to your hand in a forbidden way.

Is a Subsequent Act Encompassed in Odo B'Yado?

It follows that if a child places a *muktzeh* toy in a person's hands (question #3), *Chazon Ish* would permit moving it back to its place. However, according to our understanding of *Gra*, one should drop it; even though it didn't come into his hand in a forbidden way, it is certainly not considered that it came into his hand in a permissible way. We will soon see that *Mishnah Berurah* leans toward a third opinion that would be lenient depending on why the toy is *muktzeh*. However, there is also the opinion of *Magen Avraham* to rely on if needed, that irrespective of how *muktzeh* came into one's hand, he can move it once it's in his hands.

Eliyah Rabbah[15] permits the mohel to give the milah knife to someone else after he has finished performing the bris (following the opinion of *Rema*[16] that it's permitted to put away the knife oneself). *Machatzis HaShekel* argues that only the mohel can move the milah knife; he explains the exemption is based on *hetiro sofo mipnei techilatan.*[17] They permitted putting it away since otherwise the mohel wouldn't be willing to do the milah in the first place; this is exclusive to the mohel.

If we take on like *Eliyah Rabbah,* could we expand this to include other *muktzeh* that one is carrying permissibly? Can you give it to someone else to put away? On the one hand, one can view the second person's act as a new act of moving; that second act isn't part of the original permission granted to the first person when he picked it up *l'tzorech mekomo*. Or you can argue that the exemption that the first person has, allowing him to remove the *muktzeh* to wherever he wants, is due to Chazal viewing the entire act of moving as removing the *muktzeh* from its place. Even once he gives it over to someone else, it is still moving to vacate it from its place.

Pri Megadim has a novelty: As soon as one stops to rest, known as *omed lafush,* he must put down the *muktzeh* and can't continue with it. We can understand this as follows: As soon as one stops walking, his continued

15. 331:5.

16. *Yoreh Dei'ah* 266.

17. Also the *Taz* brings that this *heter* is the basis for moving the milah knife.

walking is a new act. Only the original act received a leniency.[18] If we hold that it is permitted to hand over the *muktzeh* to someone else, all the more so if one stops, he'll still be permitted to continue to carry the *muktzeh*. *Chochmos Shlomo* permits one who is moving *muktzeh* to give it to someone else.

Who Do We Pasken Like?

R' Akiva Eiger[19] brings a proof to *Gra* from a *Yerushalmi*. The *Yerushalmi* relates that if someone has a container of *demai*, i.e., a mixture of both *terumah temei'ah* (which is *muktzeh*) and *chullin* (non-*muktzeh*) inside, he must separate *terumos* and *maaseros* (tithes) to be allowed to consume the produce. On Shabbos it is forbidden to tithe one's produce. The Mishnah teaches a solution: One stipulates that whatever produce he leaves inside the container is the *maaser* and what he will consume is the *chullin*. One is allowed to pick up the container because it is a *bosis l'issur v'heter*. However, once one removes the *chullin* from inside, the container is now only a *bosis* for *issur*; it is only supporting the *terumah temei'ah*. If the container was already in his hand when he removed the *chullin*, he should be allowed to continue to move it based on *odo b'yado*. Nevertheless, the Gemara asks: How can you carry the *terumah temei'ah*? It's *muktzeh*! We see from the Gemara's wonderment that only when one has been given a leniency to move *muktzeh* can he continue moving it, but here the original permission didn't include a *heter* to move the *terumah*.

---

18. This *Pri Megadim* could be a nice proof to *Ohr Samei'ach*'s idea that if accidentally one picked up *muktzeh*, he can move it to where he wants, because the *issur* of *muktzeh* was made *atu hotzaah*, to protect the prohibition of carrying. An act of *hotzaah* needs an *akirah v'hanachah*. If he mistakenly picked it up, there is no reason to be *gozer atu hotzaah* since one can't be *chayav* on the *akirah*. In *Pri Megadim*'s case too, if one stops while holding the *muktzeh* and then continues walking, it is a new *maaseh akirah*, and so should be forbidden to protect *hotzaah*. However, we can't prove so from *Pri Megadim*. Perhaps all he means is that we use *gidrei hotzaah* as a measuring stick as to what is considered a new *maaseh tiltul*. Chazal were only *matir* that first *maaseh tiltul*, so the minute a new *maaseh tiltul* starts there is no longer a *heter*.

19. *Siman* 308 on *Magen Avraham*.

Mishnah Berurah[20] discusses a similar case, where one is separating challah on Yom Tov. Before one has tithed the challah, the dough is permitted to be moved, but once one has separated a piece from the dough as challah, this new piece is now *muktzeh* because one can't consume it; rather, he must burn it. Yet *Mishnah Berurah* still permits to move the challah to wherever you want. We seemingly have a clear proof that *Mishnah Berurah paskens* like *Magen Avraham,* against *Gra,* permitting any type of continuation once the *muktzeh* is in your hand.

However, R' Shlomo Zalman Auerbach refutes this proof. He explains that *Mishnah Berurah* only permits moving the challah when first you separate the dough, since only once it is in your hand do you then set it aside as challah. This is opposed to declaring a piece of dough on the table as the challah. The reason is that when you have the dough in your hand, it is not yet *muktzeh,* as you don't have to render this piece into challah; you could choose any other part of the dough to become challah. It came into your hand in a permissible manner and only later on did it became *muktzeh.* (In contrast, in R' Akiva Eiger's case from the *Yerushalmi,* the *terumah* is created retroactively based on *bereirah.* Therefore it's not considered that it became *muktzeh* in his hand, rather we view it that when he first picked up the container, there was *muktzeh* inside. Yet because it was a *bosis* to *heter* and *issur,* his act is treated as only moving the non-*muktzeh*).

Shulchan Aruch[21] *paskens* that as soon as someone lights Shabbos candles, they must drop the match: "*mashlichin hapetilos.*" *Gra* references a *Tosefta* in *Sukkah* as support to this opinion. The *Tosefta* brings the same halachah of dropping the match. The match came into your hand before Shabbos, and still you see that you must drop it once you finish lighting. This is a good proof against *Magen Avraham* and seemingly we see from *Shulchan Aruch* that he doesn't side with *Magen Avraham.*

Although *Gra* understands that moving *muktzeh* is the *issur* to which the *Tosefta* is referring to, the commentators suggest another potential

20. 506:29.
21. 263:10.

problem in moving the match: One might come to extinguish it, as opposed to allowing it to go out on its own. If so we have no conclusive proof of what *Shulchan Aruch* holds regarding the permissibility of continuation of movement once the *muktzeh* is in one's hand. This halachah of not moving the match may be totally unrelated to *muktzeh*, rather due to a worry that you may extinguish it. (Either way, the implication of "*Mashlichin*" seems to be placing it down as opposed to moving with it, but not that you have to literally drop it[22] (question #1).

Seeds and Pits

The final point to discuss is the case of one who is eating a fruit and is left with the seed or pit in his hand (question #2). What does he do? There is a third opinion, besides *Magen Avraham* and *Gra* - that of *Even HaOzer*,[23] brought in *Mishnah Berurah*[24] regarding this discussion. He explicitly discusses this question and forbids to continue carrying the pits or shells of fruits. He infers so from *Rambam*,[25] who says that when eating fruit one must throw away the pits immediately, *ochel ha'ochel v'zorek l'achorav*. *Even HaOzer* understands that Chazal only gave the *heter* of *odo b'yado* by the type of *muktzeh* which one anyway can have a reason to move, for example *kli shemelachto l'issur* that is permitted *l'tzorech gufo u'mekomo*. Since these types of *muktzeh* are lenient and we find precedence allowing one to move them in certain circumstances, so too, once they are in your hand you can continue to move them. However, in our case where you are left with the pits in your hand, these are *muktzeh machmas gufo*, as they have no use whatsoever on Shabbos, consequently they will not have a leniency of *odo b'yado*.

---

22. *Chut Shani* says that placing it down isn't considered *tiltul*, and the *poskim* chose the word *zorkin* since placing it down without a decisive act, delineating where one places it, resembles an act of throwing.

23. 266.

24. 308:13.

25. 26:16.

This is more similar to *Gra*'s understanding in the leniency of *odo b'yado* than *Magen Avraham,* yet *Mishnah Berurah* clearly brings *Even HaOzer* as a different opinion, which is concurrent with his following explanation. *Mishnah Berurah* understands that *Gra* is only giving a leniency based on starting with "permission," so there is a difference between the two opinions. And even according to the way that we presented *Gra,* the distinction between *Gra* and *Even HaOzer* lies whether you had a right to take the *kli shemelachto l'issur* or not.

R' Shlomo Zalman Auerbach holds that *Mishnah Berurah*'s opinion is like *Even HaOzer.* In Siman 308, *Mishnah Berurah,* despite bringing all three opinions, concludes like *Even HaOzer.*[26] *Magen Avraham* would disagree with *Even HaOzer* and permit taking the pits to the trash can, because whenever *muktzeh* is in your hand you may continue carrying it. However, *Gra* would hold that it's forbidden, as there never was a "permission" of *muktzeh* allowing you to carry these pits. Ideally, one should spit the pits directly in the trash can or on a plate that has other items on it (which one can then move due to the other items on the plate).

Most *poskim* forbid even taking fish bones out of your mouth with your hands, since bones are *muktzeh*; rather, one should spit them out and not have to touch them.[27] There is a support to this practice from what the Gemara records of the rabbis. They would "*zorek l'hu b'lishnah* - throw out the shells [from their mouths]." This would be true even according to *Magen Avraham.* Since you need to permit a new act of moving, being in your mouth is not "*kvar ba l'yado.*" However, if it would be embarrassing or offensive to spit it out, then it's plausible that Chazal would be lenient in such cases.

---

26. R' Shlomo Zalman Auerbach says *Mishnah Berurah*'s *psak* that on Yom Tov one can separate challah is not a contradiction, since as he explained, the dough only became *muktzeh* in one's hand, so even *Even HaOzer* would be lenient in such a case. This is not so straightforward; the way we presented *Even HaOzer,* seemingly he wouldn't permit to continue to move the dough. צ"ע what opinion *Mishnah Berurah* consistently follows.

27. R' Chaim Kanievsky is quoted to be lenient, and R' Ovadia Yosef is lenient; he says it's *derech achilah.*

Eggshells

Ben Ish Chai holds that even though eggshells are occasionally consumed by chickens, they are still *muktzeh*, as they have no regular use for a person. Accordingly, we will again be confronted with the same opinions regarding what to do with the shells once one has peeled an egg (in the event that moving them doesn't qualify for the leniency of *graf shel re'i*). According to *Magen Avraham*, if they are still in one's hands, he can take them to the trash can, while *Gra* wouldn't permit it. The suggested practice is to shell them over the trash can.

Rema[28] *paskens* that even though broken vessels under certain circumstances are *muktzeh*,[29] one can still move them if they pose a danger being left in their present state (question #4). Broken pieces are *muktzeh machmas gufo*, therefore *Gra* should limit as to where one can move them to, as the leniency of *odo b'yado* cannot apply to *muktzeh machmas gufo*. However, *Beis Yosef* explains that in situations of danger, Chazal never imposed *muktzeh* at all, so there are no limitations to where one can move them.

Summary

The *Rishonim* conclusively prove from the Gemara that the leniency Chazal gave to move a *kli l'tzorech mekomo* is not restricted to vacating the space one needs; rather, once the item is in one's hand, he can move it to wherever he wants.

The *poskim* argue about *muktzeh* that came into one's hand: What does he have to do with it? *Magen Avraham* is the most lenient opinion, holding that all *muktzeh*, regardless how it came into one's hands, one can move anywhere he wants. This is because the problem of *muktzeh* is the original handling of the *muktzeh*, but if it's already in one's hand, there is no reason to impose any sanctions. *Gra* is stringent; only if one had a "allowance" to start moving the item can he continue moving it. If one started moving this item before Shabbos, he can't continue because he didn't receive a dis-

28. 308:6 brought from *Orchos Chaim*.
29. We will elaborate on this in chapter 6.

pensation to move it. Rather, it just wasn't yet Shabbos, so there were no limitations when he began his moving of the item.

The opinion that *Mishnah Berurah* follows is that of *Even HaOzer*. Only categories of *muktzeh* that have leniencies to move in specific circumstances can one continue to move when they came into one's hand. This is because since these categories anyway have leniencies, we therefore treat them differently.

Answers

1. *Shulchan Aruch* requires a woman to drop the matches after lighting the candles. *Gra* understands this is because the match is *muktzeh* and subsequent movement is forbidden. Dropping it just means not moving with it, but if you place the match on a tray to go out, it is allowed.
2. The conclusion of *Mishnah Berurah* seems to be stringent: Since seeds and pits are *muktzeh machmas gufo*, you can't continue to carry them once they come into your hand. In awkward scenarios there is the opinion of *Magen Avraham* to rely on and you can move the seeds in your hands.
3. According to most opinions you can continue moving a *muktzeh* toy a child places in your hand. *Muktzeh* toys are *kli shemelachto l'issur*, so since leniencies apply to them; even *Even HaOzer* will permit moving them.
4. Even if the broken pieces are not in your hands, if they pose a danger left around, they can be moved to the trash can. If the item smashes while you're holding it, to the extent it is further useless and so now *muktzeh machmas gufo*, if it's not dangerous placing it down where you are, then you must put it down and not continue moving it.

Chapter 5

טלטול מוקצה לצורך מקומו

Moving Muktzeh to Vacate a Space

Questions

1. Mikey washed the pots and pans before Shabbos came in and left them out to dry on the countertop. He would like to put them away, as their presence in the kitchen bothers his wife. Can he put them back in the cupboard?
2. The kids have taken their *muktzeh* electric toys out of the cupboard. Can I put them back, since the mess of seeing them lying on the floor is bothersome?
3. If the kids placed a phone on the table, and the presence of such a non-*Shabbosdig* object on the table bothers someone, can he remove it?
4. A fan is blowing too strongly in Yaakov's direction. Can he move it to face a different angle or direction?

We have seen before[1] that at the inception of *muktzeh*, all forms of moving *keilim* were forbidden. Progressively leniencies were given. Abaye and Rava argue what Nechemiah permitted at each stage of the different leniencies. The *beraisa*[2] says, התירו וחזרו והתירו וחזרו והתירו - "They permitted and permitted furthermore and permitted a third time."

1. Introduction and chapter 1.
2. 123b.

There were three separate stages when the rabbis saw fit to relax the original decrees that Nechemiah had introduced.

Abaye explains that the first "*hetiro*," i.e., the first stage that was permitted, was a *kli shemelachto l'heter l'tzorech gufo*, moving a "permissible" vessel for the sake of using it. The second stage permitted moving a *kli shemelachto l'heter l'tzorech mekomo*, moving a "permissible" vessel for the sake of using the space it occupied. Rava argues: Why should the leniency of moving the *kli l'tzorech gufo* and the leniency of moving it *l'tzorech mekomo* be given at two separate times?[3] Rather, the first stage permitted moving for both reasons - for the sake of using the item and vacating it's space, *l'tzorech gufo u'mekomo*. However, we see from Abaye that these are two distinct cases. The way we can understand Abaye's distinction is that *l'tzorech gufo* means that one needs to use the actual object, one desires to move it for its purpose. *l'tzorech mekomo* is when one doesn't want to use it for any purpose. The space where it currently is needs to be used for something else; one is not interested in using the actual object. This a totally different sort of leniency to *l'tzorech gufo*. Why should both leniencies be encompassed in the same stage?

The Difference between a Kli Shemelachto L'Heter and a Kli Shemelachto L'Issur

Sefer HaShlamah explains the difference between a *kli shemelachto l'heter*, which is permitted to move *m'chamah l'tzel* (from the sun to shade, i.e., to protect it), and a *kli shemelachto l'issur*, which is not. The reason is that since the majority of the usages of a *kli shemelachto l'heter* can be done on Shabbos, when saving the *kli* from getting ruined there is a strong likelihood that you will end up using it on Shabbos. So in truth, it can be considered that one has moved it for the sake of Shabbos. In contrast, a *kli shemelachto l'issur* is unlikely to be used on Shabbos. Therefore, when saving it, we consider that one is saving this item for the sake of a weekday, as this is the likely time when one would use it. We can deduce from this

3. Rava's phrase is: התירו קתני מה לי צ״ג מה לי צ״מ.

Sefer HaShlamah a beautiful principle: Chazal gave permission to move an item only when the moving of the *muktzeh* is for the sake of Shabbos. (*Meiri* also uses this idea to argue on *Shitah LaRan,* who holds that *m'chamah l'tzel* has no limitation and one can move a *kli shemelachto l'heter* for any purpose. He says that a *kli shemelachto l'heter* is permitted *m'chamah l'tzel,* but not when being moved without any reason, as that is *tiltul shelo l'tzorech* and not included in the leniencies given by Nechemiah.)

Tehillah L'Dovid [4] says that if one knows that later he will require to use a *kli shemelachto l'issur* but presently it's getting ruined in the rain, one can move it inside already now. This is not a contradiction to the Gemara that says there is no leniency of *m'chamah l'tzel* by *kli shemelachto l'issur,* because this scenario is considered *l'tzorech gufo* (not that there is an exceptional leniency of *m'chamah l'tzel* in cases where one might come to use it). His novel interpretation is that the leniency to move an item in order to use it doesn't require that you make immediate use of it. Moving it in order to use at any future time on Shabbos is sufficient; it doesn't matter that right now his moving is involved in saving the object, because we view his ultimate intention to use this item at a later date to define his action, not that it's just an act of saving the item.

Abaye's Question

We can now answer our original question that Abaye asked on Rava: How can Rava encompass both *tzorech gufo* and *tzorech mekomo* in the same leniency? Surely they are two distinct dispensations? Now it makes perfect sense; the underlying idea behind permitting *l'tzorech gufo* is that the movement is for the sake of Shabbos, as this item is being required for use now on Shabbos. So once the rabbis permitted "for the sake of Shabbos," this will also include a leniency of *l'tzorech mekomo* because

---

4. 308:5.

the movement of the item, allowing you access to the space that is currently being occupied, is equally a need of Shabbos.[5] [6]

With this principle, we can perhaps lean toward being lenient when moving a *kli shemelachto l'issur*, even in a case where you don't have the classic leniency of *l'tzorech mekomo*, i.e., one doesn't intend on using the vacant space and one's sole intention is because the item's presence is bothersome. Since we can say that making the area clean is certainly considered for the sake of Shabbos, and we've explained that this is the principle behind this leniency that allows one to move something *l'tzorech mekomo*, so too in our case it can certainly be considered a movement for the sake of Shabbos, which is permitted.

Even though some *poskim* distinguish between positive benefit and passive benefit, that only a positive benefit is included in the leniency of *l'tzorech mekomo*, they say that to tidy up is just a passive benefit that would not be permitted. In many instances when the presence of an item is truly bothersome, it can be considered a positive benefit, as once tidied up, the sight of a clean area gives one a positive pleasure. This is more than something that's done which has just removed your bother.

Tosafos[7] says that one can send tefillin as a gift on Yom Tov, despite tefillin being a *kli shemelachto l'issur*. Why is this carrying considered *l'tzorech gufo*? We see from here that the very fact that it gives one pleasure to give a present to his friend is considered a *tzorech gufo*.[8] Here too, the

---

5. Why then does Rava distinguish that *m'chamah l'tzel* is not included in the original *heter*? It must be because it's not an immediate *tzorech Shabbos*.

6. This fits well with the reason brought by *Rambam* explaining why *muktzeh* is *assur*. He writes that just like there is a *din* that our speech should not be about weekday matters, but it should be clear from one's speech that today is Shabbos, similarly, our moving on Shabbos should be different than on a weekday. From what one touches on Shabbos, it should be clear it is Shabbos. Similar to speech, that when the speech is for the sake of Shabbos, it is permitted, so too there is a leniency in *muktzeh* when it is moved for the sake of Shabbos.

7. 60a, s.v. לא.

8. *Chut Shani* differs in the explanation. He says specifically that if one sends it on Yom Tov, it is permitted, because the mitzvah of *simchas Yom Tov* causes it to be considered *tzorech gufo*. R' Akiva Eiger (306, *Magen Avraham, se'if katan* 15) certainly learned our explanation. He *paskens* based on this Gemara that one can send

very pleasure in having the house tidy can be considered a positive pleasure and if we can consider the Gemara's scenario of tefillin as being *tzorech gufo*, our cases can be considered *l'tzorech mekomo*.

Machazeh Eliyahu[9] brings a (seemingly) irrefutable proof to be lenient in such cases. The Gemara in *Shabbos*[10] says that according to Rebbe Shimon,[11] once a person's *menorah* has been extinguished, he can bring it inside from the courtyard to his house in order that the non-Jews won't see that he lit the *menorah*. Even according to Rebbe Shimon, who is the most lenient regarding *muktzeh*, agrees that one can only move a *kli l'tzorech gufo u'mekomo*. Here it is not being moved in order to use the area that the *menorah* is occupying; rather, one doesn't want the item to be in this place. So why can he move it?

We can infer from this case that since the presence of the *menorah* in the courtyard concerns him, it is permitted to be moved under the leniency of *tzorech mekomo*. We see from here like we were suggesting, that the leniency of *tzorech mekomo* has broader parameters than strictly vacating the space for one's immediate use. Even if the space is not actually required, but its present location is bothersome, this is also included in *tzorech mekomo*. (*Ritva* infers from *Rashi*, who says it was dangerous; that it wasn't a case of a life-threatening danger, but rather monetary danger. We can bring a proof to this, because if it was very dangerous, why is it only permissible to move according to Rebbe Shimon? According to Rebbe Yehudah, despite it being *muktzeh machmas gufo*, it would be permitted to move if it's a life-threatening danger. It therefore must be that it wasn't a life-threatening danger.)

---

candlesticks to a *chasan* on Shabbos.

9. *Siman* 46.

10. 45a.

11. According to Rebbe Yehudah, the *menorah* is *muktzeh machmas issur*. One can't move it at all, even once the candles go out, because at *bein hashemashos* it's usage was forbidden due to the prohibition of extinguishing the flame. Rebbe Shimon doesn't hold of *muktzeh machmas issur*.

Determining whether One Really Needs to Vacate the Space

R' Falk continues in *Machazeh Eliyahu* to ask on himself a strong question from the following Gemara:[12] If a used roasting stick is on the floor, and remaining on the floor presents a danger to people, it is permitted to move, under the special leniency of *kotz bireshus harabbim*, a thorn in a public place, i.e., when the *muktzeh* is in a place which presents a danger, it is permitted to move it. Many *Rishonim*[13] explain that this roasting stick is a *kli shemelachto l'issur*. R' Falk asks: If this is the case, then why do we need to bring the special leniency of *kotz bireshus harabbim*? Why is it not sufficient to be permitted under the leniency of *tzorech mekomo*? He concludes that it must be a contradiction to the Gemara we brought earlier, allowing one to bring in the *menorah*.

However, if we look carefully, there is a significant difference between the two cases. In the case of the roasting stick, if it was anything else that was on the floor that doesn't present a danger, would one want to move it? It's only because of the potential danger that one wants to move it. He would leave a non-dangerous item on the floor. We see that it isn't the mess on the floor which bothers him; rather, it's this specific *kli* that he wants removed to avoid its potential damage. In truth, one is not interested in vacating the space per se, so it is forbidden. In a case where even if we were to substitute the *muktzeh* item that one wants to move with another item, and still one would want to move the item, this is an indication that we know he truly is interested in the vacating of the space and not just removing this specific *kli*.

Pots and Pans, and Toys

So too when moving pots and pans from the counter (question #1), it is not the specific *kli*, i.e., the pot, that is bothering a person. If there was something else in that space (which isn't normally kept there), he'd also want to move that. Once one has passed the litmus test that he is truly in-

12. *Beitzah* 28b.
13. *Rashi* and *Rashba*.

terested in the area being free, this moving can be included in the leniency of *l'tzorech mekomo*. We can still be lenient in our case, but we have lost the proof from the case of the *menorah,* since in that case he wants to move the *menorah* specifically. If anything else was there, it wouldn't bother him.[14]

The same would apply to tidying up the toys (question #2). If anything scattered on the floor bothers someone, then he can be lenient based on our broader definition of the leniency of *l'tzorech mekomo*. *Ohr L'Tzion*[15] permits removing pots that have been placed on a table because one is honoring Shabbos by having a tidy table. However, since there are those who still forbid this, they don't accept our distinction. Therefore, avoiding directly moving the toys would be recommended.

In order to forbid our case of moving something whose presence is bothersome, some bring a proof from *Baal HaMeor*.[16] The Gemara says that if an animal has a load of *keilim* (that are *kli shemelachto l'issur*) on it, and it is weighing down the animal so that one wants to remove the load, nevertheless it is forbidden to take off the load. *Baal HaMeor* explains that since one doesn't intend to make use of the place on the animal where the utensils are located, due to the fact that it is forbidden to use an animal on Shabbos, it isn't considered *l'tzorech mekomo*.[17] We must distinguish why this won't be included in our broader parameters of *tzorech mekomo*. Surely one is moving the load to vacate the space? These heavy items on the animal are causing it pain. It's the weight of the utensil itself that is

---

14. Accordingly, we must explain that the *heter* to move the *menorah* is due to *sakanah,* similar to what we learn from the case of the roasting stick in the public domain. We must then address: Why can you move it only according to Rebbe Shimon, and not also according to Rebbe Yehudah? Surely the leniencies of moving the roasting stick is according to all? צ״ע.

15. Vol. 2, 26:3.

16. *Shabbos* 154b.

17. *Meiri's lashon* is very strong: שאין צ״מ נאמר אלא שצריך מקומו ממש לישב בו — "The leniency of moving to use its place is only when you want to sit there." This does slightly indicate that *Meiri* doesn't agree to the principle we have presented. (Unless one makes a *lav davka* in his *lashon* of "*leishev bo*." Normally one would use it for sitting in, but it is equally permissible if it is just to free the area.)

bothering him, not the lack of an empty space. If the animal was loaded with feathers, one wouldn't bother taking them off. That shows that it's not vacating the area one desires, but rather to alleviate the animal's pain. Another reason to explain why it's forbidden is that one's interest in moving it is only so that the animal doesn't die. This is an interest for weekday, not Shabbos, and this is not included in the leniency of *tzorech mekomo*.[18]

The Bothersome Phone

R' Shlomo Zalman Auerbach[19] *paskens* based on this Gemara that if a *kli shemelachto l'issur* is on the table and its presence is bothersome, it is not permitted to move it. This is because it's the utensil that you want to vacate, as opposed to the place, and therefore one's movement will not be covered by the leniency of *l'tzorech mekomo*. Those who argue with R' Shlomo Zalman and permit one to move an item in such a case, where the actual place isn't required, rather its presence is not wanted, can explain that it is permitted to move because one is moving it for the sake of Shabbos. He has an immediate interest in the removal of the utensil. The correct approach would be to be stringent in our questions, since we have no proof to be lenient, but if there is a great need, then one can rely on the argument it is for the sake of Shabbos. One shouldn't move a phone that was placed mistakenly on the table on Shabbos (question #3) because it is only the phone that is bothersome. One is not interested in the empty space. According to *Ohr L'Tzion* quoted earlier, that moving for the sake of *kavod Shabbos* renders the act *l'tzorech mekomo*, a phone on a table certainly is a disdain to Shabbos, so moving it can be considered *tzorech mekomo*.

---

18. A further distinction is that in this case one's desire for the *keilim* to be removed from the animal is not for the animal's body to be vacant per se; rather, one's intention is to alleviate the load of the animal, which happens to be achieved by freeing the space. Therefore one is not moving it for the benefit of the area. In contrast, our questions are when the ultimate intention is to have an empty space.

19. *Shemiras Shabbos K'Hilchasah* 20:6.

Moving a Blowing Fan

If we accept that a fan is a *kli shemelachto l'issur,*[20] then in order to be permitted to move it when the air is disturbing someone (question #4), the act of moving would need to be classified as either *tzorech gufo* or *tzorech mekomo.* It cannot be considered that one is using the fan even though it will continue to blow air in the new direction, since this is a use one doesn't currently want to have from the fan; one is just interested that in this space there will be no fan blowing air. Because of the air that is currently being moved by the fan against one's will, we can classify that the area is, so to speak, "dysfunctional." It comes out that one's moving of the fan is for the sake of improving the place. That is included in the leniency of *l'tzorech mekomo.* Even if we disagree with our aforementioned conclusion that whenever something is being moved in order to vacate a space, it is permitted, here it's different. A person wants to make use of the area that's currently unusable due to the *muktzeh* that is there. This is classical *l'tzorech mekomo.* R' Moshe Feinstein[21] agrees that this is *l'tzorech mekomo.*

A similar idea is presumably behind *Yam Yissachar,* who permits moving tefillin out of a room if a couple wants to have relations in that room, even if tefillin are *kli shemelachto l'issur* and even though one doesn't need the exact area where the tefillin is located. This is because we take on that it's as if the tefillin are using the area of the entire room. Since the whole room is useless regarding having relations, due to the presence of the tefillin, one is considered moving it *l'tzorech mekomo* to enable the room to be used.

Summary

The most accurate way to explain the various leniencies that Chazal gave to move both a *kli shemelachto l'issur* and a *kli shemelachto l'heter* is that whenever the moving is considered *l'tzorech Shabbos,* it is permitted.

---

20. We discussed this in chapter 1.

21. Quoted in *Sefer Tiltulei Shabbos.* The same would be true regarding moving a ringing alarm clock.

When one is vacating a space not to use the area but rather so that the area will be free of the item, it can be considered that he is doing it for his Shabbos needs, so there is room to expand *l'tzorech mekomo* to encompass this movement.

We resolved conflicting sources from the Gemara with the following rule: If it is specifically this item whose current location is an inconvenience, but if something else were in its place, one wouldn't have the same wish to move it, we can't consider that he is moving it to vacate the space. The space is not what he desires; rather, the removal of this specific item. If one would want to move any item that is in this space, we can consider that he is moving the *kli l'tzorech mekomo*, to vacate the space, even though he won't actually use that specific area. Another reason to be lenient in these cases is that having an orderly house is part of the honor of Shabbos, so the act of tidying up *muktzeh* is defined as an act of moving *tzorech mekomo*.

Answers

1. *Ohr L'Tzion* permits moving the pots and pan because ensuring a tidy house is honoring Shabbos. We suggested also it can be permitted under our broader definition of *l'tzorech mekomo*, that even if Mikey just wants the space vacant, even if he is not going to use the area, it qualifies for *l'tzorech mekomo*.
2. The same answer seemingly applies to toys.
3. R' Shlomo Zalman Auerbach forbids moving the telephone. Even according to our expansive parameters of *tzorech mekomo*, moving the phone would not be permitted because one is not interested in vacating the area; rather it is the phone that bothers him.
4. Moving a fan to blow in a different direction is a classic application of *tzorech mekomo*, since Yaakov wants to use the area the fan is currently occupying.

Chapter 6, Part 1

שברי כלים

Broken Vessels

Questions

1. The handle of Shmuel's mug fell off. Can he still use the mug on Shabbos? Does the halachah differ when it broke, before or after Shabbos?
2. A child's action figure broke on Shabbos. Can an adult move the broken pieces?

The Mishnah[1] brings an argument between the *Tanna Kamma* and Rebbe Yehudah whether *shivrei keilim* (broken vessels) are *muktzeh* or not. We *pasken* like the *Tanna Kamma,* who holds that as long as the broken pieces can still serve a purpose, even if it's not a purpose that is similar to the original function (such as a bowl that has smashed and a piece of the shards can now be used as a covering for something else), it is not *muktzeh.* Rebbe Yehudah argues that only if these broken pieces still have some sort of use that is within their original function, are they permitted to be moved, e.g., if a plate smashes in half, one can still use the broken pieces to place food on them. The Gemara explains that this dispute only is relevant when the *kli* breaks *on* Shabbos. If it broke already before Shabbos, then even according to Rebbe Yehudah it would be permitted to use even broken pieces that don't have a use that is similar to their original purpose. This is because when Shabbos came in, any function that the broken pieces can serve will cause the shards to receive a *shem kli* (identity as a vessel) for that purpose.

---

1. 122b.

Different Ways in Understanding the Tannaic Dispute

The Gemara explains the reasoning behind the *Tanna Kamma* and Rebbe Yehudah, whether to allow the movement of *shivrei keilim*, broken vessels, as follows: מר סבר מוכן הוא ומר סבר נולד - "The *Tanna Kamma* holds it is prepared and Rebbe Yehudah holds it is something new." Something that in its present state was not in existence before Shabbos is considered "*nolad*." Rebbe Yehudah views the broken pieces as a new entity that previously didn't exist. Even though the physical pieces did exist, the new state renders the pieces as a new item. The *Tanna Kamma* argues that the broken pieces are "*muchan*" (prepared). This phrase is very cryptic. The commentators argue over what he means by "*muchan*." Does he hold that they are not *nolad*, in direct contrast to Rebbe Yehudah? For example, a broken piece that previously served the function of a bowl and now serves the function of a lid isn't a completely new function, and consequently it is not considered something new. Or does the *Tanna Kamma* agree that this new function of a lid is a completely new function and the shards are a new entity, hence it is *nolad*, only he holds *nolad* isn't forbidden?

There is an apparent contradiction in *Rambam*.[2] In the halachos of Shabbos he *paskens* that broken vessels are allowed to be moved even when not doing their original task, while in the halachos of Yom Tov he *paskens* that they are *muktzeh*. A simple way to resolve this contradiction is that *Rambam paskens* in accordance with the *Tanna Kamma*, with the understanding that the *Tanna Kamma* holds that broken vessels are *nolad*. However, the *Tanna Kamma* is of the opinion that *nolad* is not forbidden. Therefore, in the halachos of Shabbos, where *Rambam paskens* like Rebbe Shimon, who permits most forms of *nolad*, it will be permitted, whereas in the halachos of Yom Tov *Rambam paskens* like Rebbe Yehudah, who forbids all *muktzeh* and *nolad*, since the shards are *nolad* it will be *muktzeh*.

Pri Megadim[3] notes that the same contradiction exists in the opinion of *Shulchan Aruch*. Although we could suggest the same resolution,[4] the

2. 25:12.
3. *Eshel Avraham*, point 15.
4. I.e., *Shulchan Aruch* also *paskens* like Rebbe Shimon on Shabbos and like Rebbe

implication of *Beis Yosef*[5] is that he learns the argument between the *Tanna Kamma* and Rebbe Yehudah differently than how we explained in *Rambam*. The dispute is whether broken vessels are actually considered *nolad* or not. The *Tanna Kamma* holds it is not something new and therefore will not have any restrictions, whereas Rebbe Yehudah holds that it is *nolad*, so it will be forbidden and we won't be able to answer like we did in *Rambam*. If in truth *Shulchan Aruch* learns like this, we must answer that *Shulchan Aruch paskens* like the *Tanna Kamma* - that broken *keilim* are not *muktzeh*. In Siman 308 he is referring to when the *keilim* can still perform a function. However, in Siman 501, where he *paskens* that broken vessels are *muktzeh*, he is referring specifically to when they have no function at all. The significance of this is that *Rashba*[6] says that when something is broken to an extent that it can't be used at all anymore, this is an extent of *nolad* to which even Rebbe Shimon and the *Tanna Kamma* agree to.

New Approach of Rosh

The Gemara explains that the reason why any broken vessels are not *muktzeh* as long as they presently serve a function, is because of *huchnu agav avihen*. This means that since they originally had an identity as a *kli* when Shabbos came in, that original identity is retained. However, most *Rishonim* understand that the conclusion of the Gemara is that the broken vessels still have *shem kli*, hence they are not *muktzeh* and we don't need a new principle of *huchnu agav avihen*. *Rosh*[7] implies that broken vessels is a special dispensation; it's not permitted just due to the fact it is identified as a *kli*. When listing the different categories whereby Chazal permitted carrying *muktzeh*, *Rosh*'s seventh category is broken vessels. This must be that even though they are not identified as a *kli*, there is a unique leniency to move them since they once were a *kli*.

Yehudah on Yom Tov.

5. 308:7.

6. *Beitzah* 8a.

7. *Shu"t, siman* 25.

Broken Vessels Nowadays

However, even according to *Rosh,* who permits broken vessels even though they don't have a *shem kli,* since they once were a *kli,* nowadays broken *keilim* are likely to be *muktzeh.* Even though there seems to be more room for leniency according to *Rosh* that one doesn't need a *shem kli,* there is still a basic requirement that the broken *kli* needs to have a practical function. R' Shlomo Zalman Auerbach argues that since nowadays due to our blessed abundance no one uses any broken dish for any other use, they throw it away immediately, our broken vessels won't have a *shem kli* nor the special leniency that Chazal once gave that broken pieces of a *kli* can be moved.

We can bring a proof to R' Shlomo Zalman's *psak* from the Gemara about *krumiyos* (type of reed mat). The Gemara[8] explains that one can carry broken pieces of these mats on Shabbos because they presently serve the same function as before, namely to cover dirt. *Tosafos* explains that the Gemara is adding this reason to explain this ruling even according to Rebbe Yehudah (according to the *Tanna Kamma* it is not *muktzeh* even if it doesn't perform the original function).

However, *Rashba* argues that with these mats it's imperative that they still serve their original function, even according to the *Tanna Kamma.* The reason why this case is different is because during the week one throws away these broken mats; one doesn't usually value their current use. Only now, when they have the same function as before and they broke on Shabbos, the significance of which is that they had an identity of a *kli* when Shabbos began, can we permit them, based on the principle the Gemara brought earlier: *huchnu agav avihen.* This means that despite this item not being worthy of having an identity of a *kli* (since most people would discard of them immediately), since when Shabbos came in it was used to cover dirt and it can still be used to cover dirt, albeit in a somewhat lesser fashion, the original identity of a *kli* can continue on the *shivrei mechatzalos* (broken pieces of mat). Nowadays, we throw out broken *keilim* straight away. They are comparable to the *shivrei mechatzalos,* and

---

8. 125a.

since they don't do *me'in melachtan harishonah* (they no longer can be used even akin to their original function), we can't permit them based on *huchnu agav avihen*.

Furthermore, Rava argues that even in a public domain, a broken shard isn't *muktzeh*. The stress in this ruling is that despite its current location in the public fairway, where it is not likely to have any purpose at all, since inside the house, where there are *keilim*, the shard can be used to cover a *kli*, wherever it is located it will have an identity of a *kli*. The other *Amoraim* who argue must hold that in order for the broken piece to have an identity as a *kli*, it must have a likely use in its present location. According to everyone, the basic requirement is that it has a practical, likely function. Broken pieces of crockery nowadays have no likely use![9]

A classic illustration of this case would be if a handle falls off a mug on Shabbos (question #1). The handle has no present function, so it won't be subject to the exemption of broken vessels. However, the mug presently functions, so it should be that it would still be permitted. We need to continue the topic to clarify this.

When One Intends on Mending the Broken Pieces

The Gemara[10] says that if one's strap on his shoes breaks in a private domain, it becomes *muktzeh*. However, if it breaks in a *carmelis* (semipublic domain), since it's not safe to leave them there as someone might take them, one is likely to improvise a makeshift strap and continue wearing them. Since he will still wear them, they do not become *muktzeh*. It needs to be understood why a broken shoe in a private domain is different than broken vessels. If it can be worn, it still has a function.

---

9. There are *poskim* like *Chut Shani* and *Chazon Ovadia* who are lenient to move broken *keilim* nowadays. R' Shmuel Wosner's argument is that the broken pieces retain their status of a vessel because theoretically they can be used; if one is a pressing situation, he will use a broken piece as a covering. We have disproved this argument. Nevertheless, according to all opinions, if the broken pieces are in a location where they present a danger to people, even if they should be *muktzeh*, still Chazal never imposed *muktzeh* when it's dangerous.

10. 112a.

Raavad[11] explains that currently one doesn't intend to use the broken shoes. He is cautious not to use it for anything else and puts it aside in order to fix later. *Raavad* adds that: יצא מכלל סנדל - "it's left status of shoes," meaning once it is broken, one intends to do nothing with it until he is able to fix it to the extent that it's *not* considered a shoe currently. From here we can learn that even when the broken pieces have a function, but one doesn't want to currently use them, but rather intends to wait to fix it, the broken pieces are *muktzeh*.

This new idea - that a broken *kli* one intends to mend and therefore currently doesn't want to use the broken pieces for another function - can be relevant to toys that break. Sometimes when toys such as action figures break (question #2), they can easily be fixed, but one is worried that if they allow the children to continue playing with the broken toy, it'll reach a state where it won't be mendable. When this is the scenario, the broken toy would be *muktzeh*. However, toys that break that one doesn't intend to fix and children are still pleased to play with are classic examples of broken vessels that still have a use, so children can still play with the broken pieces.

Summary

The reason behind the opinion in the Gemara that permits one to move broken *keilim* (when they still have some sort of use) is that the broken pieces still have an identity as a *kli*, since the broken pieces can still be reused for a new purpose. Nowadays as soon as a *kli* breaks, one throws it out, so broken pieces would be *muktzeh*. If an individual doesn't usually throw away such a broken *kli*, we can still consider it as a *kli* in its broken state and thus not *muktzeh*. When a *kli* has smashed, and its pieces still have a function, but one intends to repair the pieces and is careful in the meanwhile not to continue using it, these pieces do not have the regular exception of broken vessels and are *muktzeh*.

---

11. Brought in *Ritva*.

Answers

1. If Shmuel would have thrown away such a broken mug on a weekday, then on Shabbos he must treat it as *muktzeh*. If it broke before Shabbos, it is not *muktzeh* as long as it still has a function.

2. A broken action figure that one intends on fixing after Shabbos is *muktzeh*. If one isn't intending on fixing it then, they don't become *muktzeh*, since most people don't throw out broken toys immediately.

Part 2

כלים שאין עוד שימוש בהן

Vessels that no Longer Have a Function

Questions

1. Avraham has an empty plastic container, e.g., a milk bottle, that he finished using. Must he be careful not to handle it?

2. After emptying out a packet of sugar, what should I do with the empty packet?

3. Is there any preference from the point of view of *muktzeh* to drink Coke from a bottle rather than from a can? And is an empty Coke can *muktzeh*?

Some *poskim*[12] learn that when one has finished with his disposable cutlery, the cutlery becomes *muktzeh,* similar to what we find by broken vessels. We need to determine why this is so. Asserting that since, when one has finished using the cutlery, the norm is to throw it away, disposable crockery is like a broken *kli* that has no function and so is *muktzeh* - is incorrect. Disposable *keilim,* even once used, are still fit to be used again. It's just that due to their abundance and convenience, no one bothers reusing them. From this point of view, they should still retain their identity as a *kli.* The question is that despite the *kli* not breaking, should the fact that it is destined to be thrown away cause it to lose its *shem kli* on Shabbos?

Arguments to Forbid

Those that forbid moving disposable items once one has finished using them bring the following support to their claim: They say that when something is finished its use, it's rendered *muktzeh,* from the case we find in the Gemara[13] regarding a *machat* (needle). The Gemara distinguishes between two different scenarios. One is with a sewing needle, which is comprised of a hole and a pin. If the hole breaks off, it renders the needle unfit to sew with. However, it can still be used to remove a thorn. Despite having a use, since most people throw it away when the hole breaks, the needle becomes *muktzeh* if it broke on Shabbos. The second scenario occurs if, during the needle-manufacturing process, one is at the stage whereby the pin has been made but the hole hasn't been created yet. Here, the needle is not considered to be *muktzeh* and it can be used on Shabbos. This is because people occasionally use the needle at this stage for that function - as a pin.

---

12. *Shemiras Shabbos K'Hilchasah* 22:53. (However, maybe R' Shlomo Zalman Auerbach is referring only to the disposables in his times, which could only be used once, like the old, flimsy paper plates they had. Perhaps he would agree that modern plastic disposables are different.) Also *Revivus Ephraim* quoted in *Alibah D'Hilchasah,* vol. 47.
13. 123a.

The aforementioned *poskim* who consider used disposables to be *muktzeh* explain from this Gemara, which differentiates between a needle that breaks and a needle during its manufacturing process, that even when something still retains a function, and this function is significant enough to render an unfinished needle a *kli* (in that it's not *muktzeh* at that stage), since it's not common to use the item in this manner anymore, and the *usual practice* is to discard it, this will cause it to become *muktzeh*. The argument is that despite the fact that it's still a *kli* in essence, since it's no longer destined for any further use, it is *muktzeh*![14]

Ritva[15] explains why *shiryei prozmiyos* (tattered clothes) are *muktzeh* in the same way, namely, that even though they can still be used, since the norm is to throw them out, they are *muktzeh*. He questions why the Gemara says they're *muktzeh*. Surely they are still fit to cover dirt? He answers that since they originally served an important function, despite still being fit for use (albeit to a lesser degree), in its current state, people don't actually use it and throw out it immediately. Therefore, as soon as the cloth is torn it's *muktzeh*. Used disposable dishes or cutlery are the same. They are still fit for a use in theory, yet people don't bother keeping them and instead throw them out in this state. This should cause them to be *muktzeh* like broken vessels that are no longer fit for any use.

According to this understanding, even on the very Shabbos when one finishes using a container for its designated use, if one wants to reuse the container, e.g., a cereal box or milk bottle (question #1), he won't be allowed to since unquestionably the norm is to throw it away; even to move it off the table would be in violation of *muktzeh*. Water bottles[16] are the only disposable item that one can claim that it's normal to reuse, and so can't claim that *batal datei* if one wants to move or reuse them. (R' Shlomo

14. They mention another support for this from *Shulchan Aruch* in *se'if* 28, who *paskens* that bread crumbs less than a *kezayis* is not *muktzeh* since they can be fed to animals. Without this reasoning it would be *muktzeh* because it's not destined for any use.

15. 125a.

16. I'm not clear on how to judge a bottle of soda. Is the norm to reuse them, or are only a minority of people willing to do so?

Zalman Auerbach, however, suggests an alternative reason to permit the moving of a used packet, etc., to dispose of it: Perhaps when one has finished with the bottle of milk [or any other package of food], it can be considered part of the usage of it to take the container and place it in the trach can. Without this idea, it would be forbidden to throw out the plastic bottle of milk, since it is *muktzeh* due to its lack of any function.)

Refutations of Proofs

However, neither of the aforementioned proofs that we brought to forbid used disposable items are conclusive. Firstly, one can distinguish the case of the needle is when it is broken and can now no longer perform its original function, and therefore it is considered a broken vessel. Just the *Tanna Kamma* holds that if it still has some function it can retain an identity of a *kli*. The Gemara then proposes that if the new potential use no one actually utilizes, but rather discards the needle, then it really is treated as a broken *kli* with no use and hence is *muktzeh*. In contrast, plastic containers or cutlery that can still serve their original function, and nothing has changed to the physical body of the *kli*, do not begin to enter a classification of broken vessels. We have no precedence that a *kli* like disposables, which are only disregarded due to their abundance but not because of any physical defect, loses their identity of a *kli*.

Furthermore, we can bring proof to this distinction from the case of *krumiyos* (type of reed mat) we discussed in part 1. We quoted *Rashba*,[17] who explains that because the norm is to throw out these mats once they are worn out, the Gemara must say they still perform their original function to permit using them. This is true even according to the *Tanna Kamma*, who generally only requires any use for something not to be *muktzeh*. We see that when the item currently can still serve its original function, even if it is the norm to throw it out it retains its identity of a *kli* and hence it is not *muktzeh*!

17. And *Ritva* says the same idea on 125a.

Another proof to be lenient is from *megufas chavis* (the covering of a barrel). The Gemara[18] says that even if a lid of a barrel broke on Shabbos and one subsequently throws it into the trash, displaying that it is not a *kli* in his eyes, it is still not *muktzeh*. *Ritva* explains that since this lid at *bein hashemashos* had an identity of a *kli*, one can't cause it to lose that title, because the act alone of throwing it out is not significant enough to remove its status as a *kli*.[19] If in this case, when the *kli* broke and one threw it out, it still can't lose its identity as a *kli*, all the more so in our case of disposable plates and the such, where it hasn't broke and one hasn't yet thrown it out, how can it lose its identity as a *kli*?

Why Small Disposable Containers Are Different

One can, however, differentiate between different types of disposable containers. One can argue that packets of sugar (question #2), milk bags, freeze pops in plastic casings, cans of soda, etc., are significantly different than big bags of chips; disposable cutlery, plates, bowls; and plastic bottles. The main function of the former group is when they are sealed to store the contents. Once the contents are finished, it's extremely impractical to reuse these *keilim*. They can't store as well as they previously could, and are therefore considered somewhat broken and no longer intended for their original function. A container that is broken and not fit to do its orig-

18. At the bottom of 124b.

19. Another way to understand this *Ritva*, and therefore another reason to be lenient to move disposable items, is based on the idea behind *ein muktzeh l'chetzi Shabbos*. This means that something can't become *muktzeh* on Shabbos based on *haktzaas hadaas* if the item was deemed non-*muktzeh* when Shabbos began. Unless a physical change occurs, that status remains with the item. The disposable items we are discussing have not undergone any physical change on Shabbos to render them *muktzeh*.

Let's use a bag of chips to illustrate this point. Before the contents were emptied out, the bag was a *kli*. Now that the chips are emptied out, true, the bag is no longer functioning as a container, but that is not because anything changed to the container itself; rather, something external took place. One's decision now to not use this container should be irrelevant and unable to cause it to lose the identity of a *kli* that it received when Shabbos began.

inal function is comparable to the case of the needle that is *muktzeh* because people throw it out, so these containers too are *muktzeh*. Only while the food is still inside can one move the containers *agav* the food (because that is how one moves the food). This is exactly like a pot with a cooked dish inside, which is permitted even if the pot would be *muktzeh machmas gufo*. In contrast, our previous arguments that the *kli* hasn't changed and is still fit to be used even if in actuality no one does, applies to disposable crockery, large bags of chips, and the like which can be refilled with ease despite no one doing so - hence they are not *muktzeh*.

Even though we are concluding that these small types of containers should be *muktzeh*, we can still find a reason to permit their movement. Usually even when one has finished with the small container, there still is a bit of food left inside - a few more drops of Coke (question #3), a few more grains of sugar - so maybe even without relying on the exemption of *graf shel re'i* one would be allowed to move these used packets and throw them away *agav* the food.

If one holds that used disposable containers don't become *muktzeh*, then even if one has thrown them away on Shabbos, arguably they wouldn't be *muktzeh*, because something can't lose its status as a *kli* without undergoing a change.

Our case of the mug in part 1 (question #1) depends on what the norm is to do with a broken handle from a mug. Do most people try and fix the handle, or do they throw the mug away? I think the norm is to throw the mug away. If so, based on what we have previously seen, there are grounds that the mug should be *muktzeh*. This is so despite the mug itself functioning for its original purpose; one doesn't need a handle to use a mug. Since it is a broken *kli*, coupled with the fact that one has decided to no longer use it, it loses its identity as a *kli*. However, if one is the type of person who keeps broken mugs, is that grounds to be lenient, as for him it is still a functioning *kli*, or does the normal practice of throwing out such items override his preferences? It's more plausible[20] that it depends on the individual, וצ״ע.[21]

---

20. Heard from R' Petrova.

21. Even though regarding a *kli* losing its identity we don't follow the individual.

Summary

There are opinions who prove from the Gemara that a *kli* can become *muktzeh* even on Shabbos when one *decides* to throw it away and no longer wants to use it. Hence they reason that as soon as one has finished using disposable cutlery, the cutlery becomes *muktzeh*. We presented arguments in favor of being lenient, namely when one decides to throw out disposable items, it is not because of any deficiency in the *kli* that one is relegating it to the garbage heap; rather, it is due to one's lack of interest in the continued use of this item due to the abundance of these dishes. Therefore there is no actual change in the *kli* that should cause a change in its status. Only one's new intention of throwing it out causes it to become *muktzeh*, but we have no precedence that that alone can remove an identity of a *kli*. A disposable item that is difficult to reuse, such as a torn chips bag, would be *muktzeh* because once its contents are emptied out, it is considered a broken *kli*. A broken *kli* loses its identity as a *kli* when it is the norm is to throw it out.

Answers

1. An empty container that cannot be reused should be treated as *muktzeh*. If there are still drops of liquid left inside there is room to be lenient to move it. Furthermore, there is an argument that throwing it away is the final usage of the container and hence allowed.

The Gemara says that if one throws away a coat before Shabbos, it is not *muktzeh*, while if he threw away a broken lid before Shabbos it is *muktzeh*. *Ritva* explains that the difference is that no one normally throws away a good coat, so we can evoke *batel daateh etzel kol adam*. However, some people do throw away broken lids, so one's action does determine this status of the item.

2. Ideally straight after emptying a sugar sachet you should throw it into the bin. This is permitted because moving *muktzeh* once already in one's hand is permitted. If it isn't in your hand then the answer to #1 applies.

3. The only difference between a can and a bottle is when they are empty. A bottle can be re-used and therefore there is argument it isn't *muktzeh* while a can can't be re-used so once its contents have been emptied it should be treated as *muktzeh*.

Appendix: Reasons to Permit Moving Used Disposables

Another reason for being lenient to move disposable containers is based on *Rashba*. He understands that if a needle lost its point on Shabbos it doesn't become *muktzeh*. The Gemara was only referring to when it broke before Shabbos. Since one normally throws it away in this state, when Shabbos comes in, it's not fit to be considered a *kli*. However, when it broke on Shabbos, since it can still partially do the same function it did when Shabbos came in, it retains its identity as a *kli*. He also applies this distinction by *machtzelos* (reed mats). They are only *muktzeh* if they were thrown away before Shabbos. So, regarding all our disposable items that can still serve their original function - since they had the identity of a *kli* when Shabbos came in, they can't lose that identity.

This would be a great support to be lenient if *Shulchan Aruch* would *pasken* like *Rashba*. However, R' Akiva Eiger[22] proves that *Shulchan Aruch* disagrees with *Rashba*. According to *Rashba*, there is no distinction between *machtzelos* and the needle. With both of them, only if one threw it away before Shabbos do they become *muktzeh*. Nonetheless, *Shulchan Aruch* distinguishes between the two. When bringing the halachah of a needle that is broken, he writes it open-ended. It implies that even if it

---

22. *Shulchan Aruch, os* 14. At the end he says צ"ע. I didn't understand what he means by that.

broke on Shabbos, it's still *muktzeh*. Yet by *machtzelos* he distinguishes between when one threw it away before Shabbos, and then it is *muktzeh*, while if one threw it away on Shabbos it is not *muktzeh*. *Rashba* only knew to distinguish in the case of *machtzelos* whether it broke before or after Shabbos from the case of a needle. From the distinction that *Shulchan Aruch* makes by the needle, it implies that he holds that if there isn't any practical usage once it broke, it's difficult to claim that it retains its identity as a *kli*.

Another idea to suggest in order to permit moving disposable cutlery once one has finished using it is from *Raavad*. He explains that the Gemara's case of *shiryei prozmiyos* (tattered cloths) is only referring to the worn-out threads of a prayer shawl.[23] The reason *Raavad* has this requirement is because he understands that even when one has an item that practically he doesn't use anymore, if it could be continued to be used, especially when it still does its original function, it will still retain its identity as a *kli*. A prayer shawl is different, since a person is specifically careful not to use it for anything else. Therefore once it has lost its current usage he will no longer use it for anything else, causing it to lose its identity as a *kli*. (We can bring precedence to the innovation of *Raavad* from the *sugya* of "*Minaal*,"[24] which discusses a case when the inner strap breaks off a shoe, we say that the shoe and strap become *muktzeh*. The commentators explain the reason behind this is that since one will want to fix the shoe after Shabbos, he is particularly careful not to use the broken part for anything else, even if it could serve as another function in theory.)

We can derive from this that only when there is a positive rejection, like in this case where one purposely doesn't want to use the prayer shawl for another use, an active reason not to use it anymore, does the lack of use render something *muktzeh*. However, if there is just no good reason to use it anymore, but nothing in essence holding you back from using it, it won't

23. The simple explanation why *Raavad* didn't explain like the other *Rishonim* is because he disagreed on the factual premise. He holds that people don't throw away broken rugs.
24. 112b.

become *muktzeh*. So, this a further reason to permit moving used disposable items.

Part 3

דלתות הבית והכלים

Doors of Houses and Vessels

Questions

1. If a shirt button broke off on Shabbos, can I move it to a safe place?
2. If the toilet seat comes off its hinges, can I still sit on it?
3. If the arm breaks off my glasses, can I continue wearing them?
4. If a screw falls out of an electric item, can I move the screw to keep it safe?

The Mishnah[25] distinguishes between a door of a house that falls off, whether on Shabbos or before Shabbos, which becomes *muktzeh*, and a door of a movable *kli* that fell off, which doesn't become *muktzeh*. (The difference between this Mishnah and the Mishnah discussed in part 1 of broken vessels is that here, the main object is still functional, and we are discussing the piece that has broken off, while earlier the case is where the whole *kli* broke.[26]) What is the difference between a house door and a chest door?

---

25. 122b.

26. To illustrate this distinction, a windup watch that stops working on Shabbos wouldn't be comparable to *daltos hakeilim*. Since the main *kli* isn't presently functional, it is relevant to part 1. But it is not *muktzeh* because we don't treat the watch as broken. However, a jewelry box whose lid broke off is relevant to this discussion

Shitah LaRan and *Meiri* both suggest that a door of a chest, even when broken, can still function in its previous capacity to some extent. It can cover the top of the chest, while a broken door of a house can't function at all. Accordingly, a broken piece of an object (when the original item is still intact) must presently have some function for it not to become *muktzeh.*[27]

The second opinion is that of *Tosafos* and *Ritva.* They hold that doors of a chest that have fallen off, even though they have no function at all, are not *muktzeh. Mishnah Berurah* categorically also says so. According to *Mishnah Berurah* and these *Rishonim,* what is the difference between a house and a chest? We must differentiate that since a house is not considered a *kli,* so too the crucial parts of the house, including the door, are not considered a *kli.*[28] (When attached to the house, one can open and close the door because it is *mechubar l'karka* [attached to the ground], so one isn't considered moving *muktzeh.*) In contrast, the door of the chest is considered a *kli.* It gets its identity *agav avihen,* meaning, since this door is a part of the chest, it also gets called a *kli,* and even in its present detached state it retains its identity because it most likely will be attached again onto the chest.[29]

The third opinion differentiating between a house door and chest door is that of *Tosafos Rid/Piskei Rid.* He says the difference lies in whether the case involves the *melachah* of *boneh* or not. To attach the door back onto the house would involve *boneh d'Oraisa,* even though it's not an act of craftsmanship since *yesh binyan b'karka,*[30] it is forbidden regardless. Attaching the door back to the chest doesn't require an act of craftsmanship,

---

of *daltos hakeilim.*

27. R' Shlomo Zalman Auerbach says we should reckon with this explanation even though it is not the consensus. This will be relevant when we address our questions.

28. Even though *Rambam* does call a door a *kli,* the same reason applies that the door can't be considered a *kli* based on the fact that it's part of the house.

29. The text of *Ritva* is: הרי הוכנו אגב אביהם ואינם יוצאים מהכנתם כיון שסופם לחזור שם.

30. Meaning, when one builds something that is attached to the ground, that act of building is encompassed in the Torah prohibition of building. This is in contrast to *ein binyan b'keilim,* making a utensil is not encompassed in the Torah prohibition of building.

so it's not forbidden. Therefore in the former case, Chazal said the door is *muktzeh* because the only way one could make use of it would involve a transgression.

Gezeirah Shema Yitka

We find another reason why certain broken pieces could potentially be *muktzeh,* namely a *gezeirah shema yitka* (safeguard lest one comes to fix the item). The Gemara[31] brings a dispute with a case of a three-legged oven - whether it is necessary that two legs fall off the oven to make it become *muktzeh,* or is it *muktzeh* after only one leg falls off. Rava says that already after one leg falls off, the oven is *muktzeh* because of a *gezeirah shema yitka.* Chazal were worried that if one would be allowed to move the oven, he may come to put the leg back on and thus transgress the *melachah* of *boneh.* Therefore Chazal imposed a transgression of *muktzeh* to preempt *boneh. Taz*[32] says that this only applies if the leg falls off. However, if it *breaks off* and one would need to make a new leg, it isn't *muktzeh.* This is because there is no worry that one might come to create an entirely new leg in order to fix it. Similarly, even when the leg falls off, if one of the legs gets lost, the oven will not become *muktzeh* as there is no safeguard to ensure that you will not make a replacement leg.

In *Minchas Ariel* he asks why are all doors of vessels not *muktzeh* for the same reason - that you may come and replace it? He answers[33] that only when the main *kli* can't function properly were Chazal worried that you might come to fix it. An oven with three legs doesn't function so well - you're constantly worried it will fall - and so there is a true worry, while a chest functions as storage even without its lid, thereby precluding it from this worry maybe he might come to fix it.

Rema[34] *paskens* that if a leg of a bench has fallen off, one can't move

---

31. 138b.
32. *Se'if katan* 14.
33. *Shemiras Shabbos K'Hilchasah* also brings this answer in name of R' Shlomo Zalman Auerbach.
34. *Siman* 7.

the bench. However, if one has already used (sat on) the bench once before Shabbos, it's not *muktzeh. Magen Avraham* asks: Why should sitting on it before Shabbos help? How does that get around Chazal's enactment? He answers if one has sat on it once, he won't come to fix it. According to what we've explained this makes sense, since he has shown that it can be used even in its broken stage. For him it's not similar to a broken oven therefore it is not necessary to impose any safeguards.

We can extract from *Shitah LaRan* another answer to the question why the worry one might come to fix it doesn't apply to doors. He explains that the reason behind the enactment is that it was common. It's not clear if the legs of the oven breaking was common or the likelihood of someone fixing it was high. The first option is more likely. Since this was a common scenario, Chazal felt the need to be active and impose necessary measures. Building off this, we can suggest that perhaps doors of vessels didn't break often and therefore it was not needed for Chazal to take any precautions. *Shemiras Shabbos K'Hilchasah*[35] proposes that even when the broken item can still be used, just that fixing it would be easy and involve little hassle, the safeguard would still apply. He understands that even if it doesn't have to be fixed to be used, if the norm is to fix it and it is easy to fix, Chazal's measures would still apply.

Falling Buttons

Now we can understand the halachah when a button falls off on Shabbos (question #1). Loose buttons have no function, so we can already classify them as *muktzeh* according to *Shitah LaRan*, that something that falls off when it has no use is *muktzeh*. Even according to *Mishnah Berurah*, who says that it is dependent on whether the item which this piece has broken off (in this case, the button) has a status of a *kli* or not, we can argue that it depends on the type of button. A standard white-shirt button exists in abundance and one is not careful to make sure it will be available after *Shabbos* to sew back on the shirt. So maybe we don't apply *huchnu agav*

35. 20:44.

avihen. (Meaning, despite previously being part of the shirt and so should have an identity of a *kli*, maybe now, since it won't again be part of the shirt, it loses its identity as a part of the shirt and hence its identity as a *kli*.) Yet special buttons that one is careful to put back on the shirt will be a classic application of doors of vessels that aren't *muktzeh*. *Minchas Shabbos*[36] classifies buttons and broaches that fell off as non-*muktzeh*. It must be because of our explanation.

The same way there is a *gezeirah shema yitka*, should we apply a *gezeirah shema yitfor* (safeguard lest one come to sew), which would render the button *muktzeh*? We could argue that it depends on from where the button fell off. If the piece of clothing is unwearable without the button, there is more of an argument that the enactment would render the button *muktzeh*. However, if it fell off a jacket that one can comfortably wear without the button, there is no reason the any limitations should apply. However, the issue of buttons is an old question, yet we don't find the *poskim* discussing the potential enactments lest one comes to sew. R' Yosef Shalom Elyashiv is quoted to hold that all buttons that have fallen off are *muktzeh*. There seems to be a dispute why he holds so. R' Shlomo Zafrani[37] understands that whenever putting back the broken piece will involve a *melachah d'Oraisa*, we don't apply the principle of *muchan agav avihen*. The logic is that since it takes such expertise[38] to put back the broken piece, we can't view the item as *muchan* (prepared). Sewing is Biblically forbidden; this is considered that its repair involves great expertise. *Shalmei Yehudah* explains that buttons don't have an exemption akin to doors of vessels, as this is only relevant with doors that hang on hinges and don't require a new act to fix them back in place. Such doors we can still

---

36. 88:2. He also asks a very interesting question: Before you've sewn on a button, how do we view it in halachah? Do we say that it's a *kli shemelachto l'heter* since it's destined to be part of a shirt, or do we judge it based on the fact that it now has no usage, so it should be *muktzeh machmas gufo*? This is relevant to when one has new piece of clothing and hasn't removed the spare buttons that are occasionally provided in a small bag in a pocket — can one take them out?

37. *Ayin Yedid*.

38. The extent of the expertise is judged based upon whether it falls under one of the thirty-nine *melachos* of Shabbos.

view as *muchan agav avihen*. However, a button requires a new act to fix it albeit that the button is not broken.

We can suggest that in truth, R' Elyashiv's *psak* is based on *Tosafos Rid*. The same way *Tosafos Rid* says that when *binyan d'Oraisa* is involved it's *muktzeh*, so too when sewing is involved, the item will be *muktzeh*. We can use both previous explanations to glean more depth in the distinction of *Tosafos Rid*. If a *melachah d'Oraisa* is necessary to fix this item back onto the *kli*, it loses its identity as a *kli*. If it needs a new act to fix it, that is also a reason to cause it to lose its identity as a *kli*.

If the handle of a kitchen drawer or cupboard falls off, the handle will be *muktzeh*. A kitchen is considered part of the house, since it is built-in. Therefore, parts of the kitchen that fall off, fall under *daltos habayis* and are *muktzeh*. Similarly, a toilet seat that comes apart (question #2) is part of *daltos habayis* and is *muktzeh*, as a toilet is connected to the house.

Broken Glasses and Strollers

If an arm falls off one's glasses (question #3), if it is usually still possible to fix the frame, the glasses would be *muktzeh* because of the *gezeirah shema yitka*, it is something one is likely to fix. The same is true if the lenses fall out. However, if one has already been using these glasses in their broken state before Shabbos, according to *Magen Avraham* they are not *muktzeh* because, as we've explained, you have shown that you are not going to fix them immediately. Similarly, if a wheel falls off a stroller, one seemingly wouldn't be able to move the stroller. It is *muktzeh* because he might come to fix it!

Can Items Change Their Muktzeh Status?

If a screw falls off an electric appliance (question #4), the most likely scenario is that one will want to move the screw in order to protect it from getting lost, so that after Shabbos he can fix it back in its place. If a screw is a *kli shemelachto l'heter*, then it would be permitted to be moved *m'chamah l'tzel*, i.e., to protect it. But if it was a part of a *kli shemelachto l'issur*, we don't judge the screw as an independent piece; rather, we view it as what it's a part of. However, now that it became physically separate on Shabbos, how do we view it? The essence of this question is: Can broken vessels and *daltos habayis* that should not be *muktzeh* become less *muktzeh* than the *kli* they came from? Now that it's an independent screw, can we treat it as a screw instead of a broken piece of an electrical appliance?

Sfas Emes infers from the Mishnah. It says, "*shivreihen netilin **imahen*** - its broken pieces are taken *with them.*" It's coming to teach us that only "with them," i.e., the broken vessels only have the same status as the *av* (source vessel) and not a less stringent status of *muktzeh*. There could be two different approaches to understand why the broken piece can only retain the status it had when attached to the *kli* it was part of, and not be treated as a lesser form of *muktzeh*. Firstly, like *Pri Megadim* entertains that even with a *kli shemelachto l'issur* there is *migo d'iskatzi*, meaning that throughout Shabbos, even a *kli shemelachto l'issur* keeps the status it had when Shabbos began. So a status of *muktzeh* can't change on Shabbos. The second possible way to explain this is that since the whole reason why this broken piece is not *muktzeh* is because it's destined to go back on the main *kli* and so *huchnu agav avihen*, therefore its whole identity is judged based on the main *kli*. If the source is *muktzeh*, so too any of its offshoots. According to the second explanation, there would be a distinction between broken vessels and doors of vessels. This reason only applies to the latter, whereas the reason why broken vessels are not *muktzeh* is because *now* they have their own function and thus don't lose their identity as a *kli*. Therefore they shouldn't be constrained by the identity of the *kli* they came from.

There is an implication in *Rambam*[39] that in truth the broken piece is judged based on what it can do now. *Rambam* says, שברי תנור מותר לטלטלן **והרי הן ככל הכלים שמלאכתן להיתר** - "A broken oven is permitted to move and **it is like all other** *kli shemelachto l'heter.*" Even though the oven was *kli shemelachto l'issur*, *Rambam* is saying that the broken legs can now be moved even *m'chamah l'tzel*. Based on the reason we suggested before,

39. *Hilchos Shabbos* 26:6.

maybe we can't prove from *Rambam* to doors of vessels. The broken pieces of the oven now have a permissible function of covering pots and therefore are subject to the leniencies of broken vessels.

Dispute Among the Poskim on the Above Discussion

Magen Avraham[40] learns from the halachah of *daltos habayis* to our question that the broken pieces don't change from their previous status. The unattached door of a house now has a function, e.g., you can use it as tabletop. Nonetheless, it's still restricted because it was part of the house that wasn't a *kli*. We see that the status doesn't improve. R' Akiva Eiger argues that there is no proof. The door wasn't a *kli* before it got detached, so it can't become a *kli* on Shabbos, while if a *muktzeh machmas chisaron kis* broke and now the broken piece can be used for a permissible purpose, then it can change its level of *muktzeh* and would be dependent on *migo d'iskatzi*, which Rebbe Shimon doesn't hold of.

Graz[41] *paskens* like *Magen Avraham* regarding *muktzeh machmas chisaron kis*, that even if a piece broke off and now has a function, it still is *muktzeh*. He agrees to R' Akiva Eiger's refutation of the case of the doors and accepts that it will depend on *migo d'iskatzi*, yet argues that regarding *migo d'iskatzi* we follow Rebbe Yehudah. *Graz* explains that since when Shabbos commenced one was *maktzah daas* from any *muktzeh machmas chisaron kis*, the *migo* will continue that status even if the object changes.

We can accept *Graz*'s ruling because it was said regarding *muktzeh machmas chisaron kis* and still uphold our strong inference from *Rambam*, that the pieces of a *kli shemelachto l'issur* that breaks can be treated as *kli shemelachto l'heter*[42]. However, our ruling about the screw isn't correct. Although a screw is created in order to be screwed in, which is a *melachah*,

---

40. 308, point 19.

41. *Se'if katan* 27.

42. We explained in chapter 1 that *kli shemelachto l'issur* is not, according to some, forbidden due to one's lack of decision, but rather due to a *gezeriah*. Since *migo* is based on *haktzaas hadaas*, we can argue that *kli shemelachto l'issur* is not subject to *migo*.

once it is screwed in, from then onward it doesn't actively do *melachah*. Still, the simple understanding is that it is a *kli shemelachto l'issur*.

Summary

When a cupboard door falls off, the door is not *muktzeh*, even if the door presently has no use. Since one intends on fixing it and the cupboard itself is still functional, the door retains its identity as a *kli* due to the principle of *huchan agav imo*. In contrast, a door of a house never had an identity as a *kli* while attached to the house, so when it breaks it has no identity as a *kli* to permit it being moved.

A broken item that is functional but doesn't work as well as it should is *muktzeh* because Chazal were worried that if one were to use it, he might come to fix it. If one has used this broken item in its current weakened state before Shabbos, he has shown that he doesn't mind using it even in its lesser state. Therefore, we are more certain that he won't come to fix it and this new *gezeirah* of *shema yitka* won't render it *muktzeh*. If the broken piece is lost and one can't fix it, if the main item is still presently usable, it won't become *muktzeh* for the same reason - the worry that one might repair it doesn't exist.

Answers

1. Unusual buttons that one preserves, intending to fix them, are not *muktzeh* and not subject to any restriction to ensure one doesn't come to sew them. An ordinary button that broke is *muktzeh*, but if it didn't chip, but just fell off, there are grounds to permit moving it.
2. The toilet seat is forbidden to move; Chazal were worried that one might come to fix it.

3. If the arms broke off before Shabbos and you were wearing the glasses in this broken state already, the glasses are not *muktzeh*. If it broke on Shabbos the glasses are *muktzeh*.

4. A screw is a *kli shemelachto l'issur* so can't be moved to protect it. This is even true if it was part of a *kli shemelachto l'heter* and subsequently fell off.

Chapter 7, Part 1

יחוד בכלים

Designating Vessels to be Used on Shabbos

Questions

1. Does the halachah permit protestors to throw stones on Shabbos? (I'm not getting into the *bein adam l'chaveiro* - just the potential *muktzeh* involved!)
2. Are kids allowed to play in a sandbox on Shabbos?
3. A dressmaker realizes she won't have enough tablecloths for a *Shabbos sheva berachos*. Before Shabbos, can she prepare her fabric in a way to be able to use it as a temporary tablecloth?
4. Some children like to play *chamesh avanim* (Jacks) with the pits of apricots. Is that permitted on Shabbos?

Stones, dirt, sticks, etc., are not considered *keilim*, as they don't inherently serve any purpose. Due to this total lack of beneficial use, they fall under the most severe form of *muktzeh*, referred to as *muktzeh machmas gufo*. Even Rebbe Shimon, who argues to permit most categories of *muktzeh*, agrees that this *muktzeh* can't be carried for any purpose on Shabbos. Nevertheless, Chazal enacted that if one is *meyached* (designates) such items before Shabbos to be used for a permissible function, they no longer are *muktzeh*. We will explore what consequence this "designation" achieves. Does it render the non-*kli* into a full-fledged *kli*? Or perhaps it remains a non-*kli*, yet via the designation it changes its status from something lacking preparation to something that is now prepared;

it's now part of one's collection of potential things that he might come to use on Shabbos and therefore is not *muktzeh*. Further, how does one go about designating these objects? Is it enough just to think that he now wants to use it, or is a specific act required?

The Gemara[1] brings a dispute regarding what the halachah when one uses a flat stone to function as a covering for the opening of a barrel. R' Asi holds that an insignificant act, such as placing it on the barrel opening, is sufficient to cause the stone to now be considered a covering for the barrel and one can now move the stone freely. R' Ami argues that just placing the stone isn't sufficient to designate the stone; it remains *muktzeh*. The Gemara continues to bring a case where Rebbi chanced upon a pile of large stones. He instructed his students to do an act, besides designating the stones in their mind, to enable them to be sat on during Shabbos. The same pair of *Amoraim* argue, based on their previous stance, which act Rebbi required his students to do to remove the *muktzeh* status from the stones. R' Asi held that the act was *shifshuf* - they smoothed down the stones (from the earth on them) before Shabbos, enabling them to move them. Despite this being a minor act, it suffices. R' Ami again held that a minor act doesn't suffice to upgrade the stone to be a *kli*. He explains that they were *limdum* - they arranged the stones before Shabbos so that they would be ready to sit on, thus preempting any need to move them on Shabbos, as they were already in their desired position. However, if they would have wanted to move them, a greater action of designation would have been necessary.

Chariyos Shel Dekel

The Gemara continues to bring a new dispute between the *Tannaim* about *chariyos shel dekel*: If someone chopped palm branches for firewood (which would be *muktzeh*), but changed his mind before Shabbos to use them as a mat to sit on, what action is required to change them from their original designation to prepare them for Shabbos? The Rabbanan require one to tie the branches together, while Rebbe Shimon Ben Gamliel is le-

1. 125b.

nient, saying that one only needs to have in mind before Shabbos to use them for mats. R' Asi holds: ישב אע"פ שלא חישב - "One can sit even without thought." Most *Rishonim* explain that R' Asi is the most lenient opinion. Even sitting down on the branches before Shabbos in a casual manner, i.e., even without intending through your sitting to show that this is a seat for Shabbos, it is still sufficient to designate the palm branches - all the more so if one actively thought to sit on them.[2]

Tosafos[3] asks a contradiction in R' Asi's opinion. Regarding the palm branches, he suffices with just sitting in a casual manner even without thinking, whereas with the case of Rebbi's stones, he required an act done to the item - he smoothed the stones and thought about it. Does R' Asi require a minimal act or is even less sufficient?[4] *Tosafos* concedes that it's a dispute between the two *sugyas* and there is a mistake in the Gemara. The name of the *Amora* in the case of the palm branches is R' Ashi, (who elsewhere holds one needs an act to designate an item); R' Asi always requires an act. (*Rabbeinu Tam* supports this solution because in the case of the stones, thought was needed to designate the stones, while in the case of the palm branches, thought wasn't needed.) *Baalei Tosafos* argue which statement of R' Asi the halachah is like. *Rey*[5] is lenient that R' Asi holds that a minimal action is necessary, while *Rabbeinu Tam*[6] is stringent that a significant act is needed to achieve "designation," e.g., one must tie the palm branches.

Rambam paskens like R' Ami, that a significant action is needed to prepare stones for movement. But to prepare the palm branches, *Rambam*

---

2. *Ramban* and *Baal HaMeor* argue that sitting (even casually) is more of an act of designation than thinking.

3. 125b, s.v. ואזדו לטעמייהו. Also the fact the Gemara brought both these cases on the same page, yet never connected the two disputes, indicates that there is a distinction.

4. Perhaps according to *Ramban* and *Baal HaMeor* there is no contradiction in R' Asi; he always requires a minimal act. You see from *Ritva* and *Tosafos HaRosh* brought later that they asked the contradiction in R' Asi despite holding that *yashav* is better than *chishev*.

5. 50a, s.v. רב אסי.

6. *Sefer HaYashar, Shu"t, siman* 4.

paskens like R' Asi, that even *yashav* or *chishev* helps. What's the difference?

Clearly *Rambam* doesn't hold what *Tosafos* asked is a contradiction, as he requires an action to prepare the stones, whereas the branches suffice with *machshavah*. *Maggid Mishnah* explains[7] that *chariyos* (branches) are supposed to be sat on, and are therefore easier to designate. In contrast, stones are not commonly used as covers for barrels, so a greater act is demanded to designate them as a cover.[8]

What Yichud Achieves

We can glean a better understanding from this answer of *Maggid Mishnah* of what *yichud* (designation) actually achieves: One needs to upgrade an object from its current status of not fit for any use to make it fit for use - at least to show that it's destined for one's use. Different objects require different actions to upgrade them. Palm branches are commonly used to sit on, hence they don't require a significant action to be prepared. Just thinking that one wants to sit on them is enough to prepare it; from the point of view of the object, it is already in a completed stage, nothing needs to be improved to it for it to be used. This is opposed to building stones that are not commonly used for sitting. One is required to do an actual physical change to it in order to designate it as a chair. From what the *Maggid Mishnah* says, it's implicit that the only reason that one is even required to designate the use of sitting is only to remove the negative intention one previously had - that he intended to use these branches as firewood.[9]

---

7. This is also *Tosafos*'s second answer.

8. Other *Rishonim*, *Ritva*, and *Tosafos HaRosh* answer that R' Asi doesn't need a proper act to designate an item, and it would have sufficed to sit on each stone, but that would have involved more effort than smoothing them down.

9. This notion of *Maggid Mishnah* resembles the principle behind the mishnah in *Beitzah* 10a, which says that you need to designate undomesticated chicks that you want to eat on Yom Tov. According to all opinions, an act isn't needed. Why not? We see that since a bird is a good food, you don't need to upgrade the object to make it more fitting; rather, it's *muktzeh* for a peripheral reason. It isn't considered

We see the same principle in *Ritva*. He asks a further question.[10] The Gemara earlier discusses how to designate different materials to use for *hatmanah* (insulation). For *gizei tzemer* (tufts of wool) it suffices just to do *yichud*, i.e., to have in mind to use it for this purpose and then one can cover his pot. He asks: Why by *chariyos* do we find a dispute whether we need an act or not? What's the difference between branches and fabric? *Ritva* understands the case of palm branches slightly differently, but we still see the same principles. He explains that the difference between branches and wool is that palm branches aren't suitable for sitting (unlike *Maggid Mishnah* we previously brought), while tufts of wool are an excellent insulator. Therefore one doesn't need to upgrade or change the wool. As long as one shows that he truly intends on using this wool as an insulator, that's sufficient. By placing the tufts around the food, one shows he intends on using them and has no reservation. Hence, even according to the stringent opinion of R' Ami, just warming with them is enough and no prior act is needed. However, with palm branches, since they are not suitable seats, one must do an act to clearly indicate that they are now set aside for sitting. R' Asi holds that since they are not important and of little value, one doesn't need a physical action to change them from a previous designation, hence even just sitting is sufficient, while the *chachamim* argue that a more significant action is necessary to designate them.

Yichud L'Olam vs Yichud for One Shabbos

Rashba[11] was asked: If someone wants to use a rock as a nutcracker on Shabbos, what must he do to be allowed to move it? *Rashba* answers that in order for *yichud* to work, he must designate it indefinitely to be used as

---

"prepared," so you just need to remove that. Hence intention alone is sufficient, without an act. The same is true by *nesarim shel oman*, a craftsman's poles (*Shabbos* 49b) With designation alone one can use them; a homeowner uses sticks as a regular *kli*, so you see that they have a good function. The only problem is the craftsman's negative thought, so all he needs to do is remove his care (*Shiltei Gibborim* 22b in *Dapei HaRif*).

10. 50a, s.v. איתמר, also creates a difficulty for *Ran* and *Meiri* on 50b.

11. *Shu"t*, vol. 1, *siman* 757, brought by *Beis Yosef*.

a nutcracker. This is true by all *yichud.*[12] The depth behind why *yichud l'olam* (permanent designation) is required is based on the same reasoning: This stone is originally *muktzeh machmas gufo* and one is trying to upgrade it into a *kli* without physically changing it. How does he achieve such a result? *Rashba* understands that only if you are going to use it indefinitely as a nutcracker can we halachically treat it as a nutcracker and not a stone - but if after Shabbos you're going to throw it back into the garden, then your *yichud* is meaningless. It hasn't been upgraded from a mere stone at all.

Ran asks: According to *Rashba,* you always need *yichud l'olam,* so why is it that the Rabbanan require tying the palm branches? Surely if there is a *yichud* of the branches forever, that should be sufficient without any additional act. He argues that therefore it must be the case is where he just designated these palm branches for seats for this Shabbos alone. In this instance, the dispute is whether this is enough, or you also need a physical action. *Ran* says that it follows, according to the opinion that doesn't require anything, that something which is *darko b'kach* (normal to be used for this), the duration of the designation is just one Shabbos. A stone was normal to be used as a nutcracker, so one only needs to be *meyached* for just this Shabbos. In this regard, he argues with *Rashba,* who even in these cases requires *yichud l'olam.*

Gra[13] says *Rashba* agrees that *chariyos* don't need *yichud l'olam.* If one carefully looks at the response of *Rashba,* it is apparent that *Rashba* only

---

12. *Rashba* also entertains a possibility that maybe you must use the rock for cracking nuts before Shabbos. This is in order to prove that one intends to use the item for what he designated it for because it's not inherently clear that one means to use it for cracking nuts. Precedence for this is found in Rabbeinu Yonah's *pshat* in the *sugya* of *pipcoron* (a type of bandage) in 50a. (*Rashba* himself quotes this in 50a.) This bandage only if one does an act to it, such as smearing oil on it, can one then use it on Shabbos; otherwise it's *muktzeh.* But if one wore it once before Shabbos, even if nothing has been done to the material, it is not *muktzeh.* Rabbeinu Yonah explains that just designating the fabric as a bandage is insufficient because it is unclear that the fabric is to be used for a bandage. Hence, if one has worn it once before, even without any improvement made to the fabric, it is sufficient because using it shows us clearly what one intends to use it for.

13. *Se'if* 22.

requires *yichud l'olam* in the event that the object can't have any act done to it to designate it, such as a stone. While an object that is subject to an act being done to it, then to designate it one is required to do an act. When one is doing an act to designate the item, it is irrelevant how long he intends on this item performing its new task. The act is significant enough that now we see this item is fit for the new use.

A Coin vs a Stone

The Gemara[14] rules that if one designates a stone to be used as a button (they would place a stone against one side of a coat, and tie a string around the button to hold it down), then one can move the stone. However, if one used a coin and he designated it for this purpose, it remains *muktzeh*. *Shitah LaRan* explains the difference between a stone and a coin - a coin is more important, so a *yichud* alone doesn't help. *Rashba,*[15] however, is perplexed with understanding the difference. If one can designate a stone, why can't he designate a coin? He leaves it as a difficulty. This is seemingly *Rashba* concurrent with what he holds that one must always do *yichud l'olam*. Accordingly, the Gemara must be dealing with *yichud l'olam* even for the stone, as anything less than eternal designation is insufficient. If so, surely the case must be when one is *meyached* the coin in the same fashion, so why doesn't it work? Hence he leaves the question unanswered as to what the difference is.

Ran understands, as explained by *Mishnah Berurah,*[16] that the Gemara is referring to round stone that is normal to be used as a makeshift button. Therefore *yichud* for one Shabbos works, but that's not sufficient for a coin that isn't normally used as a button (if one was to do *yichud l'olam, Ran* would agree it helps, but the Gemara is dealing with *yichud* for one Shabbos). *Chazon Ish* argues on this reasoning that a permanent *yichud* can help. He posits that a coin is different, as with a coin one will always go back to using it as a coin, so the concept of designating it forever isn't

14. 65a.
15. 65b.
16. 303:74.

applicable, as your eternal designation is a farce. In light of this logic the Gemara's distinction between a stone and a coin is understood. However, evidently from the fact *Rashba* never answered as such, he doesn't agree to this distinction.[17]

It's plausible that even *Chazon Ish* would agree that coins in a coin collection are not *muktzeh machmas gufo*. These coins are no longer set aside as currency, and won't go back into circulation. However, most coin collectors are careful about their collection and therefore they are *muktzeh machmas chisaron kis*.

Magen Avraham[18] says that if one tied a coin on a coat *before* Shabbos, one can move the coin. According to *Rashba*, how can this be permitted? You didn't designate it forever. Furthermore, the *pashtus* of the Gemara[19] is that with *muchin* and *gizei tzemer* (fabric insulators) which are generally *muktzeh*, even if one hasn't designated these fabrics to be insulators forevermore, as long as he previously used them before Shabbos for this purpose, they can be moved and are not *muktzeh*. Why according to *Rashba* is this sufficient, as there is no *yichud l'olam*?[20] Perhaps we can entertain a new reasoning to permit it. If the item is already "in the mode," i.e., it has already started functioning for this purpose, it's permissible to continue to use it. The logic is that it is already clear what this item is functioning as, so it already can be classified as *kli*. Therefore, if the coin is already functioning as a button, it's already been upgraded and nothing else

---

17. What *Gra* on 22, s.v. אא"כ, says fits beautifully with *Chazon Ish*, since *Gra* learns the Gemara as referring to a permanent designation. You therefore see that even permanent designation wouldn't help for a coin.

18. This halachah is implicit from the mishnah.

19. 49b/50a.

20. This conclusion is not conclusive. It depends on the various explanations in the back-and-forth of the Gemara. This conclusion is true according to the way *Rashba* in his *chiddushim* explains, however in his *teshuvos* he explains the Gemara significantly differently. According to how he explains it his *teshuvah*, there is no proof to this new idea of "in the mode" and one still needs to do permanent designation to use these fabrics.

is needed. It is not a disadvantage that you only intend to use it for this Shabbos![21] [22]

You Only Need to Do What Is Possible

The requirement to do a physical action in order to upgrade something to remove its status of *muktzeh machmas gufo* and give it a *shem kli* is only when it's possible to tangibly change the item. Soil can't be changed into anything, so even the Rabbanan agree that if you wish to designate this for your use, you aren't required to tie it, etc. As long as one shows clearly that he wants to use this soil, it's sufficient. The Gemara[23] suggests that one must place it in a pile in the corner of your house, as opposed to the usual practice of just scattering it on the floor. If it is scattered on the floor, it becomes part of the ground, and this doesn't suffice to designate as something that one wishes to use. Surely the disagreement between *Ran* and *Rashba* whether *yichud l'olam* is necessary wouldn't be applicable with something like soil, since every time you use the dirt for something, e.g., to cover some stain on the ground, it can never be reused. It comes out that designating for a one-off use is in effect designating it forever.

R' Akiva Eiger writes that if one wants to take writing paper to use to clean oneself on Shabbos, one needs to do a *yichud l'olam* before Shabbos. Once this paper has been used once to clean oneself, he is never going to use it again (I hope not), so why does one needs to do *yichud l'olam*? Surely there is no meaning to one's permanent designation if the usage is one-off. Even if one designates it just for this occasion, it is sufficient because that is the end of the use of this paper. Maybe R' Akiva Eiger's intention is, if

---

21. Why by the case of "stone on barrel" does "in the mode" not help? We must say that since it doesn't function as a very good cover, it's very uncommon to be used as such. Therefore, the fact that it is being used currently isn't indicative that one is treating the stone as a cover, while the round nature of a coin makes it a perfect button, but due to its worth you don't usually use it for this. צ"ע.

22. *Chazon Ish* (42:7) explains this halachah of *Magen Avraham* differently than how we've explained it. He says that if it's already tied on, then it's *tiltul min hatzad*, but not that *Magen Avraham* means the coin itself is not *muktzeh*. ע"ש.

23. 50a.

one sets aside dirt to be used, even though it's not something that can be reused, in the event that one doesn't end up using it this Shabbos, will one keep it in a pile in order to make use of it, or will he throw it back into the garden? If in the event that one didn't use it, he will just return it. This shows that you've only done *yichud* for one Shabbos, while only when you would keep it in the pile it's considered a *yichud l'olam*. So too with the writing paper. If your intention is to replace it after Shabbos in the event that it is not used, this shows that it's only a *yichud* for one Shabbos, which is insufficient to permit moving *muktzeh machmas gufo*.

The Opinion of Shulchan Aruch

Shulchan Aruch[24] brings all three opinions regarding for how long one must designate a *muktzeh* item in order to use it. First he brings *Ran*, that if one wants to use the item for a purpose that is usual, then *yichud* for one Shabbos is enough. Permitting the movement of a stone in order to break open nuts with it will suffice with a one-off designation, but *Shulchan Aruch* says it's less common to use a stone to cover a barrel or to bolt a door. Next, he brings the opinion of *Rashba*, who doesn't distinguish between these different categories and requires *yichud l'olam* even when it is somewhat a common usage that one would like to do. The last opinion brought is the opinion of *Piskei Rid* and the *Mordechai*.[25] They hold that a physical action is always necessary, but one doesn't need *yichud l'olam*.

(In *se'if* 20, *Shulchan Aruch paskens* like R' Asi regarding *chariyos*, that thinking or sitting is enough and doesn't additionally require *yichud l'olam*. According to what we suggested, *Rashba* agrees to this halachah so there is no indication from here that *Shulchan Aruch*'s main position is like *Ran*. *Gra* says that according to the third opinion, one is required to do an act with the stone in order for it to function as a button. In *siman* 303, with reference to walking outside with a coat and placing a stone button inside, *Shulchan Aruch* doesn't require any act to be done to the stone.

24. 308:22.

25. This is also the opinion of *Ritva*, *Tosafos HaRosh*.

This is a clear indication that the third opinion is not the main halachah. If *Shulchan Aruch* is discussing a scenario of *yichud* for one Shabbos, we have a proof that he holds the main halachah is like *Ran*. However, there is no indication that this is the case.)

Alternatives to Yichud L'Olam

Mishnah Berurah[26] *paskens* that *gizin* (textile insulators) need *yichud l'olam*. This *psak* is the opinion of *Bach*, and just using them casually isn't sufficient. However, he continues and says that if one has used them twice before, that is also sufficient. Yet in *Biur Halachah, Mishnah Berurah* quotes another *Bach*, who says that it doesn't help even if one previously used a stone several times for insulating. What's the difference between textile or stone insulators? A stone requires a *yichud* to fix the problem that it's not an ideal item for the job one wants it to do. Even if one has used it several times, he still may throw the stone back in the garden. Therefore it is necessary to do *yichud l'olam* to remove this worry. However, the reason why *gizin* require a *yichud* to allow them to be used for insulating is because due to their importance and value they are set aside for clothes, which puts them in the category of *muktzeh machmas chisaron kis*. Their ideal use is not to be used for insulating, however once one has used it twice for this purpose, he has shown that they are not important to him as a clothing source. This is a sufficient substitute for actual *yichud l'olam*.

Throwing Stones on Shabbos

Protestors who claim that desecration of Shabbos bothers them and hence they throw stones (question #1), themselves must learn the laws of Shabbos, since a stone isn't a *kli* - it is *muktzeh*. Even if one claims to have set it aside for this purpose, to be used as a vehicle of protest against these desecrators of Shabbos, it will still be insufficient, since stones aren't usually designated as an item of destruction, so *yichud l'olam* is needed. More-

---

26. 259:2.

over, once they've thrown the stone, they don't intend on retrieving it for the next Shabbos; rather, the stone is going to revert back to being debris on the side of street, so it's questionable whether *yichud l'olam* is even possible. (This is in contrast to soil, for which a one-off designation suffices. Whatever function one designates a stone for he can use the stone again and again, so must designate it forever. When he collects many particles of soil, these particles are used for covering the ground. Once part of the ground, they can't be recollected to form the same pile of earth. They are now as if nullified to the ground and it's as if they don't exist. Therefore the one-off designation really shows he intends on this soil functioning forever more.)

Playing in a Sandbox

When one fills a play sandbox with sand (question #2), he never intends on using that sand for any other purpose. As long as it's still fit to play with, he won't remove it. That is *yichud l'olam*, and since that no act is possible to effect a change with the sand, an act is not needed. From the point of view of the restrictions of *muktzeh*, there is no problem playing inside a sandbox.

Some *poskim*[27] want to treat a sandbox as a *kli shemelachto l'issur*, since they claim its main purpose is to dig holes. It's not clear whether this is correct. The sand is a toy for kids to play with, and any holes that are created are secondary to the child's main intention, i.e., playing. It is difficult to state that this is the main function of the sand - it's merely a tool for playing, one way of which happens to be digging, and so it should be a regular *kli shemelachto l'heter*. However, even if one allows kids to play with this on Shabbos, care should be taken not to add water into the sand to avoid issues of *losh*.

27. *Orchos Shabbos*, ch. 19, halachah 333.

Apricot Stones

Shemiras Shabbos K'Hilchasah[28] says that even though the consensus among the *poskim* is that the intention of a child doesn't help to designate something. Nevertheless R' Shlomo Zalman Auerbach says that a child putting an apricot stone into his box of apricot stones is an act of designation. Hence if a child were to put pits in his box before Shabbos, even were he not to actually have played with it yet, it would still be considered a toy. This *psak* is novel, as it's not apparent that this is an act. We saw that bringing in soil and designating it in a corner is not considered an act, nor is placing the stone in the barrel an act, so why should this be different?[29] However, if the child has already cleaned the stone, removing the residue of the fruit from it, that is an act that should be sufficient. And even though he is not going to keep it forever, and we mentioned earlier that something like a stone, which isn't destined for any use, requires *yichud l'olam*, in our case *yichud* for one Shabbos is enough. Since kids choose round pits that would be constructive for their game, one could say that they are destined for this[30] and normal for children to designate.[31]

Maybe for Sephardim *yichud* won't suffice even with an act, since *Shulchan Aruch*[32] holds that toys are *muktzeh*. *Mishnah Berurah* explains that *Shulchan Aruch* holds that playing doesn't give something an identity of a *kli*, since playing isn't a significant use. Even though most *poskim* hold

28. 16:10.

29. Maybe he held that there is no additional act to improve the stone. The only reason R' Asi said that smoothing isn't sufficient is because there is more one can do to improve the object. But he would agree in a case where there is nothing else possible to do that just placing it aside is sufficient. So perhaps R' Shlomo Zalman Auerbach felt there is nothing else possible to do to these stones. They are smooth, hence their use for the toy, so just setting aside is enough, אכתי צ"ע.

30. *Mishnah Berurah* 303:73 says that round stones are destined for buttons, so designation for one Shabbos suffices.

31. If stones were not *darko b'kach*, then we need to determine if the act of cleaning the stone is similar to *shifshuf*, because it's more or less the same act, and so practically that wouldn't be sufficient because *Shulchan Aruch paskens limdum* (arranging), implying a minor act is insufficient. צ"ע.

32. *Se'if* 45.

that *Shulchan Aruch* would agree nowadays that a toy is a *kli,* the reason being that since they are manufactured from scratch solely for that purpose, therefore they get an identity of a *kli.* However, this is only true with a manufactured, man-made *kli;* surely this logic won't apply to apricot stones (question #4). In the time of *Shulchan Aruch* they were playing such games, and it is in reference to such games that *Shulchan Aruch* said they were *muktzeh.*

The Dressmaker's Fabric

It follows that it won't suffice for the dressmaker who wants to use her fabric as a tablecloth to just designate it for this Shabbos (question #3). It's certainly not normal to designate such fabric for a tablecloth, so one needs *yichud l'olam.* If she doesn't want to permanently designate the fabric as a new tablecloth, the solution would be to do a significant act that would arranging facilitate her to upgrade this fabric to a tablecloth, albeit that she intends to reverse this act after Shabbos and use it as fabric for clothes.[33]

Summary

The reason why designating an item removes the restrictions of *muktzeh* is because via the designation one is considered to have changed the identity of this item from a non-*kli* to a *kli.* A *kli* can be moved under most circumstances. Which action is needed to designate a *kli* depends on the item. To upgrade an item for a use for which it is sometimes is used for, we have *Ran*'s leniency, that it is sufficient to designate it even for only one Shabbos. In scenarios where this item is never used for that what one intends on using it for, one must designate it for this purpose forever. Only

33. This is true even if this fabric is *muktzeh machmas chisaron kis* (since it has been designated as merchandise). This is because when one designates it before Shabbos, he is showing that he isn't careful about misusing this fabric. This removes the previous designation that other merchandise would have been treated as. A further assumption that this response is based upon is that the fabric as strips of cloth is not treated as a vessel yet — it's just raw material, hence one needs to designate it for a function for it to be treated as a vessel.

then has one shown that this item can really be considered a *kli*, as opposed to that what it appears to be - a useless item.

Answers

1. All stones are *muktzeh*. The only two ways to remove the *muktzeh* status is either by designating them forever or physically changing the stone indicating that one has designated it for use.
2. Sand is *muktzeh*. However, by placing it in a sandbox one has thereby designated it as a toy forever, so it no longer is *muktzeh*.
3. To use her fabric as a tablecloth, she would either need to designate it forever or do a significant act to the fabric to show it now will function as a tablecloth.
4. Some permit using a pit a child has designated before Shabbos, even if there is no designation forever. If the child has removed the residue off the pit and cleaned it before Shabbos, that for sure will permit the movement of the pit since that is a significant act done to the stone, showing one is interested in using it.

Appendix: Why Can't We Designate an Item on Shabbos?

From what we've seen regarding designating items, we are only discussing when it is done before Shabbos. It wouldn't work if done on Shabbos. Why can't someone designate an item on Shabbos? *Ketzos HaShulchan*[34] asks why, once a *kli* has broken on Shabbos, and its pieces are no longer fit for any use, are they *muktzeh*? Why can't one designate them *now*? We can

---

34. 109:12.

subtly infer that he purposely didn't ask our question, rather he asked specifically about a *muktzeh* item which was a *kli* when Shabbos began. It must be that the answer to our question is obvious. When Shabbos came in, the stone was *muktzeh machmas gufo* and we *pasken* that *migo d'iskatzi* - if an item is *muktzeh* when Shabbos began, it retains its status. Therefore, you can't remove the stone's *muktzeh* status.

R' Shlomo Zalman Auerbach[35] proves that in essence there is no problem in causing something to receive a *toras kli* on Shabbos. If one has an incomplete *kli*, one can decide on Shabbos that he is satisfied with the state of the *kli* and this is now the completion of the *kli* - it will now become a *kli* regarding *tumah*. So the reason why one can't designate something on Shabbos must stem from the fact that it's already predetermined that it is *muktzeh* for all of Shabbos, regardless of what one thinks.

Mishnah Berurah[36] brings down a stringency of *Eliyah Rabbah*, that when one does *yichud* to something that isn't a *kli*, he must have in mind to use it during Shabbos, as opposed to having a *stam* (general) intention for it to be a *kli* for use. The source of this halachah comes from *Rey* (one of *Tosafos*).[37] He says that if one decided to use a *muktzeh* item as a bandage and later changed his mind and decided that he is not going to use it for a bandage, but rather keep it for its original purpose, but on *erev Shabbos* he decides again that he will use it as a bandage, *Rey* says he now needs specific intention for Shabbos. *Rosh* argues with this, since we don't see from the case of designation of *chariyos* (which is the source of *yichud*) that you need to designate it for Shabbos specifically. The *Acharonim* who are stringent and require specific intent for Shabbos follow the opinion of *Rey*. However, one can follow this ruling and still need not be stringent.

The case of *Rey* is a specific case where one had previously designated this item to be used as a bandage and afterward changed his mind. He thus canceled out his previous designation, and not only did it now return to its status of *muktzeh machmas gufo* due to its uselessness, it is as if he said

35. *Shemiras Shabbos K'Hilchasah*, note 172.
36. *Se'if katan* 86.
37. *Rosh*, ch. 4, point 8.

it isn't fit for Shabbos. Against such a backdrop, if now he further changes his mind and does want to use the item, he must be extra clear that his designation is for it to be used specifically for Shabbos. *Rey* should agree that in a regular scenario, where the designation is not to go against a previous designation that declared this was not for use, but rather is just to designate a useless item to being a useful item, that even without specifying for Shabbos, he can still use them on Shabbos and doesn't need specific *yichud* that they will be seats for Shabbos. This is because since once you have upgraded this item, unless something happens to remove that intention, we still view the *yichud* as ongoing. R' Elazar Moshe Horwitz[38] also mentions this idea, that even according to *Rey*, who requires specific intent for Shabbos, this would not be the case when the original *yichud* was for general use.

Part 2

תורת כלי

The Status of a Vessel[39]

The Gemara[40] brings a dispute: If someone would like to use a wooden piece to function as a bolt for his door, what would he have to do in order to enable him to carry it on Shabbos? Is it enough to just set it aside for this specific purpose, or is one required to also tie the beam? Rebbe Shimon Ben Gamliel (*Rashbag*) is lenient and says that הזמינו אע"פ שלא קשור - he should set it aside even without tying. Rebbe Yochanan *paskens* that the halachah is like Rashbag, not like the opinion that also requires the beam to be already tied on the door.

The Gemara asks how Rebbe Yochanan can hold like *Rashbag*. The Gemara brings from elsewhere that Rebbe Yochanan requires that an

38. Found in his comments on *Rosh*.

39. This section is particularly complicated and a foundation in the *sugya* 125b/126a will aid a lot before reading it.

40. 126a.

item be a *toras kli* (in the category of a utensil) in order to be able to move it on Shabbos. Just setting the stick aside doesn't give it a *toras kli*. (*Rashbag* doesn't hold of such a requirement that one needs a *toras kli*. This is evident from the case of *chariyos*. They don't have a *toras kli*, as they aren't a specially fashioned utensil, yet *Rashbag* still holds that designating them before Shabbos to use them as seats is enough to allow one to move them.) The Gemara's answer is that Rebbe Yochanan is lenient in this case of the beam like *Rashbag*; just setting it aside is sufficient, but only when this beam has a *toras kli*. What is entailed in having a *toras kli*? *Tosafos* explains that the requirement to have a *toras kli* entails that one fashioned the item specifically for this purpose.[41]

Having seen this Gemara, the difficulty is how to fit the opinion of Rebbe Yochanan, who requires a *toras kli*, with the *dinim* we've seen of R' Ami and R' Asi, who argue in the opinion of Rebbe Yochanan what act he requires. But what about the additional requirement of *toras kli*? Does every object one designates need to have a *toras kli*?

We have seen that for certain items like soil, which can't be made into a *kli*, designation works without giving it the function of a *kli*. Therefore in such scenarios it's logical that you don't need a *toras kli*. *Baal HaMeor* says that when one has designated *chariyos*, stones on a barrel, they do have a *toras kli* because *mekoman mochiach alav* - the fact that they were already functioning before Shabbos for their purpose as a lid or a seat gives them a *toras kli*. *Baal HaMeor* holds that R' Asi, who said that the act which is necessary to designate the *chariyos* is *yashav*, meant that he specifically requires sitting. Thinking alone is not enough because how does that give it a *toras kli*? Only when it is actually functioning does it get a *toras kli*.

---

41. *Rashi* has a novel understanding that a *toras kli* status is only given to a *kli* when the *kli* has a use other than what one is now using it for. For example, a cover for a vessel will only be considered to have a *toras kli* if the cover has another function besides being a cover. That other function could be obscure, such as the cover can also function as a plate. The logic seems to be that when an item doesn't have an independent function, it is not treated as a vessel on its own; rather, it is a piece of another vessel. For example, if a door doesn't have its independent function, it is not a *kli*, but rather part of the house it is attached to. When it has an independent function, even if now it is attached it retains its identity as a vessel.

We find that *Ran*[42] suggests a similar idea, that if you use an item as a *kisui* (covering) before Shabbos, that will give it a *toras kli*. He proves this from the fact that sitting helps to give the *chariyos* a *toras kli*. It must be that when you've already used it before Shabbos, this gives it a *toras kli*. *Ran* understands that this is the opinion of *Rif* as well. *Rif* left out the requirement of *toras kli* by *pekak hachalon* (shutters). Since it is something that has to fit the size of the window perfectly, it's likely that he has used it already for such a purpose. However, *kaneh*, the piece of wood that one would like to make use of as bolt for his door, *Rif* does mention the requirement for *toras kli*, since it's just a stick of wood, which hasn't necessarily been used previously for any purpose.[43]

Milchamos answers the conundrum whether the aforementioned *sugya* discussing *yichud* of stones would also require a *toras kli* in a different way. He explains that to qualify as having a *toras kli*, it has to have a *toar kli*, the resemblance of a *kli*. He explains that R' Asi would certainly require a stone to have a *toras kli* to allow one to move it, and just placing the stone or smoothing it down doesn't give it a *toar kli*. Despite this, the reason one can use it as a lid is because the action performed with the stone prepared it for this specific function. In such a situation, there isn't a leniency to move the stone around freely, as only a *toras kli* can be moved without re-

---

42. The end of *Perek Kol HaKeilim*.

43. This contradicts the *Ran* we quoted earlier. If *Ran* holds that *chishev* is better than *yashav*, how can he prove this idea that if you previously are using it, it gets a *toras kli* from *chariyos*? He regardless must hold that *chariyos* is different and hence why *yashav* works but you can't see it gives it *toras kli*? Maybe we can answer the contradiction that in truth we're dealing with two different ideas: making something *muchan* and making something into a *kli*. To make something into a *kli*, you need to have used it before. That is his proof from *yashav* and that's what Rebbe Yochanan requires, while the earlier *Ran* was discussing what is a better way to prepare something. *Chishev* is better than *yashav*, and *l'halachah* that's only true according to *Rashbag*, who doesn't require a *toras kli*, but Rebbe Yochanan should hold that *chishev* doesn't help *l'halachah*. *Chazon Ish* gives an answer, but I don't understand it. Even in *Chiddushei HaRan* there is a similar contradiction. He proves the same idea from the case of stone on a barrel. Surely this proof contradicts what we're understanding because we don't *pasken* it's sufficient just to place it on the barrel. צ"ע.

striction. However, there is another option: to prepare an object for a specific use, in such an instance it can be moved for that purpose solely. The stone can only be used solely as a function of a lid, to be placed on and off the barrel. No other movement is permitted. Similarly, the pile of stones that Rebbi designated to be sat on can just be moved for the purpose of one's sitting. This principle is very novel - that an item is *muktzeh* regarding certain usages but not for other usages. The only precedence we find for this is from the case of soil on Yom Tov. If you brought it inside in order to cover blood of an animal, it is permitted for this use, while it remains *muktzeh* for any other usages.

Rashba also brings down this approach, as does *Baal HaMeor* as a second explanation. Accordingly they explain *l'halachah* that *Rif* does require a *toras kli* by both *pekak hachalon* (even though this is not explicit in *Rif*), and the piece of wood used as a bolt. Only once they receive a *toras kli*, achieved via doing an act to the object, would unrestricted movement be permitted. Since both of these are *keilim* whose main use is only when they are attached to the ground, which is when Rebbe Yochanan requires a *toras kli*. In contrast to *chariyos*, which are the palm branches one wants as a chair, these are detached and just *yichud* suffices.

Mordechai requires a *toras kli* with most items. The stone of the barrel and the stones for sitting are both lacking a *toras kli*. One's act of preparing them gives them a *toras kli*. It's probable that he would agree that since *chariyos* are somewhat suitable as seats, all that is necessary is to remove your previous intention of using them as fuel and that is sufficient to give it a *toras kli*. Even with *mochin* (textile insulators), we suggested earlier that the only problem is the intention to keep them as cloth for clothing, but in truth they have *toras kli*. Therefore just *yichud* to use it for the purpose of insulation might suffice, even without an act to give it *toras kli*.

Mishnah Berurah[44] *paskens*, based on a *Tosefes Shabbos*, that *yichud* alone is sufficient to prepare an item as a *kisui kli*. *Tehillah L'Dovid* asks: This is not concurrent with everything that we have learned. Intention is

44. *Se'if katan* 45.

not sufficient to confer a *toras kli*? How did *Mishnah Berurah* understand *Shulchan Aruch*?

We mentioned the case of *pekak hachalon* (a wooden window cover that comes on and off the window). *Rashbag* requires that it have a *toras kli* to permit one to move it. *Rif paskens* like Rebbe Yochanan. *Rosh* notes that this contradicts another *psak* of *Rif*, that intention is sufficient with palm branches. He answers that the main halachah according to *Rif* is that intention is sufficient, as seen by *chariyos*, hence *pekak* also wouldn't require a *maaseh tikkun* and would suffice with intention, whereas the reason that *Rif* requires a *toras kli* to remove an issue of an *issur boneh*, as otherwise it is considered adding a building material to a structure of a house, but now that it has a *toras kli* it is considered an extraneous addition. However, in order to permit *muktzeh*, just intention is enough. This is also *Raavad*'s approach to the Gemara: *toras kli* isn't needed for *muktzeh*.

Shulchan Aruch's opinion is confusing. On the one hand in *se'if* 20, regarding palm branches, he says that intention is enough. However, besides *Rosh*, no one holds that intention is sufficient, and earlier in *se'if* 10 he *paskens* like Rebbe Yochanan that *kisui keilim* requires a *maaseh tikkun* to give it a *toras kli*. Furthermore *Shulchan Aruch*[45] says that with intention alone one is able to move the window cover. If *Shulchan Aruch* learns like the aforementioned *Rosh* to some extent, we can resolve the inconsistencies. Really intention suffices, hence palm branches don't need any act and hence why *Mishnah Berurah paskens* that *yichud* alone is sufficient to designate a covering. We just are forced to explain in *siman* 308, where *Shulchan Aruch* discusses the cover of a hole and pit, he is only referring to a covering that is attached to the ground, so there is a problem of *boneh*, which requires a *toras kli* to permit it.

From what he writes in a *teshuvah*,[46] we can see *Rosh*'s stance more clearly. He explains that we only *pasken* like Rebbe Yochanan, who requires *toras kli*, regarding something that is part of the *binyan*. To move a part of a building would necessitate it to have a *toras kli*. Since one is try-

---

45. 313:1.
46. *Klal* 22, *siman* 8.

ing to change it into a *kli,* something detached that isn't functioning as a *kli* suffices with just *yichud.* This is a very logical idea. Even once one has been *yichud l'olam* a stone for some specific use, surely it won't receive *tumah.* Why not? Because it's not actually a *kli;* rather, you have now chosen a stone to function for some use. However, it is still a stone. Only something that you're trying to make into a *kli* will therefore require a *toras kli.*[47] Even though *Shulchan Aruch* doesn't mention in *se'if* 10 that the *kisui karkaos* requires a *toras kli,* which if he holds like *Rosh* surely it must because it is becoming part of something which is subject to *boneh,* maybe once these covers have a *beis achizah* (handle) (indicating that one can take this cover on and off), that provides the *toras kli.*

However, this approach, that Rebbe Yochanan only requires a *toras kli* by something which is attached to the ground, seems to oppose what the Gemara says, as we will explain. *Rashba* asks this question directly on *Raavad,* who holds that *toras kli* isn't needed for something not to be *muktzeh,* but is needed to remove the problem of *binyan.* The Gemara proves that *Rashbag* doesn't hold of the need of *toras kli* (and hence differs to Rebbe Yochanan) from the case of *chariyos.* There *Rashbag* doesn't even require to tie the branches, so surely he doesn't require *toras kli.* According to *Raavad,* even Rebbe Yochanan won't require *toras kli* by *chariyos* since they aren't attached, so what is the Gemara's proof that *Rashbag* differs with Rebbe Yochanan?

Maharshal asks the same question on *Tosafos*'s comment that *chariyos* are different, since they are *omed l'yeshivah,* hence they don't require a *toras kli.* If so, what's the Gemara's question on Rebbe Yochanan that he we see from *chariyos* there is no requirement of *toras kli*? He is forced to answer that the Gemara is only bringing from *chariyos* that you see when *Rashbag* argues against his *Tanna Kamma* his *lashon* means that one doesn't need a *toras kli.* So similarly by *nagar hanigrar* when *Rashbag* said *tiken v'lo kisher* it has the same connotation that a *toras kli* isn't required. So we

47. You see this from the text of *Rosh* that חריות לאו בני מעביד מעשה — "*chariyos* are not subject to any act," he is explaining that no act can potentially be done to make it into a *kli* because it's not being made into a *kli.* Not conclusive.

can borrow this answer to defend *Raavad*. *Milchamos* also brings up the same problem and is forced also in giving a difficult answer. ע״ש.[48]

48. *Maharsha* (126, s.v. וכ״ת) answers that *Tosafos* never meant to compare *chishev* to placing the stone on the barrel. He was only comparing *yeshivah* to *hanachah*, and in truth *chishev* doesn't give a *toras kli*; only *yashav* does. *Korban Nesanel* (point 6) asks that the Gemara in *Shabbos* 50a questions who argues on *Rashbag* and answers it's Rebbe Chanina ben Akiva, who once told his students to just think to prepare the *chariyos* to sit on and explained that his leniency was based upon the fact that it was pressing circumstances because it was either a house of celebration or a mourner's house. You see that usually he would require *kisher*, tying them up. So *Korban Nesanel* asks according to *Maharsha* what's the proof he requires tying, maybe Rebbe Chanina just requires *yashav* because that's the minimum according to what *Maharsha* requires to give it a *toras kli*? Maybe we can answer based on *Ritva* (R'Elazar Moshe on *Rosh* has a similar idea). *Ritva* asks: If Rebbe Chanina requires *kisher*, what's the basis for being lenient? He gives two approaches: Either it's just a leniency, or in truth normally Rebbe Chanina agrees that just designation alone is enough to prepare something. But if it's possible to do an act to prepare, you have to because we don't know your intention is sincere. If you are sincere, why didn't you do a real action? Therefore in these situations, when it's not possible to do more, *shaas hadechak*, nothing is lacking in his intention. According to the second approach, it only makes sense to be lenient if all that is required is to prepare the object, but if Rebbe Chanina requires an act for *toras kli*, how can he be lenient with just intention? How can that confer a *toras kli*? We see that it must be that he only needs *hachanah*, and regarding *hachanah Maharsha* agrees that *chishev* is better than *yashav*. If so, the Gemara's proof is correct. If *chishev* was only enough at *shaas hadechak*, so the only other option is that he requires generally *kisher*. The same idea could answer *Tzohar L'Binyan*'s question on *Maharsha*, ע״ש.

Chapter 8

בעלי חיים

Animals and Pets

Questions

1. Can Leah play with her pet hamster, dog, etc., on Shabbos?
2. Can Sarah stroke a guide dog?
3. Can Yonatan walk his dog in a private garden on Shabbos?

Shulchan Aruch[1] *paskens* that אסור לטלטל בהמה חיה ועוף - "it is forbidden to move animals and birds" on Shabbos. This halachah is unanimous. Most commentators explain that the reason is that animals are *muktzeh machmas gufo* (intrinsically *muktzeh* due to a lack of purpose). They are like wood and stones that have no purpose on Shabbos. (Even though during the week one does use animals for various tasks, those tasks are forbidden on Shabbos; Chazal only gave a leniency to move vessels, not animals.) *Tosafos* quotes the opinion of R' Yosef,[2] who explains that the Gemara which brings a dead chick as an example of an animal which is *muktzeh* is specifically dealing with a dead chick. If it were alive, it wouldn't be *muktzeh*. His reasoning is that while it is alive, one can give it to a child to stop his crying or even for him to play with.

---

1. 308:39.
2. He is one of the *Rishonim*. *Tosafos* 45b, s.v. הכא, quotes his opinion.

The *Rishonim* state that this contradicts a Gemara and is difficult to understand from a logical view. Firstly, the Gemara[3] discusses different ways by which one can bring an animal into its pen on Shabbos. According to R' Yosef, why didn't the Gemara suggest direct movement, if the animals are alive they are not *muktzeh*?! Secondly, if one has a beautiful-looking stone, even if one enjoys looking at its appearance and keeps it for aesthetic purposes, it is still not permitted to move. Just as it remains a stone, so too the bird should remain like a stone, i.e., *muktzeh machmas gufo*. Even though its presence can calm down a child, this purpose isn't enough to give it a status of a *kli*.[4]

The dispute between R' Yosef and the other *Rishonim* whether a chick is *muktzeh* or not doesn't seem to have bearing on the question whether pets nowadays are *muktzeh* or not. R' Yosef is not dealing with an animal that was designated for the specific purpose of being used as a pet; rather, he held that all birds have a purpose on Shabbos. He holds that this purpose is enough to remove its identity of *muktzeh machmas gufo*, while everyone else argues that all animals, despite potential side uses which may be had from them, remain *muktzeh machmas gufo*. Whether a pet which was specifically designated for one's use should not have this status of *muktzeh machmas gufo* - we still need to explore.

Designating an Animal as a Pet

We find a source that sheds light on our question whether pets are *muktzeh* or not from a question that *Ohr Zarua*[5] sent to *Rosh*. *Ohr Zarua* asked: If

---

3. 45b.

4. *Tosafos* asks why birds that die on Shabbos are not permissible to be moved because they can be classified as animal fodder. According to Rebbe Shimon, something that can be fed to an animal isn't *muktzeh*. *Tosafos* distinguishes that with a bird there is a positive designation not to feed it to an animal, in contrast to regular food, where one doesn't take care that it isn't fed to his animals. One can understand that *Tosafos* is inferring that animals are *muktzeh* because there is a positive designation. Alternatively, *Tosafos* doesn't disagree that animals are like wood and stone; rather, he is asking that still if they are fit for use, they shouldn't be *muktzeh*.

5. Responsa *Ohr Zarua, siman* 82.

one has parrots or other birds, can the owner move them? *Ohr Zarua* himself is lenient, saying that since people enjoy the chirping of these birds, they are not *muktzeh*. *Rosh* argues that since one can't play with them because Chazal made a *gezeirah*: "*Ein meshamshim b'baalei chaim* - One can't use animals,"[6] despite the fact one enjoys the sounds the birds emit, it doesn't change the fact that they are not fit for any actual use and remain *muktzeh machmas gufo*.

Our pets nowadays are certainly better than *Ohr Zarua*'s parrots. There should be more basis to permit them. Namely, pets are reared and trained for being domesticated. Surely if one can designate a stone, why can't one designate an animal? When designating both a stone and a pet, one wants to permanently use them for a purpose, which in effect allows him to use it, as he has now upgraded this item to something with a designated use.

The argument of the *Rishonim* against R' Yosef, that the animal's appearance can't count to serve as a function, doesn't necessarily apply to pets. *Tosafos* perhaps was just arguing that using a bird to calm a child isn't a use that will give it an identity as a *kli*, but could agree that when one designates a dog to be his pet evermore, this is now changing this animal into an item with a specific use. Even a use as insignificant or trivial as a pet renders it not *muktzeh*.

However, there is room to discuss whether playing with an animal is considered a sufficient use to upgrade something to have a "use." We will shortly see a dispute between *Shulchan Aruch* and *Rema* whether a ball (a crudely fashioned one, the type of which were common in previous times) is *muktzeh*. The reason why it should be *muktzeh* as explained by *Mishnah Berurah* is because playing is not considered a suitable use. If so, surely the designation of one's animal as a pet also won't help. However, maybe ac-

---

6. The original reason for this safeguard was that Chazal were worried that if one was allowed to ride an animal, he might come to remove a branch from a tree while riding the animal. Even though the reason behind the *gezeirah* doesn't apply to birds (one can't ride a bird), there is a *lo plug*, i.e., we do not differentiate which animals are encompassed in this safeguard.

cording to *Rema,* who permits toys as not being *muktzeh,* there can be more grounds to be lenient.

When R' Shlomo Zalman Auerbach[7] was asked about the *muktzeh* status of pet dogs, he replied that it is anyway forbidden to raise dogs, and if someone were to act in such an irrelevant way, we would say *batel daas* (how he practices is insignificant). He was informed that in certain non-religious circles, dogs can be more common than kids. He said that halachically we don't reckon with the behavior of such people, especially when it's against the halachah. He added that dogs are not meant for playing with, it is not their purpose. He combined two arguments to forbid moving even pet dogs. Firstly, dogs are forbidden to raise, and secondly, playing with a dog is not its purpose. If we need the combination of both arguments to forbid since the first argument is only relevant with a dog, we don't find any prohibition in raising a hamster. There might be room to be lenient in moving a pet hamster and other such pets (question #1).

A Pet Will Always Remain a Pet

We can perhaps entertain a new argument why designating won't help even for pets whose raising is not contrary to Torah law. The Gemara in *Sukkah*[8] says that a lulav is *muktzeh* even on Yom Tov. *Tosafos* explains that despite that one has designated it to be used for a mitzvah it doesn't help remove the *muktzeh* (for the sake of fulfilling the mitzvah, one can shake it). The reason why designating for a mitzvah is insufficient is since the mitzvah doesn't demand that this lulav function as anything other than a lulav, the mitzvah is only to shake a lulav. One hasn't upgraded it for any practical use, hence the designation is meaningless.[9] Similarly, when one wants to make a puppy one's pet, he isn't upgrading the dog. It is a dog and he wants it to remain a dog. Since this dog will solely be for playing

---

7. *Sefer Maadanei Shlomo,* p. 96.

8. 43a.

9. See chapter 7 for an elaboration on how *yichud* works.

and entertainment, perhaps this designation is similarly meaningless, since one is not changing anything.[10] [11]

However, the argument of *Rosh* to *Ohr Zarua*, that there is a prohibition of *shimush baalei chaim*, thus precluding any potential use one might wish to have with his animal, should apply to pets as well. The same way that *Rosh* says that the *lo plug* (we don't differentiate) encompasses even birds who don't have a concern one might come to cut off a branch, חשש שמא יבוא לחתוך זמורה,[12] so too it should be applicable with pets. However, one can infer from the aforementioned *Tosafos*, from the fact that he never asked this question on R' Yosef, that there is an prohibition to use animals, that he doesn't hold it is applicable to all animals (animals that one can't ride it won't apply to). Based on what we've presented, there are grounds for being lenient to play with one's pet, but certainly it is praiseworthy to be stringent.

---

10. The Gemara treats a shofar as a *kli shemelachto l'issur*. Even though it's a mitzvah item, it's treated as a *kli* because they used it as an instrument; it was a form of a trumpet, not just a mitzvah object. Nowadays our shofaros are only used for the mitzvah of *tekiah*, so there is a strong argument to say, based on *Tosafos*, that they should be *muktzeh machmas gufo*. They are a piece of animal horn and the fact you've designated it for a mitzvah is meaningless because the mitzvah doesn't demand it be anything other than a ram's horn. R' Shlomo Zalman Auerbach entertained only as far as to say that since nowadays, we don't use a shofar for other purposes, it's worse than a *kli shemelachto l'issur* and can't be moved *l'tzorech gufo u'mekomo*.

11. Even if pets are in actuality *muktzeh*, *Biur Halachah* nonetheless permits touching the animal's tail because it is not *tiltul b'gufo*. R' Shlomo Zalman Auerbach asked: Why is not forbidden due to *shimush b'muktzeh*, since you're using part of the animal? Simply we can answer the same way: We don't view moving the tail as *tiltul b'gufo*, a direct form of moving the *muktzeh*, and we treat the tail as a separate part other than the body of the animal. Similarly, we don't treat it as *shimush b'gufo*. It's as if one isn't using the animal's body. R' Shlomo Zalman Auerbach gives a different answer, ע"ש.

12. Chazal forbade touching an animal lest one come to ride on it and consequently snap off a branch while riding it.

Taking a Pet for a Walk

Even if pets are to be considered *muktzeh,* there is no problem at all to take them for a walk in one's garden (question #3), as long one doesn't touch the animal. In a public domain it is forbidden, since Chazal made a safeguard[13] lest one comes to lift the animal off the ground and move it four *amos.*[14] However, one needs to be careful not to move the animal in any way, nor to stroke its fur. The reason why even stroking is forbidden is because the Gemara[15] teaches that it's forbidden to shut the eyelids of a corpse due to *muktzeh.* We learn from this rule that moving part of something which is *muktzeh,* even if one doesn't move the whole item is forbidden, this is known as *tiltul muktzeh b'miktzas.* Therefore, stroking an animal, thereby causing its hair to move to and fro, is *tiltul muktzeh b'miktzas.*[16] A guide dog[17] might be different (question #2), since it is *not* considered an animal that doesn't serve a practical use. Even if by regular pet dogs the designation is ineffective because we say *batel daas* (his thoughts are deemed irrelevant against how the majority of people normally behave), here even R' Shlomo Zalman Auerbach, who strongly forbids all types of dogs, is lenient. He explains that since now it is only meant for this use - namely, to help the blind man walk - it's not *muktzeh.*

---

13. 128b.

14. In a *karmelis* (semipublic domain), it is a dispute. The argument depends on whether we enact on an *karmelis* to protect a public domain, whether Chazal encompassed in their safeguard also a *karmelis* to uphold the safeguard of the public domain. *Kaf HaChaim, se'if katan* 240, says that the opinion of *Shulchan Aruch* is stringent. Since it's carrying in the public domain, Chazal were also stringent in a *karmelis.*

15. 151b.

16. There is an exception according to *Biur Halachah* 302:11, who says that moving the tail of an animal is not *tiltul muktzeh b'miktzas* because it's not part of the body of the animal. The safeguard was only on the body, and it's logical that for the same reason it's not considered *shimush muktzeh b'miktzas.*

17. *Shemiras Shabbos K'Hilchasah,* ch. 18, note 62.

Summary

The *Rishonim* understand that animals are *muktzeh machmas gufo* because they don't have any purpose on Shabbos. The question surrounding pets is whether owning an animal solely for the sake of one's entertainment and company is considered to be a form of designation that can remove its *muktzeh* status. Despite the arguments to permit, it we leaned toward being stringent. Designating doesn't help since one is not trying to change the dog from being a dog; the only precedence we have where designation helps is when one wants to designate for use a previously useless item. Furthermore, there is a safeguard that prohibits using animals. *Rosh* is stringent that all animals are encompassed in the safeguard, hence playing even with pets such as hamsters would be forbidden. Walking an animal without touching it is permitted, but care must be taken not to move a body part of the animal because of the rule that moving part of something *muktzeh*, even if not moving the whole item, is forbidden.

Answers

1. The consensus among contemporary *poskim* is to forbid moving pet animals. Those who are lenient have what to rely on.
2. A guide dog is not *muktzeh*, so one can stroke its hair.
3. In a private domain Yonatan can walk his dog, provided he doesn't carry it.

Chapter 9

משחקים
Toys

Questions

1. Is an adult allowed to play ping-pong (table tennis) on Shabbos? Can he play with his children?
2. Is it permissible to play with wind-up cars (ones that run with a spring mechanism)?
3. Should we educate our kids that some toys are *muktzeh*?

A fundamental question regarding *muktzeh* is what's the status of toys. Are they truly *muktzeh*, or is it just not in the spirit of the day of Shabbos to play games? What is agreed upon without doubt by all the *poskim* that comment on this topic is that Shabbos is a time for connecting to Hashem, learning Torah, and singing the praises of the Creator. Whiling away one's time in games and toys is not what Shabbos was given for. Nevertheless, we need to know whether there is a halachic prohibition of *muktzeh* with toys or not.

Shulchan Aruch[1] *paskens*: אין לשחק בשבת ויום טוב בכדור - "One shouldn't play with balls on Shabbos." *Rema* argues that some permit playing with balls and testifies that the prevalent custom was to be lenient. Some modern-day *poskim*[2] are quoted to say that *Shulchan Aruch*'s *psak* wouldn't be applicable nowadays. In times gone by, a toy was a makeshift object

---

1. 308:45.
2. *Shevus Yitzchak* and *Shalmei Yehonasan*.

that was sourced from random objects found lying around the house. In reference to such a "toy," *Shulchan Aruch paskens* that it is *muktzeh* because it isn't a *kli*. Many contemporary poskim claim it is very plausible that *Shulchan Aruch* would agree that nowadays, whereby we have specifically designed and created toys that are often fully functional items - and where such importance is given by society to the toy industry - that our manufactured toys are certainly *keilim*!

However, one can certainly see room to argue with this distinction. It is seemingly clear from the Mishnah in *Keilim*[3] that even in the times of the Gemara they manufactured toys from scratch. We clearly see that such toys were in existence even back then, so certainly *Shulchan Aruch* also included such toys in his prohibition. Even without coming up with a new logic to distinguish between toys nowadays and back then, one can rely on *Magen Avraham*. *Magen Avraham* on this *se'if* references *se'if* 21. There *Shulchan Aruch* teaches that building stones are *muktzeh* and one can't sit on them unless one arranges them before Shabbos, i.e., he has previously done an act to show he intends to use these stones as a seat, so such *yichud* works for them. *Magen Avraham*'s intention in referencing the case of the stones is obvious. He must understand that *Shulchan Aruch* is not referring to a purposely fashioned ball, the likes of which the Mishnah in *Keilim* was referring to, but rather a makeshift ball that doesn't have a *shem kli*. The problem is that it's like wood and stones, it has no function of use at all. This is the reasoning behind the *muktzeh* of *Shulchan Aruch*. So *Magen Avraham* is saying that if however one did designate it forever, it won't be *muktzeh* (if playing isn't considered a use, hence it is *muktzeh* and it won't change anything by designating an item for such a certain purpose). Manufacturing an item for the specific purpose of being used for playing with from its onset is a strong form of designation forever. Surely all current toys meet these criteria and so will be classified as vessels and thus shouldn't be *muktzeh*. This *Magen Avraham* is a basis for a leniency to permit moving all of our toys.

3. 23:1.

Are Balls Permitted on Shabbos?

The source of *Shulchan Aruch*'s ruling forbidding one to move a ball is *Shibolei HaLeket.*[4] A close look at the source reveals that he is innovating a new idea. He starts off by stating that a ball is considered a proper *kli.* However, playing is not a real need. The premise to move any *kli* is that you are moving it for a purpose, and playing isn't a good enough purpose. He writes: נראה שאסור לשחק בו ולטלטלו בשבת ויום טוב שהרי **אין צריך בטילטולן** - "It is forbidden to play and move [a ball] on Shabbos and Yom Tov because there is *no need in your moving.*" He continues to ask that maybe the ball will still retain its identity as a *kli* because it is fit to cover a box, i.e., it can have a function that we consider to be purposeful. However, he rejects this possibility on the grounds that toys or balls are dirty and not fit to be used for something else.[5]

To substantiate this *psak, Shibolei HaLeket* quotes the *Yerushalmi* that Tur Shimon, a certain city, was destroyed because they played ball on Shabbos. Perhaps his intention in quoting that story is as follows: The dissenting opinion in the Gemara holds that it was destroyed because of immorality. It is difficult to understand that one opinion held that the cause was immorality, while the other held that *muktzeh* was the cause behind its destruction. Surely these two opinions should be on par with each other.[6] However, maybe based on what *Shibolei HaLeket* understood, that playing is not considered a purpose, we can explain the severity of what took place. Chazal viewed playing ball as something futile and useless, hence it's not a "need," something a Jew should be involving himself with

---

4. Section 121.

5. *Ohr L'Tzion* uses this to be lenient nowadays, since all our toys are clean so they are fit to be used as a cover. Even though we saw, in chapter 6, that nowadays, simply speaking, there is no leniency of *shivrei keilim* since we don't use broken shards to cover anything, you can distinguish that the toys we are discussing were *keilim* previously. We're determining whether they should lose that status or not, so even if in practice you won't use it to cover anything, maybe that's enough to help it not lose its identity as a *kli.*

6. The Midrash in *Eichah* does, however, say that the immorality was only committed with one woman and she was subsequently removed from the city. This mitigates the severity of what was committed.

on Shabbos. By playing ball they showed that they had lost any real connection with Shabbos and Hashem. It's an indication for the low level the people fell to.[7]

It should follow that if there is a need to play games on Shabbos, then halachically it should be considered a "need." So for children who play with toys all the time and are not yet of the age to do more meaningful things on Shabbos, it is a necessary need and for them it's permitted. (This is even without relying on the principle that kids below the age of *chinuch* have no restrictions on Shabbos. Our leniency could also apply to kids who have reached *chinuch* age.)

Surely Tur Shimon was not destroyed because kids were playing ball; rather, the adults were engaged in this futile pursuit that invoked Divine wrath. It could perhaps be argued that even for adults who are playing with their children it can be considered a need, as they aren't interested in the game, but in the entertainment that is being provided for the child. *Shulchan Aruch*'s *psak* will only pertain to those who should be engaged in spiritual matters on Shabbos instead of wasting time with games, since for such a person, playing cannot be considered a legitimate need. Therefore for them all toys are *muktzeh*.

The *poskim*[8] seem to understand that according to *Shulchan Aruch*, the problem with a ball is that it doesn't have an identity of a *kli*. It's likely that the source for this is what *Shibolei HaLeket* quoted from his brother in his *teshuvah*, that the function of playing doesn't give it a *shem kli*: הכדורים שלנו אפ׳ כלי לא חשיבי ומחשבת השחוק שחישב לשחק בו לא משוי כלי - "Our balls are not considered vessels. Even our intention to play with them doesn't confer the status of a vessel on them." To paraphrase, he is saying that even if the ball was purposely fashioned for playing with, that use is not significant enough to confer an identity of a *kli*. This is similar to what we find brought down by *Beis Yosef*[9] that people would donate candles to the shul on the occasion of the first time their son came to shul. They would accompany

7. *Rokei'ach* and *Korban HaEidah* both explain that it was because they were wasting their time with games and not involving themselves in learning Torah.

8. *Graz, Magen Avraham.*

9. *Siman* 308.

the child by carrying the (unlit) candles. Most *Rishonim* argue to forbid this custom - the candle is *muktzeh* because it is a *kli shemelachto l'issur* and what they did to designate it for moving is not a proper designation. Since it has not been designated for a usage, the candle remains *muktzeh*. The same concept would apply with our case of a ball. Since we have established that playing is not a proper designation, as it is not a functional usage of an item, it is therefore insufficient to confer the status of a *kli*.

Accordingly we can now explain the argument presented by the modern-day *poskim* to permit toys. Perhaps they mean that since nowadays toys have become such an integral part of society - it's a trillion-dollar industry - no one can claim that playing is not an important use. It is an accepted idea in society even for adults to play games. So even something whose sole purpose is to provide entertainment, nowadays would have enough significance to confer an identity of a *kli* on an object. However, this might only help for a *kli* that was manufactured originally as a toy. However, if you want to take a household item and use it as a toy, e.g., a backgammon chip went missing and you want to replace it with a button, since a button wasn't manufactured as a toy, one's designation won't help. Or one can argue that since nowadays toys have importance, there is meaning to one's designation and we won't claim *batel daas*. (The fact that any toy was manufactured solely for the purpose of entertainment shows that this purpose is important.)

According to all of the approaches we have seen until now, balls aren't singled out to be forbidden; rather, a ball is an example of a toy. But if, for whatever reason, a ball is *muktzeh*, so too other toys would be *muktzeh*.

Ohr L'Tzion has a new approach to the whole topic. He entertains that maybe *Shulchan Aruch* doesn't intend to *pasken* that *all* toys are *muktzeh*. *Ohr L'Tzion*'s argument is since there are *Rishonim* who permit all toys and some who forbid all toys, why on a rabbinic transgression would *Shulchan Aruch* choose to be stringent? It must be that the *Yerushalmi* was the deciding factor (unlike what we've presented until now, that *Shulchan Aruch* was based on *Shibolei HaLeket*). If the source is from the *Yerushalmi*, the reason for the prohibition doesn't have to be because of *muktzeh*. The Gemara is not clear that the problem was because of *muktzeh*. Furthermore, *Shulchan Aruch*[10] switches his language from the other halachos he writes regarding *muktzeh*; he says "*l'sachek*" instead of "*l'taltel*." Maybe it's a problem specifically in playing ball. The reason might be that ball games typically take place outdoors; a large group gathers to participate and this turns into a fanfare. This is a public disgrace of Shabbos and is what caused the destruction of Tur Shimon.

It follows that games other than ball games, which are played in the privacy of one's home, won't be encompassed in this prohibition. Nevertheless, he does advocate being stringent with all games. The majority of *poskim* are nonetheless lenient, even for Sephardim, and we have added further room for leniencies when one is playing with children. But one mustn't take the leniency too far, and those who are stringent have reason to continue practicing so. Playing ping-pong should be avoided according to *Ohr L'Tzion*, but one shouldn't protest at those who are lenient to do so since they have what to rely on (question #1).

Wind-Up Toys

For those who can play with toys, are they permitted to play with wind-up cars or wind-up animals, etc. (question #2)? A mechanical watch that has stopped is forbidden to wind up on Shabbos,[11] as this is considered fixing the watch. This is encompassed in the prohibition of *tikkun maneh* (fixing an item). R' Moshe Feinstein[12] is quoted to have said that it's similarly forbidden to wind up toys, yet he says that despite this they won't be a *kli shemelachto l'issur* since they are designated to be used by children who are allowed to use them.[13] However, R' Shlomo Zalman Auerbach makes

---

10. *Gra* implicitly argues on this approach. He explains that *Tosafos/Rema*, who are lenient, hold that the reason why the city was destroyed was because the citizens transgressed *hotzaah* with their ball playing, not that the ball was *muktzeh*. Implicit is that the opinion who forbids playing with games, i.e., *Shulchan Aruch*, must have understood the *Yerushalmi* simply — that it was because the ball was *muktzeh*.

11. *Mishnah Berurah* 338:15.

12. Brought in *Sefer Tiltulei Shabbos*.

13. This logic is novel and might be dependent on the reason for *kli shemelachto l'issur*. If it is because of *gezeiras keilim*, this means that there was one decree on

a very logical distinction between a watch and a toy: When one winds up a watch, he is now making it work; he has fixed it to function again until the next time it stops. However, when one winds up a car, it now has a coiled spring that can thrust it forward. It's not considered that he has fixed the *kli*; it's not now a more functional *kli*, and all you have done is made it move forward for a few seconds. This is therefore insignificant and not applicable at all to *tikkun maneh*.

Summary

Several reasons are presented to explain why *Shulchan Aruch* forbids playing with balls on Shabbos. Some explain that toys are not considered a *kli*, either because playing is not considered a use that confers the identity of a vessel, or because *Shulchan Aruch* is referring to makeshift items that were being used as toys, but not items that were made to serve the purpose of toys. From the *Yerushalmi* we see the severity of playing with balls on Shabbos. It could be not due to *muktzeh*, but perhaps for other reasons, such as transporting or a general degradation of Shabbos. Nevertheless, *Rema* is lenient and permits playing with toys on Shabbos. Even according to *Shulchan Aruch*, there are reasons why nowadays one can be lenient: playing is accepted in our society as a legitimate purpose of an item, toys have been manufactured specifically for this function and are fit to be used for other purposes as well. All these reasons will confer an identity of a vessel on a toy. Also, we understood that *Magen Avraham* holds that one can designate something as a toy and that would remove its *muktzeh* status. If there is no constructive purpose, then one should refrain from using toys, as each leniency has its difficulties. Wind-up toys can be played with because the winding is not considered fixing the toy, unlike winding up a watch, which does fix it.

---

all utensils, so it shouldn't make a difference who uses this item, ultimately it's destined for a forbidden use. However, if *kli shemelachto l'issur* is based upon the fact that one sets aside the forbidden usages of the item, then we can understand R' Moshe's idea better. See the introduction to *muktzeh* for an elaboration on this point.

Answers

1. From the point of view of *muktzeh,* there are grounds to permit playing with toys, balls included. However, there is an argument that specifically balls are forbidden to use. An Ashkenazi can certainly be lenient.
2. It is not considered fixing the toy by winding it up, so kids can play with such toys.
3. Playing with toys is a requirement of childhood. Since the consensus of *poskim* is that even *Shulchan Aruch* would agree that toys nowadays aren't *muktzeh,* children shouldn't be taught to refrain from playing.

Chapter 10, Part 1

שארית אוכל ומאכיל בהמה

Leftover Food and Animal Fodder

Questions

1. How careful must I be in moving fruit peels and pits?
2. In modern-day society, where pet dogs are prevalent, are bones *muktzeh*?

Chazal didn't establish any limitations of *muktzeh* on food, but the question is, how do we define food? Does one's own palate define what's considered food for him, or is the definition more generic and defined by what society in large consumes? Are food items that are designated for animals to eat defined as food, or do they fall into a category of their own?

The Mishnah[1] lists several items, such as raw beans, which even though in their present state are not fit for human consumption, since they are fed to animals they are not *muktzeh*. The *beraisa*[2] continues the list: mustard seeds are fit for doves, glass shards are fit for ostriches, etc. The *Tannaim* and *Amoraim* argue as to whom these halachos are applicable - only for the owner or for any Jew? One opinion holds that it depends on the animal. For common animals, such as doves, if they are frequently found in the vicinity, then there are no limits of *muktzeh* with their food, and anyone can carry it. However, if the animal is rarer, such as an ostrich,

1. 126b.
2. 128a.

then only if one owns that animal can he carry their food, as only he relates to the item as food. The dissenting opinion holds that we have a principle, "*Kol Yisrael bnei melachim* - All Jews are princes," which means that all Jews are considered to be possible to own these rare animals. Therefore, even if in actuality one doesn't own one of these more unique species, he still can carry their food, since he is still considered to have a connection to the species and thus would relate to the item as animal food.

Shulchan Aruch[3] *paskens* like the first opinion. Therefore, with types of domesticated animals and birds that are common (*Mishnah Berurah*[4] explains this to mean *matzui etzel rov*, meaning that it's common among all classes of society, not that we require that the majority of people need to own the animal), their food is not *muktzeh*. A classic example of this would be a dog, while with a less common animal, such as a hamster, only the few people in the town who own one can move its food. One can perhaps ask: For a Jew who dislikes animals and owns neither a dog nor a hamster, and has no intention of coming into any contact with these animals, what relevance does it have to him whether an animal is common or not? Surely when he finishes his chicken and is left with a bone (question #2), he doesn't entertain a notion to give it to his neighbor's dog. Therefore surely the food of commonly found animal should remain *muktzeh*?

Maybe we can suggest that this changed over time. Back in the time of *Shulchan Aruch*, even those who didn't own animals nonetheless would still relate to bones as dog food, as they would still somehow end up being eaten by dogs. But in modern society, with our modern garbage disposal facilities and general improvement in street hygiene, bones rarely end up being eaten, and hence we relate differently to bones? This question can also be asked according to those *Tannaim* who hold that all Jews are fit to be princes. What does it help if I'm fit to be a prince? Presently I have no intention of buying an ostrich, and in no way do I relate to broken glass as animal food, so why according to those *Tannaim* do we not consider it *muktzeh* for a Jew who doesn't own this animal?

---

3. 308:29.

4. *Se'if katan* 119.

What Did Chazal Qualify as Food?

It is more likely that nothing changed over time; rather, the leniency of animal food is based on what fits into Chazal's parameters of what defines "food." These items should really be *muktzeh machmas gufo,* as they are not fit for use for humans, yet Chazal said that if such an animal is common in this town that classifies this object as being animal food. Bones in general are *muktzeh,* while bones which are animal food aren't. It's irrelevant how one relates to bones; once something fits into Chazal's criteria for animal food, it's intrinsically not *muktzeh.* The other *Tannaim*'s definition of animal food was even more abstract. Even if in actuality it's not given to animals, as long as it's fit for animals, regarding the object there is nothing lacking - this is animal food. The fact that presently there are no ostriches found nearby is a technical problem, but it doesn't change the fact that this is animal food.[5]

According to this explanation that animal food is always to be considered as an object called "animal food," the distinction we made differentiating between whether it's common or not - that for something not common it is only permissible for the owner and not others - is more difficult to understand. If it's under the category of animal food, why can't everyone move it and if it's not animal food why can the owner move it. Perhaps we can say that even if it were not to be considered animal food because this item is not commonly given to most animals, the owner still has an automatic designation with these items, since during the week he uses them as fodder, despite not being considered food for the majority of animals. He therefore doesn't need to do a specific act of designation every time. For him, these items are destined for use, and for him it's obviously animal

5. The alternative way to understand the permission of animal food is: In a case where this animal is common in the city, if one has no intention of feeding the animals, he still relates to it as animal food. He recognizes that people in this city use bones to feed their dogs, so even in his eyes it's considered animal food. In contrast, when the animal isn't common, only the owner relates to this fodder as animal food, so only he can move it. For everyone else, it's *muktzeh machmas gufo,* it's not animal food. However, this way doesn't explain *Rashbag*'s halachah permitting ostrich food. No one actually relates to broken glass as animal fodder!

food. However, if this is true, the owner must only feed his animal something that is normal for that species to eat. If he feeds him something abnormal, that doesn't make it animal food, so even the owner won't have a *heter* to move it (without a specific designation before Shabbos).

Leniency of Biur Halachah

With the relatively recent invention of manufactured animal food, bones aren't used as a regular, classic dog food. Therefore it's difficult to say that bones would have an identity as animal food, as this is not a common usage of bones. The question remains: Would we have any dispensation today to move bones, since they can be used as dog food? *Shulchan Aruch*[6] says that date pits, which are "commonly fed" to animals, are not *muktzeh*. We see from the stress on the phrase "commonly fed" that the criteria is even if it is fit for animal food, it still has to be commonly used as animal food. There are those who claim that nowadays bones should be *muktzeh*, as they are no longer commonly used as dog food.

However, according to *Biur Halachah*, we might still find a leniency. He explains that date pits are different from other foods commonly used as animal fodder because they are **hard and not really fit for animal food**. For that reason - that they are not really fit, unless they are common to be used nowadays - they will be *muktzeh*. This is in contrast to other fruit pits, which are mostly possible for animals to chew on even if not commonly used, they will not be *muktzeh*. Based on this *Biur Halachah*, bones would be permitted to be moved even nowadays for the same reason: The lack of use of bones as dog food is not due to the inadequacies of bones; they are as fit as processed food, but due to convenience it has become uncommon nowadays to give a dog a bone. We can add another basis to be lenient: *Mishnah Berurah* says that if there are any remnants of meat or chicken left on the bone, it hasn't yet lost its status of food.

---

6. 308:30. (The source of *Shulchan Aruch* is a *Rif*.)

Why Dogs Are Different

Shulchan Aruch paskens[7] that one can feed his own dog, who is dependent upon its owner for his food. (Most of *Rishonim* explain that the prohibition in feeding an animal who is not dependent on you is a safeguard that one shouldn't come to trap animals on Shabbos.) *Magen Avraham* says that *Shulchan Aruch*'s leniency applies even with someone else's dog, since it's a mitzvah to feed a dog when the dog is dependent on man, as they don't find food on their own.

Magen Avraham proves so from the fact that *Rema*[8] permits one to move a bone because dogs are common. *Rema* is permitting someone who doesn't own a dog to move a bone, but if the owner of the bone is regardless forbidden to feed a dog (due to the safeguard against trapping). Since it's not his own, it follows that the owner of the food has no use with this bone and it should now be *muktzeh*, so why is *Rema* permitting it? *Magen Avraham* concludes that it must be that it's permissible to feed someone's dog. Therefore, the owner of the bone has a use for it and doesn't set it aside.

Tehillah L'Dovid[9] infers that *Magen Avraham* only permits one to feed a friend's dog due to the special mitzvah to feed a dog, since dogs don't find their own food, but he is not lenient to permit feeding someone else's animal. *Tehillah L'Dovid* asks: If so, how can *Shulchan Aruch* permit one to move other types of animal food even if one doesn't own the animal as long as the animal is common? If one can't feed someone else's animal, surely he sets the food aside and it is *muktzeh*?

Based on this question, *Tehillah L'Dovid* concludes that *Magen Avraham* meant that one can feed even a stray dog. Since there is a mitzvah to feed all dogs, all dogs are considered to be incumbent upon you to feed, and hence one can feed them on Shabbos. We can conclude that both *Tehillah L'Dovid* and *Magen Avraham* hold that when one doesn't own an animal, he can still carry their fodder and feed his friend's animal. Other

---

7. 324:11.
8. 308:29.
9. Point 14.

poskim[10] argue with this conclusion. They hold that you can't feed your friend's animal.

The premise of *Magen Avraham* and *Tehillah L'Dovid,* that if one can't feed an animal this food, it is *muktzeh,* is questionable. Even if one can't actually feed any animal this food on Shabbos since he doesn't own one, so he doesn't have the leniency to feed an animal, it's still possible to understand why the food is not *muktzeh* as we explained earlier. If animals are common, so too their food is intrinsically animal food and Chazal never restricted that. It's irrelevant whether you have or don't have a use for this; this isn't encompassed in *gezeiras muktzeh.* And if you were to claim that the owner of the food will set it aside if he can't feed anyone this food, that isn't certain; maybe he wants to use it by giving to his friend so that his friend can feed his animal.

The Stringency of R' Elyashiv

Even if we don't accept the stringency of *Tehillah L'Dovid* that the food is only not *muktzeh* in a case where one can actually feed the animal, because only then is it still considered animal food, we have a different limitation quoted from R' Elyashiv. He is quoted to say that with a species of animal that is commonly found in public but not frequent to be privately owned, their food is *muktzeh* since it's forbidden to feed them, due to the aforementioned safeguard. (For example, in England, squirrels are very common in wooded areas. However, their food, such as acorns, etc., remains *muktzeh,* as it is forbidden to feed them on Shabbos.)

We can understand this in two ways: Either that despite their food being animal food, since the only thing you can do with it is something forbidden, as it is forbidden to feed them, it is now *muktzeh,* a type of *muktzeh machmas issur*. Or perhaps he meant a more *lomdish* idea, that only food which is commonly fed to animals gets an identity as animal food, but if it's not common at present to feed them, since there is an prohibition in

---

10. *Machatzis HaShekel, Eliyah Rabbah,* and *Biur Halachah.*

doing so, it doesn't get an identity as animal food.[11] The practical relevance of this ruling, either way we explain it, is since stray cats do not belong to anyone, there is a prohibition to exert yourself in feeding them on Shabbos.

Cats in Eretz Yisrael are certainly considered common. However, most of them are strays. This should result in food one wants to give a cat being *muktzeh*. Even without the aforementioned *chiddush* of R' Elyashiv, one shouldn't be able to move food that he wants to give to the cats. (We are obviously only discussing food that is no longer fit for human consumption, and one wishes to give it to cats rather than throw it out.) This is because even during the week the norm is *not to* feed stray cats; they survive off the waste in the trash cans. We can learn from the *psak* of *Shulchan Aruch* by date pits that if it's not common to feed an animal this item, even if it is technically fit for them it doesn't get an identity of animal food. However, maybe we can argue, based on the aforementioned *Biur Halachah*, that only due to the inadequacy of the date pits must it be common to feed animals those seeds as well, that ultimately this food is fit and that's enough to confer on it an identity of animal food.

Fruit Seeds and Peels

The aforementioned *Biur Halachah* is a basis to be lenient even nowadays with a lot of fruits seeds and peels, such as watermelon seeds, orange peels, etc. (question #1). *Biur Halachah* says that since one occasionally eats apple and pear seeds while eating the fruit, we can compare them to *Rif*'s explanation of *tamri armita*. The Gemara distinguishes between two types

---

11. Maybe we can consider that if one regularly feeds a stray cat during the week, and only now since it's Shabbos he isn't allowed to feed it, maybe R' Elyashiv's halachah won't apply. Why should the current restrictions of Shabbos remove the preexisting identity of animal food? Or should it be *muktzeh* because there is now a prohibition? It's a novel *psak* that since it is unusual to feed such animals, despite the fact that they are common, the food becomes *muktzeh*. However, the theme of *muktzeh* that keeps reoccurring is that something outside of one's influence is not prepared. Since people doesn't usually feed stray cats, their food is out of his realm. ואכמ"ל.

of date pits: one you can carry, one you can't. *Rif* explains that the soft stones known as *tamri armita* are occasionally eaten with the date, so they can be moved, but the hard stones that are never consumed are *muktzeh*. These were date seeds, which were eaten with the date, so even once separate they are not *muktzeh*. Therefore, despite the norm not to eat such things, everyone knows they can be eaten and a handful of people do eat them, so we can base our leniency regarding fruit seeds and peels on this *Rif*.[12]

Summary

The food for a species of animal that is common in a specific area is not *muktzeh* for anyone. If the animal is rare, only the owner can move its food. Where an animal is commonly found, its food is classified as "animal food," and thus isn't *muktzeh*. There is a leniency to move animal food which is in essence fit for animals, but it isn't common to feed them this food. This is particularly relevant nowadays, when most traditional animal foods have been substituted with purposely produced pet food. It is questionable whether one can move food items that would be considered *muktzeh*, since regardless there is a prohibition in feeding them, and even the food they consume can't be classified as "animal food." There is reason to forbid moving food items that should be *muktzeh* and yet are consumed by animals, if the animals are not commonly privately owned, even though the species of animal might be common. This is because Chazal imposed a restriction feeding certain animals, so if such food is forbidden to feed, it might render the items *muktzeh*.

---

12. However, it's clear from the *sugya* that peels and pits are only permitted according to Rebbe Shimon, who doesn't hold of *nolad*. We treat pits and peels as part of the fruit until they are detached because they're essential for the protection of the fruit (even the stones inside ensure that the fruit doesn't go bad, *Tosafos HaRosh* 29a). So once they have been detached, they no longer can be considered as food. They are now something new, hence a potential *nolad*. So it should follow that on Yom Tov, when we *pasken* like Rebbe Yehudah and hold of *nolad*, these things would be *muktzeh*.

Answers

1. Pits that are occasionally eaten, e.g., watermelon seeds, are not *muktzeh*, but peels and stones that are not consumed, e.g., date pits or banana peels, are *muktzeh*.
2. One can be lenient to move bones to feed to a dog.

Part 2

בשר חי ופירורין

Raw Meat and Crumbs

Questions

1. My friends want to see my box of pills. Can I take them out to show them?
2. Once I have finished eating my cake, only crumbs are left on the plate. Can I move the plate?
3. I need to move the frozen raw meat in the freezer to get a challah for *shalosh seudos*. Can I move it directly?

Up till now we've discussed food items that one has no intention of eating himself; they were set aside to be given to animals. What about food that, in its present state, is only fit for an animal, but after Shabbos one intends to prepare it for himself, such as raw meat, raw mustard seeds, etc.?

The Gemara[13] explains that *demai* (un-tithed produce), despite that in its present state it is forbidden for the owner to eat, is not *muktzeh*. The

13. 127b.

reasoning is: מיגו דאי בעי מפקיר נסכיה וחזי ליה - "Since one can relinquish his possessions and be fit for it." This means that one can relinquish his assets and become a pauper who is entitled to eat *demai*. We see that even though one cannot currently make use of this food, since he has a way whereby he can make himself eligible to partake in it, it is currently treated as if it is fit for his consumption. *Tosafos*[14] asks: Why do we need this *migo* to permit *demai*? There is a more simple reason why *demai* is not *muktzeh* - one can give it to paupers; surely the ability to give it is a use that prevents a claim that this food is useless and so should be *muktzeh*. *Tosafos* says that we see a precedence for this reasoning from *terumah*; the Gemara[15] explains that *terumah* is not *muktzeh* because it can be given to a *kohen*.

The *Rishonim*, in particular *Rashba*, unequivocally reject *Tosafos*'s comparison. Since *terumah* is predestined to be given to a *kohen*, and he uses this produce in a normal way, it is not *muktzeh*. However, after Shabbos he wants to eat his fruits that are currently in a state of *demai*, only now he can't tithe his *demai*, but he has no intention of giving it to any paupers. The fact that theoretically he can give it to paupers is not a sufficient reason to claim that this produce in its present state has a regular use and shouldn't be *muktzeh*. This is why the Gemara needs to introduce the *migo* to explain why *demai* is not *muktzeh*. The principle that we can extract from *Rashba* and the other *Rishonim* is: Something that one presently can't eat but intends on eating later is *muktzeh*. Despite the fact that he can give it to someone who presently can benefit from it, that usage doesn't suffice to give it an identity as food. It retains its *muktzeh* status of *muktzeh machmas gufo* because it has no present function that will be utilized.

Ritva brings a proof to the opinion of *Tosafos* from elephant and ostrich food. We say that even if one is not actually going to give the twine and glass shards to an elephant or ostrich, the fact that they *could* be fed to them removes their status of *muktzeh*. (This is only according to certain *Tannaim*, whom we don't hold of *l'halachah*. The reason is only because we don't hold that all Jews are treated as princes. If we did hold

14. 127b, s.v. דאי.
15. 127b.

of that, it would suffice that it is possible to give to someone.) We see that for something that despite practically not having any personal use, if he could theoretically use by giving it to others, that makes it fit and thus is not *muktzeh*.

Rashba's Stance

Rashba distinguishes that twine and glass shards are *only* fit for elephants and ostriches. The owner doesn't intend on keeping them for any other use himself. In this instance, the *Rishonim* agree that the very fact it is "fit" to be consumed by something is enough to remove the *muktzeh* status. However, even though *demai* is technically fit for paupers, there is a designation from giving it to them, i.e., he positively doesn't want to give it to them; rather, he wants to keep it for himself. *Rashba* says that we find the *Tannaim* argue exactly over this differentiation. The Mishnah[16] says that mustard seeds are *muktzeh*. The opinion in the *beraisa* argues that they are not *muktzeh*. *Rashba* explains that the point of dispute is exactly this: These seeds one wants to eat himself, yet they are also fit for birds. He designates in his mind from giving it to the doves, so the *Tanna* of the Mishnah holds it's *muktzeh*, while the *Tanna* of the *beraisa* holds that since it's "fit" to give to the doves, it's not *muktzeh*.

The following Gemara[17] is easy to understand according to *Tosafos*: The Gemara says that even according to Rebbe Yehudah (who is more stringent in the laws of *muktzeh*), the raw meat of a dove can be carried because it is fit for man to chew. One can infer that this reasoning is specifically according to Rebbe Yehudah, while according to Rebbe Shimon we don't need this reason. Even if presently it is not possible for a man to chew, if it's fit for dogs, despite that it's not destined to be given to them because one wants to use it for himself, it's still not *muktzeh*. We see from here that even though it's unlikely that you will give the meat to a dog, you are keeping it for yourself. Since it's possible to be given, it won't be *muktzeh*.

16. 126b.
17. 142a.

Rashba himself asks this Gemara as a question on his own approach. He doesn't rely on something being fit for an unlikely usage, since that usage is theoretical more than practical, and is forced to explain the Gemara's case is only when it's no longer fit to chew since the meat has gone rotten, making it only edible for dogs. Since one doesn't want to keep this inedible meat for himself, the reason it's not *muktzeh* is because it is now only fit for the dogs and no longer fit for your use, so this is a likely potential usage. (Nevertheless, such meat is *muktzeh* according to Rebbe Yehudah.[18])

This dispute is relevant to anything that one personally doesn't want to use at present, but still could be used by someone else, e.g., a suit that contains *shaatnez* and the owner intends on removing the *shaatnez*. Even though now he could give it to a non-Jew, he wants to keep it for himself. It would follow that *Rashba* would hold that the suit is *muktzeh*, whereas according to *Tosafos* it should be permissible. Whom do we *pasken* like?

Psak Halachah

Taz paskens leniently like *Tosafos*, that as long as it can be given to someone else, even if you have no intention of giving it, it's not *muktzeh*, whereas *Magen Avraham* is stringent like *Rashba*. They are discussing a case of raw meat that is too hard to chew, (but not meat that has gone bad). *Taz* permits moving it since it can be given to a dog, even though you plan on keeping it for yourself, and *Magen Avraham* forbids it.

The second case they discuss is regarding raw fish. *Shulchan Aruch*[19] *paskens* that raw fish is *muktzeh* because it's not fit. The question is: For whom is it not fit? *Taz* says obviously he means it's not fit *even* for a dog,

---

18. The reason this is dependent on the dispute of Rebbe Shimon and Rebbe Yehudah is because Rebbe Shimon's stance is if an item could potentially be used for something, even if that use is extreme and unlikely, it is enough to prevent it from being *muktzeh*. This is similar to what we find by *keilim* such as *chatzosros* (trumpets), that even though they have no permissible use they are not *muktzeh* according to Rebbe Shimon because you can crack a nut with them (*Rabbeinu Tam*).

19. *Se'if* 32.

hence it has no potential use on Shabbos and therefore it is *muktzeh*. *Magen Avraham* says *Shulchan Aruch* means it's not fit for man to eat, and despite potentially being fit for animals, since your intention is to eat it yourself, the fact that it is fit for an animal won't be sufficient to permit it.

Shulchan Aruch[20] *paskens* that raw meat is not *muktzeh* since it is fit to be chewed raw. There is a vast discussion among present-day *poskim* on whether raw meat nowadays is *muktzeh* or not. Some argue that nowadays we don't ever chew raw meat, so it should be *muktzeh*, while others argue that since *Shulchan Aruch paskens* that it's permitted, we can still follow this ruling since we don't eat raw meat only because we are particularly finicky.

However, from *Rishonim* we see that it was never a common occurrence to chew raw meat. Both *Ritva* and *Rashba* say they didn't commonly eat raw meat. It wasn't a normal way to eat meat, and *Rashi* adds that those who are *daasan yafei* (of a broad disposition) ate raw meat. It is clear that it wasn't the regular practice. One can say that not much has changed even nowadays. There are still certain people who eat raw meat: blue steak, carpaccio, etc., so surely *Shulchan Aruch*'s *psak* should still be applicable. Furthermore, we can suggest another leniency to move raw meat, based on *Taz* brought by *Mishnah Berurah*.[21] (*Taz* says that for fish to be *muktzeh*, it must be unfit even for dogs. "Fit for dogs to consume" is enough for an item not to be *muktzeh*.) Since it's fit for dogs and in most societies in the diaspora dogs are commonly found, raw meat has an identity of food and is not *muktzeh*. So if there is raw meat obstructing something you need, you can move the raw meat to the side (question #3).

Crumbs on Your Plate

The Mishnah in *Shabbos*[22] lists crumbs among things that are not *muktzeh*. The Mishnah then continues to list certain other objects that are not *muktzeh* since they are animal food. One would presumably say

---

20. *Se'if* 31.
21. *Se'if katan* 127.
22. 143a.

that crumbs are like the other objects mentioned that are permitted because it can be fed to animals. If so, it follows that the *heter* of crumbs would be exclusive to places where it's common to have animals who are fed crumbs. Since nowadays it is universally uncommon to feed crumbs to any animals, it should follow that crumbs would be *muktzeh* without exception, and your plate with crumbs of cake (question #2) is a *bosis* to a *muktzeh machmas gufo*!

There is a glaring omission of this halachah in *Rambam* and subsequently in *Tur* and *Shulchan Aruch*. R' Karp[23] explains that only when animals were common was this halachah pertinent. Back then they would preserve the crumbs after a meal for their animals and so only if animals were common is it not *muktzeh*. Nowadays that animals are not common at all, we are careful even after a meal not to throw the crumbs. It follows that crumbs still retain their identity as regular food and one who wants to move them can; he is treating them in accordance of how we treat them in halachah. This explains the omission of the *poskim*.

However, *Reshimos Shiurim*[24] makes a brilliant inference in *Rambam*. When *Rambam* brings down the list of the Mishnah permitting items that are fit to be fed to an animal, he doesn't mention crumbs in the list. The inference in *Rambam* is that he understands that the *heter* of crumbs is not based on being fit to be fed to an animal. (The Gemara quotes the second item brought in the Mishnah, *se'ar shel afunin,* in reference to what the Mishnah says is fit for animals. If we say that crumbs are also included in this category, surely the Gemara should've quoted that case instead, since it is mentioned before *se'ar shel afunin*. Based on this inference, *Rambam* could have inferred that the reason why crumbs are not *muktzeh* is for a different reason).

Certainly the main halachah is that crumbs are *muktzeh* nowadays, since it's no longer common to feed them to any type of animal. One can wonder: During a meal, one can freely eat the crumbs of the challah, so why are they *muktzeh* now that the meal is over? True, the halachah ap-

---

23. *Hilchos Shabbos B'Shabbos* 2:20, insight 62.
24. R' Kalmanovitz from Bnei Brak.

plies only after the meal, once one has finished, but during the meals the crumbs are food that are fit for man's consumption - they are part of his meal. After he has finished, crumbs are no longer destined to be consumed by oneself; rather, if they are to be feed to animals they are still "food." If not, they become *muktzeh*!

Food that is forbidden to eat for a halachic reason would also be dependent on these principles. If you have some nonkosher food, under certain circumstances[25] you are allowed to give it to a non-Jew. It can be considered "a non-Jew's food," but like animal food it will be dependent upon whether it's common to be used. Here the definition of common should be more limited than just being present, because even if non-Jews are to be found in this city, the norm is that unless one has a non-Jew who works for him, such as a cleaner, people don't go around asking the non-Jews if they want some nonkosher food. Therefore, one who has a non-Jewish worker should be permitted to move nonkosher food on Shabbos.

Food that has an unreliable hechsher that doesn't fit one's usual standard would depend on how one usually acts with such foodstuffs. If he would throw it away and not even give it to someone else, as he feels it would be a *michshol* (stumbling block) to allow another Jew to eat this, it would be *muktzeh*. If however, he would pass it on to somebody who does eat this hechsher and doesn't throw it away, it wouldn't be *muktzeh*.

Moving Medicines

Another application of this halachah is regarding the moving of medicines (question #1). Someone who is sick is permitted to carry pills, and someone else is also allowed to carry them for him. The question is: Can one carry them not for the sake of a sick person? Do we compare pills to animal food? We can say that since sick people are unfortunately common, and it's common to have a headache (of the extent that one is allowed to take paracetamol on Shabbos), such pills are therefore not *muktzeh*, since their

25. There is a prohibition in giving a gift to a non-Jew. There are numerous circumstances when it is permitted. See *Rambam, Hilchos Avodah Zarah*, ch. 10, halachah 4.

use is common. Or is there a basic distinction, since all *poskim* are in agreement that medicine is not considered regular food, the fact that people commonly take them doesn't change the identity of this pill; a pill is *muktzeh machmas gufo* for a healthy person because it's not a food nor a vessel, but there is a leniency for the sick to take it. According to the stringent possibility, even if the sick patient is staying in one's house, without prior designation, i.e., placing to the side the pills which will be taken, the pills remain *muktzeh machmas gufo* and only if you're carrying for the sick person will they be permitted to move.

Perhaps it depends on the two different explanations we presented why in a case where animals are commonly found in the town their food is not *muktzeh*. If it influences how we treat this item, there is more room to make a comparison. We can argue that since it is common to consume or take these pills, they are not set aside from people's mind. If being common defines this as "animal food," hence they are permitted, and it won't help us permit pills because, as we said, pills are inherently not defined as food. So regardless of its common use, it will remain *muktzeh machmas gufo*.

The overwhelming consensus among the recent *poskim* is to permit moving pills such as Aspirin and Panadol (paracetamol). Since they are commonly taken by everyone, they are considered ready for use and not set aside. Another argument to be lenient is that when one buys pills, he does so with the intent to use them whenever he needs to. Buying them and bringing them home is an act of designation that removes the *issur* of *muktzeh*. Even if before this specific Shabbos one didn't know that he'd need them, they are considered to have been prepared from when he bought them.

Summary

In order for an item not to be *muktzeh*, it needs to have a functional use on Shabbos. The commentators dispute cases where the owner doesn't intend on using this item on Shabbos, as he can only extract benefit from it after Shabbos, but it can be given to others so that they could benefit from it today. Does the potential to give it to others suffice for us to treat the item as if it has a use, or since in actuality one won't give it to others do we treat the item as if it has no use and so is *muktzeh*? This is a reason to be lenient to move raw meat because one can give it to a dog. Another reason is that sometimes and in some places people do eat raw meat, so even now it can be considered food. Foods which the general public doesn't eat, such as stale or moldy bread, could be *muktzeh*. Crumbs are *muktzeh* after a meal. Nonkosher food depends on the practically of giving it to a non-Jew.

Answers

1. Common pills such as aspirin are not *muktzeh* and can be moved even not for the sake of a sick person. Antibiotics that have been purchased for a sick person can also be moved because one has designated them for use.
2. One should be stringent not to move crumbs on a table after a meal. However, if they are lying on a plate, you can move the plate. They are insignificant and thereby don't render the plate a *bosis* to *muktzeh* and according to some *poskim* there isn't *bosis* during Shabbos.
3. According to *Shulchan Aruch*, raw meat is not *muktzeh*. We argued this can apply even nowadays with regarding certain raw meats, even if people only rarely eat them. Certain cuts that are impossible to eat raw should be treated as *muktzeh*.

Chapter 11

פסולת על האוכל או על הבגד

Unwanted [Muktzeh] on Food and on Clothes

Questions

1. Can I remove a feather that is lying on my coat?
2. A fly fell into my cup. Can I take it out (once *borer* issues have been circumvented)?
3. If there is an ant on my skin, can I flick it off?
4. Some strands of hair accidently fall out of someone's beard. Can I pick them up?

When there is a mixture of good and bad in order to avoid transgressing *borer* (the prohibition of separating) one must take out the good (the desired object) and leave behind the bad (the undesired object). The Gemara[1] discusses the procedure of separating a mixture on Yom Tov (where *borer* is permitted). Beis Hillel holds that if there is a greater quantity of good than bad, since removing the good would involve more effort than if one were to take out the bad, one must deviate from the regular manner of taking out the good and instead take out the bad directly. *Tosafos* in passing explains how one can handle the bad. If it is "bad," surely it should be *muktzeh*? He explains that since the bad is the minority in this mixture, the bad is nullified (*batel*) to the good and thus loses its status of *muktzeh*.[2]

---

1. 142b.
2. In the event that the good is the minority, it is still considered to be significant

The Mishnah brings a case of a stone on top of a barrel. One can't remove the stone directly, since it's *muktzeh*; rather, he must tilt it off the barrel. The Gemara subsequently asks, as explained by *Tosafos*: Why can't you move the stone based on the aforementioned principle? Since the stone is insignificant relative to the barrel, it should be nullified, so it should be permitted to move the barrel with the stone. The Gemara answers that since the wine cannot be accessed without removing the stone we can't view the stone as nullified to the barrel.

The depth of this answer is that since the wine can't be retrieved without the prior removal of the stone, it's not possible to treat the stone as being insignificant relative to the wine. Only when there is something "bad" that can technically be ignored can we say that it is nullified. We see that we cannot invoke this principle of "*batel*" in all cases, but from the Gemara's question we have a proof to *Tosafos*'s principle of *bitul.*

New Principle of Chazon Ish

Chazon Ish[3] teaches a new principle based upon the aforementioned opinion of Beis Hillel. If a fly fell into one's food (question #2), even though generally insects are *muktzeh* since they have no usage, in this scenario there is no problem removing the fly (once *borer* has been circumvented, i.e., if one removes it along with some food). Since it is nullified to the food, one's act is not classified as moving *muktzeh.*[4] Instead, it's considered fixing the food. We can extend *Chazon Ish*'s principle further: Even when we are not necessarily discussing a classic mixture, we can apply *bitul* (*Chazon Ish* himself says he doesn't mean the *bitul* of *taarovos* of *issur v'heter*). Take, for example, a feather on a coat (question #1), or

---

and we don't say that it is nullified to the bad. Therefore even when it is the minority and there is a majority of bad, one can still remove it without any restrictions of *muktzeh.*

3. 47:15, 21.

4. There is an element of *l'shitaso* in this answer of *Chazon Ish,* He doesn't hold that the leniency of *tiltul min hatzad* applies to moving food with a stick, so removing a fly from a liquid with a spoon wouldn't be permitted if not for this new principle.

a label on a piece of clothing. Since the feather or the label is insignificant and therefore nullified to the clothing, one can remove it despite that these items should be classified as *muktzeh* when viewed alone, since one's act is classified as fixing the garment, as opposed to moving *muktzeh*! *Shevisas HaShabbos*[5] also thought of this idea. He uses it to explain *Rema*'s *heter*[6] to remove a feather from one's clothes. He says that despite the feather being *muktzeh*, one can remove it since it is nullified to one's clothes.[7] It follows from that if an ant is on one's skin or clothes, he can flick it off (question #3).[8]

Pri Megadim[9] discusses whether one can remove dirt or wax that is stuck onto one's clothes. He says that regarding the prohibition of *tochen* (grinding), in certain cases, i.e., when it's moist, there is no problem. He adds, however, that even when the problems of grinding are eliminated, moving the wax would be a problem of moving *muktzeh*. Surely this doesn't fit with *Chazon Ish*'s principle that insignificant items become nullified to the garment. Besides when quoting the aforementioned *Pri Megadim*, we find elsewhere that *Mishnah Berurah* doesn't seemingly hold of *Chazon Ish*'s principle. *Mishnah Berurah*[10] says that if one walked on grass and realized that some blades of grass stuck to his shoes, he can't remove them, since he'd be moving *muktzeh*. Surely *Chazon Ish* would argue that the grass is nullified to the shoe, and one is considered to be fixing the shoes, not moving *muktzeh*?!

(*Shaar HaTzion*[11] brings down from *Ohr Zarua* that one can sweep his house and needn't worry about the potential *muktzeh* of moving the dirt,

5. *Meleches Borer*, point 24.

6. *Eshel Avraham* 340:4.

7. *Ketzos HaShulchan* brings that others explain that the *heter* is because *Rema* is likely dealing with a feather that fell out of one's pillow. Therefore the feather is not *muktzeh* because it was previously designated for a use.

8. *Alibah D'Hilchasah*, p. 142. They asked R' Chaim Kanievsky this and he permitted it, according to *Chazon Ish*'s opinion. Also in *Chut Shani* (section 3, p. 144) he permits flicking an insect (question #3).

9. 340:3, s.v. שעל הקף.

10. 336:24.

11. 337, point 7.

as it is טלטול מן הצד לצורך השבת [indirect moving].[12] Again, this doesn't fit with *Chazon Ish* because according to what *Chazon Ish* says, one can sweep the floor regardless. Since the pieces of dust and waste on the floor that are *muktzeh* are nullified to the floor, one is not considered moving *muktzeh*, but rather fixing the appearance of the room. R' Chaim Kanievsky even holds that the principle of *Chazon Ish* applies even when one has collected a large pile of dirt. Even then it can be moved, and irrespective of its size it is still nullified to the ground.)

Consensus to Chazon Ish's Idea

Despite that *Mishnah Berurah* and *Pri Megadim* seemingly argue with this principle, surely they must agree to *Chazon Ish*'s principle to some extent. This is since it is otherwise difficult to understand the following *psak* of *Shulchan Aruch*: *Shulchan Aruch*[13] permits one to scrape dirt that is stuck on clothes with one's nail. We seemingly can only understand this with *Chazon Ish*'s principle. Despite dirt being *muktzeh*, now that it is on a garment, it is nullified to the garment and thus loses its status of *muktzeh* when one removes it.

Perhaps we can say that *Mishnah Berurah* could agree to the solution that we find that *Ketzos HaShulchan* suggests. *Ketzos HaShulchan*[14] discusses at length the permission to move a feather that is lying on one's garment. He first rejects the explanation of the *Shevisas HaShabbos*[15] - that the feather is nullified to the garment. He says this logic can only be true in cases when the *muktzeh* is properly attached to the clothing, as opposed to a feather, which is merely resting on top and only when one is not directly moving the *muktzeh* item. Dirt on a garment is an example of

12. *Milchamos* (48b) says there is a special exemption that we permit sweeping the floor in honor of Shabbos. When one sweeps the floor, he is doing טמה"צ לצורך דבר האסור and it should not be permitted, hence *Ramban* needs a special leniency that when one sweeps he is doing it for the honor of Shabbos.

13. 302:7.

14. 116:10 (*Badei HaShulchan*).

15. *Meleches Borer* 13.

something that is considered truly stuck, but one can't remove the soil directly. He therefore is forced to explain that the reason for the leniency is because it is *graf shel re'i*.[16] The two cases which we brought from *Mishnah Berurah*, grass on a shoe and dirt on a floor, should also not be subject to this principle of *bitul* because the *muktzeh* is not fully attached to the item, although it might depend on the circumstance.

It follows that *Mishnah Berurah*'s ruling regarding the blades of grass on one's shoes is not proof that he disagrees with *Chazon Ish*'s principle. However, *Pri Megadim*'s stringency not to peel the wax off is at odds with *Chazon Ish* and can't be disproved from *Shulchan Aruch*'s leniency to remove dirt from one's clothes.

Nullified on Its Own

In order to explain *Rema*'s *psak* regarding removing a feather, *Ketzos HaShulchan* explains that we are referring to very small feathers. He therefore suggests a new principle: Something that practically has no purpose at all is not in the realm of *muktzeh*. This sort of item wasn't included in what Chazal forbade, as it is to be considered as if it's nullified on its own; it's too insignificant to even have on it an identity of *muktzeh*! A small feather that has no purpose at all is therefore nullified on its own (unlike the previous opinion that it is nullified to the garment) and the restrictions of *muktzeh* were never applied to it. A large feather, however, will be *muktzeh* since it has a purpose - it can be used to sweep up dirt. Some medium-sized feathers will also be *muktzeh* because they are set aside for stuffing a pillow. (We must appreciate the enormity of this *chiddush*. Countless times we have seen that an insignificant item is *muktzeh machmas gufo* because it is useless. To take that negative aspect and use it as an argument to claim it is not *muktzeh* is a landmark *chiddush*.)

---

16. Presumably his intention behind this answer is not that having a bit of dirt on one's clothing is repulsive and hence qualifies for *graf shel re'i*; rather, it is disrespectful to one's honor to be seen dressed as such. Therefore it is encompassed under the principle behind *graf shel re'i*, namely *kavod habriyos*.

Graz[17] differs slightly. He says that *Rema* is only referring to feathers that previously were inside a cushion and fell out, but for a new feather, which had not yet been processed to be used inside a cushion, it would be *muktzeh* to move it from one's clothes. Again, if he holds like *Chazon Ish*, why is he forced to limit *Rema*'s *psak* specifically to certain type of feathers? We can further prove that *Graz* argues on *Chazon Ish*. He says[18] that the reason it is permitted to remove an insect off one's body is because it is uncomfortable, and Chazal didn't impose *muktzeh* restrictions when it is uncomfortable. *Chazon Ish* permits this because of *bitul*.

In light of this *Graz*, we must conclude that which we quoted earlier, that removing a feather from one's clothes is subject to dispute. Similarly, if there are a few strands of hair on the table (question #4), removing them is permitted according to *Chazon Ish*, even if it isn't a case of *kavod habriyos*. One's act is just one of cleaning, while *Pri Megadim*, *Graz*, and even possibly *Mishnah Berurah* would forbid moving the hair. In such instances, one should blow the hair away.

Summary

When an unwanted, insignificant item is located on another item, even if the unwanted item on its own would be treated as *muktzeh*, one can remove it from the item it is merged with because it is considered that one is just improving the state of the non-*muktzeh* item. It is not considered moving *muktzeh*. This principle is said in the context of removing a fly from a liquid. It is unclear to what extent *Mishnah Berurah* holds of this leniency. There are strong indications that *Mishnah Berurah* will limit the leniency to cases when the *muktzeh* is attached firmly to the non-*muktzeh*. When they are really joined it can be nullified and lose its identity of *muktzeh*. There is a stance that completely insignificant items are nullified on their own, and only regarding useless items that potentially could have a use did Chazal treat as *muktzeh machmas gufo*. Tiny feathers and the like,

17. 302:3.
18. 316:18.

which have no importance whatsoever, were never encompassed in *muktzeh*.

Answers

1. Small feathers are permitted according to all. *Ketzos HaShulchan* is stringent on large feathers; other *poskim* are lenient.
2. You can take out a fly that fell into a food or drink. Your act isn't treated as moving the *muktzeh*.
3. *Chazon Ish* would permit flicking an insect off your clothes. The opponents to this principle perhaps would forbid flicking off the insect.
4. Again, you have *Chazon Ish* to rely on to be lenient to move the hair. The other *poskim* would forbid moving it.

Chapter 12

מוקצה לאחד אם הוי מוקצה לאחרים

Muktzeh for One is Muktzeh for All

Questions

1. Can an Ashkenazi lend his Sephardi neighbor *kitniyos* on Pesach?
2. If I am Sephardi and my son-in-law is Ashkenazi, can I ask him to pass the rice?
3. According to *Shulchan Aruch*, meat that isn't *chalak* is not permitted, whereas *Rema* permits it. Can a Sephardi move such meat?
4. Can I pass my sister her university textbooks on Shabbos?
5. According to *Shulchan Aruch* that it's forbidden to play with toys on Shabbos, can I hand toys to children to play with?
6. Shmuel is stringent not to smoke on Yom Tov. Can he give a friend a cigarette on Yom Tov?

The Gemara[1] relates that Rebbi gave Rebbe Romnos permission to carry a coal pan (*machtah*) on Shabbos, even though it was filled with ash. The Gemara tries to understand how Rebbi permitted moving

1. 47a.

this item, despite it being *muktzeh* since it is a *bosis* to *issur* - ash is *muktzeh*. The first suggestion posed was that inside this coal pan there was left behind a small amount of incense. Since the incense is not *muktzeh*, it can offset the ash, thereby making the object a *bosis* to *heter* and *issur*. This approach is subsequently rejected. Since Rebbi was wealthy, he didn't place any worth in such a small quantity of leftover incense. This coal pan cannot be viewed as a *bosis* to *heter* and *issur* since in the eyes of the owner the permitted item in it was insignificant.

The principle that we can extract from here is that if something is insignificant in the owner's eyes, it is *muktzeh*, even though there are other people in society who do view it as significant. Support to this rule can be found in the following *beraisa*:[2] A piece of cloth measuring 3x3 fingers is only fit for paupers to use; a rich person would only use a cloth that is 3x3 fistfuls. If a rich man owns the smaller cloth, it's *muktzeh* because he has no use for it, despite it having a use for poor people. We see from this that despite an item having a worth for other people, if it is worthless for you, it will be *muktzeh*.

The Owner Determines the Status

The *Rishonim* use this principle to answer a difficulty raised by *Tosafos*.[3] The Gemara implies that if a woman made a vow not to eat from a loaf of bread, not only is it *muktzeh* to her as it is now *muktzeh machmas issur* (the *issur* not to transgress her vow renders it forbidden), but it is *muktzeh* even for others. *Tosafos* asks: Why is it *muktzeh* for others? Only she is forbidden from eating it. Others have no such restrictions. *Ritva, Ramban, Ran,* and others answer with the principle: מוקצה לאחד הוי מוקצה לאחרים - the owner determines the status of an item, even for others. If it is not *muktzeh* for him, it is not *muktzeh* for everyone, and if it is *muktzeh* for the owner, then it is *muktzeh* for everyone. Since the woman doesn't intend on using

2. Ibid.
3. 46b.

the bread, it becomes *muktzeh,* and this status is indiscriminate on all parties.[4]

Tosafos and *Rashba* argue with this. They hold that not only can others eat this bread, but since the woman can give it to them to eat, she herself has a use with this bread, and it therefore won't even be *muktzeh* for her! They explain that the Gemara means that since during *bein hashemashos* she couldn't eat it (due to her vow), it's subject to *migo d'iskatzi.* Even if she removes her vow, it will still be forbidden for her to eat for all of Shabbos because when Shabbos came in her vow was still in existence (but she can move the loaf).

The implication of the aforementioned *Tosafos* is that he doesn't hold of this principle, מוקצה לאחד הוי מוקצה לאחרים. If *Tosafos* did hold of this rule, why does her decision not determine the status? If our extrapolation is true, how does he learn the Gemara that explains that even when the coal pan has remnants of incense it is *muktzeh* for anyone, since due to Rebbi's wealth these remains are insignificant? Even if Rebbi might not have reused the incense, other people would. Rebbi still has a use to give it to others, which should render it not *muktzeh.*

R' Akiva Eiger[5] refers us to another *Tosafos.*[6] The Gemara there explains that *terumah* isn't *muktzeh* despite being forbidden to a Yisrael, since the Yisrael can give it to a *kohen* on Shabbos. *Demai* is also not *muktzeh,* despite being presently forbidden for the owner to eat, since the owner can give up all his possessions and become a pauper and thus be eligible to eat *demai.* Therefore we can already view it as if the owner has a use with the *demai.* (This is known as מיגו דאי בעי מפקיר לנכסיה וחזי ליה, השתא נמי חזי ליה.) This *heter* is very similar to the aforementioned *Tosafos,* who permits the moving of the bread that a woman vowed not to eat, even for herself to move, since others can benefit from it. Here too, despite the

---

4. *Chiddushei HaRan* adds something that the other *Rishonim* didn't add. That included in her vow was not to give it to others. This is the qualification he made. It is not conclusive that he argues on *Tosafos;* they just could have understood the case differently.

5. *Gilyon HaShas* 46a.

6. *Shabbos* 127a.

terumah being forbidden to the owner, since he can use it in the capacity of giving it to someone else, it's not *muktzeh*.

It All Depends Why the Owner Doesn't Use It

Tosafos asks: How does this Gemara fit with what we learned from the case of Rebbi, that something a person has no use for, despite being fit for others, is still *muktzeh*? This is the same question that we asked on *Tosafos*: Why is it that Rebbi's wealth and his subsequent lack of interest in these particles of incense would be sufficient to forbid the incense remnants for everyone? *Tosafos* reconciles the two *sugyas* as follows: It depends on why the item should be *muktzeh* to the owner. If it's because the owner doesn't see the item as *fit or purposeful*, we say that even for other people the owner doesn't see this item as fit for a use and thus he doesn't think to give it to others, i.e., he removes intention for everyone from using it. In contrast, when it is only forbidden to the owner for an *external reason*, but he still views this item as a fully usable object, since he can still give it to others for whom it isn't forbidden, he therefore doesn't reject using it. And since he can give it to others, then even for himself it isn't *muktzeh*.

One can present *Tosafos*'s answer slightly differently: Is the item in question not fit for the owner because there is a problem in the object (*cheftza*), or is the problem located in the person (*gavra*)? If in his eyes it is still a useable item, it still has an identity of a *kli* and therefore isn't *muktzeh*, whereas if in his eyes it is a totally useless object, despite that others may think otherwise and make use of it, his personal lack of use for it renders it *muktzeh*. *Tosafos* is therefore *l'shitaso*, in that he learns that the loaf of bread that the woman vowed not to eat is not *muktzeh*. This is because she still considers the bread as food. Hence *Tosafos* is forced to deviate from the simple explanation of what the Gemara means that it is *muktzeh*.

Moving Toys on Shabbos

An example of this is if one has children under the age of *chinuch* who play with toys (*Shulchan Aruch* classifies certain toys as *muktzeh*[7]), can we permit one to move these toys despite that they should be *muktzeh*, yet he has a use for them, he can give it to his kids to play with (question #5)? According to *Tosafos*, such an argument is incorrect, since the reason *Shulchan Aruch* holds that toys are *muktzeh* is because they have no inherent use. The problem is located in the item, so the fact that one's kids play with these toys doesn't impact one's intention not to use the toy. They intrinsically are useless, so they are *muktzeh*!

The other *Rishonim* don't accept such a distinction. Once the owner won't use it, it doesn't matter why, it is *muktzeh* for him and subsequently for others as well. Hence they learn the case of the woman who vowed not to eat this bread simply that it is *muktzeh* for all. However, it is difficult how these *Rishonim* will explain the Gemara that says that *terumah* is not *muktzeh* since it is fit to be given to a *kohen*. We see that despite being useless for oneself, once there is a use for others, it isn't *muktzeh*? *Shaar HaMelech*[8] explains that these *Rishonim* will distinguish that *terumah* is different because it is *intended to be given* to the *kohen*. The fact that the owner can't eat it himself is not a sufficient reason for him to set it aside. In contrast, the loaf of bread is intended for the woman; she doesn't want to give it to others. Once she can't consume it herself, she sets it aside.[9]

L'Shitaso in Understanding Demai

There is a beautiful *l'shitaso* in how the Rishonim learn the reason for the permission in moving of *demai*. As we mentioned the Gemara brings the rule of...מיגו דאי בעי מפקיר נכסיה. *Tosafos* says that this reason is not necessary, since if the owner wants to, he can give it to the poor therefore it is fit for him to use too and so not *muktzeh*. Rather, the Gemara preferred to find a way where it can be possible for a personal use. The other *Ri-*

7. Refer back to chapter 8, where it says what specific toys *Shulchan Aruch* is referring to. Simply speaking, it is referring only to balls hundreds of years ago, which were made from scraps of materials.

8. *Hilchos Sukkah* 80.

9. *Rashbag* and *Ritva* in 127b have indications like this explanation.

shonim say that the Gemara is forced to explain *demai* with this *migo* because, unlike *terumah*, one doesn't intend to give it to anyone else. One will wait until after Shabbos to separate the necessary tithes to consume it oneself. Therefore, in order to permit the moving of *demai*, the Gemara is forced to rely on this rule of *migo*. We see the consistency in their opinions. For *Tosafos* for it not to be *muktzeh* it is enough just that it can in theory be given to others, while the other *Rishonim* hold that something one intends to keep for himself, he must have a personal current use in order that it not be *muktzeh*.

(*Shiltei Gibborim*[10] and *Shitah LaRan*[11] have a different position. They hold that even when it is *muktzeh* for the owner, it is still permissible for others to move, i.e., if an affluent person owns a cloth that is 3x3 fingers, it is only *muktzeh* for him; it isn't *muktzeh* for a poor person. It follows that they must learn that Rebbe Romnos for whom we forbade the coal pan was an affluent person, and hence it was also *muktzeh* for him. This is because if only Rebbi was an affluent person, why does that affect Rebbe Romnos's right to use the incense? Alternatively, we can suggest that perhaps they hold like *Meiri*. *Meiri*[12] learns that the *sugya* of Rebbe Romnos is not dealing with מוקצה לאחד הוי מוקצה לאחרים; rather, it is dealing with *bosis*. When a *kli* is supporting both *muktzeh* and non-*muktzeh*, to determine what the base is considered a support to, we need to determine which one is more important. How do we measure importance? *Meiri* explains that the Gemara is investigating whether the non-*muktzeh* item is important for some people but not to the owner, does that still give it weight to combat the *issur*? *Meiri* concludes if one has a coal pan with ash, it is a *bosis* if the *kartin* (incense) inside is not important in the eyes of the owner, even though others give it importance. It comes out that the question of מוקצה לא' אם הוי מוקצה לאחרים is not addressed.[13])

---

10. 47a, s.v. הר"ן שלפנינו.

11. He is puzzled how can it be possible for something to be *muktzeh* to one person, but permitted to another person. He leaves it unanswered!

12. 47a, s.v. כלי הראוי.

13. Perhaps this is how *Rashi* (s.v. בגדי עשירים) also learns. *Rashi* writes, הכא נמי בי רבי בטלי קרטין — the word *batel* is, according to *Rashi*'s stance, the principle behind

The Depth behind Their Arguments

There are several ways to understand this dispute between *Tosafos* and other *Rishonim*, whether something that has a use for others but not for oneself is *muktzeh*. *Ritva* and *Rashba* understand that the owner determines the status of his object for everyone. Once he has set it aside from using it, the object's status is decided for all. *Shiltei Gibborim* and *Shitah LaRan* perhaps understand the complete opposite. The owner can't impact anyone else; if it is fit for someone and that person doesn't remove his intention, even if it doesn't belong to him it isn't *muktzeh* for him (meaning if others will use it, then for them it doesn't become *muktzeh*, not that they positively confer the status on the item). The simplest way to understand *Tosafos*'s position is that the owner determines the status. However, something that he views as fit for other people to use, he doesn't remove his intention from others using it. (Alternatively, *Tosafos* understands that the owner doesn't determine the status; rather, whether other people remove intent or not depends on what they think the owner is thinking. An item they anticipate the owner will set aside because it is not fit inherently in his eyes, they too set aside. An item they don't anticipate the owner to set aside - rather, he will not use it for external reasons - they are not *maktzah daas* from the item.)

The Advantage of Something That Is Shared

Shaar HaMelech[14] discusses someone who is stringent not to smoke on Yom Tov (question #6). (There is a dispute among the *poskim* whether smoking is considered *shaveh l'kol nefesh* [a necessity for all], one of the requirements needed for a *melachah* to be permitted on Yom Tov.) Is he is allowed to hand his pipe to his friends who are lenient to smoke?[15] He proves that according to the *Rishonim*, there are scenarios where מוקצה לא'

---

bosis. See chapter 14 on *bosis* for more on this.

14. *Hilchos Sukkah* 7:25.

15. There is another dimension to this question regarding *lifnei iver*, beyond the scope of this work.

לא הוי מוקצה לאחרים, and therefore he is lenient. It is more straightforward to permit according to *Tosafos*. Since this item is fit for use, therefore since one can give it to others to use, it won't be *muktzeh* for the owner. *Shaar HaMelech* claims that even according to *Ritva* and *Ramban* it is permissible. He says that they were only stringent with an item that one wants to keep for his personal use. However, an item that *isn't depleted with use* should be compared to *terumah* - that since it is given to others to use, it is not *muktzeh* for the owner. Similarly, this tobacco pipe on Yom Tov is meant for giving to others because the owner doesn't use it today. Even though he wants it after Yom Tov, other people's usage doesn't impinge his future usage.[16] Another precedence to this *heter* is that according to *Rashi*'s opinion, women are forbidden to shake a lulav due to *bal tosif* (since she is not commanded in the mitzvah, by performing it she is transgressing the prohibition of adding to the mitzvos). Yet we see that the lulav is not *muktzeh* for her. The Gemara[17] says explicitly that she can give it to her husband.[18]

Maaseh Choshev[19] asks an obvious question on *Shaar HaMelech*'s comparison between the tobacco pipe and *terumah*. The owner who is stringent not to smoke maintains that it has no use on Yom Tov and one should not be smoking. In other words, he holds that it is *muktzeh* for his friend too. So how can it be considered that since his friend smokes, it is not *muktzeh* for him? It should remain *muktzeh* for all, since he totally removes his intent from it?! This is unlike the case of the *terumah* where he has every intention to give it to a *kohen*. The answer is very simple: We've seen that the principle behind *muktzeh* is *haktzaas hadaas* - setting aside in one's mind. *Haktzaas hadaas* does not always follow what the halachic status

---

16. This reasoning is exclusive to a tobacco pipe. However, a cigarette is something that one wants to smoke himself. It is unlike *terumah*, whose main purpose is to give to another. Therefore, only according to *Tosafos*, one who doesn't smoke themselves on Yom Tov can give his friend a cigarette on Yom Tov, while according to *Rashba* and *Ritva* it will be *muktzeh*.

17. *Sukkah* 42a.

18. One can, however, make a distinction that a woman is bound to her husband, so his needs determine the status of the object.

19. The Steipler also asks this question.

of the item should dictate, but rather what the reality is. True, he is stringent not to smoke and hopes that others won't smoke, but he knows that they are lenient, and they will be smoking on Yom Tov. Since it is something meant for sharing, he doesn't set it aside.

The Guest Follows the Host

Tosafos[20] asks another question. The Gemara[21] says that a cloth less than 3x3 fingers is not *muktzeh*, which implies that surely a cloth of 3x3 would not be *muktzeh*. How does this fit in with the aforementioned Gemara that states that a pauper's cloths are *muktzeh*? He gives two answers: Either the Gemara that implies a cloth of 3x3 is not *muktzeh* is only in reference to a pauper, or it is said in reference to an affluent person, but only when he is in the house of the pauper. (The aforementioned *Shiltei Gibborim* learns that what *Tosafos* in his first answer means is that in all cases it's permitted for paupers even when owned by an affluent person, this is his proof for his opinion.) In the second answer, *Tosafos* is introducing us to a new principle in this *sugya*, namely, that there is an exception when the affluent person is in the house of the pauper, then it is not *muktzeh* for him too. This principle is coined "*nigrar acharav*" - follow the owner." Those residing in someone's else house follow the host. Even if generally it should be *muktzeh* for him, since he is a guest by a host for whom it is not *muktzeh*, he follows his host.[22]

This idea, that the homeowner establishes the status of his items, can fit in with either understanding that we brought earlier. If we explain that usually the owner sets the status of the object for everyone, then *Tosafos*'s new rule is qualifying that he only sets the status for those in his house. While if we explain that those people in his house subject their intention

20. 127b.

21. 125a.

22. We also find this idea in *Shitah LaRan*. *Raeh* says that a cloth of 3x3 *etzbaos*, if owned by an affluent Jew is *muktzeh* to a pauper. *Shitah LaRan* suggests that maybe *Raeh* only said that a wealthy person's cloth are *muktzeh* to the paupers inside the wealthy person's house, but outside, it is permitted to those paupers.

to his, while outsiders don't base their intention on the affluent homeowner, but once they are inthe affluent person's house they will abide with his intention.

Shulchan Aruch's Conclusion

Shulchan Aruch paskens:[23] מוקצה לעשירים הוי מוקצה גם לעניים - "That which is *muktzeh* for the rich is in result also *muktzeh* for the poor." *Bach*[24] and his son-in-law *Taz* argue over what *Shulchan Aruch* means with this *psak*. *Bach* explains that when *Shulchan Aruch* says that it's *muktzeh* for the paupers, he is only referring to paupers who are inside a house of an affluent person, whereas for paupers who are independent of an affluent person, their cloths are not *muktzeh*. (This is like what *Shitah LaRan* suggested in the opinion of *Raeeh*). *Taz* asks on this approach that if there is a distinction where the pauper is located, why would the Gemara assume that Rebbe Romnos was inside Rebbi's house, and then subsequently question the permissibility of his moving? If for paupers not in an affluent person's house it is not *muktzeh*, the Gemara should just establish that the case was that Rebbe Romnos was outside.

Taz understands that *Tosafos*'s principle that a guest follows the host's stance is exclusive when the host is a pauper, in such instances the owner establishes that this can be considered a *kli* even for someone who wouldn't usually use it. However, this only for those inside the house. If the host is an affluent person, his designation of something as being worthless impacts those outside as well. The reasoning behind this distinction is that since it is *muktzeh* because it is not fit for the owner to use, we consider it as if the owner threw it in the trash can. (The comparison to this is a broken *kli*, which we saw earlier[25] - that if it can still be used, it retains its identity as a *kli*. But as soon as the owner throws it away, it's irrelevant whether someone else would still have used it. It is now *muktzeh* for all because it loses its identity of a *kli*.) Therefore, when *Shulchan Aruch* says that when

23. The end of *siman* 308.
24. *Se'if katan* 8.
25. Chapter 6.

the affluent person's item is *muktzeh* it is *muktzeh* for the paupers, he is referring to all paupers, not only those in his house.

(*Chazon Ish*[26] has a different understanding in *Tosafos*'s resolution to the contrary implications of a 3x3 cloth, different from both *Taz* and *Bach*. He says that if something is fit for the owner, then it shouldn't be *muktzeh* for others, since the owner hasn't set it aside and it is in his sole jurisdiction to determine the status of his objects. Therefore, all pieces of cloth owned by the poor are not *muktzeh* for the affluent.[27])

Tehillah L'Dovid[28] proves that *Shulchan Aruch* holds of *Tosafos*'s distinction we mentioned earlier, whether the reason for the *muktzeh* is due to the quality of the object where we say the owner sets it aside in totality, or if there is an external reason that makes it *muktzeh* where the halachah is that it remains permitted for others. *Shulchan Aruch*[29] *paskens* that even if one doesn't own an animal, if it's common to be found in his town, that animal's food is not *muktzeh*. Surely if we follow the intention of the owner, since he doesn't own this animal, it should be *muktzeh* for him. How does it help that other people feed their animal this food? We see by cloths that are only fit for paupers that despite the fact that there are paupers who use it, that doesn't stop it from being *muktzeh* for affluent people? We must say that *Shulchan Aruch* distinguishes like *Tosafos*. This animal food is good food for the animal, but there is an external problem - I don't own this animal. This is in contrast to the case of a cloth that is only 3x3. The affluent person doesn't view this as a piece of clothing and hence

---

26. 43:20.

27. *Chazon Ish* doesn't read *Tosafos* like *Taz* and *Bach*, that *Tosafos* is giving two separate answers; rather, it is all to be read as one answer. When the Gemara implies that a 3x3 cloth is not *muktzeh*, it is referring to the cloth of a pauper. That which *Tosafos* continues *ei nami* is read as "and even" for an affluent person in the pauper's house it won't be *muktzeh*. *Tosafos HaRosh* indicates like this. He first presents *Tosafos*'s second answer, that in the pauper's house it is not *muktzeh*, and he then says: ומיהו בלאו הכי יש לפרש דאי הוו שלש על שלש יש אדם שמותר לטלטלן כגון עניים — "If it is 3x3 there is someone who it is permitted to move, namely a pauper." He is presenting a more simple explanation that when the cloth is fit for an a pauper, then it isn't *muktzeh* for anyone!

28. Point 35.

29. 308:29.

it will be *muktzeh* for him.[30] *Mishnah Berurah*[31] also *paskens,* based on *Tosafos,* that the *muktzeh* status depends on why the owner refrains from using it.[32]

Textbooks and Toys

In order to *pasken* our original questions, we need to establish with each item which category it belongs to. With the case of a textbook and toys (Questions #4, 5), for those who can't use or read them, the owner knows that the limitation to use them lies in him and not in the object. It's only because of Shabbos that he won't use them, and therefore he is not *maktzah daas.* R' Moshe is lenient in a similar case.[33] We also understand why food on Yom Kippur is not *muktzeh.* We can say that it's like *terumah,* whose purpose is to be given to a *kohen.* So too on Yom Kippur the food's purpose is to be given to children.[34] *Aruch HaShulchan paskens* that wine

---

30. From this *se'if* we can refute *Chazon Ish*'s claim that when it's not *muktzeh* for the owner it's not *muktzeh* for others. If the animal is unscommon, the halachah is that only for the owner is it not *muktzeh,* and for everyone else it is. According to *Chazon Ish,* that's not logical?!

31. 325:36.

32. However, *Be'er HaGolah* says the source of *Shulchan Aruch* is *Ran. Ran* doesn't distinguish between the cases of the cloth less than 3x3 and of the loaf of bread someone made a vow not to eat. He holds that even the loaf is forbidden for everyone. If *Be'er HaGolah* learned that this is *Shulchan Aruch*'s opinion, then in all our cases when according to the owner it is *muktzeh,* e.g., *kitniyos,* it should be *muktzeh* for all.

33. *Iggros Moshe* 5:22, point 2. His case is slightly different. He is talking about someone who is reading something forbidden, e.g., *sifrei cheshek,* literature that has ideas that are contrary to Torah ideals. Such books are forbidden to read anytime. His question is if someone, despite it being forbidden, reads such books. Are they forbidden to move? He suggests a novel idea: Something that is forbidden not due a *melachah,* but instead due to another prohibition, is only *muktzeh* if one abides by that *issur.* But it's the same principle.

34. R' Akiva Eiger and *Chasam Sofer* discuss whether we would apply *migo d'iskatzi* to food in a case where Shabbos follows Yom Kippur. Since it was forbidden to eat the food at the commencement of Shabbos, should they be forbidden all of Shabbos? ואכמ"ל.

that belongs to a *nazir* is not *muktzeh*. He explains as we've seen, that something that still has an importance to the owner, even if he can't use it, doesn't cause it to lose its identity of a *kli* and thus isn't *muktzeh*. It should follow that meat that isn't glatt would also not be *muktzeh* because the Jew who doesn't eat it can give it to others who are allowed to eat it (question #3).

Kitniyos

Dovev Meisharim[35] compares *kitniyos* on Pesach (question #1) to the pauper's cloths for affluent people, and therefore holds that for Ashkenazim *kitniyos* are *muktzeh*. Despite that, one is still allowed to feed children or a sick person *kitniyos*. *Mishnah Berurah*[36] says that since this is only in pressing situations, ideally an Ashkenazi still treats *kitniyos* as forbidden for his family and he designates it from use. This is different from food on Yom Kippur, which is permitted for children in all circumstances. It seems that *Dovev Meisharim* holds that *kitniyos* differs to a prohibition that results from a *neder*, where we saw, according to some opinions, that since one can give the bread to others, it isn't *muktzeh* even for oneself. With *kitniyos*, even though one can in theory still give it to Sephardim, since one can't feed *kitniyos* to one's family, one is *maktzah daas* from it in totality. Regarding the bread that is forbidden due to the woman's vow, she could still feed it to her family and therefore she isn't *maktzah daas*.

If one were to accept *Dovev Meisharim*'s comparison of *kitniyos* to the pauper's cloth, it will follow that if an Ashkenazi is residing in the house of a Sephardi, he will be able to move the *kitniyos*. This is as we learned from *Taz*, that in such a case the guest follows the host. *Piskei Teshuvos* learns from the *poskim* that in order to have this leniency, one must have a certain amount of permanence in the host's house. If he is just eating one meal there during Pesach, he wouldn't follow the host. Only when he is sleeping by the host would this leniency be relevant, e.g., a son-in-law who

35. Section 1, *siman* 49.
36. 253:1.

is sleeping with his in-laws. According to how *Bach* understands the *psak* of *Shulchan Aruch,* that only in the house of an affluent person is a pauper going to be limited by the affluent person's *muktzeh,* we would allow a Sephardi to go into an Ashkenazi's house and take *kitniyos*. Only for those Sephardim residing in the Ashkenazi's house is it *muktzeh,* since only these people are limited by the designation of the host.

There is a strong argument that with *kitniyos* we can't apply the rule of *nigrar acharav* (follow the owner). If the reason why we follow the intention of the host is because the guest will satisfy himself with whatever he receives from his host, i.e., he subjects his mind to the host, this is only true with something he himself is allowed to use. However, with *kitniyos,* where an Ashkenazi would in no way use this, since he holds that it is forbidden to eat, one can argue we that we can't apply the principle of *nigrar acharav*.

However, the consensus of modern-day *poskim*[37] is *not* to compare *kitniyos* to the cloth. Since *kitniyos* is dependent on who the owner is, it should be compared to *terumah* or *neder,* which we were much more liberal in permitting its movement, since it still has a valid use for a specific segment in society. Perhaps even *Dovev Meisharim* would agree that nowadays it is different. When he wrote his *psak* back then in Europe, it was extremely uncommon to find Sephardim in his surroundings, so the potential use of *kitniyos* was completely removed from an Ashkenazi's mind. However, it could be argued today that in our diverse and mixed society it's likely for one's Sephardi neighbor to knock on the door during Pesach to borrow some rice. So an Ashkenazi knows it can have potential use. So while there is an *issur* for him not to eat it, he doesn't totally reject it from use.[38]

---

37. *Shalmei Yehudah* in the name of *Risha, Shemiras Shabbos K'Hilchasah* 20:34.

38. If, however, the Ashkenazi sold his *kitniyos* to a non-Jew, the question is irrelevant. Since it doesn't belong to him, he can't impact its status.

Summary

Most *Rishonim* hold that when an owner can't use his item for whatever reason, even though it is still permitted for others to use, it is *muktzeh* for the owner, and he consequently determines the status even for others. *Tosafos* limits this rule only in a case where the reason why it is not fit for the owner is since he doesn't treat this item as a useable *kli*. However, in cases where there is an external reason why it is not fit for the owner, but he does recognize that it is a suitable item for other people, it will not be *muktzeh* for others to use. Once it is not *muktzeh* for others, it in turn is not *muktzeh* for him either, since he now has a use that he can give it to others. The other *Rishonim* conceded that items that are destined to be given to others won't be *muktzeh* only because the owner can't use them. There is a further principle learned from *Tosafos* - that the host can determine the *muktzeh* status of an item for his guests. It is disputed among the *poskim* in which specific scenarios this principle, known as *nigrar acharav*, is applicable.

Answers

1. Nowadays when Sephardim and Ashkenazim live among each other, there is an argument that an Ashkenazi doesn't set aside rice because he is aware his neighbor might ask him for it. Practically most people who don't eat rice seal it away and don't intend under any normal circumstance to use it during Pesach, so it would be *muktzeh*.

2. If your son-in-law is sleeping at your house, he follows your practices regarding *muktzeh*. Since it is not *muktzeh* for you, so too it is not *muktzeh* for him.

3. A Sephardi who has meat that he can't eat surely intends on giving it to others who can eat it. If so, it can be moved because it has a use.

4. If the textbooks can be read by the owner on Shabbos, then just like for her they are not *muktzeh* then for all they are not *muktzeh*. If the owner of the textbook is forbidden to read it, it still might not be *muktzeh*. Since it can be read by certain people, the owner has a use in giving it to others.

5. Toys are meant to be given to kids to play with. Since kids will inevitably play with them, even if the owner treats them for himself as *muktzeh* it can be argued that he isn't *maktzah daas* entirely and they can be given to kids.

6. Similarly, one is accustomed to share cigarettes with his friends. If Shmuel knows his friends are lenient, permitting themselves to smoke on Yom Tov, he doesn't remove awareness from the cigarettes and they can be moved. However, most people intend on consuming their cigarettes themselves and it's a depletable item, therefore it would be *muktzeh* - one sets it aside entirely.

Chapter 13, Part 1

טלטול מן הצד

Moving Indirectly

Questions

1. Am I required to remove *muktzeh* food items from the fridge door before Shabbos?
2. I want to take ice cream out of the freezer and there is raw meat (which can't be eaten raw at all) blocking the way. Can I squeeze my hands through and push the meat aside while taking the ice cream?

There are many ways one can carry an object indirectly: he can move it with his body, e.g., his torso, legs, head etc.; he can move it using another item; he can blow it; and so on. The Gemara only discusses moving the item indirectly by moving something else that in turn causes the *muktzeh* to be moved. This is known as *tiltul min hatzad*. The classic understanding of the term *min hatzad* is "indirectly" - one's hands are not in direct contact with the item. Accordingly, the phrase is read *min hatzad* ***shel heter*** - "from the side *of the permitted object*."

Rashi explains[1] differently. He says *k'l'acher yad*, meaning that *Rashi* understands that this is the regular *heter* of deviation (*shinui*) that we find in Shabbos. Moving *muktzeh* via a different object is an abnormal way of moving and hence subject to an exemption. (Even though elsewhere *shinui* is usually forbidden just exempt from punishment, since here there is only an rabbinic prohibition to start with, when performed through a

1. 43b, s.v. מן הצד.

shinui it is totally permitted.) We find *Rashi* elsewhere[2] also explains *min hatzad* in this way. The Gemara refers to *binyan min hatzad,* which *Rashi* explains to mean via a *shinui. Ran* understands *Rashi* this way and therefore says that one can even push a corpse across the floor with his hands, since that is also a deviation from the regular way of carrying a corpse.

The Gemara[3] brings the following case of *muktzeh* to determine if there are any permissible ways to move it. Resting on a bed is a dead body that now requires removal. If one were to tilt the bed in order to tilt the body, this should be a form of *tiltul min hatzad.* Nonetheless, the Gemara *paskens* that this is forbidden and still included in Chazal's prohibition of *muktzeh.* The *Rishonim* ask a contradiction between this *din* of corpse and the opinion of Rebbe Elazar ben Tadai. He *paskens* that if one has a dry fig buried inside a haystack, even if the dry fig is entirely concealed inside, one can still poke it out with a stick, despite that he inevitably will move the hay, which is *muktzeh.* The Gemara explains that it's permitted because it is an application of *tiltul min hatzad.* One is only moving the hay via a medium, not with his hands. We seemingly have a contradiction if *tiltul min hatzad* - is permitted or not? Most of the *Rishonim*[4] reconcile this contradiction by explaining that the distinction between these two cases is dependent on why one is moving the *muktzeh* indirectly. Is it for the sake of the *muktzeh,* or is it for the sake of the non-*muktzeh*? The corpse is *muktzeh* and one's interest is in moving the corpse. Therefore the act is *tiltul min hatzad* for the sake of the *muktzeh.* However, with the dry fig, one is only moving the straw in order access the dry fig. The fig isn't *muktzeh,* so one's act is permitted because it is directed at the non-*muktzeh.*[5]

---

2. 47b.

3. 43b.

4. *Baal HaMeor* and an opinion brought by *Ohr Zarua* hold that it's a dispute between the two Gemaras, and we *pasken* like Rebbe Elazar ben Tadai that *tiltul min hatzad* is permitted in *all* cases, they therefore permit even moving the corpse via a bed.

5. *Rif* gives another distinction. He says *tiltul min hatzad* is *mutar* with food, but for other items, e.g., stones, it's *assur.* Some *Rishonim* understand that *Rif* is giving the same distinction as *Tosafos,* that it depends on one's intention. The reason he

The Principle of Chazon Ish

Chazon Ish[6] explains this distinction. Dependent on one's intention is what defines the act which one is performing. If one is moving the item for the sake of the *muktzeh,* albeit that one is not directly touching the *muktzeh,* one's act can still be defined as *tiltul muktzeh,* moving *muktzeh.* However, if one is moving the *muktzeh* for the sake of the non-*muktzeh,* his involvement is in moving the non-*muktzeh* item. The inadvertent and indirect *tiltul* that is also taking place is insignificant to his act of *tiltul,* and therefore it is not part of Chazal's *issur* to move *muktzeh.* This novel explanation is true even though one could essentially be physically doing the same act. However, halachically they would be defined differently depending on your agenda or intention. If tilting a barrel to roll a stone off it is done in order to access the barrel's contents, this is an act of moving a barrel for something permissible, i.e., its contents, hence it is permitted. But if one is tilting the stone off the barrel so that the stone should be on the floor for whatever reason, this is an act of moving something for the need of the stone, and it is forbidden. The phraseology of the Gemara: טמה"צ לא שמיה טלטול - "indirect moving *isn't considered moving*" certainly reads very accurately according to this explanation. When *tiltul min hatzad* is permissible it's not considered an act of *tiltul* at all regarding the *muktzeh.*

---

said *tiltul min hatzad* is permissible by food is because generally that is something that one moves for the sake of the food, i.e., non-*muktzeh.* These *Rishonim* feel forced to distort the words of *Rif* because there are otherwise cases that explicitly contradict *Rif*'s distinction, e.g., it is permitted to shake a stone off a barrel. *Sefer HaMeoros* and *Sefer HaShlamah* answer *Rif* with a new principle: In the case of shaking the stone off the barrel, it isn't even considered *tiltul min hatzad.* It's a lesser degree of *tiltul* called *ni'ur* or *shomet* — you're just shaking something off and that's permitted regardless of the object. Your intention isn't to move it, just to remove it from its present place. *Tosafos* (*Eiruvin* 77b) explicitly makes this distinction, however, practically there are not many differences *l'halachah.* Even accepting this principle of *ni'ur* doesn't result in many practical differences, as it is very limited in its application and even those who don't hold of such a principle can permit the movement when it is done *l'tzorech davar ha'mutar.*

6. 47, point 22.

Other Reasons Why Tiltul Min HaTzad Is Permitted

However, this explanation is certainly not concurrent with all of the *Rishonim*. *Ritva*[7] explains the reason for the leniency of *tiltul min hatzad l'tzorech davar ha'mutar*: Since this act is being done "for the sake of Shabbos" - now that you require this non-*muktzeh* for Shabbos - it is an act of moving for your Shabbos needs. He understands that we don't need to define the specific intention of this act; rather, there is a distinct leniency when it's *tiltul min hatzad l'tzorech davar ha'mutar*. This movement is now for the sake of Shabbos since one wants to use the item that is permitted. Another case that doesn't fit with *Chazon Ish* can be found in *Ohr Zarua*.[8] He says that when one is doing *tiltul min hatzad* for the sake of the *muktzeh*, there is a worry that he might come to directly move the *muktzeh*. But if one's agenda is the movement of the non-*muktzeh*, no such worry exists. We see similarly that the intention of the act doesn't change what the act is; rather, in one instance Chazal were worried and in the other instance they weren't.

Minchas Shlomo[9] (R' Shlomo Zalman Auerbach) argues unequivocally on *Chazon Ish*'s explanation. R' Shlomo Zalman explains that one instance of *tiltul min hatzad* that the Mishnah permits is when one picks up a barrel and removes it from its surroundings in order to remove a stone cover and access the wine. Since tilting in its current place would cause the stone to smash surrounding barrels, we permit the removal of the entire barrel with the stone, since its only *tiltul min hatzad*. At the first stage when one removes the barrel, it could be interpreted that one is moving it for the sake of the non-*muktzeh*, i.e., the wine, but at the stage when one tilts the stone off the barrel, it is certainly clear that one is moving the barrel for the sake of the *muktzeh*.

R' Shlomo Zalman Auerbach therefore asks: How can we say that this act can be treated as a *tiltul* of something permitted when it's clear that one

7. 43b, 141a, and 50b.

8. *Siman* 86.

9. Section 1, *siman* 14.

is moving it for the *muktzeh*? Furthermore, the Gemara[10] permits moving, through bodily movement, straw that is lumped on a bed. Most *Rishonim* comment that this is an application of *tiltul min hatzad*. Again R' Shlomo Zalman asks: Even if your intention is to vacate the bed from the straw, it's clear that one's movements are directed at moving the *muktzeh* straw, so how can it halachically be treated as if one isn't involved in moving the *muktzeh*?![11] He therefore concludes that *tiltul min hatzad* is a special leniency. Since one is not moving the *muktzeh* with his hands, we don't consider this to be an act of *tiltul*.

Moving a Muktzeh Item for a Permitted Usage

Magen Avraham[12] posits that despite there being a prohibition of *amirah l'nochri* (asking a non-Jew to perform any forbidden *melachah*), one can ask a non-Jew to carry a lit candle into another room if the Jew wants light in that room. His reasoning is based on a general principle that anything a Jew himself is permitted to do, he is allowed to ask a non-Jew to do. This is so even when the Jew knows that the non-Jew will perform that task with a *melachah*, which, if the Jew were to do himself, he would obviously transgress a prohibition. Therefore in our case, the Jew could carry the candle himself, albeit only with *tiltul min hatzad*. Since the Jew can do this act, he can ask the non-Jew to do so, despite knowing full well that the non-Jew will carry it in a regular fashion (which the Jew himself can't do).

The apparent question is how can the Jew carry the candle *even* with *tiltul min hatzad*. Surely he's moving it for the sake of the *muktzeh*; since he now wants the candle in this room, it should be *tiltul min hatzad l'tzorech davar ha'assur*?! We must conclude that *Magen Avraham* understands that since one wants the light of the candle and that benefit is permitted, this act therefore falls under.[13] This principle of *Magen Avraham*

10. 141a.

11. This question can be answered. It doesn't appear that one is moving the straw; rather, it appears that one is trying to lie down.

12. 279:9.

13. *Beis Meir* 276:3.

is coined *tiltul min hatzad l'tzorech* ***shimush ha'mutar***. Despite that this item is *muktzeh,* since it provides one with a permitted benefit, we consider its movement for the sake of the permitted item. Surely this extension, not just to assess the situation based upon what object one is interested in carrying but also what one's ultimate intention is in carrying this object, is better understood if we learn that *tiltul min hatzad* is a special *heter* when it's for the sake of Shabbos. True, he is interested in carrying the *muktzeh* candle, but it is all for the sake of Shabbos. Since the illumination is the true motivation behind this movement, that is for sake of Shabbos. However according to the understanding of *Chazon Ish,* this *din* makes no sense. Since the only thing being carried is the *muktzeh,* how can we classify this act as something directed at moving the *heter*?

Ni'ur

Even if one were to use the shelves of the freezer door to only store frozen meat, the door still has the status of a *bosis l'heter* because it also serves to protect the contents inside that are not *muktzeh.* A door's primary importance is to serve the contents of the freezer. That importance isn't weakened because of the *muktzeh* on its shelves. When one opens the door to access food, it is *tiltul min hatzad l'tzorech davar ha'mutar* (and even though this is often how the raw meat is moved, it's not relevant to the discussion presented in part 2 below because this is not the general way that one moves meat[14]).

Despite this, R' Shlomo Zalman Auerbach[15] and R' Elyashiv say that one should try to take out the *muktzeh* from the shelves before Shabbos. Their reasoning is based on a new principle called *ni'ur. Ni'ur* literally means "shaking off." Prior to utilizing the leniency of *tiltul min hatzad,* Chazal required *ni'ur,* i.e., shaking off the *muktzeh* and preempt having to move it indirectly. *tiltul min hatzad* is only permitted when one can't do

---

14. The same way, when one pulls a dry fig out of the straw it is the normal way to move the straw in that scenario. But relative to how one normally moves this type of *muktzeh,* it is not the regular way.

15. *Shemiras Shabbos K'Hilchasah,* ch. 20, point 79.

ni'ur. An illustration of this is found in the following Mishnah.[16] The Mishnah writes that if there is a stone on a barrel and one wants to move the barrel, he must shake off the stone. If for whatever reason he can't, only then is it permitted to carry the barrel with the stone because of *tiltul min hatzad*. From this halachah of *ni'ur* we see that Chazal ideally want one not to rely on *tiltul min hatzad*. R' Shlomo Zalman Auerbach and R' Elyashiv pose that this extends even to before Shabbos, where one should see to it that he doesn't inevitably have to come to move *muktzeh* indirectly on Shabbos. A practical application is to remove the *muktzeh* items in the fridge door before Shabbos (question #1).

Moving while Walking

Returning to our original questions: If one can reach a food item without touching items in the freezer that are *muktzeh*, and pulling the desired food out will now push the *muktzeh* item out the way (question #2), this is classic *tiltul min hatzad l'tzorech davar ha'mutar*, which is permitted. If the space is tight and one will have to move the *muktzeh* with his arm while he finds his way through the freezer, some *poskim*[17] say that this is comparable to a case brought in the Gemara[18] where straw (which is *muktzeh*) is obstructing one's path, but nevertheless, while walking through he can make a passage with his feet. This is permitted because the *muktzeh* is moved indirectly while walking. All that one is doing is walking; the *muktzeh* happens to move as a result of his movement. So too here, the *muktzeh* happens to move while one is inserting his hand through the different items in the freezer. He is involved in taking out the non-*muktzeh* and is not interested in moving the *muktzeh*. Those who argue[19] say the that Gemara's *heter* is limited to when one is doing it with any body part *besides one's hand*. However, one can't move the *muktzeh* directly out the way with his hands.

---

16. 142b.
17. *Orchos Shabbos*, ch. 19, *siman* 252.
18. 127a.
19. *Hilchos Shabbos B'Shabbos* 27:17.

Summary

There is a leniency to move *muktzeh* indirectly. The classic scenario is when one moves a non-*muktzeh* item and it subsequently causes a *muktzeh* item to be moved. This is limited to when one's intention is to move the non-*muktzeh* item, but if one is trying to move the *muktzeh* item, he can't move it even indirectly. This distinction is known as *tiltul min hatzad l'tzorech davar ha'mutar* or *tiltul min hatzad l'tzorech davar ha'assur*. *Magen Avraham* extends this leniency even to a case where one is only interested in moving the *muktzeh*, yet he wants to use a permissible element of this *muktzeh* object, e.g., to move a candle indirectly to use the light it emits. This is a special leniency when it's done for the sake of Shabbos, known as *tiltul min hatzad l'tzorech shimush ha'muktzeh*.

Answers

1. The *poskim* recommend that one removes the *muktzeh* items in his fridge door before Shabbos. This is an extension of the principle of *ni'ur*; one must try to avoid relying on the leniency of *tiltul min hatzad*. If one didn't remove them he can still move the fridge.
2. If there is *muktzeh* obstructing one's way through the freezer shelf, even if one inevitably will have to move the *muktzeh* he still is allowed to push his hand through the *muktzeh* items.

Part 2

טמה"צ שדרכו בכך

Tiltul Min Hatzad When it is the Normal Way to Move it

Questions

1. After Eliyahu has used his ashtray, can he move it on Yom Tov?
2. Can I fold up and carry away a plastic disposable tablecloth that's full of trash?
3. If I realize on Shabbos that I have money in my pants pocket, can I continue wearing the pants, keeping the money in my pocket for the rest of Shabbos?

We can learn an important qualification in *tiltul min hatzad* from *Meiri*. *Meiri* establishes that if the usual way of moving this specific *muktzeh* is only via *tiltul min hatzad*, i.e., it is normal to move it via using something else, there is no *heter* of *tiltul min hatzad*. He explains that the Gemara that permits poking a dried fig out of a haystack is only when there is a hole in the haystack and one is going to thread the stick inside the hole to push out the dry fig, but if one must move the straw out of the way in order to access the dry fig, it's forbidden. This is because the normal way is to move the straw away with a stick, even during the week. This idea is repeated[20] in the case of a pot whose resting place is obstructed by insulating materials (which are *muktzeh*) and one can't move the material by jiggling the pot. *Meiri* explains: ואין זה טמה"צ, שמגע ע"י דבר אחר מגע הוא שהרי **אף דרכו בחול כן** - "This is no indirect movement because touching via an-

20. *Shabbos* 37a.

other medium is still considered directly touching, *since he also does so during the week.*" When it's normal to move the *muktzeh* in this way, that's a reflection that this *tiltul min hatzad* is an ordinary movement. This is so even though one is only moving it indirectly, through a medium of something *mutar*, since we *pasken* that: "*maga al yedei davar acher, maga hu* - moving one item via pushing another item is considered as if one moved the original item." (This insight can certainly be understood according to *Rashi* that the reason permitting *tiltul min hatzad* is because it is a deviation. Therefore in the case of *Meiri*, one hasn't changed from how he normally does this act.)

Proof to Meiri

We can bring proof to *Meiri* from the case of moving a corpse.[21] The Gemara says that if we hold that *tiltul min hatzad* is permitted, one can move the corpse to prevent it from decaying in the sun by flipping it from one bed to a second and to keep doing so. One is not holding the corpse directly, only moving it indirectly by turning it from bed to bed by flipping the beds. Why doesn't the Gemara give a simpler solution, carry the bed directly to the shade, one is thereby moving the corpse indirectly?[22] It must be since that's the normal way of moving a corpse - via carrying the bed he is resting on - one's act is not construed as indirectly moving the corpse. Since it is the normal way, it's considered directly moving the corpse![23]

---

21. 43b.

22. Even though this is *tiltul min hatzad l'tzorech davar ha'assur,* the Gemara is going according to the opinion that permits *tiltul min hatzad* regardless why one is moving it. We don't follow this opinion.

23. *Ran* says that carrying a child who is holding a stone is not *tiltul min hatzad,* rather we attribute the carrying of the stone to the person. R' Shlomo Zalman Auerbach explains that since it's a normal act of carrying a child, now that he is holding a stone doesn't cause your act of *tiltul* of the stone to be defined as *min hatzad,* and thus won't have the leniencies of *tiltul min hatzad.* This is a big novelty because it's not the normal way to carry a stone. In this scenario of a child holding an item, it's normal to carry the child with the item in his hand.

It follows in cases when it's practically impossible to move an item without the assistance of an outer body, e.g., a bag of flour, a bottle of water, etc., that we don't view it as if one is moving the water and flour *min hatzad,* via the medium of the outer packaging. The exterior is one entity to its contents. It is one act of moving the flour or water.

The Famous Taz - Cleaning a Table with a Stick

Taz[24] brings down a very common application of *tiltul min hatzad.* He says that one can sweep crumbs and shells from a table even though they are *muktzeh,* using a brush or stick, since one is only moving the *muktzeh* indirectly. (*Meiri* is not a refutation to *Taz* because it is unlikely that it is considered the normal way to move shells off a table with a stick; on a weekday one takes them off with his hand.) The obvious question on *Taz* is: Isn't this surely *tiltul min hatzad* for the sake of *muktzeh* - one wants to move the shells?[25]

We mentioned earlier the case of moving straw that is on a bed. The *Rishonim* argue what the reason for the *heter* is. *Rosh* understands that since one is moving it for the sake of the *muktzeh,* it must be a new *heter* of *tiltul b'gufo* (moving with one's body). *Ran* explains that it's *tiltul min hatzad l'tzorech davar ha'mutar.* One is moving the straw so that he can sleep more comfortably, so his intended purpose is to benefit the comfort of his bed. *Graz* explains that they are arguing whether one is shaking the straw off the bed in order to remove it, or is he trying to spread it evenly on the bed. *Rosh* understands it as the latter, hence he defined the act as moving the straw (one wants the straw to be moved into specific areas) and therefore it must be that there is a new *heter* of *tiltul b'gufo. Ran* un-

---

24. 308:18.

25. *Chazon Ish* 47:14. To be concise, *Chazon Ish* argues on *Taz* based on his *geder* of *tiltul min hatzad,* that one's intention defines what one is moving. He argues: True, one is sweeping up the shells is to make the table tidy, but what is one doing? One is moving the shells that are *muktzeh.* Therefore, one's act is defined as moving the shells, irrelevant how it came about. At the end of chapter 13, part 3, we will elaborate on *Chazon Ish*'s stance.

derstands the former (one wants the bed to be free from straw), so he defines the act as an act of moving *muktzeh*. Nonetheless it is still permitted, since one's act is ultimately for his comfort.

However, it is not ideal that we explain that the disagreement is how to understand the scenario. Furthermore, *Ran* quotes *Rashi*'s explanation on the Mishnah - that one is moving the straw to smooth out the mattress - and *Ran* doesn't seem to argue. It is therefore hard to accept the explanation of *Graz* that *Ran* holds it is an act of removing the straw from the bed.

Therefore, we can perhaps suggest that both *Ran* and *Rosh* agree that one is moving the straw to smoothen out lumps in the bed, but their argument is how to judge this action. *Ran* understands that since he's moving it to improve the state of the bed it's *tiltul min hatzad l'tzorech davar ha'mutar*, while *Rosh* understands that ultimately one wants to move the straw, so it's *tiltul min hatzad l'tzorech davar ha'assur*. *Taz* might have sided with *Ran* and thus has precedence to claim that one who is sweeping the table is doing so to improve the state of the table by enhancing its cleanliness. This can also be encompassed in *tiltul min hatzad l'tzorech* ***davar ha'mutar***.[26]

Using a Stick as an Extension of Your Hand

Graz[27] strongly argues on *Taz*. Even if it can be claimed that it is *l'tzorech davar ha'mutar*, it is a wrong application of *tiltul min hatzad*. He says that we only find *tiltul min hatzad* when one is moving an object which is *mutar* and this movement indirectly causes the *muktzeh* to move, not when the non-*muktzeh* is being used as the means which with to move the *muktzeh*. That is the literal meaning of the words, "*tiltul min hatzad* - the moving [of the *muktzeh*] takes place *min hatzad*," i.e. indirectly as a result of the

26. *Pri Megadim* 311:47:2. He asks a contradiction in *Taz* where he forbids using a stick to move *muktzeh*. *Pri Megadim* answers that when *Taz* forbids via a stick, that's when it's *l'tzorech muktzeh*, while moving the shells is *l'tzorech ha'mutar* (the table). This is a strong proof to our suggested explanation.

27. *Kuntres Acharon* 259:3.

muktzeh moving. In the case of *Taz,* one is using the non-*muktzeh* as an extension of one's hand and we hold that לקיחה ע״י דבר אחר שמה לקיחה - "taking via another medium is considered directly taking."[28]

He explains that the case of pushing out the dry fig that is buried in the pile of straw is not an example of directly pushing away *muktzeh*. The Gemara says that you use a *kush v'karkar* (a stick and a rod) to push it out. He explains that these are not random examples of sticks; rather, only these tools that specifically have a sharp end may be used. Therefore one places the sharp end inside the dry fig and pulls it out. When you pull out the dry fig, the straw falls by itself. That's what the Gemara means when it says *v'hen menaros m'aleihen,* i.e., the *muktzeh* (the straw) now moves on its own as an indirect consequence of one's action. So it is *tiltul min hatzad*! In contrast, if one takes a blunt stick to push aside the straw in order to directly be able to access the dry fig with his hands, it is forbidden, hence why the Gemara never presented this solution. Even though one is not directly moving the straw, since he is just using the stick as an extension of his hand, that is not *tiltul min hatzad*. To do that is equal to taking out the straw with one's hand. (*Graz* understands that *Taz* would permit moving the straw in such a fashion, and has therefore refuted him from this case of the dry fig.)

Graz therefore *paskens* that if one has *muktzeh* fabric insulating a pot, one can't take a stick to move it off. He must use the stick to push the lid off, which will in turn cause the *muktzeh* fabric to fall off. The stick is not functioning as an extension of one's hand to facilitate moving the *muktzeh*; rather, one is moving the lid and the *muktzeh* is falling off inadvertently to one's action. He brings support to this idea from *Tosafos*.[29] The Gemara says that if a hole in the earth that one uses to keep his pots warm is filled

---

28. The source of this principle is found by *yayin nesech* and lulav. If one is shaking the lulav with something separating his hand and the lulav, it is still considered that one has shaken the lulav, aka מגע מגע ע״י דבר אחר שמיה. In 446:3 we are taught that if one wants to remove *chametz* that he finds in his domain into the domain of a non-Jew without picking up the *chametz,* it doesn't help to move it by pushing it with a stick. This is because of this principle that the stick is just an extension of one's hand.

29. 50b, s.v. הכל מודים.

with *muktzeh* insulating material, one cannot put back the pot inside. *Tosafos* explains that even though one will be using the pot to indirectly move the insulators, this will be forbidden, even according to those who permit *tiltul min hatzad,* since one is required to jiggle the pot to and fro. *Graz* explains that this is worse than *tiltul min hatzad,* since he is using the pot as a direct means of moving the *muktzeh.* Therefore the pot is an extension of his hand and that's forbidden.

Why Is Sweeping the Floor Permitted?

If this is so, how does *Graz* understand how we can sweep the floor? (It's explicit in *Shulchan Aruch*[30] that this is permitted when there are no issues of *choresh.*) Even though it's *tiltul min hatzad,* the broom is still an extension of your hand. However, *Graz* says that this halachah is not a question, but rather a proof to his principle. If one is careful in the reading of *Ran,*[31] he says[32] that sweeping the house is permitted because טמה"צ משום כבוד יו"ט התירו - only for the sake of *honoring Yom Tov*/Shabbos did Chazal permit it." Otherwise it would not fall under the regular *tiltul min hatzad.* This is explicable with what we have established - that to actively move *muktzeh* through a non-*muktzeh* medium does not qualify as *tiltul min hatzad*

Carrying an Ashtray, Clearing a Table

It's logical that *Graz* would forbid carrying an ashtray with ash inside (question #1), even on Yom Tov, if one is moving the ashtray in order to empty out the ash. (On Shabbos it is regardless forbidden, as the ashtray is a *kli shemelachto l'issur.*) This is because one doesn't want to move the ash with his hand; rather, the ashtray is functioning as an extension of his hand to move the ash. While *Taz* would permit it because it is *tiltul min*

30. *Siman* 337.

31. *Beitzah* 12a.

32. *Beis Yosef* brings *Ran* to explain why it's permitted to sweep the floor, and he also brings the reason of *Raavad* that it is a *heter* of *graf shel re'i.*

hatzad for the sake of freeing the ashtray for further use, that is qualified under *l'tzorech davar ha'mutar.*

Perhaps even *Taz* would agree that using tongs to move *muktzeh* is forbidden. Since its entire essence is made to function as an extension of one's hand to aid moving items, one's action is clearly defined as moving the *muktzeh* directly. *Taz* only argues in a case of a stick that isn't made to function as an extension of one's hand. Then even if that is how you presently are using the stick, it is still considered *tiltul min hatzad.* Further investigation is necessary for a clear halachic conclusion.

Mishnah Berurah[33] *paskens* like *Taz,* so one can move dirty food items on a table via a non-*muktzeh* medium. However, one must be careful not to use something that is normal, e.g., a bread crumb sweeper (a small, glasses-size box with a rotating brush inside that collects crumbs). For those who have one, that is the normal way to sweep up crumbs from a table, and in chapter 10 we saw under what circumstances crumbs are *muktzeh.*

The modern-day *poskim*[34] extend *Taz*'s leniency to wiping up the dirt of the table with a cloth. It must be stressed that they only permit a cloth or a material that is actually aiding in the cleaning. However, if one doesn't want his hands to get dirty and therefore takes a tissue so that the tissue is directly touching the mess, it is not permitted as *tiltul min hatzad,* since the tissue is part of one's hand and it's as if one is touching the *muktzeh* himself just via a separation (*chatzitzah*).

Wrapping Up a Plastic Tablecloth

Some *poskim*[35] say that if one wants to wrap remnants of a meal, which are now *muktzeh,* left on a plastic tablecloth (question #2), he can't rely on *tiltul min hatzad.* Since the tablecloth has no importance of its own, we don't treat it as if one is moving non-*muktzeh* in order to move the *muktzeh,* as the tablecloth doesn't qualify as an independent

---

33. 308:115.

34. *Ohr L'Tzion,* ch. 24, halachah 27, and *Shemiras Shabbos K'Hilchasah* 22:38.

35. *Shalmei Yehonasan* 3:8:5.

non-*muktzeh kli*. We could entertain that this scenario would be contested by *Graz* and *Taz*: One is moving the *muktzeh* to empty the table, with the tablecloth functioning as an extension of one's hand, helping him move large quantities of trash in one go. *Taz* would permit and *Graz* would forbid. Even if we accept this argument, it's not so relevant since in most cases where one wants to remove this tablecloth, the tablecloth has reached a stage where it qualifies for the *heter* of *graf shel re'i* (being in a state of repulsiveness) and one is permitted to wrap it up and throw it away regardless.

Indirect Moving but in a Normal Way

We can ask a question in the parameters of *tiltul min hatzad*: When one is carrying an object indirectly, yet in a usual way, is that considered *tiltul min hatzad*? In the last few decades, every pair of pants has pockets attached. All day, every day, people walk with their phones and wallets in their pockets. What level of moving is carrying items in one's pocket considered? Is it an indirect form of moving the *muktzeh*, or perhaps, since that's the normal way to move in this situation, it's deemed regular moving? The practical application of this question is when one can't shake out (*ni'ur*) the *muktzeh* in his pocket, e.g., it will break, nor can he presently take off his pants, e.g., he is not at home. Can he continue wearing the pants despite the *muktzeh* remaining in his pocket?

Rema[36] brings that if one forgot that he was wearing a money belt when Shabbos began (and there are no issues of *hotzaah*), he can walk to a safe location and release the money belt. *Magen Avraham* explains that this is based on the *heter* of *odo b'yado*. Once *muktzeh* is already in one's hand, he can continue walking to wherever he wants with it. We can ask: Since the money belt is not in one's hand, why do we need the *heter* of *odo b'yado*? *Rema* should rather permit it due to *tiltul min hatzad* or *tiltul b'gufo*. We could infer that since it is normal to carry money in a money belt, there is neither a *heter* of *tiltul min hatzad* nor *tiltul b'gufo*. However, we can easily refute the proof. Here one's interest is in moving the money

36. 266:12.

belt. Therefore it is *tiltul min hatzad l'tzorech davar ha'assur*. So *Magen Avraham* is forced to find a new *heter*.[37]

Nor can we prove from the case of carrying a child who is holding *muktzeh*, where we forbid lifting the child indirectly but in a usual manner. The lack of proof is because, as we will see in chapter 17, that it is a form of actual carrying of *muktzeh*, and hence only permitted under extenuating circumstance. In that case, one's hands are to a large extent involved in the moving of the *muktzeh*. In contrast, when carrying something in one's pockets, one's hands are not involved at all, so it should be classified as a much lower level of moving *muktzeh*.

(Regarding *bosis*, the *poskim* distinguish between two different types of pockets. This is a potential indication that carrying in one's pocket is a less direct form of *tiltul*. (See chapter 14, part 2 for an elaboration on this point.) Since, if it is considered that one is carrying the *muktzeh* when *muktzeh* is inside a pants pocket, then surely the debate whether the pants are a *bosis* or not is immaterial. Even if it doesn't render the pants *bosis*, one can't wear them because it's as if he's carrying the *muktzeh*. This discussion of *bosis* in pants is proof that we don't consider that one is directly moving the *muktzeh* when carried in a pocket.)

Graz[38] says that besides the *heter* of *odo b'yado*, which permits one to move the money belt, it is also permitted because it is *tiltul b'gufo*! This is proof that even when it's the normal way to carry items in such a manner (similar to carrying in one's pocket), since one is not actually handling the *muktzeh*, it still qualifies as *tiltul b'gufo*. According to *Graz*, one can move

---

37. *Shemiras Shabbos K'Hilchasah* (20:279) understands from this *Rema* that carrying in one's pocket is not considered *tiltul min hatzad*. He must understand that one is not just walking to remove the money belt, but also because he needs to go to that location in his house, in which case one is doing *tiltul min ha'tzad l'tzorech davar ha'mutar*and nevertheless *Rema* is only permitting it because of *odo b'yado*. Therefore, he can deduce that *tiltul min hatzad* is not permitted. R' Shlomo Zalman Auerbach's understanding of the case doesn't fit with our explanation that one is moving the money belt for the money. If R' Shlomo Zalman Auerbach is correct, therefore our refutation falls away, based on *Graz* brought in the continuation we possibly can refute the proof.

38. 266:19. The *Minchas Shabbos* 89:14 also says it's considered *tiltul b'gufo*.

with the *muktzeh* in his pants even if it's just for the sake of the *muktzeh* (question #3). *Mishnah Berurah*[39] doesn't bring *Graz*. If the omission is because he disagrees, perhaps still *Mishnah Berurah* could agree that it is a lower level of *tiltul* and can be subject to leniencies in certain cases. For further practical application of this see chapter 14, end of part 2.

Summary

When it's normal to move a *muktzeh* item via carrying a non-*muktzeh* item, there is no leniency of *tiltul min hatzad*. *Ran* learns that if one is moving the *muktzeh* in order to use the space, one's *tiltul* can be qualified as *tiltul min hatzad l'tzorech davar ha'mutar*. We explained this is the basis of *Taz*'s *heter* to take a stick to move shells off a table. *Graz* argues that the basics of *tiltul min hatzad* is lacking in such a case. *Tiltul min hatzad* is when one is moving the non-*muktzeh* and the *muktzeh* moves inadvertently, just as a consequence of one's action - not when one is using the non-*muktzeh* to function just as an extension of one's hand.

Answers

1. We explained that moving an ashtray would be subject to the dispute discussed between *Taz* and *Graz*. *Taz* would be lenient because one is not directly moving the *muktzeh*. *Mishnah Berurah paskens* like *Taz*.
2. Some *poskim* forbid moving a plastic tablecloth that has *muktzeh* bits of trash lying inside. This is a stringency and there is an argument to permit it. Generally a dirty tablecloth will qualify for the *heter* of *graf shel re'i*, so you anyway can move it to dispose of it.
3. We presented an argument that even though it is normal to carry money in a pocket, it still can be considered a

39. *Se'if katan* 35.

mitigated form of moving. You should avoid continuing to wear the trousers, but if you can't, you have what to rely on.

Part 3

טלטול בגופו

Moving With One's Body

Questions

1. If I left my cell phone in the yard and it starts raining, can I kick it into the house?
2. When trying to create more space, can I condense the trash in the trash can with my feet?

We have previously mentioned the case of straw lying on a bed, where one is permitted to move it off with his body. The *Rishonim* ask: How can this be? Despite the fact that this is *tiltul min hatzad,* it's being done for the sake of the *muktzeh* - one is interested in moving the straw, which is not permitted. *Rosh* learns a landmark principle: We are not referring to the *heter* of *tiltul min hatzad,* but to a new *heter* of *tiltul b'gufo,* which is when one moves *muktzeh* with his body. This is permitted even when being done for the sake of the *muktzeh,* since we don't deem this to be considered an act of moving at all!

Chazon Ish[40] understands that *Rosh* is not innovating a new principle of *tiltul b'gufo*; rather, with the case of straw on the bed, *Rosh* is lenient since one's principal action is an act of lying. He also happens to be moving *muktzeh* through the lying, but since one's main intention is to lie on the

40. *Siman* 47 points 12, 14.

bed, this is how we define his action. However, if one were to purposely move *muktzeh* with his body for the sake of the *muktzeh,* this act is defined as moving *muktzeh* and *Rosh* would agree it is forbidden, even though the medium for the movement was his body and not his hands.

We see from this understanding that there is no specific *heter* of moving objects with limbs other than one's hands. When your intended action is directed at the *muktzeh,* despite that it is being moved with some body part other than your hands, it's still forbidden. *Chazon Ish* thus concludes, unlike the *psak* of *Mishnah Berurah,* that there is no unrestricted *heter* of kicking *muktzeh* with one's foot. Since your action is directed at the *muktzeh,* we view this as a direct *tiltul muktzeh*! (A general underlying principle behind *Chazon Ish*'s understanding of *muktzeh* is that the "moving" that Chazal forbade isn't limited to when one is directly moving with his hands; rather, it all depends on the intention of the individual: Does he want to be moving the *muktzeh* or not? If he is interested in moving the *muktzeh,* his act is encompassed in Chazal's enactment of *muktzeh.* This outlook is the basis for his understanding in *Rosh*; why *Chazon Ish* defined *tiltul min hatzad* how we presented in part 1; and why walking through a path flooded with *muktzeh* items is not at all relevant to *muktzeh* and is permitted because it is the way of walking [*derech hilucho*].)

Not Even an Act of Moving Muktzeh

However, from the way the *poskim* bring down this principle, it's clear that they don't learn like this. They explicitly write: טלטול בגופו אפילו לצורך דבר האסור, מותר - "Moving with one's body, even when intending on moving the *muktzeh,* is permitted,"[41] implying that there is a new *heter* of *tiltul b'gufo*: When one is moving with his body it is permitted.

The Gemara[42] says that if one has an animal that is loaded with sheaves of *muktzeh* produce and he'd like to unload the animal, he can put his head underneath the load and shake it off. *Ramban* explains that this is permitted because Chazal never enacted *muktzeh* when one moves it with his

41. *Beis Yosef,* beginning of *siman* 308, s.v. וכתב, *Shulchan Aruch* 311.
42. 154b.

body: משום שטלטול שבגופו לא גזרו בו רבנן - "Chazal never enacted *muktzeh* when one is moving with his body."[43] In this scenario, one is moving the *muktzeh* for the sake of the *muktzeh*, i.e., the sheaves, and we still see that it is permissible. It therefore must be that this is not a *heter* of *tiltul min hatzad*, but is a new *heter* of *tiltul b'gufo*.

R' Shlomo Zalman Auerbach[44] proves from *Rosh* that the understanding of *tiltul b'gufo* is that it is not considered to be a *tiltul* at all. There is an *issur* of *shimush b'muktzeh* (using *muktzeh*), so how can one use the straw on the bed? He extracts from *Graz*[45] that it is only forbidden to use *muktzeh* when, while using it, one is also thereby moving it, or at least changing its form. If *tiltul b'gufo* is not considered to be *tiltul* at all, it is understood why one can lie on the straw. It is a usage without an act of "moving" *muktzeh*, and hence it is permitted.

Condensing Trash, Moving a Cell Phone

Mishnah Berurah explicitly[46] states that the understanding of *tiltul b'gufo* is that it is not an act of *tiltul*.[47] It should follow that even if in this instance kicking the *muktzeh* is the normal way of moving it, it is nonetheless permitted. Chazal never forbade any type of moving other than with one's hands.[48] It would follow that even if the normal way of compressing the

43. The other *Rishonim* explain the leniencies to remove the bundles is because of *tzaar baalei chaim*.

44. *Minchas Shlomo*, *siman* 14, section 2.

45. 509:16.

46. *Mishnah Berurah* 308:13 and *Shaar HaTzyiun*, *se'if katan* 16.

47. *Mishbetzos Zahav* in his introduction to *siman* 308, *os* 1, infers from *Beis Yosef* that there is no *heter* to move *muktzeh machmas chisaron kis*, even *b'gufo*. According to the understanding we are suggesting, this stringency has no reasoning. Even though *muktzeh machmas chisaron kis* is a stringent form of *muktzeh*, moving with one's body is not moving, so shouldn't have any restrictions. *Mishnah Berurah* (*se'if katan* 5) does imply that the leniencies of *tiltul b'gufo* and *tiltul min hatzad* do apply to *muktzeh machmas chisaron kis*. This certainly is more logical.

48. There are *poskim* (*Orchos Shabbos*, point 254) who do forbid kicking *muktzeh* when that is the normal way to move it, e.g., a ball. They must understand that even the *heter* of *tiltul b'gufo* is based on the fact that it is a deviation (*shinui*).

trash in the trash can is with your feet, one can still do so on Shabbos despite the fact that the trash inside is *muktzeh* (question #2). Many *poskim*[49] hold that even though *tiltul b'gufo* is permitted, one should only rely on this *heter* when there is a need, e.g., a loss will occur. Certainly, if one's cell phone is left outside in the rain, that's a sufficient reason to kick it inside (question #1).

Blowing Muktzeh

Maharil[50] learns another leniency from the Mishnah about moving straw from the bed. Even though we usually say *kocho k'gufo* - "one's force is like his body" regarding damages, when it comes to *muktzeh* it's different. It depends on if it's the normal way or not. Therefore, blowing *muktzeh* is another application of this *heter*.

Summary

We follow the opinion of *Rosh*, who permits moving all *muktzeh* with one's body, even for the sake of the *muktzeh*. The reason for the leniency is that it's not considered as if one is moving the *muktzeh*. Chazal only forbade moving *muktzeh* with one's hand. Therefore blowing is permitted. *Chazon Ish* is more stringent. When one is interested in moving the

---

Therefore once this is the normal way of moving the *muktzeh*, the fact that the movement is not done with one's hand is irrelevant. Alternatively, when this is the normal way to move the item, this is an act of *tiltul* because this is the movement of this item.

49. *Iggros Moshe, Orach Chaim* 5:22, point 6. There is an inference the aforementioned *Mishnah Berurah* agrees to this. The example he gives is when one kicks the *muktzeh* so that he doesn't incur a financial loss. The emphasis is that one doesn't come to lose as a result of not moving the item. If we use the understanding that we have shown, that *tiltul b'gufo* is not movement at all, the only reason to explain the caution is because *Rosh* is nearly the only opinion who permits it, while majority of the *Rishonim* don't hold of this leniency. Even though *Shulchan Aruch paskens* like *Rosh*, we should be worried for the other *Rishonim*. Also *Chazon Ish* differs in the understanding of *Rosh*.

50. Brought by *Rema* 308:4.

muktzeh, we must define the act as moving *muktzeh* and forbid this act, despite the object being moved in an unusual manner.

Answers

1. You can kick your cell phone inside if you are worried it will get ruined.
2. According to the conventional understanding of *tiltul b'gufo* this is permitted. Even though the trash is *muktzeh,* you can move *muktzeh* for its own sake with your body. Some *poskim* would be stringent in this case because condensing with your foot is the normal way to move the trash in the trash can.

Chapter 14, Part 1

בסיס

Bosis

Questions

1. I need food from the freezer, but realize that raw meat is sitting on top of the food I need. Can I take out the food I need?
2. Sarah and Rachel took their mommy's handbag out of her room. Their mommy would like to put it back, but realizes that she left small change inside. Can she move the bag?

We have seen that certain objects are *muktzeh* due to their essential nature. Either they are inherently not purposeful, or their main function is forbidden. There is another category of *muktzeh* known as *bosis*, literally meaning a "support" or "base." The Mishnah[1] teaches us that if one mistakenly placed a stone on top of a barrel of wine and now wants to access the wine, he should tilt the barrel so that the stone falls off. If one can't tilt the stone off (it is situated between other barrels), he can carry the barrel with the stone to a place where it'll be possible to tilt the stone off. As we mentioned, this is only if the stone was inadvertently placed there - but if it was placed intentionally on the barrel, the barrel is now forbidden to be moved. Even though the barrel is a *kli shemelachto l'heter*, one still can't move it. Since it is supporting the stone, it therefore becomes a *bosis* and is now *muktzeh*!

---

1. *Shabbos* 142b.

Two Approaches to Bosis

There are two basic explanations found in the *Rishonim* how to understand the *issur* of *bosis*. One approach is that the vessel that is beneath becomes secondary to the item that it is supporting; by being a support to the *muktzeh*, it itself becomes subservient to the *muktzeh*. It is now a necessary foundation for the *muktzeh* and so will get the same restrictions (*dinim*) as the *muktzeh*.[2]

A different approach is that *bosis* is an example of *haktzaas hadaas* (one's designation based on what he doesn't intent on using on Shabbos). By placing a *muktzeh* object on top of a vessel, since one knew it is forbidden to move, one is thereby showing that he doesn't intend on moving this vessel at all since the *muktzeh* is in a position that obstructs movement of the vessel.[3] A variation in presenting the second explanation is calling *bosis* "*muktzeh machmas issur tiltul.*" While the *muktzeh* is on the

---

2. *Ritva* in 142b also uses a *lashon* of *bitul* when explaining *bosis* in 123a. The *bosis* is also *muktzeh* since it's nullified by what it is supporting.

3. If one asks: Why, by placing *muktzeh* on the top, is there a *haktzaas hadaas*? Prior to an *issur bosis*, one would be allowed to move the *kli heter* when needed, or at the very least shake the *muktzeh* off via *itltul min hatzad*. Why do we say he has removed his *daas* from its use and consequently there are restrictions of *bosis*? We must say that we reckon with the present situation. Since the *kli* is presently serving the function of holding the *muktzeh*, in the current situation we see that he doesn't intend to use the *kli* for something else. Alternatively, we've discussed that the limitation of moving *muktzeh* isn't always due to a *haktzaas hadaas*; rather, once one has set aside something for specific *shimushim* (usages), e.g., *muktzeh machmas chisaron kis*, one just sets it aside from using it, and then Chazal stepped in and forbade moving the object. Here too, we see from the fact that he placed *muktzeh* on this vessel that he doesn't intend on using it in its present state. So Chazal added a prohibition in moving it. *Eshel Avraham* (Buchach) says if the way of moving something is with one's feet, even if a *muktzeh* item is placed on top of it intentionally, one can still move the item; it hasn't become a *bosis*. The logic is based on what we've explained, that since even if the item were to become *bosis*, one can still move it with his feet because of the *heter* of *tiltul b'gufo*. Therefore, the placement of the *muktzeh* causes no further *haktzaas hadaas*. A practical difference would be if one intentionally placed a *muktzeh* item on a skateboard. One can still move the skateboard it isn't a *bosis*.

vessel, one can't move the vessel. The prohibition of *tiltul* obstructs the use of this item. This is an application of *muktzeh machmas issur,* which occurs whenever there is an alternative *issur* that makes the moving of this item forbidden.

The *issur* of *bosis* remains even after the *muktzeh* has been removed from atop. This is because the reason causing this item to be *muktzeh* was present during *bein hashemashos*. The *muktzeh* status therefore remains throughout Shabbos, regardless of whether the *muktzeh* remains on top or not, since we take on that *migo d'iskatzi l'bein hashemashos, iskatzi l'chula yoma* - "if the reason for an item being *muktzeh* went away during Shabbos, the item still remains *muktzeh* because the beginning of Shabbos is the determining time of an objects status of *muktzeh*."

The Mishnah in *Beitzah*[4] writes that if the entrance to a storehouse of fruit collapses on Yom Tov (a situation wherein otherwise it was impossible to access the fruits), the fruit inside are permitted to eat. The *Rishonim* ask: Since one wasn't able to access the fruits when Yom Tov began (their access required one to perform an act of *soser* to break open the entrance), they should be *muktzeh machmas issur* (*muktzeh* because their use inevitably requires a prohibition to be breached). *Rashi* explains that since the prohibition in breaking the wall is only *mid'rabbanan,* it doesn't render the fruits *muktzeh* because one is only *maktzah daas* when the prohibition that prevents the use of this item is a Torah prohibition. A rabbinic prohibition would not result in a *muktzeh machmas issur*. *Ramban* and *Tosafos*[5] ask on *Rashi*: If *muktzeh machmas issur* does not apply to *issur d'rabbanan,* why is *bosis* forbidden? Surely it is only a *muktzeh machmas issur* on a *d'rabbanan* - moving the *muktzeh* on top is only *issur mid'rabbanan*?!

We see explicitly that *Ramban* and *Tosafos* understand the *issur* of *bosis* in accordance with the second explanation, that *bosis* is *muktzeh machmas issur,* due to the *issur* involved in moving the *muktzeh* that is on top. They understand that even with an *issur d'rabbanan* we still apply

4. 31b.

5. *Beitzah* 31b, s.v. ונפחת.

muktzeh machmas issur.[6] *Rosh*[7] lists *bosis* among his examples of *muktzeh machmas issur,* alongside items which are attached to the ground and need *issur talish* (the prohibition of uprooting) to be used and items that can't be used without capturing, i.e., transgressing *issur tzedah*. Explicitly he learns *bosis* is due to *muktzeh machmas issur.*

Rashi's Opinion

Perhaps even *Rashi* could agree that *bosis* is forbidden because it is *muktzeh machmas issur,* even though the *issur* is only a *d'rabbanan*. This is since we can distinguish between when the *issur* is external to the actual object or directly related to it. For example, the *issur* to break down the door is not directly connected to the permissibility of the fruit inside; rather, there is an external obstacle obstructing one's access. In such a case one would say that since this *issur* is only *d'rabbanan,* one is not *maktzah daas* and therefore there is no *muktzeh machmas issur.* As opposed to a case like *bosis* where the object is directly *assur,* the support item itself is forbidden to move because it involves also moving the *muktzeh* item on top. Then, even though it is only *issur mid'rabbanan,* we still invoke *muktzeh machmas issur.*

However, there are several indications that *Rashi* holds that *bosis* is considered to become *batel* (insignificant) to the *muktzeh* itself. When discussing[8] the case of the stone that was placed on top of the barrel, *Rashi* writes, "Even the barrel is *muktzeh.*" It's implicit that the support gets the same identity of *muktzeh* as the item above. Also, in reference to a candle that the Gemara says is *bosis* to the flame, *Rashi* says[9] that the candle is *tafel* (subordinate) to the *muktzeh*. This is seemingly how we explained the first option, that *bosis* is subordinate to the *muktzeh* that it is supporting. It would then follow that we have no need to limit that which *Rashi* said that there is no *muktzeh machmas issur* when the *issur* is only

6. *Rif* also explains that *bosis* is *muktzeh machmas issur.*
7. Responsa of *Rosh, siman* 22.
8. 142b.
9. 47a.

mid'rabbanan, since the reason for *bosis* has nothing to do with *muktzeh machmas issur,* and in all cases *Rashi* would hold that *muktzeh machmas issur d'rabbanan* is not forbidden. (See appendix 1 for further discussion in *Rashi*'s understanding of *bosis.*)

Intentional vs Unintentional

We mentioned earlier the stipulation that only in cases of *meini'ach* (placing), when one placed the *muktzeh* intentionally, is a *bosis* formed. While if it was שכח, forgotten, one inadvertently placed the *muktzeh* down or even if one forgot to remove it before Shabbos started from where he placed it, no *bosis* is created. *Rabbeinu Tam* understands[10] that if one placed the *muktzeh* item before Shabbos with the intention of removing it during Shabbos (he can move it via *ni'ur* or *tiltul min hatzad*), it does not become a *bosis*; rather, it has the status of forgotten. *Beis Yosef*[11] writes that *Rashi*[12] disagrees. If during *bein hashemashos* one left the *muktzeh* there but intended on removing it later on Shabbos, still it becomes *bosis.* These two opinions are brought by *Shulchan Aruch.*[13] The opinion of *Rashi* as *stam* and *Rabbeinu Tam* as some say. Based on the known rule that in such cases the halachah is like the *stam,* we must conclude that only when there is a pressing need can one be lenient to shake off the *muktzeh* if he placed it originally with the intention to remove it during Shabbos.

What is this dispute dependent upon? In *Sefer HaYashar,*[14] *Rabbeinu Tam* explains that the principle of *bosis* is dependent on *haktzaas hadaas.* By placing the *muktzeh* on a vessel, one is showing that he doesn't intend on using this *kli. Rabbeinu Tam* says that this is only true when one placed it there to remain for the duration of Shabbos, but if one intended to remove it, he evidently hasn't set aside from using the support vessel this Shabbos. *Rashi* is align with his opinion elsewhere. Since he holds that

---

10. 123a. He uses this principle to explain several difficult Gemaras.
11. 309:4, s.v. וכתב.
12. 142b, s.v. בשוכח.
13. 309:4.
14. *Simanim* 1, 2.

the *bosis* becomes secondary to the *muktzeh,* it is regardless of how long one intended on leaving it there. Since when Shabbos came in it was supporting the *muktzeh,* it became subordinate and thus received the *muktzeh* item's status. One's intention to remove it at some point on Shabbos won't change this.[15] Beautiful!

One of *Rabbeinu Tam*'s main proofs to his opinion that there is no *bosis* when one plans on removing the *muktzeh* during Shabbos is from a Gemara[16] that mentions a *heter* to remove an unripe fig that is buried under straw, or a cake-like bread that was surrounded with embers, through poking them out with a stick. The *Rishonim* ask: Since there are embers above the cake or straw above the unripe figs, why is the fig or cake not a *bosis* to the soil? *Rabbeinu Tam* answers that presumably the figs were only placed in the straw or the cake was only placed in the embers temporarily. One's intention was to take it before the end of Shabbos in order to eat it. We see from the case of this Gemara that if one intends of removing the *muktzeh* on Shabbos, the support doesn't become a *bosis.*

Baal HaMeor argues on this, explaining that the whole principle of *bosis* is that since the base is supporting the *muktzeh,* it becomes secondary to it. One needs to establish whether the base is really supporting the *muktzeh,* or whether it just happen perchance to be below the *muktzeh,* but isn't actually supporting it. The figs aren't placed to hold up the straw; on the contrary, the straw is serving the fig. So too the cake isn't holding up the embers. Since the underlying principle of *bosis* is lacking, the fig or cake doesn't become *muktzeh.* In contrast to the case of the barrel with a stone on top, we must say that it is dealing with an expensive stone that one purposely wants the barrel to support in order to protect it. In such a case, the barrel is a *bosis* since it's functioning as a support to the stone.

---

15. *Rashba* at the beginning of *Beitzah* labels cases of *shachach* as *bosis ketzas.* This phrase certainly fits better if the explanation is *tefelus.* If it's supporting the *muktzeh,* it gets the same *dinim* as it. So even in *shachach* there is some *tefelus.* To the on looker it looks like the *kli* is supporting the *muktzeh,* while according to *haktzaas hadaas,* in cases of *shachach* there is no *haktzaas hadaas* at all, so why is it even *bosis ketzas?*

16. 123a.

According to *Rabbeinu Tam* that *bosis* is dependent on *haktzaas hadaas,* this distinction shouldn't bear any significance, since even if the support is not aimfully holding up the *muktzeh,* the positioning of the *muktzeh* still shows that one doesn't intend on moving the support and we assume there is *haktzaas hadaas.*[17] (See appendix 2 for elaboration on these two ways of understanding *bosis.*)

Happenstance Bosis

Terumas HaDeshen[18] was asked: If several items were placed on top of each other in a chest, but there is no specific interest in any specific item being on top of anything else, would this be considered a case of a placed item that would subsequently have limitations of *bosis* were the upper object to be *muktzeh*? This is known among the *poskim* as *bosis b'akrai* - there is something supporting another item, but only in a haphazard manner. Stacking items inside a freezer or fridge, occasionally without specific intention for which foods go above or below, is a common application of this principle.

The questioner holds that it doesn't become *bosis,* supporting his leniency from *Rashi,*[19] who, when explaining a case of a forgotten item writes, ששכח האבן עליה בין השמשות **ולא מדעת** - "He forgot the stone on top when Shabbos began and *he wasn't aware.*" These final two words of *Rashi* are seemingly superfluous. Surely it's obvious that if one forgot a stone on the barrel, it's without any intention. It must be that whenever there is no specific intent for the *muktzeh* item to be on top, even if he didn't forget

---

17. Both *Maharsha* 44b, s.v. בא"ד כגון, and R' Akiva Eiger make a calculation that *Tosafos* holds in the case of *maos al mitah* (when you placed money on a bed): Even if you placed the money on the bed with the intention to take it off, the bed becomes a *bosis.* Neither present an answer. Maybe the answer is that there is an extra criteria that it be *mochach* (clear) from the scenario that one intends on removing the *muktzeh.* It is not *mochach* that money on a bed is going to be taken off anytime soon. It could be left there for a while, so *al menas l'salek* doesn't remove the *bosis* status.

18. Section 2, *siman* 193.

19. 142b, s.v. שוכח.

the item, it doesn't become a *bosis*. Instead, since he didn't intend for any specific order, it'll be considered like a forgotten item.

Terumas HaDeshen argues that there is no conclusive proof from *Rashi*. Rather, all *Rashi* intends on saying is it can only be considered a true case of a forgotten item when one forgot that he placed the item there before the onset of Shabbos. In such a case it does not become *bosis*. However, in this scenario, where on the eve of Shabbos he placed the items haphazardly in the chest, and he knows that one item is above another despite that he may not have any interest in this order of placement, since he's aware that there is a situation of *bosis*, this would *not* be a case of a forgotten item. *Terumas HaDeshen* adds the key words: גם החפץ נעשה מוקצה מפני שמקצה דעתו ממנו - "The support *becomes muktzeh because one has removed it from his mind,*" meaning since it is currently a support and one is aware of that, he doesn't intend on moving it.[20]

Perhaps we can explain this dispute with the two explanations behind *bosis*. The questioner who was lenient learned like *Rashi* and *Baal HaMeor*, that it is dependent on whether the support becomes secondary to the *muktzeh*. Here we are applying it in a new manner. Since one didn't purposely intend on the *kli* below to be holding up the *muktzeh*, it cannot be considered as supporting the upper object. Hence it will be akin to a forgotten item and not *bosis*. *Terumas HaDeshen* explicitly writes like *Tosafos*, that it is dependent on *haktzaas hadaas* and it's irrelevant whether the vessel is purposely supporting the *muktzeh* or it is only a haphazard placement. As long as one is aware that it is in such a position, he is *maktzah daas*.

Taz[21] and *Magen Avraham*[22] argue whom we *pasken* like. *Magen Avraham* sides with the questioner, while *Taz* implies that he holds like *Terumas HaDeshen*. Question #1, where one needs to take food out

---

20. *Terumas HaDeshen* does agree that if one placed items in a chest without a specific order a long time before Shabbos, and before Shabbos he no longer remembers what's actually on top of what, this is considered *shachach*, even though he intentionally placed it in that location originally.

21. 309, point 1.

22. 309, point 6.

of a freezer but there is *muktzeh* food lying on top, e.g., raw meat, is subject to this dispute, but only to one who doesn't have a specific arrangement in his freezer. One who has a specific order in his freezer will be prohibited to take the food, since he made the food a support to the *muktzeh*.

When the Muktzeh Is Insignificant

Mishnah Berurah[23] brings from *Chayei Adam* a new *heter* in *bosis*. If one has a few pennies in a drawer, even though they are *muktzeh*, due to their lack of value and importance, the drawer does not become a *bosis* to it. *Bosis* is only when something is supporting something else of value or significance. The source for this is found in *Tosafos*.[24] The Gemara[25] says that one can carry a cup that has leftover wine and bread inside, despite that it is disgusting and therefore *muktzeh machmas meyus*. We see that these leftovers don't render the cup *bosis*. *Tosafos* explains that since leftovers are so insignificant, the important cup cannot be considered nullified to these *muktzeh* scraps.

Rashba[26] explains why Beis Hillel permits one to lift a table with leftovers on it, and why the table is not a *bosis* to the leftover shells and pits that are now left on it: אבל עצמות וקליפים דלא חשיבי ...אין להם תורת בסיס....ולא להצניעם מחמת חשיבותן - "Bones and shells that are not significant do not have the halachos of *bosis*..." *Chayei Adam* therefore applies this principle to small change left in a drawer, namely that if one left a few pennies in a drawer, it won't be a *bosis*. However, if one specifically wants the money to be stored in this drawer even though they are of little value, he has now attached importance to this drawer storing the money and therefore it will become a *bosis*. *Mishnah Berurah*'s application of this *heter* is when one placed some coins in his pocket or on the table: דאין אדם מבטל שולחנו ובגדו בשביל איזה פרוטות - "One doesn't nullify his pants or table for the sake of a few coins."

23. 310:30.
24. *Shabbos* 47a, s.v. בגלילא שנו.
25. 47a.
26. *Beitzah* 2a.

Question #2 is based on this leniency. If the mother doesn't normally store lose change in her handbag, but rather in a wallet, if there is only small change lying in the bag it is not a *bosis,* even if she knew before Shabbos that the money was there.

Summary

A non-*muktzeh* item can become *muktzeh* (*bosis*) if one intentionally places a *muktzeh* item on top as a support. The *bosis* will have the same status as the *muktzeh* item that it supports, either because (1) it is now subordinate to the *muktzeh* and therefore is nullified by the *muktzeh,* or (2) now that one can't move this lower item, since the *muktzeh* is infringing on it, the non-*muktzeh* becomes *muktzeh machmas issur* (due to *haktzaas hadaas*). When one mistakenly left the *muktzeh* in a position where it is a support to the non-*muktzeh,* it doesn't become a *bosis.* There is an opinion that holds that even if one purposely placed the item in that position but intends on removing it before the end of Shabbos, it also doesn't become a *bosis.*

Many practical differences are based on the two aforementioned ways of explaining *bosis.* For example, there is a dispute whether *bosis* applies in cases when one only haphazardly placed the *muktzeh* on top of the non-*muktzeh,* but there is no specific intention regarding which item should serve the other.

Answers

1. If you have no specific order how you place items in his freezer then it would be subject to the dispute whether *bosis* applies when the placing of the *muktzeh* was haphazard. *Mishnah Berurah*[27] is lenient that it is not *bosis,* but does recommend when there is not a great need to be stringent.

---

27. 309:19.

2. *Muktzeh* items that are insignificant don't render the supporting *kli* a *bosis*. If the lady normally leaves lose coins in her handbag, they have importance and this is their normal location, so they will impact the handbag. If she generally doesn't leave coins in her bag, the forgotten coins in the bag don't render the bag *bosis*.

Part 2

בסים בפמוטות

Bosis by Candlesticks

Question

1. Does placing a ring on a candle tray enable me to move the tray once the candles have been extinguished?

The Gemara[28] explains that a candle can't be moved since it is a *bosis*. A flame is *muktzeh*, which renders the wick that supports it a *bosis* and hence *muktzeh*. In turn, the oil that supports the wick becomes *muktzeh*, and finally the candlestick that supports it all also becomes *muktzeh*.

In ancient times, the custom was to have a lower tablecloth on which the challah and the rest of tableware lay upon. In addition to this, in order to cover the challah there was another tablecloth (that extended along the length of the table, unlike modern-day challah covers). The candles were generally placed on top of this upper tablecloth. Upon completion of the meal, one would remove the upper tablecloth, even though it should be

28. 44a.

a *bosis* due to the candles that were resting on top when Shabbos began.[29]

Shulchan Aruch[30] brings an opinion that placing a non-*muktzeh* item, e.g., bread, on the candlesticks before Shabbos would enable one to move them. *Shulchan Aruch* himself argues that the bread does not cause the candlestick to lose its *bosis* status, so he is stringent not to remove the tablecloth. This is because we say that the oil/flame is more important than the bread, and therefore we consider the bread to be insignificant relative to the oil, and therefore we still treat the candle as a support to the *muktzeh*. What is the basis for those who are lenient?

There is a concept known as: *bosis l'davar ha'mutar v'davar ha'assur* - "a support of two items, one permissible and one not permissible," i.e., *muktzeh*. This is when the vessel below is supporting more than one item on top. When the non-*muktzeh* items are more important in value or importance relative to the *muktzeh* items, we say that the support item, despite carrying both items, is predominantly a *bosis l'davar heter* and is therefore permitted. The reasoning is that we determine what the base is supporting solely based upon the principal item that is on top. The less important items are viewed as insignificant, to the extent that the base is not considered to be supporting them at all. Hence it becomes only a *bosis l'davar ha'mutar.*[31]

The lenient opinion must hold that when the candlesticks are sup-

---

29. *Pri Megadim* understands that only the area of the tablecloth that the candles are standing on becomes a *bosis*. The rest of the tablecloth is not *muktzeh*. He nevertheless says that if challah is placed on the tablecloth, the entire tablecloth can be moved. Surely he should be consistent and view only the area of the table where the challah is sitting to be considered a *bosis l'heter,* but how can he permit the whole tablecloth? Perhaps, generally we view the whole tablecloth as a support to that which is above it. When the *muktzeh* is only a specific area of the tablecloth and the rest of the tablecloth can be used, since it has a use that is independent to the part of the tablecloth that is covered, that vacant part doesn't become a *bosis*. When the tablecloth has two items resting on it, to determine what the tablecloth is supporting, you follow the regular criteria, i.e., which item is more important. אכתי צ"ע.

30. 279:3.

31. *Tosafos HaRid* 142a is the only *Rishon* whom we find disagrees to this principle, ע"ש.

porting both the bread and the oil, we consider it primarily a support to the bread, since the bread relative to the oil is the more important. If the bread outweighs the oil, then candlesticks remain just a *kli shemelachto l'issur*, which can be moved *l'tzorech mekomo*. Hence they could remove the candlesticks to take off the tablecloth below.[32]

Rivash[33] explains that it is insufficient to permit moving a candlestick by placing bread on it. He argues that we measure the value of the non-*muktzeh* against the oil and the wick. The oil and the wick are presently more important than the bread, since they are an essential part of the Shabbos candles that one needs greatly. This purpose of having Shabbos candles - in other words, light in the house - is more important than the bread, albeit one also needs it for his mitzvah of the Shabbos meal. Therefore, even though the candlestick would be a *bosis l'davar ha'mutar v'davar ha'assur*, it is still forbidden to move because when Shabbos began one needed the flame, wick, and oil, so the candle's status is determined as a *bosis l'davar ha'assur*.

Magen Avraham has a different reason why the placing of the non-*muktzeh* bread wouldn't help. A vessel that is specifically designed to support certain things cannot be considered as supporting something which it isn't designed to naturally support, even if the other object is of great value. Candlesticks are the perfect example. They are designated to support oil, wicks, and a flame. The candlestick is naturally a *bosis* to them, and it therefore won't help putting something, even of a much higher value, on top.

The *poskim* say, following this understanding, that even if one puts a wedding ring on top of a tray that is specifically designed and created to hold candlesticks (question #1), it would not enable him to move this tray even once the candles go out. Even if the tray is insignificant relative to the diamond ring, since it is a tray that's only meant to hold candlesticks, it's only considered to be truly supporting the candlesticks. By extension, the candle/oil and flame would cause the tray to be a *bosis l'issur* to the

32. An alternative explanation what this opinion holds is based on the principle of stipulating on *muktzeh*. We will elaborate on this in chapter 24.
33. Responsa *Rivash, siman* 93.

candlestick and its accessories. However, the ring that's also been placed on the tray doesn't cause the tray to now be considered as holding a ring, despite its higher value.

A practical difference *l'halachah* between *Rivash* and *Magen Avraham* would be if one has candlesticks as well as other items on his Shabbos table. According to the *Rivash,* since at *bein hashemashos* the most important thing is that one's candles are lit, the table is considered predominantly supporting the fire and can't be moved. While *Magen Avraham* [34] explicitly permits such a case, this is since a table isn't naturally a support for the candles more than for the other items. *Mishnah Berurah* [35] holds like *Magen Avraham,* that if there is bread that you'll be using for your *hamotzi* or wine for Kiddush on the table, they are more important than the candlesticks and the table will therefore be considered a *bosis l'heter.* [36]

We can be lenient only regarding moving a table or even a standard tray that does not have a specific purpose to be a candlestick tray. However, a tray that's specifically designated for Shabbos candles will naturally be a *bosis* for the candles, and placing a ring on it won't help to remove this *bosis l'issur.*

R' Meshulam Igra [37] makes an important observation. According to the opinion of *Rabbeinu Tam,* that if one's intention is to remove the *muktzeh* during Shabbos, then this support doesn't become *bosis,* similarly, if one is coming to prevent a *bosis* by placing a non-*muktzeh* item on it, he must intend on leaving this on the support for the entire Shabbos. It follows that if one's intention is to eat the bread he has placed on the table, then the bread can't offset the candles. The table won't be considered a *bosis l'heter* since he will remove the *heter.*

---

34. 277:8.

35. *Se'if katan* 10.

36. *Pri Megadim* goes as far to say that even other items, not even vital mitzvah-related ones, that one needs can render the table a *bosis l'heter.* This is not like our understanding of *Rivash,* that the oil and wick have importance because one needs the candle to be light for the mitzvah at *bein hashemashos.*

37. Responsa *Orach Chaim, siman* 7.

However, this *chiddush* seems to be difficult to concur with the following Gemara.[38] The Gemara permits one to move a basket of fruit with a stone inside, since we consider the basket to be a *bosis* only for the fruit, due to their importance relative to the stone. Surely the case is where he intends on eating the fruit inside, resulting in the basket just being a *bosis l'issur* and yet we see that it's a classic example of *bosis l'issur v'heter* where the *heter* outweighs the *issur* and is thus permitted.[39]

We see that R' Meshulam's halachah is contradicted from the Gemara, but how can we refute his logic? *Rabbeinu Tam* holds that *bosis* is dependent on *haktzaas hadaas*. We generally say that one's *daas* is fixed at the beginning of *bein hashemashos*, therefore when one places a permitted item even with intention that it subsequently be removed, since at the beginning of Shabbos the base is providing support for the *heter* one doesn't set aside this vessel from being moved, irrelevant that he may later take it off. Therefore, even if the bread will be taken off the table, it is not a *bosis*.

Rashba[40] asks: According to *Rabbeinu Tam*, that *daas* to remove the *muktzeh* on Shabbos cannot create a *bosis*. So why does a flame render the candle *bosis*? Surely, he doesn't intend on the flame remaining for the entire Shabbos, so it should be treated like a forgotten item. *Beis Meir*[41] answers that this case is intrinsically different from every other case where he intends on removing the *muktzeh*. With the candle, for the entire existence of the flame he intends on leaving it on the candlesticks. However, in regular cases, he intends on removing the *muktzeh* while the *muktzeh* is resting upon the *kli*. This idea can be coined *l'olamo shel hashalheves* - the candle will remain a support for the lifetime of the *muktzeh*. (*Tosefes Shabbos*[42] adds that when one intends to move the *muktzeh* on Shabbos,

---

38. 142a.

39. *Orchos Shabbos* writes that if one eats all the bread, it is considered as if the bread were on the table all of Shabbos, because that is the *l'olam* of the bread. According to this we can refute our proof. If one is consuming the fruit, this is considered that the fruit was there all of Shabbos.

40. *Beitzah* 2b.

41. 309.

42. 277:5.

he is stating that he doesn't want the support to be nullified by the *muktzeh*. But since he is leaving the flame on the candle for the duration of its existence, he wants it to be nullified.)

Alternatively, in instances such as *gizin* (insulators), once the *muktzeh* is removed from the pot, retroactively we see that the vessel never became a *bosis* for the *muktzeh*. One never intended that this pot actually be a support for the *muktzeh*. However, we never see that the candle was not retroactively a *bosis* for the flame because it is not as a result of one's action that the flame is no longer resting above.[43]

Summary

Candlesticks, despite being a *kli shemelachto l'issur*, are forbidden to move under any circumstance because they were a *bosis* for the flame, wick, and oil. The *poskim* argue whether it is sufficient to offset the *bosis* by placing bread on the candlesticks, rendering the candlesticks a *bosis l'davar ha'mutar v'davar ha'assur* which primarily is for the permitted item. *Shulchan Aruch* is stringent because one needs to keep candles alight, and therefore the flame is the more important item. Placing the candlesticks on a tray with an expensive ring on the tray to facilitate moving the candlesticks is not a suggested alternative, since a tray that is made to be a support for the *muktzeh* is naturally a *bosis* to the *muktzeh*, and even an expensive item won't offset the *muktzeh* status. When the support is holding both *muktzeh* and non-*muktzeh* items, there are various factors to determine which item the base is considered to be chiefly supporting in order to determine whether it is *bosis* or not. The solution is to measure which of the two items are more important.

---

43. This *sevara* is built upon *Tosafos Beitzah* 31b, s.v. ונפתח בא״ד ואמר הרב משה... *Tosafos* is distinguishing when we do and don't say *migo d'iskatzi* by *muktzeh machmas issur*. *Tosafos* differentiate when the *issur* is eradicated entirely to when the *issur* just moves from this item, e.g., *tevel*. Once one wrongly tithed the produce, the *issur tevel* is eradicated while *muktzeh* that is resting of an item. Even once has shaken off the *muktzeh* from the base, we still see the *muktzeh* lying next to it. וע״ש.

Answer

1. It won't help placing a ring on a candle tray to enable one to move the tray. The tray is made to support the candles and so it is naturally *bosis* to the candlesticks.

Part 3

מוכני

An Undercarriage

Questions

1. Something fell under the night table. Can I move the table in order to pick it up?
2. I need to go somewhere for *shalosh seudos*, but have to be back home right after Shabbos. Can I put my bus pass in my pocket and carry it (in a place with an *eiruv*), so I'll be able to take the bus home right away?
3. I drove to a function hall just before Shabbos and realized there was no safe place to leave my car keys overnight. Can I leave them in your pocket and carry them home?

Early *poskim* discuss the question regarding *muktzeh* items that are found in one's pocket. This is obviously connected to *bosis*, but there is an additional *sugya* that is relevant to this question. The Mishnah[44] discusses the halachos relevant to a *muchani* (wheel) that is part of a *shidah*

44. *Keilim* 18:2. Discussed in *Shabbos* 44b.

(carriage). The carriage was for storing items, while the wheel also had an area that could be used to store money.[45]

The Mishnah[46] says that if the wheel is *nishmeses* (detachable), the wheel and carriage are considered two individual items. Since the wheel is treated as a separate item, if one placed money on this wheel, it causes the wheel to become a *bosis* to the money. The wheel's status of being a *bosis* now forbids moving the carriage, since one will thereby be indirectly moving the wheel, which is *muktzeh*.[47]

Tosafos explains, however, that when the wheels are fixed on, since they are considered as one with the carriage, the carriage can be moved despite the money placed on the wheel. This is because the wheel is only a peripheral, insignificant part of this item, and therefore won't affect the item's general status. The carriage is a *kli shemelachto l'heter* and can be

---

45. The *Rishonim* argue what exactly a *muchani* is. However, there is little difference between the two explanations. *Rashi* explains that it's the wheel of a carriage, which had an area in it where they would place the money. The *Rishonim* bring the explanation of Rabbeinu Ephraim, that the *muchani* is the base of the carriage. It was normal for the carriage to have non-*muktzeh* items inside it. Therefore, if *muktzeh* is resting on the *muchani*, depending on different variables, the carriage is considered to be a *bosis* to *heter* and *issur*. For ease we will always explain the way *Rashi* explains.

Important note: Everything that we will explain is based on *Magen Avraham*'s conclusion in the *sugya*, since this is usually how *Mishnah Berurah paskens*. However, we'll try to expand on different ideas in the footnotes.

46. *Keilim* 18:2.

47. *Chazon Ish* (44:5) explains that there is no *heter* of *tiltul min hatzad* (moving indirectly) because it's considered טמה"צ לצורך דבר האסור. Since you are interested in the wheels' movement, they assist the movement of the carriage. Therefore, even though it is not possible to do *ni'ur* (shake the money out), moving the carriage is not permitted. The problem with this explanation is that it doesn't fit with *Magen Avraham*'s understanding that *tiltul min hatzad* is permitted when it is for the sake of using the *muktzeh* in a permissible manner. (See chapter 13 for an elaboration on this. *Chazon Ish* argues on this *Magen Avraham*, so *Chazon Ish* is *l'shitaso*.) Another reason why it is not *tiltul min hatzad* is that since each part serves a purpose for the other part, regarding *tiltul* we view it as one *kli*. Moving the *shidah* is also moving the *muchani*.

moved freely. Yet the wheel itself can't be moved on its own because it is a *bosis.*[48] [49]

To recap, if the wheel is firmly attached, the carriage can be moved - but the wheel cannot. However, if the wheel is not firmly attached, the carriage can't be moved because the wheel is considered a part of the carriage.

A Bedside Table

A practical example of where *muchani* is relevant nowadays is a bedside table (question #1).[50] It is comparable to a *muchani,* in that the surface of the chest is like the carriage and the drawers are like the wheels.[51] If

48. *Mishnah Acharonah* (*Keilim* 18:2) argues that even the wheel can be moved. He says the distinction whether the wheel is fixed or detachable has no bearing on the fact that the carriage is predominantly a *bosis l'heter,* so the point of contention is never the carriage itself, rather just the wheel. When the Gemara is lenient in the case where the wheel is fixed, it's in reference to moving the actual wheel. The logic in this is because the wheel loses its own identity and takes on the same identity as the carriage. This argument is an explicit *machlokes Rishonim* in the *sugya.* They argue if when the Gemara says, "you can move it" whether it is referring to the wheel or the carriage. *Ramban* and *Ritva* learn that it's referring to the wheel, but the carriage can always be moved, like *Mishnah Acharonah. Meyuchas LaRan* and *Rashba* explain like the explanation brought by *Magen Avraham,* that if the wheel is detachable even the carriage can't be moved.

49. *Nishmas Adam* 67:4 brings down that *Rosh* holds that even when it is permitted to move the *muchani,* i.e., when it is considered not a *bosis l'davar ha'assur,* since it is also supporting the carriage, which is non-*muktzeh,* the *shidah* is still forbidden to move. It seemingly makes no sense: How can the wheel, which is the actual item holding the *muktzeh,* be more lenient than the item that isn't storing the money? *Nishmas Adam* makes an *okimta* to explain Rosh, ועי"ש תירוצו. *Minchas Ariel* suggests that since the *muchani* is nullified by the *shidah,* one is allowed to move the *muchani,* as it now has the status of the *shidah.* However, when you move the *shidah,* the *muchani* is viewed as part of this *shidah.* Therefore the *shidah* is considered to have *muktzeh* on part of it. So moving the *shidah* is considered to be moving the *muktzeh.* צ"ע.

50. This is all based on the conclusions of *Magen Avraham* (above) and *Mishnah Berurah* (end of 308:31).

51. According to *Rambam* (*Keilim* 18:2, translation of "*kapach*") we don't even need to compare it to a drawer. *Rambam* explains that *muchani* is a chest of drawers and distinguishes exactly like we will explain, whether the drawer can be removed

there is a *muktzeh* item inside one of the drawers, whether the drawers are fixed into the chest or not will determine whether one can move the bedside table. This is similar to the distinction with *muchani,* where we say that if the wheels are detachable then the *muktzeh* lying on the wheel will cause it to become a *bosis* and thus forbid moving the entire *kli.*

Drawers that can slide in and out remain a separate vessel. Therefore, since the drawer is a *bosis* to the *muktzeh* one can't move the bedside table too. Since the table is supporting this drawer that is *muktzeh,* the table has in turn become *muktzeh.*[52] If there are important non-*muktzeh* items on top of the bedside table or in a different drawer, they will stop this chest from becoming a *bosis,* as it is now a *bosis* to *heter* and *issur.* However, if the drawers are fixed to the chest, they are considered a peripheral part of the chest. Therefore, despite there being *muktzeh* in the drawer, the status of the drawer doesn't impact the chest. The chest can therefore be moved even if the table is not supporting any other non-*muktzeh.*[53] [54]

---

or not. This explanation of *Rambam* is quite significant (i.e., it could have bearing on the halachah) since *Aruch HaShulchan* (*siman* 13) says we can't compare *muchani* to a set of drawers. I think what *Aruch HaShulchan* asks on this approach is: Both according to *Rashi* and Rabbeinu Ephraim the *muchani* is essential to the moving of the *shidah.* Either it is the wheels or it is the base. When one moves the carriage, one is interested in moving the *muchani,* hence it would be *assur* In all cases, when one moves the carriage, the moving of the wheels is attributed to him. In contrast, the drawers have no function to the moving of the table/chest. Even if the drawer itself is *muktzeh,* one can move the table because the moving of the drawer is not attributed to this act of moving. One is not interested in the drawers moving. It's just coincidental that they move as well. *Rambam* obviously took on that this distinction isn't true. The question is how to answer the question of *Aruch HaShulchan.* Based on *Chazon Ish* we brought in note 99, it is a very sound distinction?! וצ"ע.

52. On this point, this case is more severe than the *shidah.* Even if one can't move the *shidah,* it's only because it is considered *tiltul min hatzad* of the wheel, but the *shidah* itself does not become *muktzeh.* However, the chest is supporting the drawers, therefore the chest will become *muktzeh.* Even according to *Mishnah Acharonah* in note 100, who permits the wheel to be moved, he should agree that the table is a *bosis* to the drawer.

53. In a case where the drawer is attached, whether one can open the drawer itself or not would be subject to the dispute brought in note 100.

54. *Rashba* brings the opinion of Rabbeinu Ephraim, who holds that it is only per-

Most drawers nowadays have some type of release mechanism. Is this comparable to a removable drawer, or a fixed one? If the principle behind being "attached" is that we can consider it to be *batel* (part of) the chest, while something that can be detached can't be viewed as an intrinsic part of the chest, surely we should treat our drawers as "attached." This is because even though it is *possible* to take out the drawers, they are not designed to be used by placing them in and out. A drawer that comes out in the course of its use can't be an intrinsic part of the chest, but this logic wouldn't apply to these drawers.

However, the modern-day *poskim* hold that these drawers are considered as if they are "detached." They understand that absolute physical attachment is required to make it one unit. According to these *poskim*, if one needs to move his bedside table, one must be aware what is stored inside the drawers. If there are valuables that are *muktzeh machmas chisaron kis*, e.g., a camera or money, one can't move the table. (However, according to our logic, there is room to be lenient.)

It's important to note that this comparison between a *muchani* and a chest of drawers is only if the main purpose of the chest is the surface on top, because only then do we considered the drawers nullified to the table. (Otherwise the main vessel is the drawer, and we must judge the drawer in isolation.) *Mishnah Berurah*[55] refers to a table that had drawers. A table main's function is certainly the surface on top. Similarly, the main use of a woman's dresser with drawers, is the dresser's surface. However,

---

missible to move the *shidah* with the attached wheel when the carriage is also storing non-*muktzeh* inside, so it is a *bosis davar mutar v'davar assur*. Accordingly, he will require the chest to have something on top more important than the *muktzeh* inside the drawer. *Mishnah Berurah* entertains that maybe the drawer itself is considered a non-*muktzeh* item if it is not always used for storing the *muktzeh* item. However, the *poskim* don't bring this opinion of Rabbeinu Ephraim and so we don't need non-*muktzeh* on the chest.

On the same note, *Rashba* can answer the question of *Nishmas Adam*: Why is the wheel not considered a *bosis* for the money and the carriage? It should be *mutar*. On *Shabbos* 142a he answers that money is always considered more important.

55. 310:35.

children's drawers that store toys aren't comparable to *muchani,* since their main function is the storage of each drawer, not the surface on top.

Money in Your Pocket

A second practical example learned from *muchani* that the *poskim*[56] discuss is when one has money in his pants pocket. Do the pants become a *bosis* or not? *Rema*[57] permits moving pants even if money was left in the pocket. *Magen Avraham* distinguishes between different types of pockets: If the pocket is an entirely separate pouch that's sewn onto the garment, this can be considered a separate entity and thus subject to the *din* of *muchani,* and this is what *Rema* permits. However, a pocket that is only an opening in the garment, and its fabric is that of the main garment, would not have a separate identity and would in all cases render the entire garment a *bosis* were there to be *muktzeh* in this pocket.

R' Shlomo Zalman Auerbach[58] says that nowadays our pants pockets are similar to the pockets that *Rema* permits - no fabric of the main body of the pants is part of the pocket; the pocket is a completely separate entity. This is comparable to the carriage with *muktzeh* on its wheel - there is a main vessel, the pants, and the *muktzeh* is found on a peripheral part, the pocket. Therefore *bosis* doesn't apply since the *muktzeh* in the pocket is insufficient to forbid the main garment, i.e., the pants, similar to the *muktzeh* on the wheel that doesn't forbid the main carriage.[59]

---

56. *Shulchan Aruch* 310.

57. 310:7.

58. *Shemiras Shabbos K'Hilchasah,* ch. 20, note 241.

59. *Graz* (310:4) says that one can move pants with money in its pocket because it is *tiltul min hatzad l'tzorech davar ha'mutar,* indirect movement for the sake of a permissible item. He understands that even if the pocket is considered separate to the pants, one is still considered to be moving the money inside. To address this problem, he explains it is *tiltul min hatzad.* (This can also be the explanation why when the wheel is *einah nishmetes* one can move the carriage — because the money is only being moved *tiltul min hatzad* — while in cases when the wheel becomes *muktzeh* the *tiltul min hatzad* is for the sake of the *muktzeh.*)

Our shirt pockets are different. Since the main body of the shirt is itself part of the pocket, we can't view the shirt and the pocket separately. Hence if the pocket is a *bosis l'issur*, so too the shirt is considered a *bosis l'issur*.[60]

Rema warns that even if the pants are not a *bosis*, one still shouldn't wear pants that have *muktzeh* inside because one may come to leave his house and transgress *hotzaah*. Nowadays, in places where there is an *eiruv* it is debatable whether such a worry applies. It can be argued that there is still a worry that one might come to take it outside the *eiruv*.[61] The counterargument is that is a different worry to what *Rema* said to be worried for, so we have no proof that there should be such a safeguard in place. If we take a lenient stance, that there is no such worry in a neighborhood that has a *eiruv*, it follows that it would be permitted before Shabbos to put money or a bus pass in one's pocket if he needs to walk somewhere on Shabbos and wants to take a taxi or bus home (question #2).

Ni'ur in Cases of Muchani

Magen Avraham[62] explains, in cases of *muchani* where it would be permitted to move the main vessel despite *muktzeh* resting on a peripheral part, that the rule we usually apply before moving the *bosis l'issur v'heter* - that one must do *ni'ur* to preempt *tiltul min hatzad* - *wouldn't apply*. He says that the moving of the *muktzeh* in these cases is an even lower level of *tiltul* than *tiltul min hatzad*, and no requirement of *ni'ur* applies. However, *Mishnah Berurah*[63] brings from *Rambam* that even in such cases one must do *ni'ur*.[64]

---

60. *Mishnah Acharonah* based on his principle, discussed in note 100, says that even a shirt pocket will not impact the status of the actual shirt. However, one can hear an argument that even according to his principles the shirt will still be forbidden to move. Since we are explaining that the shirt is *muktzeh* because of regular *bosis l'issur*, the *sugya* of *muchani* would no longer be relevant.

61. *Orchos Shabbos* advocates such an argument.

62. 310:7.

63. 310:30.

64. This point is subject to a wide dispute. R' Akiva Eiger is *medayek* from *Rashba* that only in regular cases of *bosis* is there a *chiyuv ni'ur*, but not in cases of *muchani*.

If *l'chatchilah* we need to be *machmir* for *Rambam*, then do we lose this aforementioned leniency to place *muktzeh* in one's pocket before Shabbos, since before one moves the pants he has to shake the *muktzeh* out? The Mishnah[65] explicitly writes that the obligation of *ni'ur* is only when it is possible to shake off the *muktzeh*. When it is not possible, there is no obligation to shake off the *muktzeh*. The classic examples of when it is not possible to shake off the *muktzeh* is when there is no space to tilt it off physically. What if one can physically shake the *muktzeh*, but shaking it will damage the *muktzeh*? Is that rendered "not possible" to be subject to a dispensation? *Beis Meir*[66] and R' Akiva Eiger[67] argue over this. R' Akiva Eiger, is lenient.[68]

Perhaps we can be lenient to permit those who take their cars to shul before Shabbos and are afraid to leave their car keys behind in case of theft (question #3) to place their keys in their pants pockets before Shabbos. Since it isn't possible to do *ni'ur* in the shul, as otherwise they may be stolen, we can allow them to leave it in the keys pockets until they get home! However, placing a bus pass would not be ideal because according to *Rambam* one must shake it out before wearing the pants. If it is very important, under pressing circumstances one can rely on *Magen Avraham*.

Practically this *heter* is very questionable. R' Shlomo Zalman Auerbach[69] *paskens* that since ideally one must do *ni'ur*, it is logical that it is forbidden to set up a scenario whereby one will have the requirement to

---

Ramban, *Beis Yosef*, and *Tosafos* also explain like this. *Ran*, however, writes like *Rambam*. *Tehillah L'Dovid* asks that if it is considered *tiltul min hatzad*, why is it that there is no *chiyuv ni'ur*? *Magen Avraham* subtly answers that this is an even lower level of moving the *muktzeh* than regular *tiltul min hatzad*, since it is only on a peripheral part of a vessel that you are moving.

65. 141b.

66. 310.

67. *Chiddushim* on *Shabbos* 117b.

68. The question was about someone who was staying in an inn for Shabbos and had money inside his suitcase, besides other things. He was afraid to leave the bag unattended while he left the inn to pray. He asked if he can carry the bag with him. If he shakes the money out, it will be stolen. Is he still obligated to do *ni'ur*?

69. *Shemiras Shabbos K'Hilchasah* ch. 20, note 53.

do *ni'ur* but not be able to do so.[70] Furthermore, even though we proved in chapter 13 that moving *muktzeh* in one's pocket is *tiltul min hatzad,* in this scenario one is interested in moving his pants for the sake of covering himself - *davar ha'mutar* - but is also moving the pants to have the *muktzeh* car keys with him - *davar ha'assur*. How we define one's act when one has multiple interests, whether it is *tiltul min hatzad* for the sake of the non-*muktzeh* or for the sake of the *muktzeh* item, is subject to a dispute.[71] According to the explanation we suggested in the chapter on *tiltul min hatzad,* that one's act is defined based upon his intention, then even if he has multiple intentions we attribute his act of carrying to the *muktzeh* as well. These are two further reasons to forbid placing the car keys in one's pocket.

Summary

When a vessel has various components to it and the *muktzeh* is found on a certain part of the vessel, there are several criteria to determine whether this vessel can be moved in its entirety or only certain parts can be moved, and if so which parts can be moved. When the various separate parts can be treated as a single unit, since all parts are connected and dependent upon each other, then if the *muktzeh* is found on a peripheral part of the vessel, it doesn't cause the status of the main vessel to be forbidden, and only the actual part that has the *muktzeh* resting on it would be forbidden to be moved. However, if the area where the *muktzeh* is resting on is viewed as a separate area, since that piece will become a *bosis,* one can't move even the main part if in turn one will also move the *bosis* part. An example of this is a chest with drawers or a pocket. *Muktzeh* placed in a

---

70. He extracts this from *Taz* (end of *siman* 310), who permits in a case where *muktzeh* was placed in a vessel during Shabbos to subsequently place more important non-*muktzeh* items to render this vessel a *bosis l'heter* so one can move it. R' Shlomo Zalman Auerbach infers that if the vessel had *muktzeh* that one can't shake out, one can't subsequently place non-*muktzeh* to enable one to move it. ואכתי צ"ע what his inference is.

71. *Mor U'Ketziah* 308, s.v. בעל, *Chazon Ish* 47:2 and *Tehillah L'Dovid* 277:5.

pants pocket won't affect the general status of the pants. However, there are *poskim* who hold that drawers that are attached with a pull-and-lift mechanism are considered as separate objects and thus not intrinsically part of the chest. Therefore, if *muktzeh machmas chisaron kis* is to be found inside the drawer, one can't move the chest.

Answers

1. When the *muktzeh* is sitting on top of the night table, the table is a *bosis* to the *muktzeh*. If the *muktzeh* can't be moved, then subsequently the table can't be moved either. If the *muktzeh* is inside a drawer, the drawer can't be opened. Whether it renders the whole table *bosis* depends on whether the drawer is firmly attached or not. If the drawer is detachable, the table is a *bosis*. If the drawer is firmly attached, the table is not a *bosis*.
2. Pants with *muktzeh* inside the pockets are not a *bosis* to the *muktzeh*. There is room to permit this scenario according to the *poskim* who say there is no requirement of *ni'ur* in cases of *muchani*. However, there are other factors[72] why it is recommendable not to be lenient.
3. The same answer as in number 2 applies to this question. The need to put one's keys in your pocket is presumably a much greater need and would be done to prevent a financial loss. Therefore there might be more room to be lenient. A rabbi must be consulted regarding these two questions.

72. Firstly this might be an act of preparation for a weekday which is forbidden. Secondly we discussed whether the enactment not to carry in such a way applies even in a place where there is an *eiruv*.

Part 4

מוכני במכשיר אלקטרוני
Muchani for Electronic Items

Questions

1. The water level has dropped below the water spout of the Shabbos urn. Can I tilt the urn to empty the little remaining water out?
2. I require the area that the hot plate or slow cooker is occupying. Can I move the appliance?
3. Are the new Shabbos kettles (where the kettle locks onto its base) 100 percent *mehadrin*?
4. Can I move the base of the classic Shabbos lamp?

There are two basic categories of appliances relevant to our discussion of moving electrical items: those that have a red-hot element (e.g., urn, hot plate, slow cooker) and those that don't (e.g., a fan or alarm clock). We discussed in chapter 1 whether a fan is a *kli shemelachto l'issur/heter,* but the discussion was not regarding its wires. Perhaps the electricity that runs through the wires render it *muktzeh.* However, the electric current is not something tangible and surely not relevant to *muktzeh.* Therefore the cable would not be a *bosis* to anything *muktzeh.*

There is an opinion[73] that does consider the cable as a *bosis* to the electric current since he holds that an electric current would have the same *din* as fire, which is *muktzeh machmas gufo.* However, with what we learn from *muchani,* that something that is causing a *bosis* on a peripheral area of a larger *kli* does not cause the main *kli* to become *muktzeh,* here too the *bosis*

73. *Chut Shani.*

of the cable would not affect the status of the fan. The fan is the main part of the vessel and the cable is just a peripheral part, so when the *muktzeh* is found on a side part of the vessel it doesn't impact the vessel's status. R' Shlomo Zalman Auerbach[74] holds that the cable is not *muktzeh* and writes that if the electric item is turned off, one can unplug it from the socket with a *shinui* and move it *l'tzorech gufo u'mekomo*!

Many *poskim*[75] understand that a red-hot element is halachically treated as a flame, since we aren't fully aware as to the reason why a flame is actually *muktzeh*; we only know that the Gemara says explicitly that it is, even according to Rebbe Shimon. Therefore, we consider anything that has properties similar to fire to be included in the *muktzeh* of fire. Due to this, electrical items that have an element inside would be forbidden to move since the item is a *bosis* to the element. For example, an urn is considered to be supporting a flame, so even though it is a *kli*, and should be a *kli shemelachto l'heter*, it would become *muktzeh machmas gufo*, like the flame it supports. This would be so even if the element isn't currently red hot, as long as when Shabbos began it was at this level, as we say, *migo d'iskatzi l'bein hashemashos, iskatzi l'chula yoma*.

Ritva[76] explains that when there is *muktzeh* on the handle of a ladle, *muchani* doesn't apply since the ladle and its handle is one cohesive object. *Muchani* is when there are two separate *keilim* that are functioning together as one. Accordingly, these examples of electrical appliances are inherently different from *muchani*, as they too are one unified object. We can't treat it that one part is insignificant relative to another part, since it is all one entity. Hence a different logic is necessary in order to be lenient.

---

74. *Shemiras Shabbos K'Hilchasah* 33:33.

75. In chapter 27, part 2, we will elaborate extensively on why fire is *muktzeh* and all the relevant halachos to electrical appliances and light bulbs, etc.

76. Interestingly, *Shitah LaRan* does apply the principle of *muchani* in this case and permits moving the ladle. According to *Shitah LaRan*, there could be more room for leniencies in the cases of the electrical items we are discussing, but it depends on whether the red-hot element is on a secondary part of the appliance or not. If the part with the red-hot element is secondary, we can potentially compare it to *muchani*, while if the red-hot element is the main part, the vessel is more likely to be classified as a *bosis*.

R' Moshe's Principle - Some Flames Are Not Muktzeh

There is an idea entertained in a *teshuvah* of R' Moshe Feinstein that can help us assess our cases of electrical appliances. R' Moshe,[77] while discussing the use of an electric blanket on Shabbos, says that before assessing *bosis* we must determine what the electrical coils are. He says the reason why a flame is *muktzeh* is because it is not a vessel. However, even if the coils have a red-hot element that resembles fire, that still doesn't necessitate it is *muktzeh* like a *shalheves*. These electric coils are a vessel. One uses them to turn the blanket on and off, so they have a status as *kli shemelachto l'issur*. Therefore, even if we treat the blanket as a *bosis* to the coils, the blanket is only a *kli shemelachto l'issur* and can be moved *l'tzorech gufo u'mekomo*.

We can use this principle to permit moving several electric appliances, e.g., a hot plate (question #1 and #2). We wouldn't view it as a sheet of metal that supports a fire and as a *bosis* to fire; rather, a hot plate supports a vessel that is made for heating items and so is a *kli shemelachto l'issur*. Similarly, an urn isn't treated as a vessel that is supporting fire; it's a vessel that at worse is supporting an electrical heating vessel, which would render the urn a *kli shemelachto l'issur*. Therefore, in the event that something fell behind an urn or a hot plate, one can move them.[78]

The new Shabbos kettle (question #3) functions like a regular kettle, but in order to use it on Shabbos it is locked onto its base. Even once the water has boiled, it's kept on its base for the duration of Shabbos. It keeps the water hot by periodically reheating the water. Although this invention has solved the issue of boiling the water on Shabbos, since the boiling is not connected to one's action in any way, there are some who question their usage due to *muktzeh*. Since the element is inside the kettle, the kettle is a *bosis* to this, so one can't move the kettle to pour the water, rendering

---

77. *Iggros Moshe, Orach Chaim* 3:50.

78. Even though from the point of view of *muktzeh* one would be able to move the urn, there is another *issur* in tilting the urn. R' Shlomo Zalman Auerbach (*Shemiras Shabbos K'Hilchasah*, p. 22) brings from the *Yerushalmi* that there is a *gezeirah* to empty out all the water lest one come to refill it, which is forbidden due to the prohibition of cooking involved in heating water.

this invention useless. However, according to R' Moshe, the red-hot element inside is treated as a vessel in its own right, so the kettle on its own is treated as a *kli shemelachto l'heter*. Now that it is supporting the base, it becomes a *kli shemelachto l'issur* and one can be lenient to use this new kettle.

Similarly, with the invention of the Shabbos lamp (question #4) (a lamp on a stand that supports the bulb, with a cylindrical covering that slides around the casing of the box where the light sits. This cover is moved around depending on how much light you want), there were those who wished to forbid moving its cylindrical covering due to *bosis*.

Even though the covering is above the *muktzeh*, and every example of *bosis* we have discussed is the contrary, with the *muktzeh* is above the vessel, nevertheless *Pri Megadim*[79] is *mesupak* whether the geographical location of a *bosis* has to be below the *muktzeh*, or maybe even if the *muktzeh* is below, and there is something on top that is serving the *muktzeh*, this too can become a *bosis*.

(The *poskim*[80] say that if laundry is hanging on a clothespin, in a state when the clothes are *muktzeh* since they are wet and therefore *muktzeh machmas issur*, the clothespins, despite being above the *muktzeh*, become a *bosis*. It could be that *Pri Megadim*'s doubt is dependent upon the reasoning of *bosis* we discussed in part 1. If it is due to being nullified by the *muktzeh*, then the geographical location shouldn't make a difference. However, if it is based on *haktzaas hadaas*, if the *muktzeh* is below, the *kli* can be accessed without moving the *muktzeh*, even if it is serving the *muktzeh* but the way it is set up doesn't show he has set it aside in his mind, so maybe there wouldn't be the restrictions of *bosis*. If so, the clothespin would be a *bosis* even according to *Pri Megadim*, since it clasps the *muktzeh* and is clear that one doesn't intend on moving the clothespin unless he moves also the *muktzeh*, so there is *haktzaas hadaas*).

R' Elyashiv is quoted to be strict on moving a cover that is designed to shield a light. Since it serves the light, it's a *bosis*. It seems like he is stringent

---

79. *Mishbetzos Zahav*, introduction to *siman* 308.
80. *Shalmei Yehudah*, ch. 9, insight 55.

on the doubt of *Pri Megadim* and even something on top of *muktzeh* can be a *bosis*. R' Yisroel Belsky is purported to have told the company who manufactured the Shabbos lamp to design it in a way that won't inevitably cause one to move the base as well. He held that the bulb can only render the base a *bosis*, not the cover. (One can add that the cover is not serving the light; on the contrary, it is constraining the light. It serves one's need for the light to be constrained.)

Most bulbs used nowadays are florescent bulbs, which don't have a red-hot element inside; rather, they are emitting light from charged mercury particles. Fluorescents are subject to a *machlokes* among the present-day *poskim*[81] whether they are considered fire. There is certainly room to be lenient to move the cover, and even if the base is always moved while opening or closing the cover, it is still permitted to use the Shabbos lamp because the bulb is only a *kli shemelachto l'issur* according to many opinions. Therefore one can move the base while using it because that is considered *l'tzorech gufo*.

Summary

Muchani is limited to vessels that have two separate parts and are formed into one. Vessels that have electric cables or red-hot elements inside them are not treated as *bosis* to the *muktzeh*; rather, we treat them as one item. therefore it depends on the regular criteria, what type of vessel it is will determine what category of *muktzeh* it falls into. There is an opinion that *bosis* is even if the non-*muktzeh* is above the *muktzeh* but is still serving the *muktzeh*. Even if we hold of this opinion, a cover of a light can be opened and closed to remove the light when he doesn't want it or to show the light when he does want it because the cover is not serving the light; it is serving the person.

81. *Shevus Yitzchak*, section 1, p. 174, *os* 4; *Orchos Shabbos*, ch. 19, *se'if* 181, and *Iggros Moshe, Orach Chaim* 5:22, point 32.

Answers

1. Even though the urn seemingly is a *bosis* to the red-hot element inside it and that would forbid even tilting the urn. There is room to be lenient based on treating even the red-hot item in such cases as a vessel. Therefore to move it for to use it or make space would be permitted.
2. The same answer as before applies equally to a hot-plate, there is room to be lenient but to be stringent has sound basis.
3. The reason some *poskim* question the use of the Shabbos-kettle is because the base has a red-hot element inside. Therefore they claim since the base is attached to the kettle it renders in *bosis*. According to the logic we explained it is permissible to be used and the base doesn't render it *bosis*.
4. If the bulb is florescent there is much more room to permit even moving the base. If it is filament bulb then you shouldn't move the base; the bulb is *muktzeh* rendering the base to be a *bosis*.

Appendix 1: הרחבה בשיטת רש״י בבסיס – Expansion of Rashi's Stance in Bosis

The *Acharonim*[82] prove from *Rashi*[83] that he holds of *Baal HaMeor*'s principle in *bosis* - that it is dependent on the lower object serving as a support for the upper item. The Mishnah says that if one covers a pot with *gizin* (*muktzeh* insulating material), he can remove the lid, causing the *muktzeh* to fall off. *Rashi* addresses why the lid does not become a *bosis* to these in-

82. R' Akiva Eiger, *Chasam Sofer*.
83. 49a, s.v. נוטל הכסוי.

sulators. He explains: שאין עשוי אלא לכסות הקדירה - "The purpose of the lid is only to protect the contents of the pot." Its purpose is not to hold up the insulation, so it cannot become a *bosis*. We see explicitly the idea that *bosis* depends on which item is considered to be supporting the other.

However, this seemingly contradicts *Rashi* later on.[84] The Gemara brings a case where one covers a pot with a lid and insulation cloths. *Rashi* explains that if the lid is *muktzeh*, one *can't* grip the walls of the pot and tilt the pot in order for the *muktzeh* lid to fall off. Since the pot is a *bosis* due to the intentional placing of the lid on top, this will have a *din* of a placed item. We see clearly from *Rashi* that the pot can become a *bosis* despite that its main function is not as a lid carrier, so it's not accurate to define the pot as secondary to the lid.

Sfas Emes[85] asks this contradiction, and answers that the Gemara and the Mishnah are discussing two different scenarios. In *Shabbos* 51a we are discussing the pot, and on the pot is the *muktzeh*, whereas in *daf* 49a we are discussing the lid that has the *muktzeh* on top. Why does it make a difference whether we are discussing the lid or a pot? Based on a principle of *Chasam Sofer*, we can suggest an answer. *Chasam Sofer* explains that a lid only serves the pot. It keeps the heat inside and protects its contents. Hence if the *muktzeh* is on the lid, it doesn't render the lid a *bosis* to it. The lid is serving the pot, not the insulators. In contrast, a pot, aside for its main purpose of retaining its contents, also serves the lid sitting on top. If the walls of the pot don't hold up the lid, the lid can't serve its function. Hence *Rashi* is saying if the lid is *muktzeh*, the pot becomes a *bosis*.

Appendix 2: הרחבה במחלוקת בעה"מ ור"ת בגדר בסיס – Expansion of the Dispute Between Baal Hameor and Rabbeinu Tam Regarding Bosis

The Gemara[86] discusses that if a person dies on a bed on Shabbos, how to move the corpse from the bed. The Gemara concludes that the way the

84. 51a, s.v. הרי זה.
85. 51a.
86. 43b.

corpse should be moved is by placing a *kikar oh tinok* (a loaf or child, examples of non-*muktzeh* items) on the bed, thus allowing one to carry the bed. *Baal HaMeor* has a unique explanation as to why the bed that the man died on isn't a *bosis* to the corpse, "since when Shabbos began the man was alive." It isn't clear what the intention behind this is. Perhaps he means: "*Ein bosis b'emtza Shabbos* - One can't create a *bosis* during Shabbos, i.e., if it only became a support during Shabbos, once the *muktzeh* is removed the support is permitted to be moved." Regardless of the explanation, we clearly see that he took on that the dead body renders the bed *bosis* and is not treated as a forgotten item, even though he unintentionally remained there. This can be explained because when Shabbos began and he was lying on the bed, albeit alive, the bed was secondary to the body. Without such an assumption, that it isn't a case of a forgotten item. It is obvious why there is no *bosis*. It wasn't intentionally left on the bed.

It is implicit in *Tosafos*[87] and *Tosafos HaRosh*[88] that a corpse that died on Shabbos is considered to be a forgotten item. *Reshimas Shiurim* explains this dispute to be *l'shitasam*. Since this person was lying on the bed from the beginning of Shabbos, albeit he was alive, his position was in a situation where the bed was *tafel* (inconsequential) to the man, and even when he dies the bed is still in a state of supporting the body. Since *Baal HaMeor* holds that *bosis* is when the support is acting "secondary" to the *muktzeh*, this situation qualifies as *bosis*. Hence he must explain with a new principle why the bed is still permitted to be moved. (The understanding how it can be treated as a placed item as opposed to *shochei'ach* is since when Shabbos began, despite there not being a state of *muktzeh* on the bed, there is a state of an object supporting something else. This is enough to confer a status of a placed item on the object; in addition, the man decided to lie on the bed while alive.) While *Tosafos* who explains *bosis* with the principle of *haktzaas hadaas*, since he was alive when Shabbos began there was no *haktzaas hadaas*. Now that he happened to die on Shabbos,

87. *Eiruvin* 71b.
88. *Shabbos* 43b, s.v. דכ"ע.

it is akin to a case of *shachach*. This *muktzeh* was never intentionally placed on the bed.

The Gemara[89] says that if one partially covered a pot with *muktzeh* insulation, the pot is not *muktzeh*. What is the difference whether the pot is entirely covered or only partially covered? *Piskei HaRid* explains that when one only partially covers the opening, since that is not the usual way to cover a pot, it doesn't render it *bosis*. Since it is an ineffective way of retaining the heat, one has thereby shown that he intends on taking it off. Showing he intends on removing it is a reflection that there is no *haktzaas hadaas* for all of Shabbos.[90] This is in line with the opinion of *Rabbeinu Tam*.

Appendix 3: בסים של אחרים - Bosis When it Belongs to Others

Rema[91] brings from *Ohr Zarua*[92] that one is not able to render his friend's item a *bosis*. For example, if Moshe places money on Yaakov's table before Shabbos, the table doesn't become a *bosis*. This is based upon the general principle of: אין אדם אוסר דבר שאינו שלו - "a person can't forbid something that isn't his." Although this seems straightforward, *Tosafos Yeshanim*[93] brings a Gemara in *Sukkah*[94] that implies the contrary. The Beitusim (a sect of heretics who dwelled in Israel) would place *muktzeh* on top of the *aravos* (willows) of Jews to stop them from being able to use them. The Gemara records that only the ignorant would take the *aravos* to shake. The implication is that the *talmidei chachamim* held that

---

89. 51a.

90. *Meiri* also says that the pot does not become a *bosis* in this case, but doesn't explain why. It may be that his intention is like *Piskei HaRid*, that covering half the pot is not the usual manner to insulate a pot. This can be explained in two ways — either that there is no *haktzaas hadaas*, or when the pot is covered in such a way, it doesn't become subordinate to the insulators. They aren't properly resting there, so they don't become *tafel*.

91. 309:4.

92. End of *siman* 29, and *siman* 86, point 3.

93. 44b.

94. 43b.

although they owned the *aravos*, the Beitusim had successfully rendered the branches *bosis* by placing a stone on top, even though it didn't belong to them? *Tosafos Yeshanim* answers[95] that the reason why the *chachamim* desisted from using their *aravos* was because inevitably they would have to move the *muktzeh*, the stone, in order to access the *aravos* - but the *aravos* themselves were not a *bosis*.

If we understand that the reason behind *bosis* is based on *haktzaas hadaas*, it's understandable why one can't make his friend's item *bosis*. There is no *haktzaas hadaas*; the owner hasn't designated anything not to be used, since he was unaware that *muktzeh* is resting on his item. Perhaps *Tosafos Yeshanim* understood in his first answer that the reason behind *bosis* depends on the base being nullified by the *muktzeh*. Therefore, regardless who placed the *muktzeh* on top, the base is still a support to the *muktzeh* on top.

The *poskim*[96] discuss whether a gabbai of a shul can make the benches in the shul a *bosis*; whether a guest who is given a room in a house can make items in his room a *bosis*; and whether a wife at home can make household items *bosis*. The similarity between these cases is that these people do not own the objects - the shul, the host, and the husband do - yet a certain amount of jurisdiction is given over to these people. The consensus among the *poskim* is that if the owner would be content with the person placing the *kli* as a support to the *muktzeh*, then it would be a *bosis*. However, if the gabbai, guest, or wife is doing something that is not in the interest of the owner, they do not have the ability to make it *bosis*. In a case when the owner has given over this object for the other person to use, then presumably they can forbid the item, e.g., if a guest is given a bed and a drawer for his own use and the owner doesn't intend on using them while his guest uses them, it will become a *bosis*.[97]

---

95. In his first answer he argues with *Rema*. We need to understand how he can argue with *Ohr Zarua*'s rule. Surely it's built on a *Shas* principle of אין אדם אוסר דבר שאינו שלו.

96. *Orchos Shabbos*, ch. 19, insight 395.

97. *Hilchos Shabbos B'Shabbos*, ch. 25, insight 10

Appendix 4: החילוק בבסים בתחילת השבת ובסים באמצע השבת - The Difference Between Bosis Before Shabbos and Bosis on Shabbos

Beis Yosef[98] lists different categories of *muktzeh*. One is a *kli shemelachto l'heter* that had *muktzeh* on it at the onset of Shabbos. He stresses that the *muktzeh* was on top during *bein hashemashos* (the onset of Shabbos). However, there is another scenario of *bosis* that *Beis Yosef* doesn't mention - if the *muktzeh* was only placed on the vessel during Shabbos. The halachah is clear-cut. Even in this scenario, one can't move the base while the *muktzeh* is on top. We can infer from the omission of *Beis Yosef* that this is a different category of *bosis*. In *Beis Yosef*'s case where one placed the *muktzeh* before Shabbos, the *bosis* became *muktzeh* itself. This support vessel has now transformed itself to a *muktzeh* item, so it's listed as a type of *muktzeh*. In contrast, in the other case, where the *muktzeh* was only placed on Shabbos, the only reason why it is forbidden to move is that one will now also be moving the *muktzeh* that is on top. Once this *muktzeh* is removed, the base reverts back to a regular *kli shemelachto l'heter* with unrestricted movement. While the vessel is presently supporting *muktzeh*, it gets the same *dinim* as the *muktzeh*, i.e., it can't be moved, but the support doesn't change into a *cheftzah* (item) of *muktzeh*. This is opposed to something that has *muktzeh* on top of it at the onset of Shabbos, which transforms it to a *muktzeh* item for the entire Shabbos, regardless whether the *muktzeh* remains on top or not.

Perhaps we can see this distinction in *Meiri*. When discussing the case of *bosis* with the stone on a barrel, he says that the barrel becomes like the stone, i.e., it actually becomes *muktzeh*. Yet he explains the dispute between the *Amoraim*[99] whether אם יש מוקצה לחצי שבת או לא[100] is not applicable to *bosis*. Meaning, if an item only became a *bosis* on Shabbos and subsequently the *muktzeh* was removed from on top, then all would agree that

98. Introduction to *siman* 308.

99. *Beitzah* 27a.

100. This dispute is over an item that only becomes *muktzeh* on Shabbos, and then subsequently the reason for it being *muktzeh* is removed. Despite this, does it retain its *muktzeh* status?

the support is no longer *muktzeh,* even the opinion who holds *yesh muktzeh l'chetzi Shabbos.* He explains the difference with the following principle: Only with objects that are actually *muktzeh* themselves is this dispute relevant, for example, dates that have become unfit for consumption. In contrast, a bed that just has money on it temporarily would not have the *din* of *muktzeh l'chetzi Shabbos.* This is because it is not inherently *muktzeh*; rather, it is presently forbidden to move due to the *muktzeh* on top that makes the bed a *bosis. Meiri* says that this second type of *muktzeh* is not pertinent to the dispute of *yesh/ein muktzeh l'chetzi Shabbos.*[101] We see from this exclusion that a bed that only becomes a *bosis* on Shabbos is not considered to be a *muktzeh* item.

101. There is a *chiddush* found in *Mordechai, Raavya,* and *Piskei HaRid.* They all hold that once the flame of a candle has been extinguished, the candle can be moved *l'tzorech gufo u'mekomo.* We don't follow this *l'halachah* because we hold that since during *bein hashemashos* the candle was forbidden to move, *migo d'iskatzi* forbids it for the entire Shabbos. Why do they not apply *migo d'iskatzi*? *Migo d'iskatzi* is based on *haktzaas hadaas* (in chapter 21, where we discuss *migo,* we will elaborate on this). If at the beginning of Shabbos you set aside the item, then for the entire duration of Shabbos it is set aside. They seemingly understand that *bosis* works that the support gets the same *dinim* as the *muktzeh* by virtue of being subordinate to the *muktzeh.* They understand that *migo d'iskatzi* wouldn't apply to this category of *muktzeh* because there is no designation in one's mind. Therefore as soon as it is no longer supporting the *muktzeh,* it reverts back to its own *dinim,* namely, that it can be moved *l'tzorech gufo u'mekomo.*

Chapter 15

טלטול במחובר ופח אשפה

Moving Attached Items and a Trash Can

Questions

1. Am I permitted to sit on grass on Shabbos?
2. Am I allowed to open a cupboard door that has a garbage can mounted on its inside?
3. Can I step on a foot lever of a trash can, causing the lid to open?

Shulchan Aruch[1] *paskens* that after defecating, one is allowed to clean oneself with grass, even if the grass is still attached to the ground. However, one must be careful not to move the blades of grass while doing so. *Shulchan Aruch* is seemingly coming to preclude an *issur* of *shimush b'yerek* (using vegetation). This is unlike what we find by a tree that any use of it is rabbinically forbidden. Using a tree, e.g., hanging a coat on a branch or leaning against its trunk, is included in this prohibition, while a shrub or other low growth is not encompassed in this prohibition.

The commentators argue as to why *Shulchan Aruch* maintains that one can't move the grass. *Magen Avraham* explains that the grass is *muktzeh* and therefore forbidden to move. However, the majority of the commentators[2] ask on this *Magen Avraham*:[3] If it is indeed *muktzeh* and therefore

1. 312:6.
2. *Eliyah Rabbah, Aruch HaShulchan, Tosafos Shabbos,* and *Toras Shabbos.*
3. *Se'if katan* 6.

can't be moved, how can one practically wipe himself with the grass, as it will inevitably move? Furthermore, why should grass be *muktzeh*? It has a use, namely as animal fodder, and certainly can't be considered *muktzeh machmas gufo*. Only grass that became detached on Shabbos is *muktzeh*, since in its present state it wasn't prepared before Shabbos.

Rather, these commentators explain, principally *Tosefes Shabbos*, that *Shulchan Aruch* means that one must be careful not to move the grass too much, as he may come to detach it, but the blades of grass themselves are not *muktzeh*. *Mishnah Berurah*[4] *paskens*, unlike *Magen Avraham* and in accordance with the majority, that attached grass is not *muktzeh*. We see that many *Rishonim* also understand so. The Gemara[5] discusses smelling a *hadas*. The *Rishonim* explain that even if it is attached to the ground, one is still allowed to move the branch, as long as he takes care not to detach it. We see explicitly that a branch still attached to the ground is not *muktzeh* and the same applies to grass. (*Taz* learns like *Magen Avraham* that the grass is *muktzeh*. He explains *l'shitaso* that even though *Shulchan Aruch paskens* that one can smell the *hadas*, that's only if he doesn't move it.)

One explanation why all these opinions hold that grass isn't *muktzeh* is because it is *mechubar* (attached to the ground). *Beis Yehudah*[6] explains that since the whole reason for the *gezeirah* of *muktzeh* was to protect people against *hotzaah* (carrying to another domain), it is not logical that Chazal imposed *muktzeh* on something that is still attached, since one can't come to carry it. We also find in *Riaz*,[7] albeit for a different reason, that an attached item isn't subject to *muktzeh* at all. He says: מותר לקנח בעשבים מחוברים ואין לקנח בצרור אבל טלטול עשבים **אינו טלטול כיון שהם מחוברים** - "It is permissible to clean oneself with grass still attached to the ground since it is *not considered moving because it is attached.*" We see that when something is attached to the ground, *muktzeh* is not applicable because it is not considered to be a *tiltul* of the *muktzeh*!

---

4. *Se'if katan* 17.
5. *Sukkah* 37b.
6. *Siman* 11, brought by R' Ovadia and the *Menuchas Ahavah*.
7. End of ch. 4.

There are more sources to substantiate this explanation that *muktzeh* items that are attached to the ground are not considered *tiltul*.

Moving a Suspended Light

Ohr Zarua[8] brings in the name of *Rabbeinu Tam* that one can move a lamp that has a candle inside if it is suspended from the ceiling. He explains: הואיל ונר שלנו תלויה טלטול מן הצד ולא שמיה טלטול - "Since our lamp is suspended, it is *tiltul min hatzad* and isn't classified as *tiltul*." This fits with *Rabbeinu Tam*'s opinion that *tiltul min hatzad* is permitted in all cases, even when something is being moved for the sake of the *muktzeh*. (*Rabbeinu Tam* understands that *tiltul min hatzad* is not considered *tiltul*[9] at all.) Nevertheless, it is seemingly difficult to understand why he calls it *tiltul min hatzad*. Surely one is moving the lamp directly and the lamp itself is *muktzeh* since it is a *bosis* to the flame? We must say that no, since the lamp remains attached in the same place, just shaking back and forth it is only *tiltul min hatzad*. The explanation in calling it *tiltul min hatzad* seems to be: The same way we find by *tiltul min hatzad* that it is an unusual way of moving items and hence Chazal didn't extend their *issur* to include this way of moving *muktzeh*, so too when moving *muktzeh* while it remains in the same location isn't included in the normal *issur* of *muktzeh*.

Tosafos[10] and *Mordechai* record that people used to place their candles on a shelf behind the door and they still opened and closed the door. *Tosafos* explains why there is no issue of *muktzeh* with that: משום טלטול אין לאסר דבנעילת דלת לא חשיב טלטול וגם לא הוי בסיס לדבר האסור דבית חשוב ובטל [הדלת] לגבי הבית - "Even though one is moving the door, we can't forbid moving the door because the closing of the door isn't considered "moving" and the door is not considered a support to the candle because the importance

8. *Siman* 33.

9. *Ohr Zarua* comments that *Rabbeinu Tam* wasn't saying this with the intention that we follow this position that *tiltul min hatzad* is not *tiltul* in all cases; rather, because of his sharpness in learning, he said such a halachah.

10. 120b, s.v. פותח.

of the house renders the door nullified to it." *Graz*[11] explains that *Tosafos* is saying one idea: Relative to a house, the door has no independent importance, and it therefore can't become a *bosis* (support) to the candle. On the contrary: The door supports/serves the house.

Tosafos addresses why it is not considered a *tiltul* of the candle, but what actually is being moved is the door. We see that *Tosafos* holds that there is no *heter* that a door is attached. In essence an attached item would still have an issue of *tiltul,* since he still needed to explain the *heter* based on the idea that the door is serving the house. The logic behind why it would still be considered moving despite being attached is because a door is made to be moved in this way. Since this is its designated way of moving, we consider it an act of moving. *Graz* infers from the way *Tur*[12] and *Hagahos Maimoni*[13] bring down this halachah of moving a door with a candle without mentioning *bosis,* they learn that since the door is attached, one's movement has no relevance. Therefore there are no problems of *muktzeh* since there is no "moving" of the *muktzeh. Levush*[14] understands that even *Tosafos* and *Mordechai* mean to say that when it is attached there is no act of moving, i.e., because the door is part of the house it is considered attached, and when the *muktzeh* is attached to something else, since the main item is not moving, one's act of moving the *muktzeh* part is deemed insignificant, not moving.

When It Automatically Goes Back to Its Place

However, if *muktzeh* items while attached are not *muktzeh,* we have to address the following Mishnah. The Mishnah[15] says that one can use a branch of a tree that he previously cut and attached to his bucket as a handle. The Gemara infers that if the branch is still attached to the tree, he can't move

---

11. *Kuntres Acharon* 277:3.
12. 680.
13. Ch. 5, point 90.
14. 277:1.
15. 125a.

it because it is *muktzeh* (branches are *muktzeh machmas gufo*). Surely if the branch is attached, it shouldn't be relevant to *muktzeh*?

R' Shlomo Zalman Auerbach entertains that when one is moving the *muktzeh* in a way that it will go back to its original place on its own accord, there is no problem of *muktzeh*. The logic in this is that since it will go back to its original place, it's not considered that one has moved it at all. It still has an intrinsic connection to its original place. In contrast, when something is attached but its movement will remain once one has changed its place, he has moved the item. The fact that some part is still in the original location is irrelevant since we *pasken* that *tiltul b'miktzas shmeih tiltul* - "even moving part of an item is forbidden."[16]

We can now understand why it is forbidden to move the branch as a handle when it is still connected. Since this is not something that goes a back on its own to its original place, we consider this a proper act of moving. R' Ovadia gives another answer: The case is always dealing with a branch from a tree, and moving it is included in the general prohibition of *shimush b'ilan* (using a tree).

An entirely different approach to the first case of the grass we brought would be to explain that the lenient opinions who hold that the grass is not *muktzeh* is not based on a general principle that an attached item is not *muktzeh*; rather, grass, even when attached to the ground, is considered to be prepared for animal feed. Something "prepared" is not *muktzeh*. While *Magen Avraham* and *Taz,* who hold that grass is *muktzeh,* hold that until one has plucked the grass it is not prepared, despite animals being able to feed from it.

It's quoted in the name of R' Elyashiv that nowadays attached grass is *muktzeh*; it isn't considered prepared since we don't commonly feed it to animals. This *psak* is only understood according to the aforementioned explanation that the original *heter* of grass not being *muktzeh* was based on it being prepared for animals. A potentially common stringency that would follow is one who is sitting on grass on Shabbos (question #1) must be careful not to put his hands on the grass next to him. Instead, it's rec-

16. 311:3.

ommended that he put a sheet underneath him. However, even according to this explanation, there is no problem walking on grass because, as *Pri Megadim*[17] explains, it is *tiltul min hatzad*. We can even classify it as *tiltul derech hilucho* (moving while walking), which the Gemara[18] teaches is prepared.

Extending This Principle to Cupboard Doors

R' Elyashiv[19] rules that if a fridge contains forty *seah* (a halachic volume) then even if there is *muktzeh* in the fridge door, the door can be opened. According to *Levush, Tur,* and *Hagahos Maimoni* (according to *Graz*) we understand the logic behind this ruling. When one moves *muktzeh* while attached to something which is attached to the ground then it is not considered one is "moving" the *muktzeh*. Forty *seah* render even a *kli* to be considered attached to the ground, so the *muktzeh* in the fridge door one isn't "moving." (In chapter 13,we brought a stringency from R' Elyashiv and R' Shlomo Zalman Auerbach that one should empty any *muktzeh* items from the fridge door. According to this reasoning one can be lenient.)[20]

We now have a basis for being lenient when opening cupboard doors that have attached garbage cans (question #2). If there is a leniency to move anything that is attached, a cupboard door is certainly attached to the house, and therefore shouldn't have any problems even if it is *muktzeh* (because it is supporting *muktzeh*). One's act isn't considered moving *muktzeh*.

---

17. 336:4.

18. 127.

19. Brought in *Shevus Yitzchak*, ch. 12, point 2.

20. I later found a different explanation in a *sefer* called *Toras HaBosis*. The author says that R' Elyashiv's ruling even fits with *Tosafos*. The reason why he holds only if the *kli* contains forty *seah* is the door not a *bosis* is because R' Elyashiv understands that *Tosafos*'s case is exclusive to a house which has importance. He understands that the house's importance is from the fact it is attached to the ground.

Can We Be Lenient According to Tosafos?

Simply speaking, *Tosafos* didn't apply the principle of "attached" with the case of a candle on the back of a door, so it's implicit that he doesn't hold of this exemption of an attached item. Rather, since the door is considered predominantly serving the house, it is not a *bosis* to the candles. Does that same logic apply in our case with the trash can? Is the door a *bosis* to the can or not? Perhaps we claim that there is no difference between the door of a house and the door of a kitchen cupboard. Even the door of the cupboard serves another function; it predominately provides a completeness to the kitchen. Only for the sake of convenience does one attach the bin to the cupboard door. If this argument is true then any cupboard door that holds *muktzeh* can still be opened at one's leisure because serves the house not the *muktzeh* contents.

On the other hand, we can argue that a cupboard door holding a trash can is different from a door supporting a candle. The cupboard door is specifically made to hold the trash can, to the extent that it can be claimed that it is a part of the trash can and will therefore become a *bosis*. In contrast, the door is a part of the house. It's not made to support candles, it just happens to have a candle resting on it.[21] [22]

---

21. One solution would be to open the cupboard with one's foot, which is *tiltul b'gufo*. Alternatively, if the bin is empty during *bein hashemashos*, then the cupboard doesn't become a *bosis*. This is based on the principle of *ein muktzeh l'chetzi Shabbos*. According to one explanation in *Magen Avraham*, even if during Shabbos, when the *muktzeh* is inside the *kli*, the *kli* isn't nullified by the *muktzeh* and doesn't become a *bosis*. *Mishnah Berurah* 264:24 explicitly *paskens* like this *Magen Avraham*, despite *Magen Avraham*'s principle being a single opinion among the *Rishonim* who argue over this point. *Chazon Ish*, however, says from the case of the chicken coop (where one places an empty container as a stool for the chickens to climb into their coop), we see that if the *kli* is meant to hold the *muktzeh*, it can become a *bosis* during Shabbos. *Orchos Shabbos* applies this to trash cans: Even if it was empty before Shabbos, it will still become a *bosis* on Shabbos since this is the natural place of the *muktzeh*. However, it's unclear if *Mishnah Berurah* holds of this stringency. *Mishnah Berurah* references *Derech HaChaim*, who doesn't distinguish that something can't become a *bosis* on Shabbos, even when it's the *muktzeh*'s natural place. Therefore in all cases there should be no *bosis* during Shabbos.

22. There are *poskim* who give a solution to the problem of *bosis* — that prior to

A fridge or freezer door is certainly more comparable to the case of the candle hanging on the door. The fridge/freezer can't function without their door, the door is a main part of the use of the vessel. Therefore it's logical that the door is considered serving the fridge/freezer and not the *muktzeh* content that is placed on the shelves of the door. (Since *Tosafos*'s principle is regardless that the house is attached therefore there is no requirement for the fridge/freezer to contain forty *seah.*)

R' Shlomo Zalman[23] ruled that cupboard door is considered serving the house and even if it has only *muktzeh* resting on it, the door can still be moved. *Chut Shani*[24] is stringent, he argues on the comparison between any cupboard door and the door of a house that *Tosafos* is discussing. His reasoning is that only something as significant as a house does this logic apply to that the door is not considered serving what's resting on it but rather the house. A cupboard is a less significant item, so the cupboard doors are considered serving the *muktzeh* on it, it is not considered primarily serving the cupboard. He adds that even if the cupboard is forty *seah* the door will still be a *bosis* to what it's supporting.

If we accept the argument that the cupboard door is not a *bosis,* then moving such doors is only a *tiltul min hatzad* of the trash can. And even though you are opening it for the sake of the *muktzeh,* i.e., the can, which should be forbidden since it is *tiltul min hatzad l'tzorech davar ha'assur,* we can rely on *Magen Avraham*'s principle that when one wants to use the *muktzeh* in a permissible fashion it is considered *tiltul min hatzad l'tzorech davar ha'mutar.*[25] Even though one is moving the bin via the door, since

---

Shabbos one should put inside the bin a non-*muktzeh* item, so it will now be *bosis l'davar heter v'issur*. However, one can ask on this: Since the receptacle is designated for *muktzeh,* i.e., trash, its chief purpose is to be a *bosis l'issur* and the placing of a non-*muktzeh* item won't rectify it. This is similar to the logic of *Pri Megadim* regarding a candlestick tray. He says that since it is designated for *muktzeh,* it doesn't help to place a non-*muktzeh* item on it to cause it not to be a *bosis l'issur.*

23. *Shulchan Shlomo* 308, insight 13. The author brings that at first R' Shlomo Zalman ruled that the door is a *bosis* to the *muktzeh* that is hanging on it. In later years he retracted, saying we can compare cupboard doors to door of a house.

24. Ch. 44.

25. We elaborated on this in chapter 13.

depositing garbage in a trash can is a permitted usage, *Magen Avraham* would permit this *tiltul min hatzad.*[26]

If we distinguish between the cases, perhaps we even lose the basis to be lenient that we earlier based on the *heter* of an attached item - that all doors are not considered to be an independent movable item. One can differentiate that with the candle on the door, the candle hasn't actually moved from its place. It was on the door and is still on the door. However, the trash can is meant to be moved, but for convenience it's attached to a door to facilitate its movement, and therefore it is an act of moving *muktzeh*. Or perhaps we can still extract from the case of the candle that anything that is attached to a door is considered not to have been moved at all.

In the previous chapter we saw the case of *muchani*, a type of carriage, and we learn from there for scenarios where there is *muktzeh* on one part of an item but not on other parts. *Rambam*[27] explains the case differently from other *Rishonim*. He says that *muchani* is a drawer inside a chest and the *muktzeh* is in the drawer. It is permissible to open the drawer and it isn't considered that one is moving the *muktzeh* because the drawer is just a part of the chest. *Rambam* is teaching that moving *muktzeh* that is inside a drawer is not an act of *tiltul*. Although *Mishnah Berurah*[28] *paskens* that *muktzeh* inside a drawer renders the drawer *bosis* and is forbidden to move, nevertheless perhaps we can include the opinion of *Rambam* as an addition to be lenient.

---

26. The reason we don't rely on this *Magen Avraham l'chatchilah* is because it is implicit in *Shulchan Aruch* that he doesn't agree to this. In *siman* 311 he says that moving straw off a bed is only permitted because it is *tiltul b'gufo*. *Magen Avraham* himself is bothered why *Shulchan Aruch* did not permit it, since it is *tiltul min hatzad l'tzorech davar ha'mutar,* since one's intention in the moving is to clean the bed.

27. *Peirush HaMishnayos Keilim* 18:2.
'והותר לגרור את המגירה הזו בשבת ואע"פ שיש בתוכו מעות שאינו מותר לטלטלן מפני שאין המגירה הזו כלי בפני עצמו וכאשר יגרר את המגירה ובה המעות **הואיל ואינה יכולה להוציאה ולבהדילה מן השידה הרי זו כאלו לא טלטל את המעות'**

28. 310:18.

Trash Cans and Their Lids

There are those who even suggest a problem in lifting the lid of a trash can with a foot lever because of *bosis* (question #3). They claim since the lid is part of the trash can, which is *muktzeh* since it is a *bosis* to the garbage, the lid also can't be moved. There is certainly room to be lenient in this case, since even if a bin is a *bosis* to the *muktzeh* trash, surely the lid is a separate part of the bin and isn't considered a *bosis* to the garbage. The function of the trash can is to contain the trash, which is a purpose the lid doesn't serve. The purpose of the lid is to act as a partition. It contains the smell and stops insects from coming. It is therefore serving the surroundings and not the trash.

This is similar to the *heter* found permitting the movement of a spout of an urn even though the urn is a *bosis* to a *muktzeh machmas gufo* (question #1). The spout can be used even though one is moving it. Since it operates independently to the urn, each part has a separate function; since it is used independently to the body of the urn, it doesn't get the same status as the urn. Therefore, even if the lid of the bin is attached and one needs to press down on a lever to open it, since the lid has a separate function to the body of the trash can, it doesn't have the same status as it and would be permitted to open on Shabbos.

Summary

There are several indications that there is no infringement of *muktzeh* with moving something that is attached to the ground. That's one possible way to explain why it's permitted to touch grass that's still attached to the ground. Another reason could be that since grass is considered "prepared" for animals, there is reason to say that this logic doesn't apply nowadays in modern society, where we don't have animals living among us that graze. Some *Rishonim* explain the *heter* of moving a door with candles attached to it is that the door is primarily serving the house and therefore not considered a *bosis* to the candles. Both of these explanations can be used to permit opening a cupboard door that has a garbage can attached. Either way one is not considered to have moved the trash directly. Some modern-day *poskim* distinguish that a cupboard door that is designated solely to hold the trash can that is *muktzeh* can't be treated separate to the trash can and that the door is part of the can. They would nevertheless be lenient with a fridge door containing *muktzeh*. Opening the cupboard door with one's feet is recommended because it is *tiltul b'gufo*, but if it's extremely impractical there's sufficient reason to be lenient to lift open the door in the regular manner.

Answers

1. According to most opinions, grass, even when attached, is not *muktzeh*. R' Elyashiv is quoted to be stringent in moving grass. Sitting, however, is not considered directly moving the grass, so according to all you can sit on it.
2. Many contemporary *poskim* are stringent. However, we entertained several strong arguments why despite the bin being *muktzeh* the cupboard door that it is attached to isn't rendered a *bosis*. If the cupboard door isn't *muktzeh*, you can open it in order to throw something in the bin because it is *tiltul min hatzad* for sake of a permitted use, which is allowed.
3. Even if the bin is *muktzeh*, the lid doesn't get that status as it has a different purpose. The lid will remain a *kli shemelachto l'issur* and you can open it with the foot lever.

Chapter 16

כיכר או תינוק

[Placing] a Loaf or Child [to Enable the Moving of Muktzeh]

Questions

1. Yitzchak left his expensive camera on his bed and is afraid to shake it off (*tiltul min hatzad*). Can he place a different object on top of the camera to allow him to move it with his hands?
2. If, unfortunately, someone passed away on Shabbos, is there any way to move the *niftar*?
3. After serving the chicken soup, Leah wants to put the soup back in the fridge, since it could spoil if it remains on the countertop. Can she do so even though she is moving it *m'chamah l'tzel*?
4. Shmuli poured out water that was left in the kettle. Can he return the now-empty kettle to its base?

The Gemara[1] teaches us that Chazal gave a leniency to move a corpse in order to protect it from rotting in the sun, by placing a child or a loaf of bread on the corpse. This is known as "*kikar oh tinok.*" This involves placing either the child or the bread on the surface to support the corpse, or even directly on top of the corpse. This serves to qualify the act of *tiltul* as being directed at these non-*muktzeh* objects.

---

1. 43b.

The Gemara states that this leniency was *only* given regarding a corpse: לא אמרו כו״ת אלא למת בלבד. The *Rishonim* argue whether this limitation is literal or not. If it is literal, no item other than a corpse may be carried by the placing of a *kikar oh tinok*; the exclusivity would be that this is a specific *heter* to safeguard the sanctity of the deceased. If it is not literal, other items can also qualify for this leniency. We need to explain this second possibility: A corpse is *muktzeh machmas gufo* (it has no purpose). Perhaps the Gemara only meant to limit this dispensation of *kikar oh tinok* within this category of *muktzeh* to a corpse and exclude similar items that are *muktzeh machmas gufo*. However, items that are considered to have a use, but have limitations in their movement, like *muktzeh machmas issur*, would not be discussed in this statement, and therefore there is no reason to exclude any actual vessels from this leniency of *kikar oh tinok*. To understand this dispute, we first need to understand how this leniency of *kikar oh tinok* works at all.

Why Kikar Oh Tinok Helps Remove the Problem of Muktzeh

We find there to be a leniency of moving *muktzeh* under certain circumstances in an indirect way (*tiltul min hatzad*). This is where one does not touch the *muktzeh* directly with his hands, but via something else. With *kikar oh tinok* one can be actually touching the *muktzeh* with his hands (the bed itself will also be *muktzeh* since it is a *bosis* to the deceased). What is the basis for doing so? R' Akiva Eiger[2] observes that we only find that Chazal permitted one to move a corpse, in order to save it from rotting, via *kikar oh tinok* - not through *tiltul min hatzad*. However, when moving the corpse *l'tzorech mekomo* only *tiltul min hatzad* is permitted, as opposed to *kikar oh tinok*.[3]

---

2. 311:1.

3. R' Akiva Eiger is perhaps asking a question how can it be so. Surely if *tiltul min hatzad* is a more lenient form of *tiltul*, this should be the way to move a corpse. A very simple answer could be: While it is a lesser *tiltul*, since it is only permitted *l'tzorech davar ha'mutar*, if one was allowed to move a corpse to protect it using *tiltul min hatzad*, people will come to think that *tiltul min hatzad* is permitted even

One can understand the *heter* of *kikar oh tinok* in one of two ways. The simple explanation is that the placing of the *kikar oh tinok* on top of the deceased functions as a reminder that one is not really permitted to handle this *muktzeh* and that this is an exceptional case where Chazal permitted it due to honor of the deceased. *Mishnah Berurah*[4] writes: לא מנכר כל כך טלטול המוקצה - "It is not so recognizable that one is moving the *muktzeh*." With *kikar oh tinok* one is camouflaging the moving of the *muktzeh*. It is *not* halachically considered that one is only moving the non-*muktzeh* item - one is considered to be moving the corpse - but in order to "minimize" the outright handling of the *muktzeh*, we place a non-*muktzeh* item on top.

However, there is a different understanding of this *heter*. Earlier we saw the concept of *bosis*, that if a *muktzeh* item is resting on top of a non-*muktzeh* item, the item below becomes *muktzeh* as well since it is a *bosis* (support). For example, if a flame is resting on top of a candle that's on a candlestick, the flame renders the candlesticks *muktzeh* to the extent that they can't be moved at all. We explained that one understanding is because the non-*muktzeh* item becomes nullified to the *muktzeh* item by virtue of it being its support. There are those who understand that *kikar oh tinok* utilizes the underlying principle of *batel*: Due to the importance of the *kikar oh tinok*, the *muktzeh* is now serving as a support to the *kikar oh tinok*. Therefore the *muktzeh* becomes subordinate to the *kikar oh tinok*; it loses its independence and therefore one is considered to be solely moving the *kikar oh tinok*. *Rashba*[5] seemingly learns like this. He uses the word *bosis* to describe the *heter* of *kikar oh tinok*: מניח ככר על המת ומראה עצמו כרוצה לטלטל את ההיתר **ועושה לו האיסור בסיס**.[6]

---

l'tzorech davar ha'assur. Therefore Chazal gave a different *heter* despite it being more of a *tiltul*.

4. *Se'if katan* 2.

5. 143a and *Beitzah* 36b.

6. This sentence is not conclusive since the beginning of the sentence, "that it makes it look like one is carrying the *heter*," does sound like the previous way we have suggested. Adding a *kikar oh tinok* changes the way the *tiltul* is perceived. Nevertheless the ending is difficult to disregard as not being the thrust of his main intention.

Bread or Child or Any Non-Muktzeh Item

According to either way of understanding - either it minimizes the explicit carrying of the *muktzeh* or the *muktzeh* becomes subsidiary - it concurs with what the commentators explain - that the child or bread is not *specifically* required, but any permissible non-*muktzeh* item can be placed on top to enable the moving of the corpse. The proof for this is from a Gemara[7] that mentions that Abaye and Rava placed cutlery on top of *muktzeh* items in order to enable the moving of the *muktzeh*. (They themselves held that the items they were moving weren't *muktzeh* and can be handled directly. They placed something on top just so people who thought these vessels were *muktzeh* wouldn't draw the wrong conclusion.) The Gemara's choice of a loaf of bread and a child are things that are practical that are not at all *muktzeh*. Any non-*muktzeh* item can function as an indicator or can cause the corpse to be a *bosis* to it.[8]

Levush Serad[9] explains that even though *kikar oh tinok* is not specific, it still can't be a *kli shemelachto l'issur*. The reasoning is that *kli shemelachto l'issur* has a limitation of only being permitted to move *l'tzorech gufo u'mekomo* and not *m'chamah l'tzel*, i.e., one cannot move a *kli shemelachto l'issur* if it is not for the sake of using the vessel (in a permissible way). Placing a *kli shemelachto l'issur* on top to enable one to move the *muktzeh* is not considered a legitimate function of the actual *kli* and would not be included in the *heter* of *l'tzorech gufo*. *Pri Megadim* asks that even a *kli shemelachto l'heter* has a limitation of not being moved *shelo l'tzorech klal* - not to move it for no reason at all, so why is there any difference be-

---

7. 142b.

8. *Tosafos Rid* on 43b says that regarding moving a corpse, only a *kikar oh tinok* can be placed. The logic in this is: With any other item, people may think that it's being buried with the corpse, since it's now forbidden to benefit from (the Gemara in *Sanhedrin* teaches that anything that touches the bed that the deceased is going to be buried in is forbidden to benefit from; see *daf* 48a for more explanation) and that it is forbidden to move this non-*muktzeh*. They therefore won't understand Chazal's leniency. Only with a *kikar oh tinok* is it clear that it is not part of the corpse and remains not *muktzeh*.

9. 311 on *Magen Avraham, se'if katan* 15.

tween placing a *kli shemelachto l'issur* or a *kli shemelachto l'heter*? *Levush Serad* must understand that the limitation of *shelo l'tzorech klal* only excludes it from being moved when there is no constructive purpose at all in the moving of this item, e.g., moving it aimlessly from hand to hand. However, here there is a purpose, namely that one will be able to move the *muktzeh* away. While a *kli shemelachto l'issur* can only be moved when one will be using the vessel in terms of its inherent usages of a vessel, here one is not using any of the vessel's inherent usages.

Shulchan Aruch[10] brings an opinion that only when the corpse is unclothed is there a necessity to make use of a *kikar oh tinok* to carry it. If the corpse is clothed, his clothes can function as the *kikar oh tinok* to allow its movement. This is as we mentioned, that a bread or a child is not specific. R' Akiva Eiger[11] asks: If so, even if he is unclothed why can't one use the bed underneath the corpse to function as a *kikar oh tinok*?[12] *Rashash* answers that the bed is completely subordinate to the deceased and thus can't function as a *kikar oh tinok*. The leniency of *kikar oh tinok* is when something different, independent to the *muktzeh*, is placed on the *muktzeh*, but here the bed is naturally subordinate to the corpse. This is true according to both explanations; a bed doesn't appear as a distinct sign that one is relying on an extenuating *heter*, and neither can we say that the corpse appears nullified by the bed, that it's as if one is mainly carrying the bed and not the deceased.

A question one can ask on *Rashash* is how to reconcile this answer with the opinion that even clothes can function as the *kikar oh tinok*. Surely clothes are like a bed, in that they are something that is subordinate to the person. Nevertheless, there is an opinion who holds that it can function as *kikar oh tinok*. In what way do clothes differ from a bed? Perhaps only when one is alive we say that his clothing is considered subordinate to him,

---

10. 311:4.

11. *Se'if* 1.

12. *Magen Avraham* 308:51 explains the *heter* of *Shulchan Aruch* to put bread on a table that has shells on it is based on *kikar oh tinok*. R' Akiva Eiger (311:1, s.v. ואם) asks: Why do you need to put a non-*muktzeh* item on the table? Let the table itself function as *kikar oh tinok*.

but when one dies, since the clothing will be removed, they are no longer serving the function of clothing and they therefore will not remain subordinate. In contrast, the bed is still serving to support the corpse and thus would not be relevant to *kikar oh tinok.*[13]

The Location of the Kikar Oh Tinok

We see from R' Akiva Eiger's question that he holds of a *chiddush* mentioned by *Magen Avraham.*[14] *Magen Avraham* says that *kikar oh tinok* isn't specifically required to be on top of the corpse; it can even be adjacent to the corpse. It must be that R' Akiva Eiger also holds so, since he asks that the bed below the *muktzeh* should function as *kikar oh tinok.* Proof to this, that *kikar oh tinok* can be even when the *muktzeh* is below, can be found in *Tosafos.*[15] He explains the Gemara that says that Shmuel carried pits or seeds on top of bread, that the intention of this is *kikar oh tinok,* even though the bread was below. Shmuel held that these seeds were not *muktzeh* and just because he was an important person he didn't want it to seem like he was carrying *muktzeh.*[16]) This is easier to understand according to the first *pshat* of *kikar oh tinok* we mentioned, that we just need a *heker* (sign). If so, it shouldn't make a difference where the sign is, above or below. However, even *Rashba,* who understands *kikar oh tinok* to work with *bosis,* could perhaps agree. Since, as we saw earlier in the chapter on *bosis, Pri Megadim* mentions the option that *bosis* is not only if the *muktzeh* is on top, it can be even if the *heter*/non-*muktzeh* item is on top, if it is serving the *muktzeh* we can consider the upper item to be a *bosis* to the *muktzeh* beneath.[17] So too with *kikar oh tinok* we can utilize the same principle that

---

13. In *Avnei Zikaron,* a different answer is quoted in the name of R' Elyashiv. One carries a corpse via moving a bed, so a bed is not viewed as an independent item vis-à-vis the moving of the corpse. In contrast, one doesn't use clothes as a means by which to move a corpse, so vis-à-vis the act of carrying we identify one as moving two separate items, so the clothes can function as *kikar oh tinok.*

14. *Se'if katan* 1.

15. 143a, s.v. רבא מיטלטל.

16. *Tosafos* 143a, s.v. שמואל.

17. From *Rashba* in *Beitzah* 21a, it is implicit that it would help even if the *muktzeh*

the main object that one is moving is the *kikar oh tinok,* regardless of its location above or below.

There is an additional *chiddush* that we see from *Magen Avraham,* who says that *kikar oh tinok* would help even if the *kikar oh tinok* is adjacent to the corpse. Even *Pri Megadim,* who mentions the option that *bosis* is not limited to when the *muktzeh* is on top, doesn't discuss a possibility when the item is adjacent to the *muktzeh,* as this would in no way be a *bosis.* We see from this *Magen Avraham,* who explains *kikar oh tinok* even when adjacent, that he understands like we brought from *Mishnah Berurah* that the *heter* of *kikar oh tinok* is dependent on showing that one's main action isn't carrying the *muktzeh.*

Does Kikar Oh Tinok Apply to Keilim?

We mentioned earlier that whether there is an application beyond a corpse to this leniency of *kikar oh tinok* is subject to a dispute. The dispute stems from how to understand the following halachah. The Gemara[18] says that one can move a mortar with garlic inside. The mortar is *muktzeh,* as it is a *kli shemelachto l'issur,* since its main purpose is for grinding garlic, which is *tochen* (the prohibition of grinding). Yet we see that it can be moved if it has garlic inside (even though the Gemara is in accordance with Rebbe Nechemiah, who holds that a *kli shemelachto l'issur* can only be moved for its designated purpose not for secondary usages). Why? *Raavan* explains that the *heter* is based on *kikar oh tinok.* He proves from here that the Gemara's limitation of *kikar oh tinok* being only relevant to a corpse is only within *muktzeh machmas gufo.* However, all *kli shemelachto l'issur* can be moved unrestrictedly with *kikar oh tinok.* *Shulchan Aruch*[19] brings such an opinion, that even with a *kli shemelachto l'issur* there would be a *heter* of *kikar oh tinok.*

---

is on top with the *kikar oh tinok* below!

18. 123a.

19. 308:5.

R' Akiva Eiger[20] discusses according to this opinion what is unique with a *kli shemelachto l'issur* in that it is permitted in all cases to be moved with a *kikar oh tinok*. Is it because, since it can be moved *l'tzorech gufo u'mekomo*, it is a more lenient form of *muktzeh* and therefore we allow it to be moved unrestricted with a *kikar oh tinok*? Or does its leniency stem from the fact that it is a *kli*, not bearing its halachic status? The practical difference between the two is whether there is a leniency to move *muktzeh machmas chisaron kis* with a *kikar oh tinok*, since *muktzeh machmas chisaron kis* is a vessel, yet it doesn't naturally have any leniencies to be moved. *Pri Megadim*[21] asks whether one can move *muktzeh machmas chisaron kis* with a *kikar oh tinok*, and he leaves it unresolved. R' Akiva Eiger says that the implication of *Shulchan Aruch se'if* 5 (from the fact *Shulchan Aruch* specifies *kli shemelachto l'issur* as opposed to just writing *kli*) is that the *heter* is exclusive to a *kli shemelachto l'issur*.

However, the implication of *Raavan* brought by *Rosh* is that even with *muktzeh machmas chisaron kis* there is a leniency. *Rosh*[22] says that *kikar oh tinok* applies to something that has a *toras kli*. Implicit is that even a purse that is *muktzeh machmas chisaron kis* can be moved with *kikar oh tinok*.

Taz[23] asks the following contradiction in *Rosh*: *Rosh paskens* that even if one placed a *kikar oh tinok* on a lamp that was lit when Shabbos commenced, it wouldn't allow one to move it. Yet *Rosh* rules one can move a *kli shemelachto l'issur* with *kikar oh tinok*, a candle is a *kli shemelachto l'issur*, so why doesn't a *kikar oh tinok* help? (*Shulchan Aruch paskens* like *Rosh* on both these points and so this contradiction is true also in *Shulchan Aruch*'s stance.) *Taz* answers that one can differentiate between a *kli shemelachto l'issur* and a lamp. A *kli shemelachto l'issur* is permitted to be

---

20. Responsa, first edition, *siman* 22.

21. *Mishbetzos Zahav*, point 4.

22. Responsa *siman* 22. *Rosh* says that since the money is nullified by the purse, one can move it even without *kikar oh tinok*. But from the fact that he originally posited that *kikar oh tinok* was applicable indicates that he held it is applicable to *muktzeh machmas chisaron kis*.

23. 311:5.

moved *l'tzorech gufo u'mekomo* and is only forbidden *m'chamah l'tzel,* whereas the lamp has no permissible ways of moving at all since it was a *bosis* to the flame, which is *muktzeh machmas gufo* when Shabbos came in. Therefore *kikar oh tinok* wouldn't help.[24] The reason for the distinction must be that only a vessel which has *heterim* to move, does *Rosh* extend the leniency of *kikar oh tinok.* While vessels that have no *heter,* such as *muktzeh machmas chisaron kis,* for example, a purse won't be permitted. Evidently the *Taz* doesn't hold that *Rosh* permits even *muktzeh machmas chisaron kis.*

R' Akiva Eiger brings a proof in favor of permitting *kikar oh tinok* to permit moving *muktzeh machmas chisaron kis.* The Gemara that brought the leniency to move the mortar with garlic was speaking according to the opinion of Abaye, who holds that there is no *heter* to move a *kli shemelachto l'issur* even *l'tzorech gufo u'mekomo,* and yet the presence of the garlic in the mortar still functions as a *kikar oh tinok,* which allows the mortar to be moved. We see from here that the *heter* of *kikar oh tinok* can even include items that don't have any permissible ways of being moved on Shabbos. R' Akiva Eiger then rejects this proof because he proves that Abaye anyway holds that the *heter* of *kikar oh tinok* was not limited to a

---

24. *Korban Nesanel* and *Nesiv Chaim* give a similar answer. Since the *geder* of *kikar oh tinok* is that it makes it less apparent that one is carrying *muktzeh,* only for a vessel that has a *heter* of *l'tzorech gufo* where the onlooker can think it is being moved permissibly does the leniency help. For a vessel that can't be moved, what does it help to place a *kikar oh tinok*? One will still think it is being moved forbiddingly.

Perhaps even according to the alternative way *kikar oh tinok* works we can suggest another idea. Since the *geder* of *kikar oh tinok* is similar to *bosis,* it would only help if there is no additional *issur* item on top of the *muktzeh* as well. In the case of the candlesticks, one places the loaf on top, but there is also *muktzeh* on top that is trying to forbid the candlesticks.

Mori V'Rabi R' Ariav Ozer suggested a new idea in *Rosh.* Something that is *muktzeh* due to *gezeiras keilim* is permitted with a *kikar oh tinok,* while something that is forbidden because of *muktzeh,* i.e., *haktzaas hadaas,* wouldn't have this *heter.* A lamp that is alight is forbidden because it is a *bosis;* it is subject to a regular status of *muktzeh.* A mortar is a *kli shemelachto l'issur* that belongs to *gezeiras keilim,* so it can have a leniency of *kikar oh tinok.* If so, then *muktzeh machmas chisaron kis* wouldn't have the leniency of *kikar oh tinok* since it belongs to *muktzeh.* ואכמ"ל.

deceased. We do not follow Abaye, so we can't conclusively prove from Abaye's practice.

Perhaps we can bring another proof from the continuation of this Gemara. As we mentioned, the Gemara establishes the *heter* of moving the mortar even according to the opinion of Rebbe Nechemiah. He holds that one can't move anything if it is not *l'tzorech tashmish hameyuchad lo* (its designated purpose). A garlic crusher can only be moved for crushing garlic, but since that is forbidden, it can't be moved at all and yet it has a *heter* of *kikar oh tinok*. Implicit in this is that the *heter* of *kikar oh tinok* can even encompass something that doesn't have any *heter tiltul* at all.[25] *Meiri* says that according to Rebbe Nechemiah one can move anything *l'tzorech gufo* with a *kikar oh tinok*.

The Arguments in Favor and Against

To explain the argument whether *kikar oh tinok* would help even with a *kli shemelachto l'issur*, or that it's only a specific *heter* given for a corpse, due to *kavod hameis* (honor of the deceased), one could say it depends on the two aforementioned ways of understanding *kikar oh tinok*. If it is just a sign to minimize the implication of the *muktzeh* being moved, but in essence one is still moving the *muktzeh*, we should limit the leniency to where we find the Gemara mentions it, i.e., a corpse, there are no grounds to expand it further. However, if we explain that *kikar oh tinok* is a form of *bosis*, surely it can extend to include a *kli shemelachto l'issur*. The logic is that the *muktzeh* is nullified by the *heter* item on top. Perhaps we can explain the reason why *kikar oh tinok* was limited to a corpse and no other *muktzeh machmas gufo*, while all *kli shemelachto l'issur* would have this leniency. Since *keilim* are designated as objects that serve other items, it is more relevant for them to be nullified by items they are serving. Therefore they would always have the ability to be nullified by the non-*muktzeh* item on top, since their entire existence is to hold things. In contrast, items that are *muktzeh machmas gufo*, intrinsically have no

25. After I saw that *Chazon Ish* 47:11 brings this proof.

purpose at all, so it's more difficult to consider them to be nullified by something else they are carrying.

However, this cannot be true in *Rashba*. We saw earlier that he learned that *kikar oh tinok* works via *bosis*, which should translate that *kikar oh tinok* would also permit a *kli shemelachto l'issur*. Yet he argues that the only reason the mortar was moved is that when it has garlic inside it changes from being a *kli shemelachto l'issur* to being a *kli shemelachto l'heter*, namely that the mortar is now functioning as a permissible vessel for storing garlic. He rejects the opinion that the garlic can function as *kikar oh tinok*. We see that despite holding that it is a form of *bosis*, he still holds that the *heter* is exclusive to a corpse.

When a Kli Specifically Stores a Certain Item

Shulchan Aruch[26] brings the lenient opinion who holds that *kikar oh tinok* helps even with a *kli shemelachto l'issur*. *Kaf HaChaim*[27] writes that since *Taz* and *Gra* argue, ideally one shouldn't rely on this opinion. Only in a pressing situation should one rely on this opinion. If one's cookbooks are left in the rain, one can place a non-*muktzeh* item on top of the books to bring them inside because otherwise they'll get ruined. However, if one has an expensive camera on his bed (question #1), one cannot use *kikar oh tinok* to move it, since, as we noted above, there is a contradiction in the opinion of *Shulchan Aruch* and according to all four resolutions we suggested there is no *heter* to move *muktzeh machmas chisaron kis* via *kikar oh tinok*.

There is a third way to understand the Gemara we mentioned earlier that permits the mortar to be moved with the garlic inside. *Meyuchas LaRan* explains that the mortar is nullified by the garlic the same way a pot is nullified by the dish contained within. This will explain the reason permitting all movement of pots with food inside. Even though a pot is *kli shemelachto l'issur*, since the food inside is considered the main item that is being moved, the pot is nullified by that. He understands that some

---

26. 308:5.

27. 308:52.

items have an intrinsic connection to one another, and therefore they can be nullified one by the other. The mortar is *specifically* meant to store garlic inside after the garlic has been crushed, so when the garlic is inside, it's as if one is only carrying the garlic, since the mortar is nullified by it.[28]

This explanation results in even more leniencies than *Rashba*'s explanation. According to *Rashba,* the *heter* of moving the mortar is since it changes into a *kli shemelachto l'heter.* A vessel has a limitation that it can't be moved for no reason at all. However, according to this new approach, it is considered that one is only moving food, food is not subject to any limitations of *muktzeh* at all. *Graz*[29] and *Mishnah Berurah*[30] both *pasken* like this latter understanding. They say that if one has a *kli issur* that is designed for storing a non-*muktzeh* item, when the *heter* is inside it is permitted to move the *kli.* This is based on this understanding of a *kli* being nullified by the contents that it is designated to carry.

Practical Application - Moving a Soup Pot

To apply this practically: Even though a kettle is a *kli shemelachto l'issur,* when it has water inside the kettle is nullified by the water and can be moved freely, even *m'chamah l'tzel* (question #4). Similarly, a pot with chicken soup can be returned to the fridge, even though one is moving it to preserve the food (question #3), because one's act is considered only to be moving the chicken soup. (Even without the *din* of this *Ran,* the pot would still be permitted to move since it has now become a *kli shemelachto l'heter,* as *Rashba* explained.)

Summary

Chazal gave a special leniency to move a corpse on Shabbos by the placing of a *kikar oh tinok.* A child or loaf of bread are only examples of items that

---

28. This also could be what *Rashi* means when he explains that the *heter* of moving the mortar is that it is being moved "*agav*" the garlic. ע״ש.

29. 308:22.

30. 308:26.

are not *muktzeh*. Any non-*muktzeh* item can be used. We find two reasons to explain this leniency: Either the *kikar oh tinok* acts as a sign, reminding one that he is handling *muktzeh*, and only because there is an extreme need is it currently permitted to be moved. Or it functions similar to *bosis*, with the *muktzeh* becoming subordinate to the item on top. Some learn that the Gemara that states the *heter* of *kikar oh tinok* being limited to a corpse is literal - *kikar oh tinok* was instituted only for a corpse - while other commentators learn that the Gemara is only limiting *kikar oh tinok* within *muktzeh machmas gufo*, that a corpse is the only *muktzeh machmas gufo* that has the *heter* of *kikar oh tinok*. However, all vessels would also have the *heter* of *kikar oh tinok*. *Shulchan Aruch paskens* like the second opinion. We explained that the two ways of understanding the *heter* of *kikar oh tinok* can explain this dispute. If *kikar oh tinok* is a sign, then it is limited to a corpse, but if the reason is based on *bosis*, it should apply to all vessels. However, we saw that this is not necessarily conclusive. When a *muktzeh* vessel is made to store a non-*muktzeh* item, e.g., a kettle and water, we view it as if one is only carrying the item within. This has practical application regarding various kitchen vessels, that there will be no restrictions moving them when there is something inside.

Answers

1. If the camera is *muktzeh machmas chisaron kis*, there is no leniency to place a non-*muktzeh* item on top to enable Yitzchak to carry it.
2. Chazal gave a special *heter* to move a corpse, despite being *muktzeh*, by placing a non-*muktzeh* item on top of it. One can then move it, even by carrying the body.
3. A pot is a *kli shemelachto l'issur* and so can't be move to protect it. However, when it has food inside, the pot has the same status as the food and can be moved freely.
4. The same idea as the pot applies to a kettle with water inside. The kettle can be moved back to its base.

Chapter 17

תינוק ואבן בידו

[Carrying] a Child With a Stone in his Hand

Questions

1. Little Aharon is having a tantrum, refusing to leave the *kiddush*. He's clutching money he found on the floor. What can his parents do?
2. The children are playing around with markers and I'm worried they may color on the walls. Can I pick up a child while a marker is still in his hand?
3. Is it permitted to carry a baby with a dirty diaper (not in order to change him)?
4. Aharon found money on his way home from shul. Once he's picked it up, can an adult continue holding his hand to walk him home?

Certain items can become secondary to another object, so much so that regarding the prohibition of transporting it wouldn't be considered that one has carried them. For example, the Mishnah[1] writes that if one carries a person on a bed in a public domain, one is not liable at all. Regarding the person we say, "*Chai noseh es atzmo* - A live person is considered to be carrying himself" and regarding the bed we say that it is nullified by the person. So too, if one carries a person who is wearing clothes,

1. 93b.

one is not liable due to the *hotzaah* of the clothes since they are *tafel* to the person.

Carrying a Child Who Is Holding Money

The Mishnah[2] teaches us that one can carry his son (in a private domain) even if the infant is holding a stone. Rava limits the Mishnah's leniency specifically to when the infant is carrying a stone - not if he is carrying money. The novelty of the Mishnah is that even though the stone is *muktzeh*, if one is carrying an infant who is carrying the stone, it is permitted to carry the infant.

Ramban[3] explains that the Gemara originally thought that a stone would be nullified to the infant, to the extent that the father isn't considered carrying the stone at all; the moving of the stone is not attributed to the father. That explains the leniency of the Mishnah: The *muktzeh* stone is not being carried by the father. But since it's abnormal for infants to carry money, the money doesn't become secondary to the infant and it is considered that the father is moving the money. The father is really the one carrying the money; he is just "using" his child as a means to do so.

The Gemara then retracts from this - that only something that serves a person's body can be considered nullified by the person - to the extent that the one lifting the person is only considered carrying the person and not the other items, e.g., clothes or jewelry. A stone can't be nullified to a child to the extent that the father is not considered moving the *muktzeh*; rather, the stone is an independent item that the infant is carrying and in turn by the father carrying the infant, he is also carrying the stone. This form of carrying is not direct, yet it can sometimes be a normal way of carrying. Hence *Ramban* phrases it *tiltul katan* and *Rashi* calls it *tiltul shelo b'yadayim*. The father is carrying the *muktzeh*, but in a more lenient fashion.

Due to this retraction, the Gemara is forced to explain the Mishnah entirely differently. The leniency is specifically when the infant has

---

2. 141b.

3. *Ramban* 141b, s.v. אי הכי. *Rashba* also has a near-identical explanation.

gaagu'in - he is in a state of panic to the extent that he is sick; if his father doesn't pick him up to calm him down, he'll become more sick. For this level of sickness (not life-threatening) Chazal permit this lower level of *tiltul*, but not the outright moving of *muktzeh*.

The Gemara continues to ask that if this circumstance of *gaagu'in* enables us to disregard the problem of the father carrying *muktzeh*, we should also permit when the infant is holding money. What is the difference between a stone and money? The Gemara answers that we are worried the father may come to pick up the money directly were it to be dropped, and this is more severe than the indirect moving, which is what we permit while carrying the infant. But if the infant was to drop the stone, the father will leave it on the floor, so there's no worry that this leniency will lead to direct moving of *muktzeh*.

Really It's a Form of Tiltul Min HaTzad

Tosafos HaRid and *Ritva* have a similar approach in the Gemara. They explain that the *heter* is *tiltul min hatzad*, meaning that we consider it as if the father is the one who is moving the stone. It's not a movement that's disassociated from the father. Rather, since the father is not moving it directly, he is moving the child who is carrying the *muktzeh*, so the father is treated as indirectly moving the *muktzeh*. The Gemara had to establish the case where the child had *gaagu'in* because without a *tzorech* (need), one can't even do *tiltul min hatzad*. Since the child will panic without the stone, the father has a legitimate reason in carrying the stone, and since it is in an indirect manner it is permissible. (Had there not been a worry that the father would pick up the money, so even if the infant was carrying money it would have been permitted.) [4]

---

4. *Keren Orah* (142b) infers from the way *Rambam* juxtaposed this halachah with the halachah of *pugla*, that *Rambam* learns that it's a form of *tiltul min hatzad*. *Keren Orah* differs slightly to *Tosafos HaRid* in explaining why only by *gaagu'in* is it permitted. He says that really it is *tiltul min hatzad l'tzorech davar ha'assur*, just when the infant has *gaagu'in* it is *mutar* because only then do we consider the main reason the father is carrying the infant is for the sake of the infant alone.

(*Chazon Ish* seemingly argues on these *Rishonim*. He says that since in this instance the father has an active interest in moving the stone, the infant will cry if the stone is taken from him. Since it's being carried to keep the infant calm, it's *tiltul min hatzad l'tzorech davar ha'assur* - moving indirectly for the sake of something forbidden. *Tosafos HaRid* must understand that since one is not moving the stone to actively use it, he has no positive interest in the stone being in the location in which he is moving the infant. It is not considered that one is moving it for the sake of the *muktzeh*, i.e., the stone. The father's interest is in moving the infant only. His action is only directly toward the infant. It's true that he wants the infant to remain calm, and the moving of the stone is not what he wants per se; it's just the means by which he achieves this need.)

Can You Walk Holding the Child's Hand?

As we have seen, the problem with carrying an infant who is holding money is not specifically a problem of *tiltul*, but it's forbidden because of a worry that if the money falls, the father is likely to pick it up and move it directly. *Rashi* adds: It follows that to hold the infant's hand and walk with him when he has money in his (other) hand is also forbidden. The same worry exists: If it falls down, the father might come to pick it up. *Ramban* argues on *Rashi*. He asks that if so, one should never be allowed to stand in close proximity to any infant holding money. *Rashba* defends *Rashi* that the concern only applies to one's own infant, since that money belongs to him. Regarding other infants there is obviously no worry.

Ramban understands that the reason Chazal were worried that one might come to move the money directly is because one can confuse the *heter* of carrying the infant who is holding the money with direct *tiltul*. Even when carrying the child, it is a form of carrying an item, so people might mistakenly think that, flat out, all ways of moving what is in the child's hand is permitted. In contrast, if one is walking with an infant who is holding money, there is no worry if it falls the father will pick it up, because originally no form of *tiltul* was being performed that one can error in thinking that there is a leniency in moving *muktzeh* in this circumstance.

Shulchan Aruch[5] brings both opinions. First he *paskens* like *Rashi* - that it's permitted to carry an infant who is holding a stone. However, if he is carrying money, then even walking holding the infant's hand is forbidden. Then he brings the opinion of *Ramban* as "*yesh omrim,*" that only carrying an infant who is holding money is problematic. The usual rule with "*stam v'achar machlokes*" (an unauthored opinion followed by an opinion titled "some say") is that the main opinion of *Shulchan Aruch* is with the *stam*. If so, when one's infant is holding something of value, a fifty-pound bill or one's wallet with his credit cards, one wouldn't be allowed to walk holding the infant's hand.

Location Matters

In which locations would this *issur* be relevant? It's clear from *Rashi* that the case of the Mishnah is only discussing a courtyard. The Gemara explicitly writes that in a public domain there is a problem of *hotzaah,* so even if the infant is only carrying a stone, it is not permitted to carry him in a public domain. But what is encompassed in a courtyard? Did *Rashi* mean all types of private domains, or is it specifically a courtyard and similar enclosed places where the public pass through? The difference is that perhaps in one's house one is less worried about even something valuable, since it will regardless remain within his domain, and therefore there is less of a worry he may come to pick it up. However, places such as shuls or hotels, even though they are a private domain, if money falls on the floor one will come to carry it. Both according to *Rashi* and *Ramban,* perhaps there is no worry that in one's own house if an infant drops money that the father will pick it up. Therefore, as long as there is *gaagu'in* it would be permitted to lift the infant even if he is holding money. In one's house one doesn't need to be worried what he is carrying.

---

5. 309:1.

Is the Father Picking It Up for Himself, or for the Child?

We are worried that one might come to pick up the money if the infant drops it, but we need to establish for whose sake he is picking it up. Will he give it back to the infant to carry, or will the father now take it for himself? *Shevus Yitzchak* says that there is a big difference between these two options. What would the halachah be if the infant is carrying a valuable *kli shemelachto l'issur*? If we are worried that the father will do this *tiltul* to safeguard his object, perhaps he will move this *kli shemelachto l'issur* to safeguard it, which is a *tiltul* of *m'chamah l'tzel* and is forbidden. However, if the father will give it to the infant who is playing with this object, it can be considered as moving *l'tzorech gufo*. He is moving it so that it should be used and would be permitted.

The simple understanding of the *Rishonim* is that the father will pick it up to guard it for himself. *Shitah LaRan* adds a crucial word: *l'hatznio* - he will pick up the money in order to "conceal it." We saw *Ramban* explain that the concern is that one will mistake the *heter* of carrying the money via the infant with carrying the money directly. Perhaps we can deduce from this like the other option, that one is picking it up for the infant's sake. (One can ask that it is not very likely that one will confuse the carrying via the child, which is for the sake of the son, and direct carrying for his own sake. These are two very different acts. It's more likely that he will confuse carrying it for the sake of the infant indirectly and indirectly.) Therefore, according to this understanding in *Ramban*, it follows that if the child is holding a *kli shemelachto l'issur* there would be no problem with carrying him.

Mishnah Berurah[6] understands the concern is that since one wants to keep the money, he will pick it up and give it back to the infant to continue to carry. According to *Mishnah Berurah*, there could be what to rely on to carry an infant who is holding an expensive *kli shemelachto l'issur*, such as an expensive pen, since were one to pick it up, it would be to hand back to the infant to keep him happy, which is regardless permitted since it is *l'tzorech gufo*.

---

6. *Se'if katan* 5.

If an infant has a marker in his hands (question #2): Let's accept the assumption that people are particular to keep a marker, unlike a stone, but not to the extent that one will pick up a marker if it drops. So if an infant is in a state of distress and holding a marker, according to all opinions it is permissible to carry him.[7] If, however, one wouldn't leave the marker on the floor, it would be similar to money and, despite being a *kli shemelachto l'issur,* according to *Mishnah Berurah* it would be forbidden.

Does This Rule Apply beyond when He Has Gaagu'in?

A more common instance is when the child has no *gaagu'in,* yet a parent wants to pick him up. Is it permissible for a parent to move a child from where he is because he may color the walls with the marker? According to *Ramban*'s explanation,[8] when the child is holding the *muktzeh,* it's as if the father himself is carrying it, albeit in a less severe manner ; this is because it's a usual way of carrying. So only when there is *gaagu'in* did Chazal

---

7. The only indication we find from the *poskim* of this question is *Magen Avraham* 308:13. When discussing the practice they used to have, that the first time they would bring their infant to shul, the infant would accompany the father holding a candle to donate to the shul, *Magen Avraham* references *siman* 309. *Machatzis HaShekel* expounds that *Magen Avraham* means that according to the first opinion (*Rashi*), it is forbidden to even hold the infant's hand and walk with him, while according to the *yesh omrim* one can be lenient, and perhaps that's what this practice was based on. Simply, a candle is a *kli shemelachto l'issur* — if it fell, the father would pick it up — and we see that *Magen Avraham* would be stringent. It seems like the worry is he himself will safeguard it and therefore is relevant even with a *kli shemelachto l'issur,* which is forbidden to move to safeguard.

8. *Mishnah Berurah* also explains this way. What is the opinion of *Shulchan Aruch* on the following matter? *Shulchan Aruch* writes that "one is not considered carrying the stone. It is only permitted when there is *gaagu'in...*" At first thought it sounds contrary to *Ramban,* that one is not considered to be carrying it. Maybe all *Shulchan Aruch* intends is to bring part of the reason why we can be lenient when there is *gaagu'in,* because it is not a real form of *tiltul.* But without *gaagu'in* he would agree that it is forbidden because it's considered that the father is the one carrying the *muktzeh. Shulchan Shlomo* leaves the question unanswered, and in *Shevet HaLevi,* vol. 5, *siman* 43, he has a different answer.

permit this *tiltul.* Without the special of *heter* of *gaagu'in* one is deemed to being moving *muktzeh.* So obviously it is forbidden!

Even according to *Tosafos HaRid,* that carrying via a child is *tiltul min hatzad,* since in this instance the father wants to move the infant to prevent the inevitable marking of the walls, it is undoubtedly *tiltul min hatzad l'tzorech davar ha'assur.* One's intention is not that the child should be in a different location, but rather the marker. But since he can't directly handle the marker, he is moving it via moving the child. This is classical *tiltul min hatzad l'tzorech davar ha'assur.*

Is the Need to Have the Child Home Insufficient?

Another common scenario is when an infant is holding *muktzeh,* e.g., an electric toy, and doesn't want to let go of it, but the father needs the child to come with him. Can he pick up the child? Again, according to *Ramban,* since this is a manifestation of *tiltul muktzeh* there won't be room to permit it. *Tosafos HaRid* will define this as *tiltul min hatzad,* but without *gaagu'in,* can we find a scenario where it is considered *l'tzorech*? I would have thought that if one needs the infant to come home with him, then the father's carrying is being done for a need. His act in the bigger picture is defined as moving the *muktzeh* for a positive, permissible need. Yet *Graz* says that without *gaagu'in* there is no "*tzorech*" in carrying the child. Surely it depends on the case; an infant who can't walk and one needs to carry home unquestionably is a *tzorech.* As we discussed in chapter 13, if one carries *muktzeh* even via a non-*muktzeh* item, he must first try to do *ni'ur* (shake the *muktzeh* out). One must therefore shake the infant's hand until the *muktzeh* falls out, or bribe the child to take a candy in place of the *muktzeh* and then carry him. If these attempts fail, one can rely on the *tiltul min hatzad.*[9] Though, as we have noted, *Mishnah Berurah* does not follow *Tosafos HaRid* and *Graz.*

---

9. What would *Chazon Ish pasken* in this case? *Chazon Ish* explains that the ruling of the Mishnah can't be based on *tiltul min hatzad* because the infant will cry if the stone is taken from him. Therefore the father also has an interest in moving the stone, which is *tiltul min hatzad l'tzorech davar ha'assur.* If the infant won't

Nevertheless, in certain instances it will be permitted according to all opinions! In the aforementioned scenario, the child is refusing to leave a *kiddush* and is being stubborn to release the *muktzeh* (question #1), and is at the age where removing the *muktzeh* won't cause him *gaagu'in*. Nevertheless if the father left the *kiddush* without the child, that certainly will cause him to have a tantrum. Included in the *heter* of *gaagu'in* is to prevent the child's pain, so if leaving the child alone will cause him extreme panic, and one needs to go home according to all opinions, one can carry the child.

Dirty Diapers

Excrement is *muktzeh*. It's classic *muktzeh machmas gufo*, as it has no purpose, but there is a special *heter* of *graf shel re'i*, which means that something repulsive can be moved. When an infant has had a bowel movement and his diaper is still on him (question #3), are there any restrictions regarding what one can do with him? As we explained at the beginning, clothes are nullified by the body to the extent that one is not considered carry the clothes. A clean diaper is serving the body and so is treated as a piece of clothing. If the diaper is dirty, is the halachah different? On the one hand it still serves the body (in the event the child relieves himself further), but on the other hand it's now meant to be taken off and discarded - so how can it be considered part of the child's body?

If we view a dirty diaper not part of the baby and that one is doing *tiltul* on the diaper, we reenter the above discussion whether there are circumstances to permit moving the child even without *gaagu'in*. However, it's certainly more plausible that one's act of carrying is not attributed to the diaper nor the excrement. Even if it is not nullified by the infant, the parent certainly doesn't want to be carrying it. It's therefore not part of the father's act at all! Therefore, one has no reason not to carry a baby with a dirty diaper.

---

panic if one removed the item from his hand, but nevertheless one has failed in getting the child to relinquish holding the *muktzeh*, then in truth one's action is *tiltul min hatzad l'tzorech davar ha'mutar*.

Summary

The Gemara permits carrying a child who would otherwise have a tantrum, even if he has a stone in his hand, but not if he is carrying money, since there is a worry that if the money falls one will pick it up. *Rashi* extends the worry even to holding the child's hand while holding money, while *Ramban* explains that carrying a child who is holding money is tantamount to the father holding the money.

We suggested that the worry that one may pick up the money is only applicable in an area where other people walk through, as opposed to one's private home. As we inferred, the worry is that the father will pick up the money to safeguard himself. Therefore, we can't be lenient if the infant is carrying a *kli shemelachto l'issur*, as the same concern is relevant.

A question on the *sugya* was why it is not permitted simply based upon *tiltul min hatzad*. Several *Rishonim* explain that this is the normal way to carry items, so it's as if the father himself is carrying the *muktzeh* item, albeit in a slightly more lenient manner. Others explain that while it is *tiltul min hatzad*, without *gaagu'in* one is missing the prerequisite of "a need" to move *muktzeh*. *Chazon Ish*'s explanation is that the father is also interested in moving the stone to calm the child, so it is *tiltul min hatzad l'tzorech davar ha'assur*. *Mishnah Berurah* follows the first explanation, so it is unlikely that there is a room to be lenient when the child will not become sick if one doesn't carry him.

Answers

1. Even if little Aharon will get into a state of panic if his parents left him at the *kiddush*, Chazal still didn't permit carrying a child who is carrying money. However, one can walk holding the child's hand even if he has money in the other hand.

2. If the child will not panic if the markers are taken away from him, there is no room to be lenient. By carrying the child one is deemed to be carrying the marker, albeit in an indirect manner.

3. The diaper, even if soiled, is considered nullified by the child, so there is no reason to be stringent not to carry the infant.

4. Whether one can walk holding a child's hand who is carrying money is a dispute between *Rashi* and *Ramban*. *Shulchan Aruch* is stringent.

Chapter 18

נגיעה ושימוש במוקצה

Touching and Using Muktzeh

Questions

1. Dan's bike is getting ruined by rain. Can he cover it with a plastic cover?
2. Can I rest my foot on a stone in order to tie my shoelaces? Can I sit on a stone in order to tie the laces?
3. Can I lean against or sit on a parked car?
4. Rafi left a box of antibiotics on the table. Can he use it to prop up his Chumash?

Shulchan Aruch[1] *paskens* that one can touch *muktzeh*: דבר שהוא מוקצה מותר ליגע בו..., and *Rema* refers this to earlier in the *siman*, where he already maintained that it is permissible to touch *muktzeh*. *Raavad*[2] *paskens* that touching *muktzeh* is forbidden. His source is a *Yerushalmi*,[3] where it is written that one is allowed to cover a freshly laid egg with a vessel, as long as one doesn't *touch* the egg. However, *Maggid Mishnah* argues with this and states that there is no reason why one shouldn't be able to touch *muktzeh*.

---

1. 308:42.
2. Ch. 25, halachah 23.
3. *Beitzah*, ch. 1, halachah 5.

Terumas HaDeshen[4] asks: How does the aforementioned *Yerushalmi* concur with that which the earlier *Rishonim* already *paskened,* that touching *muktzeh* is permitted? He answers that similar to the distinction we find regarding *tiltul min hatzad* - that when it is done for the sake of the non-*muktzeh* it is permitted, but is forbidden when done for the *muktzeh* - similarly here: When the touching is done for the sake of the *muktzeh,* like the case of covering the egg, then it is forbidden. However, if the touching is for the sake of something *mutar,* it is permissible. *Maggid Mishnah* answers that the *Yerushalmi* is only advising not to put a *kli* on top of an egg. Since it is round, it's very likely to move when one touches it. However, something unlike an egg wouldn't be forbidden to touch. This reconciliation is also explicit in *Meiri,*[5] that the *Yerushalmi* is only giving advice to avoid moving *muktzeh.*

Gra[6] says that *Shulchan Aruch* holds like *Maggid Mishnah.* The halachah permitting one to touch *muktzeh* isn't specifically if one's intention is not for the sake of the *muktzeh,* which would be the case according to *Terumas HaDeshen.* However, *Magen Avraham*[7] explains that when *Shulchan Aruch*[8] writes that one must be careful not to touch the *muktzeh* egg when covering it, despite writing earlier that touching is permitted, this is only permitted when it is not for the sake of the *muktzeh* - unlike in the case of covering the egg, like *Terumas HaDeshen. Mishnah Berurah,*[9] despite bringing both opinions earlier, *paskens* like *Gra,* that *Shulchan Aruch* is warning not to touch an egg lest it be moved, since it is prone to move through touching, but touching regular *muktzeh* items would be permitted even for the sake of the *muktzeh.*

---

4. 67.
5. 125a.
6. 310:6.
7. 310:3.
8. 310.
9. 310:22.

Covering a Bike

Since one is permitted to touch *muktzeh,* covering a bike with a rain cover (question #1) should not pose any problems. However, one should be careful while doing not to move any part of the bike. It's very easy to accidentally move a wheel or a pedal. R' Moshe Feinstein[10] explains that a bike is a *kli shemelachto l'issur.* Since its purpose is for traveling and transporting people, its main use is forbidden. Even if this specific bike is only used inside an area with an *eiruv,* it is still designed for an forbidden use and would be a *kli shemelachto l'issur.* Accordingly, any *tiltul* of the bike *m'chamah l'tzel* (to protect it) it forbidden. (Some *poskim* claim based on *Ohr L'Tzion*[11] that a bike is a *kli shemelachto l'heter.* He explicitly says otherwise, that only a child's bicycle he says is not *muktzeh.* So covering a tricycle is permitted, even if one will move parts of the tricycle.)

Benefiting from Muktzeh

Sometimes touching *muktzeh* is not judged as just touching, but rather using the *muktzeh,* e.g., sitting on or leaning against a car (question #3; in an instance where the car would not move due to one's pressure). Even though one is only touching the *muktzeh,* and from that point of view there is no problem, maybe there is a new reason to forbid it: One is benefiting from the *muktzeh.*

Tosafos[12] proves that there is no *issur hanaah* (prohibition to derive benefit) from *muktzeh.* If one baked bread on Yom Tov with wood that was *muktzeh,* the bread is permitted. (We don't apply the principle that we find by other *issurim,* such as *kilei hakerem,* where we say that *shevach eitzim b'pas* - "the benefit of the wood is in the bread.") *Rashba*[13] proves likewise: Though it is forbidden to stoke the fire that is burning with pieces

10. Quoted in *Sefer Tiltulei Shabbos.*

11. Section 2, ch. 42, halachah 1.

12. *Pesachim* 26b, s.v. חדש יותץ.

13. *Shabbos* 29b, s.v. כי אדליק.

of *keilim* that are *muktzeh*, it is still permissible to benefit from the fire even though one is extracting benefit from the *muktzeh* vessels.

Rashba[14] learns that any form of active usage from *muktzeh* is forbidden. He extracts this principle from the Gemara[15] that forbids one to burn broken vessels on Yom Tov, even if one does not touch the actual vessels and only burns them in their place. We see that it's forbidden because one is using the *muktzeh* for his benefit. *Rashba* also forbids one to rest a bed on *muktzeh* since it is still considered to be taking benefit from *muktzeh*. He adds, however, that if the benefit comes about on its own, without one's active involvement, it is permitted to benefit from: "*hanaah d'memela shapir dami.*"

Sources Stating That Benefiting from Muktzeh Is Forbidden

The *Tanna Kamma*[16] permits returning a pot back into insulating blankets even though they are *muktzeh*. One is clearly taking benefit from the *muktzeh*, so why was the Gemara not bothered by this? Similarly, the Gemara[17] permits one to warm food in soil on the condition that one doesn't move the soil since it is *muktzeh*. Explicitly the Gemara is not bothered with the fact one is benefiting from the *muktzeh* - why?

To these questions, *Rashba* says, "*Yesh l'chalek ketzas* - One can slightly distinguish." Perhaps he means in these case one is not taking a new, direct benefit from the *muktzeh*, but the *muktzeh* is just being used to retain the heat - a more passive form of benefit. In contrast, by burning *muktzeh* firewood, one is actively taking benefit.[18]

---

14. 29a.
15. Ibid.
16. 49a.
17. 39a.
18. Alternatively, he means that a benefit that is indirect, i.e., it comes after one's act and is not performed simultaneously with one's act, is permitted. *Magen Avraham* brings a similar distinction to explain why one can burn a complete vessel. We will discuss this soon.

However, *Beis HaLevi*[19] adds further questions that he doesn't resolve. The Gemara[20] permits lying on *muktzeh*. (One can't remove the straw from the bed, but one can lie on the straw.) We see[21] that it is permitted to sit down on palm branches that are *muktzeh*.[22] We can add the question of *Ohr Samei'ach*[23] to the list: He notes that there is only a prohibition of cutting grass to feed your animal, but one is allowed to put his animal on the grass to graze, even though attached grass is *muktzeh* (according to *Magen Avraham*[24]) and the owner is thereby benefiting from *muktzeh*. These are classic examples of direct benefit from *muktzeh*, so how does it fit with *Rashba*'s principle that benefit that comes about through using is forbidden?

To further complicate matters, *Magen Avraham*[25] *paskens* that it is permitted to benefit from *muktzeh*, so one can benefit from the fire emitted from *muktzeh* wood. But one can't use *muktzeh*; burning *muktzeh* wood is forbidden. R' Akiva Eiger[26] understands that the source of *Magen Avraham* is *Rashba* that we've been discussing. So R' Akiva Eiger raises the following contradiction in *Magen Avraham*: *Rashba* forbids resting a bed on *muktzeh*, so R' Akiva Eiger presumes that according to *Rashba* surely sitting on *muktzeh* is also forbidden. Yet *Magen Avraham*[27] permits sitting on a stone?! R' Akiva Eiger leaves the contradiction unresolved.

---

19. Responsa, section 1, end of *siman* 12.
20. 141b.
21. 50b.
22. *Rashi* there explains that without an act of tying the branches together, they are *muktzeh* and can't be moved. Implicit the only problem is moving them, not sitting on them.
23. *Hilchos Yom Tov*, ch. 1, halachah 17.
24. 312:6.
25. 325:9.
26. *Gilyon R' Akiva Eiger* 325, *Magen Avraham, se'if katan* 9.
27. 308:41.

R' Elyashiv's Resolution

R' Yosef Shalom Elyashiv[28] argues on the comparison between resting on a bed and sitting on *muktzeh*. He claims *Rashba* would permit sitting on *muktzeh*. R' Elyashiv elaborates: *Rashba* only forbade one to take benefit when one's act that he is carrying out with his hand can be treated as "moving with his hands." He infers from the words "*v'afilo l'hishtamesh b'yadayim*" that *Rashba* means benefiting is forbidden when it can be construed as act of moving *muktzeh* with one's hands. One is lighting the *muktzeh* firewood with his hands, so it's as if his hands are moving *muktzeh*. Similarly, when one lifts the bed with his hands in order to rest it on the *muktzeh*, it's as if he's moving *muktzeh* with his hands. In contrast, lying or sitting on *muktzeh* is permitted since the way of use is not with one's hands, so it cannot be considered "moving with his hands." (To answer why warming the pots with the insulators is permitted, he says that since we are forbidding usage since it is a "form of moving *muktzeh*," what is forbidden is when one first begins to use the *muktzeh*, that first act of taking the benefit is deemed as moving the *muktzeh* if done with one's hands. In these cases, the pot was already insulated by the *muktzeh* from before, there was already benefit being extracted. When one now wants to return the pot to the insulators, that is not a beginning of an act of using *muktzeh* so is not deemed "moving *muktzeh*.")

R' Elyashiv's approach can be how *Magen Avraham* understands, since, as R' Akiva Eiger noted above, *Magen Avraham* permits sitting on *muktzeh*, yet holds that using *muktzeh* is forbidden. R' Akiva Eiger clearly didn't agree with R' Elyashiv's resolution and learns that *Rashba* forbids sitting on *muktzeh*.

Is Using Muktzeh Encompassed in Issur Achilah or Issur Tiltul?

Furthermore, R' Elyashiv's idea can be understood better in light of the following *Afikei Yam*.[29] He explains the halachah that *Rashba* brought out

---

28. *Kovetz Teshuvos* 3:59.
29. Section 2, *siman* 23.

from the Gemara, that to actively take benefit from *muktzeh* is forbidden, as follows: That which we find a restriction in using *muktzeh* stems from the *issur achilah* (prohibition in consuming) of *muktzeh*. As we saw in the introduction to *muktzeh*, there is an *issur achilah* on objects that are *muktzeh machmas gufo*. *Afikei Yam* explains that this doesn't only include a prohibition of eating or consuming, but even making use of the *muktzeh* is included. *Rashba* is extending the *issur* of using *muktzeh* even to a case where one doesn't move the *muktzeh*. *Afikei Yam* does note that *Mishnah Berurah* didn't learn like this. *Mishnah Berurah*[30] explains the reason why one can't burn broken vessels is: **דמעשה הדלקה שעושה בכלי שנדלקת על ידו חשוב טלטול** - "The act of burning the *muktzeh* is *as if you are moving the muktzeh*." It's clear that *Mishnah Berurah* learns that using *muktzeh* is part of Chazal's enactment of the *issur tiltul*[31] and not a part of the *issur achilah*, which, we explained in the introduction, preceded the *issur tiltul*.

Magen Avraham[32] notes that it will only be forbidden to benefit from the burning of an incomplete *kli*, but to burn a complete *kli* is *mutar*. Since while it is complete it is not *muktzeh*, even though the benefit that one gets from the vessel is at a stage where it is now *muktzeh*, it is now considered broken, as it is in the process of being burned up. However, this benefit only comes about indirectly, after one has done his action of placing the vessel in the fire, and is therefore permitted.

Graz's Distinction

Graz[33] says that we don't *pasken* like *Rashba*, forbidding one to actively take benefit from *muktzeh*. The Gemara[34] recalls that Rabban Gamliel descended on a ramp that a non-Jew built on Shabbos; the *Rishonim* explain that there is no problem of *muktzeh* to descend this ramp, even though the

30. 501:23.
31. *Shaar HaTzion* says the source of *Mishnah Berurah* is *Rashba*.
32. *Se'if katan* 12.
33. *Siman* 509, *Kuntres Acharon* 3.
34. 122a.

ramp itself is *muktzeh* since it was built on Shabbos (it is *nolad*). *Graz* understands that these *Rishonim* argue on *Rashba*, that descending the ramp is considered to be taking direct benefit from this item, even though it is *muktzeh* and yet we do *pasken* like this Gemara,[35] permitting one to descend on such a ramp.

Graz does agree that we *pasken* that it is forbidden to burn items that are *muktzeh*. He explains that the distinction why this is forbidden, as opposed to regular benefit, which is permitted: When burning the *muktzeh*, one is consuming the very essence of the object. Walking down a ramp or sitting on a stone is only using the external form of the *muktzeh*, but not actually consuming the very object itself. This is similar to that which we differentiated in the introduction to *muktzeh* between *muktzeh l'achilah* and *muktzeh l'tiltul* - the act of *achilah*, whereby the object is consumed during its use is a much more severe form of usage.

How Does Rashba Learn the Case of the Ramp?

However, it's unlikely that *Rashba* argues on the halachah of the Mishnah itself, which the *Rishonim* all *pasken*, where we permit using the ramp once the non-Jew made it for himself. So how will *Rashba* explain this case?

The principle R' Elyashiv taught will explain this as well. Walking down the ramp, even though one is using *muktzeh*, cannot be construed as a form of "moving with one's hands." Perhaps we can suggest a further variation behind the principle of *Rashba*.

As we quoted, *Rashba* himself conceded that when the benefit comes on its own it is permitted to take the benefit. This can be extended to certain actions where one is involved in one primary act and his act also involves using *muktzeh* but that is secondary. If the taking of the benefit is peripheral, we can define one's act solely as the primary act he is doing. When sitting on a rock, one's primary act is sitting; it just happens to be that he is also is benefiting from *muktzeh*. Since that is just haphazard, it doesn't define his act and the benefit is considered to be accrued on its own, which is permitted. In contrast, while resting a bed on a *muktzeh*

35. 276.

item, his act *is* one of using a *muktzeh* item as a leg. The benefit from the *muktzeh* is not just coincidental, but rather he is making the *muktzeh* a leg of his bed, which is direct benefit taken from *muktzeh*.

If this subtle distinction is true, we can apply it also to the case of the ramp. One is walking; the fact that he is only walking because of the *muktzeh* ramp doesn't change how we define his act. He is not actively taking from *muktzeh*, but rather it happens to come on its own.[36]

Ritva[37] uses a phrase to describe why it is permitted to sit on a rock despite it being *muktzeh*: דהא אין משמשות שום מעשה כי אם מעשה קרקע בעלמא. The stone isn't being used for an act, but rather we view the stone as an extension of the ground. Maybe the intention of *Ritva* is like we are suggesting: When one is sitting on a rock, we don't primarily treat it as if one is actively using the stone and hence the stone is considered being used.

Leaning on Muktzeh

Magen Avraham[38] writes that it is permitted to sit on a large stone that would not move under one's weight. It is forbidden to sit on palm branches without designating them before Shabbos because they will inevitably move under your weight. *Mishnah Berurah*[39] brings this opinion down as the final halachah. Therefore, sitting or leaning against a car that won't move is permissible (question #3).

---

36. I later saw *Chut Shani* present a similar answer (section 3, ch. 41, p. 51). This is similar to the distinction *Chazon Ish, Orach Chaim* 47:12 and 42:12, presents. He says that lying down on a bed is not indicative of using *muktzeh*. Even if the bed had no straw on it, you could still lie down. We are able to separate one's act of lying from the fact that one is benefiting from *muktzeh*. However, in a case where there is *muktzeh* on the floor and one wants to sit on it, one can't separate sitting down from using the *muktzeh*. Sitting on a rock is indicative of using *muktzeh*, so for sure one's act is attributed as *shimush muktzah*. (Still, *Chazon Ish* doesn't help us entirely; according to him it is forbidden to sit on *muktzeh*, different from how we concluded.)

37. 125b, s.v. צאו.

38. 308:41.

39. 308, point 88.

Therefore, even if we *pasken* like *Rashba,* unlike *Graz* says, one can sit on a stone to help him tie his shoelaces (question #2), since one's act isn't defined as using the *muktzeh*. However, according to all, one must make sure it's a firm stone and not one that may wobble when he rests his weight on it. Propping one's book on something that is *muktzeh* (question #4) is less straightforward. According to R' Elyashiv this is *shimush b'yadayim*. Even according to our distinction, surely the act of propping up the book can't be defined as something else; one is using the *muktzeh* and the act should be forbidden. If one is stringent for *Rashba,* one shouldn't prop up his book since it may be forbidden. However, according to *Graz* it would be permissible to raise the book on something that is *muktzeh* since he holds that we don't *pasken* like *Rashba* and that only burning *muktzeh* is *assur*.

Summary

The *Rishonim* argue whether touching *muktzeh* is permitted in all cases, or only when one's agenda is for the sake of something that is not *muktzeh,* as opposed to for the sake of the *muktzeh*. For example, sitting on a car is considered touching *muktzeh* for one's own sake. The final halachah in *Shulchan Aruch* sides with the lenient opinion.

Although there is no *issur hanaah* with *muktzeh, Rashba* proves that it is forbidden to directly benefit from it. Hence he explains why it is forbidden to burn something *muktzeh* even though one does not touch it. There are many refutations raised against this principle, and many ways suggested to answer *Rashba*. We saw from *Ritva* that items built on the ground are treated as a part of the ground. We used this idea to explain why it is permissible to descend a ramp that was built on Shabbos. It's as if one is walking on the ground, not on the ramp. Hence the *psak* of *Graz* that majority of the *Rishonim* argue on *Rashba* is not conclusive because we can permit descending the ramp yet forbid benefiting from *muktzeh*. But when necessary we can rely on *Graz* that it's permitted to actively take benefit from *muktzeh*.

Answers

1. When covering a bike, one must be careful not to move it. *Mishnah Berurah* concludes that touching *muktzeh* in all cases is permitted.

2. According to *Graz*, any form of benefit from *muktzeh* that comes on its own is permitted. Resting one's foot on a stone is a prime example of such. Even if one is stringent for the opinion of *Rashba*, we presented an argument to be lenient.

3. Leaning on *muktzeh* is permitted according to all opinions.

4. One should be stringent not to prop a book on something that is *muktzeh*. We explained that is a form of using *muktzeh* with one's hands, which is forbidden according to *Rashba*. Those who are lenient have *Graz* to rely on.

Chapter 19

גרף של רעי

Muktzeh That is Repulsive

Questions

1. Moshe's trash can has filled up. Can he throw out the bag?
2. Is it permitted to bring the garbage can to the table in order to sweep the trash that is on the table directly into the can?
3. The children emptied out a box of *muktzeh* toys all over the living room and guests are coming. Is it permitted to put the toys away?
4. Can I tidy up after a *kiddush* in a shul hall?
5. Can I put a dirty diaper in the trash can?

We learn from the Gemara in *Berachos*[1] the famous principle of *kavod habriyos* (respect for human dignity). It is so important to the extent that it even can push aside a positive mitzvah. *Graf shel re'i* literally means "a basin of excrement." It's an example of something considered by all to be repulsive. This basin is *muktzeh,* but nevertheless Chazal gave a special dispensation to move it. The *Rishonim*[2] learn that the reason of this *heter* is for the same reason: *kavod habriyos*! One can

1. 19a.
2. *Ritva* 121b and *Rashi* in *Beitzah* 36b.

ask: Why were Chazal required to make a special *heter* with *muktzeh* called *graf shel re'i*? Why didn't the regular *din* of *kavod habriyos* suffice?

Rashi says that excrement (*re'i*) is fit to be eaten by a dog. *Chazon Ish*[3] asks: Why do we need a special *heter* of *graf shel re'i*? The principle is that any items that are fit to be eaten by animals are not *muktzeh*. We can answer that while the excrement is potentially fit for animals and that can be a basis for moving it, that *heter* has specific criteria, such as the animal must be commonplace and one must regularly feed the animal these foods. While the *heter* of *graf shel re'i* is all inclusive, as long as it is bothersome, there are no other criteria or limitations.

From the scenarios of *graf shel re'i* brought by the various Gemaras, it's difficult to deduce a clear definition of which scenarios or objects are encompassed in the *heter*. The most lenient case mentioned in the Gemara[4] is dirty dishes after they have been eaten from. The Gemara asks according to Rebbe Nechemiah, who holds that objects can only be moved for their main use: הני כוסות וקערות היכי מטלטלין אותם - "How can we move used dishes?" The Gemara answers: *graf shel re'i*. One can suggest that one is not really disgusted or repulsed by dirty dishes - one is happy to leave them on the table for a while and wait until everyone has finished eating - yet the Gemara still defines this as *graf shel re'i*. Based on how we've explained that the *heter* of *graf shel re'i* is based upon *kavod habriyos*, we can understand the basis for reasoning that the *heter* is applicable beyond cases to where it disgusts a person. The very fact that it's *unpleasant* for a person that this item is currently in this place is enough to invoke the *heter*.

How to Define "Bothersome"

However, we need to establish how to apply this principle. Can we apply the *heter* of *graf shel re'i* in all instances where there is something that is bothersome, or are there any limitations? R' Bodner[5] quotes from R' Shlomo Zalman Auerbach that if there is something that would cause one

3. 48:10.

4. 123a.

5. *Sefer Tiltulei Shabbos*, responsa at the the end of the *sefer*.

to feel discomfort were a guest to walk in and see this object lying around, this would be included in the *heter* of *graf shel re'i*. It follows that small, inconsequential piece of trash, like a candy wrapper, which wouldn't bother most people even were a guest to walk in, would be forbidden to move and not have the *heter* of *graf shel re'i*. However, larger pieces of trash, such as an empty bags of chips, may very well be included in this *heter* of *graf shel re'i*, provided that its presence would bother one were a visitor to arrive.

The Heter Is Relative to the Owner

Not everyone considers toys scattered on the floor to be an unpleasant sight (Question#3). Do those who are very meticulous to always have the toys organized, and will be embarrassed if guests arrive and see the mess, have a *heter*? *Rema*,[6] in reference to moving a candle (they used to be fashioned from tallow, a putrid substance), writes that if one is an *istenis* (fastidious) he can move the candle out of the room, since it is a *graf shel re'i to him*. *Mishnah Berurah*[7] writes like this too, that the *heter* is relative to the owner. He says that if there is a pile of trash on a table, which *to him* is a *graf shel re'i*, it would be permitted to be moved. We see from this that anything that is personally unpleasant can be included in *graf shel re'i*.

Emptying a Full Garbage Bag

Taking a full garbage bag outdoors to be emptied (question #1) is a classic application of *graf shel re'i*, as the bag is extremely unpleasant. R' Shlomo Zalman Auerbach[8] is quoted to permit the removal of a garbage bag even when the trash can isn't emitting a foul odor, but one wants to throw it out simply because it is full. He explains that if one were to keep the full can inside the house, he'd now be required to hang an empty bag in the kitchen to store the future trash. That situation is unpleasant and thus justifies already emptying out the full bag of trash.

---

6. 279:1.
7. 308, point 115.
8. *Shemiras Shabbos K'Hilchasah* 22:40.

The Gemara[9] says when the *graf shel re'i* has a covering, it doesn't qualify for the *heter* of *graf shel re'i*. The logic is that since it is covered, one can't see that which is repulsive. This is not a refutation to R' Shlomo Zalman's leniency. Even if a trash can is closed and not currently in a situation of *graf shel re'i*, since the alternative option of hanging a bag in the kitchen to put future trash in is unpleasant and will be visible, he permits throwing it away. It is a preemptive usage of the *heter* of *graf shel re'i*. If one has a lid on his trash can that is withholding the smell, and it is not yet full, there won't be any leniency of *graf shel re'i* to throw out the bag.

Not Making a Graf Shel Re'i

Shulchan Aruch[10] *paskens*: אין עושין גש״ר לכתחילה - "You can't make in the first instance (or ideally) a *graf shel re'i*." We need to see the source of this halachah to understand what it means. We find this rule in two places: In *Beitzah*[11] the Gemara says that one can't invite a non-Jew to his Shabbos meal because of *ein osin graf shel re'i l'chatichilah*. It was common for people to dip their bread in their wine. If a non-Jew would do so, the wine becomes *assur b'hanaah* (forbidden to benefit from) due to the *issur* of *stam yayin*. In turn it becomes *muktzeh* because one can't do anything with this liquid. Now that it is *muktzeh*, the only leniency to move the non-Jew's used cup is under the pretext of *graf shel re'i*, since used dishes are disgusting. Since by inviting a non-Jew to dine, one is inevitably going to be required to rely on the *heter* of *graf shel re'i*. Therefore Chazal said that one should not invite a non-Jew in the first place in order not to have to rely on this leniency.[12]

---

9. *Shabbos* 47a.

10. 308:36.

11. 21b.

12. Even though *Shulchan Aruch paskens ein osin graf shel re'i l'chatichilah*, he still *paskens* (325:1) that you can invite a non-Jew on Shabbos. There are two answers found in the *Rishonim* why it's not a contradiction to the Gemara. (They ask it as a question on the Gemara, not just a contradiction in *Shulchan Aruch*.) Firstly, *Shulchan Aruch* holds that the leftover contents that are inside the cup are nullified by the cup. Therefore even the contents of the non-Jew's cup are nullified by his

The other place *ein osin graf shel re'i l'chatichilah* is mentioned is in *Shabbos.*[13] The Gemara records that while eating dates, R' Huna would make a pile of date seeds. When the pile reached the state of being repulsive, he would move them away, based on the *heter* of *graf shel re'i.* The Gemara asks: וכי עושין גש״ר לכתחילה, which means that it is not permitted to accumulate a pile of trash that will eventually reach a repulsive state enabling one to remove it. To support its claim that such an act is not permitted, the Gemara brings examples from other *Amoraim,* who, while eating nuts and fruits, would *immediately* throw the shells and peels behind their chairs in order not to make a pile that would eventually constitute a *graf shel re'i.*[14]

Should You Delegate to Someone Else to Move a Graf Shel Re'i?

From these two cases one can conclude that the meaning of *ein osin graf shel re'i l'chatichilah* is that one can't bring about a situation where he now has something disgusting and that requires a *heter* of *graf shel re'i* to remove. Since this is a weak leniency, it's better to avoid putting oneself in a situation whereby he will have to carry a *graf shel re'i.* This could be the reason behind the *psak* of *Aruch HaShulchan*[15] that if there is a non-Jew or even an infant who is available to carry this object, one must enlist them to move the *graf shel re'i* instead of doing it himself. (R' Moshe Feinstein[16] says that we should take on like this *Aruch HaShulchan.* If so, a stringency should apply that one who has a non-Jew in his house on Shabbos must ask the non-Jew to clean the table and shouldn't do so himself at all. R'

---

cup and one is considered to be only moving the cup, not the liquid (*Ran*). Secondly, we don't hold of the Gemara's distinction between *issur hanaah* and regular leftovers; neither are *muktzeh* and only something *muktzeh* can be *graf shel re'i* (*Meiri*).

13. 143a.

14. It must have been that the place where they threw it was not visible, and therefore there was no need for the peels to be collected. If what did they gain was visible, even on the floor it still constitutes a *graf shel re'i.*

15. 308:60.

16. Brought in *Sefer Tiltulei Shabbos,* point 39.

Chaim Pinchas Scheinberg[17] argues that the reason of *graf shel re'i* is *kavod habriyos,* which also demands that we show respect to non-Jews and not demand them that they do our dirty work for us. He brings a proof to this from *Chagigah* 5a.)

Normal Way of Behavior

Sfas Emes[18] asks: If we take on that *ein osin graf shel re'i l'chatichilah,* how can we go to the bathroom? (This is only relevant before flushable toilets were prevalent.) One is forcing himself to carry the *graf shel re'i* after he has finished excusing himself. We can add to *Sfas Emes*'s question: How can we eat on plates? A dirty plate is a *graf shel re'i,* as is explicit in the Gemara we mentioned above, and one will have to move it inevitably, when he's finished using it. Rather we must conclude that since this is the normal way of behavior, there isn't an issue of *ein osin graf shel re'i l'chatichilah.* The reasoning is that the problem with *ein osin graf shel re'i l'chatichilah* is to purposely bring about a situation where you will now have a *heter* of *graf shel re'i* to remove *muktzeh.* However, when one is doing a regular act that will only result in a *graf shel re'i,* this is not considered to be purposely making a *graf shel re'i.* He's just eating or using the bathroom. What happens as a result of that is inconsequential. Therefore both are permitted and not part of the *issur* of *ein osin graf shel re'i l'chatichilah.*

Dirty Diapers

When throwing out a dirty diaper (question #5), there are two possibilities: one could immediately take the diaper and throw it into the garbage can outside the house, i.e., the large bins on the streets, or he could place the diaper in the kitchen trash can and consequently, when the kitchen trash can smells, he can take that can and throw it out. Will this second option constitute a case of *ein osin graf shel re'i l'chatichilah,* since one is now

---

17. *Shalmei Yehudah, siman* 34, point 11.
18. *Beitzah* 21b.

causing his kitchen trash can to become a *graf shel re'i*? We can take this question a stage further: If someone has something smelly, is he forbidden from placing it inside the regular kitchen trash can, since this will cause a situation where he will subsequently rely on the *heter* of *graf shel re'i* to empty his kitchen trash can into an outdoor trash can?

Even if one's usual practice during the week is to throw the dirty diapers in the kitchen trash can and then take the can outside, throwing the trash in the kitchen trash can isn't permitted under the principle that we just established of "the normal way." The *Sfas Emes*'s principle was to permit an act that is performed for a different purpose but subsequently causes a *graf shel re'i*. Throwing the trash in the kitchen trash can is the very act of making a *graf shel re'i*. All the more so, those who don't usually place diapers in a trash can, but tie them in a diaper sack, would certainly not be allowed to place a diaper in a trash can if this will cause a situation where one will subsequently have to carry out the trash can.

When the Graf Shel Re'i Has to Be Created on Shabbos

The Gemara[19] asks a question on this idea - that when it's the normal practice of doing an act, it isn't a problem of making a *graf shel re'i* - when mentioning the case of the *Amoraim* who threw their pits and peels behind the bed in order to avoid a situation of creating a *graf shel re'i*. Surely they didn't behave that way during the week; during the week they would leave the trash in front of them. Since it is the norm to pile the shells and then throw them away, why were they forced to act in this way to avoid *graf shel re'i*?! The answer might be based on *Rashba*[20] (and *Shitah Mekubetzes*[21]), who implies that we *pasken* like R' Huna who did make a pile of the trash and then throw it away due to *graf shel re'i*. *Rashba* adds that it is permissible and not an issue of *ein osin graf shel re'i l'chatichilah* because it wasn't possible to do otherwise before Shabbos, i.e., the act of eating was only taking place now. Nothing was purposely left to be moved on Shabbos with a

19. *Shabbos* 143a.
20. *Beitzah* 21b.
21. Ibid.

heter of *graf shel re'i*. They only decided to eat the nuts now. We see explicitly that when it isn't possible to avoid the situation of creating a *graf shel re'i* before Shabbos, then if it is the normal way to perform this action, one can do it on Shabbos.[22]

However, this understanding of *ein osin graf shel re'i l'chatichilah* seems to be at odds with the Gemara in *Beitzah*.[23] The Gemara records that there was a leak in the millhouse of Abaye that was causing his pottery mill to disintegrate. Abaye was worried about the financial loss that the leak was causing to his mill, so Rava advised him to take his bed inside the house, and then he'd be able to move the mill out to a different place, as now the disintegrated mill's presence will be bothersome to him and he would have a *heter* of *graf shel re'i*. (Abaye was not previously using that area, so he did not yet have the *heter* of *graf shel re'i*.) The Gemara records that Abaye disregarded Rava's advice, and as a punishment his house collapsed. The *Rishonim* ask why was Abaye wrong in not listening, Abaye held *ein osin graf shel re'i l'chatichilah*, which is why he desisted from putting his bed there only in order to enable him to subsequently remove this disgusting item.

Tosafos presents two answers: Rava held either that when there is a financial loss it is permissible to create a *graf shel re'i*, or since the rain was already leaking, causing the mill to disintegrate, it is not considered to be

---

22. *Rambam* (ch. 26, halachah 15) doesn't *pasken* like *Rashba*. On the contrary, he brings down the halachah like the other *Amoraim*, requiring one to throw the pits on the floor. *Maggid Mishnah* explains that this is because *ein osin graf shel re'i l'chatichilah*. *Shulchan Aruch* recommends for an important person to treat pits as *muktzeh*. *Mishnah Berurah* (*se'if katan* 124) explains that one should spit them out on the floor with his mouth. They both don't seem to hold of this *sevara* that when it is the normal manner of eating it is permitted. Perhaps we can deflect the question: In this case it is extremely easy to avoid making the *graf shel re'i*. Once the pits are in one's mouth, he has two options: to spit them into a pile or to spit them onto the floor. *Rambam* understands that despite when in the way of eating it is permitted to make a *graf shel re'i*, since it is so easy to avoid here, it must be avoided. R' Elyashiv explained that we are not obligated to spit our seeds onto the floor because nowadays a mess on the floor is a *graf shel re'i* to us, so one has not gained anything by spitting on the floor. In the olden days it wouldn't qualify as a *graf shel re'i* if it was left on the floor, hence it was obligatory to spit on the floor and avoid the *graf shel re'i* on the table.

23. 36b.

creating a *heter* of *graf shel re'i*. According to our explanation that it is forbidden to purposely bring about a situation requiring one to make use of the *heter* of *graf shel re'i*, the second answer is difficult to understand. So what that the foul object already existed. The problem in making a *graf shel re'i* is exactly that, placing oneself in a situation where he will have to move the item, so how does our explanation fit with *Tosafos*?

We have to add slightly to our explanation. If there is already a *muktzeh* object, one can't do something that will remove its status of *muktzeh*. This is the problem of making a *graf shel re'i*. One is engaging with the *muktzeh* in the sense that he is changing its *din*, since now the regular restrictions of *muktzeh* have been lifted to allow its removal. True, once one has removed the *muktzeh* restrictions there is no longer any reason not to move it. Nevertheless, one is bringing about a *heter* to allow himself to carry items that are intrinsically *muktzeh*. Therefore, in Abaye's case the mill was already in a state whereby it was permissible to be moved. His action of bringing the bed inside wouldn't have impacted the status of the mill; it would have enabled him to actualize the *heter*. *Gra*[24] says that the opinion of *Shulchan Aruch* is one can only be lenient to purposely actualize a *heter* of *graf shel re'i* when one has *both* reasons: a financial loss and it is *bedi'eved*, i.e., the *graf shel re'i* is already in existence. Therefore, if there is a dead bird in one's yard, one can't go and sit outside just to enable himself to move the dead bird away. He has to be sitting outside already.[25]

---

24. *Siman* 308, point 84.

25. The simple explanation we first suggested, namely that one shouldn't cause oneself to rely on the *heter* given, is still true. We're just adding that the problem is true when one changes the *din*. *Magen Avraham* (*siman* 338:12) says if one makes a *graf shel re'i* but intends on leaving it, it is *mutar*. The logic is because one is not causing himself to have to rely on the special *heter* that was given. Even though he is changing the *din*, it is permitted. This halachah is prevalent toward the end of Shabbos, where one can bear the unpleasantness for a few more hours. This is further discussed in chapter 20.

Moving the Can to the Trash

Now that we understand why Chazal gave this leniency, we can entertain a novel *sevara* (logic).[26] The same way Chazal permitted one to throw away something disgusting, perhaps they would also permit bringing the trash can to the trash (question #2). Although the trash can is *muktzeh machmas gufo*, since it presumably has trash inside that it is a *bosis* to, the general *heter* of *graf shel re'i* is to remove that which is foul. Contained in this *heter* is that anything that is needed to vacate the foul item can be moved, i.e., we can move all *muktzeh* to facilitate the removal of this *graf shel re'i*. The argument against this *chiddush* is that one is allowed to vacate the area where the trash is present, but it is not permitted to carry additional *muktzeh* items. Chazal only gave a *heter* to remove trash from the table; this act of *tiltul* was permitted, nothing else.

Graf Shel Re'i Found in a Shul

We've seen that when there is excrement or any other object whose presence is disturbing, one can move the *muktzeh* since it is an affront to *kavod habriyos*. *Shulchan Aruch*[27] says this *heter* is only if the *muktzeh* is disturbing one in a courtyard he is residing in. However, excrement in the courtyard next door can't be moved. What would the *din* be in a place where one doesn't actually live, but he is presently in the vicinity of excrement? Do we say that since it's not his regular living quarters it's not really an affront to his self-respect? Or do we say that since its presence bothers him he can now move it?[28]

---

26. I found that R' Elyashiv said the same idea in *Maor Shabbos*, section 4, *siman* 15, insight 22, s.v. ואגב.

27. 308:34.

28. If someone is a guest in someone else's house, even if the excrement doesn't disturb the guest but does disturb the host, even the guest should be able to move it. This is because someone has to move it regardless. Why does it make a difference who? Since this item is a disturbance, it is permitted to be moved. If a guest is in someone's house and the host isn't currently present where the excrement is and it doesn't disturb the guest, צ"ע if the guest can move it. Although presently the

The Mishnah in *Eiruvin*[29] discusses what to do when a dead *sheretz* (rodent) is found in the Beis HaMikdash. Rebbe Akiva holds that if it was found in an area where entry in a state of *tumah* is punishable with *kareis,* it is permitted to be moved. However, if it was found in any other area (outside the Temple grounds), one must cover it with an upturned pot. *Rashi* writes that this Mishnah is discussing Shabbos, and the reason why *muktzeh* is not a problem is because of the general rule of "*ein shevus b'Mikdash* - no rabbinic prohibitions are applicable in the Beis HaMikdash." We see from here that the Mishnah treats this rodent as *muktzeh,* but that *muktzeh* is not relevant in the Beis HaMikdash.

The obvious question is that surely a dead *sheretz* is a *graf shel re'i,* so why do we need the rule *ein shevus b'Mikdash*? Even outside the Mikdash it should be permitted to be moved. *Mishnah LeMelech*[30] quotes this question from *Be'er Sheva,* who asks from the Gemara[31] where R' Ashi permitted the removal of a dead mouse by its tail because it is a *graf shel re'i.*[32] So why is this situation any different? He says that one cannot distinguish between a house and the Beis HaMikdash and say that there is no *heter* of *graf shel re'i* in the Beis HaMikdash because it wasn't anyone's dwelling place and it's like a different area. However, the *Mishnah LeMelech* himself does differentiate as such; a house is a place of dwelling. Therefore, the presence of a disgusting object will bother a person, allowing the *heter* of *graf shel re'i* to be used. However, this doesn't apply in the Mikdash.

Accordingly, we can debate whether in a shul one wouldn't be able to remove something disgusting. Even though it's a disgrace to the honor of the place and to Hashem, since the shul is not a place of dwelling, it is less bothersome to people and the *heter* wouldn't apply. On the other hand,

---

host doesn't have a *heter* to move it because he is not near it, maybe since later he will be permitted to move it, already now the guest can move it out. צ"ע.

29. 104b.

30. *Hilchos Bi'as HaMikdash* 3:20.

31. *Beitzah* 36b.

32. This Gemara is seemingly a question on the opinion (the *Iggros Moshe* we mentioned earlier) that holds that it's preferable to move a *graf shel re'i* with *tiltul min hatzad.* Surely this mouse could have been moved out in such a way, yet we seemingly permit its direct movement *l'chatchilah*?

since considerable time is spent in shul, it can be considered that now this is one's dwelling place, one is not just passing through. *Mishnah LeMelech* understands that despite the *kohanim* constantly being present in the Beis HaMikdash, it's not a disgrace to their honor and bothers them less than had it occurred in their house. Therefore they don't have the leniency of *graf shel re'i* and the Mishnah had to find a new reason to permit the removal of the insect.

Tosafos HaRid's New Understanding in Graf Shel Re'i

However, based on a *Tosafos HaRid,*[33] we can be lenient. He explains that the *heter* of *graf shel re'i* is because of *tzaar* (pain), not *kavod habriyos.* If the presence of this item is causing one anguish, he can move it. He explains that in the Beis HaMikdash they were not using the *Azarah* (courtyard). They had no legitimate claim that it was causing them anguish because they didn't have to remain there. Hence it is permitted to move the insect only because of the *tumah* it causes. We can infer that even if it is not in a dwelling place, if the *muktzeh* mess causes anguish being left there, and one must be in that location, a person can't relocate himself, so there is a basis for moving it. So after a shul *kiddush* (question #4) - especially if it was inside the shul itself, as opposed to a hall - there isn't any greater need than that to remove the leftovers. Maybe one can even be lenient if there are full trash cans in direct sight of the entrance to the shul that are causing the community members discomfort being there.

Summary

Chazal gave a unique leniency to move something that is repulsive albeit being *muktzeh.* This is very applicable nowadays, since it can extend to permit moving trash that causes one discomfort and unpleasantness if it remains where it is, e.g., empty potato chip bags scattered on the floor. The

33. *Piskei Rid* on *Eiruvin* 104b.

reason for this leniency is self-respect and not to cause discomfort on Shabbos.

One has to be justified in moving the item, i.e., he must be using the area, but this leniency is not limited to one's own house, so even messy leftovers of a shul *kiddush* may be tidied up under this pretext.

There is a qualification to this leniency: One can't create a situation whereby he will be forced to rely on this leniency. Since an item that qualifies for this leniency is intrinsically *muktzeh*, it's better not to place oneself in a situation whereby he'll have to rely on this leniency.

We saw that this never included an act performed in its regular way. One can allow a toddler to use a potty even though one will be forced to handle it; one can eat something that will create a mess and force him to rely on *graf shel re'i* to remove the leftovers even though it will be *muktzeh*, e.g., shells or pits.

Answers

1. A trash can is *muktzeh*. If there is a smell omitting from the can, Moshe can throw out the bag. If there is no repulsive smell, it then depends: If it is full and one would need to open a new bag and leave it on the floor to collect trash, if that bothers him, he can throw out the old trash bag. If it won't bother him leaving the trash bag on the floor, it's unclear whether he can throw out the bag.
2. We entertained a new logic to permit moving the trash can to the trash. Nevertheless one should be stringent when possible.
3. If the toys are spread out in such a way where one is embarrassed to entertain guests with the house in such a state, it does qualify for *graf shel re'i*. A small mess that doesn't bother someone usually can't be tied up.

4. There is an argument that in a shul a mess doesn't qualify as *graf shel re'i* because it is not a living quarter. However, we presented an argument to be lenient. Nevertheless, in a shul hall that won't be used again that Shabbos, one should be stringent.

5. If, when putting the new diaper on the baby, one leaves the soiled diaper on the floor, he can pick it up again and throw it away. Putting it in a bin which one will then need to subsequently throw out is not permitted. One is making a situation whereby he will inevitably need to rely on *graf shel re'i*.

Chapter 20, Part 1

ביטול כלי מהיכנו

Nullifying a Vessel From its Purpose

Questions

1. When eating a fruit, can I spit the seeds into an empty bowl?
2. At a *shalom zachar*, the host often puts out empty bowls for the guests to place the shells of the nuts in. Is that correct?

The Gemara[1] brings a halachah that on Shabbos it is forbidden to place a basket underneath a chicken in order to catch its egg that will be laid. R' Yosef explains that the reason behind this *issur* is because one is being *mevatel kli m'heichano*. This literally means to ruin a vessel, but it doesn't mean to physically destroy it. It means that by placing a *muktzeh* item inside this vessel, one can no longer move it and the vessel has also become *muktzeh*. This act is forbidden, as demonstrated with the prohibition of placing a basket to catch an egg.

Pri Megadim[2] explains that there are three underlying reasons why Chazal enacted the *issur* of *mevatel kli m'heichano*: 1) By rendering a *kli* unable to be moved, one has done an act similar to *boneh* - he has now fixed this moveable object to the ground. 2) He has rendered this item unmovable, similar to *soser*, destroying the *kli*. 3) One is forbidden to create

1. 42b.
2. *Mishbetzos Zahav* 265:1.

muktzeh. These three reasons are all referenced to by *Rashi* in various places throughout *Maseches Shabbos*.[3] However, the simple way of understanding *Rashi* is not that these three reasons are mutually exclusive. Rather *Rashi* is explaining the *what* and the *why*: *What* Chazal enacted was forbidding making the vessel *muktzeh*. *Why* - the *reason* this is problematic - is that Chazal saw in this act of making *muktzeh* that it is similar to an act of building or to an act of destroying.[4]

There are other reasons brought by other *Rishonim*. *Ritva* gives a new reason for this *issur*. He says that by rendering this vessel unusable, one has decreased his *kavod Shabbos* because he now has less vessels at his disposal. *Tosafos Ri HaZaken*[5] explains that the problem is since one has made a useful vessel *muktzeh*, he might come to move it, thereby transgressing *muktzeh*.

Bitul L'Shaah

The Gemara[6] teaches that if one's animal is loaded with glass vessels that are *muktzeh* (they are used for bloodletting) and they require unloading, one can do the following: Place cushions underneath to catch the glass, stopping them from smashing on impact. The Gemara asks why it is permitted to release the strings that hold these vessels, since one is thereby causing *bitul kli m'heichano*. Once these *muktzeh* vessels fall on the cushions, one can no longer move the cushions. The Gemara answers that spe-

---

3. In 128b *Rashi*, s.v. והא קא מבטל כלי מהיכנו, says *k'soser* — like destroying. In 42b, s.v. ככלי, it's implicit that *Rashi* means *boneh*. In 43a, s.v. מפני, the third reason is implicit.

4. *Pri Megadim* quotes *Pnei Yehoshua*, who explains why *Rashi* brought different reasons that it is like building or destroying. He says that placing a bowl underneath a dripping candle is not destroying the vessel. A bowl is meant for storing things and now it's doing that function. Hence *Rashi* on the Mishnah that brings this *din* explains that the issue is *boneh*. However, in the case brought by the Gemara of placing pillows and cushions to catch glass vessels, since these objects are not meant for having vessels on top, now that they can't be used for their function due to the presence of the glass vessels, this is similar to an act of destruction.

5. 47b.

6. 154b.

cifically with *shifli zutri* (small vessels) it's permitted because one will slide these vessels off the cushion to place them on the ground. One doesn't intend on leaving them on the cushions; he only placed the cushions underneath to break the impact of the glass. We can deduce from this, in contrast to *shifli ravrevi* (large vessels), which due to their size one is not able to move them off the cushions. So one will thereby forbid the movement of these pillows for all of Shabbos and it is forbidden to release them onto the pillows.[7]

Baal HaMeor proves an important *heter* from this Gemara: Whenever one intends to shake the *muktzeh* off the vessel, one has not done *bitul kli m'heichano*. All of the examples brought by the Gemara of *bitul kli m'heichano* are only when one intends on leaving the *muktzeh* on this vessel the entire Shabbos. *Beis Yosef*[8] brings a *Hagahos Ashrei* who permits putting a *kli* underneath a wax candle to catch it should it fall. Since one

---

7. The Gemara records that Rabban Gamliel had a donkey with sour honey laden on it. He left the honey on the donkey, since it is *muktzeh*, and due to the burden the donkey died. The Gemara continues to ask whether due to *tzaar baalei chaim* he should have been allowed to undo the ropes. *Rashi* explains this question as follows: We should allow him to catch these vessels of honey on a cushion. The positive command of *tzaar baalei chaim* pushes aside the rabbinic prohibition of *bitul kli m'heichano*. The Gemara answers that Rabban Gamliel held that *tzaar baalei chaim* is also *d'rabbanan*. The commentators ask on this explanation of *Rashi*: Even if *tzaar baalei chaim* is a *mitzvah d'rabbanan*, while he can't release the vessels on the pillow, he should have to release them and let them smash. It must be that *Rashi* holds that since animals were provided for our benefit, e.g., to plow a field, turn a mill, etc., using an animal is not forbidden even if it'll cause the animal discomfort, since it's not a misuse of the animal.

It follows that in a case where there is a *hefsed merubah*, if one were to just release the vessel then we can permit catching them on the pillows in combination with *tzaar baalei chaim*. We hold *l'halachah* that *tzaar baalei chaim* is *d'Oraisa*, so we can be lenient to release onto the pillows despite *bitul kli m'heichano* when there is *hefsed merubah*.

Rambam qualifies that is it permitted only when there is no alternative other than releasing the vessels onto the pillows. If, however, one can move the vessels *b'nachas*, which *Chazon Ish* explains to mean that one moves them off indirectly, i.e., release them using the ropes, then one must do that first before directly releasing them onto the pillows.

8. 265:3, s.v. ומה שכתב רבינו.

can and will shake off the wax immediately, it's not *bitul kli m'heichano.* We see that he also holds ביטול לשעה לא שמיה ביטול - destroying for a limited time is not considered destroying, and it is therefore permitted. There are other *Rishonim,* in particular *Rashba,* who argue that there is no *heter* of *bitul kli m'heichano* just because one intends to shake off the *muktzeh.* They explain the Gemara that seemingly permitted *bitul l'shaah* is since such scenarios are somewhat more lenient, therefore when there is a large financial loss at stake *bitul l'shaah* was permitted.

(*Magen Avraham*[9] explains that *Rashba* doesn't disagree with *Baal HaMeor* on the grounds that the vessel becomes *bosis* since it is now holding the *muktzeh.* Since the *muktzeh* wasn't inside during *bein hashemashos,* there is no *bosis* according to all. Rather, *Rashba* learns that since currently one can't move it, presently he has been *mevatel* the vessel from its purpose [before moving the vessel one must shake off the *muktzeh*]. *Beis Yosef* explains that *Baal HaMeor*'s stance is based on the premise that something can't become a *bosis* on Shabbos. This means that if *muktzeh* ends up inside a vessel during Shabbos, the vessel is not *bosis.* It is not forbidden to tilt the *muktzeh* out. Yet we see regarding *bitul kli m'heichano* that there is a distinction between if one intends on shaking out the *muktzeh* or not.)

The depth behind this understanding of *bitul kli m'heichano* cannot be like *Rashi* explains "*asahu muktzeh,*" that one has created *muktzeh* because

---

9. 266:2. *Beis Yosef* explains that *Baal HaMeor* holds like *Sefer HaTerumah,* who holds that if on *leil Shabbos* one placed *muktzeh* on an item with the intention of taking it off before the end of Shabbos, it's treated like *shachach* and not *bosis.* Those who argue with *Baal HaMeor* hold that it's considered *meini'ach,* so even if it is placed with the intention to shake off, it is still *bosis. Magen Avraham* argues that this dispute is not relevant here. *Sefer HaTerumah* is specifically discussing when it was placed before *bein hashemashos,* but in in our case it was only put on during Shabbos, so even those who say in that scenario it is *meini'ach* and forbidden to move will agree in our case that one can shake off the *muktzeh* if his intention isn't to leave it there. *Maamar Mordechai* affirms like *Beis Yosef.* The only significance of *bein hashemashos* is that then even if the *muktzeh* falls off the *kli* it remains *muktzeh,* but whenever *muktzeh* is on top of a *kli* one can't shake it off. So the only reason why *shifli ravrevi* is permitted to shake off is because it is a case of a large financial loss.

the vessel has not been made *muktzeh* since one has the ability to shake the *muktzeh* off. Rather we must explain according to *Baal HaMeor* that when one doesn't intend to shake out the *muktzeh* one has limited the vessel's possible usages. Since as long as the *muktzeh* is inside the vessel it cannot be used, one has effectively "destroyed it." When one intends to shake out the *muktzeh*, it's not considered he has currently "destroyed it" because he can shake it out.

We can understand this principle from the following Gemara. The Gemara asks on the opinion that forbids *bitul kli m'heichano* from a case where we permit propping up a fallen beam (which is *muktzeh*) with a bed frame, even though that the bed frame will now be unusable. The Gemara answers that if one rests this beam loosely on top of the bed, it's not *bitul kli m'heichano*. However, if one places the bed in a very firm way that he is now unable to take the beam off from the bed, that would be *bitul kli m'heichano*. *Baal HaMeor* limits it even further, saying that even if the beam is loose, it's still only permitted if one intends on taking it off on Shabbos. *Chazon Ish*[10] asks: Since it is loose, surely it can be removed, so why would it be *bitul kli m'heichano* without the intention to remove it? It must be that *Baal HaMeor* understands *bitul kli m'heichano* is not conditional upon *creating muktzeh*; rather, if with one's actions and intentions he *removed the usage* of this item, this is *bitul kli m'heichano*.[11]

---

10. 48, point 8.

11. With this we can understand a *chiddush* of *Iglei Tal*. He says that putting a *kli* on a tree is *bitul kli m'heichano*, since one is forbidden to take it down from the tree. This *kli* has not become *muktzeh*; there is an external *issur* that prevents one from using it, which is also a form of destroying the *kli*. *Magen Avraham* suggests that even with a *kli* that is already stuck to the ground, one can still be *mevatel m'heichano*. Even though one couldn't move it anyway, *Magen Avraham* understands that since its usages are now ruined it's included in the *issur*.

Unusable Even If Not Muktzeh

Some commentators explain *Rambam*[12] with this same principle. The Gemara[13] says that if an animal has fallen inside a pit in the ground and the animal can provide its own nourishment, it's forbidden to drop cushions down to help the animal climb out. It is *bitul kli m'heichano* - while the animals would be on top of the cushions, one wouldn't be able to move the cushions.[14] *Rambam* explains differently, that there is water inside the pit. Therefore, putting the pillows inside to raise the animal will soak the pillows, causing *bitul kli m'heichano*. *Maggid Mishnah* infers that *Rambam* doesn't write that the pillows become *muktzeh*, but since they are now wet they are unusable. We see from this the fact that one has now destroyed the usage of an item is sufficient to consider it *bitul kli m'heichano*.

In another scenario of *bitul kli m'heichano*, the Gemara[15] says that if a pillow gets dirty it is *bitul kli m'heichano*. Dirty cushions are not necessarily *muktzeh*, yet they have no present use and are still considered *bitul kli m'heichano*. This is seemingly another proof that rendering something unusable, even if not *muktzeh*, is *bitul kli m'heichano*. However, neither implication is conclusive. In both instances once it can no longer be used it becomes *muktzeh* and once it is *muktzeh* it's *bitul kli m'heichano*. Most

---

12. 25:26.

13. 128b.

14. *Rashba* is bothered why putting the pillows inside is *bitul kli m'heichano*. We find that it's permitted to place an upturned basket in order to allow chicks to climb up to their coop with. He answers that one can chase chicks off whenever he wishes. But one does not have this ability with a cow. Perhaps it will remain on the cushion for the duration of Shabbos. Some explain that *Rambam* was bothered with the same point and hence changed from the simple explanation. If there is water inside, that will render the *kli mevutal*, which is a certain *bitul kli m'heichano*. We see a *machlokes* between *Rashba* and *Rambam* if in cases of *safek* you are also culpable for *bitul kli m'heichano*. Perhaps we can distinguish between different cases of *safek*. In a case where the doubt is if the *muktzeh* will fall inside, *Rashba* would agree that such a *safek* is *mutar*. This case of *safek* that we forbid is different. Since the animal is definitely ascending the cushions, the doubt is if he will come off it or not. There is a certain *bitul kli m'heichano* and a subsequent doubt that it might reverse.

15. 128b.

commentators explain that the problem in *bitul kli m'heichano* is *soser* (destroying). This reason is certainly more apt to be able to forbid cases even when the item is still permitted to move yet can't be used.[16]

Tosafos HaRid[17] explains that small glass vessels can be lowered onto the pillows because since one's intent is only for a short time, the cushions do not become *muktzeh*. However, if one puts the *muktzeh* with the intent for it to remain there for the entire Shabbos, it renders the *kli* a *bosis*! We see explicitly that he understands the problem of *bitul kli m'heichano* is making the *kli* a *bosis* and making it *muktzeh*. Therefore, if one won't cause the vessel to become *muktzeh*, e.g., when one intends to shake it off, then it is permitted.

Placing Peels or Shells into an Empty Bowl

This dispute whether *bitul kli m'heichano* for a short while is permitted or not is relevant to one who intends on eating a quantity of nuts, oranges, etc., and he intends to put the peels or shells in an empty bowl (question #2). Since one doesn't want the peels and shells to remain in the bowl for the duration of Shabbos, it's only a temporary location so that one can keep the shells together and put the shells in the trash can. This is *bitul l'shaah* (temporarily ruining the bowl), so would this be permitted?

Magen Avraham[18] permits placing a vessel under a wax candle, yet also *paskens*[19] that it is forbidden to place a vessel under coals. He explains that one can shake off the wax immediately, while since the coals are still hot, one can't shake them off right away. He concludes[20] that *bitul l'shaah* is forbidden (it is permitted only for a great financial loss). *Mishnah Berurah*[21] also concludes with this distinction. If one is going to or can

16. *Hagahos M'At Tzori* (printed at the back of the *Yeshuos Malko*).
17. 154b.
18. 265:2.
19. *Se'if katan* 2.
20. 266:4.
21. 265:5 and 266:14. *Kuntres Acharon* 11 also gives such a distinction.

shake off the *muktzeh* immediately, like in the case of the birds, it is not even considered *bitul kli m'heichano l'shaah.*

The case of loosening the glass vessels so they fall off is *only* permitted when it is great financial loss. This is because it is not possible to shake off the *muktzeh* immediately. *Rashi* explains that one puts many cushions to absorb the fall and take them off one by one and each time the vessel falls onto the cushion below until it reaches the ground, so the *muktzeh* rests on the cushions for a long time. Since it is not a case of *bitul kli m'heichano l'shaah,* we need an extenuating *heter* of a large financial loss.[22] [23]

Bitul Kli M'Heichano Derech Achilah

With this we can understand the *psak* of *Ben Ish Chai.*[24] He writes, אסור להניח כלי על השולחן כדי להניח בו קליפי ביצים ואגוזים... - "It is forbidden to place a bowl on a table to put inside shells of an egg or nuts." In such a case, since one doesn't intend to shake out the shells immediately, he won't throw them away until the bowl fills up, and therefore it is *bitul kli m'heichano.* However, this doesn't seem to be the general practice. How can we explain that which people seem to be lenient? There are those who say[25] that just like with other Shabbos prohibitions, that when it is done in the way of eating there is no *issur* (like with *borer, tochen,* etc.), similarly, *bitul kli m'heichano,* which is done during the course of eating, is not forbidden.

Perhaps we can suggest a simpler justification. The distinction between the cases of *bitul kli m'heichano l'shaah* that *Magen Avraham* for-

---

22. Not all the *Rishonim* agree that this is the physical state of the cushioning. *Tosafos* learns that one is able to shake them off immediately, and the reason the Gemara needs the *heter* of *hefsed merubah* is only because the Gemara is also addressing how it fits with Rebbe Yitzchak's opinion that *ein kli nitel.*

23. *Graz* proves that *Magen Avraham's chiddush* is also true according to *Shulchan Aruch.* In *siman* 310 *Shulchan Aruch* doesn't bring catching the egg or the oil as examples of *bitul kli m'heichano* because they are *bitul* for all of Shabbos and he holds even temporarily is forbidden. We also see that from *siman* 335, catching the leak, so the *heter* of *shifli zutri* is only to avoid a large financial loss.

24. *Shanah Beis, Parshas Mikeitz, se'if* 15.

25. *Menuchas Ahavah,* section 1, ch. 14, point 21.

bids and those that he permits is not just whether they will be shaken out immediately, but if it *can* be shaken out immediately or not. Shells certainly *can* be shaken out immediately, but for convenience one doesn't shake them out of the bowl now and wait for it to fill up. This is opposed to the case of coals - one can't shake them out because they are still smoldering, and that will cause *kibui* (extinguishing a fire) as well as damage. Accordingly, shells are permitted to be disposed of in a bowl, as it is *bitul kli m'heichano l'shaah*.

However, *Graz*[26] explains that this *heter* of "immediately" (*miyad*) requires that it is clear from one's action that he intends to remove the *muktzeh* immediately. This is known as *muchach mitoch maasav*. In this case, where one puts the vessel to collect the shells, it's not *muchach mitoch maasav* that one is going to shake it out immediately. On the contrary, continuing to shell further nuts shows that one is leaving the shells inside in the meantime. Accordingly, we lose the *heter* of *miyad* since it is an act of *soser l'shaah* and we hold that *bitul l'shaah* is forbidden. In contrast, when one puts a *kli* just to catch the wax candle from falling directly onto the table, but one will immediately slide it down onto the floor, nothing he has done has shown that he intends on leaving it there. The practice of using an empty bowl for one's shells still requires further justification.

How To Preempt Bitul Kli M'Heichano

Magen Avraham[27] brings from *Hagahos Ashrei* a practical way to avoid *bitul kli m'heichano*. If inside the vessel the *muktzeh* is falling into where one has already placed a non-*muktzeh* item, it is permitted to allow the *muktzeh* to fall inside. As long as one can still move the support vessel, one hasn't done *bitul kli m'heichano*.

It is very important to stress since this leniency is based on the principle of *bosis* (chapter 13) then the criteria of *bosis l'davar ha'mutar v'davar ha'assur* are meet. Namely, the non-*muktzeh* that is already inside the con-

26. *Graz, Kuntres Acharon* 11.
27. 265:2.

tainer is more important than *muktzeh*; only then can we treat the lower vessel only carrying the non-*muktzeh* item.

Hagahos Ashrei adds a further criterion: The non-*muktzeh* item is not able to be shaken out of the container. If one can shake out the non-*muktzeh, ni'ur,* then he has no *heter* to move the support vessel since it has *muktzeh* inside; only when he can't shake it out can he move the support vessel while it holds both the *muktzeh* and the non-*muktzeh*. Again, this criteria is based on the rules of *bosis* - what this leniency is predicated on. We saw in chapter 13 a dispute between R' Akiva Eiger and *Beis Meir* whether when one can shake out the *muktzeh* item but doing so will ruin it, does he still have to do *ni'ur*? *Beis Meir*'s stringency would have further restrictions on the application of this rule of *Hagahos Ashrei*.

The contemporary *poskim* use this idea as a solution to the "shell problem." The solution often advocated is placing a food item inside the bowl beforehand and then placing the shells. However, one must digress and first learn when one must do *ni'ur* and when he is exempt from doing so, to know how to apply this halachah practically.

What Is Considered Possible to Shake Out?

We have learned that before one moves a *bosis* to *muktzeh* and non-*muktzeh,* one must do *ni'ur,* shake out the *muktzeh* or the non-*muktzeh* to avoid carrying the *muktzeh* indirectly. The Mishnah writes that if there is a stone on a barrel and one wants to move the barrel, he must shake off the stone - this is the principle of *ni'ur*. If the barrel is surrounded by other barrels, that if he is to shake the stone off another barrel will be smashed, it is permitted to carry the barrel with the stone on top and shake it off in a safe location. This comes to teach us that when it is not possible to shake off the *muktzeh, ee efshar l'na'er,* one can carry the non-*muktzeh* with the *muktzeh* on top. (The barrel itself is not *muktzeh* due to *bosis,* because the stone was not placed on the barrel, but rather was left accidently on top.)

What reasons qualify as "not possible" to shake out? From the aforementioned Mishnah already we see that even if one physically *can* shake it out, but due to an undesired direct consequence he doesn't want to shake it out, it still is categorized as "not possible."

If a basket has fruits and stones, non-*muktzeh* and *muktzeh* respectively, the Mishnah[28] permits moving the basket. The Gemara asks: Surely he must shake out the stone rather than carry it, even indirectly. So should he shake out the contents and return just the fruits to the basket? True, if they were hard fruits one must shake out the contents of the basket and then just carry the non-*muktzeh*. However, the Mishnah is dealing specifically with very soft fruits that will get ruined if shaken out onto the ground. The Gemara says that still there are insufficient grounds to carry the basket with *muktzeh* inside. One can shake the fruits to one side of the basket and isolate the stone, facilitating him to shake out just the stone. The Gemara concedes if that is possible, one must try doing so. The Mishnah's case is when the stone is attached to the basket in a way one can't shake it out.

Tosafos HaRosh says we clearly see from this Gemara the necessity to do *ni'ur*, to the extent the Gemara established the case in an obscure scenario just to justify why in this case there is no mention of *ni'ur*. He asks: Why don't you have to remove the fruits individually and place them in their own basket? He answers: That involves an effort; Chazal didn't require *ni'ur* if it is bothersome!

We now better understand why placing a large fruit, e.g., an orange, in a bowl that one intends to place shells inside is not a good solution. It is simple to remove the orange and avoid moving the *muktzeh*. Similarly, placing a ball in a bucket that a leak is falling into won't solve the *bitul kli m'heichano* because the ball can simply be removed. Placing an item that would sink would be an ideal solution, e.g., metal cutlery. One can't access the item because the water surrounding it is *muktzeh*; one can't spill the water out because he doesn't want the surrounding area to get wet.

The Gemara then discusses the second case in the Mishnah where one has a basket of *terumah* - some pieces are *muktzeh* some pieces are not *muktzeh*. Even though in this case it is simple to remove the non-*muktzeh*,

---

28. 141b.

the Gemara explains one can move the whole basket, as it is because one needs the area the basket is located on. The application of צורך מקומו is very pertinent to shelling nuts and peeling fruits on a Shabbos table. We questioned the credibility of the solution of placing a food item in the bowl beforehand because it only helps if one can't do *ni'ur*; most food items one can do *ni'ur* to. However, often one needs to vacate the table, so one doesn't have an obligation of *ni'ur* at all. The placing of the non-*muktzeh* preempts the bowl from becoming a *bosis*, so *l'tzorech mekomo* one can move the bowl.

Shells Don't Make a Bosis

A further reason to explain the common practice of placing shells in a bowl is found in *Minchas Ahavah.*[29] He quotes from *Rashba*[30] that shells are insignificant and therefore when placed inside a vessel don't render the vessel a *bosis* to the shells. If the vessel doesn't become *bosis* then one can still move it and so there is no *bitul kli m'heichano.*[31] This seemingly is what people who don't place any food item in a bowl before shelling nuts rely on. *Ramban*[32] adds: שכיון שכל עצמו אינו נעשה כן אלא לזרוקן לא הוי בסיס - "Since its purpose is only to enable one to throw it out, it doesn't become *bosis.*" Something one intends to throw and he is placing it down to help his throw away doesn't create *bosis*. This logic will equally apply to nut shells, fruit peels, etc.

---

29. *Menuchas Ahavah* by R' Moshe HaLevi, section 1, ch. 14, *halachah* 21, and *Tefillah L'Moshe,* section 1, *siman* 20.
30. *Beitzah* 2b and *Avodas HaKodesh, Shaar Beis Moed, Shaar* 2.
31. R' Shlomo Zalman Auerbach (*Shemiras Shabbos K'Hilchasah,* ch. 22, point 27, insight 51) entertains that nowadays one can purposely place something beneath a wax candle to catch the wax; even though wax is *muktzeh* since nowadays it has no significance, it's never used, so doesn't render the vessel a *bosis* to it. His precedence is from *Mishnah Berurah* (265:14), who says one can catch ash from a candle, even though ash is *muktzeh*. R' Shlomo Zalman understands the *heter* is because ash has no significance. In light of *Rashba,* there is further reasons to be lenient to catch the wax!
32. *Shabbos* 143a.

Rectifying a Situation of Bitul Kli M'Heichano

R' Akiva Eiger[33] asks: According to *Hagahos Ashrei*'s solution, why can't one always put a non-*muktzeh* item inside the vessel, even *after* the *muktzeh* has been placed inside? If this is sufficient, the *din* of *bitul kli m'heichano* is in essence void, since one can always subsequently permit the movement of the vessel, thus negating any *bitul* of the *kli*. The answer must be that placing the non-*muktzeh* after the *muktzeh* is already inside is considered a *haaramah* (deception) and would not permit the vessel that was *bosis* to the *muktzeh* to be moved. This is because the *kli* is currently *bosis* to *muktzeh* and the non-*muktzeh* item is currently in a situation without any restrictions at all. If so, one cannot put the non-*muktzeh* inside the vessel and then claim he can't shake it out and so receive a *heter* to move the vessel. Don't put it inside in the first place and the non-*muktzeh* can be moved unrestricted.[34] This is a big *chiddush* - that one cannot purposely place a *heter* object in a vessel that is *bosis* to *muktzeh* and rely on a subsequent *heter* of *bosis* to *heter* and *issur* to move it - and that if one did so it wouldn't permit the movement at all!

Summary

The classic example of *bitul kli m'heichano* is when one causes *muktzeh* to fall into an empty vessel. The problem in doing so is that one makes the vessel itself *muktzeh*. This act is comparable to *soser*, as one is destroying the vessel. The receptacle becomes *muktzeh* because it is a *bosis* to the *muktzeh* inside. *Baal HaMeor* and others explain that since a vessel can never become a *bosis* on Shabbos, if when Shabbos started it was moveable, the placing of the *muktzeh* inside doesn't change its status. The problem of *bitul kli m'heichano* is when one intends on leaving the *muktzeh* in-

---

33. *Siman* 265 on *Magen Avraham, se'if katan* 2, s.v. עוד בהג"ה.

34. In contrast, in *Hagahos Ashrei*'s case, where the *kli* that one wants to place under the candle already had the *davar ha'mutar* inside it from before Shabbos, there was already a relationship between this *kli* and the *heter*. So it's not a deception if it collects *muktzeh*, since that's not changing the *heter* to carry this *kli*.

side for all of Shabbos. This is because then one has limited the usages of this vessel on Shabbos, rendering it useless. We don't follow this opinion; rather, even if for part of Shabbos one places the *muktzeh* inside, it is *bitul kli m'heichano*. In cases where the *muktzeh* can be moved from the receptacle immediately, one hasn't "ruined" the vessel, since it will still be able to be moved upon shaking out the *muktzeh*. This is the controversy whether one can shell eggs into a bowl because although he can shake them out immediately, he doesn't intend to do so. The consensus among the *poskim* is to avoid doing so.

A solution to avoid *bitul kli m'heichano* is to place an important non-*muktzeh* item in the receptacle so it won't be a *bosis* solely for *issur*.

Answers

1. Many *poskim* are stringent, saying that placing *muktzeh* in a bowl is classic *bitul kli m'heichano* even if one intends eventually to empty out the bowl. However, if one is lenient he has what to rely on. Firstly, since one *can* shake out the seeds immediately, the case can be judged as *bitul kli m'heichano* with the intention to shake out immediately. Secondly, there is an argument that seeds don't render the bowl *bosis*. Thirdly, it is done in the process of eating.

2. Placing shells in a bowl is the same as question #1. To avoid *bitul kli m'heichano*, the *poskim* suggest placing a non-*muktzeh* item inside the bowl beforehand. Ideally it should be an item that can't easily be shaken out. Even if one can shake it out but one wants the surrounding area to be clean, then even though the bowl is a *bosis*, under the leniency of *tzorech mekomo* one can move the bowl without spilling anything out.

Part 2

התירים בביטול כלי מהיכנו

The Leniencies for Nullifying a Vessel From its Purpose

Questions

1. Can I place a dirty diaper in a regular plastic bag, or only in a specially designated bag?
2. If the air-conditioning is leaking, can I take a bowl to collect the water?

We learned in part 1 that if one doesn't cause the receptacle to become *muktzeh,* one is allowed to put the *muktzeh* inside. The practical application of this rule is when there is non-*muktzeh* inside and by placing the *muktzeh* inside the receptacle will be a *bosis* for *heter* and *issur.*

The Leniency of Grama

If there is a *bosis* to *heter* and *issur* and he now requires the non-*muktzeh* that is inside the *kli,* is one now allowed to take it out? By removing it, one subsequently will be making the *kli* a *bosis* only for *issur,* which is now forbidden to be moved. Is that a problem of *bitul kli m'heichano*? Placing a receptacle under a lamp to catch dripping oil is *bitul kli m'heichano,* since the oil is *muktzeh* and one won't be able to move the receptacle. *Maharil*[35] says that if one wants to catch the oil from a lamp hanging above, he can place a bucket underneath the table that is directly underneath the lamp, eat and use the table with the lamp above, and then, upon finishing eating,

---

35. Brought in *Beis Yosef* end of *siman* 265.

he can move the table so that the oil will drip directly into the vessel.[36] Moving the table is only causing *bitul kli m'heichano* indirectly, and since one's main motivation is for the table not to get ruined, it's treated as if he doesn't intend on the *bitul kli m'heichano*. We see from here an important leniency that *gram bitul kli m'heichano* (indirectly causing something to become *bitul kli m'heichano*) is permitted.

We must ask why this is so. Surely some of the cases mentioned in the Gemara of *bitul kli m'heichano* are cases of *grama* (caused indirectly), yet are still forbidden, e.g., placing the basket under the chicken to catch its egg and too putting the cushion in the pit so the animal can raise itself on it. In these, cases the person is not doing a direct act of *bitul kli m'heichano*. Subsequent to one's actions, the *bitul* takes place. So why are they still forbidden?

The answer is that we must measure *grama* relative to what Chazal forbade. If our case is removed from what Chazal forbade, it can be considered *grama*. The two scenarios Chazal forbade were placing *muktzeh* in a vessel and also taking a vessel and placing it under *muktzeh* that will subsequently fall inside. A case where one is not placing the vessel that will become *muktzeh*, but instead is moving an external vessel that will just result in the *muktzeh* falling into the vessel, that act is therefore a stage removed from the act that Chazal forbade and is deemed *grama*.

The *poskim*[37] say that removing a non-*muktzeh* item from a *kli* that also has a *muktzeh* inside is only *gram bitul kli m'heichano* which is per-

---

36. It is implicit from *Maharil* that this is only permitted if the *kli* was put underneath the table before Shabbos, but putting it underneath on Shabbos would be forbidden. Why is it not still considered *grama*? Perhaps we can say that from the point of view of *grama* it doesn't make a difference if it was placed before or on Shabbos. However, *Maharil* dealt with another obstacle, *miskaven* — one is doing an act with the intention that it will cause *bitul kli m'heichano*, and his *chiddush* is that this is considered *eino miskaven*, as if he didn't intend. If one puts the *kli* there just before he wants to remove the table, we can't say when one removes the table that it's *eino miskaven*, and therefore it will be forbidden. The immediate proximity of the two acts shows one's true intention. (If this is correct, it is simple to understand why the case of the forthcoming *Meiri* is permitted: It is certainly *eino miskaven*.)

37. *Shemiras Shabbos K'Hilchasah*, ch. 20, note 40.

mitted. *Meiri*[38] explicitly says like this. In explaining the Gemara's *heter* to remove the *terumah tehorah* from a basket that has both *terumah temei'ah* and *tehorah* and leave the basket just with the *muktzeh* produce inside, he writes: מ"מ כשנטל הטהורה הכלי מבטל מהכינו ונמצא **ביטול בא מאליו ולא בידיים** - "Nevertheless, when you remove the *tehorah* from the *kli*, the *kli* becomes ruined from its purpose. *This destruction came about on its own and not actively.*"[39]

Cases of Bitul Kli M'Heichano when a Graf Shel Re'i Is Involved

The Gemara[40] discusses whether one can place a bucket underneath a leak. The conclusion is only if the water that is leaking is clean enough to drink from. *Rambam* rules:[41] Only under clean water can one place a bucket, but under dirty water it is forbidden. *Tur*[42] argues. He says the Gemara only concluded that the leak needs to be clean water to explain how the Mishnah fits according to the opinion of Rebbe Yitzchak,[43] but we don't follow Rebbe Yitzchak and so are not bound by the Gemara's conclusion of clean water; even to catch dirty water one can place a bucket.

Beis Yosef explains that *Rambam*'s source is the parallel Gemara in *Shabbos*,[44] which says if the water is not clean then placing the bucket under is *bitul kli m'heichano*. Dirty water is *muktzeh*; placing the bucket will result in an inability to move it, *bitul kli m'heichano*. If this is *Rambam*'s

---

38. 142b.

39. R' Chaim Pinchas Scheinberg (brought at the back of *Shalmei Yehudah*) says that the *din* that we see from this *Meiri* permitting indirect *bitul kli m'heichano* is limited to cases where one is interested in the non-*muktzeh*. When one just wants to take out the non-*muktzeh* and intends to purposely leave the *muktzeh* inside, that is considered an active act and would be *bitul kli m'heichano*.

40. *Beitzah* 36a.

41. *Hilchos Shabbos* ch. 25, halachah 24. *Raeh* also learns so.

42. 338.

43. He holds that אין כלי ניטל אלא לצורך דבר הניטל — one can't move any vessel for the purpose of an item which is *muktzeh*, so if the water was unfit then one would be forbidden in bringing the bucket toward the water. Hence the Gemara must conclude it is clean, non-*muktzeh* water.

44. 43a.

source, why doesn't he quote this reasoning of *bitul kli m'heichano*? Furthermore, *Rambam* gives a different reason. He explains that if the water is unclean, the problem is *osin graf shel re'i l'chatichilah* (making a *graf shel re'i* intentionally). *Yam Shel Shlomo*[45] explains *Rambam*'s reasoning: One can't put himself in a situation whereby he will be forced to rely on the leniency of *graf shel re'i* to move *muktzeh*. In order to avoid this, if one catches dirty water in a bucket he must intend on leaving the *muktzeh* inside and not rely on *graf shel re'i* to move the bucket. As a result of intending on leaving the *muktzeh* inside, he inevitably is *mevatel kli m'heichano* - he has made the bucket *muktzeh* and intends on leaving it *muktzeh*. *Yam Shel Shlomo* concludes, the Gemara is giving the *issur* one is transgressing - *bitul kli m'heichano*, while *Rambam* is explaining the reason one is transgressing such an *issur* because of *ein osin graf shel re'i l'chatichilah*, he doesn't want to move the water immediately. If one was allowed to fashion a *heter* of *graf shel re'i*, he would be allowed to collect the dirty water because he wouldn't be limiting the movement of any vessel.

Taz adds that *Tur* doesn't argue fundamentally on these ideas. Rather *Tur* holds because anyway the dirty water, the *re'i*, the *muktzeh*, already exists, it's already leaking, and one is not considered to be fashioning a heter of *graf shel re'i* (akin to what *Tosafos*[46] explains Abaye held in the story with Rava[47]). If one is not transgressing *ein osin graf shel re'i l'chatichilah*, he can intend to move the bucket immediately even with the *muktzeh* inside because already there exists a *heter* of *graf shel re'i*. The result is he hasn't been *bitul kli m'heichano*.[48]

The explanation of *Yam Shel Shlomo* is very important because without it one could mistakenly think that if the leak is falling into an area where anyway it would be a state of *graf shel re'i* and one anyway would move the water, therefore there is no problem in placing the bucket in-

45. Quoted in *Magen Avraham, se'if katan* 12. I understand that this is also what *Taz* means to explainמבטל עכ"פ הכלי לענין טלטול לכתחילה.

46. *Beitzah* 36b, s.v. תיתי לי.

47. See chapter 19 for an elaboration of this point.

48. *Rashba* entertains this approach, that because the leak exists already one is not making the *heter* of *graf shel re'i*; he, however, concludes like *Rambam*.

stead underneath.[49] That isn't true because placing a bucket has an additional problem of *bitul kli m'heichano*. This is explicit in *Tehillah L'Dovid*. He says this halachah even applies in one's living quarters where anyway the leak is causing a mess on the floor; still placing a bucket is forbidden because of *bitul kli m'heichano*.

Beis Yosef's Explanation

Beis Yosef explains[50] entirely differently *Rambam*. He takes it for a given that if one will be allowed to move the vessel containing the *muktzeh* then there is no problem of *bitul kli m'heichano*. Therefore even if the leak is *muktzeh*, if one can move it subsequently because it is a *graf shel re'i*, there is no problem in placing it there in the first place. The rule of *ein osin graf shel re'i l'chatichilah* doesn't apply in one's house because anyway there is a mess which is going to be created and either way one inevitably will have to move the *muktzeh* leak.[51] It follows, that which *Rambam* wrote - the problem in placing the bucket is your making a *graf shel re'i*, is only in reference to where one doesn't live. Where one lives, even if the leak is dirty water one can place a bucket because one will be allowed to move it and regardless of him placing the bucket he will have a *heter* to move the water. (*Beis Yosef* understands that *graf shel re'i* and *bitul kli m'heichano* are independent problems in this scenario, unlike the *Yam Shel Shlomo* that says they are intertwined.)

Shulchan Aruch[52] sides with *Rambam*. Both *Magen Avraham* and *Biur Halachah* quote the explanation of *Yam Shel Shlomo* to explain *Shulchan Aruch*. Therefore, if one has a leaking air-conditioning unit and would like to place a bucket underneath to catch the water (question #3), it's perti-

---

49. Our conclusion is not like *Piskei Teshuvos* and *Orchos Shabbos*; they are lenient.

50. I've explained based on the *Perisha*. See *Tehillah L'Dovid*, point 9.

51. He says the Gemara only established the leak as being clean (not *muktzeh*) according to the questioner who understood it is a problem of making a *graf shel re'i*, but in truth there is no prohibition. Alternatively, the Gemara established it as a clean leak to resolves instances where it is not leaking in a dwelling quarter and so there is a problem of making a *graf shel re'i*.

52. 338:8.

nent to this discussion since the water is *nolad,* which makes it *muktzeh* since the water has been created on Shabbos from the air. One must first ascertain the status of the water; usually a leaking air conditioner has clean water. Even though *Shulchan Aruch* permitted putting a bucket under a clean leak he is referring to a leak that is not *muktzeh* but water being expelled from an air-conditioning unit is *muktzeh.* Unless one intends on spilling out the water immediately it is forbidden.

If the leak is disgusting, then one can't catch the water with a container. However, *Chayei Adam* [53] permits one to rely on the opinion of *Tur* when there is a very pressing situation. We can add, a further reason to be lenient is according to *Beis Yosef*'s explanation of *Rambam,* if the leak is in one's house and regardless there will be a *heter* of *graf shel re'i,* even *Shulchan Aruch* would permit it. In light of what we discussed earlier, a suggestion to collect the leak according to all opinions would be to put a ball or any other permissible object inside the bucket and then place the bucket under the leak to catch the water. [54] (The same solution we previously discussed by shells.) Due to the heter of *grama,* if you require the ball you can subsequently take it out.

If *inadvertently* one placed a bucket underneath a leak when he wasn't allowed to, he can move that bucket before it starts to overflow, creating a further mess. He has mistakenly transgressed *bitul kli m'heichano* but still can use the *heter* of *graf shel re'i* if needed.

In light of this discussion we can deduce that one can't do *bitul kli m'heichano* even when he will subsequently have a *heter* of *graf shel re'i* to move the container with the *muktzeh.* The reason is since he doesn't intend on moving the *muktzeh* so for a short time he has been *bitul kli m'heichano* and we are stringent that *bitul kli m'heichano l'shaah* is forbidden. Therefore when eating something that has waste which one wants to put in a separate bowl, even though if the waste is piled up inside it will

53. Section 2, *klal* 67, *siman* 26.

54. This solution is only good if one holds that he doesn't have to do *ni'ur* if the *muktzeh* can't be shaken out. *Beis Meir, siman* 310, against R' Akiva Eiger in his *Chiddushim* 117b.

be unpleasant and subject to the heter of *graf shel re'i,* one can't initially place it inside the container.

Shulchan Aruch[55] seemingly contradicts this conclusion. He *paskens* that if wine which hasn't yet fermented and hence not fit for consumption and is *muktzeh,* starts dripping from a barrel, one is allowed to place a container underneath to catch the wine.[56] *Magen Avraham* adds the case is when there is a significant financial loss. This qualification is the only way to resolve our contradiction - the *only* circumstance by which *Shulchan Aruch* is lenient is when a financial loss is at stake. In such scenarios *Shulchan Aruch* presumably is relying on the opinion that *bitul kli m'heichano l'shaah* is not prohibited and so even if one intends on leaving the wine for a short period of time inside the bucket it is not *bitul kli m'heichano.*[57]

Rendering the Kli Muktzeh but Not Ruining Its Use

Notwithstanding all the *heterim* we've seen in *bitul kli m'heichano,* it should still be forbidden to put trash in a trash can, since one is now rendering the can *muktzeh.* R' Elyashiv[58] says a simple idea: A prerequisite to transgressing *bitul kli m'heichano* is only when one is ruining the *kli* from the usages it usually has. However, when an object's entire purpose is to store this *muktzeh,* then on the contrary - one isn't ruining the *kli,* but rather using it for its purpose and obviously this is not part of the prohibition!

---

55. 335:4.

56. *Tehillah L'Dovid* (point 7) asks similar to what we're asking. He asks: Even if the *heter* of *graf shel re'i* encompasses preempting a *graf shel re'i* — enabling moving the bucket before it overflows — nevertheless from the inception, to catch the first few drops of the wine should be forbidden because at that stage one is *bitul kli m'heichano*? However, his answer does not fit with our conclusion from *siman* 338. He concludes that the same way Chazal waived *muktzeh* to preempt *graf shel re'i* they also waived *bitul kli m'heichano* to preempt *graf shel re'i.* וצ"ע.

57. *Gra* references 308:37. There *Shulchan Aruch* permits making a *graf shel re'i* when there is a loss at stake. It seems he is answering our problem also, like *Magen Avraham.*

58. *Shevus Yitzchak,* section 1, p. 233.

Similarly with plastic bags, one is not even required to use specially designated bags to dispose of dirty diapers (question #1). Even though regular bags are not made specifically to store dirty diapers, one who keeps plastic bags does so for all potential possible uses. Sometimes they're used for putting groceries inside and sometimes for diapers. Therefore in one's house, plastic bags are meant for this and this is not relevant to *bitul kli m'heichano*.

A similar logic is presented by the *poskim*[59] to permit placing *muktzeh* in disposable vessels. Since these vessels are only destined to have only one usage and then they are discarded, one is not destroying the usage of the item by placing *muktzeh* inside because it never had any future use that one is now terminating. R' Wosner[60] says this is why one can clean his hands on a paper towel even though he is ruining it and it can no longer be used. Even though we concluded stringently regarding placing the nut shells in a bowl, placing them in a disposable bowl would be permitted!

R' Shlomo Zalman Auerbach[61] suggests another similar logic. When one is using an object in a way that is destructive, Chazal never forbade that usage. The distinction between classic *bitul kli m'heichano* and this is that when one destroys the item he has terminated its usages; he's now left with no *kli*. Classic *bitul kli m'heichano* is when the item can still be used, just one has currently limited or curtailed its usage. An example is tearing a bag of potato chips, rendering the torn bag a broken *kli* and *muktzeh*. From the point of view of *bitul kli m'heichano*, it is permitted because the vessel no longer exists.

Summary

A solution to avoid *bitul kli m'heichano* is to place an important non-*muktzeh* item in the receptacle so it won't be a *bosis* solely for *issur*. We suggested that once subsequently the *muktzeh* falls inside, one can

---

59. *Shemiras Shabbos K'Hilchasah*, ch. 22, note 54, and R' Elyashiv quoted in *Shalmei Yehonasan* 310:20, point 4.

60. From *Beis HaLevi*, section 6, p. 46.

61. *Shemiras Shabbos K'Hilchasah*, ch. 22, note 54.

take out the non-*muktzeh* because there is a special leniency that if one is only doing the *bitul kli m'heichano* indirectly it is permissible. When placing the *muktzeh* inside a *kli* will result in a situation of *graf shel re'i,* there is disagreement whether it is permitted. On the one hand one can move the *kli* because it's a *graf shel re'i,* while on the other hand to avoid making a *graf shel re'i* one also intends on leaving it inside and not moving the *kli,* which is *bitul kli m'heichano.* One must be stringent in such cases. If the *kli* containing the *muktzeh* is disposable or is meant for holding such items, there are arguments to rely on that it is permitted to place the *muktzeh* inside.

Answers

1. Even though placing a diaper in a bag is seemingly an act of *graf shel re'i,* it is permitted. The *poskim* explain that a bag that is meant for such waste it is not considered "ruining" the bag by placing the waste inside.
2. The water being extracted from an air-conditioning unit is *muktzeh.* Therefore it is irrelevant whether the water is clean or dirty; either way placing a bucket is *bitul kli m'heichano.* When the water is dirty and if it spills it will qualify for *graf shel re'i,* there is circumstances in which it is permitted.

Appendix: היתר לנטילת ידים שחרית ומים אחרונים - The Leniency to Wash Netilas Yadayim in the Morning and Mayim Acharonim

Biur Halachah[62] quotes the explanation of *Yam Shel Shlomo* that we saw, that placing *muktzeh* water in a bucket is forbidden because one intends to leave the water inside to avoid to *osin graf shel re'i,* so in the overall pic-

62. 338:8.

ture he has done *bitul kli m'heichano*. He then asks: Why is it permitted to do *netilas yadayim* into a bowl in the morning, or *mayim acharonim*? The water rids one of the *ruach ra* from his hands and the water is no longer fit for use - so one has thereby done *bitul kli m'heichano*?!

He first answers that we rely on *Tur*. We saw *Taz* explains *Tur* holds because the dirty water already exists, one causing it to fall into a bucket that will necessitate its removal is not *osin graf shel re'i l'chatichilah*. This reason doesn't apply in this scenario because there is no water which is yet unfit, when pouring over one's hands he is "creating" the *muktzeh*, so surely even *Tur* would be stringent in this case?![63] Furthermore only when there is a great need does *Chayei Adam* permit relying on *Tur*. Is this a great need?

The second answer *Biur Halachah* presents is that the water is not *muktzeh*. There is no *issur* in using this water rendering it not fit. Physically it is fine water and so one is not making *muktzeh* and the problem of *bitul kli m'heichano* falls away, one can move this bowl. This answer is a *chiddush*. Although it is true that no *issur* forbids this water, it nevertheless has *ruach ra*. Surely one doesn't intend on using such water, one must be more careful with items which involve spiritual danger than *issur*: "*chamirah sakanta m'issura*." If so, there is reason to assert the water is *muktzeh*![64]

Shemiras Shabbos K'Hilchasah answers how we can do *netilas yadayim*, that since this water is insignificant it can be compared to sparks which you can place a bowl to catch them because they have no significance the bowl is not nullified to them. He then questions this answer; maybe because one doesn't want to spill this water on the floor because of the *ruach ra* he does

---

63. *Shemiras Shabbos K'Hilchasah*, ch. 22, note 44, raises this question.

64. Maybe *Biur Halachah* understands that even though no one will use such water anymore for the aforementioned reasons, since there is no physical change to the water it can't become *muktzeh* during Shabbos. If there would be an *issur* on the water, it would then be subject to *muktzeh machmas issur*, but since there isn't, it's just subject to the regular rules of *haktzaas hadaas*. Since *ein muktzeh l'chetzi Shabbos*, the water which wasn't *muktzeh* won't become *muktzeh*.

attach significance to the water being in the bowl and it is treated as if the bowl is supporting the water.

Perhaps we can offer the following answer: Why didn't *Biur Halachah* raise a more basic problem - surely pouring water over one's hands in the morning, even if it doesn't get collected in a bowl, is forbidden because it is *osin graf shel re'i l'chatichilah*?[65] Must be since that is one's normal routine it is not considered *osin graf shel re'i*. In chapter 19 we elaborated on this idea that in one's regular, normal behavior there is no issue of making a *graf shel re'i*. If washing one's hands in the morning and for *mayim acharonim* can be encompassed in that rule, then we have an answer. Since there is no problem in making this *re'i*, when one pours the water into the bowl despite it being *muktzeh* he doesn't need to intend purposely to leave the water inside to avoid *osin graf shel re'i* and since he can pour out the water immediately there is no *bitul kli m'heichano*!

65. The question is just theoretical because water poured onto the ground gets absorbed and won't be transported, so he hasn't created *muktzeh* he inevitably will move.

Chapter 21, Part 1

מיגו דאיתקצאי ושינויי שם מוקצה בשבת

Migo D'iskatzi and Changing a Muktzeh Status

Question

1. On Shabbos, a camera fell off the night table and it broke. Can I now give the camera to the children as a toy, or does it remain *muktzeh machmas chisaron kis*?

The Gemara[1] discusses the case of a basket that was *muktzeh* for the entire duration of *bein hashemashos* (the onset of Shabbos). Since there were chicks standing on the basket, the basket became *bosis*. Even if the chicks subsequently descend the basket, we say, *migo d'iskatzi l'bein hashemashos, iskatzi l'chula yoma* (referred to as *migo d'iskatzi* henceforth). This literally means that if something was set aside during *bein hashemashos*, it will remain set aside for the entire Shabbos. The novelty of this halachah is that even though the reason for the basket to be *muktzeh* is no longer present, since when Shabbos began it was *muktzeh*, it remains *muktzeh* for the duration of Shabbos. We need to establish whether this *din* of *migo d'iskatzi* is relevant with all categories of *muktzeh*, or perhaps there are some exceptions.

Removing Limitations on Shabbos

R' Akiva Eiger[2] and *Magen Avraham* have a famous dispute. A bris milah knife is *muktzeh machmas chisaron kis*. Due to one's reluctance to use it

1. *Shabbos* 43a.
2. Beginning of *siman* 308.

for any other use, it has a severe designation. If on Shabbos one decides that he no longer wants to keep his milah knife for bris milah and instead wants to use it as a regular knife, is it permitted for him to now freely move the knife on Shabbos? The underlying question behind this is: If one has an item that is *muktzeh machmas chisaron kis,* and on Shabbos he changes his mind for whatever reason that he no longer wants to be careful to use this item for that purpose and wants to use it for something else, can he, on Shabbos, remove this *kepidah* (designation) that rendered the item *muktzeh* in the first place?

While R' Akiva Eiger leans toward that it does help to change one's mind that this knife will now be a regular knife and one can move it like a regular *kli shemelachto l'heter, Magen Avraham*[3] disagrees.

Shulchan Aruch[4] *paskens* that raw meat that is fit to be chewed is not *muktzeh. Magen Avraham* quotes from a number of *Rishonim* that if it is not edible at all, it is *muktzeh.* R' Akiva Eiger qualifies *Magen Avraham*'s statement that such inedible raw meat is only *muktzeh* if one wishes to wait to cook this meat for himself after Shabbos. However, if he wants to feed it to a dog on Shabbos, even though it wasn't necessarily designated to be fed to an animal previously, but was left to be cooked after Shabbos, we don't say *migo d'iskatzi* and one can change his *kepidah.* Therefore, since he wants to feed an animal now, he can make it *muchan.*[5]

R' Akiva Eiger adds the reason that *migo d'iskatzi* doesn't forbid this item is because we *pasken* like Rebbe Shimon, who doesn't hold of *migo d'iskatzi.* This is seemingly *l'shitaso,* consistent with his opinion that one can change or determine an item's status even on Shabbos.

---

3. 308:19.

4. 308:31.

5. In *Tosafos R' Akiva Eiger Shabbos,* ch. 24, *os* 180, he repeats the same idea. The Mishnah says that one can chop a pumpkin to feed to animals. R' Akiva Eiger says this is true even though the pumpkin is designated to be cooked and consumed by the owner after Shabbos. There are opinions who hold that something that's designated for man, even if it is fit for an animal, is *muktzeh* if it can't be consumed now. (We brought this opinion in chapter 10.) According to this opinion, why can one feed the animal the pumpkin? Isn't it *muktzeh*? Once one has decided to feed the animals, it's become designated for them and is therefore no longer *muktzeh.*

(R' Akiva Eiger[6] brings precedence to his *chiddush* from the following *Ran.*[7] There is a dispute between Rebbe Shimon and Rebbe Yehudah regarding *muktzeh machmas meyus,* something that one doesn't intend to use due to its disgusting state. Rebbe Shimon holds that one doesn't set aside such an item, while Rebbe Yehudah holds that there is a designation not to use it, hence it is *muktzeh. Ran* explains that the root of this *machlokes* is dependent upon a general dispute whether there is a *din* of *migo d'iskatzi* or not. All cases of *muktzeh machmas meyus* are when one has a current interest in using the item, despite the item's unpleasantness. He is thus showing that now the *kepidah* that previously rendered this item unusable is no longer in existence. It should follow that the status that this item is "set aside" should disappear. Despite this, Rebbe Yehudah holds that it remains *muktzeh.* We see that Rebbe Yehudah is of the opinion that it doesn't help to change one's *kepidah* on Shabbos because of *migo d'iskatzi* - when Shabbos came in it was *muktzeh,* so that status remains for all of Shabbos even though that your *kepidah* subsequently changed on Shabbos.

According to Rebbe Shimon, who doesn't hold of *migo d'iskatzi,*[8] even though the item that is *ma'us* (repulsive) started as *muktzeh* on Shabbos, there is no reason to forbid it once one has changed his mind to use it. Once the *kepidah* is removed, the *muktzeh* status is also removed. *Ran* has eloquently illustrated to us that Rebbe Shimon and Rebbe Yehudah argue whether changing one's mind helps remove a *muktzeh* status, and this is dependent upon whether we are bound by *migo d'iskatzi* or not. This can only explain R' Akiva Eiger with a premise that he doesn't agree to a limitation of *migo d'iskatzi.* We will see further whether this is sustainable or a contradiction to the opinion of *Shulchan Aruch.*

Ran is still a *chiddush* and *Magen Avraham,* who doesn't seem to consider the option of changing an item's status on Shabbos, is not bound to have understood the *machlokes* regarding *muktzeh machmas meyus* in

---

6. *Drush V'Chiddush, Beitzah* 2a.

7. End of *Maseches Beitzah.*

8. In 46b it is explicit that Rebbe Shimon agrees to *migo d'iskatzi* only in specific cases, besides the exceptional cases where he doesn't hold of *migo d'iskatzi.*

such a way. *Magen Avraham*[9] himself explains simply that *muktzeh machmas meyus* is permitted *tzorech gufo u'mekomo*, similar to a *kli shemelachto l'issur*, i.e., that one doesn't designate this item regarding certain *shimushim*.[10])

Magen Avraham's Position

What is the context of the aforementioned *Magen Avraham*[11] that forbids changing *muktzeh* on Shabbos? The halachah is that if a *kli* breaks on Shabbos, the broken pieces are not *muktzeh* if they still have some type of function. *Magen Avraham* is *mechadesh* that if the broken *kli* was previously *muktzeh*, such as *muktzeh machmas chisaron kis*, even though now when it is broken one is no longer careful not to use it for other usages and there is no longer any care, it still can't be moved and must still be treated as *muktzeh machmas chisaron kis*. The reason is because of *migo d'iskatzi*.[12]

---

9. 279:6.

10. *Avnei Nezer* 402 explains according to *Ran* that the reason *muktzeh machmas meyus* can be moved *l'tzorech mekomo* is because if one was to decide that he wants to use the item, he would remove the *muktzeh*, so already now he can move it freely. Nevertheless, he refutes this as proof to R' Akiva Eiger. In this case one doesn't need to remove a previous designation, just the decision to use it removes its identity as *muktzeh*. In contrast in R' Akiva Eiger's case, one needs to be *mevatel* the previous designation.

11. 308:19.

12. *Magen Avraham* learns this from *Rambam*, who writes that if a door of a house, even though it's a *kli*, broke off its hinges "even" on Shabbos, it is *muktzeh* because "*eino min hamuchan* — it has not been prepared." *Magen Avraham* understands that *Rambam* means to say that since the door wasn't "prepared" for moving while it was still attached to the house, i.e., it wasn't an independent moveable item, even though it is now detached and can be moved, its movement is still forbidden. *Rambam* is teaching that since the door wasn't a moveable *kli* when Shabbos came in, even though now it is a *kli* and can now be moved, it remains *muktzeh* due to *migo d'iskatzi*. This is proof that in our case of the broken vessel, *migo d'iskatzi* is applicable and it will remain forbidden to be moved. The proof is not conclusive since it can be argued that the door is not *muktzeh* at the beginning of Shabbos. Without a *shem muktzeh* there is nothing to extend based on *migo d'iskatzi*. Yet the proof is that it can't change its status on Shabbos.

We've seen that *Magen Avraham*'s main point of argument is built upon *migo d'iskatzi*. Since it was *muktzeh* when Shabbos began, it is irrelevant what happens subsequently. What is the source that *Shulchan Aruch paskens migo d'iskatzi*?

Shulchan Aruch[13] writes that a candle that was alight when Shabbos came in is forbidden to move even *l'tzorech gufo u'mekomo*, even when extinguished. *Magen Avraham* quotes *Beis Yosef*, who explains that the candle can't be moved while alight because it is *muktzeh machmas issur* and a *bosis* to the flame. But once it goes out, neither reason applies, so why is it still *muktzeh*? He explains that we *pasken* like Rebbe Yehudah regarding *migo d'iskatzi*. Therefore since it was *muktzeh* when Shabbos entered, it remains *muktzeh* for all of Shabbos. It is explicit from this *Shulchan Aruch* that we hold of *migo d'iskatzi*. If so, which point is R' Akiva Eiger arguing on in order to permit the changing of status of *muktzeh* on Shabbos?

Large Candles vs Small Candles

The Gemara[14] writes that according Rebbe Shimon, a small lamp is not *muktzeh* (once the fire was extinguished), whereas a large lamp remains *muktzeh* for the duration of Shabbos. The Gemara explains the difference between these two cases: With a small lamp, *datei ilavei*, one expects the flame to extinguish, enabling him to have use from it. However, he expects a large lamp to remain aflame all of Shabbos and so doesn't anticipate using

---

Gra explains *Rambam* differently, saying that *eino min hamuchan* is a reference to the door in its current situation. *Rambam* is explaining that since in its present state it is not prepared as a *kli*, it is *muktzeh*.

Chazon Ish (308, point 21) also refutes the comparison. Doors are not *kli tashmish* (usable vessels) and when detached they have no use at all, similar to stones and branches. Therefore, even if the door broke before Shabbos, it'll remain *muktzeh* unless one specifically designated it. In contrast, the broken *muktzeh machmas chisaron kis* now has some sort of function.

13. 279:2.

14. 44a, s.v. אמר רבי זירא.

it. This is further clarified in the Gemara[15] which that states that a candelabra that requires two hands to move is *muktzeh* even once the flame is extinguished, also according to Rebbe Shimon. This is because "one fixes it a place." The commentaries differ in explaining why Rebbe Shimon agrees in this case, that even once the flame goes out, the large lamp is still forbidden to be moved.

Ran[16] explains that there is an exception in this case: Rebbe Shimon concedes that there is *migo d'iskatzi*. *Ritva*[17] differs, saying that when the candle is so large that it can remain alight all of Shabbos, we say the owner has been *asach daas* for all of Shabbos, meaning that one has excluded from his mind the possibility of using this on Shabbos. Lighting a large candle is effectively setting aside the candleholder by not intending on using this candleholder for the entire Shabbos.

Rebbe Shimon agrees that something is *muktzeh* when one has in mind positively not to use it. In such cases of *dichui b'yadayim*, one has in mind not to use the *muktzeh* for all of Shabbos. Therefore even if something changes and the original reason for one's *hesech hadaas* disappears, it is still forbidden because originally the entire duration of Shabbos was included in his *hesech hadaas*. Even when the candle is extinguished and the reason for the holder being *muktzeh* - the fact that it is a support to the flame - no longer applies, despite this Rebbe Shimon agrees the holder is *muktzeh* because one had set it aside for all of Shabbos, no matter what.[18]

Two Ways in Explaining Migo D'Iskatzi

This *machlokes* explaining the difference between a large candelabra and a regular case of *migo d'iskatzi* can be explained based on two different

---

15. *Shabbos* 45b.

16. *Chiddushim* 45b. He quotes from *Ramban* saying that Rebbe Shimon agrees in a specific case to *migo d'iskatzi*, and the lack of disagreement on behalf of *Ran* indicates that he agrees. (I found this *diyuk* in *Reshimas Shiurim*.)

17. 44a, s.v. אבל כוס.

18. We will elaborate more on these two explanations in chapter 30.

ways of understanding *migo d'iskatzi*. R' Aharon Kotler[19] presents one option: Since the item isn't fit to be used at *bein hashemashos,* it therefore receives a 'חלות מוקצה' (a halachic implication or status) for the duration of Shabbos. This is not because one doesn't intend to use it for all of Shabbos, but rather the decisive time to determine the item's status for the duration of Shabbos is *bein hashemashos*. If at that time it is not prepared to be used, it gets an unequivocal status of *muktzeh* and this can't subsequently be changed. *Muktzeh* means "unprepared for use," so once we classify this item as "unprepared," that identification stays with it throughout Shabbos. As we have explained,[20] we learn from the *pasuk* "*v'hechinu*" that everything must be prepared before Shabbos begins. Therefore the entrance of Shabbos is the determining time whether an item is defined as prepared or not.

The other way to understand the reason behind *migo d'iskatzi* is simpler. Since this item isn't fit for use with the onset of Shabbos, it is most likely that this person's intention was not to use it for the duration of Shabbos, his *daas* to put the object aside and not use it determines the status for Shabbos.

Ritva[21] explicitly says the explanation for *migo d'iskatzi* is like the former: We learn from "*v'hechinu*" that something one wants to have ready for Shabbos must be prepared before Shabbos. So if at the onset of Shabbos it isn't ready, this item can't be considered as prepared for Shabbos, irrelevant of what subsequently develops. With this principle *Ritva* can't explain that the reason why Rebbe Shimon agrees to prohibit a large candle is because of *migo d'iskatzi*. This is because Rebbe Shimon denies the whole principle of *hachanah* that is learned from "*v'hechinu*." He must learn that in the case of a large lamp there is a *dichui b'yadayim,* which causes a positive *haktzaah* not to use this object for all of Shabbos.

Ran, however, could learn the second explanation we brought of *migo d'iskatzi,* that at the onset of Shabbos one has in mind not to use this object

---

19. *Siman* 9.
20. In the introduction to *muktzeh*.
21. *Sukkah* 46b, s.v. אמר ר"י.

for the duration of Shabbos, and this forbids it for the entire day. Hence he explains that in specific cases where it is highly improbable for this object to become fit for use this Shabbos, Rebbe Shimon can agree that a person's intention is not to use the item at all. This would be the reason why the large candle can be an exceptional case where Rebbe Shimon agrees to *migo d'iskatzi*.

Proof We Pasken Migo D'Iskatzi

We can now suggest answering R' Akiva Eiger, who permits one to change the status of a *muktzeh machmas chisaron kis* knife, despite *Shulchan Aruch* seemingly taking on *migo d'iskatzi*. R' Akiva Eiger must learn like *Ritva*'s approach in explaining why the lamp is forbidden to be moved. If so there is no precedence from the case of candle that we *pasken migo d'iskatzi*, the reason it is *muktzeh* is because of *dichui b'yadayim*. On the other hand, *Magen Avraham* learns like *Ran*, and therefore he has proof that we *pasken migo d'iskatzi*.

However, this isn't accurate. *Magen Avraham*, unlike R' Akiva Eiger, quotes Siman 310:3, where *Shulchan Aruch* explicitly *paskens migo d'iskatzi*. *Shulchan Aruch* writes: Something which was set aside *bein hashemashos* is forbidden all the day. *Shulchan Aruch* isn't referring to any particular case where we can explain that it is a specific instance of *dichui b'yadayim*, and furthermore *Rema* Siman 309:4 and also in Siman 310:7 *paskens migo d'iskatzi*. Most explicitly in Siman 279:1 *Shulchan Aruch paskens* like Rebbe Yehudah regarding a small candle, that due to *migo d'iskatzi* once it is extinguished it is forbidden. If so, R' Akiva Eiger is in need of an explanation how he can permit one to change the status of a knife?!

Shulchan Aruch[22] *paskens* that if a cow is slaughtered on Shabbos for a sick Jew, even if that Jew was healthy at the onset of Shabbos and hence the cow was not set aside for use on Shabbos, it is permitted even for a

22. 318:2.

healthy person to eat from that (raw) meat. *Taz* explains the *chiddush* in this being that we don't say the meat is *muktzeh* since we hold like Rebbe Shimon. This is despite that when Shabbos began there was a *haktzaas hadaas* from this cow.

Taz proceeds to ask a question on *Shulchan Aruch*. Even if Rebbe Shimon himself holds that the animal is permitted once slaughtered, without any restrictions of *muktzeh*, we *pasken migo d'iskatzi* (like the opinion of Rebbe Yehudah and not like Rebbe Shimon as we proved above). If so, *Shulchan Aruch* should *pasken* that it is forbidden for the healthy person, since when Shabbos came in it was forbidden to slaughter and hence *muktzeh machmas issur*, so we should invoke *migo d'iskatzi*. (This is the same reason why we hold in Siman 279:1 that a candle is forbidden even once the flame goes out.)

Viewing the Muktzeh as Still Present

Taz answers that the *geder* (parameters) of *migo d'iskatzi* is that even when the reason for the *muktzeh* is removed, we still view it as if the original reason creating the *muktzeh* is present. For example, a lamp with a flame is *muktzeh* due to the presence of the flame; even once the flame is extinguished, thus ending the reason for the *muktzeh*, we still view it as if the flame is still alight. Something has changed, but we view it as if nothing has changed.

Taz explains that, as opposed to the case of *Shulchan Aruch*, nothing has changed with the animal from the beginning of Shabbos until now when there is a *heter* to slaughter it. Rather what has changed is that there is a now a sick person who requires this animal. But the actual animal is the same animal; it has not undergone any change. This indicates that the reason it was *assur* at the onset of Shabbos wasn't because of something intrinsic in the animal, rather the person was *masiach daas* because he didn't think he would need it. Now that someone needs the animal, it is revealed to us that this animal was never *muktzeh*. This brings us to the usual *machlokes* between Rebbe Shimon and Rebbe Yehudah about whether there is something considered *muktzeh* due to *hesech hadaas*, and on this point *Shulchan Aruch paskens* like Rebbe Shimon, not like Rebbe Yehudah.[23]

Only when There Is Dichui B'Yadayim

However, *Magen Avraham* and *Pri Megadim* give a simpler answer.[24] *Shulchan Aruch* only holds of *migo d'iskatzi* in cases where the original *muktzeh* is because of *dichui b'yadayim* (the owner set it aside). In this case of the animal, there is no *dichui b'yadayim*. Rather, the animal wasn't fit to be used at the beginning of Shabbos, and hence it was *muktzeh*.

We can now begin to understand R' Akiva Eiger. He must understand that the case in which he permitted changing the *muktzeh* status and didn't forbid due to *migo d'iskatzi* are not cases of *dichui b'yadayim*.

Let's first address the case of a smashed vessel that was previously *muktzeh machmas chisaron kis*, from where *Magen Avraham* differs with R' Akiva Eiger and *Magen Avraham* says that now it cannot be used. Some *Acharonim*[25] explain that *muktzeh machmas chisaron kis* is not due to a greater extent of designation not to use it on Shabbos any more than during the week. Rather, delicate items are *muktzeh* because they lack a halachic status of a *kli*. Precedence to this can be found from the requirement we find regarding contracting *tumah*. The Gemara[26] says that in order for something to be considered a vessel it needs to be carried *malei*

---

23. Perhaps we can suggest that the depth behind the distinction of *Taz* is based on the two ways we explained *migo d'iskatzi*. In the cases where it is *muktzeh* due to a prohibition that resides on the object, it is positively not prepared for Shabbos and relevant to the first type of *migo d'iskatzi*, due to "*v'hechinu*." We *pasken* that like Rebbe Yehudah. However, in the case of an animal, it's *muktzeh* just because one doesn't think about using it, so to forbid it for all of Shabbos would be because of the second type of *migo d'iskatzi*, where we say the natural state of mind is not to use it all of Shabbos. Regarding that, we *pasken* like Rebbe Shimon that a person's natural state of mind doesn't determine the status for all of Shabbos.

24. According to *Levush Serad* this is also the intention of *Taz*.

25. *Harerei Kedem, siman* 54; *Kuntres Shiurei R' Soloveitchik*.

26. 83b.

v'rekan (full and empty), but if the *kli* just sits in one fixed place it doesn't contract *tumah.*[27]

The Gemara[28] draws comparisons between halachos of *tumah* to halachos of *muktzeh.* We see that something being stationary is a reason for it not to be a vessel. Similarly, since a *muktzeh machmas chisaron kis* is a *kli* that isn't moved unnecessarily, and one designates a set place for it, this makes inroads into its identity as a *kli.* Perhaps R' Akiva Eiger understands that the reason why Rebbe Shimon agrees to *muktzeh machmas chisaron kis* is because the item has too few usages to be qualified as a *kli shimush.* Therefore, there is no *migo d'iskatzi* to forbid it all of Shabbos since this is not a case of *dichui b'yadayim* and once it smashes and can be used as a *kli heter* it is now permissible. (*Magen Avraham* could learn simply that there is a greater level of designation with *muktzeh machmas chisaron kis,* hence Rebbe Shimon agrees. If it is based upon designation, that's equivalent to *dichui b'yadayim,* hence *migo d'iskatzi* is applicable on *muktzeh machmas chisaron kis.*) It must be stressed that such an understanding behind *muktzeh machmas chisaron kis* is extremely novel!

We find that R' Akiva Eiger holds that there is no *migo d'iskatzi* in the case of raw meat. One can change his previous designation of keeping the meat for himself and now decide to feed it to his dogs. Again R' Akiva Eiger will answer in the same fashion. The raw meat is *muktzeh* simply because it has no function and one doesn't intend to feed it to the animal. However, if one changes his mind, there is no previous *dichui b'yadayim* that will stop him from changing the status of the raw meat.

The Mishnah[29] says that one is not allowed to take a beam of wood to use in one's fire on Yom Tov from wood that has been designated to be used in a building. *Tosafos*[30] explains that this limitation is even according to Rebbe Shimon, since these beams are *muktzeh machmas chisaron kis.*

---

27. From *Megillah* 26b it's implicit that the requirement of *malei v'rekan* is a halachah in qualifying the identity of the *kli.*

28. 123a.

29. *Beitzah* 31a.

30. 2b, s.v. אין מבקעין.

R' Akiva Eiger asks concurrent with his principle that one can remove his care: Why can't one take these beams to use as firewood - by doing so surely he is redesignating these beams to be used as firewood?[31] *Avnei Nezer*[32] explains that the care with these beams is specifically for them to remain set aside for construction and not to use them for fuel. One can't go directly against the main *kepidah* and change it on Yom Tov. This is in contrast to a milah knife, where the care is that while it remains a milah knife, one is not to use it for any other thing. There is no specific *kepidah* not to switch it to a regular knife, so it remains permitted to do so even on Shabbos.

R' Akiva Eiger concludes that perhaps it only helps to change one's care if it is accompanied with an action that shows he intends on using this knife for an alternative use.[33]

Mishnah Berurah[34] and *Tehillah L'Dovid* both *pasken* like *Magen Avraham*, that if a *muktzeh kli* breaks on Shabbos, it remains *muktzeh* even if the reason for the original *haktzaah* has now been removed. Therefore, a camera that breaks on Shabbos remains *muktzeh machmas chisaron kis* (question #1).[35]

Summary

The novelty of *migo d'iskatzi* is that even though this *muktzeh* item became fit to use on Shabbos, and there is no longer any reason why it should be

---

31. *Ohr Gadol, Beitzah*, ch. 4, asks a very similar question on R' Akiva Eiger from the first mishnah in that chapter, which says that one cannot burn firewood that is in a designated storehouse, since such firewood is *muktzeh machmas chisaron kis*. Why can one burn it? One is showing that he no longer retains his original care. Maybe this answer of *Avnei Nezer* will also address that question. ע"ש.

32. 402.

33. *Avnei Nezer* quoted in part 2 also reaches the same conclusion.

34. 310:32.

35. *Chazon Ish* (43:21) argues with *Mishnah Berurah*'s *psak*. He holds that there is a problem of *nolad* with a smashed vessel and only in scenarios when one anticipated the vessel to break according to Rebbe Shimon it is *mutar*. In cases where one never anticipated the vessel to smash, there is no anticipation, so then he agrees to the halachah of *Mishnah Berurah* that it is *muktzeh*.

muktzeh, it is nonetheless forbidden to be moved. This is because since it was *muktzeh* at the onset of Shabbos, it remains *muktzeh* for the entire Shabbos. The understanding behind this is that either the commencement of Shabbos determines an item's status for the entire Shabbos whether it is "prepared" or not, or, alternatively, a person doesn't intend on using an item that is *muktzeh* at the beginning of Shabbos for all of Shabbos. He has therefore been *maktzah daas* from using this object for the rest of the day.

Only Rebbe Yehudah holds of *migo d'iskatzi,* as opposed to Rebbe Shimon. While we *pasken* like Rebbe Yehudah in this regard, Rebbe Shimon agrees that once a candle is extinguished, the lamp remains *muktzeh.* According to the latter explanation, a candle is a situation where Rebbe Shimon consents that a person has explicit intention not to use it all of Shabbos. While according to the first explanation of *migo d'iskatzi,* the reason Rebbe Shimon agrees it is *muktzeh* for all of Shabbos is because one positively set it aside. *Magen Avraham* understands that *Shulchan Aruch* holds of *migo d'iskatzi* in all cases, even regarding *muktzeh machmas chisaron kis.* Hence one can't change the *muktzeh* status of a milah knife or merchandise, while R' Akiva Eiger holds that there is a problem of *migo d'iskatzi* only in cases of *dichui b'yadayim. Mishnah Berurah* sides with *Magen Avraham.*

Answer

1. We rule stringently, like *Magen Avraham,* that if a vessel that was *muktzeh* smashes, it remains forbidden to move. Since the camera was severely *muktzeh* when Shabbos began, it remains so throughout Shabbos.

Part 2

שיטת רשב"א והרמב"ם במחלוקת הנ"ל

Rashba's and Rambam's Opinions

Question

1. A woman sells children's clothing from her house. On Shabbos/Yom Tov morning she wishes to give her daughter a new dress. Can she go into her storage room and give her daughter one of the dresses that was set aside for selling?

Rambam[36] *paskens* that encompassed in the category of *muktzeh machmas chisaron kis* are items that are set aside to be sold, since one is careful not to use such vessels. He further *paskens*[37] regarding food that even if the food was set aside as merchandise, it is nonetheless permitted to consume it on Shabbos: שאין שָׁם אוכל שהוא מוקצה בשבת - "There is no food that is *muktzeh* on Shabbos." He learns this idea from *tamri d'iska*.[38] These dates are set aside for selling, yet if one decides to keep them for himself, he can eat them (only according to Rebbe Shimon).

In light of *Rambam* regarding food, *Maggid Mishnah paskens* that even if one has *keilim* that are designated to be merchandise and are *muktzeh machmas chisaron kis*, if one suddenly needs them for his personal use on Shabbos, he can move them. This is because we see regarding food that was designated to be sold that if one suddenly wants to eat them, he can.

Beis Yosef[39] asks: But how does this halachah fit with the earlier *Rambam* we quoted, that specified items set aside for merchandise are *muktzeh*? He answers that *Rambam* is only referring to objects that one is particular not to use lest they lose their value or get lost. However,

36. 25:9.
37. 26:14.
38. 19b.
39. 308:1.

Maggid Mishnah is referring to merchandise that one is not careful that it doesn't loses its value or is lost. When one needs to use the latter category on Shabbos, he can use them, even though they are *muktzeh*.

Avnei Nezer[40] suggests an alternative answer: *Rambam* is referring to a scenario where one wants to keep this item as merchandise, but wants to temporarily use it this Shabbos. But since he's careful that it should look unused, it remains *muktzeh machmas chisaron kis*. In contrast, *Maggid Mishnah* is referring to a case where one no longer wants to use this as merchandise, so one can remove his care. According to *Avnei Nezer*, *Maggid Mishnah* holds like R' Akiva Eiger, that even on *muktzeh machmas chisaron kis* one can change one's restriction on Shabbos and it won't be *muktzeh*. Accordingly, if one wants to take a dress for her daughter to wear from her sale rack (question #1), since the woman is no longer keeping it for trade, she is capable of changing her mind and removing the *muktzeh* status of the dress.

Avnei Nezer says the examples the Gemara gives of *muktzeh machmas chisaron kis* are only when the vessel remains designated for its particular task, as opposed to when once one uses the item for another purpose and continues using it for other purposes. The source of *Maggid Mishnah*'s ruling is a case of dates that one set aside to sell and yet he can eat them. By consuming them he has entirely removed his *kepidah* and hence it is permitted. (According to *Beis Yosef*, if these dates are meant for selling, why is one not careful that they don't lose their value?)

He further proves this from seeds that are planted. The Gemara[41] writes that if one placed wheat kernels in the ground, it's permitted to uproot them on Shabbos to eat them, provided that they have not yet taken root (and are still fit to eat). At *bein hashemashos* the kernels were designated to remain taking root in the ground. Removing them is detrimental and nevertheless Rebbe Shimon permits removing these seeds to eat. Why? It's clear that they've been designated to take root in the ground. *Avnei Nezer* concludes that when one removes his *kepidah*, the item loses it status of *muktzeh*.

---

40. 402.

41. 45a.

He proposes that *Rashba* also supports this idea of R' Akiva Eiger, that removing one's care is effective. The Mishnah[42] says that one can only move bundles of straw, wood and reeds if one designated them before Shabbos for animal fodder. Most *Rishonim* explain that the reason one needs to designate these bundles is because their main purpose is to be used as fuel for fire, which would categorize them as *muktzeh machmas gufo*.[43] Therefore one needs to prepare them for another use to remove this designation. *Rashba*[44] explains differently. He asks from the Gemara[45] that says: שווי אוכלין משוינן בשבת - "One can cause food to become prepared on Shabbos." If so, why does the Mishnah requires prior designation if one wants to use these bundles as animal food? This rule teaches us that one can make something classified as food on Shabbos. He answers that the Mishnah's requirement is only to enable one to move the reeds *l'tzorech mekomo* or to sit on them, but if one wishes to use it as animal fodder it's permitted even without prior designation. Preparing food is permissible.

The answer is very cryptic. Where have we found that for a certain purpose an item is *muktzeh* but for other purposes it is not *muktzeh*? *Avnei Nezer* understands the difference as follows: If one just wants to move these reeds, etc., or sit on them, he is retaining his original *kepidah* and hence they are *muktzeh*. But if one is consuming them, he is removing his *kepidah* and hence he can eat them.[46]

---

42. 126b.

43. See *Shevus Yitzchak*, p. 38, where he correctly shows that there is a dispute whether bundles, reeds, etc., are *muktzeh machmas gufo* or *muktzeh machmas issur*.

44. 155a, s.v. קסבר.

45. 155a.

46. We see another *chiddush* from this *Rashba*. R' Akiva Eiger entertained the following possibility: Even if something is *muktzeh* currently, since one can change his mind and decide to use the item for a new purpose, thereby rendering the item not *muktzeh* anymore, maybe even before that actual decision one can move the item *l'tzorech mekomo* since one can hypothetically bring about a *heter* of *l'tzorech gufo*. If so, already now, before in actuality taking place, one can move the item *l'tzorech mekomo*. We see contrary to this suggestion in *Rashba* because the only restriction *Rashba* is saying is moving it *l'tzorech mekomo*.

Chazon Ish[47] asks according to R' Akiva Eiger why can't one use a stone on Shabbos for any purpose? While he did not designate it for use before Shabbos, but now he wants to use it. If there is no *migo d'iskatzi* when there was no *dichui b'yadayim*, what prevents him from now using the stone via the present designation? The answer is seemingly obvious. In order to be able to use a stone on Shabbos, one needs to make it a *kli*. This is what we saw earlier,[48] that designation changes an item into being a *kli*. R' Akiva Eiger never permitted transforming something into a *kli*, so even without *migo d'iskatzi* the stone will remain forbidden throughout Shabbos because one can't change the essence of what it is. R' Akiva Eiger's *chiddush* is limited to vessels where one removes his *kepidah*.

At first glance it appears that *Rashba* doesn't fit with the answer we just suggested because he said his ruling regarding wood, straw, etc., which are all *muktzeh machmas gufo* and surely requires designation to remove their *muktzeh* status, and despite so he permitted one to change this status on Shabbos. The answer is simple: One doesn't need to designate these items for animal fodder. Rather, these items are inherently animal food and they are *muktzeh* only because one is retaining them as fuel. With removing the *kepidah* alone, it is sufficient to make them not *muktzeh* without designating them as a vessel.

Alternatively, when explaining this proof *Avnei Nezer* adds the following words: ...כיון דעכשיו מוכנים לבהמה לא חשיב מוקצה **דמעקרא נמי דעת אולי ימלך עלייהו לבהמה**- "Since these items are fit for animal fodder, *one knew originally he might change his mind and not keep it for fuel but rather feed it to the animals.*" These item always potentially could be used as animal fodder, so even though one had decided to use them for fuel, always at the back of his mind was that maybe he'll change his mind and use it for fodder, so there's no real change in designation. It should follow that we can only prove from this *Rashba* to scenarios where it is true one originally was aware that he might change his designation.

Certainly, the fact that R' Akiva Eiger didn't bring this *Rashba* in support of his *chiddush* means that he doesn't hold *Rashba* is built on the

47. 44:14.
48. In chapter 7.

same premise. The principle of *shavei ochlin mashvinan b'Shabbos* dictates that we see the potential in an item for its use as food, and one is allowed to make something into food. Therefore, while one hasn't designated these reeds, straw, etc., for animal fodder, as they are meant for fuel, they have the potential to be food so they have a partial *muktzeh* status. Regarding using them as food they are not *muktzeh,* but regarding everything else they are *muktzeh.* One's present decision to consume them on Shabbos doesn't change their status; rather, for this use they were never originally *muktzeh.* R' Akiva Eiger will agree to the same halachah that comes from *Rashba,* namely the restrictions if one hasn't prepared the reeds is only regarding moving, sitting on them, etc., but one can feed them to animals.

Summary

Maggid Mishnah suggests that the same way one can choose to consume food set aside for consuming, one can decide to use merchandise despite being *muktzeh machmas chisaron kis. Beis Yosef* limits this leniency to merchandise one is not careful about, while *Avnei Nezer* says it is specifically about merchandise one is no longer is keeping for trading, and he has now decided to consume it himself.

According to *Avnei Nezer, Rambam* is an advocate of R' Akiva Eiger's principle that one can change the *muktzeh* status on Shabbos if he decides he is no longer careful. He resolves a difficult *Rashba* based on the principle that one can decide to feed certain food items, even if they are destined to be used fuel, to an animal on Shabbos, even though it's forbidden to move them for any other constructive purpose. The proof is not conclusive because it might be a unique idea by food items - that even if they are meant for other purposes, they always retain the identity as food.

Answer

1. Once one has changed her mind to longer sell this dress, she thereby is removing its *muktzeh* status. It is not certain all agree to this idea, however one can rely on *Avnei Nezer* and R' Akiva Eiger.

Chapter 22

גמרו בידי אדם

Completed Due to Human Intervention

Questions

1. Josh put wet clothes in the dryer just before Shabbos. Can he use these clothes once they have dried?[1]

2. Ari has food in the freezer for a dinner party he's making on Sunday. Can he eat those foods on Shabbos if he wishes?

We are familiar with the principle of *migo d'iskatzi l'bein hashemashos, iskatzi l'chula yoma* - if something is set aside during the onset of Shabbos, the item remains *muktzeh*. This is even if the reason for it being *muktzeh* is removed subsequently on Shabbos. The item is still *muktzeh* because when Shabbos began it was *muktzeh*.

The Gemara in *Beitzah*[2] teaches that in cases of *gamru biyedei adam* (literally, "completed by man") we don't apply *migo d'iskatzi*. The case brought is as follows: If one's pot of food is boiling hot on the fire when Shabbos began, the food is so hot that it's currently considered inedible. Nevertheless, when one wishes to he can take the pot off the fire in order

1. Provided that no light will be switched on when opening the door. There is another issue involved with leaving a dryer running on Shabbos: It is *avshah milsa*. This prohibits one leaving his *keilim* to do work on Shabbos when they make a loud noise that is clear to all. If the dryer is silent, there is no reason to forbid putting it on just before Shabbos.

2. 27a.

to eat the food. If inedible food is *muktzeh,* why don't we say since it was *muktzeh* when Shabbos commenced the food should remain forbidden for all of Shabbos? Surely this is a classic example of *migo d'iskatzi*?

The Gemara answers that this is a scenario of *gamru biyedei adam*. This means since the current situation is one that a person can fix, he doesn't set this item aside despite the fact that it is currently not fit for use. In our case, since one can take the pot off the fire at any time and cool down the food, thereby making the state of the food edible, one doesn't avert his attention from the pot. Whenever one can rectify the reason for the current inadequacy, *migo d'iskatzi* is not evoked because there is no *haktzaas hadaas*.

Gamru Biyedei Shamayim

The Gemara contrasts this to cases of *gamru biyedei Shamayim,* scenarios where the improvement of the item is dependent upon circumstances beyond one's own control. The classic example is when one places items to dry in the sun. Since at *bein hashemashos* they are not fit to be used and their perfection is dependent upon something that is out of one's control, i.e., the drying of the sun, even if they do become fit on Shabbos they remain *muktzeh*. With this we invoke *migo d'iskatzi* since it wasn't fit at the beginning of Shabbos.

Knowledge Is Sufficent

Kol Bo[3] says if one places dates in a barrel of water so that the water absorbs the flavor of the dates, even though the water isn't yet ready to be drunk at *bein hashemashos* and the process is completed only on Shabbos itself, nevertheless the water is permitted and we do not say *migo d'iskatzi*. His reasoning is that this is because it's *gamru biyedei adam*. *Beis Yosef* disagrees with this. He argues that it is not *gamru biyedei adam*. The reason behind *Beis Yosef*'s argument presumably is since one can't complete the

3. Brought in *Beis Yosef* 310:5.

flavoring process himself, it is not in his control and therefore can't be considered *gamru biyedei adam*. However, most of the *poskim* don't agree with this claim and hold that the water is permitted to be drunk. *Derishah paskens*, and this opinion is followed by *Mishnah Berurah*,[4] that the water is not *muktzeh* since one didn't divert his attention from the water. However, how will we answer the question of *Beis Yosef*? Unlike the Gemara's example of *gamru biyedei adam*, where one can actually change it from being unfit to being fit, in this case the readiness is not in one's control.

Levush Serad[5] answers that *gamru biyedei adam* does not necessitate the ability to manually prepare the object at present, but rather when one knows without doubt that the cause of the current inadequacy of this item will be removed on Shabbos then this is considered *gamru biyedei adam*. The certainty ensures that there is no removal of consciousness. Proof of this is from the Gemara's very case of *gamru biyedei adam*, the pot cooking the raw beans and seeds. Presently at *bein hashemashos* the foods can't be fixed since they are currently still in the process of cooking; it must be since one is certain the situation will be rectified during Shabbos it still qualifies for *gamru biyedei adam*. Similarly, one who flavors his water regularly is fully aware how long it takes for the water to absorb the flavor. Therefore he can be certain the process will be completed on Shabbos and so it qualifies for *gamru biyedei adam*.

The only case where *gamru biyedei adam* is *not* relevant is when something is currently not fit for use and its rectification is not in one's hands, such as fruit that has been left out to dry and now mid-process is currently inedible. It will only be ready when fully dried and this is dependent on the sun drying it out; a cloudy day will prolong the process. Such a situation that is not in man's sphere of influence is considered a true example of *migo d'iskatzi*.

The logic behind this innovation that considers anything which one can expect or predict to be considered *gamru biyedei adam* is very simple. The reason for *migo d'iskatzi* is if something is *muktzeh* when Shabbos

---

4. *Se'if katan* 19.

5. *Rosh Yosef, Beitzah* 20b; *Maamar Mordechai*; *Graz*; and *Chemed Moshe* also hold of this idea.

commences, this status continues throughout Shabbos since you presumably removed your intention for the entire duration of the day. However, when one knows something will certainly become fit on Shabbos already before Shabbos, there is no removal of intent for all of Shabbos and hence *migo d'iskatzi* is irrelevant.

Chazon Ish[6] holds there is no removal of intent to the extent that the item is not even *muktzeh* to begin with. He proves this from the very example the Gemara brings to demonstrate the example of *gamru biyedei adam* - a boiling-hot pot. Whenever this leniency is applied, even during the initial stage where it was not yet ready, the object is not *muktzeh* and may be moved, similar to the boiling hot pot that can surely be moved even while boiling. (This is discussed further in the appendix.)

An Inevitable Result

Meiri also says this idea and adds a further dimension. Even if one doesn't directly control the final improvement, but rather it's an inevitable result of one's actions he begun, it is considered *gamru biyedei adam*. R' Shlomo Zalman Auerbach[7] illustrates this point from the case of *kedirah chaisa* - one is allowed to leave raw food on an exposed fire to cook without taking precautions with any of the restrictions of *shehiyah/chazarah* since there is no worry that he may stoke the fire, as this food would only be ready the next day regardless. Certain raw foods are *muktzeh*, e.g., tough meat, potatoes, etc., yet one is allowed to eat them once they are cooked despite being eligible to be classified as *muktzeh* when Shabbos came in. We see that this principle is true. Whenever one knows with certainty that the cause for the *muktzeh* will go away, the item is not subject to *migo d'iskatzi* since it is considered *gamru biyedei adam*.

---

6. *Magen Avraham, se'if katan* 16.

7. *Minchas Shlomo,* section 1, *siman* 10, point 2. He adds that if one ate meat right before Shabbos and now he is forbidden from eating dairy products, would anybody think that dairy products would now be forbidden to eat for the duration Shabbos since during *bein hashemashos* they were forbidden? Obviously not. Since one knew the *issur* was temporary there is no lack of awareness.

Levush Serad finishes off with a question on this principle. A candle whose flame goes out is *muktzeh* even according to Rebbe Shimon due to *migo d'iskatzi*. However, *migo d'iskatzi* shouldn't be applicable since one knows for sure that it will go out. Surely he is aware how long the candle/oil will last? The contemporaries of *Meiri* asked him this question and based on this they argue with his principle. However, *Meiri* answers them that this only applies when that what is inevitable is the improvement of the item. One has in mind for an improvement that will take place, but when the removal of the reason for the *muktzeh* is actually detrimental as in the case of the candle, the reason for the removal of the *muktzeh* is the extinguishing of the flame. One didn't light the candle so that it should go out. In such an instance we do invoke *migo d'iskatzi* since there is a removal of awareness and we don't say that one had the usage in mind after the completion of the candle.

Meiri doesn't name those who argue on his principle. However, *Shitah Mekubetzes* explains the reason the candle is not considered to be *gamru biyedei Shamayim* is because one can't extinguish the flame. The implication is that *Shitah Mekubetzes* learns simply that *gamru biyedei adam* is only when one himself can remove the reason of the designation. Perhaps *Beis Yosef* would also hold like this, hence why he is bothered with the aforementioned *Kol Bo*. However, it is not conclusive. *Beis Yosef* could alternatively hold that one can never be certain that the water will absorb the flavor within a specific time. Therefore in the case of the water it lacks the necessary certainty, but *Beis Yosef* would agree in scenarios where there is absolute certainty.[8]

Clothes That Dried on Shabbos

There is a difficulty in *Mishnah Berurah*'s opinion regarding this *chiddush*. He *paskens*[9] that if one had clothing that was very wet when Shabbos be-

8. *Beis Meir* explains that *Beis Yosef* holds that when the water absorbs the flavor, it is something new and considered *nolad*; *gamru biyedei adam* may not help with *nolad*, as we see in 325:4 regarding bread baked by a non-Jew on Shabbos.
9. 308:63.

gan, even if they dry on Shabbos they remain *muktzeh*. When the clothes are wet, one can't move them in case one may squeeze water out and thus they are *muktzeh*. This causes a *migo d'iskatzi* to forbid these clothes even once dry. Surely if one knows the clothes will dry, it is similar to the dates in the water, which *Mishnah Berurah* explicitly permits? R' Shlomo Zalman Auerbach and others say we have to answer that *Mishnah Berurah* is referring to a case where they are so wet that it's not certain they will dry this Shabbos. Practically, the consensus of the *poskim* after *Mishnah Berurah*[10] is to be lenient. Clothes which are in a dryer that one knows will dry when the cycle finishes can be worn on Shabbos (question #1).

R' Shlomo Zalman Auerbach[11] addresses a problem with this idea. There is a halachah that an egg that is laid on the first day of Yom Tov is *muktzeh* for that day, but permitted to be eaten on the following day of Yom Tov or if the following day is Shabbos. *Tosafos*[12] asks in several places: During *bein hashemashos* following the first day of Yom Tov this object is still *muktzeh*, so why do we not say *migo d'iskatzi* to forbid it for the second day? In essence, when the second day started it is *muktzeh*, so why don't we apply *migo d'iskatzi*? *Tosafos* answers that when the reason for the *muktzeh* is due to the previous day, we don't apply *migo d'iskatzi*. This is phrased, "*mukzeh machmas yom she'avar lo amrinan*." According to the principle we have learned that when the item will without doubt become permissible for use on Shabbos, there is no *migo d'iskatzi*. Why doesn't *Tosafos* answer simply based on this principle?

Exceptions to the Rule

R' Shlomo Zalman Auerbach distinguishes that in these cases there is a previous designation. On the first day of Yom Tov the egg was *muktzeh*; therefore during *bein hashemashos* there is already a status of *muktzeh* that continues to forbid the egg on the second day. Therefore we can't apply the principle that since one expects something to become permitted he

---

10. E.g., *Ohr L'Tzion, Iggros Moshe,* and *Shevet HaLevi.*

11. Responsa *Minchas Shlomo,* section 2, *siman* 31.

12. *Beitzah* 4a s.v נימא.

doesn't remove his intent, since there already was a full removal of intent prior to *bein hashemashos* based on its original *muktzeh* status. This is why *Tosafos* is required to answer with a new principle.

R' Shlomo Zalman proves another exception to this rule. The Gemara[13] says that if one places a basket as a step for chickens to climb into their coop, if there are chickens on the basket during *bein hashemashos* then the basket is *muktzeh* for all of Shabbos. The basket is a *bosis* to the chicken, who are *muktzeh. Tosafos*[14] asks: Surely it is *gamru biyedei adam* since one can shoo the birds off the basket. Why is it different to the pots of not yet fully cooked food which are on the fire that are not subject to *migo d'iskatzi*? *Tosafos* answers that in the case of the pot of food, one wants the food to cook without any interruption. In contrast, one specifically wants the birds to be on the basket and thus sets it aside. This is a very difficult answer to understand. What is the difference between the two cases?!

R' Shlomo Zalman Auerbach explains *Tosafos*'s intention beautifully: Regarding the pots of food, one hasn't "pushed away" the pots while they are cooking on the fire. On the contrary - this is how they become fit. However, one has "pushed aside" the baskets from any use during *bein hashemashos* despite being able to shoo away the birds. Since one actively wants the birds to climb up on it at present, this negates any other potential use and there is a designation. In cases where there is a *dichui b'yadayim* (one positively sets aside), the designation is much stronger and we don't apply the logic that since one had the ability to remove the cause of the *muktzeh* it will not be subject to *migo d'iskatzi*. This is since one sets this aside at the beginning of Shabbos with a full removal of his intent, this is the principle of *muktzeh* and it will remain so for the rest of Shabbos.

In cases when this item is not fit for external reasons (i.e., cooking food causes the food to be inedible temporarily, but one doesn't necessarily want that stage per se; it's just a natural consequence of what is happening), but not because one has positively "pushed it aside," then if those ex-

---

13. *Shabbos* 43a.
14. S.v. בעודן עליו.

ternal reasons are in one's control or are known to be only short lived, we don't apply *migo d'iskatzi.*

Frozen Cooked Food

Frozen cooked food is not *muktzeh* even though it is currently inedible. It can be defrosted and then used, a practical application of *gamru biyedei adam*. In cases when one has set aside the frozen food for an event on Sunday (question #2), perhaps these foods should be treated as *muktzeh* because one positively set them aside. We saw in cases of *dichui b'yadayim* that the principle of *gamru biyedei adam* doesn't help. However, in *Sefer Tiltuli Shabbos* the author says that according to Rebbe Shimon, whenever food is fit to be consumed there is no positive designation. He learns this from *tamri d'iska*. These are dates that one sets aside to sell. Merchandise is usually considered *muktzeh machmas chisaron kis* since one is careful not to use such objects, but they are not *muktzeh*. We see that one's original intention for what he will do with the food is irrelevant if he can potentially make it fit on Shabbos. Therefore we still can apply *gamru biyedei adam*!

Summary

Gamru biyedei adam is a reference to a category of cases where we don't invoke the regular rule of *migo d'iskatzi*. The consensus among the *poskim* is that this rule applies not only to a case where one can remove the reason why the item is *muktzeh* himself, but also to cases where one knows with certainty that the reason for the *muktzeh* will terminate on Shabbos. The example we saw was the case of water that absorbs a fruit's flavor. The reasoning is because one doesn't divert his attention in such cases, to the extent we saw that already from the inception of Shabbos the item is not *muktzeh*. The *poskim* proved several exceptions to this rule. One important rule is that we apply *gamru biyedei adam* only when the eventuality is an improvement to the item. This is in contrast to a candle, whose extinction, despite being inevitable, is not an improvement of the item - it's the termination of the candle.

Answers

1. *Mishnah Berurah* is stringent, holding the clothes are *muktzeh*. However, we saw this halachah is not widely agreed on and one can be lenient, especially when it was known before Shabbos that the clothes would dry during Shabbos.

2. Since the food is edible, one's intention not to consume it doesn't render the food to be positively set aside. Therefore even if the food couldn't have been consumed at the commencement of Shabbos, it isn't *muktzeh* because of *gamru biyedei adam* - since one can defrost it, he doesn't remove his mind from the food.

Appendix: What is Gamru Biyedei Adam Ketzas?

Magen Avraham[15] raises a contradiction in *Tosafos*. We quoted *Tosafos*, who holds that the birds on the basket is not considered to be *gamru biyedei adam* since at the time when the birds were on the basket there was an active *haktzaas hadaas*. However, *Tosafos*[16] says elsewhere that according to the opinion of "*ein muktzeh l'chetzi Shabbos*" (see footnote for explanation[17]) that if one placed money on a bed during Shabbos, causing the bed to be a *bosis* with the intention of having the money removed later that day, it *is* considered to be *gamru biyedei adam* and the bed does not remain *muktzeh* despite that there was an active designation at the time when the money was on the bed. *Magen Avraham* answers that it is *gamru biyedei adam* **ketzas**.

---

15. 325:10.

16. *Shabbos* 44b, s.v. יש.

17. The *Amoraim* argue over when something was fit when Shabbos came in and then during Shabbos became unfit, and subsequently became fit again, whether we say that since it was once *muktzeh* on Shabbos it remains *muktzeh* for the rest of Shabbos even if it becomes fit again. This is a form of *migo d'iskatzi* continuing a *muktzeh* status from during Shabbos. *L'halachah* we hold *ein muktzeh l'chetzi Shabbos* and it does not remain *muktzeh*.

The explanation of this is as follows:[18] *Tehillah L'Dovid*[19] holds that *gamru biyedei adam* only helps that after the reason for the *muktzeh* disappears the item will not be *muktzeh* despite it being *muktzeh* at the onset of Shabbos - while it is set aside it is *muktzeh*! Many *poskim*, in particular *Graz*[20] and *Chazon Ish*,[21] argue that even while the item is not fit it is not *muktzeh*. This is as we saw earlier that *gamru biyedei adam* is since one can move the item now, there is therefore no lack of awareness; he is always thinking about this item. Proof is from the quintessential case of *gamru biyedei adam*, the boiling pot on the fire. The only reason there is no *migo d'iskatzi* is because he can remove the pot from the fire whenever he wants, thereby cooling down the food and making it edible. If the pot were to remain *muktzeh* while the food is not yet fit, despite it being *gamru biyedei adam*, how can one actually remove the boiling pot from the fire to cool it down? At present it is not yet fit! We must conclude, that since one can remove the cause of the *muktzeh*, i.e., by cooling it down, its *gamru biyedei adam* and that is dependent upon that **already now it is not even *muktzeh* at all.**[22]

We have seen[23] that one explanation for the rule of *migo d'iskatzi* is because preparation is needed before Shabbos, as we learn from the *pasuk* of "*v'hechinu*" that the weekdays must prepare for Shabbos. The opinion that holds *yesh muktzeh l'chetzi Shabbos* holds that even though it was prepared when Shabbos started, since it became not fit on Shabbos, that nul-

---

18. Heard from Mori V'Rabi R' Ariav Ozer.

19. 259, point 10.

20. 325:6.

21. 41:16.

22. This fits nicely with what R' Elchanan Wasserman, *Kovetz Shiurim, Beitzah, siman* 6, explains that *gamru biyedei adam* only helps when the item is in essence permitted, just that now it is not fit. But an item which is essentially forbidden (i.e., if we were to *pasken* that *muktzeh machmas yom she'avar* is forbidden), even if the *issur* will certainly be removed, currently the item is *muktzeh* so there will be *migo d'iskatzi*. He is implicitly understanding that in order for *gamru biyedei adam* to work we must achieve that it is not *muktzeh* now. This is only possible with something that intrinsically is permitted and is only unfit at present for a temporary reason.

23. See the previous chapter.

lifies the original preparation. When it becomes fit again, that is considered a new preparation, not a preparation that came from Friday. So there is a difference between the two concepts: *migo d'iskatzi* is due to a lack of preparation, while *muktzeh l'chetzi Shabbos* is due to a removal of the preparation.

With this introduction we now can explain the answer of *Magen Avraham* that the case of removing the money from the bed is considered *gamru biyedei adam* **ketzas.** *Magen Avraham* agrees that for *gamru biyedei adam* the item needs now not to be *muktzeh.* If an item remains *muktzeh* at *bein hashemashos* it is not considered prepared and hence it would be subject to *migo d'iskatzi.* The basket is a *bosis* and the fact one can shoo the birds away doesn't change the fact that presently the basket is *muktzeh.* Hence it's only *gamru biyedei adam* **ketzas** because one's actions don't have the full ability to remove the current *muktzeh,* so there isn't any positive preparation. In the case of the money on the bed, the same problem exists. One's ability to ask the non-Jew to remove the money doesn't stop the bed from being *muktzeh* while it is a *bosis* to the money. Therefore the case is also qualified only as *gamru biyedei adam* **ketzas.**

Since this partial *gamru biyedei adam* **ketzas** is not the true application of *gamru biyedei adam,* it is only enough to consider that there is no removal of the preparation that was previously in place. The bed was prepared when Shabbos came in, despite *muktzeh* being placed on it subsequently. Since it can be taken off, we don't consider that the original preparation of the bed has been nullified despite the temporary state of the bed actually being *muktzeh.* In contrast, the basket with the chicks is not considered prepared when Shabbos commences despite one being able to shoo off the birds because the basket is a *bosis* presently, so *gamru biyedei adam* **ketzas** will not stop it being *muktzeh.* (The idea behind this distinction is that having a lack of something is easier than positively having something. This weak form of *gamru biyedei adam* can be rendered insignificant resulting in a lack of preparation. However, to consider this weak *gamru biyedei adam* a positive act of destroying the preparation is demanding too much.)

Chapter 23

מוקצה מחמת יום שעבר

Muktzeh Due to the Previous Day[1]

Questions

1. On Shemini Atzeres, is it permitted to smell the *hadassim* one had previously been using for the mitzvah of *daled minim*? (See Appendix: נוי סוכה והדסים.)

2. Are there any limitations on what can be cooked on a Yom Tov that immediately follows a Shabbos? (Since during *bein hashemashos* many cooking substances such as raw eggs and flour are *muktzeh*, as one can't cook on Shabbos, during *bein hashemashos* preceding Yom Tov these items were surely *muktzeh*. Do they become permitted for use on Yom Tov?)

3. In Eretz Yisrael, if Shabbos falls immediately following the last day of Pesach, can I eat *chametz* on that Shabbos?

4. Yosef placed exotic fruits as a decoration in his sukkah and on Simchas Torah he wishes to serve these fruits. Can he take them down and serve them? (See Appendix: נוי סוכה והדסים.)

1. Disclaimer: This chapter requires a prior understanding of chapters 21 and 22 and is relatively more complex to understand than other topics in *muktzeh*.

We have seen the principle of *migo d'iskatzi,* whereby something that is forbidden at the onset of Shabbos remains forbidden throughout the duration of Shabbos. This is even if its status changes and becomes fit for use on Shabbos. Regarding this halachah we follow[2] the opinion of Rebbe Yehudah, who holds that this *migo d'iskatzi* forbids the item for the entire Shabbos.

The Gemara[3] says that on the seventh day of Sukkos an esrog that was used for the mitzvah is forbidden to be eaten, even after one has completed his use with it. The reason is that it was set aside for the mitzvah at the onset of this day and therefore *migo d'iskatzi l'bein hashemashos, iskatzi l'chula yoma.* However, on Shemini Atzeres, the eighth day of Sukkos, one is permitted to eat it.

On the eighth day there is no longer a mitzvah to shake the *daled minim.* However, during *bein hashemashos* of the eighth day it is *muktzeh,* since we are stringent that this time period is still part of the previous day and the designation of the mitzvah encompasses all of day seven. *Tosafos*[4] therefore asks: If it is *muktzeh* during *bein hashemashos,* surely we should invoke *migo d'iskatzi* for the following day too?

Tosafos answers that even though it is *muktzeh* during *bein hashemashos,* we don't apply *migo d'iskatzi* because the reason it is *muktzeh* is *machmas yom she'avar,* and in such cases *migo d'iskatzi* doesn't apply. Simply put, when the reason it is *muktzeh* during *bein hashemashos* is because of a reason that is only applicable on the previous day, but is not a reason that would forbid it the following day, we don't apply *migo d'iskatzi.* Here the esrog is only forbidden during *bein hashemashos* because it may still be the seventh day. However, were it to be the eighth day, it wouldn't be forbidden since the eighth day is removed from the obligation to shake the *daled minim.* Therefore, yesterday's cause of *muktzeh* can't forbid the following day, even if during *bein hashemashos* it was technically still *muktzeh.*

---

2. 279:2.
3. *Sukkah* 46b.
4. 10b, s.v. עד.

Tosafos brings other examples where we find this principle. Here is one such example: During two days of Yom Tov in *chutz la'aretz*, if an egg is laid on the first day, it is *muktzeh/nolad* on this day, but it's nevertheless permitted to be eaten on the second day. Surely during *bein hashemashos* between days one and two it was *muktzeh*, so how can it be permitted on the second day? Why don't we apply *migo d'iskatzi*? Again, since it's forbidden only due to a reason causing it to be forbidden on the first day, since that is the only day when the *issur nolad* is relevant - as opposed to the following day - we don't invoke *migo d'iskatzi*.

Migo D'Iskatzi Follows the True Time

The logic why we don't say *muktzeh machmas yom she'avar* is very simple. *Migo d'iskatzi* is when an item that was *muktzeh* at the beginning of Shabbos retains that status and is then forbidden for the rest of Shabbos. In these cases of *machmas yom she'avar*, whenever the second day *truly starts*, this item is not forbidden. The reason we have to treat it as *muktzeh* during *bein hashemashos* is only because *bein hashemashos* is a doubt whether it is still the preceding day or the following one. Perhaps it is still the previous day and thus still *muktzeh*. If we truly knew when the previous day finishes and the following day begins, we wouldn't continue treating it as *muktzeh*. Therefore in actuality on the following day it was never *muktzeh* to begin with to extend throughout the following day!

If one asks: But why should we follow the ultimate *din*? Surely *muktzeh* is based on one's mind, and since we don't practically distinguish within the time of *bein hashemashos*, but rather treat it as a *muktzeh* for all of *bein hashemashos*, regardless when the next day started, he has set it aside at the beginning of the following day and so *migo d'iskatzi* should apply?! *Yeshuos Yaakov*[5] explains this is an application of the prin-

5. *Siman* 513. *Chazon Ish* (49:13) also alludes to this explanation. The language of *Ritva* strongly indicates that he understands like *Yeshuos Yaakov/Chazon Ish*. He says: שלא אמרינן מיגו אלא במה שמוקצה ממש מדין עצמו אבל זה מוקצה מפני ספיקו כיון שעבר ביה״ש נתברר שהוא שמיני, נסתלק ספיקו ובא יום שמיני בהכנתו. This is very different from the way *Tosafos* in *Beitzah* 4a, s.v. נימא, presents it, ע״ש.

ciple of מוקצה בטעות לא שמיה מוקצה - "A designation that is made inadvertently is not effective."

The Gemara[6] says that if one placed *grogeros v'tzimukim* (figs and dates) to dry before Shabbos/Yom Tov, if they dried before Shabbos commenced, even though one wasn't aware of this, even though one set them aside in his mind when Shabbos started, they are nonetheless *mutar* - because in truth they were not actually *muktzeh*. From here we see this rule that מוקצה בטעות לא שמיה מוקצה, if one mistakenly thought something was *muktzeh* and hence set it aside but it was due to a wrong assumption, it is not *muktzeh*.[7] *Yeshuos Yaakov* argues that in this case as well, had one known when the day switched over, he wouldn't have set it aside for all of *bein hashemashos*. Therefore it is a designation based on misinformation.

R' Shlomo Zalman Auerbach[8] argues on the comparison between our case and the Gemara's case where the fruits dried before Shabbos without one's awareness. In the Gemara's case, the owner is just lacking the requisite information, but had he wished, he could have found out. However, in our case of *bein hashemashos*, it is a doubt when the previous day ends and the next day begins, and this doubt is equal to all. No one can actually verify this information. It is an inherent a lack of knowledge and this is not considered a *hakzaah b'ta'us* since there is nothing more to expect that he should have known. We see from this understanding that the *heter* of *muktzeh b'ta'us* is only when the designation was done due to a lack of verifiable information. Then we say that this *haktzaah* was meaningless. However, if he designated based on a doubt, where there was no way of clarifying whether or not this item can be fit for use, it is considered a valid *haktzaah*.

---

6. *Beitzah* 26b.

7. The *poskim* give other examples of this, e.g., if one thought a certain item was *muktzeh* and during Shabbos someone taught him that in truth it is permitted. Even though he set it aside at the beginning of Shabbos, it wasn't really halachically *muktzeh* and therefore is *mutar*. Similarly, if one thought that something wasn't *muktzeh* and he found out it is *muktzeh*, he needs to treat it as *muktzeh* even though previously it wasn't *muktzeh* in his eyes.

8. *Minchas Shlomo*, section 2, *siman* 17, point 1, s.v. אך עדיין.

R' Shlomo Zalman Auerbach proves this from *Maharsha*.[9] A newborn calf is only permitted to be eaten after eight days have passed since its birth. If the eighth day falls on Yom Tov, *Maharsha* holds that it is forbidden to slaughter it that day. This is since when Yom Tov began in the night, it wasn't yet clear whether it would live until the eighth day. Therefore it was *muktzeh* when Yom Tov started and there is *migo d'iskatzi*. *Tzelach* argues. He compares this scenario to fruit that was left outside to dry and became fit before the onset of Shabbos. One's mind-set was based on a lack of information, so once one realizes this, he doesn't have to treat it as *muktzeh* anymore. Similarly, the calf was only designated based on the lack of knowledge of whether it will live today, but now that one knows that it lived eight days, it shouldn't be *muktzeh* and may be eaten. How will *Maharsha* refute the proof from the Gemara? It must be this distinction is true. Namely, since nobody can know at the start of the eighth day whether this calf would live through the night, therefore there is a proper designation at the onset of Yom Tov and so the calf is *muktzeh*. It is not similar to the Gemara's case of *muktzeh b'ta'us*, where one was just lack information.

In Cases of Kedei Sheyaasu We Don't Apply Migo D'Iskatzi

R' Akiva Eiger raises a question on *Shulchan Aruch*, but the question raises a fundamental problem with the explanation we have so far suggested behind why *muktzeh machmas yom she'avar lo amrinan*. *Shulchan Aruch*[10] *paskens* that if a non-Jew brings a Jew a gift on Yom Tov from fruit that could have been harvested on Yom Tov, the fruits are *muktzeh* and the Jew can't benefit from them. Aside from being forbidden for that day of Yom Tov, Chazal also extended the *issur* until *kedei sheyaasu* (the time it takes to accomplish this act) of the second day. However, once the time it took the non-Jew to do the *melachah* has elapsed into day two, it will be permitted. R' Akiva Eiger asks: Why is it permitted on the second day? Not

9. *Beitzah* 6a.
10. 515:1.

only is it forbidden during *bein hashemashos,* but even beyond that time. If there is an independent reason why it's forbidden at the beginning of the second day, surely *migo d'iskatzi* must be applied in this case?

R' Akiva Eiger understands that *kedei sheyaasu* is a new reason, not connected to the previous day, that forbids the fruit. Hence he says that even if *muktzeh machmas yom she'avar lo amrinan,* it won't help in this case. However, the *Rishonim*[11] explain based on this principle, *muktzeh machmas yom she'avar,* why it is not forbidden on the second day. What is the understanding? In this case, when the second day of Yom Tov began, it was certainly forbidden and we should apply *migo d'iskatzi*?!

Ritva[12] asks this question explicitly. If the restriction of *kedei sheyaasu* forbids an item into the following day, why does *migo d'iskatzi* not then extend the *issur* for the whole day? He answers that we only apply *migo d'iskatzi* when it was forbidden during the *bein hashemashos* of Shabbos or Yom Tov, but when it is forbidden during the *bein hashemashos* of Yom Tov Sheni, we don't apply *migo d'iskatzi.* The explanation is as follows: Since there is a *safek* (doubt) whether or not the second day of Yom Tov is actually a Yom Tov, even if we have to treat this item as forbidden with certainty including the *kedei sheyaasu* (time it takes to do the act) of the second day, the principle of מחמת יום שעבר, namely that the previous day can't forbid the following day, is still applicable. This is because there is a *memah nefshach* (in any rate it is not *muktzeh*) to permit this. If the first day is the real day of Yom Tov, the second day is not Yom Tov, so there is no reason to forbid it on the second day since today is really *chol*! Whereas if the second day is the actual day of Yom Tov, this means it was not actually forbidden on the first day, and therefore is not forbidden *kedei sheyaasu* since there were no restrictions regarding this first day at all. True, we don't know which is the real day of Yom Tov and are thus required to treat both days as *safek Yom Tov,* but were all the facts to be known, there would be no reason to consider this *muktzeh.* As we saw earlier, we follow the truth or actuality in *muktzeh.*

---

11. *Ritva* and *Rashba* quote from *Tosafos Beitzah* 4b and *Sukkah* 10b that *Tosafos* is answering this question.
12. *Eiruvin* 39b.

Rashba[13] quotes the opinion of *Raavad,* who gives the same answer regarding there not being an issue of *migo d'iskatzi* from one day of Yom Tov to Yom Tov *Sheni in chutz la'aretz.* He proves this from the Gemara[14] that writes that an esrog is forbidden on the eighth day, i.e., Shemini Atzeres, since during the *bein hashemashos* preceding it, it was a *muktzeh* due to the preceding day. However, on the ninth day (for those in the diaspora) it is permitted. The difference is that the ninth day is only a doubt[15] and we have the *memah nefshach* to permit it.

The New Understanding in Light of Rashba

Rashba asks on this approach: If so - that we only permit one day of Yom Tov to the next when it's followed by a Yom Tov that is only a doubt whether or not it is the real day - in a case of Yom Tov followed by a Shabbos or vice versa, we would not permit this *muktzeh* item on the second day, since this *memah nefshach* is not relevant. However, this explicitly contradicts numerous Gemaras that seemingly permit even such scenarios.

After rejecting this answer, *Rashba* himself answers quoting *Tosafos*'s principle of *muktzeh machmas yom she'avar lo amrinan.* Implicit is that *Rashba* understands that this principle explains even such cases when the *issur* of the previous day for sure continues into the following day, with our current understanding of this rule, why is there no *migo d'iskatzi*?[16]

---

13. Ibid. 40a.

14. *Sukkah* 46b.

15. Can we infer from the fact that *Raavad* didn't answer with the principle of *muktzeh machmas yom she'avar* that he doesn't hold of such a rule? No, he could agree with our understanding that because it was a *safek* if it is forbidden during *bein hashemashos,* that's enough not to invoke *migo d'iskatzi.* Yet he needed this new idea of *mimah nefsach* for cases of a two-day Yom Tov (when the fact *bein hashemashos* is a *safek* is irrelevant). צ"ע. *Reshimos Shiurim, siman* 79.

16. Similarly, *Ritva* presents two answers to his question, first the idea of *Raavad* and then the idea of *Tosafos.* It is clear that *Tosafos*'s principle alone answers the question without needing the assistance of the principle of *Raavad.*

Mori V'Rabi R' Ariav Ozer explains as follows: The essence of *migo d'iskatzi* is not just when something is forbidden at the beginning of Shabbos, it is forbidden throughout Shabbos. Rather, when something is *not prepared* at the beginning of Shabbos, due to its lack of preparation for Shabbos it becomes forbidden throughout Shabbos. However, there are some items that are forbidden due to their status of *muktzeh* and that is not necessarily a reflection that they are not prepared. When the reason why something is forbidden during *bein hashemashos* is entirely connected to yesterday, that is a reflection that this is an external *issur* unrelated to the true preparedness of this object. An *issur* that is external does not change the fact that this item is prepared.

The source for this idea can be found in *Ramban*:[17] שהמוכן שקפץ עליו איסור שבת, ועל כרחן של מכין אסרו עליו לא יצא מכלל הכן - "Whenever something is prepared and an *issur Shabbos* forbids its use, it doesn't remove its status of being prepared." *Ramban* explains this idea at length and does limit it, but it certainly is the basis for our idea. Since this item is prepared for this day, and there is just an external *issur*, we don't invoke *migo d'iskatzi*.

The Stringency of Shaar HaMelech

R' Shlomo Zalman Auerbach[18] gives a similar explanation and with so answers a strong question on *Shaar HaMelech*. We mentioned earlier the opinion of *Maharsha* based on *Tosafos*, that if a calf's eighth day falls out on Yom Tov it is *muktzeh*. *Shaar HaMelech*[19] asks: Why is it not permitted, since we don't apply *muktzeh machmas yom she'avar*? *Shaar HaMelech* deduces from here that when the reason for it being *muktzeh* is due to an *issur d'Oraisa* we don't apply the *heter* of *muktzeh machmas yom she'avar*.[20] If this *chiddush* is true, how can we slaughter an animal on a Yom Tov that follows Shabbos, since during *bein hashemashos* preceding Yom Tov there is an *issur d'Oraisa* that forbids this animal? Similarly, how can we be al-

---

17. Brought in chapter 30. *Beitzah, Dapei HaRif* 11a.
18. *Minchas Shlomo*, section 2, *siman* 17, points 2 and 5.
19. *Hilchos Yom Tov* 1:24.
20. R' Akiva Eiger *Beitzah* 6a, s.v. וכי, gives another answer to this question.

lowed to bake on a Yom Tov that falls on Sunday, since during the *bein hashemashos* of the Yom Tov it was biblically forbidden to bake?

R' Shlomo Zalman defends *Shaar HaMelech* with our new explanation. Only on an *issur d'Oraisa* that renders this item unprepared did *Shaar HaMelech* say we don't invoke the leniency of *muktzeh machmas yom she'avar lo amrinan*. The prohibitions to bake and slaughter are considered external prohibitions that don't affect the inherent usability of this item. Were one to slaughter the animal, it would be permitted to be eaten. There is only an external *issur* preventing the access to this object, so this prohibition is insufficient to consider the item unprepared for the following day. In contrast, the prohibition of eating a calf before its eighth day is an intrinsic *issur* and therefore *migo d'iskatzi* is applicable.[21]

The consensus among the latter *poskim*[22] is unlike *Shaar HaMelech*, that even when the prohibition is *d'Oraisa* we apply the leniency of *muktzeh machmas yom she'avar*. It follows that if the last day of Pesach falls out on Friday, *chametz* would be *mutar* to eat on the following Shabbos (question #3).[23] *Shaar HaMelech* would forbid such a case because the prohibition lies in the actual bread. According to all, one can bake and slaughter on Yom Tov that falls out on Sunday.

Why We Don't Need to Fast the Day Following Yom Kippur

The Steipler[24] asks: According to the *Tannaim* that Yom Kippur can fall on Friday, if it does, it should be forbidden to eat on Shabbos, since not only during *bein hashemashos* is the food *muktzeh*, but since there is a mitzvah of *tosefes Yom Kippur* it's also forbidden for part of the next day, i.e., Shabbos. Yet no one would suggest the food is forbidden on Shabbos. Why not? (This is a very similar question to our case of *kedei sheyaasu*.)

---

21. See R' Akiva Eiger, *Drush V'Chiddush Beitzah* 16b, for another answer why one can cook on Yom Tov that follows a Shabbos.

22. *Chazon Ish*, R' Shlomo Zalman, *Chasam Sofer*, and others.

23. *Chazon Ish* (49:15) *paskens* that it is permissible to eat the bread.

24. *Beitzah, siman* 2.

The Steipler gives a similar answer to what we have suggested. In both these cases one knows for sure that the *issur* will soon go away. *migo d'iskatzi* is only invoked in cases where the *issur* is indefinitely, e.g., the oil in the candle might burn for all of Shabbos or the beam that fell might never have fallen, but in cases when it's certain that the *issur* is limited to a short period of time, we don't apply *migo d'iskatzi*. He explains *migo d'iskatzi* is applied to something that is currently *muktzeh*, but if the *issur* that would render this item *muktzeh* is just temporary, this item is not called "*muktzeh*." Rather it's just currently "*assur*." We don't apply *migo d'iskatzi* to the status of *assur*.

He draws a parallel between this and what we have seen in the previous chapter. In cases of *gamru biyedei adam*, since one knows that the reason for the designation will terminate on Shabbos, there is no *migo d'iskatzi*. To the extent we showed that many opinions hold that the item is not even *muktzeh* from the beginning of Shabbos, even while the designation is in place. Similarly here, when one knows the *issur* will shortly be removed, the item doesn't become *muktzeh*; it is temporarily *assur*.[25]

Summary

The *Rishonim* prove the following principle: When the reason an item is *muktzeh* only applies to the day before, but not the day ahead, even though the item is *muktzeh* during the *bein hashemashos* of the second day, we don't apply *migo d'iskatzi*. This is known as *muktzeh machmas yom sh'avar lo amrinan*. The simple explanation is based on a principle that if one designates something under a false assumption, despite the *hesech hadaas*, it is not *muktzeh*.

---

25. *Tosafos* says his principle of מחמת יום שעבר לא אמרינן explains why an egg that was hatched on the first day of Yom Tov is permitted on the second day. Surely, according to the Steipler's principle, since the egg is *assur* during *bein hashemashos* and that *issur* will shortly be removed, isn't it a case where we should invoke *migo d'iskatzi*? The Steipler explains that since on the first day this egg was hatched it had a status of *muktzeh*, that status remains during *bein hashemashos*. Since it is *muktzeh* during *bein hashemashos*, *migo d'iskatzi* is applicable. This forced *Tosafos* to answer with his new rule.

In these scenarios the item is only *muktzeh* during the first day, and since he doesn't know when the first day finishes, he practically treats it as *muktzeh* for all of *bein hashemashos*. But it never was *muktzeh* at the start of the second day to evoke *migo d'iskatzi*. We disproved this understanding from a case when an item a non-Jew brings is forbidden *kedei sheyaasu* into the second day and nevertheless, after that times elapses, it is permitted. It's explicit that even when the *muktzeh* status extends into the second day of Yom Tov, if it's due to the previous day, we still apply this rule of *muktzeh machmas yom sh'avar lo amrinan*?!

The explanation we presented was when the reason for the item being *muktzeh* is a reason exclusive to the day before, that is a reflection that regarding the following day this item is "prepared," just temporarily forbidden, and not really *muktzeh*. *migo d'iskatzi* is invoked when something wasn't prepared, not when something happened to be *assur* that rendered it *muktzeh*.

Answers 2, 3

2. According to *Shaar HaMelech* it should follow that it would be forbidden to bake on a Yom Tov that follows Shabbos. However, we saw that even he could agree in this case that we wouldn't invoke *migo d'iskatzi* and according to all it is not *muktzeh*.

3. *Chametz* on the Shabbos that immediately follows the seventh day of Pesach would be subject to a dispute. *Shaar HaMelech* would forbid it, but the halachah follows the majority of *poskim* who argue on the premise of *Shaar HaMelech*. Accordingly, *chametz* is not *muktzeh* that Shabbos.

Tosafos[26] notes an exception to this rule of *muktzeh machmas yom sh'avar lo amrinan*. The Gemara says that a sukkah on the eighth day is forbidden to derive benefit from, i.e., *muktzeh machmas mitzvah*. The original designation of the sukkah is only for seven days. Therefore during *bein hashemashos* of the eighth day it is *muktzeh*, so *migo d'iskatzi* forbids it all day. Surely the *muktzeh* during *bein hashemashos* is only due to the previous day? The *Rishonim*[27] answer: "*Muktzeh machmas mitzvah* ***shani*** - If it is *muktzeh* because it has been designated for a mitzvah, *it is different*."[28] *Tosafos* says the reason sukkah is different is based on what the Gemara[29] explains. If one wants to eat during *bein hashemashos*, despite possibly being the eighth day he still has to eat in the sukkah.

Both answers are very ambiguous. Surely the only reason one must eat inside the sukkah during *bein hashemashos* is because it might still be the seventh day? The depth behind the answer is when an item's status of *muktzeh* is due to its designation for a mitzvah, that *issur* is not external and the sukkah is deemed "prepared;" rather, the very essence of this item is designated and the item is "not prepared." *Tosafos* explains that even though an esrog is *muktzeh* during *bein hashemashos*,[30] we don't invoke *migo d'iskatzi* because one doesn't fulfill his mitzvah of esrog during *bein hashemashos*, so in essence it's not designated for the mitzvah at this time. Just since it was *muktzeh* on the seventh day, even for the *bein hashemashos* of the seventh day it remains *muktzeh*.

Explicit in the Gemara is that the decorations of the sukkah are subject to *migo d'iskatzi* and will be *muktzeh* on the ninth day, Simchas Torah

---

26. *Sukkah* 10b.

27. *Rashba and Ran* on *Beitzah* 2a.

28. A variation of the answer is: "*Muktzeh machmas mitzvah hechmiru bo* — They were more stringent with *muktzeh machmas mitzvah*."

29. *Sukkah* 46b.

30. *Ran* explains that since on the last six days of Sukkos it is only a *mitzvah d'rabbanan* to shake the *arba minim*, so during *bein hashemashos* of the seventh day one cannot make a *berachah*, so originally when one designated the lulav for the time of the duration of the mitzvah, he didn't intend to include *bein hashemashos*.

(question #4). There is a dispute regarding if the ninth day falls on a Friday, whether the sukkah and its decoration are *muktzeh* on Shabbos. *Rosh*[31] and *Ran pasken* that it is not *muktzeh*. The logic is since the only reason to forbid it on Shabbos would be because of *migo d'iskatzi* and on the ninth day it is also only forbidden because of *migo d'iskatzi*, we don't stretch *migo d'iskatzi* twice, i.e., forbidding two consecutive days.

Tosafos[32] recalls a custom not to benefit from the decoration if Shabbos falls after Simchas Torah. *Tosafos* explains that since it was forbidden before Shabbos and on Shabbos it should become permitted, it is deemed that Yom Tov prepared for Shabbos, which is akin to *nolad* (formed today) and so the sukkah is *muktzeh*. *Shulchan Aruch*[33] doesn't decide between these two opinions, so if it is a pressing situation one can be lenient and presume it is not *muktzeh*. On Simchas Torah itself, all agree it is *muktzeh*.

It is forbidden to smell the *hadas* while it is set aside for the mitzvah (question #1). The same way we have seen that an esrog is permitted on the eighth day and we don't apply *migo d'iskatzi*, this equally applies to the *hadassim*. *Chazon Ish*[34] queries whether it is permitted even to move a *hadas* during *bein hashemashos*. When we say something is not *muktzeh* because it is *muktzeh machmas yom she'avar*, is the *heter* only after it becomes fit, or is it even retroactively? The practical difference lies in whether it will be permitted to move the *hadas*. If the *heter* is only post-factor, once *bein hashemashos* has finished, now during *bein hashemashos* it is not fit to smell and will be forbidden to move. But if the *heter* is retroactive, *memah nefshach* it is permitted to move the *hadas*. If *bein hashemashos* is the seventh day, it is not yet *muktzeh* and not forbidden to move. If *bein hashemashos* is the eighth day, it is permitted to smell. So even though because of the doubt one currently can't benefit from the *hadas*, he can move it!

---

31. *Beitzah*, end of *siman* 1.

32. *Beitzah* 30b, s.v. עוד.

33. *Siman* 667.

34. 49:13.

Answers 1, 4

1. We don't apply *migo d'iskatzi* in this scenario and one can smell the esrog.

4. The sukkah decorations are *muktzeh* even on Simchas Torah. Yosef can partake of the fruit hanging in his sukkah.

Chapter 24, Part 1

תנאי במוקצה

Stipulating on Muktzeh

Questions

1. While I know in advance that on Shabbos day I'll need to move the Shabbos candles from the table, I still want to light on the table in order to fulfill the mitzvah in the best fashion. Does it help to verbally stipulate that after the candles go out, I'll remove them?
2. Levi has a silver *chanukiah* that he lights outside his door on Chanukah. He usually brings it inside after the candles extinguish so that no one steals it. What should he do on Shabbos night in order to protect his *chanukiah*?
3. Yehudah has lights on a timer that will keep them on from 6 p.m. to 12 a.m. This suits him on Friday, but on Shabbos day he wants the lights off from 6 p.m. On Shabbos morning, can Yehudah move the switches of the timer so that the light won't turn on? (This question is more relevant on a two-day Yom Tov.)

The *beraisa*[1] recalls an argument between Rebbe Shimon and Rebbe Chiya whether one can make use of the wood from a sukkah that fell on a regular Yom Tov during the year, or is it *muktzeh*. To explain why there is no *migo d'iskatzi* that forbids the sukkah, the Gemara establishes that it was a weak sukkah from before Yom Tov. Rebbe Shimon holds that

---

1. *Beitzah* 30b.

since one anticipated that it would fall since it already was very weak, it isn't *muktzeh*. Rebbe Chiya (who takes on like Rebbe Yehudah) holds that since the wood was forbidden to remove when Yom Tov began due to an *issur soser* (prohibition to destroy), *migo d'iskatzi* extends that *muktzeh* status even once it has fallen down.

The *beraisa* continues that Rebbe Shimon agrees that the wood of a sukkah that falls during the festival of Sukkos is *muktzeh* (previously was discussed when it fell during the rest of the year). The *beraisa* concludes: ואם התנה עליה הכל לפי תנאו - "If you stipulate regarding it then it is bound by one's conditions."

What is this last phrase referring to? Is it referring to the first half, which is discussing *muktzeh machmas issur*? The wood of the sukkah is *muktzeh* because there is an *issur soser* in removing the wood. If this last phrase is referring to this, then we're being taught that Rebbe Yehudah agrees in this instance that one can stipulate that he intends on using the wood, thus negating the *muktzeh*. Or is it referring to the latter section, which is referring to *muktzeh machmas mitzvah*? If this last phrase is referring to this scenario, we are being taught that one can stipulate to negate *muktzeh machmas mitzvah*.

Is the Kedushah of a Sukkah Unavoidable?

The Gemara explains that during Sukkos the sukkah has *kedushah* (derived from a *pasuk* that implies it should be a continual seven-day *kedushah*). The *kedushah* prevents one from stipulating, because had the stipulation worked, the *kedushah* would cease, but this *kedushah* must be continual for seven days. The Gemara is therefore forced into establishing that the *beraisa* that says a condition helps is only regarding a sukkah that doesn't have *kedushah*, i.e., a year-round hut, but not a sukkah during Sukkos.

The Gemara asks from edible sukkah decorations, where we find that even though they also have a status of *kedushah*, one is able to stipulate that when one wants to take these foodstuffs down for his own personal benefit he can do so. The Gemara answers that with these decorations, one stipulated that he is not separating himself from them from the beginning of the *chag*: איני בודל מהם כל בין השמשות, thereby the *kedushah* is never applied to these items from the inception. This is in contrast to a sukkah; the sukkah itself had *kedushah* applied to it and so is *muktzeh*. One can't subsequently subject it to be permitted with a condition.

We can now ask a question on the conclusion of this Gemara. Are we differentiating between the very essence of decorations and a sukkah, whereas in the former it is possible to make a condition and in the latter it is not possible? Or are we only explaining a difference in the cases, with decorations one usually stipulates from the onset of Yom Tov, however with a sukkah one does not, but were one to actually make a condition with a sukkah at *bein hashemashos* it would be sufficient to permit it?

There are two main approaches found among the *Rishonim* how to understand this. *Rashi* explains that the Gemara's conclusion is that a condition cannot help with a sukkah that is being used for a mitzvah. The difference between a sukkah and decorations is that at the onset of Yom Tov one is forced to separate himself from the sukkah. Since there is regardless an *issur soser* (prohibition in taking down the sukkah), when Yom Tov commences the *kedushah* is automatically applied to the sukkah, as the Gemara learns through a *limud* (derivation) from a *pasuk* that a sukkah has *kedushah*. Once something is designated for a mitzvah and the *kedushah* is *chal* (being applied), one cannot remove the resulting *kedushah* and it will be *muktzeh machmas mitzvah*.

In contrast, there is no independent *issur* involved in removing decorations from the sukkah. Rather, when Yom Tov begins, they are attached to the sukkah and thus become part of it and receive the same *kedushah*. However, a condition helps since one is thereby stipulating that he is not relinquishing his mind over the decoration and that he can access them whenever he wishes. He is in essence saying that this decoration shouldn't be part of the actual sukkah, despite looking like part of the sukkah. He has thereby preempted the *muktzeh* from applying by stopping the *kedushah* from being *applied*.

Rif's Conclusion of the Gemara

Ran explains *Rif* differently, based on a different text *Rif* had in the Gemara. *Rif* doesn't explain that the *beraisa* that permits one to make a condition is dealing only with a hut of all year round. The *beraisa* was only ever discussing a sukkah that is being used for a mitzvah. To resolve the contrary implications whether one can or cannot make a condition, the Gemara explains that once the *kedushah* is *chal* it's too late to change anything. *bein hashemashos* of Yom Tov determines the status for all of Shabbos/Yom Tov and this is when a condition does not help. However, were one to stipulate *prior* to the onset of *bein hashemashos,* a condition would help even with a sukkah that is being used for a mitzvah.

Ran further clarifies: The only condition that works for decorations is when one stipulates with the words איני בודל מהם ביה״ש. This causes the decorations not to be nullified to the sukkah. In contrast, were he to stipulate: "*K'shetipol ani yetaltel* - When the decorations fall I will use them for my needs," that is problematic, because until it falls one intends on it being nullified to the sukkah and once it begins at the beginning of Yom Tov in such a state it can't be changed for the duration of the seven days. Similarly, if one was to stipulate in reference to the sukkah: איני בודל מהם כל בין השמשות, this stipulation will work for the sukkah and he can use the sukkah for his personal needs. (Practically on Yom Tov he will be limited in using the material of the sukkah because there is an *issur soser* in taking it down. The condition will enable him on Chol HaMoed to use the sukkah or if the sukkah falls to then use the building material.)

In light of *Ran,* we can understand the depth behind where *Rashi* and *Rif* differ. According to *Rif,* the essence of the stipulation is that the incoming *kedushah* shouldn't come into existence. Even though practically one is limited to what he can do with this sukkah other than use it for the mitzvah, it is still not a contradiction to have a sukkah without *kedushah.* In other words, he has stipulated that this should be a booth devoid of any *kedushah.* It looks like a sukkah and he is treating it as a sukkah since he is still fulfilling his mitzvah with it, nevertheless, he can preempt the *kedushah* from being activated. If there is no *kedushah* it isn't *muktzeh. Rashi* holds that since one needs to keep the sukkah erect when Yom Tov begins, his stipulation that this shouldn't be a sukkah is void. Since he can't do a specific act to show that it is not a sukkah, he can't disassemble it, and therefore the *kedushah* comes against his will and forbids his sukkah for all seven days.

Let's summarize the main points we learn from this Gemara: According to *Rif* we can learn that one's stipulation against *muktzeh machmas mitzvah* is effective provided it is done in a fashion that preempts the *kedushah* from being activated, while regarding *muktzeh machmas issur* there is no mention in the Gemara whether a condition is effective or not. According to *Rashi*, due to the *kedushah* that is active, inevitably a sukkah isn't subject to conditions. Nevertheless, the last phrase of the *beraisa*, "it all follows the condition," is referring to a booth all year. Despite it being *muktzeh machmas issur*, one can stipulate that if it falls he can use the sukkah. It follows according to *Rashi* that there is a precedence that a condition works against *muktzeh machmas issur*.

Stipulations for Candlesticks

Tosafos[2] assumes that one cannot stipulate that once the flame on a candle has been extinguished he will use the candlestick (question #1). He differentiates between this *muktzeh machmas issur* and the *muktzeh machmas issur* we have seen from the Gemara in sukkah that one can stipulate that once the booth falls he can use the material (we will elaborate on his distinction later).

Shulchan Aruch[3] *paskens* that one can make a condition on a candlestick. If one stipulates, "Once the flame goes out, the candlesticks should be permitted for me to move," this is sufficient to permit its movement, even though while alight the candlestick was *bosis*. *Rema* brings an opinion that a condition does not help and he writes that this is the *minhag*.

From where did *Shulchan Aruch* know that a condition is effective against a candle? *Ramban* quotes a *Yerushalmi* that explicitly says that a condition helps in enabling one to move a candle once the flame is extinguished, even according to Rebbe Yehudah. However, another source

2. 44a, s.v. שבנר.
3. 279:4.

could be the conclusion of the aforementioned Gemara in *Beitzah* based on what we can extract according to *Rashi*'s way of learning. The same way that a condition helps a sukkah all year despite *muktzeh machmas issur*, so too this holds for a candle. We could also understand why *Rema* would argue. If he had the same text of *Rif*, there is no precedence that with *muktzeh machmas issur* a condition is effective.

Not only is there no precedence according to the opinion of *Rif* that a condition can help, we even find opinions in the *Rishonim* that explicitly hold that a condition doesn't help with *muktzeh machmas issur*. The Gemara originally answers that the *beraisa* that holds a condition helps to remove the *muktzeh* status of the sukkah is referring to a sukkah of all year round. In reference to this stage, *Tosafos*[4] explains that the Gemara could have refuted this suggestion since we don't find that one can make a condition with *muktzeh machmas issur*, but since the Gemara is anyway going to conclude with a different explanation it didn't need to refute it now. This *Tosafos* clearly holds that a condition doesn't help to combat *muktzeh machmas issur*. *Ritva*[5] and *Meyuchas LaRan* also all learn that a condition doesn't help with *muktzeh machmas issur* and they explain that one cannot stipulate with a candlestick that when the flame is extinguished he will move the candle.

How Does a Condition Work?

We first need to understand how a condition works and then we can reach an understanding on what point the *Rishonim* are arguing over. The first question to ask is: How can a condition help according to Rebbe Yehudah? If something is *muktzeh* at the beginning of Shabbos, since Rebbe Yehudah holds and this is how we *pasken* that *migo d'iskatzi* (once it is *muktzeh* at the beginning of Shabbos then it remains *muktzeh* for all of Shabbos), it should be irrelevant whether one makes a condition. Even once the *issur* goes away it remains *muktzeh*?! *Beis Yosef*[6] quotes *Rivash*,

---

4. *Beitzah* 30b, s.v. עד מוצאי.
5. *Shabbos* 44a.
6. 279.

who raises this problem. (*Beis Yosef*[7] entertains in according to *Rambam* that there will be a distinction between Rebbe Shimon and Rebbe Yehudah regarding the effectiveness of a condition.)

We have seen earlier[8] that there are two approaches how to understand *migo d'iskatzi*. One explanation is that when the reason for the designation exists at *bein hashemashos*, i.e., the onset of Shabbos, we claim that a person's mind for all of Shabbos is based on this status that was present at the beginning of Shabbos. He has set it aside from use for all of Shabbos.

Accordingly, we can understand how a condition can work. The owner is simply revealing to us that this object is not subject to the standard intention we claim people usually have. He has explicitly said he *is interested* in this object during Shabbos, so by default we can't invoke *migo d'iskatzi*. This is the *lashon* of *Rashba*:[9] דע״כ לא קאמר ר״י מיגו דאיתקצאי ביה״ש אלא בדאיתקצאי סתם, הא בשהתנה לא - "It has to be Rebbe Yehudah only said *migo* when the *haktzaah* was *stam*, not when one stipulated."[10]

There is another way of understanding *migo d'iskatzi*, based on the *pasuk* of "*v'hechinu*," which teaches us that items must be prepared before Shabbos if they are to be used on Shabbos. Something that isn't prepared for use on Shabbos at *bein hashemashos* receives a (status of *muktzeh*), even if it subsequently becomes fit during Shabbos. This is because the object's status for the entire day is decided based upon the first moments of Shabbos.

We can suggest that those who learn a condition doesn't help with *muktzeh machmas issur* understand *migo d'iskatzi* the latter way. How can a condition prevent *migo d'iskatzi* from applying? Even with the condition the item has a status of *eino muchan*. This certainly fits with the opinion

---

7. *Siman* 518. *Raavad Hasagos* on *Rif* in *Beitzah* also says a condition won't help according to Rebbe Yehudah because of *migo d'iskatzi*.

8. Chapter 20.

9. *Beitzah* 30b.

10. *Magen Avraham* comments on *Shulchan Aruch* that only by a candle does a condition help because "*asui l'chabos* — inevitably it will be extinguished." He understands like we are suggesting, that by stipulating one is showing that he intends

of *Ritva*. He learns *migo d'iskatzi* is because of "*v'hechinu*" and he also holds that *muktzeh machmas issur* is not subject to being permitted with a condition.

Those who follow the opinion of *Shulchan Aruch* can make a condition and stipulate that they want to remove their candlesticks from the table once the flame goes out. While those who follow *Rema* won't be allowed to remove their candlesticks based on a condition, nonetheless there is a custom to be lenient to ask a non-Jew to remove the candles once they go out since we consider asking a non-Jew to be as if one stipulated, i.e., it is not presently *muktzeh.*[11]

Bringing in a Chanukiah

Bringing in a *chanukiah* from outside (question #2) should be dependent on the same *machlokes*. However, there is a slight difference between the two cases. In the latter case one is bringing it in to *safeguard* it, while the candlesticks are most likely being removed from the table in order to use the table. Based on how we've explained how a condition works - that it removes the reason for the candle to be *muktzeh machmas issur* once the flame has gone out, but the candlestick remains a *kli shemelachto l'issur* and so would be limited in that it may not be moved *m'chamah l'tzel* - the condition isn't an override button that removes entirely all the limitations imposed by *muktzeh*. Therefore, one wouldn't be allowed to move the can-

---

on using the item. *Magen Avraham* is adding that this is true only in cases when it is inevitable the *issur* will be removed. The context in which *Magen Avraham* is saying this is in answering *Rivash*'s question. He argues on the answer *Beis Yosef* brings that a condition is said in cases of *bosis*. We will elaborate on this alternative answer in part 2.

11. *Bikrei Yosef* (point 5) quotes from the Responsa *Chut HaMeshulash* (*Tashbatz*) that one can make a condition one time for the whole year. The stipulation is: "Every candle I hereby light I intend on using once it is extinguished." *Tashbatz* even suggests that since the *minhag* is to move the candle with a condition, when one lights the candles, he lights *al daas haminhag* — with the intention to uphold the *minhag*. So even if one didn't make a condition, he can still move the candlesticks. He adds that placing the bread on the candles is a *zecher* (resemblance) of the *minhag*, like an impetus that one is lighting based on this preexisting *minhag*.

dlestick in order to protect it. *Magen Avraham*[12] writes explicitly that one is, however, allowed to ask a non-Jew to move the candlestick even to protect it from theft.

Magen Avraham's reasoning for suggesting so is that since even without a condition one is allowed to ask a non-Jew to move a candle *l'tzorech gufo u'mekomo* (as he can move it himself were he to do it with a *tiltul min hatzad*), why does *Rema* write that it is permitted to ask a non-Jew, as it's considered like he made a condition? It must be the "considered" condition helps so that one can ask the non-Jew to carry it even *m'chamah l'tzel.*

Classifying Candlesticks

R' Akiva Eiger raises a difficulty with this. How can one can ask the non-Jew to move the candlestick even for its protection, since the condition hasn't removed the fact that it is a *kli shemelachto l'issur*? He answers that there is a known dispute whether a candlestick is a *kli shemelachto l'issur* or a *kli shemelachto l'heter*. *Rashba* holds the latter, since one doesn't actively *do issur* with the candle; *issur is done with it.*[13] He writes that even though we don't *pasken* like *Rashba,* perhaps we can rely on his opinion regarding asking the non-Jew to carry the candlestick. The implication of R' Akiva Eiger is that according to *Shulchan Aruch,* when the Jew will be carrying the candlestick himself we cannot rely on *Rashba*. Accordingly, it will not be permitted to move the *chanukiah* to inside the house.[14]

---

12. 279:9.

13. We elaborated on this dispute in chapter 1.

14. R' Ovadiah Yosef (*Chazon Ovadiah,* section 3, p. 190) permits moving the *chanukiah* even *m'chamah l'tzel* and brings *Birkei Yosef,* who also is lenient. But after seeing R' Akiva Eiger it is difficult to be lenient. His claim that the implication of the *lashon* of *Shulchan Aruch* — *"mutar l'taltalo"* — is that it is permitted *m'chamah l'tzel* is also incorrect because in *se'if* 6, *Shulchan Aruch* uses the same *lashon* and there he clearly means that you can only move it *l'tzorech gufo u'mekomo.* Knesses HaGedolah permits moving the *chanukiah* inside if the non-Jews do not allow it to remain outside, as long as one has stipulated. This seems to support *Birkei Yosef*; however, maybe it is different. Moving it inside is due to a necessity that the non-Jews want this space vacant and therefore it is considered *tzorech mekomo.* We elaborated on this in the chapter on *tzorech mekomo.* The Gemara

Aruch HaShulchan says that this halachah is not relevant nowadays. The "*ner*" *Shulchan Aruch* was referring to is a utensil that they would use for various tasks, unlike our modern-day candlesticks that have no use besides supporting the flame on top. Whether a *kli shemelachto l'issur* that has no permissible functions is still classified as a *kli shemelachto l'issur* or is relegated to a form of *muktzeh machmas gufo* is a vast dispute. In chapter 1 we elaborated on this point. According to those who are stringent, *Aruch HaShulchan* is correct in his ruling. However, we brought proof that there is room to be lenient, so our candlesticks can be classified as *kli shemelachto l'issur*.

Chazon Ish's Criteria That One Will Use the Muktzeh

Nevertheless, *Aruch HaShulchan*'s observation that our candlesticks are inherently different from what *Shulchan Aruch* is discussing raises another potential problem. *Chazon Ish*[15] asserts that a condition only helps when one intends on actually using the *muktzeh* item. If one only intends to *move* the item, a condition won't help. The logic seems to be that if one isn't going to use it, he hasn't prepared the item for the eventual time when the *issur* is removed, i.e., the condition has no meaning to it. Accordingly, a condition won't help for our candlesticks. One is only stipulating to move them because we don't use our candlesticks.[16]

---

discusses an identical scenario and we showed from the commentators that this can be included in *tzorech mekomo*. Therefore, with a condition the *chanukiah* remains a *kli shemelachto l'issur* so there is a *heter of tzorech mekomo*, but not *m'chamah l'tzel*.

15. *Siman* 43, point 13.

16. *Chazon Ish* is very cryptic. He says: בעינן תנאי להשתמש בו ולא תנאי לטלטל מיהו כיון דראוי להשתמש ועומד לכך כיון שמתנה שאין מקצהו לכל השבת שפיר מהני... I understood this as follows: "Even though a condition to move the *muktzeh* should not be sufficient, since one *could* use the item and the item is one that is meant for using, one's condition, despite his intention, is sufficient." He then says: דדין זה תלוי לפי מקום וזמן דבמקום שאין משתמשין בנר לצ״ג כלל דמי לסיכי...וכלוהו איסרית וצ״ע — "This halachah is dependent according to the place and time; in a place where they don't use a candle for its own sake then it is similar to a knife and is forbidden." The

According to how we explained why there is no *migo d'iskatzi* when one makes a condition, that one has announced he has intention to use this item for Shabbos, so even when one has *daas* just to move this item we can argue that his *daas* is sufficient for us not to evoke *migo d'iskatzi*. Furthermore, *Rema* says they made a condition so the non-Jew would *move* the candle, explicit that the condition was to move the item and yet worked![17]

Shabbos Timers

There are many other potential *issurim* (such as *gram maavir/kibui*) involved in changing the switches of a timer (question #3), but from the point of view of *hilchos muktzeh*, certainly with a condition one would be able to move the switches - even if one is only interested in saving money by keeping the light off. This is permitted because one is moving the switches for a current purpose of the timer, which is considered *l'tzorech gufo*.

Summary

There are two ways, one is found in *Rashi* and the other in *Rif*, to understand a Gemara that discusses condition, stipulating that when the *issur muktzeh* is removed one will use the item. The novelty in a condition is

---

direct connection between this half and what he just brought before is unclear. Does he just mean the argument *Aruch HaShulchan* presented? I think he is saying that even though in actuality a condition to move it does work because one can use the item, that is only true when one actually uses the item. In cases such as candlesticks nowadays, when one doesn't use them for anything, one's condition is only to move the item and so the condition won't help. *Chazon Ish* would argue that even if nowadays one stipulates that he wants to use the candlesticks, it won't suffice, because *batel daas* (his intentions are in vain against the accepted practice), and it really is only interpreted as a condition to move, which is insufficient.

17. Based on our previous footnote, we can suggest why *Chazon Ish* never felt this *Rema* was a refutation to his idea. Since the candle *Rema* was referring to had usages, even if presently one is only stipulating so that the non-Jew can remove it from the table, he can use this item for other purposes and it is meant for other purposes, so there is no designation and his condition is effective.

that even though the item was *muktzeh* when Shabbos started, so *migo d'iskatzi* should forbid the item for all of Shabbos, nevertheless a condition helps because one is declaring that he is not averting his attention from this item, so when the current reason for it being *muktzeh* is removed, it's free to be handled. *Shulchan Aruch* holds that a condition works to move a candle once the flame is extinguished. *Rema* argues; he only relies on a condition regarding enlisting a non-Jew to move the candle. Besides a Gemara *Yerushalmi* being the source of *Shulchan Aruch,* we suggested that according to *Rashi*'s conclusion of the Gemara, a condition helps regarding a sukkah all year round. *Shulchan Aruch* extrapolated that the same way *migo d'iskatzi* on *muktzeh machmas issur* is circumvented via a condition, so too by a candle. *Rema* can understand like *Rif,* according to which there is no precedence that a condition is effective against *muktzeh machmas issur.*

Answers

1. *Shulchan Aruch* permits one to rely on a stipulation to move a candle once it has been extinguished. *Rema* forbids it, the candlesticks remain *muktzeh.*
2. Even though *Shulchan Aruch* permits stipulating, we showed that only helps to remove the *muktzeh machmas issur.* The candlesticks still remain a *kli shemelachto l'issur.* The same applies to a *chanukiah;* therefore bringing it inside is problematic because it is moving to safeguard, which is forbidden.
3. From the point of view of *muktzeh,* if Yehudah stipulates that he wants to move the switches in a time switch, he is allowed to do so. *Rema* would be stringent here too. There are potentially other *issurim* involved, beyond the scope of this work.

Part 2

המשך ביאור ע"פ שיטת רש"י

Continuation in Rashi's Stance

Until now we have understood that the essence of a condition was effective by stipulating that one is preparing this object for later on, when it will be available for use. Even if the item is *muktzeh* when Shabbos begins, we don't evoke *migo d'iskatzi* because one has prepared the item for the eventual time it will be permitted, so there is no designation for all of Shabbos. This is how we answered the question *Rivash* raised against the effectiveness of condition.

We conceded that if one understands *migo d'iskatzi* is based on "*v'hechinu,*" the item must be prepared when Shabbos begins. Otherwise it's identified come as "unprepared" for all of Shabbos. Then *Rivash* is correct in his problem - why should a condition help? And true, many *Rishonim* learned that condition is not effective.

However, we've seen, simply speaking, that *Rashi* learns a condition does help with *muktzeh machmas issur* even according to Rebbe Yehudah, yet *Rashi* also explains [18] that *migo d'iskatzi* is based on this understanding of "*v'hechinu.*" How does *Rashi* understand the essence of a condition? How can it override the problem that at *bein hashemashos* it is *muktzeh* and we should therefore apply a *migo d'iskatzi*?

The truth is, *Gra* [19] argues on our explanation of the two opinions found in *Shulchan Aruch* whether a condition helps for candles or not. He agrees that learning the Gemara we first started with is dependent on the two ways of *Rashi* and *Rif*, but the complete opposite to how we suggested. According to *Rif*, the same way one can make a condition by a sukkah, surely one can make a condition by a candle. However, according to *Rashi*, the

---

18. *Beitzah* 26b, s.v. ואי דלא אחזו.

19. 279:4.

conclusion of the Gemara was that one can't make a condition for a sukkah, so surely one can't make a condition for a condition.

Gra explains that the dispute is dependent upon two opinions mentioned in the aforementioned Gemara. According to *Rif*, the conclusion was that a condition can help for *muktzeh machmas mitzvah*, so presumably according to *Rif* it can also work with *muktzeh machmas issur*. Whereas according to *Rashi* the Gemara says one cannot make a condition by a sukkah because there is an *issur* infringing on his condition, so by all *muktzeh machmas issur* the *issur* should infringe the condition from working.[20]

The difficulty in *Gra*'s suggestion is apparent. We clearly saw that according to the text of *Rashi* the *beraisa* teaches that a condition helps for a hut of all year round. This law, permitting one to make such a condition, is true even according to the opinion of Rebbe Yehudah (according to Rebbe Shimon this hut is permitted even without a condition, so the condition must only be necessary for Rebbe Yehudah). If so, there is no proof that the opinion brought by *Shulchan Aruch* permitting one to make a condition with a candle is limited to *Rif*. Even *Rashi* agrees that with *muktzeh machmas issur* Rebbe Yehudah permits a condition!

According to our explanation we don't understand *Rashi*'s opinion, nor according to *Gra* do we understand *Rashi*. Evidently there must be a new explanation to unravel this confusion.

A Condition - Making It Considered Prepared Now

Until now the understanding was that the essence of a condition was effective by stipulating that one is preparing this object for later on when it

---

20. *Shulchan Aruch* 273 brings two opinions whether a woman can make a condition before she lights the Shabbos candles that she is not accepting Shabbos with the lighting of the candles. *Gra* says this dispute is based on the same *machlokes* whether one can make a condition or not with *muktzeh*. The suggestion seemingly is that according to *Rif* a condition helps even by *muktzeh machmas mitzvah*, so it will presumably work also with an actual mitzvah, while according to *Rashi* it doesn't work by *muktzeh* so neither by mitzvos. The comparison is certainly novel and not so simple. ואכמ"ל.

will be available for use. However, *Rashi* must learn that via a condition one actually makes the item prepared *now*. Without the condition, the *issur* that currently limits the item's use renders it "unprepared." Via stipulating that one will be using this item, one is in effect declaring that this object is *now* prepared. From the point of view of the object, it's ready to be used. There is just a temporary external *issur* that prevents its present use. However, since the item is prepared there is no reason to evoke *migo d'iskatzi*.[21] This will reconcile our approach how *Rashi* can hold that condition helps yet learn that *migo d'iskatzi* is based on "*v'hechinu*."

Beis Yosef quotes that *Rashbatz* rejects *Rivash*'s question of how a condition can ever help. Surely *migo d'iskatzi* should forbid it for the duration of Shabbos. *Rashbatz* explains that those who permit making a condition only do so by *ner* and the like; *ner* is different and *migo d'iskatzi* will not prevent one from making a condition to permit it. This is because it is not something that is inherently *muktzeh*; it is only *muktzeh* because it is a *bosis* to the flame. With this we say that one can make a condition that will circumvent the *migo d'iskatzi*. However, items that are *muktzeh mitzad atzman* (contained within themselves the reason to set them aside) such as sukkah decorations (the *kedushah* is inherent in the item), we will invoke a *migo d'iskatzi* and one can't make a condition.

The understanding behind the difference why something that is *muktzeh* due to external reasons can have a condition, whereas something that is *muktzeh mitzad atzman* cannot can be based on what we've explained according to *Rashi*, that the essence of a condition is to make the object prepared now. If the reason causing this *muktzeh* exists presently in the item, one can't say it is prepared and that just something external is curtailing its usage. The item is inherently not prepared. Stipulating otherwise is disregarding the actuality that this is *muktzeh*. On the other hand,

---

21. Toward the end of chapter 22, we elaborated on this principle in the name of the Steipler. This idea is similar to what we find by *tevel*. The Gemara 43a says it's מוכן אצל שבת דאי בעי — "prepared regarding Shabbos since if..." Until he tithes the produce it is *muktzeh*. Nevertheless there is no *migo* because we view this produce as prepared and there is just a side problem. Once that *issur* is removed it is permitted.

something like a candlestick is only *muktzeh* because it is a *bosis*. This reason for *muktzeh* is only because one has set it aside to serve something else, i.e., the flame. When its identity as *muktzeh* is not inherently linked to this object, one can stipulate that he is not setting aside this candlestick to be subservient to the flame and it's prepared for when he needs. Without any designation we can't evoke *migo d'iskatzi*.

Does Shulchan Aruch Always Permit Making a Condition?

We mentioned that *Shulchan Aruch* sides with the opinion that condition works with a *muktzeh machmas issur*, unlike *Rema*, who brings down that the custom is not to rely on such a condition. *Magen Avraham* questions the omission in *Hilchos Yom Tov*[22] that a condition can help regarding a flimsy sukkah all year round. Surely if *Shulchan Aruch* holds that a condition helps, why didn't he state so again?! *Mateh BiYehudah*[23] says *Shulchan Aruch* didn't need to repeat himself; he relied on what he wrote by a candle. *Magen Avraham* holds the implication is that a condition doesn't help. What's the difference that regarding a candle he does permit a condition, while by sukkah he doesn't? *Magen Avraham* answers that with regards to the halachos of Shabbos we *pasken* like Rebbe Shimon regarding *muktzeh*, while in *Hilchos Yom Tov* we *pasken* like Rebbe Yehudah. *Magen Avraham* proposes that according to Rebbe Shimon one can make a condition, as opposed to according Rebbe Yehudah.[24] He then raises a question with this answer: Regarding *muktzeh machmas issur*, such as the case of the candle, *Shulchan Aruch* follows Rebbe Yehudah to consider it *muktzeh*, yet *Shulchan Aruch* still permits one to make a condition?

---

22. *Siman* 518.

23. Quoted in *Biur Halachah, siman* 518.

24. *Beis Yosef siman* 518 understands the same idea in the opinion of *Rambam*. According to Rebbe Shimon a condition helps, while not according to Rebbe Yehudah. *Raavad Hasagos* on *Rif* in *Beitzah* also says that a condition won't help according to Rebbe Yehudah because of *migo d'iskatzi*.

We can answer based on *Rashbatz,* who says that a candle is different. The reason it's *muktzeh* is not inherent to the vessel, so a condition can work. *Shulchan Aruch* requires that the condition render it now prepared and this is possible to achieve with the candlestick, since the *muktzeh* is not inherent to this object. However, a sukkah is inherently *muktzeh,* since it is forbidden to dissemble, and therefore a condition won't help.

(*Minchas Ariel* answers that while we *pasken* like Rebbe Yehudah in cases of a candle but not for the same reasoning as Rebbe Yehudah, only when there it is also *dichui b'yadayim* [positively set is aside] does *Shulchan Aruch* follow the halachah in accordance with Rebbe Yehudah. Making a condition renders it as if there is no *dichui b'yadayim,* since by stipulating that one wishes to use it at a later date one is revealing that he hasn't set it aside. It follows that *Magen Avraham*'s original suggestion is true. The candle is only forbidden because there is also *dichui b'yadayim.* The stipulation results in the only reason to forbid the item is because it is *muktzeh machmas issur.* We *pasken* cases of only *muktzeh machmas issur* like *shitas Rebbe Shimon* that there isn't *migo d'iskatzi,* so once the candle is extinguished it is permitted. While on Yom Tov we *pasken* entirely like Rebbe Yehudah, *muktzeh machmas issur* on its own is forbidden even without *dichui b'yadayim.* Therefore even if condition removes the *dichui b'yadayim,* there is still a reason to evoke *migo d'iskatzi.*)

Scenarios Where Even Tosafos Agrees One Can Stipulate

Perhaps *Tosafos*[25] understands the essence of condition along the same lines. Even though he holds that a condition doesn't help for a candle, he still agrees that a condition does help with a flimsy sukkah. *Tosafos* distinguishes that by a candle there is a *dichui b'yadayim,* which means that there is an action that was done to this candlestick to make it not prepared, whereas with a flimsy sukkah "one is awaiting when the sukkah will fall down." The explanation is that a condition is required to make this object prepared at present and not *muktzeh.* Therefore *Tosafos* ar-

25. *Shabbos* 44a, s.v. נר.

gues that whenever there is *dichui b'yadayim*, no stipulation will help to consider it not *muktzeh* at this moment, since for the time being you have actively set it aside and want it to temporarily be unavailable. This is a true reflection that it is *muktzeh*.

In contrast where there is no *dichui b'yadayim*, by stipulating that at the moment when it will be permitted for use one wishes to make use of it, one renders it now already not *muktzeh*. However, there is currently an external *issur* preventing one from disassembling the sukkah, but he is not interested in this temporary state so it is not removed from his mind and from his point of view it is now prepared. There is just an external barrier that needs to be lifted for him to actualize what is currently prepared. The essence of the condition is to create a preparation now, for the moment when the object will be usable. This is implicit from what *Tosafos* writes: ביה"ש אינו בודל, meaning even at the beginning of Shabbos, when the sukkah was erect, he didn't temporarily remove it from his mind that he will use it.

Gra's Understanding of the Topic

Now we can perhaps understand how *Gra* learns.[26] One is making the same condition to preempt the *kedushah* from coming onto the sukkah. איני בודל מהן ביה"ש is the same condition that *Shulchan Aruch* requires one to make to remove the *issur muktzeh*. According to *Rashi*, one isn't able to stipulate that he is not distancing himself from the sukkah because he has to distance himself from the sukkah when Shabbos begins. Similarly, one must leave the lights alight when Shabbos begins for the mitzvah of Shabbos candles (or even if these lights are not the Shabbos candles but one wants them alight during *bein hashemashos*). One can't stipulate on a situation that he's forced into against his will. While according to *Rif*, from the Gemara we have precedence even when one is forced to distance himself from the *muktzeh*. If one stipulates איני בודל מהן ביה"ש, it is effective. The need for this specific wording of the condition is better understood

26. *Dameshek Eliezer*. Some ideas are based on what he discusses.

according to how we now are understanding condition. If a condition works that one is revealing that he has intention to use this item when it comes available and there is no *stam daas* not to use it for all of Shabbos, why does he need to state that from the beginning of Shabbos he has a connection to the item? While if the item now needs to be considered prepared for the condition to be effective, this requirement that one must stipulate from the beginning of Shabbos that he is not distancing himself from the item is better understood.[27]

This understanding can help explain a strong question asked by *Keren Orah.*[28] The *Yerushalmi* says that one cannot make a condition on *muktzeh machmas meyus,* i.e., it is ineffective to say when this item changes and is no longer repulsive, it will be permitted to me. Asks *Keren Orah*: According to the opinion of *Ran* that the reason Rebbe Yehudah holds that something repulsive is *muktzeh* is because he holds of *migo d'iskatzi.*[29] (Since now that he wishes to use the object, the repulsive factor is no longer relevant. However, there is a *migo d'iskatzi* that prevents its use.) Why can't one stipulate, since we have precedence from *muktzeh machmas issur* that a condition can override a *migo d'iskatzi*? We can answer that a condition can only help when it is now making it prepared. Something that is repulsive is intrinsically not currently prepared and therefore the condition is meaningless. Stipulating that this object will be fit for use at a later period does not negate its current state of repulsiveness. However, when you do decide to use this repulsive vessel, this is something new; it's a completely new designation.

Tehillah L'Dovid asks: Why can't the condition help to enable one to move the candle even when it is still alight? Since by stipulating that the candlestick does not become *muktzeh,* one can hold the candle, regarding the flame he is doing *tiltul min hatzad l'tzorech davar ha'mutar* under cir-

---

27. *Gra* must understand like *Tosafos* distinguished between the case of a flimsy sukkah and the candle. Therefore, even though according to *Rashi* the conclusion of the Gemara is that a condition helps by a flimsy sukkah, that is not a reason why he should hold a condition should work by a candle.

28. *Shabbos* 45a.

29. We elaborated on this *Ran* in chapter 21.

cumstances where it is not possible to do *ni'ur*. So why does *Shulchan Aruch* only permit moving it once it goes out? According to one approach to condition we have presented, it is not considered that one is preparing the item now; rather, he intends on using it later. However, according to the other understanding, that a condition essentially makes the object prepared right away, the question has a firm basis. Perhaps we can answer this with an understanding of *bosis*. True, one is saying that this candlestick is prepared and not subservient to the flame, but since in reality the candlestick is still holding the flame and a flame isn't something that be carried on its own, the way to carry it is via holding a candlestick. Therefore holding the candlestick is not an indirect form of moving the flame; it's the regular way of transporting the flame and it cannot be considered טלטול מן מצד.

Summary

Beis Yosef answers that a condition helps by a candle despite *migo d'iskatzi* because it's only *muktzeh* due to *bosis*. This answer is better understood according to our new understanding how a condition works - it renders the item prepared, from the beginning of Shabbos. The restrictions in using the item are just considered external, but not a reflection that the item is not prepared. *Beis Yosef* is saying that *bosis* is a prime example of this. The candlesticks are prepared, so there is no reason to evoke *migo d'iskatzi*. Just because they are a support to the flame, there is an external restriction moving them. We used this principle to defend how *Rashi* could learn that *muktzeh machmas issur* is subject to a condition yet simultaneously learn that *migo d'iskatzi* is due to an item being not *muchan* when Shabbos begins.

Shulchan Aruch doesn't write that one can make a condition on a flimsy sukkah. Based on *Beis Yosef* we answered that since the *issur* is not external, one can't render the actual sukkah prepared.

Appendix: שיטת בעה"מ בתנאי – Opinion of Baal Hameor Regarding a Stipulation

Baal HaMeor has a very interesting opinion, different from the opinions we've seen till now. He explains that a condition only helps by a flimsy sukkah because it is *muktzeh machmas issur d'rabbanan,* as opposed to *muktzeh machmas issur d'Oraisa.* He explains that once the structure is already weak, there is no longer any *issur d'Oraisa* in the destruction of the building. It is only forbidden *mid'rabbanan* to take down such a structure since it is *michzi k'soser* (appears to be an act of destruction). *Baal HaMeor* is *mechadesh* that there's a difference whether the *issur* that renders something *muktzeh* is *d'rabbanan* or *d'Oraisa.* If the sukkah is a solid structure and involves a *issur d'Oraisa* in disassembling it, it is *muktzeh* even according to Rebbe Shimon. This is because one doesn't think at all that it may fall and that one will have the opportunity to use the wood on Shabbos or Yom Tov. It's therefore considered to be a case of something that is *eino chazi* (not fit) as well as *dichui b'yadayim,* which are the requirements that Rebbe Shimon has in order for something to qualify as *muktzeh.* When there is a *issur d'rabbanan* to disassemble the sukkah, according to Rebbe Shimon it isn't *muktzeh* if it falls, since the rabbinic prohibition is insufficient to consider it sufficiently removed from his mind. However, according to Rebbe Yehudah it is *muktzeh* even once it falls, but according to Rebbe Yehudah one can make a condition!

Meiri brings examples where we find there is no *muktzeh* when there is only an *issur d'rabbanan* that would render this item *muktzeh.* His first example is from the Mishnah[30] earlier that discusses if one had fruit inside a house that was entirely sealed and the only way to access the fruit was through destroying the house. Even though the fruit could be considered *muktzeh machmas issur,* since their usage is bound in a transgression, since the case is when it is only forbidden rabbinically to destroy the house, if the house falls down the fruit are permitted. We don't treat them as *muktzeh machmas issur,* since they were only ever *muktzeh due to* a *issur d'rabbanan.*

Another example is *tevel* (un-tithed produce). If on Shabbos someone mistakenly tithes the produce, they are permitted. We don't say that since they were forbidden to tithe previously they are *muktzeh machmas issur.*

---

30. *Beitzah* 31b.

Explains *Meiri*: Since it is only a *issur d'rabbanan* to tithe on Shabbos we don't apply *muktzeh machmas issur*.

Meiri understands that these examples are even according to Rebbe Yehudah. If so, why does Rebbe Yehudah hold of *muktzeh machmas issur* by a flimsy sukkah? He answers that all agree that there is no *muktzeh machmas issur* only for food items that have an *issur d'rabbanan*. General items whose usage is limited because of an *issur* like the sukkah are subject to the general *machlokes* between Rebbe Yehudah and Rebbe Shimon. Still Rebbe Yehudah does concede that a condition does help in such scenarios. We have precedence[31] that food is less *muktzeh* than other items, since a person's mind is much more reliant on the potential usage of the food. If something can be consumed, one always thinks that he may need to eat it. Therefore even if the possibility of eating it will involve a *issur d'rabbanan*, a person still thinks about it.

31. *Shulchan Aruch* 310:2 writes: אין שום אוכל תלוש הראוי לאכילה מוקצה — "Food is never subject to an *issur muktzeh*."

Chapter 25, Part 1

מוקצה מחמת מצוה

Muktzeh Due to a Mitzvah

Questions

1. Naftali wants to remove a pomegranate that's hanging as a decoration from his sukkah roof. May he do so? If yes, is he permitted to eat it now? Is it forbidden even on Chol HaMoed, not just Shabbos?
2. Can I move a decoration hanging in a sukkah? Can I put it in storage on Chol HaMoed?

There is a *beraisa*[1] that teaches us a law regarding the *kedushah* of a sukkah. The *pasuk* writes: חג הסוכות שבעת ימים לה׳.[2] We learn from here that just like an animal that is designated for a *korban chagigah* receives *kedushah* and as a result of this *kedushah* one cannot use the animal for any other purpose, similarly once the festival of Sukkos begins, the sukkah receives *kedushah*. The resulting *kedushah* forbids the sukkah to be used for any purpose other than the fulfillment of the mitzvah.

Disgracing a Mitzvah

The Gemara[3] discusses a number of actions that are forbidden due to the prohibition of *bizui mitzvah* (disgracing a mitzvah). One of the issues

1. *Beitzah* 30b.
2. *Vayikra* 21.
3. *Shabbos* 22a.

mentioned is that one can't take benefit from (edible) sukkah decorations (question #1) because of *bizui mitzvah*. The source of *bizui mitzvah* is from *kisui hadam*: One can't cover the blood of a slaughtered animal using one's feet; using one's feet instead of his hands is a disrespectful manner of carrying out the mitzvah. The Gemara continues to learn that so too consuming one's sukkah decoration is considered a disgrace to the mitzvah. The Gemara gives another example of *bizui mitzvah*: Counting money using the light from the *chanukiah* is an affront to the Chanukah lights.

Tosafos[4] notes that the Gemara in *Shabbos*[5] implies the reason why one can't use the decorations of the sukkah for other purposes is because they are *hoktzah l'mitzvah* (designated for the fulfillment of a mitzvah). The Gemara in *Shabbos* discusses one who hangs various fruits as decoration in his sukkah. The Gemara says one can't benefit from the fruits throughout the festival of Sukkos since the decorations have been designated for the mitzvah. This is seemingly a new category of *muktzeh* - being set aside for the use of a mitzvah is a designation that renders the item *muktzeh*.

Is the Muktzeh Status Applicable on Chol HaMoed?

We need to establish two points: Will this *muktzeh* status that's conferred on the sukkah and its decorations be applicable only for the days of Yom Tov, or is it even applicable on Chol HaMoed? We also need to establish whether this *issur* is only a prohibition to make use of or consume, or does it also encompass an *issur tiltul*?[6]

Tosafos asks: Why do we need the reason of *hoktzah l'mitzvah* if there is the reason of *bizui mitzvah*? Both forbid using the decorations (and structure) of the sukkah. We can ask further: If there are two reasons already to forbid using the decorations of the sukkah for any other purpose, and similarly the actual structure of the sukkah would be bound by these limitations, what is the teaching from the *korban chagigah* adding?

---

4. Ibid., s.v. סוכה.

5. Ibid. 45a.

6. This is more relevant to the *muktzeh* of decorations on Chol HaMoed.

Tosafos explains that the concept of *muktzeh* is only applicable to Shabbos and Yom Tov, not Chol HaMoed (presumably because the *pasuk* "*v'hechinu*," which teaches us the requirement of items being prepared, is only said regarding these days). While *bizui mitzvah* only forbids making use of the decorations of the sukkah while they're still hanging, once they have fallen down and are not functioning as a mitzvah item, it is not considered a disgrace to benefit from them, so there is no mitzvah one is disgracing. Due to the designation for mitzvah the decorations of the sukkah are *muktzeh* for the duration of Yom Tov, including Chol HaMoed, regardless of whether they are attached or fallen.

What does *Tosafos* hold in the event the decorations fell on Chol HaMoed? *Maharsha* and *Hagahos Ashrei* understand simply that neither reason applies to fallen decorations on Chol HaMoed. *Muktzeh* doesn't apply because it is not Yom Tov and there is no disgrace to the mitzvah since it is not presently serving a mitzvah purpose. So they explain *Tosafos* holds it is permitted to benefit from them. However, *Taz*[7] and *Gra*[8] argue that even if the decorations fall on Chol HaMoed, it's forbidden to benefit from them. They bring from *Rosh*,[9] who writes explicitly that even on Chol HaMoed there is a problem of *muktzeh* even once fallen.[10]

How is this *muktzeh* relevant even for Chol HaMoed? *Tosafos*'s presumption in his question was that *muktzeh* doesn't apply to weekdays, even Chol HaMoed. *Rosh* explains since were the sukkah to fall one must rebuild it, if one were to take the wood for other uses he would be annulling the mitzvah. This applies even on Chol HaMoed, so the *haktzaah l'mitzvah* of the sukkah is applicable all seven days! This *haktzaah l'mitzvah* forbids depleting the material of the sukkah. By depleting, one is thereby severing the mitzvah. Even according to *Tosafos*'s presumption that *muktzeh* is only forbidden on Yom Tov, it means only regarding for-

---

7. 21:2.

8. 638:2.

9. Responsa *siman* 24, point 9, and in *Shabbos* 22a.

10. *Levush Serad, siman* 21, who explains that seven though each reason on its own doesn't forbid fallen decorations on Chol HaMoed. Since both reasons are partially applicable on Chol HaMoed, together they can forbid when the decorations fall.

bidding *tiltul*, while this *muktzeh* that forbids depletion is not limited to Shabbos/Yom Tov. Precedence for this is from esrog. Due to the *haktzaah l'mitzvah* it is forbidden to eat all seven days; Chol HaMoed is included in the prohibition because the esrog is a mitzvah item throughout the seven days, thereby eating it even on Chol HaMoed is depleting the mitzvah.

This reasoning, that benefiting from the material that is designated for the mitzvah is considered an annulment of the mitzvah, doesn't apply to decorations because consuming the decorations doesn't prevent one's fulfillment of his mitzvah of eating in a sukkah. Therefore *Tosafos* holds that *muktzeh l'mitzvah* is not relevant to the decorations on Chol HaMoed. On Yom Tov the *haktzah l'mitzvah* forbids *tiltul* of the decorations.

After clarifying these two principles, *Rosh* explains why even though each principle on its own won't forbid fallen decorations on Chol HaMoed, it is still forbidden. Since on Chol HaMoed there is *bizui mitzvah*, we artificially treat it as if there is a *haktzaah l'mitzvah* even on Chol HaMoed. Once there is a *haktzaah* at the beginning of Chol HaMoed, we can evoke *migo d'iskatzi* and when they fall they will also be forbidden.[11]

Ran[12] gives a slightly different explanation why the decorations are forbidden even once they fall. Even though only *bizui mitzvah* is applicable to the decoration, since the decorations are serving and secondary to the sukkah they become nullified by the sukkah and receive the same halachos as the sukkah, that even once it falls it'll be forbidden, and one will transgress *bizui mitzvah* if he benefits from the fallen decoration.

Shulchan Aruch[13] *paskens* that it's forbidden to consume the decorations of the sukkah all eight days, even once they have fallen. *Shaar HaTzion*[14] says the source is *Rosh*. *Rema* adds to *Shulchan Aruch* that on Shabbos/Yom Tov it is forbidden to even move the decoration. As we've

---

11. In responsa he is very concise, and his full intent is unclear. Our explanation is based on what is presented in *Chiddushim Shabbos* 22a, ואכתי צריך ביאור.

12. *Beitzah, Dapei HaRif* 17a.

13. Ibid.

14. Point 17.

seen, this is specifically due to *haktzaah l'mitzvah*, which applies only on Shabbos/Yom Tov.

Is Removing without Depleting Also a Disgrace to the Mitzvah?

The *poskim*[15] discuss whether one can remove decorations entirely from the sukkah on Chol HaMoed (question #2). That which *Rema* adds, that on Shabbos/Yom Tov one must not even *move* the decoration, implies that on Chol HaMoed one can *move* the decoration. Is moving not a disgrace to the mitzvah because one is *not consuming* the item? Regardless of where it is moved to, one could always still use this for the mitzvah of adorning the sukkah, or perhaps moving the decoration within the sukkah is not a disgrace to the mitzvah because it's still adorning the sukkah. However, were one to actually remove the decoration from the sukkah, this would constitute *bizui mitzvah* despite the ability to still use these items for the mitzvah, since temporarily one has removed the beauty of the sukkah.

Whether one can put his decoration in storage on Chol HaMoed (question #2) will be dependent on the aforementioned investigation, if moving the decoration out of the sukkah is a disgrace. According to the first option, as long as one doesn't deplete the decorations he can put them away in storage for next year. But if the second option is correct, one can't take the decoration out of the sukkah, since that disgraces the mitzvah.

Shulchan Aruch writes that one can make a condition before Yom Tov that he wishes to eat from his decorations whenever he wishes. *Rema* says that the custom is not to make such a stipulation with decorations hanging from the roof. However, the custom is that one can remove tapestries that are attached to the wall to save them from the rain, even without a condition. He adds that nonetheless it is still better to make a condition. We see from here that even regarding just removing decorations, even without consumption, *Rema* still prefers one to make a condition.

Megillas Sefer[16] is adamant that it is not forbidden to remove decorations even without a condition. He says *Rema* is referring only to Yom Tov.

15. Responsa *Sho'el U'Meishiv* and he brings more *poskim* there.
16. *Siman* 51.

On Yom Tov one can take down the decoration only if a condition is made. The condition preempts the decoration becoming *muktzeh machmas mitzvah*, while on Chol HaMoed the only issue is *bizui mitzvah*. Therefore, as long as one doesn't nullify the mitzvah it is permitted. *Mishnah Berurah* is unclear when commenting on these halachos. If he understands *Rema* like *Megillas Sefer*, he should have explained so. R' Shlomo Zalman Auerbach[17] concurs with those who permit removing the decoration on Chol HaMoed, even without making a condition. ואכתי צע"ג.

Summary

Tosafos establishes that the rabbinic prohibition of *bizui mitzvah* only applies while the decoration are hanging, i.e., the mitzvah is being performed. The *haktzaah l'mitzvah* only applies on Shabbos/Yom Tov when *muktzeh* applies, not on Chol HaMoed.

From *Rosh* we saw that the meaning that *haktzaah l'mitzvah* only applies on Shabbos/Yom Tov is only regarding moving the item, but even on Chol HaMoed it is forbidden to deplete the sukkah because it was designated for the mitzvah. In addition, *Rosh* forbids benefiting from the decorations on Chol HaMoed even once they have fallen. Whether removing decorations from the sukkah is encompassed in *bizui mitzvah* is subject to a dispute between the contemporary *poskim*. One is not depleting the mitzvah, yet it might be a disgrace to the mitzvah. R' Shlomo Zalman Auerbach is lenient.

Answers

1. Naftali can't even move the decoration on Yom Tov, let alone eat it. Eating is more stringent that it is even forbidden on Chol HaMoed.

---

17. *Minchas Shlomo*, section 2, *siman* 58, point 36.

2. To put the decorations away is a dispute; one can be lenient. On the one hand the decorations still exist and their role of adorning the sukkah can still be actualized, yet removing them from the sukkah is currently an act of disgracing the mitzvah.

Part 2

מוקצה מחמת מצוה לגבי סוכה

Muktzeh Machmas Mitzvah Pertaining to a Sukkah

Questions

1. Dovid is going away on Chol HaMoed and wishes to dismantle his sukkah. Is he permitted to take it down on Chol HaMoed?
2. There is a custom[18] for pregnant women to bite off the *pitom* on Hoshana Rabbah. Is this a correct custom?
3. There is a decoration with a pleasant odor hanging in the sukkah. Can I smell it?

There is confusion surrounding whether one is allowed to dismantle his sukkah on Chol HaMoed (question #1). In addition to *bizui mitzvah* and *muktzeh l'mitzvah*, the Gemara learns from *korban chagigah* that the sukkah has *kedushah* all seven days. The general question is: What restrictions do these designations place on the sukkah? Does the *kedushah* forbid one to make use of the material of the sukkah or does it only forbid one from stopping this mitzvah from existing?

---

18. Brought in *Likutei MaHariach* and *Moed L'Kol Chai, siman* 24, point 25.

What does it mean that there is *muktzeh* on a weekday? The simple explanation is that *muktzeh* is a borrowed term that means "set aside." Since this item is designated for a mitzvah, it's forbidden to use. The designation is manifested in a *issur hishtamshos* (prohibition to use it), not a prohibition in moving it. To rephrase our previous question according to these *Rishonim*: What does the *issur muktzeh* (in other words, the *issur hishtamshos*) encompass?

Taz[19] explains that the teaching from "*chag laHashem,*"[20] which teaches us that a sukkah has *kedushah* for seven days, doesn't teach us that it is forbidden to take any benefit from the sukkah at all. Rather, acting in a way that is nullifies the *kedushah* of the actual sukkah is forbidden; one can't ruin the mitzvah. However, a benefit that doesn't cause a *bitul* of the mitzvah such as leaning against it or resting something against it is permitted. (The main purpose of the *derashah* is to teach us that for all seven days it is *kadosh.*) Therefore, if one were to take down his sukkah, while the mitzvah has not been terminated indefinitely because he can rebuild it, he has removed the *kedushah* from this structure. *Shoel U'Meishiv*[21] understands that the *issur* is further encompassing. He forbids even taking the *sechach* off from one sukkah to put onto another one. His claim is that "*chag laHashem*" forbids all aspects of using the sukkah, even in a manner where one still can fulfill the mitzvah.

Rema says that one can't take a piece of wood from the sukkah to use as a toothpick. In light of this *Taz,* we understand the choice of the addition of *Rema*. Taking a piece off the sukkah, one can still fulfill the mitzvah of sitting inside a sukkah. But he has ruined the *kedushah* on that piece of the sukkah that he removed. So we see that the *kedushah* is on each and every part, and each part is judged independently, so one is breaching the *issur* of treating the sukkah with respect even by removing an insignificant part. Also, in light of *Taz, Rema*'s example is specifically something one will not return to the sukkah, hence it is a depletion of the *kedushah*.

---

19. 638:3. *Mishnah Berurah, se'if katan* 4, *paskens* this *Taz.*

20. *Vayikra* 23.

21. *Mehudara Teleisa,* section 3, *siman* 28.

(The *Rishonim* argue which parts of the sukkah the *pasuk* of "*chag laHashem*" is referring to as receiving the *kedushah*: Is it only the *sechach*, or also the walls? *Tosafos*[22] holds that the *sechach* and the essential walls (two and a bit) receive the *kedushah*. *Rambam*[23] equates the *issur* of using the *sechach* with the walls. *Taz*[24] quotes *Rosh* as understanding that this means that even the walls are subject to a *kedushah*. This could either be similar to *Tosafos*, referring only to the essential walls, or perhaps he means all of the walls. However, *Taz* himself argues that the opinion of *Rambam* is not that the walls receive *kedushah*, but rather that they are forbidden to be used similar to *sechach*, albeit for an alternative reason. The walls are simply *muktzeh machmas issur* (*soser*). *Rosh*[25] himself holds explicitly that only the *sechach* receives this *kedushah* as opposed to any of the walls. *Shulchan Aruch*, following *Ran*,[26] holds that only parts of the sukkah that are essential to the fulfillment of the mitzvah receive the *kedushah*, i.e., the first two and half walls and the *sechach*. This is only if one built a two-and-half-walled sukkah and then subsequently added a wall. The additional wall doesn't have *kedushah*. However, if one built four walls at the same time, the *kedushas sukkah* applies on all the walls. He *paskens* any part that has *kedushah* can be dismantled, if we hold the walls don't have kedushah they can be dismantled.)

Rain in the Sukkah

Armed with this principle from *Taz*, that the only benefit that is forbidden because of the *kedushah* is one that is nullifies the mitzvah/*kedushah*, we can answer the famous question of the *Oneg Yom Tov*:[27] If "*chag laHashem*" teaches us that the sukkah is forbidden to benefit from other than for the mitzvah, when it rains it is surely forbidden to remain sitting

22. *Beitzah* 30b, s.v. אבל עצי סוכה.
23. 7:15.
24. 638:1.
25. *Sukkah*, ch. 1, point 13.
26. *Beitzah* 17a, s.v. ועצי.
27. *Siman* 49.

inside the sukkah because one is benefiting from the sukkah while not fulfilling the mitzvah. The Steipler[28] answers that the essence of mitzvah of sukkah is that it should be a place of dwelling, so the designation for the mitzvah and the subsequent *kedushah* causes it to be a place of dwelling. Even when it rains, one is still using the sukkah as a place of dwelling; what the *kedushah* forbids is to use it for anything other than a place of dwelling.

According to *Taz* we have a more simple answer. Sitting inside the sukkah when it's raining in no way causes the mitzvah to be nullified. Therefore there's no reason to forbid this action. There is proof to *Taz* from *Tosafos*.[29] He asks: Why does the Gemara not bring the *issur* to make use of the structure of the sukkah, which we learn out of "*chag laHashem*" as the source from which we learn *bizui mitzvah*? He answers that if we were to learn from sukkah, the Gemara could have refuted it because "*chag laHashem*" is forbidding a situation where there is a *bitul* of a mitzvah. We are now learning a different type of *bizui mitzvah* even to instances where one is not ruining the mitzvah. We see explicitly that the *issur* of "*chag laHashem*" is teaching us that only when one is ruining the mitzvah is it forbidden.[30]

Dismantling the Sukkah

Shulchan Aruch[31] forbids, based on a Gemara,[32] dismantling the sukkah on the seventh and final day of Sukkos. The Gemara explains that one needs to keep it erect in case he wants to eat something and will still need the sukkah. *Tzitz Eliezer*[33] wonders: If there is a problem in dismantling the sukkah because one is removing the *kedushah*, why does the Gemara need to come onto a new reason - that one might still need it - to forbid

---

28. *Sukkah, siman* 7.

29. *Shabbos* 22a, s.v. אבוהון. We find this also in *Rashba* and *Tosafos HaRosh*.

30. *Oneg Yom Tov* address what this *Tosafos* says and he explains that it's only a suggestion but not true in *Tosafos*'s conclusion. ע"ש.

31. *Siman* 666.

32. *Sukkah* 36b.

33. Section 13, *siman* 38.

dismantling the sukkah? Furthermore, if there is such a reason, that one is removing the *kedushah,* this should have been mentioned by one of the commentaries. Due to these questions he suggests that from the point of view of removing the *kedushah* from the sukkah, there are no issues in dismantling. The sukkah itself doesn't have proper *kedushah.* In halachah we treat the sukkah as *tashmishei mitzvah,* not *tashmishei kedushah.* Therefore, he concludes, if one knows with certainty that he won't need the sukkah again, e.g., he has another one or he is traveling abroad, it would be permitted to dismantle the sukkah.

R' Shlomo Zalman Auerbach[34] also says that in truth there is no problem in taking down a sukkah. They must understand, similar to how we concluded in part 1 regarding sukkah decorations, that *muktzeh l'mitzvah* just forbids benefit that annuls the mitzvah. Since one can always rebuild it, that is not considered depleting the mitzvah.

In contrast, our understanding of *Taz* is that the sukkah has unique properties of *kedushah* that forbid any removal of the *kedushah,* even temporarily, (this is what the connection to *korban chagigah* taught us). Alternatively, all agree the *kedushah* forbids *bitul* mitzvah, nullifying the mitzvah. The point of contention is whether dismantling is considered a proper nullification.

Potentially we can bring support to our understanding that taking down the sukkah is included in *bitul* mitzvah even though the building material still exists and can be used. *Rema* says that in order to protect the decorative drapes and sheets that are adorning the walls of the sukkah, the practice is to rely on the opinions who permit one to stipulate that when he wants he can remove the drapes.[35] Even if he didn't stipulate, *Rema* is lenient to removes the drapes if it's raining because we can rely on the opinions that the *kedushah* is only on the *sechach,* not on the walls. We see *Rema* is trying to find leniencies to permit taking off the decorations even though they are only being taken off *temporarily.* Right after it rains he will adorn the sukkah with them again. If *bitul* mitzvah even

---

34. *Minchas Shlomo,* section 2, *siman* 8, point 36.

35. See chapter 24 for elaboration on the principle of condition.

encompasses disassembling, then we understand why *Rema* needs to explain the *heter* to remove the drapes is either if one stipulated or because we can rely on those who hold there is no *kedushah* on the walls.

Despite *muktzeh l'mitzvah* not forbidding to dismantle the sukkah, *Tzitz Eliezer* agrees that *bizui mitzvah* prohibits taking down the sukkah. As we will encounter in part 3, the prohibition of *bizui mitzvah* is far encompassing. Even once one has already fulfilled the mitzvah, there are still rules regarding how he must treat the mitzvah item. *Tzitz Eliezer* therefore only permits dismantling the sukkah when one needs the material to build another sukkah. There is no disgrace to the mitzvah - on the contrary, one is involved in ensuring the fulfillment of the mitzvah.

Eating and Smelling the Four Species

The Gemara[36] permits one to smell an esrog that was designated for a mitzvah but not a *hadas*. What's the difference? If designation for a mitzvah forbids smelling, why is an esrog different? The Gemara explains that the designation only forbids using the mitzvah item for its main *shimush* (use), hence an esrog is designated from eating but not from smelling it. In contrast, a *hadas* is meant for smelling, so when one sets aside a *hadas* to fulfill the mitzvah, he is designating it from smelling it. Many *Rishonim*[37] extend this *issur* to smell even a *hadas* one is not using for the *daled minim*, but that he has placed as decoration in the sukkah (question #3). Other *Rishonim*[38] hold that such a *hadas* is different. One only designates this *hadas* from burning; not smelling it is not part of the designation.[39] According to *Taz*, why can't one smell the *hadas* that's hanging in the sukkah, since even if it is part of the sukkah, smelling is not depleting the mitzvah nor the *kedushah*?[40]

---

36. *Sukkah* 37b.

37. *Ran*. *Rema*, *siman* 638, brings both opinions.

38. *Ritva* holds so and *yesh omrim* brought in *Ran*.

39. In a similar vein, *Taz* says based on this that one can lean against the walls of a sukkah since that benefit is considered peripheral and therefore not forbidden.

40. Even according to those who permit smelling a *hadas* that is hanging in the sukkah,

Tur,[41] when listing examples of restrictions due to *bizui mitzvah*, lists both eating an esrog and smelling a *hadas*. We can explain that *Tur* understands like we've seen, that *muktzeh l'mitzvah* only forbids depleting the mitzvah, so he is forced to find a new reason why generally one can't smell a *hadas*. When one uses a mitzvah item for the use that it is inherently meant for (had it not been set aside for a mitzvah), that shows the fact that he's designated it for the mitzvah is not true in his eyes, and that is the greatest disgrace to the mitzvah. While taking a peripheral benefit is not an affront to the fact this item is designated for a mitzvah, even when it has its natural function, one takes side benefit, e.g., smelling an esrog is not an affront to the fact this esrog has been designated as part of the *daled minim* since even when the esrog is used as fruit that one consumes, one smells it.

So according to *Tur*, the restriction in smelling a *hadas* is due to *bizui mitzvah*. We can answer the problem we raised on the principle of *Taz*, of why it is forbidden to smell a *hadas* hanging in a sukkah. True, due to *haktzaah l'mitzvah* there is no problem because there is no *bitul* mitzvah (depletion of the mitzvah), there is still a rabbinic problem of *bizui mitzvah*. *Taz* was only discussing what restrictions the *derashah* of "*chag laHashem*" impose on the sukkah and the decorations that become part of the sukkah. This supports the conclusion of *Tzitz Eliezer*, that even if there are no restrictions due to *haktzaah l'mitzvah* in taking down the sukkah, nevertheless *bizui mitzvah* will prevent the dismantling.

If we are correct in our understanding of *Tur*, it follows that *bizui mitzvah* is applicable when one is using the mitzvah item specifically for what it's generally meant for, but if one were to extract a peripheral benefit, it would be forbidden. *Taz* permits leaning against the sukkah walls. It must be that it is not a disgrace to do so to the mitzvah because leaning is a very peripheral benefit to what the walls usually provide. (If the wall is made out of wood, they can be used as fuel.)

---

it's only because of an external reason that the designation doesn't encompass not smelling it. According to *Taz*, there is a more fundamental reason since smelling doesn't detract from the mitzvah regardless of the extent of the designation.

41. *Siman* 21.

If one wishes to remove a pomegranate that is hanging from his sukkah roof on Yom Tov, it is totally forbidden to even move it. On Chol HaMoed, however, there is no *issur* in moving it. However, it's forbidden to eat and even removing it from the sukkah, which now causes a loss of this particular decoration, may fall under the category of *bizui mitzvah*. If one hangs a candle for adornment purposes and it happens to be emitting an fragrance, it is subject to the two opinions brought in *Rema* whether one can purposely approach it to smell it. However, it is permitted to enjoy the pleasant fragrance that is emitted in the sukkah.

Biting Off the Pitom

Based on what we've seen, the practice of pregnant women biting off the *pitom* from the esrog on Hoshana *Rabbah* (question #2) seems to be very wrong. For all seven days there is a mitzvah to shake the esrog, so it is designated for the mitzvah. Surely the *haktzaah l'mitzvah* forbids eating or destroying it!

As a *limud zechus* for this custom of biting the *pitom*, perhaps those who had such a practice stipulated before Yom Tov that the esrog was designated for the mitzvah *only* until they finished their mitzvah; after they shook the esrog on the morning of Hoshana *Rabbah* the designation of it being an esrog of mitzvah was removed and they could then eat it. Alternatively, during *bein hashemashos* of Shemini Atzeres, the esrog is not designated for the mitzvah, so maybe this custom can be carried out during *bein hashemashos*.

Summary

There are three reasons why it may be forbidden to take benefit from a mitzvah object: (1) *Muktzeh machmas mitzvah*, which is caused by the designation of it as a mitzvah object; (2) *Bizui mitzvah*; and (3) with a sukkah there is also a *kedushah* that is learned from the *pasuk* of "*chag laHashem.*"

Taz explains that the *kedushah* on the sukkah does not forbid all benefit from the sukkah. It is forbidden only when one will benefit in a manner that depletes and ruins the mitzvah. Even though *Mishnah Berurah paskens* like *Taz*, some of the later *Acharonim* understand that dismantling the sukkah is not considered a nullification of the mitzvah, while we suggested that even if it is temporary it is forbidden. Even when there is no *issur d'Oraisa* from the *kedushah*, one always needs to reckon with the rabbinic prohibition of *bizui mitzvah*. Disgracing the mitzvah even when not depleting the mitzvah is forbidden. *Tur* learns this is the reason behind the prohibition in smelling a *hadas*. *Tosafos* says that *muktzeh* is only applicable on Shabbos/Yom Tov, so the restriction in *moving* a mitzvah item is limited to Shabbos/Yom Tov, while on a weekday *muktzeh l'mitzvah* manifests in that it forbids *consuming* the mitzvah item.

Answers

1. Even if we are to follow the opinions who hold that since one can always still rebuild the sukkah, dismantling it is therefore not a breach of the designation for the mitzvah. Nevertheless it is a disgrace to the mitzvah and would be forbidden.
2. On Hoshana Rabbah the designation for mitzvah still applies it is therefore forbidden to bite the esrog.
3. You can benefit from a decoration that is giving off a pleasant smell. *Rema* brings two opinions whether one can approach such decoration to smell it. Those who forbid argue it is a disgrace to the decoration, which are now a mitzvah item.

Part 3

ביזוי מצוה

Disgracing a Mitzvah

Questions

1. Can I take a photograph with a *chanukiah* alight in the background?
2. Can I throw away the used wicks and leftover oil from the Shabbos candles?
3. Besides the halachic issues in causing another discomfort, are there any other issues with annoying one's little brother by tickling his ear with tzitzis strings?

The Gemara[42] brings the opinion of R' Asi, who forbids counting money using the light of the *chanukiah*. *Baal HaMeor* explains that R' Asi only forbids using this light for a mundane purpose, but if one wants to use the candle for another mitzvah it is permitted. The vast majority of the *Rishonim* argue. They explain that R' Asi singled out counting money because it is a one-off use, i.e., it is a short-span consumption and the candles immediately revert back to solely being used for the *chanukiah*, so we could have thought that is less of a disgrace and permitted. The reason why it is forbidden taking this benefit even for a mitzvah is because it's demonstrating that the first mitzvah is not important. They nonetheless permit lighting one candle of the *chanukiah* from another. This is because when the new mitzvah that one is performing is similar to the original one, this doesn't demonstrate a lack of care for the original mitzvah.

Shmuel permits counting money in front of the *chanukiah*. Shmuel reasons that since there is no *kedushah* on the candles, deriving benefit

42. *Shabbos* 22a.

is permitted. This is unlike a sukkah, which has a *pasuk* indicating to us that it has *kedushah* that forbids benefit. It follows from Shmuel that only *tashmish* (using) the mitzvah item is forbidden, but not *hanaah* (benefiting from it). R' Yosef disproves Shmuel's assertion from *kisui hadam*. The blood doesn't have *kedushah* and still there is a prohibition of *bizui mitzvah* (as one is forbidden to kick the dirt with his feet). If *bizui mitzvah* is applicable even when the mitzvah is devoid of *kedushah*, *bizui mitzvah* will forbid benefiting from the Chanukah lights!

Tzitzis Strings

Tur[43] quotes a *She'iltos*, who holds that one can't use any item that he is using to fulfill a mitzvah with for mundane purposes. He learns this from the *din* of *bizui mitzvah*. Among his examples are eating an esrog and tying something with tzitzis strings. *Tur* himself suggests that perhaps there is a distinction between *bizui mitzvah*, which is learned from *kisui hadam* that it's forbidden to do so with one's foot, and using the tzitzis as string. With covering the blood, the actual mitzvah is being carried out in a disgraceful manner. This is as opposed to using the strings of the tzitzis, where there is no belittlement in the act of the fulfillment of the mitzvah itself.

Beis Yosef defends *She'iltos*. He says there is no distinction whether the disgrace comes through the actual fulfillment while one is fulfilling the mitzvah, or an act unrelated to the fulfillment of the mitzvah. He argues that since we learn from *kisui hadam* that *bizui mitzvah* is forbidden, surely this should include any type of disgrace. Furthermore, according to the reasoning of *Tur*, why should it be forbidden to eat one's esrog or benefit from the sukkah or from the Chanukah lights, but it's permitted to benefit from the tzitzis strings? In these cases one is not disgracing the mitzvah during its fulfillment, but because these objects were set aside for a mitzvah, any benefit from the mitzvah is considered an affront to the mitzvah. So too, since the tzitzis is set aside for a mitzvah, it is a disgrace to use them for one's personal needs!

---

43. *Orach Chaim, siman* 21.

Taz defends the opinion of *Tur*. We mentioned earlier the opinion of *Tosafos*[44] that *muktzeh machmas mitzvah* doesn't apply on weekdays, and hence we are required to add the element of *bizui mitzvah* to forbid sukkah decorations on Chol HaMoed. Therefore, the only reason to forbid using tzitzis strings is *bizui mitzvah*. He asserts that *bizui mitzvah* is only when one is disgracing the mitzvah while simultaneously trying to fulfill the mitzvah. With Chanukah lights one wants the flame to be continuously serving his mitzvah purpose, since were he to wish to pause the mitzvah during the crucial timespan of the fulfillment of the mitzvah, he'd be required to relight it. Therefore, during this period of time benefiting from the light of the candles is disgracing the light of the mitzvah. With this understanding, he has drawn closer the different cases of *bizui mitzvah*. By *kisui hadam*, one is performing the mitzvah in a disgraceful manner. Similarly, one is trying to fulfill his mitzvah of Chanukah lights in a disgraceful manner, while simultaneously using them for his own benefit.

In contrast, one can use tzitzis strings for mundane string. This is because when one is using the tzitzis as string, it's as if, at that moment, he doesn't want it to function as a garment of a Mitzvah. Therefore, the moment one is using the strings in a mundane manner is not an affront to any mitzvah since there's no mitzvah taking place![45]

The Steipler[46] takes a similar approach to explain *Tur*. Obviously *Tur* agrees that *bizui mitzvah* forbids one from depleting a mitzvah item. Therefore eating an esrog and burning the sukkah decorations is forbidden. Using tzitzis strings for tying is therefore not akin to this *bizui mitzvah*. Neither is benefiting from Chanukah lights depleting the mitzvah and yet it is encompassed in *bizui mitzvah*? He says Chanukah lights is an exceptional case. They are light for *pirsumei nisa* (publicizing the miracle). When one uses the light, it's no longer clear that these were lights for Cha-

---

44. *Shabbos* 22b, s.v. סוכה.

45. I never fully understood this answer because there is a problem in wearing a four-cornered garment without tzitzis. If one doesn't want the strings to function as tzitzis while one uses them, is it not considered that one has a four-cornered garment lacking tzitzis?

46. *Shabbos, siman* 18.

nukah. That is an act of detracting from the mitzvah; since by benefiting from the lights the actual mitzvah item is affected, Chazal included this in *bizui mitzvah.*[47]

Shulchan Aruch paskens like *She'iltos* that it's forbidden to use tzitzis strings for tying. Is tickling kids' ears with tzitzis also a *bizui mitzvah,* or is it permitted since it's only being done in a joking manner and it's not a real usage that one is using the tzitzis for? (question #3) צ"ע.

Leftover Oil

The *Rishonim*[48] argue whether one can use the leftover oil from the Chanukah candles for regular usages (question #2). If we're to judge it from the aspect of *bizui mitzvah,* everyone agrees that once the mitzvah has ended there is no longer any problem. *Tosafos*[49] differentiates between leftover oil from the Shabbos candles, which is permitted to use, and leftover oil from the *chanukiah,* which we say that one should burn and not use. Since the oil for the Shabbos candles is lit for one's benefit (on Shabbos), one therefore is not *maktzah daas* from its benefit. This is as opposed to the oil for the *chanukiah,* which is not there for one's benefit, but rather for publicizing the miracle. Therefore, due to the importance of the miracle one totally removes his mind from using it.

In light of what we've seen, we should conclude that it is permitted to take a photo with the Chanukah lights as the background (question #1) because one is not detracting from the mitzvah. The only precaution[50] is

---

47. There are opinions that hold that *muktzeh machmas mitzvah* is even applicable during a weekday. According to these opinions, the Steipler explains why using the tzitzis strings is not subject to *muktzeh machmas mitzvah.* We saw at the end of part 2 that one can smell an esrog because, the Gemara explains, when the benefit is peripheral to what the item is usually used for, the designation for the mitzvah doesn't forbid peripheral benefit. The Steipler says *Tur* understands that threads on a garment are meant for sewing, not stringing items, so using the tzitzis as string is not encompassed in the designation that forbids other uses. While *She'iltos* agrees to this principle only when one is passive, e.g., smelling the esrog, any act is forbidden regardless of the main designation, e.g., tying with the tzitzis strings.

48. *Ritva* 22a, *Rif, Ran,* and *Tosafos Rid* 44a.

49. *Shabbos* 44a, s.v. שבנר.

50. R' Yitzchak Zilberstein, *Aleinu L'Shabei'ach,* section 2, *teshuvah* 3.

that the light emanating from the candles is not providing the illumination of the people in the photo because it is forbidden to directly benefit from this light.

Summary

The *Rishonim* argue whether the prohibition of *bizui mitzvah* extends to using one's tzitzis strings for mundane purposes. We learn from the case of counting one's money with the light of the Chanukah candles that even without actively debasing the mitzvah, the prohibition still forbids one in how one treats the mitzvah. The prohibition is not limited to only when one simultaneously performs the mitzvah. Even items that don't have *kedushah* are subject to this prohibition. *Tur* distinguishes between *kisui hadam,* the prime example of *bizui mitzvah,* where while performing one's obligation one is degrading the mitzvah, and using the tzitzis, where after fulfilling the mitzvah one is degrading the mitzvah - the latter is permitted. The *Acharonim* give specific explanations to answer the case of Chanukah candles according to *Tur,* since it seemingly contradicts his principle. One has fulfilled the mitzvah, yet benefiting ex postfacto is considered *bizui mitzvah.* The Steipler's explanation is that benefiting from the Chanukah lights is detracting from publicizing the miracle and so it is comparable to *kisui hadam,* where the actual fulfillment is done degradingly.

Answers

1. You can take a picture with the *chanukiah* provided the candles are not purposely illuminating the photo.
2. The leftover wicks and oil from Shabbos candles are not subject to any limitations. They can be reused or discarded.
3. From the aspect of *bizui mitzvah,* it is questionable whether poking in a lighthearted manner is a disgrace to mitzvah.

Chapter 26

מוקצה של גוי

Muktzeh Belonging to a Non-Jew[1]

Questions

1. A non-Jew came into my house on Shabbos and I wished to take his jacket from him to hang, but it had *muktzeh* inside the pockets, e.g., money, car keys, etc. Can I take the coat from him?
2. The Goldbergs' cleaning lady left her phone in their dining room and they're worried the children will break it. Can they move it to keep it safe?
3. The Ganzes' non-Jewish neighbor entrusted them to look after his pets while he goes away for the weekend. Can the Ganzes move these dogs and rabbits on Shabbos?

---

1. Prior to learning this chapter, it's important to understand that it is the owner who establishes the status of a *muktzeh* object. If one has an object that he is particularly careful with, it is now *muktzeh machmas chisaron kis*. This *muktzeh* status is also applicable even to a person who wouldn't be careful with such an object, since it is the owner who sets the *muktzeh* status of his possessions. This is the reason why "*muktzeh l'ashirim harei muktzeh l'aniyim*," as *paskened* by *Shulchan Aruch* 308:52. Here too it is the non-Jew who decides the status of his personal possessions. See chapter 12 for a more detailed discussion of this topic. See *Eshel Avraham* 310:2, who explains this principle as the foundation of these halachos.

The *Yerushalmi*[2] brings a dispute whether the concept of *hachanah* (preparation) is applicable to a non-Jew or not. *Kol Bo*[3] *paskens* from this Gemara that one can move a non-Jew's dates that are set aside for sale (known as *tamri d'iska*), as well as a non-Jew's figs and raisins (*grogeros v'tzimukim*) that have been set aside to dry, since there is no concept of preparation with a non-Jew. Were these items to belong to a Jew, they would be *muktzeh* since they have not been prepared for use on Shabbos.[4]

Ein Hachanah L'Goy

Mishnah Berurah[5] brings *Beis Meir,* who takes issue with this halachah. *Beis Meir* asks: The reason why figs and raisins are *muktzeh* is due to the fact that while they are in the process of drying out, they are not fit for any use at all. So why should we distinguish whom they belong to? The non-Jew does not have in mind to eat them any more than a Jew. *Beis Meir* explains that the opinion of *ein hachanah l'goy* only means to explain that a non-Jew thinks to use everything he could. As a non-Jew, his mind is not as limited, unlike a Jew, as to which objects he can potentially use. Hence even though we say that a Jew has diverted his attention from his merchandise, even if edible, since he is forbidden to make a sale on Shabbos, we say that a non-Jew has intention to use them if he needs, so his merchandise is not *muktzeh*. In contrast, something that intrinsically is not fit for use is *muktzeh* for a Jew to move, regardless of whom it belongs to.

Mishnah Berurah proceeds to quote from *Griz,*[6] who also is bothered with this issue. *Griz* explains that *Kol Bo*'s halachah is referring to a case

---

2. *Shabbos,* ch. 1, halachah 7, and *Beitzah,* ch. 3, halachah 2.

3. Brought in *Rema* 310:2.

4. *Beis Yosef* asks that we *pasken* like the opinion of Rebbe Shimon that date merchandise are *mutar* to be moved, since a person never removes his mind from food. It follows that the only novelty of *Kol Bo* is what he says by figs and raisins. However, *Kol Bo* is found in *Hilchos Yom Tov,* and on Yom Tov we follow Rebbe Yehudah, so even date merchandise are a *chiddush* that they are permitted. I found that *Maamar Mordechai* gives the same answer to explain *Kol Bo*.

5. Point 13.

6. 310:3.

where the *grogeros v'tzimukim* are partially ready. These semi-prepared dates are the ones *Kol Bo* permits if they belong to a non-Jew. Since there is a potential that these fruits may be fully ready to be eaten soon, we say that a non-Jew has his mind on everything. It's as if he prepared them and hasn't set them aside. This qualification is a reference to the halachah brought in *se'if* 5 that if dried figs are in a state where only certain people are ready to eat them, while other people will wait for them to further improve, then if one prepared them to eat before Shabbos they no longer are *muktzeh*. This requirement is only with a Jew with whom we say if something is not necessarily prepared for use, he must designate it explicitly, However, there is no such requirement with a non-Jew, so it is always considered prepared.

This understanding of *ein hachanah l'goy*, that a non-Jew's items are not bound by a limitation with objects that are lacking a designation or preparedness, is in contrast to the conventional understanding. One could have learned that there is a special halachah that there is no concept of a *muktzeh* on a non-Jew's possessions. Our understanding can also be found in *Ran.*[7] *Ran* quotes from the *Yerushalmi*: *ein hachanah l'goy*, yet he says if something was attached to the ground and the non-Jew detached it on Shabbos, the object is *muktzeh*. So too if a non-Jew cooked something on Shabbos, the dish is only not *muktzeh* if the raw ingredients were already fit to be eaten raw, but if they were previously inedible then they are *muktzeh*, since there is *issur muktzeh* on Shabbos because item is "*lo chazi*." Explicit in *Ran* is that the opinion of *ein hachanah l'goy* does not intend to permit an object belonging to a non-Jew which should be *muktzeh* because it was not fit for any use at the onset of Shabbos. The concept of *ein hachanah l'goy* is only sufficient to permit something whose sole inadequacy is a lack of preparation. In the continuation he writes, לפי שאין הגוי מקצה כלל דדעתו על הכל - "A non-Jew doesn't designate it and his mind is open to everything."

7. *Dapei HaRif* 46b.

Lacking Preparation vs Intrisincally Not Ready

The Mishnah[8] says that animals that graze in the fields far away from a settlement are *muktzeh* on Yom Tov, so one cannot slaughter them. *Ran*[9] writes that if a non-Jew was to own such an animal it wouldn't be *muktzeh*. *Ohr Zarua LaTzaddik* states that this is a contradiction to the aforementioned *Ran*, who said *muktzeh* is possible by a non-Jew. The answer is already obvious. These animal are *muktzeh* not because they are not fit - there is nothing intrinsically lacking with them - rather they are so far away, they are completely removed from one's conscious as such that even Rebbe Shimon holds that such an item is *muktzeh*. However, since a non-Jew isn't limited by a lack of preparedness, even these animals can be considered prepared for him. There is no intrinsic deficiency in them, so they are not *muktzeh*. *Ran* doesn't reveal to us what he holds regarding figs and raisins belonging to a non-Jew, but it must follow that if they are in the stage where they are not fit at all they will be *muktzeh*, but if they are partially ready and are only limited by a lack of designation, since this is not relevant with a non-Jew then they are not *muktzeh*.

The majority of the *Rishonim* learn along these lines that something intrinsically not ready is *muktzeh* even if it belongs to a non-Jew. However, we assess that a non-Jew does intend on using items that are not fully prepared. *Baal HaMeor*[10] says a non-Jew's item can't be forbidden for a Jew to move if it is fit to use. It's *muktzeh* only if the non-Jew diverted his attention. *Ramban* and *Ritva* both mention this distinction between something that is only lacking preparation and something that is intrinsically removed from potential use. The Mishnah[11] permits descending on a ramp that a non-Jew built on Shabbos (and therefore should be forbidden to move because of *nolad*), even if one moves the ramp. Since the wood was in the possession of a non-Jew, he didn't divert his intention from using it. So the ramp is not subject to the rules of *muktzeh* since there

8. *Beitzah* 40a.
9. On *Rif* at the end of *Beitzah*.
10. Beginning of *Beitzah*, ch. 3.
11. *Shabbos* 122b.

is no problem of there being a lack of preparation with it. These *Rishonim* consent that something that is still attached to the ground would be *muktzeh*. The reason behind this is that these objects are more than just lacking preparation - they are inherently removed from current use.[12]

It would follow that fruits that a non-Jew removes from a tree on Shabbos/Yom Tov are *muktzeh* because they are not fit while attached. This explains why the Mishnah[13] that forbids consumption of freshly caught fish doesn't distinguish between who caught it. Even if a non-Jew did catch it, while it was in the water it is totally removed from any state of consciousness and therefore isn't considered to be in a fit state. This case has a novelty we have not yet come across. Picked fruit, caught fish, etc., are *muktzeh* for a Jew because of *muktzeh machmas issur*. There is an *issur* involved in their preparation; since that *issur* doesn't apply to a non-Jew, one could have thought if belonging to a non-Jew they are therefore not *muktzeh*. We are being taught that since a significant act is needed to prepare these items, even a non-Jew doesn't think to use his fruit on his tree or the fish swimming in the water. Since the non-Jew also has these items excluded from his mind, these items are also subject to *muktzeh* when they belong to him.

Muktzeh Doesn't Apply to a Non-Jew's Possesions at All

There are opinions that learn that *Kol Bo* holds that even something that isn't fit is not *muktzeh* if it belongs to a non-Jew. The aforementioned

---

12. *Meiri* in *Chiddushim* on *Beitzah* 24b (not *Beis HaBechirah*) explicitly also writes this explanation: Fruits that a non-Jew brings are not *muktzeh* because there is no *issur* restricting the non-Jew in preparing them, just generally a person doesn't intend on eating them hence if they belonged to a Jew they would be *muktzeh*. He develops this thought, *ein hachanah l'goy* doesn't demand the non-Jew prepare these fruits for use, since they are intrinsically fit.
Orchos Chaim, *Hilchos Yom Tov, siman* 33, presents this approach as follows: Items that a Jew needs to prepare for them not to be *muktzeh*, if they belong to a non-Jew, they are not *muktzeh*, regardless whether the non-Jew actually prepares them before Shabbos or not.
13. *Beitzah* 24a.

Mishnah, after bringing the opinion that one may not benefit from animals that were trapped on Yom Tov, proceeds to bring a story of Rabban Gamliel, who received a present of fish from a non-Jew on Yom Tov and permitted its consumption. The Gemara asks: Surely this contradicts the previous halachah, that one may not benefit from fish caught on Yom Tov? The Gemara answers that it was a doubt when they were caught and Rabban Gamliel permits cases of doubt.

Pnei Moshe explains that the opinion of *ein hachanah l'goy* is concurrent with the opinion of Rabban Gamliel in the Mishnah (i.e., without the Gemara's qualification) that permits the fish. Since they were caught by a non-Jew and *ein hachanah l'goy,* none of his items are *muktzeh*! *Pnei Yehoshua*[14] also seems to understand that the opinion brought by the *Yerushalmi* holds that all items of a non-Jew are not *muktzeh,* even freshly caught fish. He understands that the *Bavli* argues on the *Yerushalmi,* hence to the aforementioned *Bavli* had to explain Rabban Gamliel's actions, who permitted the fish, was only because it was a case of doubt. He claims that this is why we don't find that any of the main *poskim* - *Rambam, Rif, Rosh,* and *Tur* - bring the rule of *ein hachanah l'goy* because they followed this *Bavli* which indicates that *muktzeh* is equally applicable to a non-Jew as much as it is to a Jew. If *muktzeh* didn't apply to a non-Jew, the Gemara should have answered the question on Rabban Gamliel like this, that a non-Jew's objects aren't *muktzeh.*

Perhaps we can explain that these commentators who understand that there is no *muktzeh* with any objects of a non-Jew hold that since all *muktzeh* is rooted in the *pasuk* of "*v'hechinu*" - which teaches that items must be prepared before Shabbos if they are to be used, and if not they become *muktzeh* - and this *pasuk* is not said regarding a non-Jew, his items regardless of their state are never lacking anything relative to "being prepared" because there is no such requirement. Since there is never a requirement to be prepared, there are no ramifications of *muktzeh* if something is unprepared. Even in the stage where the figs and raisins are

---

14. Ibid., s.v. מעשה לסתור. Based on the distinction we see from *Ritva* and *Ramban,* that something that needs the non-Jew to do a *melachah* to prepare is considered "not fit," we can answer *Pnei Yehoshua*'s question, ע"ש.

not edible and they should be *muktzeh machmas gufo,* since we don't have a requirement of "being prepared" there is nothing lacking in the item. The fact they are useless shouldn't render them *muktzeh,* and they are permitted.

Shulchan Aruch's Conclusion

Pri Chadash[15] says that we see from *Shulchan Aruch* in numerous places that he also holds that a non-Jew's items are not *muktzeh. Shulchan Aruch*[16] permits eating bread that was baked by a non-Jew (flour is *muktzeh* for a Jew) since it was in the capacity of the non-Jew to bake the flour. His flour is not *muktzeh* and subsequently neither is his fresh bread. *Shulchan Aruch*[17] writes explicitly that there is no *muktzeh* by a non-Jew, and animals that are far from civilization that belong to a non-Jew are permitted for Yom Tov, as opposed to those of a Jew. *Rema*[18] brings the halachah of *Kol Bo* that *ein hachanah l'goy* as *"yesh omrim"* (some say), which implies that *Rema* understands *Shulchan Aruch* doesn't hold of this i.e., that he holds *muktzeh* is applicable by a non-Jew. Yet we just saw *Shulchan Aruch* does agree! *Pri Chadash* concludes that *Rema* was not careful with his choice of words, prefixing with *"yesh omrim"* was inaccurate; even *Shulchan Aruch* agrees.

Beis Meir argues on *Pri Chadash,* saying that *Rema* is exact is his wording. The examples where we proved *Shulchan Aruch* holds of the opinion that *ein hachanah l'goy* are all cases when the item is in essence fit at the moment, but there is a designation that would make it *muktzeh.* Flour is a final product in its own right; it is not lacking any act to complete it. The wheat was already grinded and made into flour, just due to it having no use a Jew designates it. So too animals that are situated far from civilization are inherently fit for use, just a person usually removes his mind from them. *Shulchan Aruch* holds that if they belong to a non-Jew, since he al-

15. 507:15.
16. 325:4.
17. 498:3.
18. 310:2.

ways has intention for anything and doesn't divert from anything, they are not *muktzeh*. In contrast, *Rema* is referring to figs and raisins, which are *not fit at all*, so *Rema* is holding that nothing belonging to a non-Jew is *muktzeh*. *Shulchan Aruch* doesn't agree to this! It follows that *Rema* is accurate in bringing this halachah in the name of a "*yesh omrim*."[19]

Beis Yosef, when bringing *Kol Bo*, equates it with the opinion of *Ran*. We saw explicitly that *Ran* learns that when something is not fit, it is *muktzeh* even if it belongs to a non-Jew. This is a strong indication in favor of how *Beis Meir* is reconciling the opinion of *Shulchan Aruch*. It follows that the opinion of *Shulchan Aruch* is in accordance with what he writes in *Hilchos Yom Tov*: *ein hachanah l'goy*. This does not mean to permit all *muktzeh* items, rather objects that are lacking only in designation.

If *Rema* only means to permit *grogeros v'tzimukim* which are partially edible as *Griz* explains, and that *Shulchan Aruch* agrees to, the choice of wording of "*yesh omrim*" is inaccurate. It is not a new opinion; it is what *Shulchan Aruch* himself holds. However, *Eliyah Rabbah* claims that when *Rema* chooses to write "*v'yesh omrim*" with a *vav*, *Rema* holds this opinion is in disagreement with *Shulchan Aruch*; a "*yesh omrim*" without a *vav* is when this opinion is in agreement but for whatever reason *Shulchan Aruch* didn't feel it necessary to write. Here *Rema* brings it without a *vav*, which demonstrates that they are in agreement and the choice of wording is not a slip of the pen. This reconciliation is in accordance with *Pri Chadash* without his *dochuk* (difficulty).

It follows, according to both *Rema* and *Shulchan Aruch*, something that isn't fit for any current use is *muktzeh*, even if it belongs to a non-Jew. However, if it's something that is technically considered fit, but it is something that by a Jew we would say that he set it aside from in his mind,

---

19. Even if *Rema* is more lenient, it is not likely he means to the extent that nothing a non-Jew owns is *muktzeh*. There is no precedence in the *Rishonim* for such and also it is not logical that if something intrinsically is not fit for use, just because it belongs to a non-Jew it shouldn't be subject to *muktzeh*. Rather, items such as *grogeros v'tzimukim* even though presently are not fit, since they were once fit for consumption and the non-Jew did something to render them unfit, then *Rema* will hold that the non-Jew's act can't confer a status of *muktzeh* because it was previously prepared. This is the most reaching leniency we find in the *Rishonim*.

since it is something that just is set aside, we say that a non-Jew doesn't set aside and therefore it would not be *muktzeh.*

A Non-Jew's Muktzeh Machmas Chisaron Kis

Which category does *muktzeh machmas chisaron kis* fall under - something that isn't fit for any use, or something that can be used but we say that one usually sets aside? We have seen[20] that there are different ways to understand the reason behind *muktzeh machmas chisaron kis.* The simplest way and most conventional understanding is due to one's extreme care to only use it for its specific purpose and not for anything else on sets it aside. In this case, a non-Jew's *muktzeh machmas chisaron kis* won't be *muktzeh* because a non-Jew doesn't designate any of his objects not to be used at the onset of Shabbos. This is how *Chazon Ish*[21] and *Pri Megadim*[22] *pasken.*[23]

In chapter 3 we explained that the way most people treat their phones is not like something that is *muktzeh machmas chisaron kis,* but as *kli shemelachto l'issur. If* one's phone is *muktzeh machmas chisaron kis,* it would be subject to the previous conclusion we posed.

The status of a non-Jew's *kli shemelachto l'issur* is more complicated If the prohibition of moving a *kli shemelachto l'issur* is due to a designation, due to its inherent lack of Shabbos-related permissible usability one designates it for usages besides those that are permissible. Therefore, a *kli shemelachto l'issur* belonging to a non-Jew will not have any limitation since *ein hachanah l'goy* tells us that he doesn't set aside something that is fit. (A *kli shemelachto l'issur* is obviously still fit for a non-Jew since he isn't bound by any such *muktzeh*-related prohibitions!) It follows that if

---

20. In chapter 21.

21. 44:9.

22. Introduction to *Hilchos Yom Tov.*

23. However, if we learn that the reason behind *muktzeh machmas chisaron kis* is since it is considered as if one has set this item in a fixed place due to his care not to use it, which causes it now to have limited usage, it is akin to wood and stones which are *muktzeh machmas gufo* since they have no use; even those of a non-Jew would be *muktzeh.*

one's cleaning lady left her phone lying around (question #2), one would be able to move it to a safer location.

However, if the reason prohibiting *kli shemelachto l'issur* is because of *gezeiras keilim,* that should apply equally to a non-Jew's *keilim* and it would be forbidden to move it. We brought in chapter 1 that *Mishnah Berurah* learns the former way, that a *kli shemelachto l'issur* is forbidden due to a *haktzaah,* and if so one can be lenient.

Money Is Not Subject to the Regular Rule of Muktzeh Machmas Gufo

When there is money in a non-Jew's jacket (question #1), since money is *muktzeh machmas gufo* we should conclude that one can't move the jacket. However, in truth, money is inherently different from the classic *muktzeh machmas gufo* we have so far discussed, e.g., sticks and stones. *Rashi*[24] says money is *muktzeh* because it is not *chazi* (fit). We can add that it is also not a vessel, so it's classified as *muktzeh machmas gufo.* Yet for a non-Jew it is fit, there is no designation, so it should not be *muktzeh.* Proof to this can be brought from the very case of flour of a non-Jew. *Shulchan Aruch paskens* that it's not *muktzeh.* Flour belonging to a Jew is categorized as *muktzeh machmas gufo,* despite being inherently useful, because a Jew sets it aside, we see precedence that certain items are not *muktzeh* when belonging to non-Jew, even if they are categorized as *muktzeh machmas gufo,* based on the reoccurring principle we've seen that a non-Jew doesn't designate his items.[25]

Are a Non-Jew's Animals Muktzeh?

We saw in earlier chapters that the reason animals are *muktzeh* is that they are considered to be like stones and wood; they have no beneficial use. We brought a dispute among the contemporary *poskim* whether pets nowa-

---

24. *Shabbos* 44b, s.v. ההיא ר"ש.

25. This is all not in accordance with *Shaar HaTziyun* 310:10, who groups money with stones and sticks.

days are *muktzeh* or not. According to those who forbid even domesticated pets, would it be different if they belong to a non-Jew (question #3)? According to *Ran* and how we concluded in the opinion of *Shulchan Aruch,* even a non-Jew's pets will be *muktzeh* because they are something that is inherently not fit, they are *muktzeh* because they have no purpose. According to the way *Beis Meir* understands *Rema,* there would be no deficiency that the animal is not fit. He understands that *Rema* holds that *muktzeh* doesn't apply at all to objects belonging to non-Jews, so a pet belonging to a non-Jew would be *mutar.*

Summary

The *Yerushalmi* brings an opinion, which *Kol Bo paskens* like, that *ein hachanah l'goy.* The simple way to understand this is that none of the limitations of *muktzeh* apply to a non-Jew's possessions. We follow the owner, so a Jew can move anything belonging to a non-Jew. Many understand differently, that this opinion holds that anything that is *muktzeh* due to a הקצאת הדעת, if owned by a non-Jew, we say that the non-Jew didn't designate this item and intends to use it, and hence it is not *muktzeh.* In contrast, items that are *muktzeh* because they intrinsically are not fit are *muktzeh* regardless of the owner, since *muktzeh* requires that items be prepared and these are not prepared. This halachah is quoted both by *Rema* and *Shulchan Aruch.* It is subject to a dispute whether they agree to the same scenarios or whether *Rema* is permitting all types of *muktzeh* that belong to a non-Jew, whereas *Shulchan Aruch* only permits items that lack a designation but aren't inherently lacking any purpose. We concluded according to the opinions that both *Shulchan Aruch* and *Rema* are referring to the same scenario and both only permit an object of a non-Jew that is lacking only in designation.

Answers

1. Money in a coat normally renders the coat *muktzeh*, due to it being a *bosis* to the money, which is *muktzeh machmas gufo*. However, a non-Jew doesn't designate money; on the contrary, he intends on using it. Therefore it has a purpose and so won't be *muktzeh*.
2. If a telephone is a *kli shemelachto l'issur* then one can move the non-Jew's phone to protect it. Even though this is *m'chamah l'tzel*, which is forbidden by a regular *kli shemelachto l'issur*, since *Mishnah Berurah* explains *kli shemelachto l'issur* is based on designation, a *kli shemelachto l'issur* would therefore be encompassed in the rule of *ein hachanah l'goy* - a non-Jew's items are not *muktzeh*.
3. A pet is not fit for any use and hence is *muktzeh*. While there are opinions one could rely on to move a non-Jew's pet, it is recommended to be stringent.

Appendix 1: ישוב דברי הכל בו – Explanation of Kol Bo

Based on *Griz*, we suggested an answer to *Beis Meir*'s problem of how can *Kol Bo* permits raisins and figs of a non-Jew. Since they are inherently not fit for use, what difference does it make that they belong to a non-Jew? They also aren't fit for him and he has no intention of using them. He says that *Rema* is referring to raisins and figs that are partially ready. However, the answer is not so easy to fit in. *Rema*'s addition is in *se'if* 2, where *Shulchan Aruch* was talking about regular raisins and figs that are *muktzeh*. If *Rema* means to refer specifically to a case when they are partially ready, surely he should have waited until *se'if* 5, where *Shulchan Aruch* discusses this exact case.

Maybe we can suggest a different answer. The novelty of raisins and figs is that even if they fully dry out and now become ready on Shabbos they are still *muktzeh*. The simple reason for them being *muktzeh* even once they are ready is because of *migo d'iskatzi*. Presumably when *Rema* says that raisins and figs belonging to a non-Jew are not *muktzeh*, he is referring to when they are in a state where they are fit to be eaten. Otherwise, why would someone want to eat them? If this assumption is true, we can understand why they are not *muktzeh*. *migo d'iskatzi* is based on *haktzaas hadaas*, that even when it will be fit he has diverted his attention for this item. A non-Jew does not divert his attention and anything which can now be eaten is not *muktzeh*. However the Mishnah says if a non-Jew catches a fish on Shabbos or harvests fruits, they are *muktzeh*. Now they are fit to be eaten, so why are they *muktzeh*? It must be that we do apply *migo d'iskatzi* when things were not fit at *bein hashemashos*. Therefore this suggestion must be wrong.[26]

Appendix 2: עוד שיטות ראשונים באין הכנה לגוי - Further Explanations in the Rishonim

There is another explanation in "*ein hachanah l'goy*." *Raavad*[27] understands that all "*ein hachanah l'goy*" comes to permit are the fruits, etc., of a non-Jew. Since one might think that a non-Jew's produce would be considered like the animals of a Jew, which are far from civilization and thus *muktzeh*, since they are removed from one's mind, so too a non-Jew's produce might be considered removed from the Jew's mind and consequently *muktzeh*. This is what the *din* of "*ein hachanah l'goy*" permits.

---

26. *Pri Megadim*, brought in *Biur Halachah*, says if a non-Jew lights a candle, the candle can be moved once the flame goes out. *Chazon Ish* (44:12) asks: If it is forbidden to move while it is alight, it should be forbidden even once it goes out. From what we have seen, *Chazon Ish*'s question is correct. Something that is not fit, even if it belongs to a non-Jew, has *migo d'iskatzi*. *Pri Megadim* might understand that since the candle is a *bosis* during *bein hashemashos*, and *bosis* is forbidden because of designation, the support is now auxiliary to the *muktzeh* so you set it aside as part of the *muktzeh*. So for a non-Jew, *bosis* is not applicable. Maybe, even though he didn't say so, *Pri Megadim* held that even once it's alight there would not be a *din bosis* with something belonging to a non-Jew. וצע"ג.

27. *Tamim Deiyim*, *siman* 121, and *Hasagos* on *Baal HaMeor*, *Beitzah* 24b.

The understanding behind this may be similar to how we spoke in the first footnote, that it is the owner who fixes the status of his objects, regardless of another person's association with this item. Therefore, even though one certainly didn't have in mind to use the fruit of a non-Jew, this is not a problem since it was never in one's realm whether to have or not have in mind to use. Aside from this, if the non-Jew's item would be *muktzeh* if it belonged to a Jew, it is *muktzeh* even though it belongs to a non-Jew, e.g., wheat that were planted are *muktzeh* even if belonging to non-Jew.

Another explanation is brought in the same *Raavad,* and *Orchos Chaim*[28] and *Sefer HaMichtam*[29] also mention this approach. Any item that is *muktzeh* even it belongs to a non-Jew is *muktzeh* regardless of why it is normally *muktzeh,* even if due to lack of preparation. The *Amoraim* argue over what the halachah is by *safek muktzeh.* If the non-Jew brought something that could potentially be *muktzeh,* e.g., it potentially could have been harvested today or slaughtered today, do we need to be stringent and worry whether it is *muktzeh* or not? The opinion that holds *ein hachanah l'goy* holds that one doesn't need to worry. The way it fits into the phrase *yesh hachanah l'goy* or *ein hachanah l'goy* is: Can a non-Jew prepare something, thereby making it not *muktzeh*? *ein hachanah l'goy* - a non-Jew can't prepare something, so we must be worried that anything he has on Shabbos/Yom Tov has been prepared just now, not previously. So according to *Raavad,* the opinion that holds *ein hachanah l'goy* is a stringency, not a leniency. This is opposite to how *Ran* and company explained. (This halachah is in contrast to a Jew who brings another Jew a gift on Yom Tov. Since the Jew can't prepare anything, there is no reason to assume it is *muktzeh.* However, a non-Jew can do what he wants, so there is a likelihood what he brings you is *muktzeh.*)

---

28. *Hilchos Yom Tov, siman* 33.
29. *Beitzah* 24b.

Chapter 27, Part 1

מוקצה ביו״ט ואיסור נולד

Muktzeh on Yom Tov and Issur Nolad

Questions

1. Can I stoke the coals of a BBQ on Yom Tov?
2. If a blender or other electric appliance is blocking the children's Shabbos treats, can the appliance be moved out of the way?
3. Can I move raw meat, inedible vegetables, etc., a short time before the end of Yom Tov?

We have mentioned many times that Rebbe Shimon and Rebbe Yehudah argue whether there is an issue of *muktzeh* or not. The Gemara's[1] conclusion is that we follow the lenient opinion of Rebbe Shimon, that there is no *muktzeh* besides *muktzeh machmas issur* - "when due to the prohibition involved in the item's use one sets it aside." R' Nachman[2] adds that since the halachah generally follows the *stam* (unattributed) *Mishnah*, we find that the *stam mishnayos* throughout *Shabbos* reflect the opinion of Rebbe Shimon. However, the *stam mishnayos* in *Maseches Beitzah* reflect the opinion of Rebbe Yehudah, who holds of *muktzeh*. If we follow Rebbe Shimon, why are these *mishnayos* like this? R' Nachman reconciles this difficulty: שבת דחמירי ולא אתי לזלזולי בה סתם לן כר״ש דמיקל, יו״ט דקיל ואתי לזלזלי ביה סתם לן כר״י דמחמיר

1. *Shabbos* 157a.
2. *Beitzah* 2a.

- "Since Shabbos is integrally more stringent relative to Yom Tov, Chazal didn't feel a need to be stringent in the area of *muktzeh*; the general stringency of Shabbos will keep one from coming to disgrace the Shabbos. Since Yom Tov is more lenient, Chazal felt it was necessary to set an extra precaution and be more strict in the area of *muktzeh*. Thus they *pasken* like Rebbe Yehudah on Yom Tov."

Rambam[3] learns this Gemara simply: On Yom Tov we *pasken* like Rebbe Yehudah, so the halachos of *muktzeh* are more stringent. *Rif*[4] also learns the Gemara literally, that on Yom Tov we follow Rebbe Yehudah. As an example, food items that have been set aside for merchandise, i.e., *tamri d'iska*, are *muktzeh* on Yom Tov even though we can eat them on Shabbos.

There Is No Distinction between Yom Tov and Shabbos

There are many *Rishonim* who argue with this, foremost *Rashi*. The Gemara[5] *paskens* that dry wood that is meant for burning is not *muktzeh*, while moist firewood is *muktzeh* since it is not fit for burning. *Rashi* comments that this halachah is only according to the opinion that holds of an *issur muktzeh*. However, we follow Rebbe Shimon, and consequently all firewood, dry and moist, is not *muktzeh*. *Rashi* is explicitly saying that even on Yom Tov we follow Rebbe Shimon! (This is obviously regarding Yom Tov since it's discussing using a fire, which is only permitted on Yom Tov).[6]

---

3. *Hilchos Yom Tov* 1:17.
4. End of *Maseches Beitzah*.
5. *Beitzah* 33a.
6. If this is *Rashi*'s opinion, how does he explain the following mishnah in *Beitzah* 33a? The mishnah records a dispute whether one can use a small piece of wood as a toothpick. Rebbe Eliezer permits taking such a piece, whether from a courtyard or from inside the house, whereas the *chachamim* forbid it. *Rashi* explains that they forbid any usage of wood from a courtyard (due to exertion) and the usage for a toothpick even from a house, since wood is designated as firewood. *Tosafos* asks that according to *Rashi* it follows that the *chachamim* don't hold like Rebbe Shimon. According to Rebbe Shimon, if one has any single potential use the item it is not

Rosh[7] brings that *Rabbeinu Tam* and Rebbe Yehudah agree with *Rashi* regarding *paskening* like Rebbe Shimon even on Yom Tov. These opinions are also quoted by *Tur*.[8] *Rosh* explains that these opinions argue that we never find any *Amora* besides R' Nachman who holds there is a distinction between Yom Tov and Shabbos. The only reason R' Nachman made such a distinction was to uphold his qualification that he made in the first mishnah in *Beitzah*, that the Mishnah forbidding an egg that is laid on Yom Tov is dealing with a chicken that is meant for laying eggs. The other opinions in the Gemara don't make such a qualification and so are not forced to learn that the *mishnayos* in *Maseches Beitzah* are going according to Rebbe Yehudah. R' Nachman is a lone opinion who holds there is a distinction, but we are not forced to follow him. There are other *Amoraim* whom we can follow who didn't distinguish as such!

Shabbos Can't Be Less Stringent than Yom Tov

Baal HaMeor[9] also argues on *Rif* and *Rambam*, who entirely side with Rebbe Yehudah's opinion on Yom Tov, yet concedes there are some *muktzeh* categories that do apply on Yom Tov. He asks from the Gemara[10] that says that there is no stringency on Yom Kippur that is not found on Shabbos: מי איכא מידי דשבת שרי וביוה"כ אסור. From here we learn that there also can't be any stringency on Yom Tov that doesn't apply on Shabbos. This source is the thrust of the opinion of *Baal HaMeor*. *Baal HaMeor* ex-

---

muktzeh for anything. Following his opinion, why should the wood be *muktzeh* for the purpose of being a toothpick? It follows that this mishnah is not in accordance with the halachah. From what we've seen according to *Rashi*, this is a very strong question because even if the mishnah is dealing with Yom Tov, it must go according to Rebbe Shimon since this is the halachah. צ"ע how *Rashi* will answer this question. We can extract from the fact that *Tosafos* never rejected the assumption that the Mishnah that is discussing Yom Tov must fit with Rebbe Shimon that he also holds the halachah is like Rebbe Shimon on Yom Tov!

7. End of *Maseches Beitzah*.

8. 495:4.

9. Beginning of *Beitzah*.

10. 18b.

plains that R' Nachman, who says that on Yom Tov we *pasken* like Rebbe Yehudah, is referring to types of *muktzeh* which would be forbidden on Shabbos regardless, due to the prohibitions of Shabbos that lies within. These items require the *muktzeh* of Rebbe Yehudah to forbid them for Yom Tov. The result is that Shabbos and Yom Tov have equal stringencies.

He brings several examples to illustrate this rule. Firstly, a beam that falls off a celling is *muktzeh* on Shabbos because there is no use for it other than as firewood. Burning is a *melachah* on Shabbos, so it's *muktzeh*. On Yom Tov it is permitted to burn, so in truth it should not be *muktzeh* on Yom Tov, but in these cases we will *pasken* like Rebbe Yehudah. (Rebbe Yehudah holds that since it was set aside at the commencement of Yom Tov, because it is part of the house, it is *muktzeh* when it falls down.) Since on Shabbos one can't slaughter animals that graze far away from civilization, these animals are *muktzeh*. One is allowed to slaughter on Yom Tov, so in truth they should not be *muktzeh*, but since it is something that is forbidden on Shabbos because it involves a *melachah* on Yom Tov, we follow Rebbe Yehudah, who forbids it. (Rebbe Yehudah holds that these animals are *muktzeh* because they are so far away from the town. One doesn't have in mind the possibility to slaughter them, even though technically he can.) Besides the aforementioned category of *muktzeh*, *Baal HaMeor* will agree to *Rashi* that items that have no use or items that one sets aside are not *muktzeh* on Yom Tov since we follow Rebbe Shimon in these categories on Yom Tov like on Shabbos. Therefore, fruit pits and nutshells (which can be fed to animals) can be moved on Yom Tov according to *Baal HaMeor*, but not according to *Rambam*.

Only Stringent with Regard to Nolad

The final opinion is that of Rabbeinu Chananel[11] and *Bal Halachos Gedolos*. They explain R' Nachman's statement that we *pasken* like Rebbe Yehudah on Yom Tov differently. When R' Nachman says the halachah is like Rebbe Yehudah, it is only regarding *nolad*. R' Nachman brought the

11. Brought in *Beis Yosef*, quoted from *Rosh*.

Mishnah that teaches that if a beam falls off the celling, it is *muktzeh*; one can't use it for firewood. *Rif* understands that it is a regular form of *muktzeh* and that can only fit according to Rebbe Yehudah. Rabbeinu Chananel learns the problem with the beam is that it is *nolad* (it was created) on Yom Tov and from here he concludes that we follow Rebbe Yehudah regarding *nolad*.

Practical Differences between Rebbe Shimon and Rebbe Yehudah

Shulchan Aruch[12] follows *Rambam* and *Rif*, that we follow Rebbe Yehudah entirely on Yom Tov. Accordingly, one is not allowed to move any shells, even ones which could be consumed by an animal. (These are not *muktzeh* according to Rebbe Shimon because it they are fit for dogs.) *Rema* brings down that one can rely on the lenient opinions that there is no *muktzeh* on Yom Tov, so such shells would be permitted for an Ashkenazi to move.

Another area where there is a large split between Rebbe Shimon and Rebbe Yehudah is regarding a *muktzeh machmas meyus*. If something is repulsive but one is not using the surrounding area where it is located, there is no *heter* of *graf shel re'i* to move it since it is not bothering him if he is not nearby. Nevertheless, if we *pasken* like Rebbe Shimon, there is a different *heter* (allowance) that one is allowed to move something repulsive.

Another ramification is moving a *kli shemelachto l'issur* that has no permissible purpose. We discussed earlier[13] that the *Rishonim* argue when a *kli* has no permissible use at all if it retains its status as a *kli shemelachto l'issur* or not and rather is *muktzeh machmas gufo*. Even those who are lenient only permit so according to Rebbe Shimon, but according to Rebbe Yehudah it is clear[14] that such a *kli* is *muktzeh machmas gufo* and there is no room to be lenient to move it. It follows that to move a blender or other electric appliance would be forbidden, even though one requires to vacate the space it is occupying and even though on Shabbos one can be lenient.

12. 495:4.
13. Chapter 1.
14. *Shabbos* 35b.

Nevertheless, if one needs to get the children's Shabbos treats (question #2), there may be a new *heter*...

Once Muktzeh Is Waived for Food Preparations, It's Waived Entirely

Tosafos[15] is *mechadesh* that one can move *muktzeh* for the sake of *ochel nefesh* (preparing food). It is permitted to move ash from an oven to put food inside, even though ash is *nolad*. Since one is moving it for the sake of *ochel nefesh*, it is permitted. The proof is from the case[16] of a storehouse that falls down - one can move the bricks to access the food. The bricks are *muktzeh*, yet they can be moved because one needs to get to the food. So, if there are treats that are inaccessible without moving the blender, it can be moved.

Koheles Yaakov[17] suggests the following. The same way that carrying is permitted for the sake of *ochel nefesh*, and subsequently it's also permitted to carry for the sake a mitzvah (i.e., non-*ochel nefesh*), based on the famous principle of *mitoch*,[18] we can also apply *mitoch* and permit moving *muktzeh* on Yom Tov for the sake of a mitzvah. He supports this claim from the fact that *muktzeh* is forbidden because of carrying, so if carrying is permitted even not for the sake of *ochel nefesh*, then *muktzeh* should be permitted too.[19]

Imrei Binah[20] argues that even according to *Koheles Yaakov*'s logic, we can only permit cases that weren't possible to move before Yom Tov.[21]

---

15. *Beitzah* 8a, s.v. אמר רב יהודה.

16. See *Tosafos Beitzah* 31b, s.v. אמר ר' זירא שם.

17. *Baal HaChavas Daas*, printed at the end of *Toras Gittin*, *Hilchos Yom Tov*, *se'if* 15.

18. This literally means "since." The basic idea is that since this *melachah* is permitted partially, Chazal further permitted it entirely when there is a need.

19. I don't know why he doesn't go as far to assert that *mitoch* will permit even moving *muktzeh* when it is not for the sake of the mitzvah. After I saw in *Beis Yaakov Kisvos* 7, s.v. מתוך (also written by *Chavas Daas*) that he phrases the question in this way, if *muktzeh* is permitted for *ochel nefesh* then surely for any small need it should be permitted?!

20. *Dinei Yom Tov*, *siman* 12.

Imrei Binah permits cases such as ash, which should be *muktzeh,* to cover the blood of a freshly slaughtered animal. In this scenario, moving the ash was not possible to do before Yom Tov since the purpose of this act of moving was only present after Yom Tov. When one finds *chametz* on Yom Tov, he must cover it with a vessel and wait until after Yom Tov to burn it. *Tosafos*[22] explains that even though burning is permitted on Yom Tov because *muktzeh* is simultaneously transgressed when burning, one can't burn the *chametz* on Yom Tov. According to *Koheles Yaakov,* why can't we evoke *mitoch* to also override the *issur muktzeh*? According to *Imrei Binah,* since one has an obligation to destroy *chametz* before Yom Tov, moving *chametz* is only categorized as *machshirin* (preparation) and is not an obligation of the day. Therefore *mitoch* won't apply.

Koheles Yaakov concedes that *Tosafos,* who permits *muktzeh* for the sake of *ochel nefesh,* only permits moving but not using. We have elaborated elsewhere that there are two components to the *issur muktzeh*: an *issur tiltul* and an *issur shimush.* The former is a safeguard for the prohibition of carrying and the latter is learned from "*v'hechinu.*" Only the former is permitted based on *mitoch* since this is what the *mitoch* is permitting - something that has a relevance to carrying - but not an *issur shimush,* since this was never forbidden due to a problem of carrying.

Maharsha[23] (many other *Acharonim* also explain this idea) says that even according to the opinion of *Tosafos,* who permits moving *muktzeh* for food-related purposes, this would only be in a case where the removal

---

21. *Imrei Binah* explains that *mitoch* is only applied on something that one has to do today, "*chovas hayom,*" but an obligation that one was aware existed before Yom Tov are like *machshirin* (preparations) that could have been done before Yom Tov and *mitoch* doesn't permit even *machshirin.* He adds that even if one only became aware of the existence of the ability to perform the mitzvah on Yom Tov itself, but since he knew he had such an obligation prior to Yom Tov, it is still classified as *machshirin.* His example is *aravos* that are *muktzeh* because they were plucked on Yom Tov itself. They can't be moved for the sake of fulfilling one's mitzvah of *arba minim* because even though these *aravos* were not ready before Yom Tov, since one was aware of the obligation to shake *arba minim,* it is classified as *machshirin.*

22. *Kesubos* 7a.

23. *Beitzah* 33a.

of the *muktzeh* is necessary to allow access to the food. However, if the moving of the *muktzeh* is being carried out for the sake of using the *muktzeh* itself (*shimush muktzeh*), it would be forbidden, since this is considered like *achilah* (consumption), which is forbidden. If so, burning wood is considered using *muktzeh*. The simple reason is because one uses its purpose through the burning of the wood.

Wood on Yom Tov - an Anomaly to the Rules of Muktzeh

It follows that there would be no leniency to stoke the coals of a BBQ on Yom Tov (question #1) and thus help them burn better, even though one is doing it for א"נ. However, there is a more basic *heter*: Wood is not *muktzeh* on Yom Tov regarding burning it. It would only be *muktzeh* if one wishes to use it for a purpose other than as fuel. This is a unique form of *muktzeh* that only partially forbids the item. If one wants to use wood for anything other than fuel, it is *muktzeh*. However, moving it for firewood is permitted. Similarly, coals are meant to be burned, so one can stoke them while in a BBQ since they were never set aside for the purpose of burning. However, were one to wish to use something *muktzeh* as fuel, which wasn't obviously set aside for burning, such as discarded newspapers, magazines, etc., this would be forbidden since through the burning it's considered that one is using the *muktzeh*.

When There Is Not Enough Time to Cook

Even though inedible raw meat, inedible vegetables, flour, etc., are *muktzeh* on Shabbos, they are not *muktzeh* on Yom Tov since they have a purpose: One can cook them today. Assuming it takes thirty minutes to boil potatoes, one is not allowed to boil these potatoes thirty minutes before the end of Yom Tov because the cooking is now being done for the weekday (question #3). Do the potatoes become *muktzeh* during that period? R' Shlomo Zalman Auerbach[24] says that there is a general principle:

24. *Shemiras Shabbos K'Hilchasah*, ch. 21, note 17.

"*lo natnu devarecha l'shiurin*" - Chazal didn't make decrees dependent on many factors; they enacted the halachah in a uniform manner. If this food were to be treated as *muktzeh*, its status would depend on how fast the food cooks, on how fast the individual intends cooking it, and many other considerations. It is not logical Chazal would make a decree that varies; rather, since one can cook on Yom Tov it is not *muktzeh* throughout Yom Tov.

Chut Shani[25] argues that they do become *muktzeh*. He brings that *Rambam* stresses that the leniency to move such things is when it is *l'tzorech achilah*. We see regarding the halachah of actually cooking that one can't cook something that won't be ready in time. There is no uniform halachah that all *bishul* (cooking) is permitted; rather, the leniency in each act of cooking is dependent upon various factors. Surely this is a question on R' Shlomo Zalman's argument. If cooking is restricted, shouldn't the moving of the food items also have restrictions? Maybe *Rema*'s understanding of *ein muktzeh l'chetzi Shabbos* applies here. We elaborated on this elsewhere.[26] Briefly *Rema* holds if the reason for the item to be *muktzeh* is because of a designation from use that was only was performed during Shabbos, however this item hasn't undergone a change, the designation has no bearing. Applying to our case, these food items never underwent any physical change on Yom Tov to cause it to be inherently *muktzeh*. The reason for the *muktzeh* is not coming from anything intrinsic to the item; it is the designation of the owner that now he has no use for them. That alone can't turn something into *muktzeh* during Yom Tov itself.

Yom Tov Falling on Shabbos

The commentators argue about what happens when Yom Tov falls on Shabbos. We usually would impose all the halachos of Shabbos on this day, since generally Shabbos is more stringent than Yom Tov, but according to *Shulchan Aruch*, who *paskens* like Rebbe Yehudah on Yom Tov and not on Shabbos, regarding *muktzeh* it is the reverse: Yom Tov is more strin-

---

25. *Yom Tov*, ch. 9, p. 93, point 3.
26. Chapter 28.

gent than Shabbos. Is the rule that we follow the more stringent of the two, and we'll now be stringent and forbid *muktzeh* like Rebbe Yehudah, or does Shabbos usually override Yom Tov because the *kedushah* of Shabbos is greater, so it "dwarfs" Yom Tov, so to speak? If so, are only the halachos of Shabbos applied even if it were to come out more lenient than those of Yom Tov?

The majority of the *poskim*[27] are stringent, but those who are lenient[28] have a strong case. They say that the reason why we are stringent with *muktzeh* on Yom Tov is only because Yom Tov is more lenient and therefore people may come to be lenient. If this day of Yom Tov is also Shabbos, there are none of the regular Yom Tov leniencies, such as carrying and cooking. Therefore there is no reason that one would come to be lenient, and there is no reason to forbid *muktzeh*.

Summary

The *Rishonim* argue how to interpret the Gemara's statement that we follow Rebbe Yehudah, who forbids all *muktzeh*, regarding the rules of *muktzeh* on Yom Tov. *Shulchan Aruch* explains it literally. Consequently, he would forbid moving nutshells and other *muktzeh machmas meyus*. Based on the claim of the *Rishonim* brought by *Tur*, that Yom Tov is not more stringent than Shabbos, *Rema paskens* that there is no *muktzeh*. However, we are stringent regarding *nolad* on Yom Tov.

There is a unique leniency of moving *muktzeh* for the sake of *ochel nefesh*, but this is limited only to moving and not "using" the *muktzeh*. Burning something *muktzeh*, even if one doesn't actually move it in the process, is considered "using" the *muktzeh*. But wood is not considered *muktzeh* on Yom Tov since it is permitted to make a fire on Yom Tov. Therefore it would only be forbidden to burn something that is regardless *muktzeh* for some other reason, such as discarded paper, waste, and the like.

---

27. *Orchos Shabbos*, *Tzitz Eliezer*, and *Elef Lecha Shlomo*.
28. *Ben Ish Chai*, *Shanah Alef*, *Bamidbar*, *os* 11; *Sho'el U'Meishiv*, section 1, *siman* 1.

Answers

1. You can stoke the coals of a BBQ on Yom Tov. This is a unique leniency that coals are not *muktzeh* when being used as fuel.
2. Even a *kli* that is *muktzeh machmas gufo* can be moved to access food on Yom Tov. This is a leniency exclusive to Yom Tov.
3. Moving raw food during a time when one won't have sufficient time to prepare them even if he would try cook them is a dispute between the contemporary *poskim*. There are grounds for being lenient. Once Chazal said this food isn't *muktzeh*, that status can't vary depending on the time and type of food.

Part 2

שלהבת

A Flame

Questions

1. Can I move an electric torch on Shabbos/Yom Tov?
2. After the Yom Tov candles extinguish, is it now permitted to move the candlesticks?

There are several opinions among the *Tannaim*[29] whether a lamp and leftover oil contained within is *muktzeh* or not.

29. *Shabbos* 44a.

Rebbe Yehudah holds that any lamp that has been previously used is *muktzeh* due to its state of repulsiveness. Rebbe Meir doesn't hold of *muktzeh machmas meyus* and therefore his opinion is that only a lamp that has been used *this Shabbos* is forbidden to be moved. Rebbe Shimon holds that only a lamp that is currently alight is *muktzeh*. However, it may be moved once extinguished. The Gemara also quotes a *beraisa* that the leftover oil is forbidden to be used according to both Rebbe Yehudah and Rebbe Meir, not Rebbe Shimon. The Gemara[30] explains Rebbe Shimon holds that a lamp is *muktzeh* when the flame is lit since it is a *bosis* to the flame, which is *muktzeh*: הנח לנר שמן ופתילה הואיל ונעשה בסיס לדבר האסור.

The conclusion of the Gemara[31] is that the case of a lamp is the exceptional case where we don't follow Rebbe Shimon, but rather Rebbe Yehudah (not that it is *muktzeh machmas meyus,* rather like the opinion of Rebbe Meir that the candle is forbidden even once it has been extinguished). *Ran* explains that the *issur* in consuming the leftover oil is due to *muktzeh machmas issur,* since when it was alight any usage of the oil will cause a *kibui* (extinguishing) of the flame. Once this *muktzeh machmas issur* was present at *bein hashemashos* we apply the rule of *migo d'iskatzi* and therefore even after the flame is extinguished it is forbidden to handle the oil. *Ran* categories this as *muktzeh machmas issur* and also says it fits with the Gemara that states the oil and wick are a *bosis* to the flame. *Mishnah Berurah*[32] explains since *bosis* is a form of [33]*muktzeh machmas issur* and therefore although the Gemara gives two explanations why one can't move the lamp and its oil, it's really giving different aspects of the same answer.

Shulchan Aruch[34] *paskens* like *Rambam* and the *beraisa*: Any lamp that was lit this Shabbos is *muktzeh,* as well as any leftover oil. *Magen Avraham,* in explaining why the leftover oil is *muktzeh,* quotes *Ran* as saying that at *bein hashemashos* when it was alight, there was an *issur kibui*

30. 47a.
31. 157a.
32. 279:1.
33. We elaborated on this *geder* in chapter 14.
34. 279:1.

and we now apply a *migo d'iskatzi*. However, the simple understanding why the lamp itself is *muktzeh* is due to an *issur bosis* as is explicit in the aforementioned Gemara.[35]

Leftover Oil of Yom Tov Candles

Does this reason also forbid one from using the leftover oil from the Yom Tov candles? The Mishnah[36] says in reference to oil that dripped from a lamp on Shabbos: ואין נאותין ממנו בשבת לפי שאינו מן המוכן - "One can't benefit from the oil since it is not prepared." The simple understanding of this rule is similar to what we have spoken out. Since the oil was *muktzeh* at the onset of Shabbos, since its removal would be a violation of the *issur kibui*, this *muktzeh* status remains even once the reason forbidding it is removed, since we apply *migo d'iskatzi*. If this is the case, there should be no reason to differentiate between Shabbos and Yom Tov since extinguishing is equally relevant to both. However, *Tosafos*[37] says that this halachah does not include Yom Tov.

Beis Meir[38] writes: Obviously *Tosafos* doesn't mean that one can take the oil on Yom Tov when it is still alight. There is also a prohibition of extinguishing on Yom Tov. Forced by this problem, he deviates from the simple reading of *Tosafos*.[39] However, *Beis Meir* retracts from this deviation since he found written explicitly in *Shitah Mekubetzes* like the simple reading of *Tosafos*. Rabbeinu Peretz[40] is also clear that the intention is that *only* on Shabbos one can't use this leftover oil; on Yom Tov he can. However, how do we address *Beis Meir*'s problem that extracting the oil involves extinguishing even on Yom Tov and if so, this oil should remain *muktzeh* due to *migo d'iskatzi*? צע"ג.

---

35. 47a.

36. 42b.

37. *Beitzah* 6a.

38. *Chiddushim* on *Beitzah* and *Shabbos* 45a, s.v. אין מוקצה לר"ש.

39. He entertains that *Tosafos* means the Mishnah is excluding Yom Tov because there is no reason to differ between Shabbos and Yom Tov.

40. Brought in *Shitah Mekubetzes, Beitzah*.

Levush Serad asks on the aforementioned *Magen Avraham* who quotes *Ran* as explaining the reason forbidding *moving* the oil since it was *muktzeh machmas issur* of extinguishing. *Levush Serad* asks that this reason is only necessary to explain the prohibition of *consuming* the oil. However, surely there is also a prohibition of *moving*, and the reason is since it was a *bosis* to the flame, as the Gemara we quoted earlier writes, why did *Magen Avraham* not suffice with saying *bosis*? He answers that the reason of *muktzeh machmas issur kibui* is applicable even on Yom Tov, so we would apply *migo d'iskatzi* and the leftover oil would also be forbidden to consume. On Yom Tov, the lamp and the oil don't become *bosis* since a flame is not *muktzeh* on Yom Tov, so once the flame goes out, if not for this *muktzeh machmas issur* of extinguishing, one would have been able to *use* the oil. So *Magen Avraham* is bringing the more encompassing reasoning.

Another Reason for Muktzeh - Muktzeh Machmas Mitzvah

Magen Avraham says that according to *Ran* one should be able to use the leftovers of a wax candle on Yom Tov. The candle was not a *bosis* to the flame (since fire is not *muktzeh* on Yom Tov) and there is no prohibition of extinguishing since one can remove the bottom of the candle even while alight since one is not diminishing the flame with this act. However, *Magen Avraham* rejects this because there is another reason mentioned in the Gemara why the oil is *muktzeh, muktzeh machmas mitzvah*. The oil is designated for the mitzvah of lighting candles. So too a wax candle is forbidden in its entirety, since at the onset of Yom Tov it was all designated for the mitzvah. (Even though there are opinions who hold that there is no mitzvah of *hadlakas neros* on Yom Tov, we *pasken* that there is.)

Even accepting the final conclusion of *Magen Avraham* forbidding the use of even a leftover candle due to *muktzeh machmas mitzvah*, we can still take a practical application from all of this discussion. An electric torch can be moved on Yom Tov even while switched on (question #1). There is no *bosis* and no *haktzaah l'mitzvah*.[41] The oil or candle that is left over from Yom Tov candles can't be used because they are *muktzeh*

41. R' Shlomo Zalman Auerbach is lenient in several places (*Shulchan Shlomo* 495:9).

machmas mitzvah. However, moving it is permitted since there was no *bosis* to a flame at the onset of Yom Tov. Fire isn't *muktzeh* on Yom Tov and the designation for the mitzvah does not forbid moving, only a usage that expends it.

Whether or not one can move a torch on Shabbos depends on the reason why a flame is considered *muktzeh*. The Gemara[42] is implicit that a flame is *muktzeh*, but the underlying reason is not so clear. Whatever explanation is given, we need to address the difference - why on Yom Tov it is not *muktzeh* while on Shabbos it is.

Chazon Ish[43] presents the explanation beautifully: The oil and the wick themselves are not *muktzeh* on Yom Tov since they have a use, i.e., serving the candle. If so, why should the flame be different? Just because it is serving the candle, that shouldn't render it *muktzeh*. To summarize the answer very concisely: *Chazon Ish* explains that the problem with fire is that people don't want to move the flame, since if it goes out one can't relight it. Therefore on Shabbos[44] people naturally refrain from moving a candle, hence it's as if one has designated it a set place that will cause it to be *muktzeh*. He explains alternatively that once one has lit a candle, he doesn't usually move it. Its purpose is to remain fixed in place. Something that isn't meant to be moved on Shabbos is *muktzeh*. Another suggestion from *Chazon Ish* based on a *chiddush* from the Gemara in *Berachos*[45] is that the flame is considered *nolad*. R' Shlomo Zalman Auerbach[46] and R' Moshe Feinstein[47] have slight variations explaining the reason why, but both

---

Chut Shani, Yom Tov, ch. 9, is stringent; since the way of using a torch involves switching it on and off, one shouldn't move it.

42. 47a.

43. 41:16.

44. This is how R' Shlomo Zalman Auerbach in *Minchas Shlomo*, section 1, *siman* 14, explains *Chazon Ish*'s intention.

45. 53a. The flame is considered to be recreated each moment. The Gemara explains that one can make the *berachah* of Havdalah on a candle that a non-Jew lights because the flame is considered something that renews itself constantly. This must be considered severe nolad, as Rebbe Shimon agrees that a flame is *muktzeh*.

46. *Minchas Shlomo*, section 1, *siman* 14.

47. *Iggros Moshe, Orach Chaim* 3:50.

hold that the main issue of a flame is that it is not considered a *kli*.

Most our lights nowadays are not actual fire (this is only relevant with incandescent or filament bulbs). They are either LEDs, fluorescents, electric, etc. Some *poskim* hold that since we don't know clearly the real reason why a flame is considered to be *muktzeh*, we must be stringent and treat all of our lights as completely *muktzeh* even though they are not actual fire.

However, most of the reasons we suggested that explain why fire is *muktzeh* only apply to the actual fire, not a vessel that contains fire. Both R' Moshe Feinstein[48] and R' Shlomo Zalman Auerbach[49] hold the absolute halachah is that it is permitted to move a torch even on Shabbos. Even though they don't encourage sharing this leniency to all, since it can lead to a lax attitude regarding Shabbos as it appears like one is acting in a weekday fashion, it is nonetheless important to know the real halachah for necessary scenarios. For example, if there is a power outage on Shabbos and reserve battery-powered lights get switched on, one might need to move them to reassure people's fears. Or if a nurse is serving a patient and needs extra light, this allowance becomes relevant. In such pressing cases one can (and sometimes should) rely on the opinion that permits unrestricted movement of any such torch.

Summary

There are several reasons why a lamp or candlestick that was alight at the onset of Shabbos is *muktzeh*. The flame is *muktzeh* and consequently the wick, oil, and candlesticks are a *bosis* to the flame. Alternatively, the oil is *muktzeh machmas issur*, as one extinguishes the flame by removing the oil. In addition, it is *muktzeh machmas mitzvah*. According to some opinions, none of these reasons apply to an electric light, only to fire, and therefore modern-day torches can be moved.

---

48. Quoted in *Halachos of Muktza* by R' Yisroel Pinchos Bodner (Feldheim).

49. *Minchas Shlomo*, section 1, *siman* 14, s.v. ואמרתי. The author of *Halachos of Muktza* also brings this *psak*.

Answers

1. You can move an electric torch on Yom Tov. A halachic authority must be quoted to know if this halachah practically applies in a specific scenario.
2. Since the flame itself is *muktzeh*, the candlesticks are a *bosis* to *muktzeh*. So even once the flame is extinguished, the candlesticks are forbidden from moving. On Yom Tov the flame isn't *muktzeh*, hence the candlesticks have no actual limitations in being moved; one must ensure he doesn't extinguish the fire.

Part 3

נולד

Nolad

Questions

1. Is it permitted to move the water that drips from an air-conditioning?
2. Is mother's milk *muktzeh*?
3. Binyamin had a beautiful esrog, but unfortunately it became *pasul* on Yom Tov. Can it now be eaten?

We quoted earlier that *Rema* is lenient regarding *muktzeh* on Yom Tov, in that he *paskens* like Rebbe Shimon. *Rema* also *paskens* like Rabbeinu Chananel and *Behag* that *nolad* is forbidden. What does *nolad* encompass?

The Gemara[50] concludes that the opinion who holds of *muktzeh* also holds of *nolad*. The opinion who doesn't hold of *muktzeh* doesn't hold of *nolad*. However, at one stage the Gemara did entertain that they are not conditional upon each other. *Rashi* and *Tosafos* explain the logic to distinguish between the two, Rebbe Shimon doesn't hold of *muktzeh* because the item is present, it is fit for some use and one doesn't set aside something that has a use, while items of *nolad* didn't exist at all prior to Yom Tov, therefore one doesn't have any intention about that which he doesn't know.

Even according to the conclusion of the Gemara that Rebbe Shimon holds that both *muktzeh* and *nolad* are permitted, there are scenarios of *nolad gamur* (severe *nolad*) that Rebbe Shimon agrees to. The Gemara[51] brings a dispute between Rebbe Shimon and Rebbe Yehudah whether one can use vessels that break on Yom Tov as fuel for a fire. These pieces were not in this state of being fit for fuel when Yom Tov began. They were not meant for this purpose, but rather to be vessels, hence now that they are broken they are considered to be *nolad*. *Tosafos* says this is the *nolad* that is subject to the dispute between Rebbe Shimon and Rebbe Yehudah. The item existed in some form before Yom Tov, but it has now changed. severe *nolad* is when the *item didn't exist at all* before Shabbos/Yom Tov. The first opinion in the Gemara thought a hatched egg is considered something entirely new and hence even Rebbe Shimon would forbid it. Then R' Nachman, the second opinion, argues that it belongs to regular *nolad* and Rebbe Shimon would permit handling the egg.

Rainwater: A More Severe Case of Nolad

Tosafos's proof that there exists a form of *nolad* that Rebbe Shimon agrees to is from *Eiruvin*.[52] The Gemara assumes that while rainwater is held in the clouds, it is absorbed in the clouds and doesn't exist. Based on this assumption, the Gemara asserts according to all opinions that the rainwater

---

50. *Beitzah* 2a.
51. *Shabbos* 29a.
52. 45b.

will be *nolad*. This water doesn't exist, so it is a more severe case of *nolad*, which Rebbe Shimon agrees to.[53] This is as opposed to vessels that break on Yom Tov. The material previously existed at the beginning of Shabbos, but subsequently changed its form to allow it to be used in an entirely different way. According to Rebbe Shimon we can consider this new form to be encompassed in the original designation.

Another example is ash that was formed on Yom Tov via burning wood. Ash, relative to its previous existence of wood, is something entirely new. (It is not comparable to vessels that break; ash undergoes a complete structural and molecular change from its previous existence.) Hence it is *nolad gamur*.[54]

Nolad vs Severe Nolad

The difficulty in this area is to discern what is considered just *nolad* and what is severe *nolad*. *Shulchan Aruch* and *Rema* both permit using shoes that a non-Jew completed making on Shabbos.[55] Why do neither of them hold it is severe *nolad*? It must be since the raw material existed before Shabbos, it is not considered to be something entirely new; rather, it's the original material of leather, just in a new form. If so, it is regular *nolad*, which would be subject to a dispute between Rebbe Yehudah and Rebbe Shimon. Regarding Yom Tov, even regular *nolad* is forbidden, since we *pasken* like Rebbe Yehudah, at the least regarding *nolad*. Hence *Magen Avraham*[56] says that chicken bones are forbidden to move on Yom Tov, since when they were whole with chicken meat they were considered one entity of food, whereas now they are in a new state of being trash (unless it is a case of *graf shel re'i*).

---

53. The conclusion of the Gemara in *Eiruvin* 46a is that it is not *nolad* (even according to Rebbe Yehudah) because we consider the water to already exist in the clouds. The proof of *Tosafos* is from the Gemara's assertion based on the assumption that the water is absorbed in the clouds and doesn't exist separately.

54. *Tosafos Beitzah* 8a, s.v. אמר.

55. They differ whether it is permitted when the non-Jew made it for a specific Jew, or only when the non-Jew made it to sell to someone.

56. 495:7.

Meiri asserts that a condition (stipulation) can't help to remove even regular *nolad*. (The condition would be, "When this item comes to existence, I intend on using it.") He explains that there are two problems in *nolad*: Firstly, it is not prepared; and secondly, a person has no awareness he might use it. Even if we can consider that a stipulation circumvents the second problem since one is claiming he known this chicken will lay an egg tomorrow, it is still insufficient because there is still no preparation possible in something that doesn't exist. It is not in his hands to prepare it.

Practical Examples of Nolad

An esrog is *muktzeh machmas mitzvah*. It has been designated solely for the purpose of using for the mitzvah of *daled minim*, therefore it is forbidden to consume. If, unfortunately, it becomes *pasul* on Yom Tov (question #3), although the designation is now removed by default, it can no longer be handled. Since it became "prepared" on Yom Tov into its present state, it is considered *nolad*.[57]

We mentioned that the Gemara distinguishes between the eggs of different types of chickens - one that is reared for its eggs and one that is being kept for consumption. If the chicken is reared for consumption, we consider the egg *ochleh d'ifrasa*, which means that it is food that has been separated from food, i.e., the egg from the chicken meat. Therefore, this is not considered to be something new and is not *nolad/muktzeh*. It can be treated as if one food item is being detached from another food item it previously was a part of. However, if an egg hatches from a chicken that is kept to hatch eggs, we view the food as a new entity that came into existence; it is inherently different from its source, i.e., the mother chicken.

Magen Avraham[58] learns that the Gemara retracts from this sugges-

57. *Orchos Shabbos*, part 2, p. 48, mentions a similar scenario: If one is very careful to not even smell his esrog and then it becomes *pasul*, he says it will also be forbidden to smell because of *nolad*. There is an element of *chiddush* in this *psak*. Normally an esrog is not forbidden to smell; it seems if one is careful not to smell it then his care even forbids smelling.

58. 505:1.

tion and both types of eggs are permitted, even from an egg-reared chicken. Following from this, he says one can milk both a cow that is designated for eating and a cow that is kept for her milk (provided it is done under the permitted circumstances to preempt *sechitah,* e.g., into food, etc.). *Nesiv Chaim* explains that *Magen Avraham* learns that all animals are considered to be food, regardless of what they are currently kept for. So the milk, being food, is not considered something new that has come into existence. It follows even according to *Magen Avraham* breast milk is *nolad* (question #2). It is something new that has come into existence. If a woman is expressing her milk into a bottle, she must be careful to move the bottle with a *shinui* (deviation) since the bottle is a *bosis* to the milk.[59]

An air-conditioning unit produces clean water as waste. It extracts the moisture from the air, which condenses into water. Some institutions run this outlet pipe of the water into toilet tanks for economic reasons. This water that drips out is severe *nolad;* it didn't exist before Shabbos in this form. Nevertheless, those who place the water in the fill valve can flush the handle of the toilet, even though they are thereby moving the water. This is because it is not considered that the person has moved the water, rather he released the dam and the water came flowing out on its own.[60]

Summary

Regular *nolad* is permissible according to Rebbe Shimon because the item existed in some form before Shabbos and therefore one didn't designate it. *Rema* is stringent on Yom Tov and forbids even regular *nolad,* in accordance with Rebbe Yehudah. Rebbe Shimon concedes to cases of severe *nolad,* i.e., when the item came into existence *entirely* on Shabbos. The

---

59. See *Piskei Teshuvos, siman* 330.

60. Even though regarding *Chosen Mishpat,* if a person releases a dam and the water damages property, he is culpable, it is deemed *koach rishon,* see *Sanhedrin* 77b. Nevertheless, moving *muktzeh* is not determined based on what is considered in *Chosen Mishpat* as one's act. *Rema* permits blowing *muktzeh,* while in *Chosen Mishpat* one is culpable if he blew something and it caused damage. So presumably here too, releasing the flush is not regarding moving *muktzeh;* it's treated as if one directly moved *muktzeh* with his hands.

classic example is a laid egg. Two problems cause the severity of *nolad*: Firstly, the item is not "prepared"; and secondly, one doesn't intend on using something that is not yet in existence. Breast milk and air-conditioning waste water are considered new entities that have come into existence, so even on Shabbos they are forbidden to be moved.

Answers

1. Even on Shabbos this water is deemed to be *nolad* and forbidden to move.
2. According to many opinions mother's milk is an example of severe *nolad*.
3. An esrog which becomes *pasul*, since now it is fit for consumption while previously it had a different purpose, is considered a new item. This form of *nolad* would only forbid it on Yom Tov.

Chapter 28

טלטול מוקצה במקום מצוה

Moving Muktzeh for the Sake of a Mitzvah

Questions

1. If I find money or some other *muktzeh* object on Shabbos, can I pick it up in order to return it to the owner?
2. Ariel found a piece of bread on Pesach. Can he pick it up so that he can burn it or rid himself of it, in order to fulfill the mitzvah of *tashbiso*?

The *issur* of *muktzeh,* despite being only rabbinic is still very severe, to the extent that we find Chazal upheld *muktzeh* even at the expense of a *mitzvah d'Oraisa* (we shortly will bring the case from *Rosh Hashanah* 32b where we see this). Yet there are some sources which indicate that *muktzeh* is waived when it will enable the fulfillment of a mitzvah. There are differing sources and we will see if a rule exists delineating when there is a leniency to move *muktzeh* for the sake of a mitzvah.

Gra[1] brings a proof that *muktzeh* is waived to fulfill a mitzvah. The Gemara[2] says that one can bring *nesachim* (libations) from wine which is *muktzeh,* e.g., wine which was designated to be sold; the Gemara contrasts it to *tevel, tevel* is a *issur cheftza* (intrinsic *issur*) and it can't be used for *nesachim* as opposed to *muktzeh* which is not an intrinsic *issur* in the wine,

1. 586:22.
2. *Pesachim* 48a.

rather "*issur acher gorem lah* - something external forbids the wine," namely because today is Shabbos. This is the reason why it can be brought as *nesachim* notwithstanding that it is *muktzeh*. We see explicitly that despite the wine being *muktzeh* it can be moved or used for the fulfillment of the mitzvah.

Mordechai[3] brings this as a proof to his opinion that there is a *heter* to move *muktzeh* for the sake of a mitzvah. He holds that if a non-Jew fashioned a shofar on Yom Tov, i.e., he cut the ram's horn, despite being *muktzeh* since it wasn't prepared before Yom Tov and it is *nolad*, if one needs to use it to fulfill his mitzvah he can do so.

Is There Proof to Shulchan Aruch's Opinion?

Shulchan Aruch[4] *paskens* that if a non-Jew brings a shofar from outside the boundary or if he fashioned a shofar on Yom Tov it is permitted to use. *Gra* quotes from *Hagahos Ashrei* that when *Hagahos Ashrei* discusses the first scenario, i.e., when the non-Jew brought a shofar, he explains that despite the shofar brought for a specific Jew and therefore forbidden for him to benefit from still he can fulfill his mitzvah! This is because the halachah is that the shofar is permitted to be used by other people since the *melachah* wasn't done for them; if other people can use the shofar even for the one whom it was brought for it is not *muktzeh* because he has a use with it, namely he can give it to others, rather it is only forbidden for him *to benefit* from the shofar. Since we *pasken* "*mitzvos lav l'hanos nitnu* - benefit from a mitzvah is not deemed to be benefit," so even the one for whom it was brought for can use it to fulfill his obligation. *Hagahos Ashrei* doesn't permit *muktzeh* for the sake of a fulfillment of a mitzvah; and *Gra* contrasts this opinion with that of *Mordechai*. Therefore, there is no conclusive proof from the first halachah in *Shulchan Aruch* with regards to what he holds about *muktzeh* being waived for a mitzvah.

---

3. *Sukkah*, point 747. *Mordechai* himself doesn't address why this shofar is not a problem of *muktzeh*. The explanation we're presenting seems to be how *Gra* understands it.
4. 585:22.

Also the second halachah of *Shulchan Aruch* can be explained like we have seen from *Gra* that *muktzeh* can be waived to fulfill a mitzvah. But again it isn't conclusive proof since the commentators offer other explanations why the shofar fashioned by a non-Jew isn't *muktzeh*. *Magen Avraham*[5] explains *Shulchan Aruch* holds there is no *issur nolad* on Yom Tov hence the fashioned ram is not *muktzeh*. Alternatively, *Shulchan Aruch* is referring to when the non-Jew is removing the shofar from his own animal hence it is not considered to be *muktzeh*, the non-Jew's possessions are not subject to *nolad* when it is *gamru biyedei adam* (completed by the actions of man).

Covering the Blood after Slaughtering on Yom Tov

The Mishnah[6] says that it is forbidden to move a pile of rubble (because it is *muktzeh*[7]) in order to access a shofar which is stuck underneath, even if it is the only shofar available. This is the most explicit source that *muktzeh* is not waived even at the expense of a *mitzvah d'Oraisa*! How does that Gemara fit with the halachah we just learned that a shofar which was created by a non-Jew, i.e., he cut off a ram's horn on Rosh Hashanah is permitted, even though such a shofar is *muktzeh*? What is the difference between the two scenarios?

The opinion of Beis Hillel[8] is that unless one has specifically prepared soil before Yom Tov one is not allowed to slaughter an animal; subsequent to slaughtering an animal one must fulfill the mitzvah of *kisui hadam* (covering the blood), soil that has not been designated for this purpose is *muktzeh*. The Mishnah continues that even according to Beis Hillel if one went ahead and slaughtered this bird one can use ash from an oven to fulfill his requirement of covering the blood, since ash is considered prepared

5. *Se'if* 25.

6. *Rosh Hashanah* 32b.

7. This is the reasoning of *Rashba*, *Ran*, and *Tur*. Others explain the reason is because one is transgressing *chofer*.

8. *Beitzah* 2a.

for use (and therefore not *muktzeh*). The Gemara[9] subsequently substantiates that this is only relevant to ash which was created before Yom Tov, however ash created on Yom Tov would be *muktzeh*. *Tosafos*[10] proves that the opinion of the *Bavli* is that even if one went and wrongly slaughtered a bird he is still not allowed to cover the blood with freshly created ash, as the ash is *muktzeh* since it was not prepared before Yom Tov. (He adds that creating ash is considered a level of *nolad* that even Rebbe Shimon agrees to.)

Tosafos however brings the opinion of the *Yerushalmi* which holds that if one did go and slaughter fowl one can now use freshly produced ash, even though it wasn't prepared and cover the blood. We presumably see that the *Yerushalmi* holds that it is permitted to move *muktzeh* for the sake of fulfilling a mitzvah! *Rosh*[11] *paskens* explicitly like the *Yerushalmi*. He explains that even though regarding soil the Mishnah writes that even *bedi'eved* - "after one already did it (slaughtered)," we still don't permit him to use unprepared soil unless there was a shovel already stuck in to the earth, this is because there are two problems with soil that hasn't been prepared. In addition to *muktzeh* there is a problem of digging a hole, which even though it is only a *melachah she'eno tzrichah l'gufa* since the hole isn't required, it nonetheless is still an *issur d'rabbanan*. The Mishnah is referring to when there are these two issues to overcome, hence we cannot permit digging the soil, while the *Yerushalmi* is talking about ash which was created on Yom Tov, that only involves *muktzeh*, we can waive *muktzeh* alone for the fulfillment of a mitzvah.

Besides *Rambam*[12] the *Rishonim* side with *Rosh* over *Tosafos* and the consensus among the *Rishonim* is *bedi'eved* we do say that *muktzeh* is permitted to be moved in order to fulfill covering the blood, however one shouldn't slaughter in the first instance. *Shulchan Aruch*[13] follows these opinions.

---

9. Ibid. 8a.
10. Ibid., s.v. אמר רב יהודה.
11. Ibid. *siman* 10.
12. *Hilchos Yom Tov* 3:1.
13. 498:15.

Reconciling Contrary Sources

If so why is it permitted to move the ash to cover the blood but not the stones to access the shofar? The commentators[14] suggest several distinctions. The most obvious is that it depends what one is moving, the ash is the "mitzvah" item (i.e., it is an integral part of actual fulfillment of the mitzvah), whereas the heap of stones is not the "mitzvah" item, rather the stones are completely *muktzeh*, rather one's ultimate intention in moving them is to enable the retrieval of the mitzvah object. An item which is intrinsically part of the fulfillment of the mitzvah was permitted to be moved to fulfill the mitzvah, not an item which happens to be in this scenario essential to move to fulfill the mitzvah. If with moving the *muktzeh* object alone one fulfils this specific mitzvah, in such scenarios Chazal never upheld the *issur muktzeh*. This also answers our original question why it is permitted to use the *muktzeh shofar*, again, the mitzvah item itself is *muktzeh* and one is simultaneously fulfilling the mitzvah when he handles the *muktzeh* so Chazal never prohibited such scenarios.[15]

---

14. *Shaar HaMelech, Hilchos Yom Tov*, ch. 2, halachah 18, and the *Marcheshes*.

15. *Chayei Adam, siman* 446 (*klal* 2, point 27) rules when the moving of the *muktzeh* will only enable one *subsequently* to perform a mitzvah, it is not permitted to transgress *muktzeh*. He brings an example: If one's *sechach* on the sukkah is dripping with water and preventing one from eating inside, you can't move the *sechach* to shake out all the water. That act of moving the *sechach* isn't a mitzvah; it just subsequently enables a mitzvah. When the moving of the *muktzeh* involves the actual performance of the mitzvah, he permits it, e.g., covering blood. He does qualify this principle to only when the reason it is *muktzeh* is for a regular reason, e.g., designation from use and not because of a rabbinic enactment. A lulav a non-Jew detaches from the ground can't be used for the mitzvah of shaking lulav. He explains that while attached to the ground the lulav was *muktzeh* lest one come to detach it, not because of a designation, but because of the *gezeirah*. Chazal upheld their own enactments even at the expense of a *mitzvah d'Oraisa*. His source is *siman* 655. I don't know what he learns from there. צ"ע.
The Gemara explicitly says one could carry *mei chatas* (purity water for a *korban*) despite its *muktzeh* status. *Chayei Adam* asks: The sprinkling of this water is not a mitzvah; it just enables the *korban* to be fit to be offered — doesn't this fit with the rules he concluded above? Further he asks the same question we've seen from *chametz* found on Pesach: One can't move it to destroy despite that being a mitzvah? He offers difficult answers. Really the *mei chatas* is not *muktzeh* and only with burn-

This answer doesn't seem to fit with *Tosafos.*[16] *Tosafos* holds that if one found *chametz* on Pesach he isn't allowed to burn it (question #2). Even though there is a mitzvah to destroy the bread, it is not permitted to move the bread which is *muktzeh* for the sake of the fulfillment of the mitzvah. Seemingly this doesn't fit with the distinction we made, permitting one to move *muktzeh* if the movement is the actual fulfillment of the mitzvah, since in this case the actual moving of the *muktzeh* is the way by which the mitzvah is fulfilled?![17]

The Gemara[18] in *Rosh Hashanah* asks why is it that one cannot move the rubble to access the shofar, blowing shofar is a positive command and that should override the *issur d'rabbanan* of *muktzeh*?! It answers that violating Yom Tov is both a positive and negative command, violating both is not permitted for a positive command alone. *Ran* explains the reason why we consider moving the rubble to be equivalent to a positive and negative command, despite that *muktzeh* is only *issur d'rabbanan* is because "*asu chizuk l'divreihem,*" which means that just like a regular *issur* of Yom Tov would not be permitted in order to uphold a positive command, so too with a *d'rabbanan* they upheld certain Rabbinical *issur* even in scenarios where one will be passively annulling a Torah commandment.

---

ing does one perform mitzvah of burning *chametz. Shulchan Aruch* (446:2) brings an opinion that permits destroying *chametz* found on the second day of Yom Tov. *Chayei Adam* learns from here that any form of moving *muktzeh* for a mitzvah is permitted on the second day of Yom Tov.

16. *Kesubos* 7a.

17. The answer that seems most apparent is that burning *chametz* is different because one can fulfill his obligation tomorrow. Therefore there is no need for Chazal to waive *muktzeh* on Yom Tov. There are two problems with such a distinction. Firstly, if the blood is still visible, one can cover the blood even after Yom Tov. So the same argument should be advanced in this case, yet we know one can cover the blood. Furthermore, *Tosafos* in *Pesachim* 5a classifies burning *chametz* as a *tzorech hayom*. The explanation is: If one doesn't burn the *chametz,* he is delaying his mitzvah of *tashbiso*. That's enough of a reason to perform the mitzvah now, albeit that one who intends on burning the *chametz* isn't considered transgressing the prohibition of seeing and possessing *chametz.*

18. 32b.

Steipler's Approach

The Steipler[19] explains *Ran*'s statement "*asu chizuk l'divreihem*" to mean that Chazal gave *muktzeh* the strength of a negative command, not that they considered *muktzeh* to have the strength of a *melachah* which carries with it a positive and negative command.[20] With this assumption he has gained that we can work with the regular rules of *aseh docheh lo taaseh* (a positive command can push side a negative command), so why doesn't the positive push aside the negative? He brings a fundamental principle from *Piskei Tosafos*[21] that any stage necessary in the process of a mitzvah, even if one is not actually performing the mitzvah at that time is considered *b'idna* (simultaneous) (for *aseh docheh lo taaseh* to take place it needs to be *b'idna*). For example, eating the *moach* (a part of the meat of the *korban Pesach*) is not possible without breaking the bone, so even though the mitzvah is the actual eating but since the breaking of the bone is a necessary stage to facilitate the mitzvah, we consider the mitzvah to be taking place simultaneous that one is breaking the bone hence it is permitted. Regarding covering the blood, moving the dirt is a necessary part of the mitzvah, without it the mitzvah can't be performed therefore the moving of the dirt is always considered simultaneous and we can evoke *aseh docheh lo taaseh* to permit moving the soil. In contrast, moving rubble is not a necessary stage in the fulfillment of the mitzvah of *shofar*, in this situation it happens to be one can't otherwise fulfill his mitzvah but generally it is not required therefore moving the rubble is not considered part of the actual mitzvah and we can't evoke yet *aseh docheh lo taaseh*.

R' Shlomo Zalman[22] also suggests a similar answer why it is forbidden to move the stones to access the shofar, even if one was incapable of getting

---

19. *Beitzah, siman* 6.

20. When one breaches one of the thirty-nine *melachos* of Shabbos, he has transgressed both a negative commandment and has not fulfilled a positive commandment. Certain *dinei d'rabbanan* are given the same framework, meaning from the viewpoint of the *d'rabbanan* it's as if one transgressed a negative commandment and failed to keep a positive commandment.

21. *Zevachim* 37a.

22. *Minchas Shlomo* on *Maseches Beitzah,* end of the *sefer, siman* 2.

the shofar out of the rubble before Shabbos it is still is treated as *machshirin* that was possible before Yom Tov just it was out of his control, therefore it is subject to the general rule that *machshirin* - anything which could have been done before Yom Tov is not permitted to do on Yom Tov.[23]

These last two answers seemingly are insufficient. They resolve the difference between covering the blood and the shofar in the rubble, however according to their principles it should be forbidden to use a shofar that the non-Jew fashioned on Yom Tov since the Jew had the obligation of shofar beforehand it therefore is not considered simultaneous and so we can't evoke *aseh docheh lo taaseh*?[24]

The Stance of Rashba

However, both the Steipler's answer and R' Shlomo Zalman answer can explain the opinion of *Rashba*. *Rashba*[25] forbids using a shofar or lulav that a non-Jew fashioned on Yom Tov, he says moving *muktzeh* is not permitted even for the sake of a mitzvah. Yet *paskens* like the *Yerushalmi* that one can use soil that is *muktzeh* for covering the blood; moreover, he argues on *Tosafos* we quoted earlier that forbids burning *chametz* on Yom Tov and says if one hasn't done *bitul*, i.e., he will be transgressing an *issur*

---

23. R' Shlomo Zalman Auerbach notes another difference: In the case of covering the blood, if one leaves the blood uncovered he has transgressed an *issur*. The Torah doesn't want the blood left uncovered, so one can't slaughter knowing he doesn't have soil to cover the blood and after slaughtering the animal claim that he is *oness* (not responsible) since what the Torah desired, i.e., covered blood, is not being kept. When there is a mitzvah and an *aveirah* at stake, Chazal permitted *muktzeh*. By covering the blood, by permitting moving the *muktzeh* one is fulfilling a mitzvah and saving himself from transgressing an *aveirah*. (R' Shlomo Zalman fits only with *Magen Avraham* that one can't use a *muktzeh* shofar.) Even though burning the *chametz* also involves an *aseh* and a *lo taaseh*, the reason *muktzeh* is not waived in that scenario is because one only transgresses the *aveirah* in a passive manner. However, *Shaar HaMelech* already entertained this suggestion but rejected it because he proves that by covering the blood it's also as if one transgresses the *issur* only passively.

24. After I saw R' Shlomo Zalman raise this question on the Steipler.

25. Responsa, section 1, *siman* 297.

d'Oraisa of בל יראה (not to have *chametz* in one's possessions) he can burn the *chametz* on Yom Tov. The apparent resolution is that *Rashba* permits moving *muktzeh* when one will not only thereby fulfill a mitzvah but also not transgress a negative command. This can be explained simply that together the positive and negative commands can override the *issur muktzeh* or can be explained using *aseh docheh lo taaseh* with either variation of the Steipler or R' Shlomo Zalman.[26]

In light of this *Rashba* we can return to the original answer of *Shaar HaMelech* that those commentators who permit using a shofar a non-Jew fashioned despite being *muktzeh* is because when one is fulfilling the actual mitzvah while transgressing *muktzeh* then Chazal waived *muktzeh*. We previously rejected this answer in light of the case of burning *chametz* which *Tosafos* forbids. Now we see that halachah is subject to a dispute, we can reinstate *Shaar HaMelech*'s answer, those *Rishonim* who permit using the shofar will hold like *Rashba* who permits burning the *chametz*. While *Tosafos* who forbids burning the *chametz* could hold like *Tosafos* in *Beitzah* says that the *Bavli* doesn't sanction moving the soil which is *muktzeh*.

Returning a Lost Muktzeh Item

Chasam Sofer[27] asks if one can return a lost item on Shabbos even if the lost item is *muktzeh*, is there a *heter* to move *muktzeh* in order to fulfill the mitzvah (question #1)? He says even though one begins the mitzvah of returning a lost item already when he picks it up and it is considered simultaneous, at the same time that one is moving the *muktzeh* he is also fulfilling the mitzvah, (this is the opinion of the *Nemukei Yosef*) nonetheless in this specific case of a lost item he says we can't be lenient. Firstly, he brings a proof from *Rashba*, *Rashba* considers announcing even a lost

---

26. *Shaar HaMelech* also raises this contradiction in *Rashba* and says an enormous *chiddush*, that *Rashba* only intends on forbidding to use the *aravos* on the second day, which is *d'rabbanan*, but *muktzeh* is overridden to fulfill a *mitzvah d'Oraisa*. See ibid. how he fits this approach into the actual words of *Rashba*.

27. Responsa, *siman* 82.

muktzeh item on Shabbos to be permitted speech and not forbidden as weekday matters, the reasoning is because such speech is classified as *cheftzei Shamayim* (spiritual matters) which is certainly permitted on Shabbos. If the returning of a lost *muktzeh* item is in itself permitted then the speech facilitating this is certainly also permissible speech in itself, why would *Rashba* need to come onto the special *heter* of *cheftzei Shamayim*, we can deduce that it is forbidden to return a lost item![28]

(*Chasam Sofer* brings another beautiful proof. We learn from the Torah that if one's parents tell him to transgress Shabbos one doesn't need to abide, from this halachah we can learn that it is incumbent upon every member of Klal Yisrael to ensure that his fellow Jew keep Shabbos and one can't allow his fellow Jew to transgress Shabbos for his benefit. Applying this to our case, the owner of the lost item must forgo the right of having his lost item returned and hence the one who found it can't violate *muktzeh* in order to return it.)

R' Shlomo Zalman[29] asks if the lost *muktzeh* item is a *kli shemelachto l'issur* why can't one return the lost item, is carrying it to fulfill a mitzvah not considered moving for the sake of the item, encompassed in *l'tzorech gufo*? Precedence for such a comprehensive understanding of what is encompassed in צ"ג is found in *Tosafos.*[30] He permits sending shoes which are forbidden to be worn and thus *muktzeh* as a gift on Yom Tov, even though neither the recipient nor the sender are actually using the actual *guf* (body) of the shoe. It must be that moving something for the objects own good is still considered as *tiltul l'tzorech gufo*. Consequently, carrying the item to enable oneself to fulfill a mitzvah would also be considered *tzorech gufo*. In light of this we must conclude *Chasam Sofer* who forbids

---

28. *Pri Megadim* (introduction to *siman* 308) says according to *Rambam*'s reasoning explaining that *daber davar* (correct speech on Shabbos) is the reasoning behind *muktzeh*. Just like one's speech should be different on Shabbos, so too one's touching should be different. It should follow that the leniency of speaking matters of mitzvos should also apply to *muktzeh*. Moving *muktzeh* for the sake of a mitzvah should be *mutar*. However, he brings *Magen Avraham*, who *paskens* like the mishnah in *Rosh Hashanah* that it is forbidden to move rocks to access a shofar.

29. *Minchas Shlomo* on *Maseches Beitzah*, end of the *sefer*, *siman* 2.

30. *Shabbos* 60a, s.v. לא.

to return a lost item must only be referring to an item which is completely *muktzeh* and not subject to a *heter* of *l'tzorech gufo.*[31]

Summary

There is a dispute between the *Bavli* and *Yerushalmi* whether if one slaughtered on Yom Tov without having previously prepared soil for the covering of the blood can one move the soil despite it being *muktzeh*. The *Yerushalmi* is lenient and seems to permit moving *muktzeh* to fulfill a mitzvah. Those who follow the *Yerushalmi* despite having other proofs that *muktzeh* is waived for the fulfillment of a mitzvah, must reconcile the Mishnah that forbids removing stones to access a shofar. The simplest distinction is that the *issur muktzeh* is only waived when the moving of the *muktzeh* is part of the actual process of fulfilling the mitzvah, otherwise even though one will lose the opportunity to fulfill the *mitzvah d'Oraisa* the rabbis gave extra weight to *issur muktzeh* and upheld it in such scenarios. Though generally there is room to be lenient to move *muktzeh* for a mitzvah, *Chasam Sofer* shows that returning a lost item is different and may be forbidden. However, if the lost item is a *kli shemelachto l'issur* then it is permitted since it is considered to be moving the item *l'tzorech gufo*.

Answers

1. If the lost item is a *kli shemelachto l'issur* then you can move it to fulfil the mitzvah because that is moving *l'tzorech gufo*. If the item is completely *muktzeh* then you are not allowed to move it, even at the expense of the mitzvah.

---

31. One could perhaps even extend this *Tosafos* to permit someone wishing to demonstrate to a student a *kli shemelachto l'issur* as a prop on Shabbos, to illustrate what he is teaching. He can take a hammer and wave it, explaining, "This hammer is a *kli shemelachto l'issur*." However, one could differentiate that giving a present is an action that has more significance than an act of just showing an item and maybe *Tosafos* would not say this qualifies under *tzorech gufo*. צ"ע לדינא.

2. *Tosafos* forbids moving *chametz* to burn since it is *muktzeh*. This is despite that one will thereby lose the opportunity to fulfil a positive mitzvah.

Appendix: The Opinion of Ritva[32]

Ritva brings a new source that *muktzeh* can't be transgressed to fulfill even a Torah *mitzvah*. The Mishnah[33] lists what items one can move from your house to make space to enable more people to come inside to learn Torah or for the sake of hosting more guests. Both purposes, hosting guests or learning Torah, are mitzvos from the Torah and nevertheless the Mishnah says if one wants to move *muktzeh* items, e.g., *maaser* and *tevel*, one can't move them. Explicit that even at the expense of a *mitzvah d'Oraisa* Chazal imposed *muktzeh*. He does add that if a *mitzvah* is permanent, i.e., it has a fixed time, *mitzvah kavua*, Chazal didn't impose *muktzeh* if it will result in a lack of fulfillment of the mitzvah. His example is the mitzvah of lulav: Even if a lulav would be treated as *muktzeh* it won't be forbidden to shake it because Chazal would have waived their restrictions of *muktzeh* for one to fulfill such a mitzvah. He says when the mitzvah is rabbinic then Chazal upheld their prohibition of *muktzeh* even at the expense of the fulfillment of the mitzvah.

32. *Sukkah* 42b.
33. 126b.

Chapter 29

טלטול לולב ושופר בשבת ויו"ט

Moving a Lulav and Shofar on Shabbos and Yom Tov

Questions

1. Can someone take his lulav home after shul even if there's no one at home who needs to use it?
2. Shimon was practicing blowing the shofar before Rosh Hashanah and forgot to put it away. Can he move it on the night of Rosh Hashanah?
3. Someone didn't listen to the *rav*'s request for everyone to take home their lulavim before Shabbos, and there's a lulav lying over several chairs. Can it be moved on Shabbos?

Maggid Mishnah[1] infers from *Rambam* that since nowadays we don't shake the lulav on Shabbos, it would be considered *muktzeh* on Shabbos. *Rambam* writes that a woman can take the lulav from her husband on Shabbos. (The *chiddush* is that even though she herself won't use it, since it is not *muktzeh* for the owner it isn't *muktzeh* for anyone.) However, *Rambam* stipulates that this is only relevant when it was the practice to shake lulav on Shabbos (during the time of the Beis HaMikdash). *Maggid Mishnah* understands that implicit in the reasoning of *Rambam* is that nowadays, when we don't shake on Shabbos, it is forbidden for her to take it because it is *muktzeh*.

---

1. *Hilchos Lulav* 7:25

Beis Yosef brings this ruling from *Rosh,* that on Shabbos a lulav is *muktzeh,* and he adds that the lulav is like a stone regarding moving it, i.e., it is *muktzeh machmas gufo. Darchei Moshe*[2] quotes *Maggid Mishnah* and adds that *Ran* is also in agreement. In *Shulchan Aruch, Rema*[3] also says that a lulav is forbidden to move, like a stone. He has seemingly labeled a lulav on Shabbos as *muktzeh machmas gufo,* that it intrinsically is *muktzeh* because it is now considered like a branch taken from a palm tree.[4] The most explicit source we find in the Gemara that a lulav should be treated as *muktzeh* is from *Sukkah* 42b. The Gemara first entertains the reason why the Mishnah forbids carrying the lulav on Shabbos is because it is *muktzeh.*

The *Tosefta*[5] recalls that the practice in Yerushalayim was to walk to shul holding the lulav, to ascend to the reading of the Torah while holding the lulav, and to hold the lulav while visiting the sick. In other words, they

---

2. 654.

3. 658.

4. Many of the *poskim,* including *Tosefes Shabbos* and *Eshel Avraham* 308:12, understand *Rema* means that it is *muktzeh machmas chisaron kis.* One is normally extremely careful when handling a lulav since he doesn't want it to become *pasul.* It's plausible that this applies even nowadays, despite the abundance of lulavim, that we are also careful and so it will have the status as *muktzeh machmas chisaron kis.*

5. *Sukkah* 41b. *Gra, siman* 658, brings this as an additional source to *Rema*'s halachah that a lulav is *muktzeh. Gra* also brings the following *Tosefta* (ch. 2, halachah 13) that says once one has finished using the lulav on Yom Tov he can't move it because it is *muktzeh. Gra* has a different text in this *Tosefta.* His text reads that it is specifically when Yom Tov falls out on Shabbos, it is *muktzeh* after the completion of the mitzvah. We can extract from the fact that it was forbidden to pick up after completion of the mitzvah that the lulav is *muktzeh.* However, it is unclear why according to *Gra*'s text this rule is uniquely only on Yom Tov and Shabbos together. If the *Tosefta* is referring to even in the times of the Beis HaMikdash when they shook the lulav on Shabbos, why specifically on Shabbos can't they continue to move the lulav, since the reasoning is equally applicable regardless what day Yom Tov is? On Shabbos the only difference is that *hotzaah* (transportation) is forbidden. That difference must be the distinction. Since one can't carry the lulav, his usage, relative to a Yom Tov on a weekday, is severely limited. Once one has finished his mitzvah, there is no purpose to it anymore, while on Yom Tov one can carry the lulav so that other people can fulfill their mitzvah, so there is still a purpose to the lulav as a mitzvah object and it doesn't revert to being *muktzeh.* ואכתי צ"ע.

carried the lulav as much as they could, not only while they were fulfilling the main mitzvah. The *Yerushalmi*[6] adds that once they put down their lulav on the floor upon completion of the mitzvah, they were then forbidden to take them again since it became *muktzeh*. This status is presumably the same as a lulav on Shabbos, which we've seen is *muktzeh*.

Ein Muktzeh L'Chetzi Shabbos

Rema in *Darchei Moshe*[7] is perplexed: How can the lulav become *muktzeh* on Yom Tov itself, if we *pasken* that *ein muktzeh l'chetzi Shabbos* - "something can't become *muktzeh* during Shabbos or Yom Tov"?

The Gemara[8] brings the following scenario: One had ripe fruits at the beginning of Shabbos, and on Shabbos he decided to make them into dry fruits and he left them out in the sun to dry. If the process happens quickly and on Shabbos they became fit to eat again, are they permitted? In the interim, they are not edible while drying in the sun, so they became *muktzeh* on Shabbos. The opinion who holds *ein muktzeh l'chetzi Shabbos* holds that even though they became *muktzeh*, if they subsequently become edible they revert back to their original status of being permitted. The other opinion holds *yesh muktzeh l'chetzi Shabbos*. Once something becomes *muktzeh*, it can no longer subsequently revert to being non-*muktzeh*. Since we *pasken* like the former opinion, *ein muktzeh l'chetzi Shabbos, Rema* asks: Why does the lulav become *muktzeh* upon completion of use? We hold something can't become *muktzeh* on Yom Tov![9]

---

6. *Sukkah*, ch. 3, halachah 11.

7. 652:1.

8. *Beitzah* 26b.

9. From *Rema* we can suggest a connection between halachah 24 and halachah 25 in *Rambam*. He first brings this practice of the men of Yerushalyim and then he brings the halachah about a woman taking the lulav from her husband. Perhaps *Rambam* understands there is a *chiddush* in the practice of these Jews. Surely since a lulav is in essence just a palm branch it should therefore be *muktzeh*, and one can only carry it for the sake of the fulfillment of the mitzvah. It must be that the *Tosefta* is praising these Jews to whom the mitzvah of lulav was so precious in their

Only if It Reverts Back to Not Being Muktzeh Is It Permitted

Magen Avraham[10] and *Taz*[11] both explain the principle of *ein muktzeh l'chetzi Shabbos* in a manner that would *not* be relevant to permit our case of a lulav that one has finished using for his mitzvah. *ein muktzeh l'chetzi Shabbos* permits an item *only when it subsequently becomes fit again,* such as a situation where it was fit for use at the onset of Yom Tov, but a subsequent change in circumstances caused the item to be unfit and hence one removed his mind from it. If it reverted back to a state of preparedness, we now permit the item and we don't say that it remains *muktzeh,* since the *muktzeh* state was only in being during Shabbos/Yom Tov itself. This is similar to what we saw from the Gemara that when the fruits have finished drying out they are permitted, but while they are not edible, all agree they are currently *muktzeh.*

However, if there is an object that usually is *muktzeh,* but there is also a specific circumstance that allows one to use the item at present. *ein muktzeh l'chetzi Shabbos* would not permit its use for the duration of Shabbos. An example of this is a milah knife; it is usually *muktzeh machmas chisaron kis* due to one's care not to use it for anything other than circumcision. If one has a bris milah to perform on Shabbos, he may certainly use the knife for this purpose since he was never *maktzah daas* from this use. However, any subsequent movement is not permitted since the reason for the *muktzeh* was always present, and there was a technical *heter* that permitted its use (that you use it for its intended purpose). Even if we hold *ein muktzeh l'chetzi Shabbos,* it won't remove the current reason for it to be *muktzeh.* All this principle does is stop a perpetuation of a *muktzeh* sta-

---

eyes that they carried the lulav wherever they went as a display of their affection to the mitzvah. The *Tosefta* is singling them out that only they are allowed to move the lulav when they wanted. (It is all considered a continuation of the mitzvah even though they have fulfilled their main obligation.) The next halachah follows that a woman can carry the lulav when it is for the sake of the mitzvah, i.e., to preserve it in water, but otherwise it is *muktzeh* and hence on Shabbos she shouldn't move it.

10. 331:5.

11. 310:3.

tus the was once effective on Shabbos *if* the status of the object subsequently changes.

They bring proof to this is from the halachah[12] found with a certain type of chopping board that one is allowed to move for the fulfillment of one's *simchas Yom Tov,* despite the board being *muktzeh machmas chisaron kis* (they only used it for grinding a specific food). Once one has finished using this chopping board for his meat, the board continues being *muktzeh* and one cannot move it. *Magen Avraham* and *Taz* prove from here that when something has a present reason to be *muktzeh,* even though when Shabbos came in it wasn't *muktzeh,* the current reason prevails. It is now *muktzeh,* regardless of the fact that we hold *ein muktzeh l'chetzi Shabbos.*[13]

Applying this to our case, while one needs to fulfill his mitzvah of lulav, there is full permission to move it. But once the mitzvah has finished and it now is useless, its status reverts back to what it intrinsically is, namely *muktzeh.* Once it is *muktzeh,* it remains so for the duration of the day. Since now it no longer has a use, it doesn't help that it had a function previously.

Where Rema Differs in His Understanding

Rema seemingly understands that *ein muktzeh l'chetzi Shabbos* tells us that anything that at the onset of Shabbos was not *muktzeh* cannot become *muktzeh* subsequently during this same day. This is even with something that usually is *muktzeh,* and in this instance there are special circumstances that negate the *muktzeh,* such as the lulav, which under normal circumstances would be a useless branch and hence *muktzeh.* However, on Sukkos it has a use for the mitzvah and therefore is permitted to be moved.

---

12. This is from the Gemara in 122a s.v. עלי לקצב עליו הבשר, and *Beitzah* 11a.

13. *Mishnas HaShabbos* quotes the *Eliyah Rabbah* 331:5 to answer on behalf on *Rema* why this case is not a proof. The *ali* (chopping board) is only permitted for the sake of *simchas Yom Tov* and really at the onset of Shabbos it is *muktzeh.* However, the milah knife is not *muktzeh* at all *bein hashemashos* because one knows in advance that he will need to use it. Since it is not *muktzeh* at all, it can't subsequently become *muktzeh.* (צ"ע if this difference is also relevant with a lulav.)

Therefore, even once the mitzvah has been completed and the lulav should now be considered to be a useless branch and *muktzeh,* the rule of *ein muktzeh l'chetzi Shabbos* permits it for the entire day.

Rema[14] uses the same argument to explain that one who performs a bris on Shabbos is permitted to continue carrying the milah knife for the rest of the day. Although usually a milah knife is *muktzeh machmas chisaron kis,* as we previously explained, in this instance where the mohel was aware of the impending milah he was due to perform, the knife is not *muktzeh* when Shabbos commences. Since it was not *muktzeh* at the onset of Shabbos, we say that *ein muktzeh l'chetzi Shabbos* means that it can't subsequently become *muktzeh. Taz* and *Magen Avraham* also argue on this *Rema* for the same reason. After one has used the knife, there is no intrinsic reason why it should not be *muktzeh,* so *ein muktzeh l'chetzi Shabbos* isn't pertinent to permit moving it freely. Proof against *Rema* is from the fact that we find lengthy discussions among the *poskim* what to do with the knife after one completes the actual bris - whether one must drop it immediately or perhaps there is a leniency that since the knife is already is one's hand, he may therefore continue holding it until he puts it down.[15]

We can understand why many *poskim* discuss what to do with the knife, since there is a strong argument that it is *muktzeh.* However, we don't find such lengthy discussions what to do with a lulav subsequent to completing its use. If we refute *Rema,* who wished to extend *ein muktzeh l'chetzi Shabbos* even in this instance, surely a lulav should be *muktzeh* upon completion of its use (provided there is no one else to give it to to use)?

A Mitzvah Item Becomes a Kli

One direction to explain why the lulav will still be permitted to move after fulfilling the mitzvah is based upon the following *Taz.*[16] *Rema,* concurrent with what we've seen, says the lulav is *muktzeh* only on Shabbos, when one has no use for it at all. *Taz* asks: Surely the same way *Rema* holds that a

14. *Yoreh Dei'ah* 266.

15. Discussed at length in chapter 4.

16. 658:2.

shofar is permitted to be moved *l'tzorech gufo u'mekomo* on Shabbos because it is a mitzvah item, so too a lulav should be permitted to be moved *l'tzorech gufo u'mekomo*?

Taz extrapolates a principle from *Rema*'s definition of a shofar as a *kli shemelachto l'issur* that any item that one designates for the performance of a mitzvah receives an identity of a *kli*. Before Yom Tov begins, one puts aside this branch as his mitzvah item. This is treated as a designation that this branch will serve a purpose and this is sufficient to turn it into a vessel. It follows accordingly to *Taz* that from the beginning of Yom Tov the lulav's movement is never entirely restricted, so even once the mitzvah is finished it just reverts back to this status of being like a vessel that is permitted to be moved.

Chemed Moshe[17] questions the comparison. The reason a shofar is a *kli shemelachto l'issur* is because it is an actual vessel. Even without the shofar enabling the fulfillment of his mitzvah, it's purposeful, it's an instrument, and the Gemara[18] says they would use it as a bottle to feed a baby. This is the reason it is permitted *l'tzorech gufo u'mekomo*; it qualifies as a typical *kli shemelachto l'issur*. It is a *kli* whose main use is forbidden but nonetheless has potential permitted usages. Therefore, there is no precedence from which to extrapolate that every mitzvah item is a *kli*. It depends on whether the item has a purpose all year round. A lulav has no purpose - it is a merely a branch - one just happens to have a use with it for the mitzvah.

Even according to *Taz*'s assumption that if it is used for a mitzvah, the item is designated as a vessel, it's not clear why it is a *kli shemelachto l'issur*. A regular branch has no purpose at all. Once there is a designation and it is effective why doesn't it become a *kli heter* (*kli shemelachto l'heter*), it has no forbidden purpose?[19] We can also question that surely the mitzvah

17. 658:2.

18. *Shabbos* 39b.

19. I later saw *Chemed Moshe*, who says that a shofar on Yom Tov is a *kli shemelachto l'heter* for two reasons. *Taz* holds that even after one has fulfilled his mitzvah he is permitted to blow all day of Rosh Hashanah, so the shofar has a use after performing the mitzvah and, secondly, one might have to blow the shofar for others. Again this shows that the shofar still has a use. He says neither reason applies with a lulav, so one can no longer use it after fulfilling his mitzvah.

doesn't demand that this stick change its status to anything more than a stick. The mitzvah is just to shake a stick; why should the fact that one is using it for a mitzvah upgrade its status?

Upholding Rema

If we don't follow *Taz,* who considers a lulav to be a *kli shemelachto l'issur,* and the consensus of *poskim*[20] is unlike *Taz,* to permit moving a lulav after completing the mitzvah we must rely on *Rema*. To do so we first must answer why a lulav after use is relevant to *ein muktzeh l'chetzi Shabbos*. There is a striking difference between the lulav and the Gemara's case of dried fruit. In the Gemara's case, the fruit underwent a physical change during Shabbos, both causing it to become *muktzeh* and to subsequently permit it. However, the lulav hasn't undergone any physical change precipitating its *muktzeh* status. Rather, one has just finished without any potential use he may wish to use it for.

The significance between the different causes of the *muktzeh* status is as follows: When one places the fruit to dry on Shabbos, they become *muktzeh* because they presently are not fit for any use, and as a direct result of their unusable state there is a removal of one's consciousness. When they subsequently become edible, there is no longer any reason for them to remain *muktzeh*; they are edible. The only potential reason for them to retain their status of *muktzeh* is because there was once a removal of awareness. The opinion of *yesh muktzeh l'chetzi Shabbos* holds that once there was a designation, even though it only took place after the commencement of Shabbos, it still affects the rest of Shabbos and it's as if he removed his intent for the entire Shabbos.

However, we *pasken* like the opinion *ein muktzeh l'chetzi Shabbos*. *Rema* evidently understands this opinion to hold that the designation that occurs on Shabbos does not have any effect on the item, thus explaining why fruit are not *muktzeh* once they become edible. The reason is that since the fruit are currently fit for use, there is no problem that the owner

20. See *Biur Halachah* there.

previously removed his intent, since a designation on Shabbos has no bearing on the item now that it is prepared.

Rema applies this too to a lulav that has completed its use. Before one fulfilled his mitzvah, this lulav is not *muktzeh,* and once one has finished the mitzvah nothing changed in the actual lulav. The same preparation of the object exists; the only reason to forbid moving the lulav is that since one now has no use for it anymore, he sets it aside in his mind. To address this claim, *Rema* brings the principle of *ein muktzeh l'chetzi Shabbos,* which demonstrates that one's actions or mind during Shabbos has no effect of causing a *muktzeh* based upon a *haktzaas hadaas*. The only way it can become *muktzeh* during Shabbos is when accompanied by a lack of physical preparation in the item that makes it no longer fit for use.[21]

It follows that according to *Rema,* even after one has finished his mitzvah he can still take the lulav home (question #1). (In scenarios where there is a possibility that someone among his household will still need to use the lulav, even without all we've discussed it is permitted to move the lulav, since it's still needed for the sake of the mitzvah.) *Hilchos Chag B'Chag*[22] suggests that since nowadays it has become the practice to take one's lulav to and from shul, regarding this we are like *anshei Yerushalayim* (those who had the practice to carry everywhere the lulav) and the movement is considered a continuation of the mitzvah.

Rema forbids moving the lulav on Shabbos, so if one accidently left his lulav in shul (question #3), he can't move it, even if it might get ruined by remaining in shul. Even according to *Taz,* who holds that a lulav is a *kli shemelachto l'issur,* moving it so that it doesn't get ruined or stolen is a problem, since such movement (to save the object itself) is considered *tiltul m'chamah l'tzel,* which is not permitted with a *kli shemelachto l'issur*.

---

21. *Magen Avraham* and *Taz* don't argue on the parameters of *ein muktzeh l'chetzi Shabbos*. They understand that with the case of the lulav there is a problem inherent with the item. The lulav itself is a reason to be *muktzeh* since in essence it is only a branch, even without not intending to move it. However, while there is a mitzvah, there is a special leniency to move it to ensure the fulfillment of the mitzvah (Chazal waived *muktzeh* to ensure the fulfillment of the *mitzvas lulav*), but after accomplishing the mitzvah the lulav reverts to being intrinsically not fit.

22. *Arba Minim* 15:7.

What About an Esrog?

All we have discussed until now applies only to a lulav, not to an esrog. Since an esrog is a food item, and even though it has been designated for the mitzvah and can't be consumed during the seven days of Sukkos, one can still benefit from it through smelling its aroma. Therefore its identity as a food is not lost and it will not become *muktzeh* even upon completion of use. Even if one is extremely careful that the esrog doesn't become *pasul,* food doesn't become *muktzeh machmas chisaron kis.*

Moving a Shofar

We saw earlier that *Rema* holds that a shofar can be moved *l'tzorech gufo u'mekomo* on Shabbos. *Mishnah Berurah*[23] explains that on a regular day of Rosh Hashanah, the shofar can't be used for any potential purpose other than for the mitzvah. This is because it is *muktzeh machmas mitzvah,* it is designated for the mitzvah. On Shabbos Rosh Hashanah, the mitzvah isn't practically applicable since Chazal forbade blowing on a Shabbos lest one come to carry it in a public domain. So the shofar is no longer considered to be designated for the mitzvah and is thus permitted to be used *l'tzorech gufo,* e.g., one can use it to feed water to a baby, etc.

Pri Megadim[24] uses this idea to refute *Taz*'s comparison we mentioned earlier between a shofar and a lulav. *Taz* claimed that both are permitted to be moved *l'tzorech gufo u'mekomo.* A shofar on Shabbos is not considered to be designated for the mitzvah at all. Today there is no mitzvah of blowing the shofar, so it is not subject to *muktzeh machmas mitzvah.* This is opposed to a lulav, which is designated for the mitzvah for all seven days. Therefore even when today is Shabbos, since there are still other days that will require its use, it remains *muktzeh machmas mitzvah. Pri Megadim* even entertains that when the first day of Sukkos is Shabbos, it still has been designated for the mitzvah that Shabbos, and

23. 688:15.
24. *Siman* 658.

not only when you have used it for the mitzvah previously. We see that there are further reasons to restrict a lulav that don't apply to a shofar.

We see that a shofar on Shabbos can be moved like a *kli shemelachto l'issur*, since it has no designation for a mitzvah, while a lulav is still considered *muktzeh machmas mitzvah* even on Shabbos. *Pri Megadim* doesn't explain what the difference between a shofar and lulav is. If regarding a shofar there is no longer a designation for a mitzvah on Shabbos, when the mitzvah doesn't practically apply, why is a lulav still considered designated for the mitzvah on Shabbos? A potential answer might be dependent on the reason behind *muktzeh machmas mitzvah*. Do we say that the reason why it is *muktzeh* is due to your removal of intent to use since it is an object designated for a mitzvah, or perhaps we can suggest an alternative explanation. The actual *kedushah* of the mitzvah is what gives this object its *muktzeh* status. Since there is a mitzvah that defines the usage of the object, there are therefore no other permissible usages.[25]

If we follow the second explanation, although it is very novel, we can perhaps understand *Pri Megadim*'s difference between a shofar and a lulav. Since *d'Oraisa* the mitzvah of shofar is only for one day, it is not considered to be designated for a mitzvah of two days. Even though we practically keep two days, the second day is only due to a doubt over when the actual day of Rosh Hashanah is. Therefore, the *kedushah* doesn't designate the shofar for two days since in essence it is only a one-day mitzvah. This answer is still innovative, as we find that the Gemara[26] treats שתי ימים של ר"ה כקדושה אחת - "both days of Rosh Hashanah as one cohesive day." We see that Rosh Hashanah is treated as one long day. Perhaps we can add that we can say that *memah nefsach* (whichever way you view it), there is only one day of Yom Tov. If the true day of Rosh Hashanah is on Shabbos then on that day Chazal decreed a prohibition to blow, and the following day is not Yom Tov either, hence there is no *muktzeh machmas mitzvah*. In the event that the first day is not the true Yom Tov, but rather it is to-

25. See chapter 24, where we elaborated on this in greater detail.
26. *Beitzah* 4b.

morrow, certainly today there is not yet a *muktzeh machmas mitzvah* restricting moving the shofar.

We could also suggest that since a shofar has other potential uses, its use as a mitzvah item and subsequent designation for a mitzvah only overrides its regular status as a vessel while it is in actual use for a mitzvah. Otherwise it reverts back to being a vessel. For this reason the shofar on Shabbos is a regular *kli shemelachto l'issur*. However, a lulav is not used for anything other than the mitzvah. It is not a *kli*, so its designation for the mitzvah includes even the days when the mitzvah doesn't practically apply, commencing from the first day, even if that falls on Shabbos. צ"ע.

Perhaps we can extend this ruling even to the night of Rosh Hashanah. Since the mitzvah is only relevant during the day, the designation for the mitzvah that limits the use of the shofar only for the sake of the mitzvah won't apply at night and you can move the shofar at night like a regular *kli shemelachto l'issur*.[27] Even without this innovation it is permitted to move a shofar at night because, as we've seen, it is a *kli shemelachto l'issur* and even if it is already designated for the mitzvah it is still permitted to move *l'tzorech mekomo*.

Summary

Rema holds that a lulav is not *muktzeh* even after one has finished performing the mitzvah himself *and* even if no one else may need to use his lulav. His reasoning is: *ein muktzeh l'chetzi Shabbos*, i.e., something cannot become *muktzeh* due to a designation of mind during Shabbos/Yom Tov. *Taz* argues that *ein muktzeh l'chetzi Shabbos* is only relevant to permit an item that was unfit and then the item subsequently becomes fit again. However, the lulav is in essence a branch; it intrinsically should be *muktzeh*. *Taz* suggests that the designation of this "branch" for the sake of a mitzvah upgrades it to a *kli shemelachto l'issur*. This would permit

---

27. In *Shemiras Shabbos K'Hilchasah*, ch. 22, note 67, R' Shlomo Zalman Auerbach suggests that since nowadays we don't use our shofaros during the year, they don't have the status of a *kli*. Yet he says that since on Rosh Hashanah day it is used, it becomes a *kli* and even from the night it becomes treated as a *kli*.

moving a lulav that is occupying needed space on Shabbos. However, we defended the opinion of *Rema* that when there is no physical change in the item causing a state of *muktzeh,* rather a designation of mind, we learn from *ein muktzeh l'chetzi Shabbos* that if the item was not *muktzeh* when Shabbos commenced. So this change in one's mind cannot impact the status of the item. On Shabbos Sukkos (and all year round) the lulav reverts back to being intrinsically *muktzeh* since it has no current purpose, referred to as *muktzeh machmas gufo.*

Answers

1. According to *Magen Avraham* and *Taz,* when one is sure there is no further need for the lulav, one can no longer move it. *Rema* is lenient, for all of Yom Tov he holds it remains not *muktzeh.*
2. A shofar even on Shabbos Rosh Hashanah is a *kli.* One can therefore move it for its sake and to make space.
3. Nowadays that we don't shake lulav on Shabbos, our lulav becomes *muktzeh machmas gufo* and one can't move it. According to the *Taz* there might be grounds to be lenient to move it *l'tzorech gufo* and *l'tzorech mekomo,* but in a case where one wants to move it to protect the lulav, one can't be lenient.

Chapter 30, Part 1

שיטת ר' שמעון

Rebbe Shimon's Opinion

To what extent does Rebbe Shimon agree to *muktzeh*?

Throughout the Gemara [1] we find the phrase ר' שמעון לית ליה מוקצה - "Rebbe Shimon doesn't hold of *muktzeh*." This is difficult to understand at face value since we find that the halachah follows Rebbe Shimon [2] and yet the halachos of *muktzeh* span over five *simanim* in *Shulchan Aruch*. We need to understand to what extent Rebbe Shimon argues on Rebbe Yehudah and when he agrees to *muktzeh*. Then we can come back to understand the true intent behind the Gemara's phrase.

Beis Yosef[3] provides a list of categories of *muktzeh* to that Rebbe Shimon agrees to:

1) *Muktzeh machmas gufo*. This is the quintessential *muktzeh* item - an object that has no functional use on the day of Shabbos, e.g., stones, pebbles, money. Such items have the most stringent rules of *muktzeh* governing them.

2) *Muktzeh machmas chisaron kis*. This type of *muktzeh* is set aside only to be used for its specific use due to its value or fragility. We've seen *muktzeh machmas chisaron kis* is an extreme case of *muktzeh*; even during the week one doesn't use this item for any given use, but rather just for what it's specifically designed for. Therefore the designation is so strong even Rebbe Shimon agrees to it. [4]

---

1. On more than ten occasions we find this phrase, including: *Shabbos* 43b, 44a, 44b, 45a, 45b, 46b, 127a, and 143a; *Beitzah* 2a and 30b.

2. *Shabbos* 156b brings a dispute about this. The consensus of the *poskim* is with the opinion that *paskens* like Rebbe Shimon.

3. *Siman* 310.

4. This is explicit in 157a.

3) *Grogeros v'tzimukim.* Dates and grapes that one placed on the roof to dry are *muktzeh.* Since they lose their fitness for consumption during the drying process, they become *muktzeh.* This status remains even if they finish drying and are now ready on Shabbos. The reason is since through the act of putting them to dry one has actively begun a process that will cause them to become unfit (*dichui b'yadayim*), this act coupled with the fact that they are currently unfit for use is considered a great act of *haktzaah.*[5]

4) A lit candle. The Gemara[6] says Rebbe Shimon agrees that a lit candle is *muktzeh.* The conclusion of the Gemara is that since the candle is supporting the wick, which in turn is supporting the flame, and the flame is *muktzeh,* the lamp becomes a *bosis* to the flame.

5) *Muktzeh machmas issur.* He also agrees that any object whose use is unattainable due to an *issur* that prevents its use is *muktzeh.* The severity of this *muktzeh* is that even if the *issur* is removed on Shabbos, the item still remains *muktzeh.* (We will see whether this is specifically when one doesn't anticipate the *issur* to be removed, known as *eino yoshev u'metzapeh,* or if this is only when in addition one positively sets aside the item, known as *dichui b'yadayim.*) An example of this is *kos v'ashashis* (lanterns and a cup), where, due to the large amount of oil one puts inside them, he doesn't anticipate being able to use the vessel or the oil on Shabbos. So even if the flame is extinguished, the leftover oil and vessel are *muktzeh.*

6) *Muktzeh machmas mitzvah.*[7] A candle that is functioning as one's Shabbos lights is *muktzeh* because it is designated for the mitzvah of Shabbos candles.

7) *Nolad.* Although it is not brought by *Beis Yosef* in his list, it is explicit[8] that Rebbe Shimon agrees to certain scenarios of *nolad.* In chapter 27, part

5. This is a unique category; unlike the other exceptions, which all are categories of *muktzeh* that Rebbe Shimon agrees to, this is not a category of *muktzeh* but rather a specific case.

6. *Shabbos* 44a.

7. Ibid. 45a.

8. *Eiruvin* 45b.

3, we elaborated on this category of *muktzeh* and why Rebbe Shimon agrees to it in specific situations.

Can we find any similarities between these cases? *Meiri*[9] explains that there are more than fifty subcategories of *muktzeh*. Thus, when the Gemara claims that Rebbe Shimon doesn't hold of *muktzeh*, that just implies that of all the opinions among the *Tannaim* he is the most lenient; he holds of the fewest types of *muktzeh*.

Two Categories of Muktzeh

Meiri[10] categorizes different groups of *muktzeh*, saying there are two main umbrella categories: *muktzeh gamur/muktzeh b'etzem* and *muktzeh machmas hachanah*. The former is when the reason for the item to be *muktzeh* is due to something inherent in the item, e.g., its value causes one to treat the item carefully, or the item hasn't yet been manufactured to serve as a vessel and so it is currently useless. Rebbe Shimon agrees to this category of *muktzeh*.

Rebbe Shimon agrees that *grogeros v'tzimukim* are *muktzeh*. The Gemara explains that this is when they are in a state where they are not fit to be consumed as they are still in the process of drying. *Meiri* shows why Rebbe Shimon concedes: The reason for these fruits to be *muktzeh* are inherent; they are currently not good fruit and therefore belong to the former category of *muktzeh gamur*, which Rebbe Shimon agrees to.

Muktzeh machmas hachanah is when there is no inherent reason why this item should be *muktzeh*. There is no flaw in the item itself, but rather the object has another purpose it is meant for besides the use applicable to Shabbos. For example, dates set aside for selling are themselves fit; no

---

9. Found in his introduction to *Maseches Beitzah*.

10. *Beis HaBechirah* of *Meiri Maseches Beitzah* 2a:

״ומ״מ *מוקצה* שאנו עסוקין בו עכשו הוא מוקצה מצד שאדם מסיח דעתו ממנו לא מחמת איסור ולא מחמת מיאוס ולא מחמת סבות אחרות אלא **שהוא דבר שמן הסתם אין דעתו של אדם עליו לאכילה** ונאסר מ״מ אא״כ הכינו מערב יום טוב וגלה דעתו שלבו עליו **והוא הנקרא מוקצה מחמת הכנה** כגון תמרים העומדים לסחורה ושורים העומדים לחרישה ותרנגולת העומדת לגדל ביצים אף על פי שהביצים עומדים לאכילה ועז לחלבה ומוקצה זה אסור לדעת ר׳ יהודה בין ביום טוב בין בשבת ולדעת ר׳ שמעון מותר בין ביום טוב בין בשבת״

inherent flaw forces one to think he will not use these dates on Shabbos, but they are designated for a specific purpose - selling. Rebbe Yehudah holds that since the item is designated for a specific purpose that is not Shabbos related the owner doesn't treat this item as prepared for Shabbos. Since he perceives it as unprepared, it's treated as *muktzeh*. However, Rebbe Shimon holds that since the object itself doesn't trigger a person to remove his mind from using it, the item itself is considered prepared and hence not *muktzeh*.[11]

Beis Yosef's Presentation of Rebbe Shimon

Beis Yosef presents the same idea in a slightly different manner. He says that when there is a reason inherent to the use of the object that causes it to be *muktzeh*, in such instances Rebbe Shimon agrees to it being *muktzeh*. He says this explains why Rebbe Shimon agrees to *muktzeh machmas gufo*. Such items have a total lack of potential use; the inherent flaw is so great to the extent that Rebbe Shimon agrees a person doesn't think to use such

11. *Talmid HaRamban* (*Shabbos* 157a) says when the Gemara concludes the that halachah is like Rebbe Shimon with the exception of *muktzeh machmas issur*, the Gemara alternatively could have said: הלכה כרבי יהודה בר ממוקצה סתם. He is saying that this phrase, "*muktzeh stam*," encapsulates all the cases Rebbe Shimon doesn't agree to *muktzeh*. The reason for the item being *muktzeh* is "*stam*," i.e., there is no inherent reason. This is the same division of categories of *muktzeh* we are seeing explicit in *Meiri*.
This can explain the phrase: ר׳ שמעון לית ליה מוקצה — "Rebbe Shimon doesn't hold of *muktzeh*." It means that Rebbe Shimon doesn't hold of any cases of *muktzeh stam*. All the cases he agrees to are *muktzeh* due to the item not being prepared. That is a different reason for *muktzeh* that the Gemara is not alluding to when making this statement.
Derishah (*siman* 310, point 2) brings a different text to that which we have in our *Beis Yosef*. Our text reads that Rebbe Shimon agrees to *muktzeh machmas issur*, and then *Beis Yosef* goes on to list examples, such a *muktzeh machmas gufo*. It doesn't seem accurate; why is *muktzeh machmas gufo* classified as *muktzeh machmas issur*? Rather, *Derishah*'s text reads that Rebbe Shimon agrees to *muktzeh machmas muktzeh*. This phrase means to say that anything that should be *muktzeh* because of the general, simple reason of *muktzeh*, i.e., the item is intrinsically not prepared, Rebbe Shimon agrees to this category.

an item. We can also explain that this is why Rebbe Shimon agrees that a *kli shemelachto l'issur* is also *muktzeh*. The *issurim* that limit the object from being used for its regular purpose render the item to have an intrinsic flaw, so it is *muktzeh*. (However, Chazal treated this *muktzeh* leniently and permitted its movement *l'tzorech gufo u'mekomo*.)[12]

He further says that this explains Rebbe Shimon's concession by *muktzeh machmas mitzvah*. This is an object that is presently being used for the sake of the mitzvah, such as a sukkah during Sukkos. We say that there is a current designation that is limiting one's unabridged use of the object, hence it is *muktzeh* even according to Rebbe Shimon. So too with certain *muktzeh machmas issur*, such as a large lamp filled with enough oil to remain burning for the duration of Shabbos. Its use can only come about through extinguishing the flame, which is forbidden on Shabbos. There is presently an *issur* tied into the usage of this item, which causes a designation due to its inevitable unobtainable status, hence it is *muktzeh*.

Furthermore, Rebbe Shimon permits moving a regular candle once extinguished, even though it was burning when Shabbos commenced and at that time it was *muktzeh*. *Beis Yosef* explains that we see a further dimension in Rebbe Shimon's opinion: Even if something isn't currently fit for use, but one has in mind for a later eventuality that may cause it to become fit, that mind-set is sufficient to remove *muktzeh*. **The depth behind Rebbe Shimon's stance is that as long as there may be a potential use this item can be used for, even if it's an extremely unlikely one, one is always open to that possibility and thus he doesn't remove his intention.**

A further example to this is that according to one opinion[13] Rebbe Shimon permits feeding a carcass to an animal, even if the animal sud-

---

12. This is different from how we explained in the introduction to *muktzeh* why Rebbe Shimon agrees to *kli shemelachto l'issur*. We brought that it is a dispute between the *Rishonim* whether Rebbe Shimon agrees to this category at all. Those who say he does agree explain this based on the principle of the *Acharonim* that there are two different types of *muktzeh*; *kli shemelachto l'issur* belongs to *gezeiras keilim*, which is agreed upon by Rebbe Shimon.

13. *Beitzah* 27b, s.v. מר בריה דרב יוסף.

denly died on Shabbos. When Shabbos began the animal was *muktzeh*, it had no permissible use. Nevertheless one anticipates that maybe the animal might die. Therefore in the unlikely eventuality that it does suddenly die, one can use the carcass and it is no longer *muktzeh*.

This explanation has now clarified, and limited, the leniencies of Rebbe Shimon to be relevant only with cases of *muktzeh* that are not *muktzeh gamur*. In general, Rebbe Shimon understands that a person is more open to using items, to the extent that unless the item intrinsically isn't fit or one has no anticipation that he will need the item it is not *muktzeh*.

This approach can be demonstrated with the following example: *muktzeh machmas meyus* is an object that under usual circumstances one would not use due to its disgusting state. However, despite it being disgusting, one *could* make use of it in desperate circumstances, even though under regular circumstances it's unlikely one will use it since it is nonetheless possible. According to Rebbe Shimon it isn't *muktzeh*. *Rabbeinu Tam* captures the essence of this principle as follows: ר"ש סבר דעתו על הכל - "Rebbe Shimon holds that one's mind encompasses everything."[14]

We can further illustrate this understanding of Rebbe Shimon with the following *Taz*.[15] *Shulchan Aruch*[16] rules that raw meat is not *muktzeh* since it can be eaten raw. *Sach* points out that the Gemara discusses only raw goose meat, not all meat. He answers that there are two criteria that determine whether something is *muktzeh* or not: (1) if it is fit for use; (2)

---

14. This understanding of Rebbe Shimon's opinion may be another example of Rebbe Shimon *l'shitaso*. We know Rebbe Shimon doesn't necessarily follow the current status of the item whether or not to consider something *muktzeh*, but rather he considers the future possibilities too. We also find throughout *Shas* that he holds of the rule: "*Kol ha'omed... dami* — Since this item is destined for X, we already treat it as if X took place." He looks beyond the present even when assessing the present situation and evaluates even based on what is not apparent to the eye. Perhaps this is another example of such thinking. We take into account what is hidden in a person's mind; he is prepared to use it if necessary. Rebbe Shimon looks at what will be. In the future it will be permissible if the *issur* is removed, so we can already judge it now based on that.

15. 308, point 20.

16. 308:31.

if it is commonly used for this purpose. Rebbe Yehudah, who argues with Rebbe Shimon, holds that both of these criteria are necessary in order for something to be permitted. Hence the Gemara that establishes that only raw goose meat is permitted is going according to Rebbe Yehudah, since goose meat is the only meat commonly eaten raw. However, according to Rebbe Shimon, there is no need for it to be commonly used, as long as it is technically fit for use. We say that it is not *muktzeh*. Therefore all types of raw meat could technically be eaten raw and so are not *muktzeh*. This explains why *Shulchan Aruch*, who *paskens* according to Rebbe Shimon, is correct in permitting all types of raw meat, for the sole reason that they could theoretically be consumed raw.

Why Does Rebbe Shimon Disagree with Migo D'Iskatzi?

A regular candle that is extinguished on Shabbos remains *muktzeh* according to Rebbe Yehudah. Even though there is no current reason why it should be *muktzeh*, since it was *muktzeh* when Shabbos commenced we evoke *migo d'iskatzi* to forbid it all of Shabbos. If Rebbe Shimon agrees that while the candle is burning it is *muktzeh*, why doesn't he hold that *migo d'iskatzi* forbids it for all of Shabbos?

As elaborated in previous chapters,[17] *Rashi*[18] explains the reason we say *migo d'iskatzi* is because "*muchan l'Shabbos b'inan* - we need it prepared for Shabbos." Chazal learn from the *pasuk* of "*v'hechinu*" that objects must be prepared for use before Shabbos commences. Hence they decreed that something that isn't ready for use is forbidden to move, known as *muktzeh*. Something that isn't prepared at the beginning of Shabbos gets a title of being *eino muchan* (not prepared) and that status remains on the object throughout the duration of Shabbos even if it subsequently gets prepared on Shabbos, and thus it remains forbidden.

We explained that Rebbe Shimon holds that a person is open to any possibility that might occur. If there is a possibility that the *issur* will be

---

17. Chapters 20, 23.

18. *Beitzah* 26b, s.v. ואי דלא – אי דלא אחזו בין השמשות ודאי אסורין דאין כאן הכנה מבעוד יום ומאן דאית ליה מוקצה הכנה מבעוד יום בעי.

removed, one doesn't remove his intention, Based on this we can explain that for that eventual outcome the item is treated as already prepared. This is because one anticipates this outcome and it doesn't need his intervention to occur. If Rebbe Shimon treats these items as prepared, there is no ability for *migo d'iskatzi* to perpetuate the *muktzeh* status throughout Shabbos.

We can see the correlation between the points upon which Rebbe Shimon argues on Rebbe Yehudah. Arguing on *migo d'iskatzi* and the several categories of *muktzeh* he permits are based upon the same idea that Rebbe Shimon doesn't consider things as set aside as long as they have some potential function.

Rashba's Connection between Migo and Rebbe Shimon

We can extrapolate from *Rashba* and *Ran* that they deviate slightly from how we've explained the two disputes of Rebbe Shimon. *Ran* explains that Rebbe Yehudah always follows *stam daas* (the natural mind-set). For example, with *tamri d'iska* (dates designated for merchandise), the regular attitude is that one won't take from them for personal use. Therefore, he determines that it is *muktzeh* based on the natural mind-set. *Rashba*[19] also says *migo d'iskatzi* is based on the natural mind-set of a person. If at the beginning of Shabbos one doesn't intend on using this item on Shabbos because it is not fit, we presume that he doesn't intend to use it the entire Shabbos, even if it becomes possible to use. *migo d'iskatzi* isn't a rule based on a lack of preparation like we saw in *Rashi*. Rather it's part of the designation in one's mind; a person bases his thoughts for the entire Shabbos based on the beginning of Shabbos.

Afikei Yam[20] also discusses why Rebbe Shimon does not hold of *migo d'iskatzi*. He asks: Is it because he doesn't require preparation and hence there is no ground for it to be *muktzeh*, or does he agree to the teaching from the *pasuk* of "*v'hechinu*" that items must be prepared? Rather he

---

19. *Beitzah* 30b.
20. Section 2, *siman* 19.

holds that even if something requires preparation at the onset of Shabbos, if subsequently on Shabbos it will become prepared, that is sufficient to consider it already prepared now.

He posits that since we find[21] that Rebbe Shimon agrees to cases of *muktzeh,* such as certain types of large lamps, it's more logical that he agrees there is a requirement of preparation. Rebbe Shimon holds that even when something is *muktzeh machmas issur* and we would invoke *migo d'iskatzi,* if one is *yoshev u'metzapeh* (anticipates the removal of the *issur*), it is not *muktzeh. Afikei Yam* explains that with awaiting it can be considered as if the item is prepared.[22]

Another proof we find that "anticipation" causes something to become prepared can be learned from the rule of *tenai* (stipulation) by *muktzeh.*[23] The *Rishonim* explain that such a stipulation works even according to the opinion of Rebbe Yehudah. How can the stipulation change the object from not being prepared to being prepared? It must be that when one stipulates that he wishes to use it when possible, this has the same effect as "anticipation" according to Rebbe Shimon. This causes there to be the necessary preparation. So too a stipulation according to Rebbe Yehudah affords the necessary preparation.

(Some[24] explain that there are two ways one can prepare something: the object itself is lacking, one thereby physically prepares it for use (*hachanah mitzad hachefetz*), or the object isn't physically lacking in readiness but one has to do an act to show he is prepared to use the item (*hachanah mitzad hagavra*). They explain that Rebbe Shimon and Rebbe

---

21. *Shabbos* 44a.

22. *Afikei Yam* explains that with this investigation we can understand Ulah's opinion (mentioned in *Shabbos* 44a), who holds that even in cases of large lamps and lanterns, where one doesn't anticipate the flame to be extinguished, i.e., there is no anticipation, even so Rebbe Shimon holds it is not *muktzeh.* Ulah holds that Rebbe Shimon doesn't require any form of preparation. Hence even without anticipation now that the source of *muktzeh* is removed, it is not lacking anything.

23. A stipulation is relevant to an object whose cause of *muktzeh* is expected to be removed at some point. One stipulates that he wishes to use the object when the cause of *muktzeh* is removed.

24. *Harerei Kedem, siman* 54, and I heard like this from Mori V'Rabi R' Ariav Ozer.

Yehudah are arguing over what type of preparation is necessary to prepare an item. Rebbe Yehudah requires *hachanah mitzad hagavra* and Rebbe Shimon only needs *hachanah mitzad hachefetz*. Dates set aside for sale are something the owner intends not to use, since he has set them aside for sale. He hasn't prepared them for his use on Shabbos even though from the point of view of the fruits they are good dates, ready to be consumed. According to Rebbe Yehudah the preparation that is incumbent upon the person hasn't been done, so it is *muktzeh*. However, according to Rebbe Shimon's requirements it shouldn't be *muktzeh* because there is no *hachanah mitzad hachefetz* lacking, and the lack of personal preparation is irrelevant.)

It's All One Dispute

Ran[25] explains that Rebbe Shimon and Rebbe Yehudah are arguing over only one point: *migo d'iskatzi*. He explains that every case of *muktzeh machmas meyus* is where there is a disgusting vessel, but nonetheless one wants to use it now. In effect the owner is saying the reason it was originally *muktzeh*, i.e., the fact it was disgusting, is no longer relevant since he is presently prepared to use it. *Ran* explains that this is the point on which Rebbe Shimon and Rebbe Yehudah disagree. Even though now there is no positive reason causing it to be *muktzeh*, it nonetheless remains so because of *migo d'iskatzi*. Therefore, Rebbe Shimon, who doesn't hold of *migo d'iskatzi*, permits *muktzeh machmas meyus* once the owner decides he wishes to use it. The dispute by *muktzeh machmas issur* is a result of the same reasoning. Since now there is no reason for it to be *muktzeh*, as the *issur* has been removed, the only reason to forbid is due to a *migo d'iskatzi* since it wasn't ready when Shabbos came in. So again, Rebbe Shimon permits because he doesn't hold of *migo d'iskatzi*, while Rebbe Yehudah does. *Afikei Yam* infers that *Beis Yosef* learned Rebbe Shimon in the same fashion, *Beis Yosef* only writes that the dispute is whether we say *migo d'iskatzi*. He extrapolates from this inference that this is the only

---

25. End of *Maseches Beitzah*.

area of dispute and therefore *Beis Yosef* will explain like *Ran*. We earlier suggested a different understanding in *Beis Yosef*.

Part 2

What's the Necessary Ingredient - Anticipation or Setting Aside?

In the opinion of Rebbe Shimon, there is a distinction between a small candle and a large candle. The Gemara[26] explains that a small candle is *datei ilavei* - "his intention is to use it." In other places the Gemara[27] says: אדם יושב ומצפה מתי תכבה נרו - "A person sits anticipating his candle to be extinguished so he can use it." These two phrases reveal to us that that the person needs to have a positive interest in the object despite it being temporarily forbidden to move in order for the item not to be *muktzeh* subsequently on Shabbos. Similarly, regarding a sukkah, the Gemara draws the same distinction. Even Rebbe Shimon concedes that a sturdy sukkah that falls down on Yom Tov remains *muktzeh machmas issur*, since a person doesn't anticipate it to collapse. However, a person waits for a flimsy sukkah to collapse, hence if it does fall the material is permitted: אדם יושב ומצפה מתי תפול סוכתו.

The *Rishonim* argue over what is the key factor in these two scenarios causing Rebbe Shimon to concede. Is it the fact that one doesn't anticipate the removal of the *muktzeh*, or is it that one actively sets the *muktzeh* aside? Presented differently, does Rebbe Shimon hold something is not *muktzeh* only when one is *yoshev u'metzapeh* (anticipates the reason for the *muktzeh* to be removed), or even if one doesn't anticipate but as long as he doesn't actively set it aside?

Rosh, Maggid Mishnah, and *Rashi* learn that not *yoshev u'metzapeh* (not yearning) alone is insufficient of a reason for Rebbe Shimon to con-

---

26. 44a.
27. 46b.

cede. Rebbe Shimon agrees it is *muktzeh* only when it is coupled with a *dichui b'yadayim* (active setting aside). However, *Rashba, Ran,* and *Baal HaMeor* learn that a lack of anticipation alone renders the item *muktzeh.*

Chullin 15a

This dispute is brought out from the following Gemara.[28] Rebbe Yitzchak Bar Ada *paskens* that if one slaughters an animal for a sick person, it's forbidden for anyone else to use the meat since it is *muktzeh.* R' Dimi *paskens* that if one slaughters for a sick a person, it is permitted for others to consume since it is not *muktzeh.*

Rashi learns that there is no dispute between these two sages. Rebbe Yitzchak is referring only to when the sickness developed on Shabbos. So when Shabbos began one didn't anticipate any potential usage with the live animal, hence he set it aside and it remains *muktzeh.* R' Dimi is referring to when the sickness developed prior to Shabbos. Since one anticipated a potential use with the animal, it is not *muktzeh.*

Rif only quotes the halachah brought by R' Dimi, without any qualification, unlike *Rashi. Rosh*[29] infers that *Rif* understands this Gemara is according to Rebbe Yehudah (hence why it is *muktzeh* even if one was sick prior to Shabbos). However, we *pasken* like Rebbe Shimon that unless there is a positive rejection it is not *muktzeh.* Even if the sickness developed only on Shabbos, one didn't do any positive act to show his disinterest in the animal and therefore there is no reason for it to be *muktzeh.* There is no anticipation that someone will be sick, yet it is not *muktzeh* because there is no positive dismissal. We see that *Rif* learns that Rebbe Shimon demands two criteria for something to be *muktzeh.*

Ran[30] argues on *Rif.* He agrees with *Rashi* that R' Dimi only permits if he was sick prior to Shabbos. We can suggest that he argues because he learns the key factor to preempt *muktzeh* is that one anticipates the use

---

28. *Chullin* 15b.
29. Ibid., point 20.
30. *Shabbos, Dapei HaRif* 17a.

of the item, so unless someone was already sick, one doesn't await the use of the animal and it remains *muktzeh*.

Rashba[31] mentions these two possibilities: whether Rebbe Shimon requires both a positive setting aside and that there is no anticipation in order for there to be *muktzeh*, or it may be enough that there is no anticipation even without an active rejection. He says a difference that follows is whether an animal that was slaughtered on Shabbos is *muktzeh*. In such cases there is no positive setting aside of the animal when Shabbos began, yet there is a lack of anticipation that the animal will be prepared. If Rebbe Shimon requires both criteria, it won't be *muktzeh*, but if he requires just a lack of anticipation it will be *muktzeh*.

The Status of an Animal That Was Slaughtered on Shabbos

Rambam[32] and *Raavid* argue over this case. *Rambam* writes that if an animal is slaughtered on Shabbos for a sick person, a healthy person can eat the raw meat, as it is not *muktzeh*. However, *Raavid* qualifies this halachah to a case where the patient was sick already before Shabbos began. *Maggid Mishnah* explains *Rambam* holds that without positive rejection it isn't *muktzeh*, while *Raavid* holds there must be anticipation for it not to be *muktzeh*.[33]

---

31. *Chullin* 15a, s.v. עד כאן ו, s.v. לענין, גם בתוה"ב ב"ר ש"ד.

32. *Hilchos Shabbos* 2:9.

33. In *Hilchos Yom Tov* 2:16, *Rambam* only permits if the animal was sick prior to Shabbos. The apparent difference is presumably because in *Hilchos Yom Tov Rambam* follows Rebbe Yehudah, and certainly Rebbe Yehudah is stricter on his requirements for something not to be *muktzeh*.
In *Avi Ezri, Hilchos Shabbos* 2:9, he raises the following problem: If *Raavid* is arguing with *Rambam* and *paskens* like Rebbe Yehudah, then why when *Rambam* permits feeding a carcass to an animal does *Raavid* not further qualify that it is only true if the animal was already sick prior to Shabbos? Furthermore, *Rambam* permits using a vessel that smashed on Shabbos, even if the new function available is not akin to what the vessel originally performed. This *psak* is not in accordance with Rebbe Yehudah, so why doesn't *Raavid* not argue again? R' Sach concludes that certainly *Raavid paskens* like Rebbe Shimon, hence the last two cases he agrees to *Rambam*. So why does he require the patient to be sick prior to Shabbos in the case of a slaughtered animal?

(*Tosafos*[34] differs with *Rashba*. He understands that even if Rebbe Shimon requires anticipation, a healthy animal that was slaughtered can still be permitted. He says one anticipates that maybe a child or mentally ill person might slaughter the animal: אדם יושב ומצפה שמא ישחטנה חרש שוטה וקטן.[35] It's a novelty that one anticipates even something so unlikely. We will address this point later.)

Gra[36] lists the different opinions: *Rashi*,[37] *Raavid, Tosafos, Ramban,* and *Ran* are stringent. They hold that Rebbe Shimon is only lenient when

Ramban (*Chullin* 15a, s.v. אבל שוחט וגם מלחמות ביצה דף כא.) posits that an item which requires one's intervention for the possibility of using it on Shabbos is not considered prepared when Shabbos comes in. That is even true when it is permitted to do such an act of preparing. An animal that needs to be slaughtered to consume is not considered prepared, hence it is *muktzeh*. These are the only cases of *muktzeh machmas issur*. Even if one will have a *heter* to slaughter the animal for a sick person, since it still requires one's involvement to prepare it, we treat it as if the prohibition is constantly on the animal and not removed even once he slaughters it.

In contrast, something that doesn't require one's intervention to become prepared, but just happens on its own, is considered prepared when Shabbos began. This is true even though Shabbos imposes a restriction on using the item. That does change the fact that the item is treated as prepared. The *issur* of Shabbos is viewed as external and doesn't change the essence that this is a prepared item. An animal that dies becomes permitted on its own. The animal is prepared when Shabbos began despite being forbidden to use. That *issur* is just peripheral to its status, so when it suddenly dies there is no longer any *issur* in using the item and it is not forbidden due to *muktzeh* because it was never lacking preparation.

Based on his explanation of *Ramban*, R' Sach suggests this is what *Raavid* holds. Only in a case such as slaughtering the animal, where the possibility to use it came about via one's intervention, is it considered to still be forbidden. However, an animal that just dies suddenly or vessels that just smash are not considered unprepared and can be used when they die or smash respectively.

34. *Chullin* 14a, s.v. מחתכין.

35. Providing an adult is watching over the slaughtering, the animal is kosher. However, the commentators are bothered why there isn't an additional problem of *maaseh Shabbos*.

36. 318, point 4.

37. There are conflicting implications in *Rashi*. In *Beitzah* 26b, s.v. ואי, he says the opinion that holds of *muktzeh* needs preparation, while the opinion that doesn't hold of *muktzeh* doesn't need preparation. If Rebbe Shimon doesn't need preparation, surely he doesn't require anticipation. ואכתי צ"ע.

there is anticipation. However, *Rif, Rambam, Rosh,* and Rabbeinu Yonah are all lenient and unless there is also a positive rejection it is permitted. *Shulchan Aruch* twice[38] rules in favor of the lenient opinion. He permits feeding a carcass to dogs even if the animal was in full health when Shabbos began. Furthermore, he permits this when the sick person whom an animal was slaughtered for only became sick on Shabbos. We clearly see that he follows the opinion that Rebbe Shimon does not require anticipation to permit the *muktzeh.*

Tur in *Hilchos Shabbos*[39] *paskens* that an animal which dies on Shabbos can be fed to the dogs. He doesn't qualify that it is only if it was sick before Shabbos. However, in *Hilchos Yom Tov,*[40] he does qualify that if it was healthy before Shabbos then Rebbe Shimon agrees that it is *muktzeh.* According to what we've seen, these two halachos are contradictory. Does *Tur* require anticipation or rejection? *Preisha*[41] raises this contradiction and resolves that *Tur* relied on what he added in *Hilchos Yom Tov* and intended that also in *Hilchos Shabbos.* Accordingly, *Tur*'s opinion is one needs anticipation for Rebbe Shimon to hold it isn't *muktzeh.*

The Status of Animal That Dies on Shabbos

The Gemara[42] writes that Rebbe Shimon holds that one can feed his dog the carcass of an animal that died on Shabbos. The ensuing dispute between Mar Bar Ameimar and Mar Bar R' Yosef is whether this leniency is only when the animal was already sick before Shabbos and therefore one anticipated the death, or whether it's even if the animal died unexpectedly. Mar Bar Ameimar holds that since the animal is *muktzeh* (because you can't slaughter the animal; it's *muktzeh machmas issur*), unless one anticipates the *muktzeh* status to be removed, the status conferred on the animal at the onset of Shabbos will forbid it throughout Shabbos, even if it

38. 318:2 and 324:7.
39. 324:4.
40. *Siman* 518.
41. 324, point 4.
42. *Beitzah* 27a.

dies. Therefore, Mar Bar Ameimar learns that the only scenario Rebbe Shimon permits feeding the carcass is when the animal was sick prior to Shabbos, thereby one anticipated the eventual use. Mar Bar R' Yosef argues that Rebbe Shimon permits using the carcass even if the animal was fully healthy when Shabbos began.

Rashba explains that the only reason Mar Bar R' Yosef holds that an animal which dies on Shabbos is not *muktzeh* according to Rebbe Shimon is that since death is common, and therefore there is anticipation that the *issur* will be removed: אדם יושב ומצפה מתי תמות בהמתו. Implicit, he would hold that an animal that is slaughtered on Shabbos is *muktzeh* since there is no anticipation. (Mar Bar Ameimar argues there is no anticipation even for death, hence the animal must be sick prior to Shabbos.) So surely this Gemara is a refutation to those who hold Rebbe Shimon requires also a setting aside for it to be *muktzeh*. Both the *Amoraim* here just require there to be anticipation for it not to be *muktzeh*. The dispute is just whether there is anticipation or not.

Those *Rishonim* could explain that the dispute between the sages is exactly this point: What does Rebbe Shimon require? Mar Bar R' Yosef holds Rebbe Shimon requires rejection, which by an animal there isn't and hence it is not *muktzeh*. Mar Bar Ameimar holds Rebbe Shimon requires anticipation and one doesn't await for an animal to die. If this is how these *Rishonim* are learning, they must *pasken* like Mar Bar R' Yosef that one can feed any carcass to his animals.[43]

The Gemara[44] says that fruit plucked by a non-Jew on Shabbos is *muktzeh*, and even Rebbe Shimon agrees with this. According to those who require anticipation, it is understood; one doesn't anticipate a

---

43. This answer is alluded to by *Gra, siman* 324, point 8. *Afikei Yam* also explains this idea that the dispute between the *Rishonim* is in essence whom we *pasken* like. In part 1 we mentioned *Afikei Yam*'s investigation whether Rebbe Shimon requires preparation or not. He suggests those two possibilities can explain this dispute. Mar Bar Ameimar, who holds there is no need for the animal to be sick, also holds that there is no requirement of any preparation. However, Mar Bar R' Yosef holds that we say that the necessary preparation before Shabbos is not lacking only with a sick animal when one anticipates its death.

44. *Beitzah* 24b.

non-Jew to pluck fresh fruits to give to Jews and hence it's *muktzeh*. However, according to those who also require rejection, just like there is no rejection with an animal, surely that criteria is missing by fresh fruits?

Ran needs just a lack of anticipation for something to be *muktzeh*. In line with this he explains simply that anything plucked is *muktzeh* because one doesn't anticipate grass or fruits to be plucked.

Rashi[45] provides us with an answer for the other *Rishonim*. *Rashi* posits that since one could have theoretically plucked the fruits himself before Shabbos, not doing so is as if he pushed them aside! This is even relevant with a non-Jew's fruit, since we don't differentiate between one's own fruits and a non-Jew's. In contrast, an animal is much more difficult to slaughter, so we *can't* extract from the fact that he didn't slaughter it before Shabbos that he has set it aside. *Rashba*[46] also explains the fruits are *muktzeh* since one set it aside by not plucking them before Shabbos. We can deduce from *Rashi* and *Rashba* that they deviated from the simple explanation, like that of *Ran*, because they hold that for something to be *muktzeh* one must set it aside as well.

Shulchan Aruch's Conclusion

Until now we've seen Rebbe Shimon's opinion and how the *Rishonim* differ in their conclusions when exactly Rebbe Shimon agrees and disagrees. When applying this to practical halachah, an extra complication arises. The Gemara[47] *paskens* like Rebbe Shimon's opinion, but not entirely: בכל השבת כולה הלכה כרבי שמעון לבר ממוקצה מחמת איסור ומאי ניהו נר שהדליקו בה באותה שבת - "In cases of *muktzeh* due to an *issur* encroaching the usage of the item, we do not follow Rebbe Shimon. An example of such is a candle that is extinguished on Shabbos." In light of this Gemara, when *paskening* like Rebbe Shimon we must be conscious that we can't follow all aspects of Rebbe Shimon's opinion.

---

45. Ibid., s.v. אם יש מאותו מין.

46. End of 122a, s.v. גמרא הא דתניא.

47. *Shabbos* 157a.

With this introduction, we can appreciate *Taz*'s[48] problem with *Shulchan Aruch*. *Shulchan Aruch* permits a healthy animal that was slaughtered for someone who only fell ill on Shabbos. *Taz* asks: This seemingly contradicts an earlier *psak* from *Shulchan Aruch*[49] that a lamp that was lit but is now extinguished is *muktzeh*. The reason is that since we *pasken migo d'iskatzi*, this forbids any item that was *muktzeh* at the onset of Shabbos (unlike the opinion of Rebbe Shimon, who permits even in such a case). If so, why is this animal now permitted? At the onset of Shabbos in its state of full health, it was *muktzeh*, so *Shulchan Aruch* should apply *migo d'iskatzi*!

To substantiate the question, we can add the following *Milchamos*.[50] *Ramban* says that since we *pasken* like Rebbe Yehudah by *muktzeh machmas issur*, we must *pasken* that if the patient fell ill on Shabbos the slaughtered animal will be *muktzeh* for others. *Ramban* adds the reason *Behag* and *She'iltos pasken* an animal that was slaughtered for a sick person is *muktzeh* under all circumstances is because we *pasken* like Rebbe Yehudah in such cases. We see like *Taz* is suggesting, that *l'halachah* it is *muktzeh*, so why does *Shulchan Aruch pasken* otherwise?

Taz answers that the parameters of *migo d'iskatzi* is that something that was *muktzeh* because of an *issur* encroaching the usage of this item, even when there is a development to the item at hand resulting in the disappearance of the *issur* in using this item, we view it is as if nothing developed from the state it was in when Shabbos began. For example, even once the candle is extinguished we still view the flame burning; even once the sukkah falls we view it as still upstanding, hence it's as if the *issur* still forbids the usage.

In contrast, nothing has developed in the cow; rather, now that there is someone who needs it and is allowed to slaughter the animal, the constraints of *muktzeh* on the cow are removed. Had the person been sick when Shabbos commenced, the animal wouldn't have been *muktzeh* from

48. 318:2.

49. 279:1.

50. *Chullin* 15b. He writes this also in *Chiddushim* there.

the onset of Shabbos. In such instances the only reason to forbid the item is because a person had a removal of awareness at the beginning of Shabbos. He didn't know the *muktzeh* status would be removed from the item. *Shulchan Aruch* follows Rebbe Shimon's opinion that it is irrelevant what the person was thinking, as long as the item is not *muktzeh* it is permitted only with matters pertaining to *hesech hadaas*. When the reason for the *muktzeh* pertains to the item being fit or not, *Shulchan Aruch paskens* like Rebbe Yehudah and disregards any development to the item.

The simplest answer to *Taz*'s question is given by *Pri Megadim*. He answers that the Gemara is only concluding to follow Rebbe Yehudah in cases when there is a positive setting aside, but when there is no positive setting aside, we still follow Rebbe Shimon, and as we've seen, *Shulchan Aruch* sides that a lack of anticipation alone doesn't render it *muktzeh*. The candle was set aside during *bein hashemashos*, so in such instances we follow Rebbe Yehudah and must evoke *migo d'iskatzi*, while the animal is not set aside. So even though it is *muktzeh* when Shabbos began, we follow Rebbe Shimon's stance on this object and if the *muktzeh* is removed one can use the item.[51] (*Taz*, who didn't answer, must understand that when the Gemara concludes that we follow Rebbe Yehudah in *muktzeh machmas issur* it means we *pasken* anticipation doesn't ever help, not just when there is an accompanying rejection. This is seemingly also how the aforementioned *Milchamos* learns, as he *paskens* in accordance with what *Taz* was asking.)

A Glaring Contradiction in Both Rashba and Rosh

Rosh[52] *paskens* that if one slaughters an animal for a sick person, even if he only became sick on Shabbos, it is still permitted for other people to eat and is not considered *muktzeh* according to Rebbe Shimon. The rea-

51. *Rashba* doesn't ask this question, but from what he explains in *Chullin* 14a, this idea is also apparent that only when there is a designation, like by a candle, does the Gemara *pasken* like Rebbe Yehudah. Also, *Tosafos* in *Shabbos* 157a says the Gemara is only following Rebbe Yehudah when there is also designation.

52. *Chullin*, ch. 1, point 20.

son is that we say that unless there is a rejection it is not *muktzeh,* even if there was no anticipation. *Gra*[53] says that *Rosh* contradicts himself; he *paskens* like Mar Bar Ameimar that Rebbe Shimon agrees that if a healthy animal dies on Shabbos it *can't* be fed to the dogs since there was no anticipation.[54] In this latter *psak* he requires anticipation for it not to be *muktzeh,* while before he requires just be no rejection for it not to be *muktzeh.*

The same contradiction exists in the opinion of *Rashba.* He *paskens* like Mar Bar Ameimar[55] that a carcass is *muktzeh,* yet is lenient that a slaughtered animal can be fed to an animal.

Afikei Yam recalls that he once saw the question of *Gra* but doesn't recall *Gra*'s answer (and laments that he doesn't have the explanation of *Gra* with him to check again). He therefore suggests his own answer instead. He says that *Tosafos* holds that an animal that is slaughtered on Shabbos is not *muktzeh* since we say: יושב ומצפה שמא ישחטנו חש"ו - "There is anticipation it will be slaughtered by a child, etc." This results that when it is available for use, it is not *muktzeh.* However, that specific anticipation only permits a case if the animal is slaughtered, not a case when the animal dies. The distinction is simple; we only apply *yoshev u'metzapeh* as a reason to negate a rejection when one wants that outcome. Having a kosher slaughtered animal is in one's interest. Therefore if it is actually slaughtered we can claim he was always awaiting this outcome. On the other hand, it is undesired for an animal to die. It is now forbidden for consumption and is only fit for dogs. Being consumed by animals is not what it was designated for originally and therefore without anticipation *Rosh* holds it is *muktzeh.* He brings a support to this from Abaye: מי דמי התם מעיקרא מוכן לאדם והשתא מוכן לכלבים, הכא מעיקרא מוכן לאדם והשתא מוכן לאדם. See the foot-

53. *Shulchan Aruch* 324:7.

54. *Gra* infers this from a subtle addition of *Rosh. Rosh* brings a Gemara that says a chicken cage is *muktzeh. Rosh* adds that when there is a dead chicken it is *muktzeh.* From the lack of qualification, *Gra* infers that *Rosh* holds that a chicken that dies suddenly is *muktzeh.*

55. *Avodas HaKodesh, shaar* 5.

notes for elaboration.[56] [57]

Gra suggests a similar answer: When the animal is slaughtered it is now available for human consumption. In contrast, when it dies, it can only be consumed by dogs and מוכן לאדם לא הוי מוכן לכלבים - something that is designated for human consumption is not prepared for dogs." Therefore, this state as a carcass is *muktzeh* since there was never any dismissal for this use. However, he rejects this as he asserts the rule מוכן לאדם לא הוי מוכן לכלבים is only true according to Rebbe Yehudah, but according to Rebbe Shimon we say, מוכן לאדם הוי מוכן לכלבים - even in its present state as a carcass it is considered to have been prepared, so it is not *muktzeh*.

Always Prepared for Its True Purpose

Chazon Ish[58] explains the opinion of Rebbe Shimon with great simplicity and with it the contradiction in *Rosh* falls away. He asks: What is the reason behind the opinion we mentioned earlier, that even if an animal dies suddenly it is not *muktzeh*? Why is it different from a large lantern, which Rebbe Shimon holds is *muktzeh*? Rebbe Shimon agrees that a strong hut

---

56. The Gemara suggests that Rebbe Yehudah, who holds that if an animal dies it is forbidden to feed the carcass to other animals, is the opinion brought in the Gemara that forbids eating on Shabbos an animal that was slaughtered for a sick person. To which Abaye refutes such a suggestion with the following distinction: Maybe Rebbe Yehudah only considers a dead animal not prepared for animals because prior to its death it was meant for man to consume and now it can be only consumed by animals. That is an outcome it wasn't prepared for. However, if the animal was slaughtered and so he himself can benefit, since it was originally meant for man to benefit from, and man can still benefit from it, Rebbe Yehudah can consider it prepared.

57. *Chullin* 14a. *Rashba* (s.v. אביי) asks: Even if it was meant for man, now that Shabbos arrived there was a prohibition in slaughtering it, which stopped one from using this animal for anything. If so, how could we ever entertain מוכן לאדם הוי מוכן לכלבים to permit its use, since it is not "prepared" for man? He answers that in this case there is no rejection that comes from a person; rather, there is just an *issur Shabbos* that has now stopped one from using it. Once the *issur* disappears without transgressing Shabbos, its state of preparation returns and it will be permitted.

58. *Kuntres HaMuktzeh, siman* 41, points 4 and 12, and see *siman* 43, point 7.

that falls down is *muktzeh* since there was no anticipation. Why is an animal different? He answers that anticipation is only necessary to permit a case where one wishes to use the object for a purpose it generally is not designated for. Regarding a purpose that is the usual purpose of this item, the item is always considered prepared for that specific purpose. If the item is prepared, it is not *muktzeh*. As we showed, Rebbe Shimon doesn't treat an item as *muktzeh* if it is prepared, regardless of whether one thinks he will use the item.

Let's apply this principle to a fallen hut where one wishes to now burn the firewood. A hut's general purpose is for shelter, not to burn, so the wood is considered unprepared regarding this use. If one was to anticipate the sukkah falling and the possibility of using the wood for burning, he makes it prepared, but without such an anticipation Rebbe Shimon agrees it is *muktzeh*.

Similarly with a lamp filled with a large quantity of oil. That oil's purpose is to burn, so using it for any other purpose is not considered prepared for. So even if the flame is extinguished, it is *muktzeh* because it is not prepared for this new purpose.

Determining what something is designated or destined for is based on seeing what one does with this item on a weekday. During the week, one slaughters an animal in order to consume it, so even on Shabbos it's considered designated for slaughtering. The fact that you can't practically go ahead and actualize that designation doesn't change what the item is meant for. The restrictions of Shabbos that often prevents actually using an item is treated as just external. The *issur* impacts what one thinks, but doesn't change the essence that the item is considered prepared.

Anticipation is necessary to display that this item, despite not being designated for this purpose on a weekday, in the owner's eyes it is designated for such a purpose.

Mar Bar Yosef, who permits an animal that dies suddenly to be fed to animals, holds that even on a weekday, since death is common, an animal is considered destined to be fed as a carcass to other animals. Therefore, even if there is no anticipation for it to die because that is not the ideal result one desires, but nevertheless that's what this animal is destined for, if that is what it was "meant for," it is not *muktzeh* in the eventual circumstance. Mar Bar Ameimar argues that a healthy live animal is not considered to be "meant" for dogs, so one must anticipate its death for it to be considered prepared and holds that one only anticipates a sick animal will die.

In the same vein, during the week an animal is meant for slaughtering, so even on Shabbos it is treated as destined for this. Therefore there is nothing lacking in the preparation of the item and it shouldn't be *muktzeh*. The fact that you don't anticipate the possibility it of it being slaughtered is irrelevant; that eventuality is what it is "meant for."

Similarly, the Gemara records that money on one's bed during *bein hashemashos* renders the bed unusable (due to *bosis*). If the money was subsequently removed, Rebbe Shimon holds that the bed is permitted to be used even though one didn't anticipate nor expect the money to be removed. *Chazon Ish* explains that a bed is always considered meant for using. The fact that this bed practically couldn't be used when Shabbos began doesn't change what we consider it meant for. It follows that when subsequently the *muktzeh* is removed, the bed can be used even though one didn't anticipate such an outcome.

We can now answer the earlier question on *Rosh*. *Rosh paskens* that a healthy live animal is only designated for human use. Therefore unless the animal was sick before Shabbos, whereby we say there is anticipation, even according to Rebbe Shimon it is *muktzeh* when it dies, since it can now only be fed to dogs, which it was never "meant for." However, an animal that is slaughtered on Shabbos for a sick patient, even if he only fell ill today and there was no anticipation, since the animal is now fit for human consumption, which it always was designated for, it may now be used indiscriminately. The same would hold in *Rashba*.

Rejection of Proofs That Rebbe Shimon Needs Anticipation

We presented a vast dispute whether Rebbe Shimon demands two criteria for an item to be *muktzeh*: you don't anticipate the removal of the *issur* and in addition you set aside the item, or whether the former alone renders it *muktzeh*. Those who argue that Rebbe Shimon agrees without anticipation it is *muktzeh* bring strong proofs to their case. *Baal HaMeor* brings support from the following case:[59] The halachah is that a firstborn animal can't be slaughtered to eat. If it develops a blemish, it can be slaughtered. Rebbe Shimon holds that if the animal only developed the blemish on Yom Tov, one can't slaughter it. He explains this is because one didn't anticipate such an occurrence. Explicit we see that Rebbe Shimon requires anticipation for it not to be *muktzeh*?![60]

Mordechai[61] quotes another explicit source.[62] Rebbe Shimon agrees that a sturdy sukkah that collapses on Yom Tov is *muktzeh* because one doesn't anticipate it falling.[63]

---

59. *Beitzah* 26b.

60. The Mishnah says: בכור שנולד בו מום אינו מן המוכן — "A firstborn animal that develops a blemish is not considered prepared." The phrase "*eino min hamuchan*" normally is a way of connoting that the item is *muktzeh*. However, *Rashi* deviates from that usual translation and says it means you can't check the blemish on Yom Tov. Clearly *Rashi* is bothered with how this fits with Rebbe Shimon. He doesn't normally require anticipation. *Rashi*'s explanation has preempted our question.
The *Afikei Yam* in *siman* 19, s.v. ולא, also gives an answer. His answer is that there is a designation because the person didn't take the animal to be checked before Shabbos. Not doing so is akin to designating it, ע"ש.

61. Beginning of *Beitzah, simanim* 247and 642.

62. *Beitzah* 30b.

63. *Magen Avraham* holds that this is such a strong source to the extent that he deviates from the simple understanding of *Shulchan Aruch*'s opinion. As quoted earlier, twice *Shulchan Aruch* indicates that he holds Rebbe Shimon holds that even without anticipation it is not *muktzeh*. However, *Magen Avraham* 501:2 says the reason *Shulchan Aruch* permits in both cases is because there is anticipation maybe a child or a deaf or a dumb person will slaughter the animal. *Magen Avraham* proves this from the Gemara in *Beitzah* 30b. The Gemara asks: Why is the wood of a fallen booth not *muktzeh* if it fell on Shabbos? The Gemara answers that only if the booth was flimsy is it permissible, since one anticipates it to fall. Asks *Magen Avraham*: According to the opinions that even without anticipation it is permitted according to Rebbe Shimon, what forces the Gemara to make a presumption that it is flimsy? Alternatively, the Gemara could answer that this statement is going according to the opinion that holds that Rebbe Shimon permits even in a case where the animal was healthy before Shabbos since anticipation is not a requirement. From the fact that the Gemara didn't answer this, it's clear that all opinions agree that this case is *muktzeh* since there is no anticipation that one's beam will fall down.
Also *Pri Megadim* 501:2 explains the only reason Mar Bar Ameimar holds an animal that dies is permitted is because one anticipates death. He also says the only reason

Mori V'Rabi R' Ariav Ozer answers these two questions with the principle we learned from the aforementioned *Chazon Ish*. A firstborn animal is not meant to be slaughtered on a weekday. Its purpose is to be brought as a *korban*. So since it is not meant to be consumed, all agree that unless one anticipates the outcome it is *muktzeh*. The *Rishonim* who permit a slaughtered animal and don't require anticipation specifically rule so in cases when the use you want to take from the item is something it was destined for originally. A sukkah is not meant to be burned. While upright and firm it is meant to function as a booth, so unless you anticipate it to fall down, all will agree that Rebbe Shimon will treat those beams as *muktzeh* because this is not a purpose they were "prepared for."[64]

Following the above, the explanation why setting an item aside renders it *muktzeh* is because you are thereby making it only "meant for" what you have designated it for. Even for its natural purpose it is subsequently considered not prepared, e.g., an animal which is designated is no longer considered prepared for slaughtering, even though that's its weekday purpose, so even once it is slaughtered it is *muktzeh*.

When Does One Anticipate a Certain Outcome?

Tosafos[65] explains there is no problem of *muktzeh* with an animal since a person anticipates that a minor or mentally ill person will slaughter the animal on Shabbos. R' Akiva Eiger[66] implicitly says that the chances of that

---

those who permit using a slaughtered animal is because one anticipates that maybe a child will slaughter the animal. He says the above sources are a clear indication that Rebbe Shimon requires anticipation.

64. I later found that *Ohr Samei'ach, Hilchos Yom Tov* 2:3, s.v. לכן, gives the same answer. He says that to determine what an item is prepared for, we need to look whether one anticipates the same result during the week. In such instances the item is already considered prepared, so it doesn't need a further practical anticipation. One example he gives is a candle. During the week people extinguish their candles so they can have remaining oil to use another time. Therefore you don't need to anticipate the potential use you might have from the oil. The oil is considered already prepared. Something prepared doesn't need anticipation.

65. *Chullin* 14a, s.v. מחתכין.

66. Ibid., s.v. אבל.

occurring is highly unlikely. What does *Tosafos* mean that a person anticipates such an event? R' Akiva Eiger explains that according to Rebbe Yehudah even if the animal is sick before Shabbos, if it dies it still can't be fed to the dogs. Why not? Surely one thinks it is likely to die and one will be able to feed it to the animals. However, since until it dies one wants to slaughter the animal as quick as possible so that he can eat it himself, from the point of view of the person, even a sick animal is not prepared for dogs. As we've explained earlier, Rebbe Shimon argues on the requirement of preparation from the person's actual viewpoint. He just requires the object itself to be prepared. Anticipation is just a reflection that the item is prepared for this outcome and nothing is lacking. Since this possibility of a child slaughtering, even though unlikely, could nevertheless potentially occur, that's a reflection that the item is already prepared. That is sufficient preparation according to Rebbe Shimon even if one doesn't think it will occur. ואכתי צע"ג.

This is how *Magen Avraham*[67] must understand this principle of *yoshev u'metzapeh*. He applies *Tosafos*'s anticipation that a child or mentally ill person might slaughter the animal even to a case when the animal dies, an outcome which is undesired. This is not how *Afikei Yam* understands the opinion of *Rosh*, since he distinguishes between cases of slaughtering and death, and we explained previously he understands we consider the owner to have anticipated the result only if the result is desired. Death, however, is undesired and the only way we can understand why it is permitted and considered to have anticipation is like we saw from *Tosafos*.

Rashba explains the opinion that holds Rebbe Shimon permits even if the animal was healthy and suddenly died on Shabbos is because since death is common, there is anticipation it might die. *Afikei Yam* asks, *l'shitaso*: How can there be anticipation on an outcome one doesn't desire? However, since according to Rebbe Shimon only the object is required to be prepared for it not to be *muktzeh*, not that there is an active preparation performed by the owner, then since death is a common oc-

67. 501:2.

currence it is considered that the animal itself is prepared for such an outcome.

This thought can also explain *Rashba*'s answer to *Rabbeinu Tam.*[68] The Gemara writes that if money falls off a bed on Shabbos, one can move the bed. According to *Rabbeinu Tam,* in order for the bed to be a *bosis,* the case must be when the money was placed with the intention for it to remain there all of Shabbos; only then is it classified as "placed." If so, according to those who require anticipation according to Rebbe Shimon, why is it not *muktzeh* even after the money fell off, since surely there was no anticipation for the money to randomly fall off? *Rashba*[69] answers that sometimes the money accidentally falls off. The explanation of his answer is since that result sometimes occurs, the bed is considered to be prepared for use. The owner's anticipation is just to show he recognizes the essence of what the bed is prepared for.

Appendix: האם מוכן לאדם הוי מוכן לבהמה? - Is Something Meant for Man's Consumption Considered Prepared For Animals?

We saw that *Gra* rejected his suggestion in resolving the contradiction in *Rosh* since Rebbe Shimon holds מוכן לאדם הוי מוכן לכלבים. There are certain scenarios where Rebbe Shimon concedes that despite the item being meant for human consumption it is not considered prepared for animals.

Shulchan Aruch[70] *paskens* that raw meat is not *muktzeh* because it can be consumed raw. We saw that the commentators ask about the Gemara saying explicitly only raw goose meat can be eaten raw. Another question asked is why is it not sufficient that the raw meat can now be fed to the dogs to remove its status of *muktzeh*? Why do we need to say that it can be eaten raw by man? Forced by these problems, *Bach* differs with *Shulchan Aruch* and says that since we *pasken* like Rebbe Shimon, *all* raw meat is permitted because מוכן לאדם הוי מוכן לכלבים.

68. *Shabbos* 44b.

69. *Beitzah* 2a, s.v. ומפני הדחק.

70. 308:31.

However, *Taz* and *Magen Avraham* support *Shulchan Aruch*. They explain that even according to Rebbe Shimon, who holds מוכן לאדם הוי מוכן לכלבים, that principle is not relevant here. We only say this rule when one intends on giving it to his animals. However, he doesn't intend on giving his dog something he wants to eat himself. The fact that a dog theoretically can consume this raw meat doesn't change the fact that he himself wants to consume it and isn't willing to waste it on an animal. For this reason *Shulchan Aruch* requires that it is edible for a man. *Magen Avraham* quotes a host of *Rishonim* who hold this same point, that even in the opinion of Rebbe Shimon if you want to eat the meat yourself, when in its inedible state it is *muktzeh* and we don't reckon with the fact that a dog can eat it.

Although *Bach* doesn't bring anyone in support of his stance that according to Rebbe Shimon anything that is prepared for man is also considered prepared for animals, such a stance is explicit in *Meiri*[71] and *Rashba*.[72]

71. *Shabbos* 142b.

72. *Chullin* 14a. Albeit only according to Mar Bar R' Yehudah, who holds that Rebbe Shimon even argues on a healthy animal that dies.